Fundamentals of
Social Research

First Canadian Edition

Earl Babbie
Chapman University

Lucia Benaquisto
McGill University

THOMSON
★
NELSON

**Fundamentals of Social Research,
First Canadian Edition**

by Earl Babbie and Lucia Benaquisto

Editorial Director and Publisher:
Evelyn Veitch

Executive Editor:
Joanna Cotton

Marketing Manager:
Karen Howell

Developmental Editor:
Su Mei Ku

Production Editor:
Julie van Veen

Production Coordinator:
Hedy Sellers

Creative Director:
Angela Cluer

Cover Design:
Peter Papayanakis

Interior Design Modifications:
Peter Papayanakis

Cover Images:
PhotoDisc

Copy Editor/Proofreader:
Erin Moore

Compositor:
Carol Magee

Printer:
Webcom

National Library of Canada Cataloguing in Publication Data

Babbie, Earl R.
    Fundamentals of social research

1st Canadian ed.
Includes bibliographical references and index.
ISBN 0-17-616838-9

1. Social sciences—Research. 2. Social sciences—Methodology. I. Benaquisto, Lucia II. Title.

H62.B32 2001   301'.07'2
C2001-902570-X

Dedication

Sheila Babbie

Jessie and Cresanzo Benaquisto

About the Authors

Earl Babbie

Writing is my joy, sociology my passion. I delight in putting words together in a way that makes people learn or laugh or both. Sociology is one way I can do just that. It represents our last, best hope for planet-training our race and finding ways for us to live together. I feel a special excitement at being present when sociology, at last, comes into focus as an idea whose time has come.

I grew up in small-town Vermont and New Hampshire. When I announced I wanted to be an auto-body mechanic, like my dad, my teacher told me I should go to college instead. When Malcolm X announced he wanted to be a lawyer, his teacher told him a coloured boy should be something more like a carpenter. The difference in our experiences says something powerful about the idea of a level playing field. The inequalities among ethnic groups run deep.

I ventured out into the outer world by way of Harvard, the USMC, U.C. Berkeley, and 12 years teaching at the University of Hawaii. Along the way, I married Sheila two months after our first date, and we created Aaron three years after that: two of my wisest acts. I resigned from teaching in 1980 and wrote full-time for seven years, until the call of the classroom become too loud to ignore. For me, teaching is like playing jazz. Even if you perform the same number over and over, it never comes out the same twice, and you don't know exactly what it'll sound like until you hear it. Teaching is like writing with your voice.

At last, I have matured enough to rediscover and appreciate my roots in Vermont each summer. Rather than a return to the past, it feels more like the next turn in a widening spiral. I can't wait to see what's around the next bend.

Lucia Benaquisto

Both education and communication have always been very important in my life. My father was deaf and without the advantages of special education. Therefore, innovative ways of making oneself understood were part of my world. Education was something that both my mother and father stressed, because neither of them had the opportunity to gain higher education. While their individual reasons were different— my mother had to leave school when her father's illness left her as the sole support for her family—their structural circumstances were similar. Both of my parents were children of immigrants who moved to a new land to create a better life for themselves and their children. It simply took one generation longer than they had hoped. I, therefore, was lucky to be given the opportunity to obtain a position in life that has allowed me to combine what is important to me in the art of teaching—communicating knowledge. This brings me great pleasure.

My interest in studying such things as how people relate to and communicate with one another, who ends up holding what positions in society and what factors affect which places they get, as well as people's perceptions of their place and how they got there, is endless. I find learning about these and many other aspects of life in social groups both rewarding and exciting.

I began university nearly five years after high school. I didn't leave my hometown, however, until I began my graduate studies. Shortly before leaving I met Steven Rytina, who was passing through as an instructor while completing his Ph.D. We developed a strong tie, but I was leaving for Harvard to begin my post-graduate work and experience the larger world. When I arrived there, it was indeed a strange world to me—yet another place to untangle through observation, participation and analysis. Steve and I maintained our relationship at a distance, but, as fate would have it, Harvard offered him a job. So a year later he joined me in Cambridge, MA, and we have never been apart since. We share a love for sociology and a love for each other. We left Cambridge together to join the McGill faculty where we remain today. We enjoy the excitement of Montreal and the beauty of the country. Our country home on Lake Champlain is a great place to write and think. The beauty of our surroundings is at times unbelievable. To have been given the opportunity to be together in two such different, wonderful places is a luxury that I never take for granted. I am forever grateful for what I was allowed to obtain in life.

Contents in Brief

Contents in Detail

Preface

I* have enjoyed teaching research methods for over a dozen years now. As a graduate student at Harvard, I learned from James Davis that making research methodology and data analysis accessible is the key to making it enjoyable. Therefore, when I searched for a text to use in my course, I chose *The Practice of Social Research* by Earl Babbie, because his approach exemplified these qualities. I used the book for over a decade in teaching social inquiry at McGill.

The text served me very well. There was one problem that I had to continually face, however. It was not written for a Canadian audience. In teaching research methods I have learned that while methodological issues and techniques are not necessarily culturally specific, interest and excitement are more easily aroused by using examples and illustrations that are familiar and close to home. Relevant research questions and issues of interest for Canadian society are not only useful in helping students to learn about the practice of social research but also communicate knowledge and information about their social world. In addition, there are a number of issues in social research that are specific to a given society, for example, the rules and guidelines governing research ethics, what governmental research agencies exist, what types of official statistics are available, and what types of datasets have been collected and are readily accessible. Finally, raising topics and issues that are relevant to the society in which students live helps to raise their consciousness and interest in pursuing such issues in a variety of ways, including conducting research.

I therefore provided supplemental course material with Canadian examples, relevant research questions, and issues of interest for Canadian society. Nonetheless, my students often expressed a desire to read a book written from the perspective of Canadians. For these reasons, when Nelson approached me two years ago about writing the first Canadian edition of the *Fundamentals of Social Research* in collaboration with Earl Babbie, I found it hard to resist. I felt that the strengths of his approach and style combined with Canadian content would fill a need expressed by many students and instructors, including myself.

Thus, the book in front of you has been written from a Canadian perspective. A majority of examples used for illustration concern Canadian issues and research. Discussion of available data— existing statistics—and datasets available for secondary analyses are now oriented toward a Canadian audience. Ethical issues and much more are now focused on what is happening in Canada. The book contains international examples as well, for researchers are often interested in reading about, evaluating, and conducting studies that concern issues beyond their national boundaries. The book is not parochial in its perspective, but it does place Canada at its core.

Fundamentals of Social Research maintains the basic style, organization, and content of *The Basics of Social Research*, yet there have also been additions, revisions, and extensive adaptation to meet the needs of the Canadian audience.

*The first person singular in this preface refers to Benaquisto, while the first person plural refers to Babbie and Benaquisto.

Reviewers' suggestions from the very start included more than simply the transformation of this book into a Canadian text. As the writing and revisions developed, the goals continued to expand. The movement in the past two decades to the increased use of qualitative research methods and the heightened concern with ethical considerations in research called for greater attention to these subjects. Further, there were those who felt that the addition of the elaboration model would provide a useful vehicle for the teaching of multivariate analysis. Thus, we incorporated all of these suggestions into *Fundamentals of Social Research*.

There are four major features and a number of smaller changes that distinguish this book: Canadian orientation and content; greater attention to qualitative research methods; a greater focus on and integration of ethical issues; and the addition of the elaboration model.

Canadian Orientation and Content

As noted above, this book has been written for the Canadian reader. In addition to a vast number of minor changes, numerous examples have been changed and updated in each of the chapters to reflect Canadian research and issues. As you will see below, examples of experiments, surveys, secondary analysis, existing statistics, historical/comparative research, sampling designs, question wording, units of analysis, nomothetic versus idiographic explanations, inductive versus deductive theory, field research, case studies, focus groups studies, oral history, qualitative data analysis, the elaboration model, ethical dilemmas, and much more make use of research conducted to shed light on Canadian society. We also introduce students to Statistics Canada and the numerous resources that it has to offer, and to the Tri-Council Policy Statement, a joint policy created by three major Canadian granting agencies concerning ethical conduct in research involving human subjects.

Greater Attention to Qualitative Research Methods

To reflect the increased use of qualitative methods over the past two decades, greater attention to

qualitative research has been incorporated throughout the book. Two new chapters, 12 and 14, covering such approaches to research and data analysis have been added, and Chapter 11 on qualitative field research has been extensively revised and updated. These changes, along with the reorganization of Parts 3 and 4 of the book, create a more balanced coverage of qualitative and quantitative approaches to research.

Throughout the book we note that many issues and concerns in social research equally apply to qualitative and quantitative research methods. We also discuss some basic distinctions between these two approaches to research and data. Although both qualitative and quantitative data may be gathered using nearly any of the modes of observation discussed in Part 3, some observational techniques are more suitable to generating qualitative data and others to generating quantitative data. Therefore, we have reorganized this section of the book so that the chapters are roughly divided on this basis. Chapters 8 and 9 cover experiments and survey research, methods that lend themselves to gathering quantitative data. In Chapter 10 unobtrusive methods of observation are covered. Existing statistics concern quantitative data; however, content analysis and historical/comparative research methods are equally suitable to the generation of both qualitative and quantitative data. Chapters 11 and 12 cover field research and in-depth interviewing techniques, modes of observation that are well suited for generating qualitative data. Finally, Chapter 13 focuses on evaluation research and discusses both quantitative and qualitative approaches.

Following the coverage of modes of observations in Part 3, in Part 4 of the book we discuss what to do with the data collected. Approaches to analysis of qualitative data are quite different from approaches to quantitative data. Therefore, we now have a chapter (14) devoted to techniques used in qualitative data analysis.

Greater Focus on and Integration of Ethical Issues

Given the importance of the ethical dimension of social research, coverage of this topic has been expanded and integrated into the main body of the book. As we emphasize in several places throughout the text, the phases of social research are highly interconnected. Issues of ethics must be considered during all phases of the research process. We foreshadow key ethical concerns in Chapter 1, discuss the role of ethics in the context of creating a research proposal in Chapter 4, and discuss ethical issues as they concern devising and developing measures in social scientific inquiry in Chapter 5. It is in the introduction to Part 3, however, where ethical considerations are covered in depth. In Part 3 we focus specifically on ways of gathering data, and it is in this phase of research where human subjects are directly encountered. Therefore, many ethical issues become more salient in the context of discussing modes of observation and are readily illustrated. We bring to life many ethical issues by providing both real and hypothetical examples—asking the readers to imagine themselves in the place of the researcher. In the majority of chapters in Part 3, separate sections on ethics have also been added or existing sections have been revised and expanded.

Addition of The Elaboration Model

The elaboration model offers one of the clearest available pictures of the logic of causal analysis in social research. It also lays the foundation for understanding more complex multivariate statistical techniques. Developed using contingency tables, the logic of the elaboration model is readily illustrated. Thus, this comparatively accessible multivariate technique maintains continuity of subject and is one of the simplest ways to introduce some of the more complex outcomes researchers might run across when analyzing data. We revisit the idea of a spurious relationship, talk about indirect effects, and introduce the idea of interactions in a very basic way. In short, with the addition of the elaboration model, we extend the coverage of contingency tables for those who desire a further exploration of multivariate analysis. While the topics discussed in the section on the elaboration model are primarily associated with quantitative research, the logic and techniques involved can also be valuable to qualitative researchers.

Other changes have been incorporated throughout the book as well. Some topics have been updated and some discussions have been revised in an attempt to bring greater clarity to the subject. For example, in discussing randomization in Chapter 8 on experiments, we distinguished this technique from probability samples such as the simple random sample because a number of instructors indicated that students often confuse these concepts. Another illustration is the expanded and updated discussion of the feminist paradigm in Chapter 2 and revisions to a number of other discussions of paradigms.

For those who have used any of Earl Babbie's texts in the past, you will be able to recognize the similarities in style, approach, and content. You will also be able to recognize what is different—the revisions and additions. In a very general way, much of the focus of the first three sections of the book concerns how we observe and measure things for a variety of purposes. In order to do this well, we need to know something about the determination of relationships and the notion of causality. The final section of the book focuses on how we bring order to and make sense out of what we observe.

Instructor Resources

Instructor's Manual with Test Bank

Margaret Jendrek and Danielle Soulliere have prepared an excellent instructor's manual to help instructors write examinations. In addition to the usual multiple-choice, true-false, and essay questions, the manual provides resources for planning lectures and Internet exercises. Also included is a listing of print, film, and Internet resources for instructors, as well as a concise user guide for *Infotrac College Edition*.

MicroTest III for Windows

MicroTest allows instructors to create, deliver, and customize tests (both print and online) in minutes with this easy-to-use assessment and tutorial system.

Readings in Social Research
by Diane Kholos Wysocki

The concepts and methodologies of social research come to life as students read the compelling articles in this unique collection. Wysocki includes an interdisciplinary range of social science readings that focus on important methods and concepts typically covered in the social research course.

Student Resources

SPSS Student Version 10.0 CD-ROM

This new CD-ROM includes SPSS software and preloaded data files to provide students with all the tools they need to use SPSS software at their own computers for a fraction of the cost of the commercial version. This SPSS student version features the same functionality as the SPSS commercial version with very few limitations. The first two preloaded GSS data files include 2,500 cases and 62 variables (500 cases for each of these years: 1978, 1983, 1988, 1993, and 1998). The third and fourth files include 1,500 cases (approximately 300 cases per year) and contain 50 variables.

SPSS Companion for Research Methods
by Robert Griffith Turner

This booklet is a great partner to the text and to the SPSS Student Version 10.0 CD-ROM. This concise, user-friendly guide is correlated with the CD-ROM to help students learn basic navigation in SPSS. It includes chapter-specific exercises as well as information on how to enter data; create, save, and retrieve files; produce and interpret data summaries, and much more.

A Simple Guide to SPSS for Windows, Versions 8.0, 9.0 & 10
by Lee A. Kirkpatrick and Brooke C. Feeney

Perfect for first-time users of SPSS, this concise, straightforward book teaches students what they need to know to perform such procedures as stem-and-leaf displays, t-tests, multiple regressions, scatterplots, and other basics.

Multimedia Resources

Online GSS Data

(www.fundamentalssocialresearch.nelson.com)
With this Canadian edition we have sought to provide up-to-date computer support for students and instructors. As there are so many excellent programs available for analyzing data, we have provided data from Statistics Canada's most recent General Social Survey on our Web site. We created a dataset that offers students data from 1,500 respondents throughout Canada in 2000.

The *Fundamentals of Social Research, First Canadian Edition* Web site also contains several other useful resources, including online study quizzes for each chapter, links to relevant resources, a statistics primer, and more continuously evolving social resource aids.

InfoTrac College Edition

To supplement the readings listed at the end of each chapter, students will be able to access *InfoTrac College Edition*, an online library of full-text magazine and journal articles. To use the resource students visit the Web site (www.fundamentals socialresearch.nelson.com) and check the *InfoTrac College Edition* student exercises.

The Practice of Social Research Video

A lecture-launching video featuring Earl Babbie includes six ten-minute segments introducing traditionally challenging concepts—operationalization, sampling, experimental design, formulation of theory, ethics, percentages/indexes, and variables.

Acknowledgments

It would be impossible to acknowledge adequately all the people who have influenced this book. My earlier methods text, *Survey Research Methods,* was dedicated to Samuel Stouffer, Paul Lazarsfeld, and Charles Glock. I again acknowledge my debt to them.

I also repeat my thanks to those colleagues acknowledged for their comments during the writing of the first, second, and third editions of *The Practice of Social Research. The Basics of Social Research* still reflects their contributions. Further, many other colleagues helped me with this book. I particularly want to thank the following instructors for their reviews and helpful suggestions: Rae Banks, Syracuse University; Roland Chilton, University of Massachusetts, Amherst; M. Richard Cramer, University of North Carolina, Chapel Hill; Cristine Delnevo, University of Medicine and Dentistry of New Jersey; Shaul Gabbay, University of Illinois, Chicago; Sue Garfin, Sonoma State University; Marcia Ghidina, University of North Carolina, Asheville; Jeffrey Jacques, Florida A&M University; Barbara Keating, Mankato State University; James Kluegal, University of Illinois–Urbana; Wanda Kosinski, Ramapo College, New Jersey; Manfred Kuechler, CUNY Hunter College; Joan Morris, University of Central Florida; Terry Russell, Frostburg State University; Beth Anne Shelton, University of Texas, Arlington; Ron Stewart, SUNY Buffalo; Randy Stoecker, University of Toledo; Theodore Wagenaar, Miami University, Ohio; Greg Weiss, Roanoke College; and Jerome Wolfe, University of Miami.

Over the years, I have become more and more impressed by the important role played by editors in books like this. While an author's name appears on the book's spine, much of its backbone derives from the strength of its editors. Since 1973, I've worked with six sociology editors at Wadsworth, which has involved the kinds of adjustments you might need to make in six successive marriages. Happily, this edition of the book has greatly profited from my partnership with Eve Howard. While Eve brings a wealth of publishing experience to the project, she also knows the cutting edge of new technologies and pedagogies and how to take advantage of them.

Ted Wagenaar has contributed extensively to this book. Ted and I coauthor the accompanying study guide, but that's only the tip of the iceberg. Ted is a cherished colleague, welcomed critic, good friend, and altogether decent human being.

I have dedicated this book to my wife, Sheila, who has contributed greatly to its origin and evolution. Sheila and I first met when she was assigned to assist me on a project I was supervising at U.C. Berkeley's Survey Research Center.* We have worked on numerous research projects during a third of a century of marriage, and I suppose we'll do more in the future. My gratitude to Sheila, however, extends well beyond our research activities. She is a powerful partner in life. Her insight and support take me always to the horizon of my purpose and allow me to look beyond. There's no way to thank her adequately for that.

Earl Babbie

---

*This means Sheila married her boss, no matter what she says today.

The development and evolution of this book owes a great deal to the many reviewers who contributed their time and energy to shaping its contents at every stage. They are: Bruce Arai (Wilfrid Laurier University), Patricia Churchryk (University of Lethbridge), Lawrence Felt (Memorial University), Paul Gingrich (University of Regina), Shelley Goldenberg (University of Calgary), Wendi Hadd (John Abbott College), Fiona Kay (Queen's University), Tracy Peressini (University of Toronto), James Richardson (University of New Brunswick), James Teevan (University of Western Ontario), and Russell Westhaver (Simon Fraser University). The text has benefited a great deal from their many thoughtful and detailed suggestions for additions and reorganization of material. I also want to thank my colleagues with whom I have spoken about this book. Their ear and their advice have been invaluable. Thanks especially to Steven Rytina for reading numerous chapters of this text and providing many comments and insights.

I am grateful to Kimberley Ducey who was not only twice a great teaching assistant for my undergraduate research methods course, but who also provided me with valuable and spirited research assistance for many months while I was working on this book. Thanks also to David Guimond who assisted me in the later stages of preparing the text.

I want to express my gratitude to the numerous people at the McGill Library for their aid. Very special thanks to Anastassia Khouri, who is a fabulous data librarian. Her knowledge and efficiency are remarkable. Thanks also to Susan Hook Czarnocki for her help in creating the datafile from Statistics Canada's General Social Survey, Cycle 14. I also want to express appreciation to those at Statistics Canada who have been so cooperative in providing us access to data. Thanks especially to Sunita Kossta and Marie Brodeur.

The people at Nelson Thomson Learning have been terrific. They welcomed me into their group. It's been a joy to work with people who are facilitative, congenial, and effective. Special thanks and appreciation to Joanna Cotton, Julie van Veen, Erin Moore, and Su Mei Ku. They not only helped me in numerous ways but put up with my frequently unwarranted optimism about deadlines with kindness and grace.

Finally, I want to express my deep-felt appreciation for the unconditional support and guidance I have always received from my family. I dedicate this book to my parents, Jessie and Cresanzo Benaquisto, from whom I have learned the value of hard work combined with care and concern for others. I could not have asked for better role models. Thank you for bringing me up in a house filled with love and laughter. Thanks also to my nieces, Nicole Dooley and Danielle and Ariana Hiller, for the pleasure of their company and their inspiration to have fun during those much-needed breaks while I was working on this book. I owe much to their parents too, with whom I share wonderful memories and whose company I enjoy immensely. To Steven Rytina, for both his emotional and intellectual support, words can't express my gratitude. Thanks for believing in me and always being there for me. I am a lucky person to have found someone with whom to share my life in such a complete and satisfying way.

Lucia Benaquisto

Prologue:
The Importance
of Social Research

In many ways, the twentieth century wasn't one of our better periods. Except for the relatively carefree twenties, we've moved from World War I to the Great Depression to World War II to the Cold War and its threat of thermonuclear holocaust. The thawing of the Cold War and the opening of Eastern Europe was a welcome relief, though it has in many ways heightened concern over the environmental destruction of our planet. And the thawing of the Cold War has hardly meant an end to war in general, as residents of Bosnia, Rwanda, and many other nations can attest. In our move into the twenty-first century there has been no dramatic change away from all of this. People throughout the world now worry ever more about the threat and reality of war and terrorism.

A case could be made that these are not the best of times. Many sage observers have written about the insecurity and malaise that characterized the past century. All the same, the twentieth century generated countless individual efforts and social movements aimed at creating humane social affairs, and most of those arose on university campuses. Perhaps you find these kinds of concerns and commitments in yourself.

As you look at the flow of events in the world, you can see the broad range of choices available if you want to make a significant contribution to future generations. Environmental problems are many and varied. Prejudice and discrimination are with us still. Millions die of hunger, and wars large and small circle the globe. There is, in short, no end to the ways you could demonstrate to yourself that your life matters, that you make a difference.

Given all the things you could choose from—things that really *matter*—why should you spend your time learning social research methods? We want to address this question at the start, because we're going to suggest that you devote some of your time to such things as social theory, sampling, interviewing, experiments, computers, and so forth—things that can seem pretty distant from solving the world's pressing problems. Social science, though, is not only relevant to the major problems we've just listed—it also holds answers to them.

Many of the *big* problems we faced in the last century, and that we still face, have arisen out of our increasing technological abilities. The threat of nuclear terrorism is an example. Not unreasonably, we have tended to look to technology and technologists for solutions to those problems. Unfortunately, every technological solution so far has turned out to create new problems. At the beginning of the twentieth century, for example, many people worried about the danger of horse manure piling up in city streets. The invention of the automobile averted that problem. Now, no one worries about manure in the streets; we worry instead about a new and deadlier kind of pollutant in the air we breathe.

Similarly, in years past, some countries attempted to avoid nuclear attack by building better bombs and missiles so that no enemy would dare attack. But that only prompted potential enemies to build ever bigger and more powerful weapons. Now, while countries like the United States and Russia are exhibiting far less nuclear belligerence, similar contests elsewhere in the world could escalate. Is there a technological end in sight for the insane nuclear weapons race?

The simple fact is that technology alone will never save us. It will never make the world work. We are the only ones who can do that. *The only real solutions lie in the ways we organize and run our social affairs.* This becomes evident when you consider all the social problems that persist today despite the clear presence of viable, technological solutions.

Overpopulation, for example, is a pressing problem in the world today. The number of people currently living on earth severely taxes our planet's life support systems, and this number rapidly increases year after year. If you study the matter you'll find that we already possess all the technological developments needed to stem population growth. It is technologically possible and feasible for us to stop population growth on the planet at whatever limit we want. Yet, overpopulation worsens each year.

Clearly, the solution to overpopulation is social. The causes of population growth lie in the forms, values, and customs that make up organized social life, and that is where the solutions are hidden. Those causes include beliefs about what it takes to be a "real woman" or a "real man," the perceived importance of perpetuating a family name, cultural tradition, and so forth. Ultimately, only social science can save us from overpopulation.

Or consider the problem of hunger on the planet. Some 13 to 15 million people die as a consequence of hunger each year. That amounts to 28 people a minute, every minute of every day, with 21 of them children. We all agree that this condition is deplorable; all would prefer it otherwise. But we tolerate this level of starvation in the belief that it is currently inevitable. We hope that perhaps one day someone will invent a method of producing food that will defeat starvation once and for all.

When we actually study the issue of starvation in the world, however, we can learn some astounding facts. First, the earth currently produces *more than enough* food to feed everyone. Moreover, this level of production does not even take into account farm programs in some countries that pay farmers not to plant and produce all the food they could.

Second, there are carefully planned and tested methods for ending starvation. In fact, since World War II, more than 30 countries have actually faced and ended their own problems of starvation. Some did it through food distribution programs. Others focused on land reform. Some collectivized; others developed agribusiness. Many applied the advances of the Green Revolution. Taken together, these proven solutions make it possible to eliminate starvation totally.

Why then haven't we ended hunger altogether on the planet? The answer, again, lies in the organization and operation of our social life. New developments in food production will not end starvation any more than earlier ones have. People will continue to starve until we can *command* our social affairs rather than be enslaved by them.

Possibly, the problems of overpopulation and hunger seem distant to you, occurring somewhere "over there," on the other side of the globe. To save space, we'll simply remind you of the conclusion, increasingly reached, that there is no "over there" anymore: There is only "over here" in today's world. And regardless of how you view world problems, there is undeniably no end to the social problems in your own back yard—possibly even in your front yard: crime, unemployment, homelessness, cheating in government and business, child abuse, prejudice and discrimination, pollution, drug abuse, increased taxes, and reduced public services.

We can't solve our social problems until we understand how they come about, persist. Social science research offers a way to examine and understand the operation of human social affairs. It provides points of view and technical procedures that uncover things that would otherwise escape our awareness. Often, as the cliché goes, things are not what they seem; social science research can make that clear.

Many of the things social scientists study—including all the social problems you've just read about—generate deep emotions and firm convictions in most people. This makes effective inquiry into the facts difficult at best; all too often, researchers manage only to confirm their initial prejudices. The special value of social science research methods is that they offer a way to address such issues with logical and observational rigor. They let us all pierce through our personal viewpoints and take a look at the world that lies beyond our own perspectives. And it is that "world beyond" that holds the solutions to the social problems we face today.

At a time of increased depression and disillusionment, we are continually tempted to turn away from confronting social problems and retreat into the concerns of our own self-interest. Social science research offers an opportunity to take on those problems and discover the experience of making a difference after all. The choice is yours; we invite you to take on the challenge. Along with your instructor, we would like to share the excitement of social science with you.

Fundamentals of
Social Research

First Canadian Edition

Part 1
An Introduction to Inquiry

An Introduction to Inquiry

1 Human Inquiry and Science
2 Paradigms, Theory, and Research
3 The Idea of Causation in Social Research

Science is a familiar word used by everyone. Yet images of science differ greatly. For some, science is mathematics; for others, it's white coats and laboratories. It's often confused with technology or equated with tough high school or university courses.

Science is, of course, none of these things per se. It's difficult, however, to specify exactly what science is. Scientists, in fact, disagree on the proper definition. For the purposes of this book, we'll look at science as a method of inquiry—a way of learning and knowing things about the world around us. Contrasted with other ways of learning and knowing about the world, science has some special characteristics. It is a conscious, deliberate, and rigorous undertaking. We'll examine these and other traits in this opening set of chapters where it will become clear to you before you've read very far that you already know a great deal about the practice of scientific social research. In fact, you've been conducting scientific research all your life. From that perspective, the purpose of this book is to help you sharpen skills you already have and perhaps to show you some tricks that may not have occurred to you.

Part 1 of this book is intended to lay the groundwork for the rest of the book by examining the fundamental characteristics and issues that make

science different from other ways of knowing things. In Chapter 1, we'll begin with a look at native human inquiry, the sort of thing you've been doing all your life. In the course of that examination, we'll see some of the ways people go astray in trying to understand the world around them, and we'll summarize the primary characteristics of scientific inquiry that guard against those errors. We'll also introduce the ethical dimension of social research.

Chapter 2 deals with social theories and the links between theory and research. We'll look at some of the theoretical paradigms that shape the nature of inquiry, largely determining what scientists look for and how they interpret what they see.

In their attempt to develop generalized understanding, scientists seek to discover patterns of interrelationships among variables. Often these interrelationships take a cause-and-effect form. Chapter 3 addresses the nature and logic of causation in regard to social research. This theoretical chapter forms the basis for the chapters on analytical techniques.

The overall purpose of Part 1 is to construct a backdrop against which to view the specifics of research design and execution. After completing Part 1, you'll be ready to look at some of the more concrete aspects of social research.

Chapter 1

Human Inquiry and Science

All of us try to understand and predict the social world. Science—and social research in particular— are designed to avoid the common pitfalls of ordinary human inquiry.

In this chapter . . .

Introduction

This book is about knowing things—not so much *what* we know as *how* we know it. Let's start by examining a few things you probably know already. You know the world is round. You probably also know it's cold on the dark side of the moon, and you know people speak Chinese in China. You know that vitamin C prevents colds and that unprotected sex can result in AIDS.

How do you know? Unless you've been to the dark side of the moon lately or done experimental research on the virtues of vitamin C, you know these things because somebody told them to you, and you believed what you were told. You may have read in *National Geographic* that people speak Chinese in China, and that made sense to you, so you didn't question it. Perhaps your physics or astronomy instructor told you it was cold on the dark side of the moon, or maybe you read it in a magazine.

Some of the things you know seem absolutely obvious to you. If you were asked how you know the world is round, you'd probably say, "Everybody knows that." There are a lot of things everybody knows. Of course, at one time, everyone "knew" the world was flat.

Most of what you know is a matter of agreement and belief. Little of it is based on personal experience and discovery. A big part of growing up in any society, in fact, is the process of learning to accept what everybody around you "knows" is so. If you don't know those same things, you can't really be a part of the group. If you were to question seriously whether the world is really round, you'd quickly find yourself set apart from other people. You might be sent to live in a hospital with other people who question things like that.

Although it's important to realize that most of what we know is a matter of believing what we've been told, there's nothing wrong with us in that respect. It's simply the way human societies are structured. The basis of knowledge is agreement. Because we can't learn all we need to know through personal experience and discovery alone, things are set up so we can simply believe what others tell us. We know some things through tradition, some things from "experts."

There are other ways of knowing things, however. In contrast to knowing things through agreement, we can know them through direct experience—through observation. If you dive into a glacial stream flowing through the Canadian Rockies, you don't need anyone to tell you it's cold.

You notice it all by yourself. The first time you stepped on a thorn, you knew it hurt before anyone told you.

When our experience conflicts with what everyone else knows, though, there's a good chance we'll surrender our experience in favour of the agreement.

For example, imagine you've come to a party at one of our homes. It's a high-class affair, and the drinks and food are excellent. In particular, you're taken by one of the appetizers brought around on a tray: a breaded, deep-fried tidbit that's especially zesty. You have a couple—they're so delicious! You have more. Soon you find yourself subtly moving around the room so that you'll be wherever the person next arrives with a tray of these nibblies.

Finally, you can't contain yourself any more. "What are they?" you ask. "How can I get the recipe?" And you are let in on the secret: "You've been eating breaded, deep-fried worms!" Your response is dramatic: Your stomach rebels, and you promptly throw up all over the living room rug. Awful! What a terrible thing to serve guests!

The point of the story is that both of your feelings about the appetizer would be quite real. Your initial liking for them, based on your own experience, was certainly real. But so was the feeling of disgust you had when you found out that you'd been eating worms. It should be evident, however, that this feeling of disgust was strictly a product of the agreements you have with those around you that worms aren't fit to eat. That's an agreement you entered into the first time your parents found you sitting in a pile of dirt with half of a wriggling worm dangling from your lips. You learned that worms are not acceptable food in our society when they pried your mouth open and reached down your throat for the other half of the worm.

Aside from these agreements, what's wrong with worms? They're probably high in protein and low in calories. Bite-sized and easily packaged, they're a distributor's dream. They are also a delicacy for some people who live in societies that lack our agreement that worms are disgusting. Some people might love the worms but be turned off by the deep-fried breading.

Here's a question you might consider: "Are worms *really* good or *really* bad to eat?" And here's a more interesting question: "*How could you know* which was really so?" This book is about answering the second kind of question.

The rest of this chapter looks at how we know what is real. We'll begin by examining inquiry as a natural human activity, something we all have engaged in every day of our lives. We'll look at the source of everyday knowledge and at some kinds of errors we make in normal inquiry. We'll then examine what makes science—in particular, social science—different. After considering some of the underlying ideas of social research, we'll conclude with an initial consideration of issues in social research.

Looking for Reality

Reality is a tricky business. You probably already suspect that some of the things you "know" may not be true, but how can you really know what's real? People have grappled with this question for thousands of years.

One answer that has arisen out of that grappling is *science*, which offers an approach to both agreement reality and experiential reality. Scientists have certain criteria that must be met before they'll accept the reality of something they haven't personally experienced. In general, a scientific assertion must have both *logical* and *empirical* support: It must make sense, and it must not contradict actual observation. Why do earthbound scientists accept the assertion that it's cold on the dark side of the moon? First, it makes sense, because the moon's surface heat comes from the sun's rays, and the dark side of the moon is dark because it's turned away from the sun. Second, the scientific measurements made on the moon's dark side confirm this logical expectation. So, scientists accept the reality of things they don't personally experience—they accept an agreement reality—but they have special standards for doing so.

More to the point of this book, however, science offers a special approach to the discovery of reality through personal experience. In other words, it offers a special approach to the business of inquiry. *Epistemology* is the science of knowing; *methodology* (a subfield of epistemology) might be called the science of finding out. This book is an examination and presentation of social science methodology, or how social scientists find out about human social life.

Why do we need social science to discover the reality of social life? To find out, let's first consider what happens in ordinary, nonscientific inquiry.

Ordinary Human Inquiry

Practically all people, and many other animals as well, exhibit a desire to predict their future circumstances. Humans seem predisposed to undertake this task using *causal* reasoning. We generally recognize that future circumstances are somehow caused or conditioned by present ones. We learn that getting an education will affect how much money we earn later in life and that swimming beyond the reef may bring an unhappy encounter with a shark. As students we learn that studying hard will result in better examination grades.

Second, people, and seemingly other animals, also learn that such patterns of cause and effect are *probabilistic* in nature. That is, the effects occur more often when the causes occur than when the causes are absent—but not always. Thus, students learn that studying hard produces good grades in most instances, but not every time. We recognize the danger of swimming beyond the reef without believing that every such swim will be fatal. As we'll see throughout the book, science makes these concepts of causality and probability more explicit and provides techniques for dealing with them more rigorously than does casual human inquiry. It sharpens the skills we already have by making us more conscious, rigorous, and explicit in our inquiries.

In looking at ordinary human inquiry, we need to distinguish between prediction and understanding. Often, we can make predictions without understanding—perhaps you can predict rain when your trick knee aches. And often, even if we don't understand why, we're willing to act on the basis of a demonstrated predictive ability. A race-

track buff who discovers that the third-ranked horse in the third race of the day always seems to win will probably keep betting without knowing, or caring, why it works out that way. Of course, the drawback in predicting without understanding will be powerfully evident when one of the other horses wins and our buff loses a week's pay.

Whatever the primitive drives or instincts that motivate human beings and other animals, satisfying them depends heavily on the ability to predict future circumstances. For people, however, the attempt to predict is often placed in a context of knowledge and understanding. If you can understand why things are related to one another, why certain regular patterns occur, you can predict better than if you simply observe and remember those patterns. Thus, human inquiry aims at answering both "what" and "why" questions, and we pursue these goals by observing and figuring out.

As we suggested earlier in the chapter, our attempts to learn about the world are only partly linked to direct, personal inquiry or experience. Another, much larger, part comes from the agreed-upon knowledge that others give us, those things "everyone knows." This agreement reality both assists and hinders our attempts to find out for ourselves. To see how, consider two important sources of our secondhand knowledge—tradition and authority.

Tradition

Each of us inherits a culture made up, in part, of firmly accepted knowledge about the workings of the world. We may learn from others that eating too much candy will decay our teeth, that the circumference of a circle is approximately twenty-two-sevenths of its diameter, that masturbation will blind us, or even that most people on welfare are lazy. We may test a few of these "truths" on our own, but we simply accept the great majority of them. These are things that "everybody knows."

Tradition, in this sense of the term, offers some clear advantages to human inquiry. By accepting what everybody knows, we are spared the overwhelming task of starting from scratch in our search for regularities and understanding. Knowledge is cumulative, and an inherited body of information and understanding is the jumping-off point for the development of more knowledge. We often speak of "standing on the shoulders of giants," that is, of previous generations.

At the same time, tradition may hinder human inquiry. If we seek a fresh understanding of something everybody already understands and has always understood, we may be marked as fools for our efforts. More to the point, however, it rarely occurs to most of us to seek a different understanding of something we all "know" to be true.

Authority

Despite the power of tradition, new knowledge appears every day. Quite aside from our own personal inquiries, we benefit throughout our lives from new discoveries and understandings produced by others. Often, acceptance of these new acquisitions will depend on the status of the discoverer. You're more likely to believe the medical researcher who declares that the common cold can be transmitted through kissing, for example, than to believe your uncle Pete.

Like tradition, authority can both assist and hinder human inquiry. We do well to trust in the judgment of the person who has special training, expertise, and credentials in a given matter, especially in the face of controversy. At the same time, inquiry can be greatly hindered by the legitimate authorities that err within their own province. Biologists, after all, make mistakes in the field of biology. Moreover, biological knowledge changes over time.

Inquiry is also hindered when we depend on the authority of experts speaking outside their realm of expertise. For example, consider the political or religious leader with no medical or biochemical expertise who declares that marijuana can fry your brain. The advertising industry plays heavily on this misuse of authority by, for example, having popular athletes discuss the nutritional value of breakfast cereals or having movie actors evaluate the performance of automobiles.

Both tradition and authority, then, are double-edged swords in the search for knowledge about the world. Simply put, they provide us with a starting point for our own inquiry, but they can lead us to start at the wrong point and push us off in the wrong direction.

Errors in Inquiry and Some Solutions

Quite aside from the potential dangers of tradition and authority, we often stumble and fall when we set out to learn for ourselves. Let's look at some of the common errors we make in our casual inquiries and look at the ways science guards against those errors.

Inaccurate Observations Frequently, we make mistakes in our observations. For example, what was your methodology instructor wearing on the first day of class. If you have to guess, it's because most of our daily observations are casual and semiconscious. That's why we often disagree about what really happened.

In contrast to casual human inquiry, scientific observation is a conscious activity. Simply making observation more deliberate helps reduce error. In trying to recall what your instructor was wearing on the first day of class, you'd probably make a mistake. However, if you had gone to the first class with a conscious plan to observe and record what your instructor was wearing, you'd be far more likely to be accurate.

In many cases, both simple and complex measurement devices help guard against inaccurate observations. Moreover, they add a degree of precision well beyond the capacity of the unassisted human senses. Suppose, for example, that you had taken colour photographs of your instructor that day.

Overgeneralization When we look for patterns among the specific things we observe around us, we often assume that a few similar events are evidence of a general pattern. That is, we overgeneralize on the basis of limited observations. (Think back to our now broke racetrack buff.)

Probably the tendency to overgeneralize is greatest when the pressure to arrive at a general understanding is high. Yet it also occurs without such pressure. Whenever overgeneralization does occur, it can misdirect or impede inquiry.

Imagine you are a reporter covering an animal-rights demonstration. You have orders to turn in your story in just two hours, and you need to know why people are demonstrating. Rushing to the scene, you start interviewing them, asking for their reasons. If the first three demonstrators you interview give you essentially the same reason, you may simply assume that the other 3,000 are also there for that reason. Unfortunately, when your story appears, your editor gets scores of letters from protesters who were there for an entirely different reason.

Scientists guard against overgeneralization by committing themselves in advance to a sufficiently large and representative sample of observations. The **replication** of inquiry provides another safeguard. Basically, replication means repeating a study and checking to see whether the same results are produced each time. Then, as a further test, the study may be repeated again under slightly varied conditions.

Selective Observation   One danger of overgeneralization is that it may lead to selective observation. Once we have concluded that a particular pattern exists and have developed a general understanding of why it exists, we tend to focus on future events and situations that fit the pattern and ignore those that don't. Racial and ethnic prejudices depend heavily on selective observation for their persistence.

Sometimes, a research design will specify in advance the number and kind of observations to be made, as a basis for reaching a conclusion. If we wanted to learn whether women were more likely than men to support freedom to choose an abortion, we'd commit ourselves to making a specified number of observations on that question in a research project. We might select a thousand carefully chosen people to be interviewed on the issue. Alternately, when making direct observations of an event, such as attending the animal-rights demonstration, social scientists make a special effort to find "deviant cases"—precisely those who do not fit into the general pattern.

Illogical Reasoning   There are other ways in which we often deal with observations that contradict our understanding of the way things are in daily life. What statisticians have called the *gambler's fallacy* is an illustration of illogic in day-to-day reasoning. Often we assume that a consistent run of either good or bad luck foreshadows its opposite. An evening of bad luck at poker may kindle the belief that a winning hand is just around the corner. Many a poker player has stayed in a game much too long because of that mistaken belief. Conversely, an extended period of good weather may lead you to worry that it is certain to rain on the weekend picnic.

Although all of us sometimes fall into embarrassingly illogical reasoning, scientists try to avoid this pitfall by using systems of logic consciously and explicitly. Chapter 2 will examine the logic of science in more depth. For now, it's enough to note that logical reasoning is a conscious activity for scientists and that other scientists are always around to keep them honest.

Science, then, attempts to protect its inquiries from the common pitfalls in ordinary inquiry. Accurately observing and understanding reality is not an obvious or trivial matter. Indeed, it's more complicated than we've suggested.

What's Really Real?

Philosophers sometimes use the phrase "naive realism" to describe the way most of us operate in our daily lives. When you sit at a table to write, you probably don't spend a lot of time thinking about whether the table is really made up of atoms, which in turn are mostly empty space. When you step into the street and see a city bus hurtling down on you, it's not the best time to reflect on methods for testing whether the bus really exists. We all live with a view that what's real is pretty obvious—and that view usually gets us through the day.

We don't want this book to interfere with your ability to deal with everyday life. We hope, however, that the preceding discussions have demonstrated that the nature of "reality" is perhaps more complex than we tend to assume in our everyday functioning. Here are three views on reality that will provide a simplistic and schematic philosophical backdrop for the discussions of science to follow. They are sometimes called *premodern, modern*, and *postmodern* views of reality (Anderson 1990).

The Premodern View This view of reality has guided most of human history. Our early ancestors all assumed that they saw things as they really were. In fact, this assumption was so fundamental that they didn't even see it as an assumption. No cavemom said to her cavekid, "Our tribe makes an assumption that evil spirits reside in the Old Twisted Tree." No, she said, "STAY OUT OF THAT TREE OR YOU'LL TURN INTO A TOAD!"

As humans evolved and became aware of their diversity, they came to recognize that others did not always share their views of things. Thus, they may have discovered that another tribe didn't buy the wicked tree thing; in fact, the second tribe felt the spirits in the tree were holy and beneficial. The discovery of this diversity led members of the first tribe to conclude, "some tribes I could name are pretty stupid." For them, the tree was still wicked, and they expected some misguided people to be moving to Toad City.

The Modern View What philosophers call the *modern* view accepts such diversity as legitimate, a philosophical "different strokes for different folks." As a modern thinker, you would say, "I regard the spirits in the tree as evil, but I know others regard them as good. Neither of us is right or wrong. There are simply spirits in the tree. They are neither good nor evil, but different people have different ideas about them."

It's probably pretty easy for many of us to adopt the modern view. Some might regard a dandelion as a beautiful flower while others see only an annoying weed. To the premoderns, a dandelion has to be either one or the other. If you think it is a weed, it is really a weed, though you may admit that some people have a warped sense of beauty. In the modern view, a dandelion is simply a dandelion. It is a plant with yellow petals and green leaves. The concepts "beautiful flower" and "annoying weed" are subjective points of view

imposed on the plant by different people. Neither is a quality of the plant itself, just as "good" and "evil" were concepts imposed on the spirits in the tree.

The Postmodern View Increasingly, philosophers speak of a *postmodern* view of reality. In this view, the spirits don't exist. Neither does the dandelion. All that's "real" are the images we get through our points of view. Put differently, there's nothing *out there;* it's all *in here.* As Gertrude Stein said of Oakland, "There's no there, there."

No matter how bizarre the postmodern view may seem to you on first refection, it has a certain ironic inevitability. Take a moment to notice the book you're reading; notice specifically what it looks like. Since you're reading these words, it probably looks like Figure 1-1A.

But does Figure 1-1A represent the way your book "really" looks? Or does it merely represent what the book looks like from your current point of view? Surely, Figures 1-1B, C, and D are equally valid representations. But these views of the book are so different from one another. Which is the "reality"?

As this example illustrates, there is no answer to the question, "What does the book really look like?" All we can offer is the different ways it looks from different points of view. Thus, according to the postmodern view, there is no "book," only various images of it from different points of view. And all the different images are equally "true."

Now let's apply this logic to a social situation. Imagine a husband and wife arguing. When she looks over at her quarreling husband, Figure 1-2 is what the wife sees. Take a minute to imagine what you would feel and think if you were the woman in this drawing. How would you explain later to your best friend what had happened? What solutions to the conflict would seem appropriate if you were this woman?

Of course, what the woman's husband sees is another matter altogether, as shown in Figure 1-3. Take a minute to imagine experiencing the situation from his point of view. What thoughts and feelings would you have? How would you tell your best

Figure 1-1
A Book

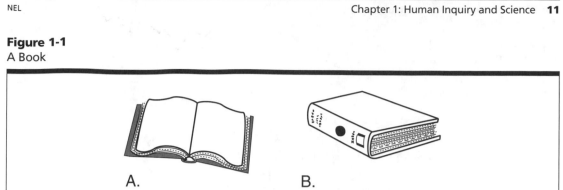

A.

B.

C.

D.

Figure 1-2
Wife's Point of View

Figure 1-3
Husband's Point of View

friend what had happened? What solutions would seem appropriate for resolving the conflict?

Now, consider a third point of view. Suppose you're an outside observer, watching this interaction between a wife and husband. What would it look like to you now? Unfortunately, we can't easily portray the third point of view without knowing something about the personal feelings, beliefs, past experiences, and so forth that you would bring to your task as "outside" observer. (Though we call you an *outside* observer, you are, of course, observing from *inside* your own mental system.)

To take an extreme example, if you were a confirmed male chauvinist, you'd probably see the fight pretty much the same way the husband saw it. On the other hand, if you were committed to the view that men are unreasonable bums, you'd see things the way the wife saw them.

But imagine that instead you see two unreasonable people, quarrelling irrationally with one another. Would you see them both as irresponsible

jerks, equally responsible for the conflict? Or would you see two people facing a difficult human situation, each doing the best he or she can to resolve it? Imagine feeling compassion for them and noticing how each of them attempts to end the hostility, even though the gravity of the problem keeps them fighting.

Notice how different these several views are. Which is a "true" picture of what is happening between the wife and the husband? You win the prize if you notice that the personal viewpoint you bring to the observational task will again colour your perception of what is happening.

The postmodern view represents a critical dilemma for scientists. While their task is to observe and understand what is "really" happening, they are all human and, as such, bring along personal orientations that will colour what they observe and how they explain it. There is ultimately no way people can totally step outside their humanness to see and understand the world as it "really" is—that is, independently of all human viewpoints.

Whereas the modern view acknowledges the inevitability of human subjectivity, the postmodern view suggests there is no "objective" reality to be observed in the first place. There are only our several subjective views.

You may want to ponder these three views of reality on your own for awhile. We'll return to them in Chapter 2 when we focus on more specific scientific paradigms. Ultimately, two points will emerge. First, established scientific procedures sometimes allow us to deal effectively with this dilemma—that is, we can study people without being able to view "reality" directly. Second, different philosophical stances suggest a powerful range of possibilities for structuring our research.

Let's turn now from general philosophical ideas to the foundations of the social scientific approaches to understanding in particular. A consideration of these underpinnings of social research will prepare the way for our exploration of specific research techniques.

The Foundations of Social Science

Science is sometimes characterized as logico-empirical. This ungainly term carries an important message. As we noted earlier, the two pillars of science are logic and observation. That is, a scientific understanding of the world must (1) make sense and (2) correspond with what we observe. Both elements are essential to science and relate to three major aspects of the social scientific enterprise: *theory, data collection,* and *data analysis.*

To oversimplify just a bit, scientific **theory** deals with the logical aspect of science, whereas data collection deals with the observational aspect. Data analysis looks for patterns in observations and, where appropriate, compares what is logically expected with what is actually observed. Although this book is primarily about data collection and data analysis—that is, how to conduct social research—the rest of Part 1 is devoted to the theo-

retical context of research. Parts 2 and 3 then focus on data collection, and Part 4 offers an introduction to the analysis of data.

Underlying the concepts presented in the rest of the book are some fundamental ideas that distinguish social science—theory, data collection, and analysis—from other ways of looking at social phenomena. Let's consider these ideas

Theory, Not Philosophy or Belief

Today social theory has to do with what is, not with what should be. For many centuries, however, social theory didn't distinguish between these two orientations. Social philosophers liberally mixed their observations of what happened around them, their speculations about why, and their ideas about how things ought to be. Although modern social scientists may do the same from time to time, as scientists they focus on how things actually are and why.

This means that scientific theory—and, more broadly, science itself—cannot settle debates about values. Science cannot determine whether capitalism is better or worse than socialism. What it can do is determine how these systems perform in terms of some set of agreed-upon criteria. For example, we could determine scientifically whether capitalism or socialism most supports human dignity and freedom only if we first agreed on some measurable definitions of dignity and freedom. Our conclusions would then be limited to the meanings specified in our definitions. They would have no general meaning beyond that.

By the same token, if we could agree that suicide rates, say, or giving to charity were good measures of the quality of a religion, then we could determine scientifically whether Buddhism or Christianity is the more effective religion. Again, our conclusion would be inextricably tied to our chosen criterion. As a practical matter, people seldom agree on precise criteria for determining issues of value, so science is seldom useful in settling such debates. In fact, questions like these are so much a matter of opinion and belief that scientific inquiry is often viewed as a threat to what is "already known."

We'll consider this issue in more detail in Chapter 13, when we look at evaluation research. As you'll see, researchers have become increasingly involved in studying programs that reflect ideological points of view, such as pay equity for women or affirmative action. One of the biggest problems they face is getting people to agree on criteria of success and failure. Yet, such criteria are essential if social research is to tell us anything useful about matters of value. By analogy, a stopwatch can't tell us if one sprinter is better than another unless we first agree that speed is the critical criterion.

Social science, then, can help us know only what is and why. We can use it to determine what ought to be only when people agree on the criteria for deciding what outcomes are better than others—an agreement that seldom occurs.

As we indicated earlier, even knowing "what is and why" is no simple task. Let's turn now to some of the fundamental ideas that underlie social science's efforts to describe and understand social reality.

Social Regularities

In large part, social research aims to find patterns of regularity in social life. Although that aim is shared by all science, it is sometimes a barrier for people when they first approach social science.

Certainly at first glance the subject matter of the physical sciences seems to be more governed by regularities than does that of the social sciences. A heavy object falls to earth every time we drop it, but a person may vote for a particular candidate in one election and against that same candidate in the next. Similarly, ice always melts when heated enough, but habitually honest people sometimes steal. Despite such examples, however, social affairs do exhibit a high degree of regularity that can be revealed by research and explained by theory.

To begin, a vast number of formal norms in society create a considerable degree of regularity. For example, nearly all Canadians obey traffic laws and drive on the right side of the road rather than the left. In the Canadian military, until recently only men could participate in combat. (It was not until 1989 that the Canadian Forces were directed to remove any employment restrictions that remained based on sex, with the exception of submarine duty.) Such formal prescriptions regulate, or regularize, social behaviour.

Aside from formal prescriptions, we can observe other social norms that create more regularities. University professors tend to earn more money than do unskilled labourers. Men tend to earn more than women, and so on.

What about Exceptions? The objection that there are always exceptions to any social regularity does not mean that the regularity itself is unreal or unimportant. A particular woman may earn more money than most men, but that will be a small consolation to the majority of women, who earn less. The pattern still exists. Social regularities, in other words, are probabilistic patterns, and they are no less real simply because some cases don't fit the general pattern.

This point applies in physical science as well as social science. In genetics, for example, the mating of a blue-eyed person with a brown-eyed person will *probably* result in a brown-eyed offspring. The birth of a blue-eyed child does not destroy the observed regularity, because the geneticist states only that the brown-eyed offspring is more likely and, further, that brown-eyed offspring will be born in a certain percentage of the cases. The social scientist makes a similar, probabilistic prediction—that women overall are likely to earn less than men. Once a pattern like this is observed, the social scientist has grounds for asking why it exists.

Aggregates, Not Individuals

Although social scientists often study motivations that affect individuals, the individual as such is seldom the subject of social science. Instead, social scientists create theories about the aggregate behaviour of many individuals. Similarly, the objects of their research are typically aggregates, or collections, rather than individuals.

Sometimes the collective regularities are amazing. Consider the birthrate, for example. People have babies for any number of personal reasons. Some do it because their own parents want grandchildren. Some feel it's a way of completing their womanhood or manhood. Others want to hold their marriages together, enjoy the experience of raising a child, or perpetuate their family name. Still others have babies by accident.

If you are a parent, you could probably tell a much more detailed story. Why did you have the baby when you did, rather than a year earlier or later? Maybe you lost your job and had to delay a year before you could afford to have the baby. Maybe you felt that being a family person would demonstrate maturity.

Everyone who had a baby last year had her or his own reasons for doing so. Yet, despite this vast diversity, and despite the idiosyncrasy of each individual's reasons, the overall birthrate in a society (the number of live births per 1,000 population) is remarkably consistent from year to year. Here are some recent birthrates for Canada.

1995–1996	12.6
1996–1997	12.0
1997–1998	11.5
1998–1999	11.2
1999–2000	10.9

From July 1 of one year to June 30 of the next year.
Source: Statistics Canada, CANSIM, Matrix 5772 and Catalogue no. 91-213-XB.
Statistics Canada's Internet Site (December 13, 2000)
http://www.statcan.ca/english/Pgdb/People/Population/demo04b.htm

If the Canadian birthrate were 16.2, 36.5, 8.8, 24.2, and 15.9 in five successive years, demographers who study such issues would begin dropping like flies. As you can see, however, social life is far more orderly than that. Moreover, this regularity occurs without society-wide regulation. No one plans how many babies will be born or determines who will have them. You don't need a permit to have a baby; in fact, many babies are conceived unexpectedly, and some are borne by unwilling mothers.

Social scientific theories then, typically deal with aggregated, not individual, behaviour. Their purpose is to explain why aggregate patterns of behaviour are so regular even when the individuals participating in them may change over time. It could be said that social scientists don't even seek to explain *people.* They try to understand the *systems* in which people operate, the systems that explain why people do what they do. The elements in such a system are not people but *variables.*

A Variable Language

Our most natural attempts at understanding usually take place at the level of the concrete and idiosyncratic. That's just the way we think.

Imagine that someone says to you, "Women ought to get back into the kitchen where they belong." You are likely to hear that comment in terms of what you know about the speaker. If it's your old uncle Harry who, you recall, is also strongly opposed to daylight saving time, postal codes, and personal computers, you are likely to think his latest pronouncement simply fits into his rather dated point of view about things in general.

If, on the other hand, a male politician who was trailing a female challenger in an election race made the statement, you would probably explain his comment in a completely different way.

In both examples, you're trying to understand the behaviour of a particular individual, but *social research seeks insights into classes or types of individuals.* Social researchers would want to find out about the kind of people who share that view of women's "proper" role. Do those people have other characteristics in common that may help explain their views?

Even when researchers focus their attention on a single case—such as a community or a juvenile gang—their aim is to gain insights that would help people understand other communities and other juvenile gangs. Similarly, the attempt to fully understand one individual carries the broader purpose of understanding people or types of people in general.

When this venture into understanding and explanation ends, social researchers will be able to make sense out of more than one person. In understanding what makes a group of people hostile to women who are active outside the home, they gain insight into all the individuals who share that characteristic. This is possible because, in an important sense, they have not been studying antifeminists as much as they have been studying antifeminism.

It might turn out that uncle Harry and the politician have more in common than first appeared.

Antifeminism is spoken of as a **variable** because it varies. Some people display the attitude more than others. Social researchers are interested in understanding the system of variables that causes a particular attitude to be strong in one instance and weak in another.

The idea of a system composed of variables may seem rather strange, so let's look at an analogy. The subject of a physician's attention is the patient. If the patient is ill, the physician's purpose is to help the patient get well. By contrast, a medical researcher's subject matter is different: the variables that cause a disease, for example. The medical researcher may study the physician's patient, but for the researcher that patient is relevant only as a carrier of the disease.

That is not to say that medical researchers don't care about real people. They certainly do. Their ultimate purpose in studying diseases is to protect people from them. But in their research, they are less interested in individual patients than they are in the patterns governing the appearance of disease—in essence, the patients are relevant only for what they reveal about the disease under study. In fact, when they can study a disease meaningfully without involving actual patients, they do so.

Social research, then, involves the study of variables and their relationships. Social theories are written in a language of variables, and people get involved only as the "carriers" of those variables.

Variables, in turn, have what social researchers call **attributes** or values. Attributes are characteristics or qualities that describe an object—in this case, a person. Examples include female, Asian, alienated, conservative, dishonest, intelligent, and farmer. Anything you might say to describe yourself or someone else involves an attribute.

Variables, on the other hand, are logical groupings of attributes. Thus, for example, male and female are attributes, and *sex* or *gender* are the variables composed of these two attributes. The variable *occupation* is composed of attributes such as farmer, professor, and truck driver. *Social class* is a variable composed of a set of attributes such as upper class, middle class, and lower class. Sometimes it helps to think of attributes as the "categories" that make up a variable. (See Figure 1-4 for a schematic review of what social scientists mean by variables and attributes.)

The relationship between attributes and variables lies at the heart of both description and explanation in science. For example, we might describe a university class in terms of the variable *gender* by reporting the observed frequencies of the attributes male and female: "The class is 60 percent men and 40 percent women." An unemployment rate can be thought of as a description of the variable *employment status of a labour force* in terms of the attributes employed and unemployed. Even the report of *family income for a city* is a summary of attributes composing that variable: $10,980; $35,000; $85,470; and so forth.

The relationship between attributes and variables is more complicated in the case of explanation and gets to the heart of the variable language of scientific theory. Here's a simple example involving two variables, *education* and *prejudice.* For the sake of simplicity, let's assume that the variable *education* has only two attributes: educated and uneducated. Similarly, let's give the variable *prejudice* two attributes: prejudiced and unprejudiced.

Now let's suppose that we have 20 people—10 are educated and 10 are uneducated. Let's also supposed that 90 percent of the uneducated are prejudiced, and the other 10 percent are unprejudiced, and that 30 percent of the educated people are prejudiced, and the other 70 percent are unprejudiced. This is illustrated graphically in Figure 1-5A.

Figure 1-5A illustrates a relationship or association between the variables *education* and *prejudice.* This relationship can be seen in terms of the pairings of attributes on the two variables. There are two predominant pairings: (1) those who are educated and unprejudiced and (2) those who are uneducated and prejudiced. Here are two other useful ways of viewing that relationship.

First, let's suppose that we play a game in which we bet on your ability to guess whether a

Figure 1-4
Variables and Attributes

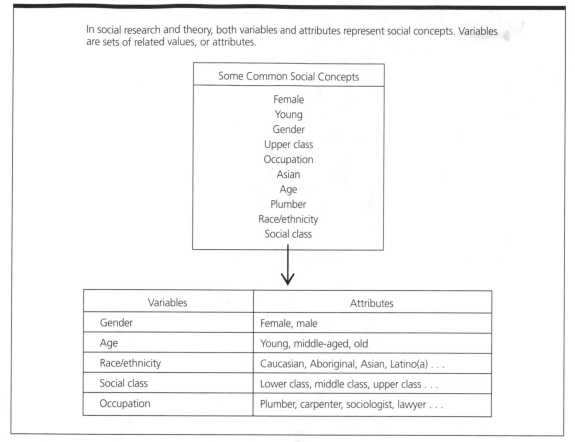

In social research and theory, both variables and attributes represent social concepts. Variables are sets of related values, or attributes.

Some Common Social Concepts

Female
Young
Gender
Upper class
Occupation
Asian
Age
Plumber
Race/ethnicity
Social class

Variables	Attributes
Gender	Female, male
Age	Young, middle-aged, old
Race/ethnicity	Caucasian, Aboriginal, Asian, Latino(a) . . .
Social class	Lower class, middle class, upper class . . .
Occupation	Plumber, carpenter, sociologist, lawyer . . .

person is prejudiced or unprejudiced. We'll pick the people one at a time (not telling you which ones we've picked), and you have to guess whether each person is prejudiced. We'll do it for all 20 people in Figure 1-5A. Your best strategy in this case would be to guess prejudiced each time, since 12 out of the 20 are categorized that way. Thus, you'll get 12 right and 8 wrong, for a net success of 4.

Now let's suppose that when we pick a person from the figure, we have to tell you whether the person is educated or uneducated. Your best strategy now would be to guess prejudiced for each uneducated person and unprejudiced for each educated person. If you followed that strategy, you'd get 16 right and 4 wrong. Your improvement in

guessing prejudice by knowing education is an illustration of what it means to say that variables are related.

Second, by contrast, let's consider how the 20 people would be distributed if education and prejudice were unrelated to each other. This is illustrated in Figure 1-5B. Recall that half the people are educated, and half are uneducated. Also notice that 12 of the 20 (60 percent) are prejudiced. If 6 of the 10 people in each group were prejudiced, we would conclude that the two variables were unrelated to each other. Then, knowing a person's education would not be of any value to you in guessing whether that person was prejudiced. Those who are educated are equally as prejudice as those who are uneducated.

Figure 1-5
Illustration of Relationship between Two Variables (Two Possibilities)

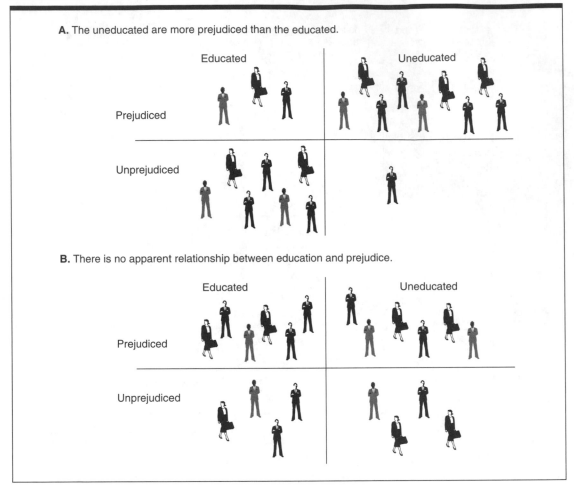

A. The uneducated are more prejudiced than the educated.

Educated

Uneducated

Prejudiced

Unprejudiced

B. There is no apparent relationship between education and prejudice.

Educated

Uneducated

Prejudiced

Unprejudiced

We'll be looking at the nature of relationships between variables in some depth in Part 4. In particular, we'll explore some of the ways relationships can be discovered and interpreted in research analysis. For now, though, a general understanding of relationships is important so you can appreciate the logic of social scientific theories.

Theories describe the relationships we might logically expect among variables. Often, the expectation involves the idea of causation. That is, a person's attributes on one variable are expected to cause, predispose, or encourage a particular attribute on another variable. In the example just

illustrated, we might theorize that a person's being educated or uneducated causes a lesser or greater likelihood of that person seeming prejudiced.

As we'll discuss in more detail later in the book, *education* and *prejudice* in this example would be regarded as **independent** and **dependent variables**, respectively. These two concepts are implicit in causal, or deterministic, models. In this example, we assume that the likelihood of being prejudiced is determined or caused by something. In other words, *prejudice* depends on something else, and so it is called the dependent variable. What the dependent variable depends on is an independent variable, in this case *education*. For the purposes of this study, *education* is an "independent" variable because it is independent of *prejudice* (that is people's level of education is not caused by whether or not they are prejudiced).

Of course, variations in levels of education, can, in turn, be found to depend on something else. People whose parents have a lot of education, for example, are more likely to get a lot of education than are people whose parents have little education. In this relationship, the subject's education is the dependent variable, and the parents' education is the independent variable. We can say the independent variable is the cause, the dependent variable the effect.

Returning to our first example, the discussion of Figure 1-5 has involved the interpretation of data. We looked at the distribution of the 20 people in terms of the two variables. In constructing a social scientific theory, we would derive an expectation regarding the relationship between the two variables based on what we know about each. We know, for example, that education exposes people to a wide range of cultural variation and to diverse points of view—in short, it broadens their perspectives. Prejudice, on the other hand, represents a narrower perspective. Logically, then, we might expect education and prejudice to be somewhat incompatible. We might, therefore, arrive at an expectation that increasing education would reduce the occurrence of prejudice, an expectation that would be supported by the observations.

Since Figure 1-5 illustrates two possibilities—that education reduces the likelihood of prejudice or that it has no effect—you might be interested in seeing some real data. As one measure of prejudice, in a survey of Edmonton, Alberta students in 1992 (seven years after graduating high school), each was asked to express how he or she felt about the opinion that "Too many immigrants have been getting jobs in Canada." The students used a scale that ranged from (1) strongly disagree to (5) strongly agree (with 3 indicating a neutral position). The researchers combined question responses of 1 and 2 to create the category of positive attitudes toward immigrants and responses of 4 and 5 to create a category of negative attitudes toward immigrants. Those whose response was 3 were categorized as holding neutral attitudes. About 38 percent of the sample held positive attitudes, 31 percent negative attitudes, and 31 percent neutral attitudes.

This data comes from an analysis conducted by Sorensen and Krahn (1996) to test whether higher education produces more liberal attitudes toward immigrants. As we'll see later in the book, their analysis was more complex than the data we present here displays. For now, however, let's look at a partial result from their report.

Table 1-1 presents an analysis of those data, grouping respondents according to their levels of educational attainment. The easiest way to read this table is to focus on the last column of percentages: those holding negative attitudes. Negative attitudes toward immigrants were held by over 50 percent of the respondents with no postsecondary education, while only about 23 percent of those with postsecondary education expressed negative attitudes toward immigrants. This finding supports the view that education reduces prejudice, as prejudice was measured here.

Table 1-1

Education and Attitudes toward Immigrants

Educational Level of Respondents	Attitudes toward Immigrants			
	Positive	Neutral	Negative	
No Postsecondary Education	19.7%	29.5%	50.8%	100% (121)
Postsecondary Education	44.9	31.7	23.4	100% (276)

Adapted from Sorensen and Krahn, 1996:10.

Notice that the theory has to do with the two variables *education* and *prejudice,* not with people as such. People are the carriers of those two variables, so the relationship between the variables can only be seen when we observe people. Ultimately, however, the theory uses a language of variables. It describes the associations that we might logically expect to exist between particular attributes of different variables.

Some Dialectics of Social Research

There is no one way to do social research. (If there were, this would be a much shorter book.) In fact, much of the power and potential of social research lies in the many valid approaches it comprises.

Four broad and interrelated distinctions, however, underlie the variety of research approaches. Although these distinctions can be seen as competing choices, a good social researcher learns each of these orientations. What we mean by the "dialectics" of social research, therefore, is that there is a fruitful tension between the complementary concepts we are about to describe.

Idiographic and Nomothetic Explanation

All of us go through life explaining things. We do it every day. You explain why you did poorly or well on an exam, why your favourite team is winning or losing, why you may be having trouble getting dates you enjoy. In our everyday explanations, we engage in two distinct forms of causal reasoning, though we do not ordinarily distinguish them.

Sometimes we attempt to explain a single situation exhaustively. Thus, for example, you may have done poorly on an exam because (1) you had forgotten there was an exam that day, (2) it was in your worst subject, (3) a traffic jam made you late for class, (4) your roommate had kept you up the night before the exam with loud music, (5) the police kept you until dawn demanding to know what you had done with your roommate's stereo—and what you had done with your roommate, for that matter, and (6) a wild band of coyotes ate your

textbook. Given all these circumstances, it's no wonder that you did poorly.

This type of causal reasoning is called an **idiographic** explanation. *Idio-* in this context means unique, separate, peculiar, or distinct, as in the word *idiosyncrasy.* When we have completed an idiographic explanation, we feel that we fully understand the causes of what happened in this particular instance. At the same time, the scope of our explanation is limited to the single case at hand. While parts of the idiographic explanation might apply to other situations, our intention is to explain one case fully.

Now consider a different kind of explanation. (1) Every time you study with a group, you do better on the exam than if you study alone. (2) Your favourite team does better at home than on the road. (3) Fraternity and sorority members get more dates than members of the biology club. This type of explanation—labelled **nomothetic**—seeks to explain a class of situations or events rather than a single one. Moreover, it seeks to explain "economically," using only one or just a few explanatory factors. Finally, it settles for a partial rather than a full explanation.

In each of these examples, you might qualify your causal statements with such words or phrases as "on the whole," "usually," or "all else being equal." Thus, you usually do better on exams when you've studied in a group, but not always. Similarly, your team has won some games on the road and lost some at home. And the attractive head of the biology club may get lots of dates, while the homely members of fraternities and sororities may spend a lot of Saturday nights alone reading. Such exceptions are accepted in the trade-off for a broader range of overall explanation. As we noted earlier, patterns are real and important even when they are not perfect.

Both the idiographic and the nomothetic approaches to understanding can be useful to you in your daily life. The nomothethic patterns you discover might offer a good guide for planning your study habits, for example, while the idiographic explanation might be more convincing to your parole officer.

By the same token, both idiographic and nomothetic reasoning are powerful tools for social research. Consider first idiographic reasoning. The researcher who seeks an exhaustive understanding of the inner workings of a particular juvenile gang, a particular criminal actor, or the particular reasons why a given region desires to secede from or join a country engages in idiographic research: She or he tries to understand that particular group, individual, or event as fully as possible.

David Mackenzie (1986), for example, undertook an in-depth study of the reasons behind Newfoundland's entrance into confederation in 1949—both why Canada accepted Newfoundland and the decision of Newfoundland to join. He detailed all the intricate aspects of this specific union, for instance the evolution of Canadian policy toward Newfoundland, the key political actors involved, and the major role that World War II played. His goal was to fully understand the history of the decision in this particular case. His was an idiographic approach to understanding.

One might also undertake a study of the specific and detailed reasons behind the actions of a single criminal actor, for example, the serial killer Paul Bernardo who was caught and convicted in Ontario in the 1990s. An attempt to fully understand his particular behaviour would be an idiographic approach.

Often, however, researchers aim at a more generalized understanding across a class of events, even though the level of understanding is inevitably less complete with respect to any one case. In other words, they seek a nomothetic explanation. For example, researchers who seek to uncover the chief factors leading to juvenile delinquency are pursuing a nomothetic inquiry. They might discover that children from broken homes are more likely to be delinquent than those from intact families. This explanation would extend well beyond any single child, but it would do so at the expense of a complete explanation of any one child's delinquency.

In contrast to Mackenzie's idiographic approach to the study of Newfoundland, Susan Tiano (1994) sought to understand the overall impact of Third-World industrialization on the status of women. Does the movement by women into the industrial labour force signify liberation or oppression? Her survey of women factory workers in Mexico illustrates the nomothetic approach to understanding.

Excessive attachment to any one approach to a given issue arguably limits our understanding of it. In 1989, Laxer critiqued the current level of understanding of Canadian political economy on this ground. He critiqued what he saw as two dominant approaches to understanding Canadian political economy. Each side, he said, was wedded to extreme opposite positions—"the two ends of the pole of idiographic and nomothetic inquiry" p. 186.

> The two perspectives share few common assumptions. For many Marxists, Canada is largely a place in which to demonstrate the workings of general Marxist laws. They are the nomothetic 'internationalist' theorists. On the other side, the new political economists start from nationalist and historical assumptions and emphasize the uniqueness of Canadian political and economic structures. Issues are explained by external influences and factors which are peculiar to Canada. They are the idiographic historians.
>
> (p. 179)

He ultimately argues that each approach would benefit from dialogue with the other—that a balance between these two approaches would provide a better understanding of Canadian political economy. As he says,

> There are ways to bridge the bifurcation of the uniqueness versus general laws approaches in Canadian political economy. The comparative-historical method is a promising approach. Instead of assuming that either everything in Canada is unique or else that nothing in Canada is unique, we can do comparative work on a whole range of questions to see in what ways events and patterns in Canada are similar to and different from those in other countries.
>
> (p. 188)

Thus, a combination of approaches can also prove very useful in many instances.

As you've just seen, social scientists can access two distinct kinds of explanation. Just as physicists sometimes treat light as a particle and other times as a wave, so social scientists can search for broad patterns of relationships today and probe the narrowly particular tomorrow. Both are good science, both are rewarding, and both can be fun.

Inductive and Deductive Theory

Like the idiographic and nomothetic forms of explanation, inductive and deductive thinking both play a role in our daily lives. They, too, represent an important variation in social research.

There are two routes to the conclusion that you do better on exams if you study with others. On the one hand, you might find yourself puzzling, halfway through your university career, why you do so well on exams sometimes but poorly at other times. You might list all the exams you've taken, noting how well you did on each. Then you might try to recall any circumstances shared by all the good exams and by all the poor ones. Did you do better on multiple-choice exams or essay exams? Morning exams or afternoon exams? Exams in the natural sciences, the humanities, or the social sciences? Times when you studied alone or . . . SHAZAM! It occurs to you that you have almost always done best on exams when you studied with others. This mode of inquiry is known as *induction.*

Inductive reasoning, or **induction**, moves from the particular to the general, from a set of specific observations to the discovery of a pattern that represents some degree of order among all the given events. Notice, incidentally, that your discovery doesn't necessarily tell you *why* the pattern exists—just that it does.

On the other hand, you might arrive at the same conclusion about studying for exams in a very different way. Imagine approaching your first set of exams in university. You wonder about the best ways to study—how much you should review the readings, how much to focus on class notes. You learn that some students prepare by rewriting their notes in an orderly fashion. Then you consider whether to study at a measured pace or pull an all-nighter just before the exam. Among these kinds of musings, you might ask whether you should get together with other students in the class or just study on your own. You could evaluate the pros and cons of both options.

Studying with others might not be as efficient, because a lot of time might be spent on things you already understand. On the other hand, you can understand something even better when you've explained it to someone else. And other students might understand parts of the course you haven't gotten yet. Several minds can reveal perspectives that might have escaped you. Also, your commitment to study with others makes it more likely that you'll study rather than decide to watch the music video channel.

In this fashion, you might add up the pros and cons and conclude, logically, that you'd benefit from studying with others. It seems reasonable to you, the way it seems reasonable that you'll do better if you study rather than not. Sometimes, we say things like this are true "in theory." To complete the process, we test whether they're true in practice. For a complete test, you might study alone for half your exams and study with others for the other exams. This procedure would test your logical reasoning.

This second mode of inquiry, known as deductive reasoning or **deduction,** moves from the general to the specific. It moves from (1) a pattern that might be logically or theoretically expected to (2) observations that test whether the expected pattern actually occurs. Notice that deduction begins with "why" and moves to "whether," while induction moves in the opposite direction.

These two very different approaches are both valid avenues for science. Moreover, they often work together to provide ever more powerful and complete understandings.

Notice, by the way, that the distinction between deductive and inductive reasoning is not necessarily linked to the distinction between nomothetic and idiographic modes of explanation. These four characterizations represent four possibilities, in everyday life as much as in social research.

For example, idiographically and deductively, you might prepare for a particular date by taking into account everything you know about the person you're dating, trying to anticipate logically how you can prepare—what kinds of clothing, behaviour, hairstyle, oral hygiene, and so forth are likely to produce a successful date. Or, idiographically and inductively, you might try to figure out what it was exactly that caused your date to call 911.

A nomothetic, deductive approach arises when you coach others on your "rules of dating," when you wisely explain why their dates will be impressed to hear them expound on the dangers of satanic messages concealed in rock and roll lyrics. When you later review your life and wonder why you didn't date more musicians, you might engage in nomothetic induction.

We'll return to induction and deduction in Chapter 2. Let's turn now to a third broad distinction that generates rich variations in social research.

Quantitative and Qualitative Data

The distinction between quantitative and qualitative data in social research is essentially the distinction between numerical and nonnumerical data. When we say someone is attractive, we've made a qualitative assertion. When we say he or she is a "9" on a scale from 1 to 10, we are attempting to quantify that qualitative assessment. Similarly, when an ice skater's performance is evaluated as an "8" on a scale of 10, the judge is attempting to quantify her or his qualitative assessment of the performance.

Every observation is qualitative at the outset, whether it is our experience of someone's attractiveness, our assessment of someone's artistic or athletic ability, the location of a pointer on a measuring scale, or a check mark entered in a questionnaire. None of these things is inherently numerical or quantitative, but sometimes it is useful to convert them to a numerical form.

Quantification often makes our observations more explicit. It also can make it easier to aggregate, compare, and summarize data. Further, it opens up the possibility of statistical analyses, ranging from simple averages to complex formulas and mathematical models.

Quantitative data, then, have the advantages that numbers have over words as measures of some quality. On the other hand, they also have the disadvantages that numbers have, including a potential loss of richness of meaning. For example, a social researcher might want to know whether university students aged 18–22 tend to date people older or younger than themselves. A quantitative answer to this question seems easily attained. The researcher asks a number of university students how old each of their dates has been, calculates an average, and compares it with the age of the subject. Case closed.

Or is it? While "age" here represents the number of years people have been alive, sometimes people use the term differently; perhaps for some "age" really means "maturity." Though your dates may tend to be younger than you, you may date people who act more maturely and thus represent the same "age." Or someone might see "age" as how young or old your dates look or maybe the degree of variation in their life experiences and worldliness. These latter meanings would be lost in the quantitative calculation of average age. In short, qualitative data can be richer in meaning than quantified data. This is implicit in the cliché, "He is older than his years." The poetic meaning of this expression would be lost in attempts to specify *how much* older.

On the other hand, qualitative data can have the disadvantages of purely verbal descriptions. For example, the richness of meaning we just mentioned is partly a function of ambiguity. If the expression "older than his years" meant something to you when you read it, that meaning arises from your own experiences, from people you have known who might fit the description of being "older than their years" or perhaps the times you have heard others use that expression. Two things are certain: (1) the expression probably doesn't mean exactly the same thing to you as it does to either of us (2) you don't know exactly what either of us means by the expression and vice versa.

Earl Babbie has a young friend, Ray Zhang, who was responsible for communications at the 1989 freedom demonstrations in Tiananmen Square, Beijing. Following the Army clampdown, Ray fled south, was arrested, and then released with orders to return to Beijing. Instead, he escaped from China and made his way to Paris. Eventually, he went to the United States, where he resumed the graduate studies he had been forced to abandon in fleeing his homeland. Ray has had to deal with the difficulties of getting enrolled in school without any transcripts from China, studying in a foreign language, meeting his financial needs, all on his own, thousands of miles from his family. Ray still speaks of one day returning to China to build a system of democracy.

You'll probably agree that Ray is someone who seems to be "older than his years" and worldly in his experiences. This qualitative description, while it fleshes out the meaning of the phrase, still does not equip us to say *how much older* or even to compare two people in these terms without the risk of disagreeing as to which one is more "worldly."

It might be possible to quantify this concept, however. For example, we might establish a list of life experiences that would contribute to what we mean by worldliness, for example:

Getting married
Getting divorced
Losing a parent to a lingering, fatal illness
Seeing a murder committed
Being arrested
Being exiled
Being fired from a job
Becoming homeless

We might quantify people's worldliness as the number of such experiences they've had: the more such experiences, the more worldly we'd say they were. If we thought of some experiences as more powerful than others, we could give those experiences more points. Once we had made our list and point system, scoring people and comparing their worldliness on a numerical scale would be straightforward. We would have no difficulty agreeing on who had more points than whom.

To quantify a nonnumerical concept like worldliness, then, we need to be explicit about what the concept means. By focusing specifically on what we'll include in our measurement of the concept, however, we also exclude any other meanings. Inevitably, then, we face a trade-off: Any explicated, quantitative measure will be less rich in meaning than the corresponding qualitative description.

What a dilemma! Which approach should we choose? Which is better? Which is more appropriate to social research?

The good news is that we don't need to choose. In fact, we shouldn't. Both qualitative and quantitative methods are useful and legitimate in social research. Some research situations and topics are most amenable to qualitative examination, others to quantification, and still others that would be best studied by using a combination of both approaches.

At the same time, you'll find that these two approaches call for different skills and procedures. As a result, you may feel more comfortable with—and become more adept in—one or the other. You'll be a stronger researcher, however, to the extent that you can effectively use both approaches. Certainly, all researchers, whatever their personal inclinations, should recognize the legitimacy of both.

Finally, you may have noticed that the qualitative approach seems more aligned with idiographic explanations, while nomothetic explanations are more easily achieved through quantification. Although this is true, these relationships are not absolute. Moreover, both approaches present considerable "grey area." Recognizing the distinction between qualitative and quantitative research doesn't mean that you must identify your research activities with one to the exclusion of the other. A complete understanding of a topic often requires both techniques.

Pure and Applied Research

From the beginning, social scientists have shown two distinct motivations: understanding and application. On the one hand, they are fascinated by the nature of human social life and are driven to explain it, to make sense out of apparent chaos. *Pure* research in all scientific fields finds justification in "knowledge for knowledge's sake."

At the same time, perhaps inspired by their subject matter, social scientists are committed to having what they learn make a difference—to see their knowledge of society put into action. Sometimes they focus on making things better. If one of us studies prejudice, for example, we'd like what we discover to result in a more tolerant society.

This is no different from the AIDS researcher trying to defeat that disease.

Applied social scientists, however, put their research into practice in many immediate and direct ways as well. Experiments and surveys, for example, can be used in marketing products. In-depth interviewing techniques can be especially useful in social work encounters. Chapter 13 of this book deals with evaluation research, by which social scientists determine the effectiveness of social interventions.

As with each of the other dialectics just discussed, some social scientists are more inclined toward pure research, others toward application. Ultimately, both orientations are valid and vital elements in social research as a whole.

The Ethics of Social Research

Most of this book is devoted to the logic and skills of doing social research, the various techniques preferred by social researchers and the reasons why researchers value them. There are, however, some vital nonscientific concerns that shape the activities of social researchers. A key concern is the matter of ethics in research.

We'll deal extensively with research ethics in Part 3, when we cover modes of observation. Other parts of the book will refer to ethical issues as appropriate. Here, we want to introduce two basic ethical issues to keep in mind as you read the first two sections of the book, because ethical considerations affect decisions at all levels of the social research process.

No Harm to Subjects

The foremost ethical rule of social research is that it brings *no harm to research subjects.* This rule is one that everyone would agree with in principle, however, it's sometimes difficult to follow it absolutely.

Suppose, for example, some of the people that researchers interview about their religious views realize for the first time that they have doubts about their religion. Or suppose a study of treatment of women in a society leads some women to become unhappy with their jobs or marriages. When does investigating a subject do harm by affecting the people who take part in the study?

As you'll see, abiding by this seemingly simple ethical rule requires vigilance on the part of researchers. In designing your own studies, be sure to ask yourself whether your research could harm the people you intend to study. Since everything we do in life *could possibly* harm someone else, all researchers must weigh the relative risk against the importance and possible benefits of the research activity.

Social researchers have many ways to guard against harming people. For example, we are careful to respect the privacy of subjects. Research often requires our learning private details of people's lives, and we are committed to maintain the *confidentiality* of what we learn. Often we collect information *anonymously*, so there is no way of identifying the individual with the information they voluntarily provide, thus preventing even the accidental release of information.

You'll see that while deception is often necessary in the execution of some kinds of research projects, researchers are committed to avoiding deception except when it's inescapable. (For example if you introduce a survey or experiment by saying, "We want to learn how prejudiced you are," the subjects will likely modify what they do and say, so as to appear unprejudiced.) When it's deemed necessary to deceive people as to our research purposes, however, we must ask whether the potential value of the research justifies the act of deception.

Voluntary Participation

Another basic ethical rule of social research is that *participation should be voluntary.* Again, in principle, this appears to be a pretty simple rule to follow. A researcher who forced people to participate in the experiment or survey would be roundly criticized. When someone calls and asks you to participate in a telephone survey, you're free to refuse.

Yet things are not always so clear-cut. When we formally observe a campus demonstration, we do not ask for permission from all the participants. When a researcher pretends to join a religious cult to do research on it, those being observed have not volunteered for the research project. Social researchers often debate whether a particular research design did or did not violate established research ethics.

The issue of voluntary participation can arise even when you ask for and receive written permission from your participants. I (Benaquisto 2000), for example, conducted a study concerning views on issues of crime, punishment, and sentencing. I sought full and informed consent from each participant. Each was given a sheet of paper that explained the study's purpose and a consent form to sign giving me permission to obtain some personal information about them and indicating their agreement to voluntarily participate in the study. They were also told that they were free to withdraw from the study at any time. The people I studied, however, were male prison inmates in Canadian federal institutions. Given the population I was studying, it was very important to keep in mind a number of issues that might interfere with obtaining true voluntary participation. For instance, one central concern was the possibility that some of the inmates were illiterate, and many people who are unable to read are reluctant to admit it. In terms of the study, this not only raises ethical concerns but also could have significant impact on the outcome. First, to what extent can someone who signs a consent form without knowing what it says be participating voluntarily? Second, unable to read the form and embarrassed to admit it, the person may refuse the study rather than sign a form he or she doesn't understand. Therefore, having gained some information about the group under study before beginning the interviews, I was aware of such potential problems and attempted to avoid them by having the forms read to the inmates as a matter of course, rather than giving them the form to read and sign on their own. In addition, the inmates were encouraged to ask questions and an attempt was made to determine that they understood what they were being told.

Another concern regarding voluntary participation that this study illustrates has to do with unsaid expectations. It's often a concern that people in controlled environments, such as prisons or

mental asylums, might believe that cooperation and participation in a research study would somehow benefit them personally—or that non-participation will produce negative consequences for them. It was therefore very important that every inmate be told that participating in the study would in no way help him personally and that the research was completely independent of the prison administration (this helps to guarantee them confidentiality as well). It's impossible to know with certainty the reasons someone volunteers to participate in a study, however, when possible, we as researchers have a responsibility to do all we can to try to insure true voluntary participation.

As we continue examining the many aspects of social research, you'll see the great complexity of ethical issues and the seriousness of ethical concerns. This seriousness is evident in the codes of ethics created and published by professional associations whose members engage in social research and by government agencies that fund such research. It is a topic that certainly deserves your attention and one that will be taken up at length in Part 3.

These, then, are some of the foundations of social research. We hope this discussion has helped to show how social science is anything but routine or boring. At its best, it is a vibrant, exciting, and important activity. All we need is an open mind and a sense of adventure.

Main Points

- This book's subject is how we find out about social reality.
- Inquiry is a natural human activity. Much of ordinary human inquiry seeks to explain events and predict future events.
- Much of what we know, we know by agreement rather than by experience. Two important sources of agreed-upon knowledge are tradition and authority. However, these useful sources of knowledge can lead us astray.
- When we understand through direct experience, we make observations and seek patterns of regularities in what we observe.

- Science seeks to protect against mistakes we make in day-to-day inquiry.
- Whereas we often observe inaccurately, researchers seek to avoid such errors by making observation a careful and deliberate activity.
- Sometimes we jump to general conclusions on the basis of only a few observations, so scientists seek to avoid overgeneralization by committing themselves to a sufficient number of observations and by replicating studies.
- In everyday life, we sometimes reason illogically. Researchers seek to avoid illogical reasoning by being as careful and deliberate in their reasoning as in their observations. Moreover, the public nature of science means that others are always there to challenge faulty reasoning.
- Social theory attempts to discuss and explain what is, not what should be. Theory should not be confused with philosophy or belief.
- Social science looks for regularities in social life.
- Social scientists are interested in explaining human aggregates, not individuals.
- Theories are written in the language of variables. A variable is a logical set of attributes. An attribute is a characteristic, such as male or female. Gender, for example, is a variable made up of these attributes.
- In causal explanation, the presumed cause is the independent variable, while the affected variable is the dependent variable.
- Idiographic explanations seek to understand specific cases fully, whereas nomothetic explanations seek a generalized understanding of many cases.
- Inductive theories reason from specific observations to general patterns.
- Deductive theories start from general statements and predict specific observations.
- Quantitative data are numerical; qualitative data are not. Both types of data are useful for different research purposes.
- Both pure and applied research are valid and vital parts of the social scientific enterprise.
- Ethics is a key consideration in the design of social research. Two fundamental ethical guidelines are that participation in social research be voluntary and that no harm should come to research subjects.

Review Questions and Exercises

1. Review the common errors of human inquiry discussed in this chapter. Find a magazine or newspaper article, or perhaps a letter to the editor, that illustrates one of these errors. Discuss how a scientist would have avoided it.
2. List five social variables and the attributes they comprise.
3. Go to one of the following Web sites and find examples of both qualitative and quantitative data.
   a. National Archives of Canada – Archives nationales du Canada
      http://www.archives.ca/
   b. UN High Commissioner for Refugees
      http://www.unhcr.ch/
   c. National Library of Australia
      http://www.nla.gov.au/
   d. Inter-University Consortium for Political and Social Research (ICPSR)
      http://www.icpsr.umich.edu

Continuity Project

To demonstrate the interconnections among the various elements of social research, you might want to apply the materials of each successive chapter to a single research project. We'll suggest here the topic of *gender equality/inequality*, but your instructor may suggest something different.

In the context of this first chapter, you might consider how this topic could be approached with a qualitative or a quantitative orientation. What would be some quantitative indicators of the equality or inequality of men and women? How could you observe indicators of equality/inequality qualitatively?

Additional Readings

Babbie, Earl. *The Sociological Spirit.* Belmont, CA: Wadsworth, 1994. This book is a primer in some sociological points of view. It introduces you to many of the concepts commonly used in the social sciences.

Becker, Howard S. *Tricks of the Trade: How to Think about Your Research while You're Doing It.* Chicago: University of Chicago Press, 1997. This very approachable book offers an excellent "feel" for the enterprise of social scientific research, whether qualitative or quantitative.

Gallup, George Jr., Burns Roper, Daniel Yankelovich, et al. "Polls that Made a Difference." *The Public Perspective,* May/June 1990, pp. 17–21. Several public opinion researchers talk about social research polls that have had an important impact on everyday life.

Hoover, Kenneth R. *The Elements of Social Scientific Thinking.* New York: St. Martin's Press, 1992. Hoover presents an excellent overview of the key elements in social scientific analysis.

Steele, Stephen F., and Joyce Miller Iutcovich, eds. *Directions in Applied Sociology,* Arnold, MD: Society for Applied Sociology, 1997. This book contains the presidential addresses of 11 presidents of the Society for Applied Sociology and provides an excellent overview of the issues involved in the application of social science knowledge.

InfoTrac: You can find further relevant readings on the World Wide Web at

http://sociology.wadsworth.com

Chapter 2

Paradigms, Theory, and Research

Social scientific theory is an interplay of theory and research, logic and observation, induction and deduction—and the fundamental frames of reference known as paradigms.

In this chapter . . .

Introduction

"Research findings" based only on the observation of patterns are insufficient. Unless we can offer logical explanations for such patterns, the regularities we've observed may be mere flukes, chance occurrences. If you flip coins long enough, you'll get 10 heads in a row. Scientists might adapt a street expression to describe this situation: "Patterns happen."

Theories seek to provide logical explanations of these patterns. Theories function three ways in research. First, they prevent our being taken in by flukes. If we can't explain why polls like Ma's Diner have been so successful in predicting elections, we run the risk of supporting a fluke. If we know why it has happened, we can anticipate whether or not it will be successful in the future.

Second, theories can shape and direct research efforts, pointing toward likely discoveries through empirical observation. If you were looking for your lost keys on a dark street, you could whip your flashlight around randomly, hoping to chance upon the errant keys—or you could use your memory of where you had been to limit your search to more likely areas. Theories, by analogy, direct researchers' flashlights where they are most likely to observe interesting patterns of social life.

Finally, theories make sense of observed patterns in a way that can suggest other possibilities. If we understand the reasons why broken homes produce more juvenile delinquency than intact homes—lack of supervision, for example—we can take effective action, such as after-school youth programs in this case.

While theories seek to provide logical explanations, not all social science research seeks to explain. Some research is conducted for the purpose of description—for example, what is social life like in an Inuit community—or to determine if a social program is effective or not. Still other research may be conducted to find out the general public's opinion on an issue. Therefore, not all research is tightly linked to theory. Nonetheless, many researchers do seek to explain—they want to know why. Theory is directly relevant to "why" questions. Therefore, in this chapter, we're going to explore some specific ways theory and research work hand in hand during the adventure of inquiry into social life. We'll begin by looking at some fundamental frames of reference, called *paradigms*, that underlie social theories and inquiry.

Some Social Science Paradigms

There is usually more than one way to make sense of things. Different points of view usually yield different explanations. In daily life, for example, liberals and conservatives often explain the same phenomenon—the existence of homeless people, for example—quite differently. So might atheists and Christians. But, underlying these different explanations, or theories, are **paradigms**—the fundamental models or frames of reference we use to organize our observations and reasoning.

Paradigms are often hard to recognize as such because they are so implicit, assumed, taken for granted. They seem more like "the way things are" than like one possible point of view among many. Here's an illustration of what we mean.

Where do you stand on the issue of human rights? Do you feel that the individual human being is sacred? Are there some things that no government should do to its citizens? More concretely, how do you feel about using civilians as human shields in wartime to protect military targets or organized programs of rape and murder in support of "ethnic cleansing"?

Those of us who are horrified and incensed by such practices will probably find it hard to see our individualistic paradigm as only one of many possible viewpoints. Yet, many cultures view the Western commitment to the sanctity of the individual as bizarre. Historically, it is decidedly a minority viewpoint. There are those who believe that the "rights" of families and society at large, for example, should be held in higher regard than those of individuals. As some world leaders point out, adhering to a belief in the sanctity of individuals has its costs in their view—for instance the high crime rates and social disorganization that Western societies experience.

We are not trying to change your viewpoint on individual human dignity. It's useful, however, to recognize that our views and feelings in this matter are the result of the paradigm in which we have been socialized; they are not an objective fact of nature. All of us operate within many such paradigms. For example, the traditional Western view of the actual world as an objective reality distinct from our individual experiences of it is a deeply ingrained paradigm.

There are benefits in recognizing that we are operating within a paradigm. First, we are better able to understand the seemingly bizarre views and actions of others who are operating from a different paradigm. Second, we can sometimes profit from stepping outside our paradigm. It opens our eyes to new ways of seeing and explaining things. That's not possible if we mistake our paradigm for reality.

Paradigms play a fundamental role in science, just as they do in daily life. Thomas Kuhn (1970) drew attention to the role of paradigms in the history of the natural sciences. Major scientific paradigms have included such fundamental viewpoints as Newtonian mechanics, Einstein's relativity, Darwin's theory of evolution, and Copernicus's conception of the earth moving around the sun (instead of the reverse). Which scientific theories "make sense" depends on which paradigm scientists are maintaining.

While we sometimes think of science as developing gradually over time, marked by important discoveries and inventions, Kuhn says scientific paradigms typically become entrenched, resisting any substantial change. Thus, theories and research alike take a certain fundamental direction. Eventually, however, as the shortcomings of a particular paradigm became obvious, a new one emerges and supplants the old one. The seemingly natural view that the rest of the universe revolves around the earth, for example, compelled astronomers to devise ever more elaborate ways to account for the motions of heavenly bodies that they actually observed. This paradigm was eventually supplanted by the view that the earth and other planets revolve around the sun. This was nothing less than a revolutionary change in perspective that fundamentally altered the direction of theory and research. Kuhn's classic book on this subject is titled, appropriately enough, *The Structure of Scientific Revolutions.*

Social scientists have developed several paradigms for understanding social behaviour. The fate of supplanted paradigms in the social sciences, however, has differed from what Kuhn has observed in the natural sciences. Natural scientists generally believe that the succession from one paradigm to another represents progress from a false view to a true one. No modern astronomer believes that the sun revolves around the earth, for example.

In the social sciences, on the other hand, theoretical paradigms may gain or lose popularity, but they're seldom discarded completely. The paradigms of the social sciences offer a variety of views, each of which offers insights the others lack—but ignores aspects of social life that the others reveal.

Thus, each of the paradigms we are about to examine offers a different way of looking at human social life. Each makes certain assumptions about the nature of social reality. For our purposes, we'll briefly discuss the paradigms in a general fashion, focusing on some of the key assumptions that characterize and distinguish them. (When you come to examine such paradigms as presented by various authors, you will discover that there are variations and amendments within each of the general perspectives we are about to discuss.) Ultimately, paradigms are not true or false; as ways of looking, they are only more or less useful. Each can open up new understandings, suggest different kinds of theories, and inspire different kinds of research.

Macrotheory and Microtheory

Let's begin with a distinction concerning focus that stretches across many of the paradigms we'll discuss. Some social theorists focus their attention on society at large, or at least on large portions of it. Topics of study for such **macrotheory** include the struggle among economic classes in a society, international relations, or the interrelations among major institutions in society, such as government, religion, and family. Macrotheory deals with large, aggregate entities of society or even whole societies.

Some scholars have taken a more intimate view of social life. **Microtheory** deals with issues of social life at the level of individuals and small groups. Dating behaviour, jury deliberations, and student-faculty interactions are apt subjects for a microtheoretical perspective. Such studies often come close to the realm of psychology, but whereas psychologists typically focus on what goes on inside humans, social scientists study what goes on *between* them.

The distinction between macro- and microtheory cuts across the paradigms we'll examine. Some of them, such as symbolic interactionism and ethnomethodology, are more often limited to the microlevel. Others, such as the conflict paradigm, can be pursued at either the micro- or the macrolevel.

Early Positivism

When the French philosopher Auguste Comte (1798–1857) coined the term *sociologie* in 1822, he launched an intellectual adventure that is still unfolding today. Most important, Comte identified society as a phenomenon that can be studied scientifically. (Initially, he wanted to label his enterprise "social physics," but that term was taken over by another scholar.)

Prior to Comte's time, society simply *was.* To the extent that people recognized different kinds of societies or changes in society over time, religious paradigms generally predominated in explanations of such differences. The state of social affairs was often seen as a reflection of God's will. Alternatively, people were challenged to create a "City of God" on earth to replace sin and godlessness.

Comte separated his inquiry from religion. He felt that religious belief could be replaced with scientific study and objectivity. His "positive philosophy" postulated three stages of history. A "theological stage" predominated throughout the world until about 1300. During the next five hundred years, a "metaphysical stage" replaced God with philosophical ideas such as "nature" and "natural law."

Comte felt he was launching the third stage of history, in which science would replace religion and metaphysics by basing knowledge on observations through the five senses rather than on belief or logic alone. Comte felt that society could be observed and then explained logically and rationally, and that sociology could be as scientific as biology or physics.

Comte's view that society could be studied scientifically came to form the foundation for subsequent development of the social sciences. In his optimism for the future, he coined the term *positivism* to describe this scientific approach—in contrast to what he regarded as negative elements in the Enlightenment. As we'll note later in this discussion, only in recent decades has the idea of positivism been seriously challenged.

Conflict Paradigm

Another social science paradigm arose from a radically new view of the evolution of capitalism. Karl Marx (1818–1883) suggested that social behaviour could best be seen as the process of conflict: the attempt to dominate others and to avoid being dominated. Marx primarily focused on the struggle among economic classes. Specifically, he examined the way capitalism produced the oppression of workers by the owners of industry. Marx's interest in this topic did not end with analytical study. He was also ideologically committed to restructuring economic relations to end the oppression he observed.

The conflict paradigm is not limited to economic analyses. Georg Simmel (1858–1918) was particularly interested in small-scale conflict, in contrast to the class struggle that interested Marx. Simmel noted, for example, that conflicts among members of a tightly knit group tended to be more intense than those among people who did not share feelings of belonging and intimacy.

In a more recent application of the conflict paradigm, when Michel Chossudovsky's (1997) analysis of the International Monetary Fund (IMF) and World Bank suggested that these two international organizations were increasing global poverty rather than eradicating it, he directed his attention to the competing interests involved in the process. In theory, the chief interest being served should be the poor people of the world or perhaps the impoverished, Third World nations. The researcher's inquiry, however, identified many other interested parties who benefited: the commercial lending institutions who made loans in conjunction with the IMF and World Bank and multinational corporations seeking cheap labour and markets for their goods, for example. Chossudovksy's analysis concluded that the interests of the banks and corporations tended to take precedence over those of the poor people, who were the intended beneficiaries. Moreover, he found many policies were weakening national economies in the Third World, as well as undermining democratic governments.

Whereas the conflict paradigm often focuses on class, gender, and ethnic struggles, it would be appropriate to apply it whenever different groups have competing interests. For example, it could be fruitfully applied to understanding relations among different departments in an organization, fraternity and sorority rush weeks, or student-faculty-administrative relations, to name just a few.

Symbolic Interactionism

In his overall focus, Georg Simmel differed from Marx. Whereas Marx chiefly addressed macrotheoretical issues—large institutions and whole societies in their evolution through the course of history—Simmel was more interested in how individuals interacted with one another. His interests were therefore with "micro" issues, focusing attention on aspects of social reality that are not visible in Marx's theory. He began by examining dyads (groups of two people) and triads (of three people), for example. Similarly, he wrote about "the web of group affiliations."

Simmel was one of the first European sociologists to influence the development of sociology in North America. His focus on the nature of interactions particularly influenced George Herbert Mead (1863–1931), Charles Horton Cooley (1864–1929), and others who took up the cause and developed it into a powerful paradigm for research.

Cooley, for example, introduced the idea of the "primary group," those intimate associates with whom we share a sense of belonging, such as our family, friendship cliques, and so forth. Cooley also wrote of the "looking-glass self" we form by looking into the reactions of people around us. If everyone treats us as beautiful, for example, we conclude that we are.

Notice how fundamentally the concepts and theoretical focus inspired by this paradigm differ from the society-level concerns of Marx.

Mead emphasized the importance of our human ability to "take the role of the other," imagining how others feel and how they might behave in certain circumstances. As we gain an idea of how people in general see things, we develop a sense of what Mead called the "generalized other."

Mead also had a special interest in the role of communications in human affairs. Most interactions, he felt, revolved around the process of individuals reaching a common understanding through the use of language and other symbolic systems, hence the term *symbolic interactionism*.

This paradigm can lend insights into the nature of interactions in ordinary social life, but it can also help us understand unusual forms of interaction, as in the following case. Emerson, Ferris, and Gardner (1998) set out to understand the nature of "stalking." Through interviews with numerous stalking victims, they came to identify different motivations among stalkers, stages in the development of a stalking scenario, how people can recognize if they are being stalked, and what they can do about it.

Ethnomethodology

While some social scientific paradigms emphasize the impact of social structure on human behaviour (for example, the effect of norms, values, control agents, and so forth), other paradigms do not. From Harold Garfinkel's (a contemporary sociologist) perspective, people are continually creating social structure through their actions and interactions—they are, in fact, creating their realities. Thus, when you and your instructor meet to discuss your term paper, even though there are myriad expectations about how you both should act, your conversation will differ somewhat from any of those that have occurred before, and how you each act will somewhat modify your future expectations. That is, discussing your term paper will impact the interactions each of you have with other professors and students in the future.

Given the tentativeness of reality in this view, Garfinkel suggests that people are continuously trying to make sense of the life they experience. In a way, he suggests that everyone is acting like a social scientist: hence the term *ethnomethodology,* or "methodology of the people."

How would you go about learning about people's expectations and how they make sense out of their world? One technique ethnomethodologists use is to *break the rules,* to violate people's expectations. Thus, if you try to talk to your professor about your term paper and he or she keeps talking about football, this might reveal the expectations you had for your professor's behaviour. We might also see how you make sense out of his or her behaviour. ("Maybe he or she's using football as an analogy for understanding social systems theory.")

In another example of ethnomethodology, Johen Heritage and David Greatbatch (1992) examined the role of applause in British political speeches: How did the speakers evoke applause, and what function did it serve (for example, to complete a topic)? Communications have often been the focus of research within the ethnomethodological paradigm.

There's no end to the opportunities you have for trying on the ethnomethodological paradigm. For instance, in one of my (Benaquisto) seminar courses on the topic, I begin by sitting down and throwing something across the room (either chalk, a book, or a pen). The class usually responds by giggling somewhat uncomfortably. If I wait a few seconds without saying anything, the students look around the table at each other not knowing quite what to do. Has she snapped? Is she angry about something? Should we be scared? Once I explain the reason for my action, the discomfort begins to subside and many act like they knew all along there was nothing to be concerned about.

You might try a few experiments of your own. When you are standing in line at the grocery store (or any number of other places), stand in line facing the person behind you instead of looking at the back of the head of the person in front of you. The next time you get on an elevator don't face front watching the floor numbers whip by (that's the norm or expected behaviour). Just stand quietly facing the rear (Bernard McGrane 1994). See how others react to your behaviour. Just as important, notice how you feel about it. If you try these experiments a few times, you should begin to develop a feel for the ethnomethodological paradigm.

At this point you may be asking yourself whether engaging in such experiments is ethical. If you aren't, you should be. We should consider the potential ethical issues that may arise in any of our attempts at social scientific inquiry. Given our preliminary discussion of ethics in Chapter 1, you may be questioning whether you should seek permission of the people in the elevator or the grocery store line before you try your experiment? One obvious problem with this is that if you told the people in the elevator or the line what you were planning to do and asked their permission, there would be little point in undertaking the experiment. You might next ask yourself whether such experiments would be likely to cause harm to those unwittingly a part of them? If you attempted such an experiment, should you end it at the point when one person shows discomfort or several people? Or do you wait until someone becomes visibly upset and agitated by your action? These issues, in addition to many others, must be considered. And, as you'll see in Part 3, there is often disagreement over what is or is not ethically acceptable in social science research. For now, you may want to discuss these potential experiments in class or with your peers to gain their perspective on the ethics of undertaking such actions.

Structural Functionalism

Structural functionalism, sometimes also known as "social systems theory," grows out of a notion introduced by Comte and others: A social entity, such as an organization or a whole society, can be viewed as an *organism*. Like other organisms, a social system is made up of parts, each of which contributes to the functioning of the whole.

By analogy, consider the human body. Each component—such as the heart, lungs, kidneys, skin, and brain—has a particular job to do. The body as a whole cannot survive unless each of these parts does its job, and none of the parts can survive except as a part of the whole body. Or consider an automobile, composed of tires, steering wheel, gas tank, spark plugs, and so forth. Each of the parts serves a function for the whole; taken together, that system can get us across town. None of the individual parts would be of much use to us by itself, however. The view of society as a social system, then, looks for the "functions" served by its various components.

Social scientists using the structural functional paradigm might note that the function of the police, for example, is to exercise social control—encouraging people to abide by the norms of society and bringing to justice those who do not. Notice, however, that they could just as reasonably ask what functions criminals serve in society. Within the functionalist paradigm, we might say that criminals serve as job security for the police. In a related observation, Emile Durkheim (1858–1917) suggested that crimes and their punishment provide an opportunity to reaffirm society's values. By catching and punishing a thief, we reaffirm our collective respect for private property.

To get a sense of the structural-functional paradigm, suppose you were interested in explaining how your college or university works. You might thumb through the institution's catalogue and begin assembling a list of the administrators and support staff (such as president, deans, registrar, campus security, maintenance personnel). You might then figure out what each of them does and relate their activities and roles to the chief functions of your institution, such as teaching or research? This way of looking at an educational institution would clearly suggest a different line of inquiry than, say, a conflict paradigm, which might focus upon the clash of interests between people who have power in the institution and those who don't.

People often discuss "functions" in everyday conversations. Typically, however, the alleged functions are seldom tested empirically. Some people argue, for example, that welfare, intended to help the poor, actually harms them in a variety of ways. For example, it is sometimes alleged that welfare encourages single women to have more children in order to increase their benefits and this only serves to increase their dependency. However, according to Mooney et al. (2001:346), "[r]esearch consistently shows that receiving welfare does not significantly increase out-of-wedlock births (Albeda and Tilley 1997)."

Feminist Paradigms

When Ralph Linton concluded his anthropological classic, *The Study of Man* (1937:490), speaking of "a store of knowledge that promises to give man a better life than any he has known," no one complained that he had left out *women*. Linton was using the linguistic conventions of his time; he implicitly included women in all his references to men. Or did he?

When feminists first began questioning the use of masculine pronouns whenever gender was ambiguous, their concerns were often viewed as petty, even silly. But, in all honesty, when you read Linton's words, did you picture a genderless human being, both men and women, or a male persona?

Researchers looking at the social world from a feminist paradigm have called attention to aspects of social life that are not revealed by other paradigms. In part, feminist theory and research have focused on gender differences and how they relate to the rest of social organization. These lines of inquiry have drawn attention to the oppression of women in a great many societies, which in turn shed light on oppression generally.

Feminist paradigms have also challenged the prevailing notions concerning consensus in society. Most descriptions of the predominant beliefs, values, and norms of a society are written by people representing only portions of society. In North America, for example, middle-class white men have typically written such analyses—not sur-

prisingly, they have written about the beliefs, values, and norms they themselves share. Because men and women have had very different social experiences throughout history, they have come to see things differently, with the result that their conclusions about social life vary in many ways. Though George Herbert Mead spoke of the "generalized other" that each of us becomes aware of and can "take the role of," feminist paradigms question whether such a *generalized* other even exists.

Further, whereas Mead used the example of learning to play baseball to illustrate how we learn about the generalized other, Janet Lever's research suggests that understanding the experience of boys may tell us little about girls.

> Girls' play and games are very different. They are mostly spontaneous, imaginative, and free of structure or rules. Turn-taking activities like jumprope may be played without setting explicit goals. Girls have far less experience with interpersonal competition. The style of their competition is indirect, rather than face to face, individual rather than team affiliated. Leadership roles are either missing or randomly filled.
>
> (Lever 1986:86)

Social researchers' growing recognition of the general intellectual differences between men and women led the psychologist Mary Field Belenky and her colleagues to speak of *Women's Ways of Knowing* (1986). In-depth interviews with 45 women led the researchers to distinguish five perspectives on knowing that challenged the view of inquiry as obvious and straightforward.

Among the perspectives on knowledge that were derived from their interviews were *subjective knowledge*—the idea that knowledge may derive from personal, subjective experiences, including intuition—and *constructed knowledge*—described by the authors as a "position in which women view all knowledge as contextual, experience themselves as creators of knowledge, and value both subjective and objective strategies for knowing" (Belenky et al. 1986:15).

These forms of knowledge are particularly interesting in the context of our previous discussions. The positivistic paradigm of Comte would have a place neither for "subjective knowledge" nor for the idea that truth might vary according to its context. The ethnomethodological paradigm, on the other hand, would accommodate these ideas. The value of subjectivity and context became increasingly important as a means of allowing the voice and experience of women to be heard and understood. If social science research was to incorporate women, then the methodology itself must be adapted to allow for women's voices. Some feminist researchers, therefore, advocated that positivist research was one of the roadblocks to the study and understanding of issues pertaining to women and their position in society.

Thus, out of feminist thought rose feminist methodology. For many, traditional, mainstream, positivist sociology—with its emphasis on objectivity and rationality—was inadequate for the study of women's issues. British sociologist Ann Oakley (1981), for example, argued that the traditional, scientific approach that emphasizes objectivity and rationality in interviews runs contrary to "feminist research requiring openness, engagement, and the development of a potentially long-lasting relationship" (Reinharz 1992:27). Dorothy Smith (1987) and others have stressed that the understanding of social life and its institutions has been represented from the standpoint of men. The social sciences must include women's experiences and standpoint as well and acknowledge men's overall dominance in society and the impact of their power and privilege. Such perspectives are an attempt to provide counters to the male worldview that dominates in theory and research.

Despite this general discussion of feminism, it is important to recognize that there is no single voice that can represent the feminist paradigm. There are a number of distinctions made within this paradigm that represent variation in feminist philosophies, such as liberal feminism, Marxist feminism, radical feminism, and cultural feminism. And, as Shulamit Reinharz (1992:4) writes in the introduction to her book, *Feminist Methods in Social Research,* there are a "multitude of feminist research voices." In essence, the very idea of trying to say "what feminist research is" runs counter to many feminist researchers' philosophy of recognizing difference and incorporating the under-

standing of diversity into social inquiry. Thus, researchers conducting research from a feminist perspective "have used all existing methods and have invented some new ones as well."

The different, and often contrasting, views set forth by social scientists indicates the influence of paradigms on research. These fundamental viewpoints shape the kinds of observations we are likely to make, the sorts of facts we seek to discover, and the conclusions we draw from those facts. Paradigms also help determine which concepts we see as relevant and important.

Rational Objectivity Reconsidered

Our discussion of paradigms began with Comte's assertion that society can be studied rationally and objectively. Since his time, the growth of science and technology, together with the relative decline of superstition, have put rationality more and more in the centre of social life. As fundamental as rationality is to most of us, however, some contemporary scholars have raised questions about it.

For example, positivistic social scientists have sometimes erred in assuming that social reality can be explained in rational terms because humans always act rationally. No doubt your own experience offers ample evidence to the contrary. Yet, many modern economic models fundamentally assume that people will make rational choices in the economic sector: They will choose the highest-paying job, pay the lowest price, and so forth. This assumption ignores the power of such factors as tradition, loyalty, image, and other factors that compete with reason and calculation in the determination of human behaviour.

A more sophisticated positivism would assert that we can rationally understand and predict even nonrational human behaviour. An example is the famous "Asch Experiment" (Asch 1958), where a group of subjects is presented with a set of lines on a screen and asked to identify the two lines that are of equal length.

Imagine yourself a subject in such an experiment. You're sitting in the front row of a classroom in a group of six subjects. A set of lines (see Figure 2-1) is projected on the wall in front of you.

Figure 2-1
The Asch Experiment

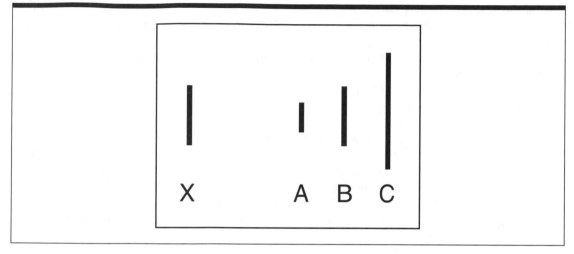

The experimenter asks you, one at a time, to identify the line to the right (A, B, or C) that matches the length of line X. The correct answer (B) is pretty obvious to you. To your surprise, however, you find that all the other subjects agree on a different answer!

The experimenter announces that all but one in the group has gotten the correct answer. Since you're the only one who chose B, that's equivalent to saying that you've gotten it *wrong*. Then a new set of lines is presented, and you have the same experience. What seems to be the obviously correct answer is said by everyone else to be wrong.

As it turns out, of course, you are the only *real* subject in the experiment—all the others are working with the experimenter. The experiment's purpose is to see whether you will be swayed by public pressure to go along with the incorrect answer. In one-third of Asch's initial experiments, he found that his subjects (all male) did just that.

Choosing an obviously wrong answer in a simple experiment is an example of nonrational behaviour. But, as Asch went on to show, experimenters can examine the circumstances that lead more or fewer subjects to go along with the incorrect answer. For example, in subsequent studies Asch varied the size of the group and the number of "dissenters" who chose the "wrong" (that is, the correct) answer. Thus, it is possible to study nonrational behaviour rationally and scientifically.

More radically, we can question whether social life abides by rational principles at all. In the physical sciences, developments such as chaos theory, fuzzy logic, and complexity have suggested that we may need to rethink fundamentally the orderliness of events in the physical world. Certainly the social world might be no tidier than the world of physics.

The contemporary challenge to positivism, however, goes beyond the question of whether people behave rationally. In part, the criticism of positivism challenges the idea that scientists can be as objective as the positivist ideal assumes. Most scientists would agree that personal feelings can and do influence the problems scientists choose to study, what they choose to observe, and the conclusions they draw from their observations.

There is an even more radical critique of the ideal of objectivity. As we glimpsed in the discussions of feminism and ethnomethodology, some contemporary researchers suggest that subjectivity might actually be preferred in some situations. Let's take a moment to return to the dialectic of subjectivity and objectivity.

To begin, all our experiences are inescapably subjective. There is no way out. We can only see through our own eyes, and anything peculiar to our eyes will shape what we see. We can only hear things the way our particular ears and brain transmit and interpret sound waves. Therefore, each of us, to some extent, hears and sees different realities.

Despite the inescapable subjectivity of our experience, we humans seem to be wired to seek an agreement on what is *really real,* what is *objectively* so. Objectivity is a conceptual attempt to get beyond our individual views. It is ultimately a matter of communication, as we attempt to find a common ground in our subjective experiences. Whenever we succeed in our search, we say we are dealing with objective reality. This is the *agreement reality* discussed in Chapter 1.

While our subjectivity is individual, our search for objectivity is social. This is true in all aspects of life, not just in science. While each of us may prefer different foods, we must agree to some extent on what is fit to eat and what is not, or else there could be no restaurants or grocery stores. The same argument could be made regarding every other form of consumption. Without agreement reality, there could be no movies or television, no sports.

Social scientists as well have found benefits in the concept of a socially agreed-upon objective reality. As people seek to impose order on their experience of life, they find it useful to pursue this goal as a collective venture. What are the causes and cures of prejudice? Working together, social researchers have uncovered some answers that hold up to **intersubjective** scrutiny. Whatever your subjective experience of things, for example, you can discover for yourself that as education increases, prejudice generally tends to decrease. Because each of us can discover this independently, we say that it is objectively true.

From the 17th century through the middle of the 20th, the belief in an objective reality that was independent of individual perceptions predominated in science. For the most part, it was not simply held as a useful paradigm but as *The Truth.* The term *positivism* has generally represented the belief in a logically ordered, objective reality that we can come to know better and better through science. This is the view challenged today by postmodernists and others.

Some say that the ideal of objectivity conceals as much as it reveals. As we saw earlier, much of what was agreed on as scientific objectivity in Western social science in years past was actually an agreement primarily among white, middle-class, European men. Equally real experiences common to women, to ethnic minorities, to non-Western cultures, or to the poor were not necessarily represented in that reality.

Thus, early anthropologists are now criticized for often making modern, Westernized "sense" out of the beliefs and practices of nonliterate tribes around the world—sometimes by portraying their subjects as superstitious savages. We often call orally transmitted beliefs about the distant past "creation myth," whereas we speak of our own beliefs as "history." Increasingly today, there is a demand to find the native logic by which various peoples make sense out of life and to understand it on its own terms.

Ultimately, we'll never be able to distinguish completely between an objective reality and our subjective experience. We cannot know whether our concepts correspond to an objective reality or are simply useful in allowing us to predict and control our environment.

So desperate is our need to know what is really real, however, that both the positivists and the postmodernists are sometimes drawn into the belief that their view is real and true. There is a dual irony in this. On the one hand, the positivist's belief in the reality of the objective world must ultimately be based on faith; it cannot be proven by "objective" science, since that's precisely what's at issue. And the postmodernists assert that their faith—that objectively is an illusion and that everything is ultimately subjective—is the only true faith.

As social researchers we are not forced to align ourselves entirely with either of these approaches. Instead, we can treat them as two distinct arrows in our quiver. Each approach compensates for the weaknesses of the other by suggesting complementary perspectives that can produce useful lines of inquiry.

In summary, a rich variety of theoretical paradigms can be brought to bear on the study of social life. Useful theories can be constructed with each of these fundamental frames of reference. We now turn to some issues involved in theory construction, which are of interest and use to all social researchers, from positivists to postmodernists and all those in between.

Elements of Social Theory

As we have seen, paradigms are general frameworks or viewpoints: literally "points from which to view." They provide ways of looking at life and are grounded in sets of assumptions about the nature of reality.

Theories, by contrast, are systematic sets of interrelated statements intended to explain some aspect of social life. Thus, theories flesh out and specify paradigms. Whereas a paradigm offers a way of looking, a theory aims at explaining what we see.

Let's look a little more deliberately now at some of the elements of a theory. As we said earlier, science is based on observation. In social research **observation** typically refers to seeing, hearing, and—less commonly—touching. A corresponding idea is **fact**. Although for philosophers "fact" is as complex a notion as "reality," social scientists generally use it to mean some phenomenon that has been observed. For example, it is a fact that the Liberal party, headed by Chrétien, won the 2000 election.

A **theory** is a systematic explanation for the observations that relate to a particular aspect of life. For example, someone might offer a theory of juvenile delinquency, prejudice, or political revolution. Explanation is a function of theory. Concepts are used in theories to explain observations—they are the "basic building blocks of theory" according to Jonathon Turner (1989:5). **Concepts** are abstract elements representing classes of phenomena within the field of study. The concepts relevant to a theory of juvenile delinquency, for example, include *juvenile* and *delinquency* for starters. Another relevant concept is *peer group*—the people you hang around with. *Social class* and *ethnicity* are undoubtedly relevant concepts in a theory of juvenile delinquency. *School performance* might also be relevant.

A **variable** is a special kind of concept. In Chapter 1 we noted that each variable comprises a set of attributes; thus, delinquency, in the simplest case, is made up of delinquent and not delinquent. A theory of delinquency would aim at explaining why some juveniles are delinquent and others are not.

Axioms or **postulates** are fundamental assertions, taken to be true, on which a theory is grounded. In a theory of juvenile delinquency, we might begin with axioms such as "Everyone desires material comforts" and "The ability to obtain material comforts legally is greater for the wealthy than the poor." From such assertions one might proceed to **propositions,** specific conclusions about the relationships among concepts that are derived from the axiomatic groundwork. For example, from our beginning axioms about juvenile delinquency, we might reasonably construct the proposition that poor youths are more likely to break the law to gain material comforts than rich youths.

Hypotheses can then be derived from propositions. A **hypothesis** is a specified, testable expectation about empirical reality that follows from a more general proposition. Thus a researcher might formulate the following hypothesis: "Poor youths have higher delinquency rates than rich youths." Research is designed to test hypotheses. In other words, research will support (or fail to support) a theory only indirectly by testing specific hypotheses that are derived from theories and propositions.

Let's look more closely at how theory and research come together.

Two Logical Systems Revisited

In Chapter 1, we introduced deductive and inductive reasoning, with a promise that we would return to them later. It's later.

The Traditional Model of Science

Most of us have a somewhat idealized picture of "the scientific method" that we've gained from science instruction throughout our years in school. Although this traditional model of science tells only a part of the story, it's useful to understand its logic.

There are three main elements in the traditional model of science, typically presented in a chronological order of execution: *theory, operationalization,* and *observation.* We're already quite familiar with the idea of theory. According to the traditional model of science, scientists begin with an interest in something. They have a theory from which they derive testable hypotheses. As social scientists, for example, we might have a theory about the causes of juvenile delinquency. Let's assume we've arrived at a hypothesis that as social class goes up we expect delinquency to go down. In other words, that delinquency is inversely related to social class.

To test any hypothesis, we must specify the meanings of all the variables involved in it in observational terms. In the present case, the variables are *social class* and *delinquency.* To give *delinquency* specific meaning, we might define it as "being arrested for a crime," "being convicted of a crime," or in some other plausible way. *Social class* might be specified in terms of family income for the purposes of this particular study.

After defining our variables, we need to specify how we'll measure them. (Recall that the classical ideal of science depends on measurable observations.) **Operationalization** literally means specifying the exact operations involved in measuring a variable. There are many ways we can go about testing our hypothesis, each of which allows for different ways of measuring our variables.

For simplicity, let's assume we're planning to conduct a survey of high school students. We might operationalize delinquency in the form of the question: "Have you ever stolen anything?" Those who answer "yes" will be classified as delinquents in our study; those who say "no" will be classified as nondelinquents. Similarly, we might operationalize social class by asking respondents, "What was your family's income last year?" and providing them with a set of family income categories: under $15,000; $15,000–$44,999; $45,000–$74,999; and $75,000 and above.

Notice that someone might take issue with the way we have operationalized our variables in this simplistic example. Both delinquency and social class can mean something different from or be viewed as more than merely having stolen something or simply family income, for example. Nonetheless, for the researcher testing a hypothesis, the meaning of variables is exactly and only what the **operational definition** specifies.

Scientists have to be masters of their operational definitions for the sake of precision in observation, measurement, and communication. Otherwise, we would never know whether a study that contradicted ours did so only because it used a different set of procedures to measure one of the variables and thus changed the meaning of the hypothesis being tested. Of course, this also means that to evaluate a study's conclusions about juvenile delinquency and social class, or any other variables, we need to know how those variables were operationalized.

There are other problems in the operationalizion of our variables that we might consider as well. Perhaps some respondents will lie about stealing, in which cases we'll misclassify them as nondelinquent. Some respondents will not know their family incomes and will give mistaken answers; others may be embarrassed and lie. Part 2 will deal with these types of issues more in depth. For the purposes of this example, we'll use the operationalizations described above.

Our operationalized hypothesis now is that the highest incidence of delinquents will be found among respondents who select the lowest family income category (under $15,000); a lower percentage of delinquents will be found in the $15,000–$44,999 category; still fewer delinquents will be found in the $45,000–$74,999 category; and the lowest percentage of delinquents will be found in the $75,000 and above category. We can finally move to the last step in the traditional model of science—observation. Having developed theoretical clarity and expectations and having created a strategy for looking, all that remains is to look at the way things actually are.

Let's suppose our survey produced the following data:

Figure 2-2
The Traditional Image of Science

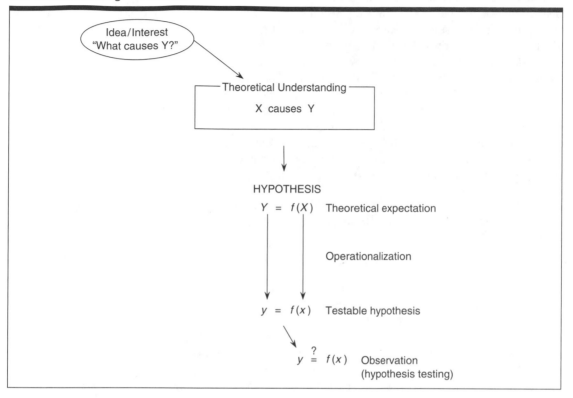

	Percentage delinquent
Under $15,000	20
$15,000–$44,999	15
$45,000–$74,999	10
$75,000 and above	5

Observations producing such data would confirm our hypothesis. But suppose our findings were as follows:

	Percentage delinquent
Under $15,000	15
$15,000–$44,999	15
$45,000–$74,999	15
$75,000 and above	15

These findings would disconfirm our hypothesis regarding family income and delinquency. *Discon-*

firmability—the possibility that observations may not support our expectations—is an essential quality in any hypothesis. There must be some possible observations that would contradict our expectations.

Figure 2-2 provides a schematic diagram of the traditional model of scientific inquiry. In it we see the researcher beginning with an interest in some phenomenon, like juvenile delinquency. Next comes the development of a theoretical understanding, for example what factors (like social class) might explain or account for it. The theoretical considerations result in an expectation about what should be observed if the theory is correct. The notation $Y = f(X)$ is a conventional way of saying that Y (for example, delinquency) is a function of (is in some way caused by) X (for example, social class). At that level, however, X and Y still have rather general meanings that could give rise to quite different observations and measurement. Operationalization specifies the procedures that will be used to measure the variables. In other words, the general concepts are translated into specific indicators. In Figure 2-2, the lowercase x, for example, is a precisely measurable indicator of capital X. This operationalization process results in the formation of a testable hypothesis: for example, self reported theft is a function of family income. Observations aimed at finding out whether this statement accurately depicts reality are part of what is typically called **hypothesis testing.**

An Illustration of Hypothesis Testing: Discrimination in Canada

Now let's look at an example of hypothesis testing in a real research study. Does employment discrimination based on race exist in Canada? The proposition that discrepancies in access to employment can be accounted for by racial discrimination can be tested. According to Henry and Ginzberg (1988), many could be sceptical of the "indirect measures of discrimination" (such as census data, reports by those who experienced such discrimination, and studies that assess people's attitudes on the subject) often used to demonstrate that racial discrimination has been practised in Canadian employment. It is difficult to test this directly, but Henry and Ginzberg devised a clever quasi-experimental research design (experiments are discussed in Chapter 9) that sent real people into the field: the Toronto labour market.

The key concepts, in other words variables, in this hypothesis are employment, discrimination, and race. These can refer to a wide variety of indicators. Therefore they defined their terms and provided specific measures of them. Employment refers to gaining and maintaining a job. As they noted, there are many stages in the process of employment where discrimination could occur, such as screening, selection, or promotion. They decided to focus on the critical moment of obtaining a job. Therefore, they operationalized the variable employment by looking at the point of

entry or employee selection. Is the job offered to the individual or not?

They defined discrimination in employment "as those practices or attitudes, willful or unintentional, that have the effect of limiting an individual's or a group's right to economic opportunities on the basis of irrelevant traits such as skin colour rather than an evaluation of true abilities or potential" (p. 215). They operationalized discrimination by whether a job was offered or not and by differential treatment such as rudeness or claiming the job had already been filled. Finally, for at least one part of their study, race was operationalized as black versus white.

Thus their study focused on two questions. Do White and Black applicants—with experience and qualifications that are similar—differ in the number of jobs they are offered when they apply for the same jobs? Second, are these White and Black applicants treated differently when they apply for these jobs? They used both in-person and telephone testing in the field; however, we'll stick to the in-person testing for the sake of this illustration.

What's tricky in this study is trying to isolate the impact of race. They had to make sure that any differences in response that they observed were due to race and not to other factors. As you'll see below, it is done comparatively in terms of comparable individuals applying for jobs, and to the extent possible, varying only their race to see if there is a difference in the applicants' treatment and outcomes.

As you move through this book, you'll notice the many details that researchers have to attend to in the implementation of their studies. We will limit ourselves here to only some of the key issues of concern for Henry and Ginzberg. For instance, a Black individual and a White individual both had to apply for the same job, with similar credentials like experience and education. Therefore, they created the résumés for the applicants so they would be as similar as possible. The applicants also had to be similar in many other traits like sex, age, physical appearance, and personality. By such steps they tried to insure that the sole difference that could account for different treatment was race—Black versus White.

The researchers chose a range of jobs that required more or less experience. They therefore created two teams of applicants, a senior and junior team. The senior team was a set of professional actors. The researchers felt that they "would be more convincing in playing the many roles required for this project." "The younger teams were composed of high-school and university students who would normally be applying for the same types of jobs that they applied for in the testing situation" (p. 216).

Another issue they were concerned with was the timing of the applications. The researchers chose jobs the evening before and had the testers try to apply for the jobs the next day. They wanted the interviews to be close together in time, within about half an hour, to limit the likelihood of a job being legitimately filled, and most of the time they had the Black applicant go first. Finally, in an attempt to eliminate the potential impact of sex discrimination, men were sent to apply for the traditionally male jobs and women for traditionally female jobs. Both male and female teams applied for jobs without clear gender typing, but men and women never applied to the same job. They were trying to isolate the impact of race as best they could.

What were the results of the in-person testing? Over a 3 1/2 month period, 402 applications were made (201 jobs) by the testers. Their overall results showed

> that offers to Whites outweigh offers to Blacks by a ratio of 3 to 1. We had thought that the nature of the job might influence whether Black or Whites would be hired. Only Whites received offers for managerial positions or jobs as waiters and waitresses or hosts and hostesses in the restaurant trade. A Black was offered a job in the kitchen when he had applied for a waiter's job!
>
> (p. 217)

Other large differences in the treatment of Blacks and Whites were also found. Some Black testers were told the job had been filled when only a half hour later a White tester was offered the job or given an application form to complete. In a few instances where the Black and the White appli-

cants were offered the same job, less pay was offered to the Blacks. Rude or hostile treatment was another form of differential treatment. In 36 cases of differential treatment, only once was it favourable to a Black. They stated

> These results indicate that Black job seekers face not only discrimination in the sense of receiving fewer job offers than Whites but also a considerable amount of negative and abusive treatment while job hunting....
>
> Racial discrimination in employment, either in the form of clearly favouring a White over a Black, even though their résumés were equivalent, or in the form of treating a White applicant better than a Black, took place in almost one-quarter of all job contacts tested in this study.
>
> (p. 218)

Henry and Ginzburg therefore concluded that their study supported their hypothesis and demonstrated that racial discrimination in Canadian employment did exist.

Deductive and Inductive Reasoning: An Illustration

As you probably recognized, the traditional model of science described above uses deductive reasoning. From a general theoretical understanding, the researcher derives (deduces) expectations and finally testable hypotheses. It's neat and clean. Nonetheless, in reality inductive reasoning is also used in science. W. I. B. Beveridge (1950:113), a philosopher of science, describes these two systems of logic in a way that should already seem familiar to you:

> Logicians distinguish between inductive reasoning (from particular instances to general principles, from facts to theories) and deductive reasoning (from the general to the particular, applying a theory to a particular case). In induction one starts from observed data and develops a generalization which explains the relationships between the objects observed. On the other hand, in deductive reasoning one starts from some general law and applies it to a particular instance.

Let's consider a real research example as a vehicle for comparing the deductive and inductive linkages between theory and research. Years ago, Charles Glock, Benjamin Ringer, and I (Babbie) (1967) set out to discover what caused differing levels of church involvement among U.S. Episcopalians. Several theoretical or quasi-theoretical positions suggested possible answers. We'll focus on only one here, what came to be called the "Comfort Hypothesis."

In part, we took our lead from the Christian injunction to care for "the halt, the lame, and the blind" and those who are "weary and heavy laden." At the same time, ironically, we noted the Marxist assertion that religion is an "opiate for the masses." Given both, it made sense to expect the following, which was our hypothesis: "Parishioners whose life situations most deprive them of satisfaction and fulfillment in the secular society turn to the church for comfort and substitute rewards" (Glock et al. 1967:107–8).

Having framed this general hypothesis, we set about testing it. Were those deprived of satisfaction in the secular society in fact more religious than those who received more satisfaction from the secular society? To answer this, we needed to distinguish who was deprived. The questionnaire, which was constructed for the purpose of testing the Comfort Hypothesis, included items that seemed to offer indicators of whether parishioners were relatively deprived or gratified in secular society.

To start, we reasoned that men enjoyed more status than women in our generally male-dominated society. Though hardly a novel conclusion in itself, it laid the groundwork for testing the Comfort Hypothesis. If the hypothesis was correct, women should appear more religious than men. Once the survey data had been collected and analyzed, the expectation about gender and religion was clearly confirmed. On three separate measures of religious involvement—*ritual* (such as church attendance), *organizational* (such as belonging to church organizations), and *intellectual* (such as reading church publications)— women were more religious than men. On the overall measure, women scored 50 percent higher than men.

In another test of the Comfort Hypothesis, we reasoned that in a youth-oriented society, old people would be more deprived of secular gratification than would the young. Once again, the data confirmed our expectation. The oldest parishioners were more religious than the middle-aged, who were more religious than the young adults.

Social class, measured by education and income, afforded another test of the Comfort Hypothesis. Once again, the test was successful. Those with low social status were more involved in the church than those with high social status.

The hypothesis was even confirmed in a test that went against everyone's commonsense expectations. Despite church posters showing worshipful young families and bearing the slogan, "The Family That Prays Together Stays Together," the Comfort Hypothesis suggested that parishioners who were married and had children—the clear American ideal at that time—would enjoy secular gratification in that regard. As a consequence, they should be *less* religious than those who lacked one or both family components. Thus, we hypothesized that parishioners who were both single and childless should be the most religious; those with either spouse or child should be somewhat less religious; and those married with children, representing the ideal pictured on all those posters, should be least religious of all. That's exactly what we found!

Finally, the Comfort Hypothesis would suggest that the various kinds of secular deprivation should be cumulative: Those with all the characteristics associated with deprivation should be the most religious; those with none should be the least. When the four individual measures of deprivations were combined into a composite measure, the theoretical expectation was exactly confirmed. Comparing the two extremes, we found that single, childless, old, lower-class female parishioners scored more than three times as high on the measure of church involvement than did young, married, upper-class fathers. Thus was the Comfort Hypothesis confirmed.

This research example clearly illustrates the logic of the deductive model. Beginning with general, theoretical expectations about the impact of social deprivation on church involvement, it was possible to derive concrete hypotheses linking specific measurable variables, such as age and church attendance. The actual empirical data could then be analyzed to determine whether the deductive expectations were supported by empirical reality.

This example shows how it was possible to do it that way, but, alas, we've been fibbing a little bit just now. To tell the truth, although the study began with an interest in discovering what caused variations in church involvement among Episcopalians, it wasn't actually begun with a Comfort Hypothesis, or any other hypothesis for that matter. (In the interest of further honesty, Glock and Ringer initiated the study, and I (Babbie) joined it years after the data had been collected.) A questionnaire was designed to collect information from parishioners that *might* shed some light on why some participated in the church more than others, but questionnaire construction was not guided by any precise, deductive theory. Once the data were collected, the task of explaining differences in religiosity began with an analysis of variables that have a wide impact on people's lives, including gender, age, social class, and family status. Each of these four variables was found to relate strongly to church involvement in the ways already described. Indeed, they had a cumulative effect, also already described. Rather than being good news, this presented a dilemma.

Glock discussed his findings with colleagues. Once he had displayed the tables illustrating the impact of each individual variable as well as their powerful composite effect, a colleague asked, "What does it all mean, Charlie?" Glock was at a loss. Why were those variables so strongly related to church involvement?

That question launched a process of reasoning about what the several variables had in common, aside from their impact on religiosity. Eventually there was recognition that each of the four variables also reflected differential status in the secular society, and then the thought developed that perhaps the issue of comfort was involved. Thus, the inductive process had moved from concrete observations to a general theoretical explanation.

A Graphic Contrast

Theory and research can usefully be done both inductively and deductively. Figure 2-3 shows a graphic comparison of the two approaches applied to an investigation of study habits and exam performance. In both cases, we are interested in the relationship between the number of hours spent studying for an exam and the grade earned on that exam. Using the deductive method, we would begin by examining the matter logically. Doing well on an exam reflects a student's ability to recall and manipulate information. Both of these abilities should be increased by exposure to the information before the exam. In this fashion, we would arrive at a hypothesis suggesting a positive relationship between the number of hours spent studying and the grade earned on the exam. We say *positive* because we expect grades to increase as the hours of studying increase. If increased hours produced decreased grades, that would be called a *negative*, or inverse, relationship. The hypothesis is represented by the line in part 1(a) of Figure 2-3.

Our next step would be to make observations relevant to testing our hypothesis. The shaded area in part 1(b) of the figure represents perhaps hundreds of observations of different students, noting how many hours they studied and what grades they received. Finally, in part 1(c), we compare the hypothesis and the observations. Because observations in the real world seldom if ever match our expectations perfectly, we must decide whether the match is close enough to consider the hypothesis confirmed. Put differently, can we conclude that the hypothesis describes the general pattern that exists, granting some variations in real life? To determine this, it is sometimes necessary to conduct a statistical analysis (Part 4).

Now suppose we used the inductive method to address the same research question. In this case we would begin with a set of observations, as in Figure 2-3, part 2(a). Curious about the relationship between hours spent studying and grades earned, we might simply arrange to collect relevant data. Then we'd look for a pattern that best represented or summarized our observations. In part 2(b) of the

Figure 2-3
Deductive and Inductive Methods

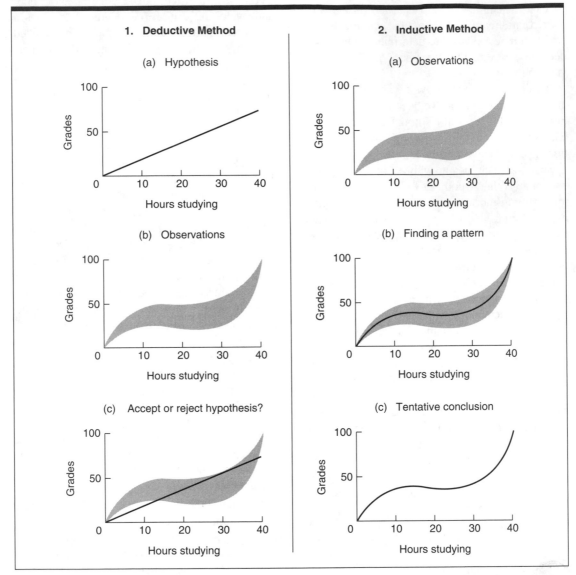

1. **Deductive Method**

(a) Hypothesis

(b) Observations

(c) Accept or reject hypothesis?

2. **Inductive Method**

(a) Observations

(b) Finding a pattern

(c) Tentative conclusion

figure, the pattern is shown as a curved line running through the centre of the curving mass of points.

The pattern found among the points in this case suggests that with 1 to 15 hours of studying, each additional hour generally produces a higher grade on the exam. With 15 to about 25 hours, however, more study seems to slightly lower the grade. Studying more than 25 hours, on the other hand,

results in a return to the initial pattern: More hours produce higher grades. Using the inductive method, then, we end up with a *tentative* conclusion about the pattern of the relationship between the two variables. The conclusion is tentative because the observations we have made cannot be taken as a test of the pattern—those observations are the *source* of the pattern we've created.

Figure 2-4
The Wheel of Science

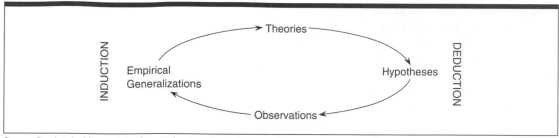

Source: Reprinted with permission from Walter L. Wallace. *The Logic of Science In Sociology.* (New York: Aldine de Gruyter) Copyright © 1971 by Walter L. Wallace, Copyright © renewed 1999.

In actual practice, theory and research interact through a never ending alternation of deduction and induction. Walter Wallace (1971) has represented this process nicely as a circle, which is presented in a modified form in Figure 2-4. Emile Durkheim's classic work on suicide ([1897] 1951) provides a good example of this. When he pored over table after table of official statistics on suicide rates in different areas, he was struck by the fact that Protestant countries consistently had higher suicide rates than Catholic ones. Why should that be the case? His initial observations led him to create, inductively, a theory of religion, social integration, anomie, and suicide. His theoretical explanations then led deductively to further hypotheses and further observations.

In summary, the scientific norm of logical reasoning provides a two-way bridge between theory and research. Scientific inquiry in practice typically involves alternating between deduction and induction. During the deductive phase, we reason *toward* observations; during the inductive phase, we reason *from* observations. Both approaches involve an interplay of logic and observation, and both are routes to the construction of social theories.

While both inductive and deductive methods are valid in scientific inquiry, individuals may feel more comfortable with one approach than the other. Consider this exchange in Sir Arthur Conan Doyle's *A Scandal in Bohemia,* as Sherlock Holmes answers Dr. Watson's inquiry (Doyle [1891] 1892:13):

"What do you imagine that it means?"

"I have no data yet. It is a capital mistake to theorise before one has data. Insensibly one begins to twist facts to suit theories, instead of theories to suit facts."

Some social scientists would more or less agree with this inductive position, while others would take a deductive stance. Most, however, concede the legitimacy of both approaches.

Now that we've completed our overview of the deductive and inductive linkages between theory and research, let's look a little deeper into how theories are constructed using these two different approaches.

Deductive Theory Construction

What's involved in deductive theory construction and hypothesis testing? Let's look at how you might go about constructing such a theory.

Getting Started

The first step in deductive theory construction is to pick a topic that interests you. It can be very broad, such as "What's the structure of society?" or narrower, as in "Why do people support or oppose a woman's right to an abortion?" Whatever the topic, it should be something you're interested in understanding and explaining.

Once you've picked your topic, you should undertake an inventory of what is known or thought about it. In part, this means writing down your own observations and ideas. Beyond that, it means learning what other scholars have said about it. You can talk to other people, and you'll want to read the scholarly literature on the topic.

Your preliminary research will probably uncover consistent patterns discovered by prior scholars. For example, religious and political variables will stand out as important determinants of attitudes about abortion. Findings such as these will be very useful to you in creating your own theory.

In this process, don't overlook the value of introspection. If you can look at your own personal processes—including reactions, fears, and prejudices—you may be able to gain important insights into human behaviour in general. We are by no means saying that everyone thinks like you, but introspection can be a useful source of insights that may inform our inquiries.

Constructing Your Theory

With knowledge of previous work on the topic, you can begin constructing your theory. Although theory construction is not a lockstep affair, the following steps should help organize the activity for you.

1. Specify the topic.
2. Specify the range of phenomena your theory addresses. Will your theory apply to all of human social life, will it apply only to Canadian citizens, only to young people, or what?
3. Identify and specify your major concepts and variables.
4. Find out what is known (propositions) about the relationships among those variables.
5. Reason logically from those propositions to the specific topic you are examining.

We've already discussed items (1) through (3), so let's focus now on (4) and (5). As you identify the relevant concepts and discover what has already been learned about them, you can begin to create a propositional structure that explains the topic under study.

Let's look now at an example of how these building blocks fit together in actual deductive theory construction and empirical research.

An Example of Deductive Theory

A topic of central interest to scholars is the concept of *distributive justice,* people's perceptions of whether they're being treated fairly by life—whether they are getting "their share." Guillermina Jasso describes the theory of distributive justice more formally, as follows:

> The theory provides a mathematical description of the process whereby individuals, reflecting on their holdings of the goods they value (such as beauty, intelligence, or wealth), compare themselves to others, experiencing a fundamental instantaneous magnitude of the justice evaluation (J), which captures their sense of being fairly or unfairly treated in the distributions of natural and social goods.
>
> (Jasso 1988:11)

Notice that Jasso has assigned a symbolic representation for her key variable: J will stand for distributive justice. She does this to support her intention of stating her theory in mathematical formulas. Though theories are often expressed mathematically, we'll not delve too deeply into that practice here.

Jasso indicates that there are three kinds of postulates in her theory. "The first makes explicit the fundamental axiom which represents the substantive point of departure for the theory." She elaborates as follows:

> The theory begins with the received Axiom of Comparison, which formalizes the long-held view that a wide class of phenomena, including happiness, self-esteem, and the sense of distributive justice, may be understood as the product of a comparison process.
>
> (Jasso 1988:11)

Thus, your sense of whether you are receiving a "fair" share of the good things of life comes from comparing yourself with others. If this seems obvious to you, that's not a shortcoming of the axiom. Axioms are the taken-for-granted beginnings of theory.

Jasso continues to lay the groundwork for her theory. First, she indicates that our sense of distributive justice is a function of "Actual Holding (A)" and "Comparison Holdings (C)" of some good. Let's consider money, for example. A person's sense of justice in this regard is a function of how much she actually has, compared with how much others have. By specifying the two components of the comparison, Jasso can use them as variables in her theory.

Jasso then offers a "measurement rule" that further specifies how the two variables, A and C, will be conceptualized. This step is needed because some of the goods to be examined are concrete and commonly measured (such as money) whereas others are less tangible (such as respect). The former kind, she says, will be measured conventionally, whereas the latter will be measured "by the individual's relative rank . . . within a specially selected comparison group" (1988:13). The theory will provide a formula for making that measurement.

Jasso continues in this fashion to introduce additional elements, weaving them into mathematical formulas to be used in deriving predictions about the workings of distributive justice in a variety of social settings. Here is just a sampling of where her theorizing takes her (1988:14–15).

3. Other things [being] the same, a person will prefer to steal from a fellow group member rather than from an outsider.

4. The preference to steal from a fellow group member is more pronounced in poor groups than in rich groups.

5. In the case of theft, informants arise only in cross-group theft, in which case they are members of the thief's group. . . .

9. Persons who arrive a week late at summer camp or for freshman year of college are more likely to become friends of persons who play games of chance than of persons who play games of skill.

14. In wartime, the favorite leisure-time activity of soldiers is playing games of chance. . .

17. A society becomes more vulnerable to deficit spending as its wealth increases. . . .

22. Societies in which population growth is welcomed must be societies in which the set of valued goods includes at least one quantity-good, such as wealth.

These propositions should provide a good sense of where deductive theorizing can take you. To gain a sense of how she reasons her way to these propositions, let's look briefly at the logic involved in Propositions 3 and 5 relating to theft within and outside one's group.

Beginning with the assumption that thieves want to maximize their relative wealth, ask yourself whether that goal would be best served by stealing from those you compare yourself with or from outsiders. In each case, stealing will increase your Actual Holdings, but what about your Comparison Holdings? If you think about it, you'll see that stealing from people in your comparison group will *lower* their holdings, further increasing your *relative* wealth.

To simplify, imagine there are only two people in your comparison group: you and Sally. Suppose each of you has $100. If you steal $50 from someone outside your group, you will have increased your relative wealth by 50 percent compared with Sally: $150 versus $100. But if you steal $50 from Sally, you will have increased your relative wealth 200 percent: $150 to Sally's $50. Your goal is best served by stealing from within the comparison group; hence, Proposition 3.

Regarding Proposition 5, can you see why it would make sense for informants (1) to arise only in the case of cross-group theft and (2) to come from the thief's comparison group? This proposition again depends on the fundamental assumption that everyone wants to increase his or her relative standing. Suppose you and Sally are in the same comparison group, but this time the group contains more people. If you steal from someone else in your comparison group, Sally's relative standing in the group does not change. Although your wealth has increased, the average wealth in the group remains the same (because someone else's wealth has decreased by the same amount), so Sally's relative standing remains the same. Sally has no incentive to inform on you.

If you steal from someone outside your comparison group, however, your nefarious income increases the total wealth in your group. This means that Sally's wealth relative to that total is diminished. Since Sally's relative wealth has suffered, she's more likely to bring an end to your stealing by informing on you. Therefore, cross-group theft produces informants.

This last deduction also begins to explain why these informants are more likely to come from within the thief's comparison group. We've just seen how Sally's relative standing was decreased by your theft. How about members of the other group (other than the person you stole from)? Each of them would actually profit from the theft, since you would have reduced the total with which they compare themselves. Thus, they have no reason to inform on you. Hence, the theory of distributive justice predicts that informants arise from the thief's own comparison group.

This brief and selective look at Jasso's derivations should give you some sense of the enterprise of deductive theory. Of course, the theory doesn't guarantee any of the given predictions. The role of research is to test each of them empirically to determine whether what makes sense (logic) actually occurs in practice (observation).

There are two important elements in science, then: logical integrity and empirical verification. Both are essential to scientific inquiry and discovery. Logic alone is not enough, but on the other hand, the mere observation and collection of empirical facts does not provide understanding—the telephone directory, for example, is not a scientific conclusion. Observation, however, can be the springboard for the construction of a social scientific theory, as we'll now see in the case of inductive theory.

Inductive Theory Construction

Quite often, social scientists begin constructing a theory through the inductive method by observing aspects of social life, and then seeking to discover patterns that may point to relatively universal principles. Barney Glaser and Anselm Strauss (1967) coined the term *grounded theory* in reference to this method.

Field research—the direct observation of events in progress—is frequently used to develop theories through observation. A long and rich anthropological tradition has used this method to good advantage.

Among contemporary social scientists, no one was more adept at seeing the patterns of human behaviour through observation than the Alberta born sociologist Erving Goffman:

> A game such as chess generates a habitable universe for those who can follow it, a plane of being, a cast of characters with a seemingly unlimited number of different situations and acts through which to realize their natures and destinies. Yet much of this is reducible to a small set of interdependent rules and practices. If the meaningfulness of everyday activity is similarly dependent on a closed, finite set of rules, then explication of them would give one a powerful means of analyzing social life.
>
> (1974:5)

In a variety of research efforts, Goffman uncovered the rules of such diverse behaviours as living in a mental institution (1961) and managing the "spoiled identity" of disfiguration (1963). In each case, Goffman observed the phenomenon in depth and teased out the rules governing behaviour. Goffman's research provides an excellent example of qualitative field research as a source of grounded theory.

As indicated by the search for causes of church involvement, qualitative field research is not the only method of observation appropriate to the development of inductive theory. Here's another detailed example to illustrate further the construction of inductive theory using quantitative methods.

An Example of Inductive Theory

Why some Jews outmarry was a subject of considerable attention in the 1960s and 1970s in

North America. Countless explanations were being offered as to why some abide by their faith's prohibition against marrying non-Jews and others do not.

This issue drew the attention of Werner Cohn (1976) at the University of British Columbia. He noted that most often people looked to background factors like education and religion to account for the differences and to factors like Jewish community size. In fact, he said that it became "a cliché of the previous literature on inter-marriage to assert that there is a linear, negative relationship between the size of the local Jewish community and its outmarriage rate" (p. 99). In other words, the smaller the Jewish community, the higher the rate of intermarriage. Testing this claim over a 50-year period in Canada, he found "almost no linear relationship" (p. 100).

He did, however, observe a pattern of regional differences in the rate of Jewish outmarriage in Canada. This gave him a different perspective on the problem.

Taking some liberty with his more elaborate and nuanced argument, we'll look at certain aspects of his research study for the sake of illustration. Cohn noticed that Jewish outmarriage varied geographically from east to west, tending to be lowest in the east and highest in the west. As he said, there was "Quebec at one extreme and British Columbia at the other" (p. 91). with regions in the middle lying somewhere in between. He then found the same pattern for Catholic outmarriages. Further, he recognized a number of other patterns that followed this east to west gradient.

A series of social indicators in the general population, such as suicide, drug use convictions, crimes, divorce, and mental disease were found to "parallel the geographic patterns of Jewish and Catholic outmarriage." The rates of each of these indicators tended to increase as one went westward and were found to be the highest in British Columbia. He termed this pattern of relationships the "Canadian syndrome of polarities." Cohn discovered a powerful pattern of relationships before he had an explanation for that pattern.

What do these patterns of Jewish outmarriage and the rate of suicide or crime have in common

other than this east-west gradient? Looking at all of these observed relationships, what might help account for the shared pattern of regional variation across each of these factors? Cohn recognized that outmarriage by Jews is a violation of a norm—but so is committing suicide, committing a crime, and getting a divorce. A commonality among these is norm violation. Each can be regarded as a "manifestation of *anomie*"—"a condition of relative normlessness" (p. 91). This recognition of a previously unsuspected common denominator illustrates inductive reasoning.

Now the question is, what factors common to each of these regional patterns of norm violation might explain the set of them, and even other similar patterns that have yet to be observed? He looked at the possible impact of economic factors to explain these "Canadian patterns of anomie" and concluded that purely economic factors couldn't account for them.

He then observed that each of these measures of anomie were closely related to a measure of geographic mobility—"the percentage of persons in each province who, although born in either Canada or the United States, now (at the time of the 1971 census) live in a province in which they were not born" (p. 97). Quebec had the smallest proportion of migrants and British Columbia had the highest proportion. Further, geographic mobility among Jews in Canada showed the same general pattern as that of the general population, western provinces having higher percentages of Jewish migrants than eastern ones. In short, the general pattern of mobility was highly correlated with Jewish outmarriage and these other indicators of social disorganization.

These observed patterns suggested to him "a relationship of causality between geographic mobility and norm violation" (p. 98). "[S]uch mobility is related to a breakdown in traditional social restraints and this...breakdown results in relatively higher rates of norm violation" (p. 91).

The relatively higher rates of suicide, mental disease, rape, drug convictions, crime, and divorce which mark the Canadian West and go together with the presence of a relatively higher proportion of geographically mobile persons...may reasonably be interpreted as signs of an environment of looser social ties and weaker social restraints. It seems reasonable to expect that when people have come from elsewhere in relatively greater numbers, they have fewer extended family ties and that the absence of such ties exposes them more often to the normlessness familiar to students of Durkheim.

(pp. 102–03).

The second inductive step was the recognition that geographic mobility is a plausible cause of anomie (the common denominator he inductively recognized earlier). His second induction meshed well with his first because of the theoretical link between geographic mobility and anomie—it is highly plausible that geographic mobility loosens social bonds while anomie (normlessness) has been attributed to loosened social bonds by many theorists, including Emile Durkheim who coined the term. Thus a tight knit of plausible linkage runs from geographic mobility, as cause, to anomie, as effect.

In short, from his data he derived a general explanation of a relationship between geographic mobility and anomie that plausibly accounts for the pattern of relationships he observed. With "fewer family ties to bind" and a community "less tightly connected by personal contacts and family networks," there is "greater freedom from traditional constraint" (pp. 103–04). In other words, social disintegration is more likely to be present when such ties are weak, and as one moves westward in Canada, geographic mobility is greater.

Overall, then, a "social integration/disintegration" theory was offered as the explanation for observed regional differences in the rate of normative violations. Looser social ties and weaker social constraints result in higher rates of social disorders. Thus regions where the proportions of migrants are higher are more likely to experience higher rates of Jewish outmarriage, crime, divorce, etc. It bears repeating that the researcher had no thought about such a theory when his research began. The theory developed from an examination of the data.

We want to conclude this chapter with a brief statement on the relationship between theory and research in social scientific inquiry. We have discussed the idealized, logical models of induction and deduction. These are highly useful, but in practice social scientific research has developed many variations on these themes. As you will see, sometimes theoretical issues are introduced merely as backdrop for empirical analyses. Other studies cite selected empirical data to strengthen theoretical arguments. In neither case is there really an interaction between theory and research for the purpose of developing new explanations. Not all social science research is tightly linked to social theory—sometimes theory is more implicit. For example, some studies are conducted in order to determine if a social program is effective or to find out the general public's opinion on any number of issues, like abortion or who is likely to win the next election. Still other research, like descriptive ethnography, is done to provide useful information and insights. Most often, however, social science researchers are conscious of the implications of their research for social theories and vice versa. In practice, there are many ways of going about social inquiry and linking theory and research.

There's no simple recipe for conducting social science research. It is far more open-ended than the traditional view of science suggests. Ultimately, science rests on two pillars: logic and observation. As you'll see throughout this book, they can be fit together in many patterns.

Main Points

- Social scientists use a variety of paradigms to organize how they understand and inquire into social life.
- A distinction between types of theories that cuts across various paradigms is macrotheory (theories about large-scale features of society) versus microtheory (theories about smaller units or features of society).
- The positivistic paradigm assumes we can scientifically discover the rules governing social life.

- The conflict paradigm focuses on the attempt of persons and groups to dominate others and to avoid being dominated.
- The symbolic interactionist paradigm examines how shared meanings and social patterns are developed in the course of social interactions.
- Ethnomethodology focuses on the ways people make sense out of social life in the process of living it, as though each were a researcher engaged in an inquiry.
- The structural functionalist (or social systems) paradigm seeks to discover what functions the many elements of society perform for the whole system.
- Feminist paradigms, in addition to drawing attention to the oppression of women in most societies, highlight how previous images of social reality have often come from and reinforced the experiences of men.
- The longstanding belief in an objective reality that abides by rational rules has been challenged by some contemporary theorists and researchers.
- In the traditional image of science, scientists proceed from theory to operationalization, to observation. However, this image is not an accurate picture of how scientific research is actually done.
- Social scientific theory and research are linked through two logical methods:
  — *Deduction* involves the derivation of expectations or hypotheses from theories.
  — *Induction* involves the development of generalizations from specific observations.
- In practice, science is a process involving an alternation of deduction and induction.
- In practice, there are many possible links between theory and research and many ways to conduct social inquiry.

Review Questions and Exercises

1. Consider the possible relationship between education and prejudice (mentioned in Chapter 1). Describe how that relationship might be examined through (a) deductive and (b) inductive methods.
2. Select a social problem that concerns you: for example, war, pollution, overpopulation, prejudice, poverty. Identify the key variables involved in the study of that problem, including variables that may cause it or hold the key to its solution. Feel free to draw on others' theoretical and empirical work.
3. Using one of the many search engines (such as Google, Netscape, WebCrawler, Excite, or Yahoo), find information on the Web concerning at least three of the following paradigms. Give the Web locations and report on the theorists discussed in connection with the discussions you found.

Functionalism	Feminism
Conflict theory	Positivism
Interactionism	Postmodernism
Ethnomethodology	

Continuity Project

Show how three of the paradigms discussed in this chapter might structure your inquiry into the topic of gender equality/inequality. What aspects of the subject would the paradigm lead you to focus on? How might you interpret evidence of inequality within each paradigm?

Additional Readings

Chafetz, Janet. *A Primer on the Construction and Testing of Theories in Sociology.* Itasca, IL: Peacock, 1978. One of the few books on theory construction written expressly for undergraduates. Chafetz provides a rudimentary understanding of the philosophy of science through simple language and everyday examples. She describes the nature of explanation, the role of assumptions and concepts, and the building and testing of theories.

Devault, Majorie L. *Liberating Method: Feminism and Social Research.* Philadelphia: Temple University Press, 1999. This book elaborates on some of the methods associated with the feminist paradigm and is committed to both rigorous inquiry and the use of social research to combat oppression.

Kuhn, Thomas. *The Structure of Scientific Revolutions.* Chicago: University of Chicago Press, 1970. An exciting and innovative recasting of the nature of scientific development. Kuhn disputes the notion of gradual change and modification in science, arguing instead that established "paradigms" tend to persist until the weight of contradictory evidence brings their rejection and replacement by new paradigms. This short book is at once stimulating and informative.

Lofiand, John and Lyn H. Lofiand. *Analyzing Social Settings: A Guide to Qualitative Observation and Analysis.* Belmont, CA: Wadsworth, 1995. An excellent text on how to conduct qualitative inquiry with an eye toward discovering the rules of social life. Includes a critique of postmodernism.

McGrane, Bernard. *The Un-TV and 10 mph Car: Experiments in Personal Freedom and Everyday Life.* Fort Bragg, CA: The Small Press, 1994. Some excellent and imaginative examples of an ethnomethodological approach to society and to the craft of sociology. The book is useful for both students and faculty.

Reinharz, Shulamit. *Feminist Methods in Social Research.* New York: Oxford University Press, 1992. This book explores several social research techniques (such as interviewing, experiments, and content analysis) from a feminist perspective.

Shaffir, William B. and Robert A. Stebbins. eds. *Experiencing Fieldwork: An Inside View of Qualitative Research.* Newbury Park, CA: Sage, 1991. The authors in this collection focus on the relatively neglected social and emotional aspects of field research.

Tomm, Winnie. ed. *The Effects of Feminist Approaches on Research Methodologies.* Waterloo, ON: Wilfrid Laurier University Press, 1989. The authors of the essays come from a variety of disciplines. They discuss the overall concept of feminist methodology and its impact, as well as its interdisciplinary character.

Turner, Jonathan H., ed. *Theory Building in Sociology: Assessing Theoretical Cumulation.* Newbury Park, CA: Sage, 1989. This collection of essays on sociological theory construction focuses specifically on the question posed by Turner's introductory chapter, "Can Sociology Be a Cumulative Science?"

InfoTrac: You can find further relevant readings on the World Wide Web at

http://sociology.wadsworth.com

Chapter 3

The Idea of Causation in Social Research

Explanations in social science rest on the idea of causation. A solid understanding of what causation means and how it is established in social research is needed in order to conduct research and to evaluate others' research conclusions.

Introduction

One of the chief goals of researchers—social or other—is to explain why things are the way they are. Typically, they do that by specifying the causes of the phenomena they observe: What things are caused by other things.

The idea of causation has been implicit in much of our discussion so far. Now we'll delve more deeply into this concept, especially as it applies to social research. We'll begin by looking at the role of determinism in social science as contrasted with the idea of free will. Then we'll look at causation in the context of the idiographic and nomothetic modes of explanation introduced in Chapter 1. After considering the criteria for deciding that one thing causes another, we'll conclude by examining some common errors that people make in reasoning about causation.

Determinism and Social Science

Scientific explanations rest on the idea that events and conditions have causes. Once we understand these causes, we know why things are the way they are: Given the occurrence of their causes, they could not be any other way. In philosophical terms,

this perspective is called *determinism*. Events are determined, or caused to happen; they are not "free" to happen any other way.

In social science, this deterministic perspective contrasts with the idea of free will that all of us take for granted in our daily lives. As such, students of social research can find this basic scientific assumption troubling. The fundamental issue is this: Is our behaviour the product of our freely chosen decisions and whims, or is it the product of forces and factors in the world that we can't control and may not even recognize?

Let's begin our explanation of this issue by looking at causation in the natural sciences. Then we'll consider how this basic concept is used in the social sciences.

Causation in the Natural Sciences

The deterministic model of explanation is exemplified throughout the natural sciences. In the science of living things, growth, for example, is caused by several factors. We can affect the growth of plants by varying the amount of light, water, and nutrients they receive. These factors, among others such as genetic inheritance, determine how the plants will grow. We also know that the growth rate of human beings is affected by the nutrients they receive. The desire to grow or not to grow is as irrelevant for humans as it is for plants. We acknowledge that genetics and nutrition greatly overshadow our free will in this matter.

The cause-and-effect, deterministic model of the natural sciences is often applied to human beings, as well as to plants and inanimate objects. For the most part, we accept the deterministic model as appropriate in such cases. We recognize that our free will is limited by certain constraints.

Finding Causes in Social Science

Essentially the same model is used in the social sciences. It's usually so implicit that we may forget the nature of the model we are using, so let's illustrate how social science depends on a deterministic model.

Imagine that you've managed to obtain a million-dollar grant from the Social Science and Humanities Research Council to find out the causes of prejudice. You hope that what you discover will lead to ideas for reducing prejudice. This is certainly a laudable aim, and various government and private foundations are often willing to support such research. Let's suppose you received the money, completed the research, and sent your report to the foundation. Here's how it reads:

> After an exhaustive examination of the subject, we have discovered that some people are prejudiced, and the reason is that they choose to be prejudiced. Other people are not prejudiced, and the reason is that they don't choose to be prejudiced.

Why would the foundation reject this conclusion as unsatisfactory? Your project aimed at finding out what causes prejudice, but your conclusion doesn't explain *why* prejudice happens. It simply pushes the explanation back into a mysterious black box labelled "choice." We have no more understanding of prejudice now than we did before you began.

When we look for the causes of prejudice, we look for the reasons, or factors, that make some people prejudiced and others not. If the "explanation" is that people choose their attitudes, then we want to know why people make different choices. Satisfactory reasons might include economic competition, religious ideology, political views, childhood experiences, and amount and kind of education. Research shows, for example, that education tends to reduce prejudice. That's the kind of useful, causal explanation we accept as the end product of social research.

Let's look at the logic of such an explanation a little more closely. What does an explanation of prejudice in terms of education and other factors say about the people who were the subjects of study? Fundamentally, it says that they turned out prejudiced or unprejudiced as a result of factors they did not control or choose. It's as though they came to a fork in the road—one path leading to prejudice and the other to the absence of prejudice—and they were propelled down one or the other by forces such as childhood experiences, level of education, economic competition, and similar factors they neither controlled nor even recognized as causing their attitudes. That is, to the extent that these factors account fully for prejudice, they turned out prejudiced or unprejudiced for reasons beyond their control.

When social scientists study juvenile delinquency, the basic model is the same: Delinquency is caused by factors other than the delinquent's free choice. They further assume that those factors can be discovered and perhaps modified, so as to produce fewer delinquents in the future.

The same model applies when social scientists study behaviours that they or others consider socially desirable. What are the factors that cause a person to be altruistic, considerate, responsible? If we knew the answers, we could arrange things so that more people turned out that way, or so the implicit reasoning goes.

Reasons Have Reasons

Sometimes people protest this line of reasoning by arguing that individuals do choose those things that determine how prejudiced, delinquent, or altruistic they are. For example, let's say you're quite unprejudiced, and researchers conclude that your lack of prejudice is probably a function of all the education you've received. Didn't you choose to go to school? Aren't your own choices, therefore, the root cause of your being unprejudiced?

The problem with this view is that reasons have reasons. Why did you go to school? Initially it was because somebody probably made you go. But there was a point when you decided to continue your education at least through university. Let's say you wanted to learn about the world around you, and you thought university would be a good way to do it. That makes sense.

It makes so much sense in fact that we might even say your desire to learn about the world caused you to continue going to school. Given that you had such a desire, how could you not go to university?

"I might not have gone if I hadn't had enough money," you might say. True, that factor would have forced you to stay out of school. But then suppose your desire to learn about the world around you was so powerful that you overcame the lack of money—maybe you got a scholarship or went to work for a while. In that case, we're back to your powerful desire as the cause of your going to university.

Ah, but why did you have such a strong desire to continue your education as a way of learning about the world around you? You could have saved money to tour the world instead. Perhaps you grew up in a family where everyone had gone to university generation after generation, and you'd have felt you were letting your family down if you didn't go to university. Or perhaps you come from a family where nobody had ever gone to university before, and they were all proud of the fact that you might be the first. In both cases, there were factors that caused your powerful desire to go to university, and that powerful desire caused you to go. Assuming that going to university caused you to be free of prejudice, this fortunate effect is ultimately produced by factors you didn't choose.

Clearly, this example oversimplifies the multiple reasons why one does something like go to university, but you can apply this line of thinking for yourself and see that there were reasons behind your behaviour that explain why you did what you did. Moreover, no matter what reason you had at any specific step in the process, that reason would

have a reason. The ultimate implication of this discussion is that our attitudes and behaviours can be traced back through a long and complex chain of reasons that explain why we turned out the way we have. If this were not the case, we would not be able to give the kinds of explanations we do in social science and see them validated by research.

Whenever we undertake explanatory social science research, then, we implicitly adopt a model of human behaviour that assumes people have little individual freedom of choice. Are we therefore committed to the view that there is no such thing as free choice? Instead of answering this question with a simple yes or no, let's put the assumption of determinism in perspective.

Determinism in Perspective

The issue of determinism and freedom is quite complex—one that philosophers have debated for thousands of years and will probably debate for thousands more. It is perhaps one of those "open questions" that are more valuable asked than answered. Certainly, we are not going to resolve the issue here.

Nevertheless, as social researchers we need to recognize the role of determinism in social research and grapple with its implications. New researchers often harbour a concern about whether they're learning to demonstrate that they themselves have no free will, no personal freedom in determining the course of their own lives. To the extent that this concern grows and festers, it interferes with learning analytical skills and techniques. Therefore, it's important to confront the issue head-on.

Although explanations in social science rest on a deterministic model, we need to be clear about what is *not* part of the model. First, social scientists do not have to believe that all human actions, thoughts, and feelings are determined, nor do they lead their lives as though they believed it. But when they seek to explain things that lend themselves to social scientific study, they necessarily use the ideas of cause and effect. Second, as we've already suggested, the deterministic model does not assume that causal patterns are simple. Nor does the model assume we are all controlled by the same factors and forces: Your reasons for going to university (and the reasons for those reasons) surely differ somewhat from each of ours. Third, the deterministic model at the base of explanatory social science does not suggest that we now know all the answers about what causes what or that we ever will. In fact, much useful research is designed to reveal associations, or relationships, between variables without attempting to demonstrate causation.

Finally, as we mentioned earlier, social science typically operates on the basis of a causal model that is probabilistic. Rather than predicting, for example, that a particular person will attend university, research predicts that certain factors make attending university more or less likely within groups of people. Thus, high school students whose parents attended university are more likely to attend university themselves than those students whose parents didn't attend university. This does not mean that all of the former and none of the latter will attend university.

To summarize, the kind of understanding social scientists seek when they construct causal explanations inevitably involves a deterministic model of human behaviour. This model implicitly assumes that the characteristics and actions under study are determined by forces and factors that can be identified through research. Social scientists don't need to believe that all aspects of human life are totally determined, but they do need to be willing to use deterministic logic in seeking explanations for the phenomena that interest them.

Causation in Idiographic and Nomothetic Models of Explanation

The preceding discussions, with their emphasis on the multiplicity of reasons that can account for a specific behaviour, illustrate the idiographic model of explanation. This model aims at explanation through the enumeration of the many reasons that lie behind a particular event or action. Although in practice we never truly exhaust such reasons, the idiographic model is frequently employed in many different contexts.

Traditional historians, for example, tend to use the idiographic model, enumerating all the special causes of the French Revolution or World War II. Clinical psychologists may employ this model in seeking an explanation for the aberrant behaviour of a patient. A criminal court, in response to a plea of extenuating circumstances, may seek to examine all the various factors that played a role in the defendant's behaviour. As Chapter 1 indicated, social researchers sometimes use this model as well.

When Charles Payne (1995) detailed the processes leading to 33 Mississippi lynchings between 1930 and 1950, he intended more to have the reader fully understand each case on its own merits than to develop a generalized theory of race violence. While the separate accounts contain common themes, the researcher's focus was more idiographic than nomothetic.

While the idiographic model of explanation is often used in daily life and in social research, other situations and purposes call for the nomothetic model of explanation. This model does not involve enumerating all the considerations that result in a particular action or event. Rather, it is designed to discover those considerations that are most important in explaining general classes of actions or events.

Suppose we wanted to find out why people voted for or against the 1995 referendum on sovereignty held in Québec. Each individual we talked to could give a great many reasons why he or she voted Yes or No. Suppose someone gave us 99 different reasons for voting Yes. We'd probably feel we had a pretty complete explanation for that person's vote. In fact, if we found someone else with those same 99 reasons, we would feel pretty confident in predicting that that person also voted Yes. This approach represents the idiographic model of explanation.

The nomothetic model of explanation, on the other hand, involves the isolation of those relatively few considerations that will provide a partial explanation for the voting behaviour of many or all people. For example, most of those sharing the attribute Anglophone probably voted No, while more of those sharing the attribute Francophone probably voted Yes. Realize, however, this single linguistic consideration (mother-tongue) would not provide a complete explanation for all voting behaviour. Some Anglophones voted in favour of Québec sovereignty and some Francophones voted against it. The nomothetic model of explanation aims at providing the greatest amount of explanation with the fewest number of causal variables to uncover general patterns of cause and effect.

The nomothetic model of explanation is inevitably probabilistic in its approach to causation. Naming a few considerations seldom if ever provides a complete explanation for complex behaviours. For example, we might discover that everyone who believed the referendum was best for Québec and Canada voted Yes, but that would not be a very satisfying explanation. In the best of all practical worlds, the nomothetic model indicates a very high (or very low) probability that a given action will occur whenever a limited number of specified considerations are present. Adding a larger number of specified considerations to the equation typically increases the degree of explanation, but it also makes explanations more complex—perhaps so much so that they cease to be useful.

Krahn and Bowlby (1997) were interested in overall satisfaction of students with their university experience. They were interested in finding variables that would make a difference in general rather than specific cases. Analyzing data they collected from graduates of the University of Alberta, showed that, as you might expect, "positive perceptions of teaching had a strong impact on satisfaction" (p. 157). But the researchers were also interested in seeing how and to what extent satisfaction levels were affected by other factors such as faculty of enrolment, GPA, satisfaction with academic resources on campus, degree of improvement in career-related skills, age, and sense of personal development/fulfillment. The nomothetic intent was to discover which variables had the strongest impact on university satisfaction.

In another illustration of nomothetic explanation, notice the language of causation when Sorensen and Krahn (discussed in Chapter 1) "test two possible explanations for why people hold positive or negative attitudes toward immigrants" (1996:14) in Canada. These derive, they say, from two theories that are dominant in the literature on intergroup relations. "The first proposes that exposure to higher education leads to more liberal attitudes toward immigrants and visible minority groups." "A second theory, realistic group conflict theory (or scarce resources theory), explains that negative attitudes toward visible minorities arise from competition over scarce resources" (1996:5). When discussing their findings they state:

> In other words, although high school graduates who are more positive toward immigrants are also more likely to pursue postsecondary education, participation in postsecondary education itself leads to more positive attitudes toward immigrants. Conversely, none of the economic security variables appears to be an important predictor of attitudes toward immigrants, controlling on baseline attitudes, postsecondary education, and other control variables.
>
> (p. 11)

Phrases like "leads to," "arise from," and "predictor of" signal causal explanations. Notice also how they are trying to empirically determine which of a limited number of factors have an impact in order to provide useful general patterns of cause-effect relationships that hold for a wide range of cases.

If researchers were to approach an explanation of prejudice idiographically, they would be trying to understand why a given person is prejudiced, noting that a large number of idiosyncratic circumstances and experiences have contributed to their views. In the nomothetic case, as in the above example, they look for factors that affect levels of prejudice in general, for example, those with more education are generally less prejudiced than are the less well educated.

Social scientists are sometimes criticized for dehumanizing the people they study. This charge is lodged specifically against the nomothetic model of explanation; the severity of the charge increases when social scientists analyze matters of great human concern. Religious people, for example, often feel robbed of their human individuality when a social scientist reports that their religiosity is largely a function of their gender, age, marital status, and social class. Any religious person will quickly report there is much more than that to the strength of his or her convictions. And indeed there is, as the use of the idiographic model in the case of any individual person would reveal. Is the idiographic model, though, any less dehumanizing than the nomothetic model?

If a characteristic like being religious (or unprejudiced) is a product of prior considerations, is it any more dehumanizing to seek partial but general explanations using only a few of those considerations than to seek a total explanation using them all? Logically speaking, a complete account of any individual's religiosity would still imply that it is a function of other causes—only there might be a great many of them. Perhaps what really underlies the discomfort with nomothetic explanations is that this model is more obviously deterministic. However, a careful listing of all the reasons why a particular person is religious, or votes for Candidate X, or is without prejudice, involves a deterministic perspective. In this respect, the idiographic model is no less deterministic than a model that allows us to specify the four variables most important in causing religiosity among people in general.

The distinction between qualitative and quantitative data we introduced in Chapter 1 relates to the difference between idiographic and nomothetic explanation also. Qualitative data often provide a greater depth of detailed information, readily lending themselves to idiographic explanations. On the other hand, quantitative data are more appropriate to nomothetic explanations. For example, an in-depth interview with one homeless person might yield a full (idiographic) understanding of the reasons for that person's fate, whereas a quantitative analysis might tell us whether education or gender was a better (nomothetic) predictor of homelessness.

In summary, the idea of causation is present in both the idiographic and nomothetic modes of explanation. Both are legitimate and useful. What we learn in individual cases, moreover, can suggest general, causal relationships among variables, just as those general relationships can help to focus analyses of a particular case. Most useful of all is a combination of the two approaches—if

not in the same study, then by the research community collectively.

Criteria for Causality

As we've indicated, much—but by no means all—social research is ultimately geared to revealing the causes of social phenomena. But, the mere fact that variables are observed to have some relationship does not establish that the relationship is one of cause and effect. If we found that people affiliated with the Liberal party prefer strawberry to vanilla ice cream, we'd be right to suspect that their party preference probably doesn't cause them to like strawberry more than vanilla, and still more that their preference for strawberry doesn't cause them to be Liberals. Most likely, any such observed association between these variables would be a coincidence.

By the same token, we might find that people with higher levels of education are more likely to own luxury cars than are people with less education. Owning a luxury car doesn't cause a person to receive more schooling, and there's no obvious reason why greater schooling, in and of itself, would cause people to own luxury cars. You might notice at this point that people with more education tend to have greater earning power than people with less education and that this could explain the greater percentage of educated people who own luxury cars. This indeed is a plausible causal explanation. We'll come back to this distinction between observed associations and underlying causal explanations. The point here is that to establish causal connections, something more is required than a mere association of variables.

Science involves both observation and logic. In these examples, logic suggests that the observed relationships, or associations, are not causal by nature. What criteria, then, do social scientists use to determine that one thing causes another?

Looking first at idiographic explanations, Joseph Maxwell (1996:87–88) says the main criteria for judging the validity of an explanation are (1) its credibility or believability and (2) whether alternative explanations ("rival hypotheses") were seriously considered and found wanting. The first criterion relates to logic as one of the foundations of science: We demand that our explanations make sense, even if the logic is sometimes complex. The second criterion reminds us of Sherlock Holmes' famous dictum: when all other possibilities have been eliminated, the remaining explanation must be the truth.

If you offer a seemingly thorough explanation of someone's criminality, your account passes the first test if it makes sense. But, if you haven't considered other explanations, perhaps we will offer you one that is equally credible. Unless one of these explanations is found wanting, none of us can claim to have found the "true" one. Perhaps the most accurate and complete explanation will combine features of both.

Regarding nomothetic explanation, we'll examine three specific criteria for causal relationships among variables as suggested by Paul Lazarsfeld (1959). (In Part 4, we'll see the use of these criteria in research practice.) The first requirement is that the cause precede the effect. It makes no sense to imagine something being caused by something else that happened later on. Clearly, a bullet leaving the muzzle of a gun does not cause the gunpowder to explode; it works the other way around. Owning a luxury car doesn't cause one to earn enough money to afford one.

As simple and obvious as this criterion may seem, you'll discover that it generates endless problems in the analysis of social science data. Often, the order of two variables is simply unclear. Which comes first: prejudice or the trait known as authoritarianism (excessive submissiveness to authority, accompanied by rigid thinking)? Even when the time order seems essentially clear, exceptions can often be found. For example, we would normally assume that the educational level of parents would be a cause of the educational level of their children. Yet, some parents may return to school as a result of the advanced education of their own children.

The second requirement in a causal relationship is that the two variables be empirically correlated (*empirically* means "in actual experience"). A **correlation** exists between variables when they are observed to be related—that is, when one occurs or changes, so does the other. It would make no sense to say that exploding gunpowder

causes bullets to leave muzzles of guns if, in observed reality, bullets did not come out after the gunpowder exploded (or they came out even when it didn't explode).

Again, social science research can run into difficulties with this apparently obvious requirement. At least in the probabilistic world of nomothetic explanations, there are few perfect correlations—that is, as one variable takes on different values so does some other variable, in perfect lockstep and without a single exception. Most Anglophones voted against the Québec Referendum in 1995, but some didn't. We are forced to ask, therefore, how strong an empirical relationship must be for that relationship to be considered causal.

The third requirement for a causal relationship is that the observed empirical correlation between two variables cannot be explained in terms of some third variable. We already saw an example of the possible "third variable" explanation in the case of education and ownership of a luxury car. To take another example, there is a positive correlation between ice cream sales and deaths due to drowning: the more ice cream sold, the more drownings, and vice versa. However, there is no direct link between ice cream and drowning. The third variable at work here is season or temperature. Most drowning deaths occur during summer, the peak period for ice cream sales. These are examples of **spurious relationships**—relationships that aren't genuine. The observed association (correlation) between ice cream sold and drownings is real enough, but a causal linkage between these variables would be spurious. In reality, a third variable explains the observed association.

Another example of a spurious relationship is the positive correlation between shoe size and math ability among school children. Here, the third variable that explains the puzzling relationship is age. Older children have bigger feet and more highly developed math skills, on average, than do younger children. There will be further discussion of spurious relationships in Part 4. The box entitled "Correlation and Causality" illustrates the point that correlation alone does not establish a particular causal relationship. The mere fact of association does not tell us which variable causes the

Correlation and Causality

By Charles Bonney
Department of Sociology, Eastern Michigan University

Having demonstrated a statistical relationship between a hypothesized "cause" and its presumed "effect," many people (sometimes including researchers who should know better) are only too eager to proclaim "proof" of causation. Let's take an example to see why "it ain't necessarily so."

Imagine you have conducted a study on university students and have found an inverse (negative) correlation between marijuana smoking (variable M) and grade point average (variable G)—that is, those who smoke tend to have lower GPAs than those who do not, and the more smoked, the lower the GPA. You might therefore claim that smoking marijuana lowers one's grades (in symbolic form, M→G), giving as an explanation, perhaps, that marijuana adversely affects memory, which would naturally have detrimental consequences on grades.

However, if an inverse correlation is all the evidence you have, a second possibility exists. Getting poor grades is frustrating; frustration often leads to escapist behaviour; getting stoned is a popular means of escape; ergo, low grades cause marijuana smoking (G→M)! Unless you can establish which came first, smoking or low grades, this explanation is supported by the correlation just as plausibly as the first.

Let's introduce another variable into the picture: the existence and/or extent of emotional problems (variable E). It could certainly be plausibly argued that having emotional problems may lead to escapist behaviour, including marijuana smoking. Likewise it seems reasonable to suggest that emotional problems are likely to adversely affect grades. That correlation of marijuana smoking and low grades may exist for the same reason that runny noses and sore throats tend to go together—*neither* is the cause of the other, but rather, both are the consequences of some third variable ($E \lesssim_G^M$). Unless you can rule out such third variables, this explanation too is just as well supported by the data as is the first (or the second).

Then again, perhaps students smoke marijuana primarily because they have friends who smoke, and get low grades because they are simply not as bright or well prepared or industrious as their classmates, and the fact that it's the same stu-

other, or, indeed, whether there is any causal relationship between them.

As John and Lyn Lofland (1995:138–39) caution, it is important to distinguish the testing of causal relationships from conjecture about it. While it is perfectly acceptable to report our hunches or untested hypotheses about the causal processes at work in what we observe, we distinguish between such suspicions and proven conclusions.

In review, if we say that there is a negative (also referred to as inverse) correlation between education and prejudice, this means that higher levels of education are associated with lower levels of prejudice and vice versa. We are saying nothing about causality here, merely that the two variables are

associated. If we say that higher levels of education are a <u>cause</u> of decreases in prejudice, we are saying that there is a negative (inverse) <u>causal</u> relationship between education and prejudice. If we say that there is a positive (also referred to as direct) correlation between levels of crime and levels of punishment, we are saying that higher levels of crime are associated with higher levels of punishment and vice versa. If we say that higher amounts of crime are a <u>cause</u> of higher amounts of punishment, we are saying that there is a positive (direct) <u>causal</u> relationship between levels of crime and punishment.

Most social researchers consider two variables to be causally related if (1) the cause precedes the dents in each case in your sample is purely coincidental. Unless your correlation is so strong and so consistent that mere coincidence becomes highly unlikely, this last possibility, while not supported by your data, is not precluded either. Incidentally, this particular example was selected for two reasons. First of all, *every one* of the above explanations for such an inverse correlation has appeared in a national magazine at one time or another. And second, *every one* of them is probably doomed to failure because it turns out that, among university students, most studies indicate a direct (positive) correlation, that is, it is those with higher GPAs who are more likely to be marijuana smokers! Thus, with tongue firmly in cheek, we may reanalyze this finding:

1. Marijuana relaxes a person, clearing away other stresses, thus allowing more effective study; hence, M→G.

    or

2. Marijuana is used as a reward for really hitting the books or doing well ("Wow, man! An 'A'! Let's go get high!"); hence, G→M.

or

3. A high level of curiosity (E) is definitely an asset to learning and achieving high grades and may also lead one to investigate "taboo" substances; hence, $E \lessgtr {}^M_G$.

or

4. Again coincidence, but this time the samples just happened to contain a lot of brighter, more industrious students whose friends smoke marijuana!

The obvious conclusion is this: If *all* of these are possible explanations for a relationship between two variables, then no one of them should be too readily singled out. Establishing that two variables tend to occur together is a *necessary* condition for demonstrating a causal relationship, but it is not by itself a *sufficient* condition. It is a fact, for example, that human birthrates are higher in areas of Europe where there are lots of storks, but as to the meaning of that relationship . . . !

effect in time, (2) there is an empirical correlation between them, and (3) the relationship is not found to be the result of some third variable. People sometimes apply inappropriate criteria in reasoning about causality, as we'll discuss shortly. Therefore, it's important to remember that only relationships satisfying all three criteria are causal.

Necessary and Sufficient Causes

An error some people make is to assume that causation requires a perfect correlation between variables. In fact, a perfect association is not a criterion of causality in social science research, or in science generally for that matter. Put another way, excep-

tions do not necessarily disprove a causal relationship. In probabilistic models, exceptions to the posited relationship almost always exist. Even though not all Anglophones voted against the Québec Referendum and not all Francophones voted for it, these cases do not deny the general causal relationship between mother-tongue and voting in the referendum.

Within this probabilistic model, it's useful to distinguish between necessary and sufficient causes. A *necessary cause* represents a condition that *must* be present for the effect to follow. For example, it is necessary for you to take university courses in order to get a degree—without the courses, the degree never happens. But, simply

Figure 3-1
Necessary Cause

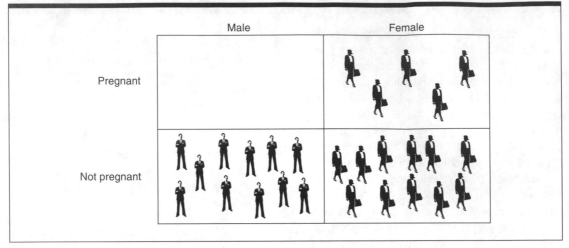

taking the courses is not a sufficient cause of getting a degree. You need to take the right ones and pass them.

Similarly, being female is a necessary condition of becoming pregnant, but it is not a sufficient cause. Otherwise all women would get pregnant. Figure 3-1 illustrates this relationship, showing the possible outcomes of combining the variables of gender and pregnancy.

A *sufficient cause*, on the other hand, represents a condition that, if it is present, guarantees the effect in question. This does not mean that a sufficient cause is the *only* possible cause of a particular effect. For example, skipping an exam in this course would be a sufficient cause for failing it, though students could fail it other ways as well. Therefore, a cause can be sufficient but not necessary. Figure 3-2 illustrates the relationship between taking or not taking the exam and either passing or failing it.

The discovery of a cause that is both necessary and sufficient is, of course, the most satisfying outcome in research. If juvenile delinquency were the effect under examination, it would be nice to discover a single condition that (1) must be present for delinquency to develop and (2) always resulted in delinquency. In such a case, you would surely feel that you knew precisely what caused juvenile delinquency.

Unfortunately, we never discover single causes that are absolutely necessary and absolutely sufficient when analyzing the nomothetic relationships among variables. It is not uncommon, however, to find causal factors that are either 100 percent necessary (you must be female to become pregnant) or 100 percent sufficient (pleading guilty will result in your conviction).

In general in social science, demonstrations of either necessary or sufficient causes—even imperfect ones—can be the basis for concluding that variables are causally related.

Errors in Reasoning about Causation

Cause and effect, as we've seen, is essential to scientific explanation. It is also fundamental to our day-to-day lives. However, we commonly make errors in our assessment of causation. Here are some examples of such errors. See if you can detect the faulty reasoning about causation before reading our explanation.

Early in the history of the AIDS epidemic, the San Francisco Chronicle carried an article reporting research that claimed a link between AIDS and fluoridation of the water. In part, the claim hinged on the assertion that "while half the country's communities have fluoridated water supplies and half do

Figure 3-2
Sufficient Cause

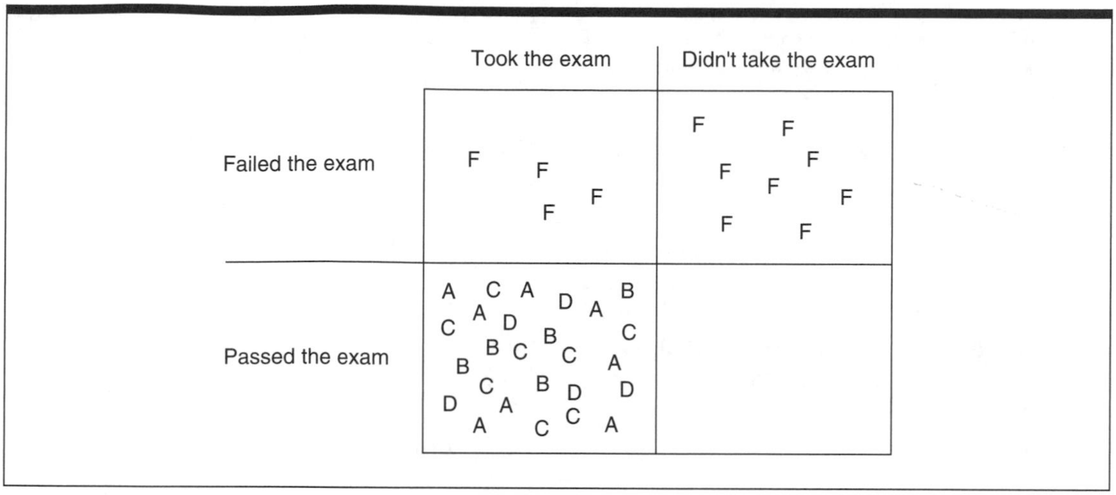

	Took the exam	Didn't take the exam
Failed the exam	F F F F	F F F F F F F F
Passed the exam	A C A D A B C A D B C B C B C A B C B D D D A C A A C C A	

not, 90 percent of AIDS cases are coming from fluoridated areas and only 10 percent are coming from nonfluoridated areas." Can you see any flaws in this reasoning? Think about it for a minute before continuing.

To begin, we should always beware when data about communities are used to draw conclusions about individuals. In this instance, "half the communities" may not contain half the population. Indeed, we might imagine that large cities would be more likely to fluoridate their water than small, rural towns. Logically, it would be possible for the fluoridated communities to have 90 percent of the nation's population, in which case they should have 90 percent of the AIDS cases even if there were no relationship between AIDS and fluoridation.

Second, progressive social values more common to cities than to small towns might affect both (1) lifestyles associated with AIDS and (2) the decision to fluoridate the water supply. In that case, AIDS and fluoridation could be statistically correlated without being causally linked.

The problems of faulty causal reasoning are not limited to statistical analyses. The examination of historical processes is equally vulnerable. Consider this example: At a news conference on August 5, 1985, then-U.S. President Ronald Reagan noted the 40th anniversary of the atomic bombing of

Hiroshima by saying that that terrible example of nuclear destruction had served as "a deterrent that kept us at peace for the longest stretch we've ever known, 40 years of peace." Many people who supported an immediate end to the nuclear arms race were quick to deny the causal relationship asserted by the U.S. president, saying it was not the bombing of Hiroshima that had kept the peace. Can you spot another flaw in the causal assertion?

What seems most subject to question was not the causes of the "40 years of peace" but its very existence. The period in question includes the U.S. conflict in Korea (often referred to as the Korean War) as well as the Vietnam War—not to mention scores of other confrontations around the world. It's difficult to maintain that the bombing of Hiroshima caused a period of peace when there was no consistent peace.

Sometimes it's possible to detect failures of causal reasoning on logical grounds alone, even when there is no possibility of examining empirical data. Again, concern about AIDS offers an example. Some have argued that the AIDS epidemic represents God's displeasure with certain human behaviours: specifically, homosexuality and drug use. The evangelist Don Boys spoke on the sexual issue in a guest editorial in *USA Today* (October 7, 1985):

The AIDS epidemic indicates that morality has broken its mooring and drifted into a miasmic swamp, producing disease, degeneracy, and death. . . . God's plan is for each man to have one woman—his wife—for a lifetime, and be faithful to her.

The flaw in this case is not that AIDS has become increasingly common among heterosexual, married couples or that some hemophiliac young people have contracted AIDS through tainted blood transfusions. It's legitimate to use a probabilistic model of causation in this context, and homosexual men are, in fact, more likely to contract AIDS than heterosexual men (at least in North America). However, if AIDS is an indication of "God's plan," then lesbians must be the most favoured of all, because AIDS is rarest among them.

None of these illustrations of faulty causal reasoning is intended as an indictment of the perpetrators. All of us fall into such errors. It has been said that the problem with "common sense" is that it's not all that common. The purpose of these examples has been twofold. First, such examples help sensitize us to faulty causal reasoning by revealing some of the ways it shows up in daily life. Developing an awareness of such flawed reasoning can help us to recognize errors in others' reasoning and avoid making similar errors ourselves. Second, these examples serve as a backdrop for understanding the power of careful, scientific reasoning. Although scientists are not immune to logical error, the procedures of science offer some degree of protection.

Although no one can give you a neat set of rules for logical reasoning, an excellent book, Howard Kahane's *Logic and Contemporary Rhetoric* (1992), outlines many of the errors people commonly make. Here are some of the pitfalls Kahane discusses.

Provincialism

All of us look at the world through glasses framed by our particular histories and current situations. There is always a danger, then, that researchers will interpret people's behaviour in ways that make sense from the researchers' own points of view.

The world can look quite different to men and women, to people who grew up in different social classes, to religious and nonreligious people, and so on. This problem is particularly evident in cross-cultural research.

At the same time, Harry Wolcott (1995:164–65), in discussing "the art of fieldwork," suggests that our personal and cultural biases can work for the good. They can lend focus to an inquiry and provide insights by involving a point of view different from that of the participants being observed. The key is to be conscious of our particular views and remain open to broadening our perspectives by recognizing that others' views may be equally valid.

Hasty Conclusion

Researchers as well as other people are susceptible to drawing hasty conclusions. Whenever a researcher offers an interpretation of data, be sure to evaluate the "weight" of evidence leading to that interpretation. Is the conclusion essentially inevitable given the data lying behind it, or are other conclusions just as reasonable? We also need to consider all the alternative conclusions that could follow from our own data.

Questionable Cause

Whenever it seems to you that X caused Y, ask yourself if that is necessarily the case. What else could have caused Y? Kahane (1992:63) gives several economic examples. If a business goes bankrupt, people often conclude that the company's president lacked business skills—even when the bankruptcy occurred during a severe recession, marked by a great many business failures. It's sometimes easy to come up with plausible causal explanations, but establishing the true cause requires eliminating other possible explanations.

Suppressed Evidence

Field researchers amass a great deal of information through direct observations, interviews, library work, and so on. To reach conclusions requires dismissing information as much as selecting it. On the whole, a researcher will dismiss information

Chapter 3: The Idea of Causation in Social Research   **71**

that is "not relevant"; however, that in itself is obviously a matter of judgment.

When reading research reports, attend to observations you've noted that do not figure in the conclusions, as well as observations not mentioned that you can reasonably assume were made. For instance, suppose a researcher concludes that members of a neo-Nazi group were hostile to aboriginals out of a fear of economic competition. If this conclusion is correct, we would expect most members to be working class or lower-middle class. But if the researcher has not indicated the occupations of the group's members, we might well question whether the evidence supports the conclusion.

More generally, you should always be careful whenever the report of a study fails to provide details of the methods employed. For example, suppose you were told that a "survey" of voters revealed the following opinions on the job that the prime minister was doing:

40% Very good job
40% Good job
10% Bad job
10% Very bad job

If the report did not disclose the number of respondents represented by the data (these percentages could equally represent 10 people or 1000 people), plus some indication of how those respondents were selected, you should be wary.

False Dilemma

Research conclusions, like nonscientific opinions, often represent the selection of one position from among alternatives. Selecting one often seems to rule out all others, but this need not be the case. A false dilemma is a choice that seems to be forced but really is not. Kahane offers this example: "Economics, not biology, may explain male domination." This bold assertion seems to rule out the influence of politics, education, custom, religion, and a host of other possibilities. As Kahane puts it:

> This statement suggests that there are just two possibilities: either biology explains male domi-

nance (note the begged question!), or economic success does. And it suggests that the second possibility, economic success, "may" (weasel word) be the true explanation of male domination. Yet there are many other possibilities, such as social custom, religious conviction, and various combinations of economic and biological factors. By tempting us to think of the cause of male domination as either economics or biology, the quote leads us to overlook other possibilities and thus to commit the fallacy of false dilemma.

(1992:42)

This warning is echoed by David Silverman (1993:205), in saying a basic rule in the analysis of qualitative data is "never appeal to a single element as an explanation." Always look for alternative or additional causes. We should be wary of this pitfall in reading the works of others but also be wary of falling into it ourselves.

The various discussions of this chapter should have given you a sense of the explanatory purpose of social research. Though it's not the only purpose of research, we very often wish to explain why people think and act as they do. Typically, we ask what causes what. Sometimes we seek an in-depth, idiographic explanation that lets us fully understand a particular case; sometimes we look for a more general, though partial explanation that applies to a broad class of cases. Both are legitimate approaches in social science that support each other.

We've introduced the notion of causation early in the book, so that you can hold it as a backdrop for the discussions that follow. The process of determining the association between variables—the nature of their relationship—however, is intimately linked with how the variables are measured. We must measure variables before we can determine if they are associated and then how they are associated. In practice, this is not always easy. There are many practical problems that arise in this process. As we saw in Chapter 2, when we attempt to operationalize concepts such as juvenile delinquency, the indicators we choose are approximations and therefore the operationalization of concepts is often ambiguous. For example, if we use arrest data as a measure of delinquency, we run the risk that we have not fully captured the concept of delinquency with this indicator. Some juveniles may have been falsely arrested and some juveniles who have engaged in delinquent behaviour may not have been arrested. Therefore, all empirical indicators have some defects. Researchers are constantly seeking to improve the measures they use. (Concepts and measurement will be discussed at length in Chapter 5.) Thus, while we discuss aspects of the research process in stages in this book for pedagogical reasons, it's important to keep in mind that in practice these steps are interrelated and often handled simultaneously. It's best to think of the researcher as moving back and forth among them rather than moving from one to the other.

Similarly, we have said little about ethical concerns in Chapters 2 and 3. In practice, however, ethical considerations are an integral part of the research process from start to finish. For example, some ways of measuring variables may be ethically questionable and therefore not used by a researcher on ethical grounds. Yet, for expository reasons, these concerns are more readily addressed in Part 3 when we take up issues of observation and data gathering.

Main Points

- Explanatory scientific research depends implicitly on the idea of cause and effect.
- Explanatory social scientific research depends implicitly on a deterministic model of the human behaviour it seeks to explain.
- Both idiographic and nomothetic models of explanation rest on the idea of causation. The idiographic model aims at a complete understanding of a particular phenomenon, using all relevant causal factors. The nomothetic model aims at a general understanding—not necessarily complete—of a class of phenomena, using a small number of relevant causal factors.
- In idiographic explanations, the principal criteria for establishing a causal relationship are (1) the credibility of the explanation and (2) a

demonstration that alternative explanations should be rejected.
- There are three basic criteria for establishing causation in nomothetic analyses: (1) The variables must be empirically associated, or correlated, (2) the causal variable must occur earlier in time than the variable it is said to affect, and (3) the observed effect cannot be explained as the effect of a different variable.
- Mere association, or correlation, does not in itself establish causation. A spurious causal relationship is an association that in reality is caused by one or more other variables.
- A perfect statistical relationship between two variables is not an appropriate criterion for causation in social research. We may say that a causal relationship exists between X and Y, then, even though X is not the total cause of Y.
- Most explanatory social research uses a probabilistic model of causation. X may be said to cause Y if it is seen to have some influence on Y.
- There are two important types of causes: necessary and sufficient. X is a necessary cause of Y if Y cannot happen without X. X is a sufficient cause of Y if Y always happens when X happens. The scientifically most satisfying discovery is a necessary and sufficient cause.
- Researchers need to guard against several common kinds of errors in reasoning about causation, including provincialism, hasty conclusions, questionable identification of causes, suppressed evidence, and false dilemmas.

Review Questions and Exercises

1. Describe the conditions that would allow you to conclude that education was
   a. a necessary cause of reduced prejudice
   b. a sufficient cause of reduced prejudice
   c. a necessary and sufficient cause of reduced prejudice
2. In 1997 women working full-time earned 73 percent as much as men in Canadian society (*The Daily*, September 14, 2000). What do you

suppose "causes" that difference? Describe the procedures by which you might test your conjectures.

3. Use the Web to locate several reports of scientific findings concerning causes of the difference between men and women's earnings. State what variables the researchers used and how they operationalized and tested them. State their findings and discuss whether or not you accept the conclusions they reported and why.

4. Why did you choose to attend the university you are now attending? Create an idiographic explanation by detailing all the factors that led to your choice. How would this compare with a nomothetic approach that explained the choices of many other university students besides yourself? What might be gained and lost from the nomothetic explanation compared with your idiographic account?

Continuity Project

Apply the logic of idiographic and nomothetic explanations to the case of gender equality/inequality. First, write a detailed idiographic explanation for why a particular woman receives less pay than a male coworker. Second, provide a nomothetic explanation by identifying a variable that affects gender income differences in general. Base your statements in fact if possible, or make up hypothetical information if necessary. The key is to illustrate the two explanatory models.

Additional Readings

Davis, James A. *The Logic of Causal Order*. Beverly Hills, CA: Sage, 1985. Davis examines the log-ical and statistical dimensions of causality in social research.

Hirschi, Travis, and Hanan Selvin. *Principles of Survey Analysis*. New York: Free Press, 1973, especially Part II. Excellent statements on causation within a practical framework. One of the very best discussions of causation within the context of particular research findings. The book is readable, stimulating, and generally just plain excellent.

Lazarsfeld, Paul. Foreword. In Herbert Hyman, *Survey Design and Analysis*. New York: Free Press, 1955. A classic and still valid statement of causation in social science. In the context of the elaboration model, Lazarsfeld provides a clear statement of the criteria for determining causation.

Shaver, Kelly G. *The Attribution of Blame: Causality, Responsibility, and Blameworthiness*. New York: Springer-Verlag, 1985. Shaver discusses many of the aspects of causality presented in this chapter and shows how they relate to the notions of responsibility and blame.

Wallace, William A. *Causality and Scientific Explanation*. Ann Arbor: University of Michigan Press, 1972. In case you developed an interest in the question of causality, this two-volume work provides a full examination of the history of the concept within science, from medieval times to the present.

InfoTrac: You can find further relevant readings on the World Wide Web at

http://sociology.wadsworth.com

Part 2
The Structuring of Inquiry

The Structuring of Inquiry

Posing problems properly is often more difficult than answering them. Indeed, a properly phrased question often seems to answer itself. You may have discovered the answer to a question just in the process of making the question clear to someone else.

Part 2 considers the posing of proper scientific questions—the structuring of inquiry. Part 3 will describe some of the specific methods of social scientific observation.

Chapter 4 addresses the beginnings of research. It examines some of the purposes of inquiry, units of analysis, and reasons scientists get involved in research projects.

Chapter 5 deals with the specification of what it is you want to study—the processes of conceptualization and operationalization. It looks at some of the terms we use quite casually in everyday life—*prejudice, liberalism, happiness,* and so forth—and shows how essential it is to clarify what we really mean by such terms when we do research. This process of clarification is called *conceptualization*. Once we clarify what we mean by certain terms, we can then measure the referents of those terms. The process of devising steps or operations for

measuring what we want to study is called *operationalization*.

To complete the introduction to measurement, Chapter 6 breaks with the chronological discussion of how research is conducted. In this chapter, we'll examine techniques for measuring variables in quantitative research through the combination of several indicators: indexes, scales, and typologies. Although such measures are constructed during the analysis of data (see Part 4), the raw materials for them must be provided for in the design and execution of data collection.

Finally, we'll look at how social scientists select people or things for observation. Chapter 7 addresses the fundamental scientific issue of generalizability. As you'll see, we can select a few people or things for observation and then apply what we observe to a much larger group of people or things. This chapter examines techniques that increase the generalizability of what we observe.

What you learn in Part 2 will bring you to the verge of making controlled research observations. Part 3 will show you how to take that next step.

Chapter 4

Research Design

A wide variety of research designs are available to social science researchers. Designing a study involves specifying exactly who or what is to be studied when, how, and for what purpose.

In this chapter . . .

Introduction

Science is an enterprise dedicated to "finding out." No matter what you want to find out, though, there will likely be a great many ways of doing it. That's true in life generally. Suppose that you want to find out whether a particular automobile—say, the new Burpo-Blasto—would be a good car for you. You could, of course, buy one and find out that way. You could talk to a lot of B-B owners or to people who considered buying one and didn't. You might check the classified ads to see if there are a lot of B-Bs being sold cheap. You could read a consumer magazine evaluation of Burpo-Blastos, and so on. You might combine several of these ways of finding out. A similar situation occurs in scientific inquiry.

Ultimately, scientific inquiry comes down to making observations and interpreting what you've observed, the subjects of Parts 3 and 4 of this book.

Before you can observe and analyze, however, you need a plan. You need to determine what you're going to observe and analyze: why and how. That's what research design is all about.

Although the details vary according to what you wish to study, there are two major tasks in any research design. First, you must specify as clearly as possible what you want to find out. Second, you must determine the best way to do it. Interestingly, if you can handle the first consideration fully, you'll probably handle the second in the same process. As mathematicians say, a properly framed question contains the answer. Of course, issues of ethics are integral to your determination of the best way to do it as well.

Let's say you're interested in studying corruption in government. That's certainly a worthy and appropriate topic for social research. But, what do you mean by *corruption*? Specifically, what kinds of behaviours do you have in mind? And what do you mean by *government*? Whom do you want to study: all public employees? elected officials? civil servants? Finally, what is your purpose? Do you want to find out *how much* corruption there is? Do you want to learn *why* corruption exists? These are the kinds of questions that need to be answered in the course of research design.

This chapter provides a general introduction to research design, while the other chapters in Part 2 elaborate on specific aspects. In practice, all aspects of research design are interrelated. How these parts interrelate will become clearer as you move through Part 2.

We'll begin by briefly examining the three main purposes of social research that help to define what kind of study to undertake. Then we'll consider units of analysis: the what or whom you want to study. Next we'll consider alternative ways of handling time in social research. Some studies examine a static cross section of social life, but others follow social processes over time. We then turn to how to design a research project. This overview of the overall research process serves two purposes. In addition to describing how you might go about designing a study, it gives you a map of the remainder of this book.

Finally, we'll look at the elements of research proposals. Often the actual conduct of research needs to be preceded by a detailing of your intentions in order to obtain funding for a major project or perhaps to get your instructor's approval for a class project. You'll see that this offers an excellent opportunity for you to consider all aspects of your research in advance.

Purposes of Research

Social research, of course, serves many purposes. Three of the most common and useful purposes are *exploration, description,* and *explanation.* Although a given study can have more than one of these purposes—and most do—examining them separately is useful because each has different implications for other aspects of research design.

Exploration

Much of social research is conducted to explore a topic, or to begin to familiarize the researcher with that topic. This approach typically occurs when a researcher examines a new interest or when the subject of study itself is relatively new.

As an example, let's suppose that widespread taxpayer dissatisfaction with the government erupts into a taxpayers' revolt. People begin refusing to pay their taxes, and they organize themselves around that issue. You might like to learn more about the movement: How widespread is it? What levels and degrees of support are there within the community? How is the movement organized? What kinds of people are active in it? You might undertake an exploratory study to obtain at least approximate answers to some of these questions. You might check figures with tax-collecting officials, collect and study the literature of the movement, attend meetings, and interview leaders.

Exploratory studies are also appropriate for more persistent phenomena. Suppose you're unhappy with your university's graduation requirements and want to help change them. You might study the history of such requirements at the university and meet with university officials to learn the reasons for the current standards. You could talk to several students to get a rough idea of their sentiments on the subject. Though this last activity would not necessarily yield a precise and accurate picture of student opinion, it could suggest what the results of a more extensive study might be.

Sometimes exploratory research is pursued through the use of *focus groups,* or guided small-group discussions. This technique is frequently used in market research; we'll examine it further in Chapter 12.

Exploratory studies are most typically done for three purposes: (1) to satisfy the researcher's curiosity and desire for better understanding, (2) to test the feasibility of undertaking a more extensive study, and (3) to develop the methods to be employed in any subsequent study.

Exploratory studies are quite valuable in social scientific research. They're essential whenever a researcher is breaking new ground, and they almost always yield new insights into a topic for research. Exploratory studies are also a source of grounded theory, as discussed in Chapter 2.

The chief shortcoming of exploratory studies is that they seldom provide satisfactory answers to research questions, though they can hint at the answers and can give insights into which research methods could provide definitive answers. The reason exploratory studies are seldom definitive in themselves has to do with representativeness, that is, the people studied in exploratory research may not be typical of the larger population of interest. (Representativeness is discussed at length in Chapter 7.) Once you understand representativeness, you will be able to know whether a given exploratory study actually answered its research problem or only pointed the way toward an answer.

Description

A major purpose of many social scientific studies is to describe situations and events. The researcher observes and then describes what was observed. Because scientific observation is careful and deliberate, however, scientific descriptions are typically more accurate and precise than casual ones.

The Canadian Census is an excellent example of descriptive social research. The goal of the census is to describe accurately and precisely a wide variety of characteristics of the Canadian population, as well as the populations of smaller areas such as provinces and cities. Other examples of descriptive studies are the computation of age-gender profiles of populations done by demographers, the computation of crime rates for different cities, and a product marketing survey that describes the people who use, or would use, a particular product. A researcher who carefully chronicles the events that take place on a labour union picket line has, or at least serves, a descriptive purpose. A researcher who computes and reports the distribution of wages for men and women over several decades also fulfils a descriptive purpose.

Many qualitative studies aim primarily at description. An anthropological ethnography, for example, may try to detail the particular culture of some preliterate society. At the same time, such studies are seldom limited to a merely descriptive purpose. Researchers usually go on to examine *why* the observed patterns exist and what they imply.

Explanation

The third general purpose of social scientific research is to explain things. Descriptive studies answer questions of what, where, when, and how—explanatory studies, of why. So when William Sanders (1994) set about describing the varieties of gang violence, he also wanted to reconstruct the process that brought about violent episodes among the gangs of different ethnic groups.

Reporting the voting intentions of an electorate is a descriptive activity, but reporting why some people plan to vote for Candidate A and others for Candidate B is an explanatory activity. Reporting the crime rates of different cities is a case of description, but identifying variables that explain why some cities have higher crime rates than others involves explanation. A researcher who sets out to discover *why* an antiabortion demonstration ended in a violent confrontation with police, as opposed to simply describing what happened, has an explanatory purpose.

Similarly, a study of the wage differentials between men and women might serve a worthwhile descriptive purpose by simply reporting the earnings of men versus women annually, in full-time jobs, part-time jobs, in different occupational groups, and so forth. Or a researcher might be interested in discovering what factors account for the "gender wage gap." That is "why" do women, on average, earn less per hour and have lower annual incomes than do men? Marie Drolet (1999) conducted an explanatory analysis using the Survey of Labour and Income Dynamics data to examine factors that might account for the differences in wages between men and women in Canada. She looked at the potential impact of factors such as education level, major field of study, work experience, job tenure, job skills, job-related responsibilities, full versus part-time employment, and a number of other factors. She found, for example, that gender differences in work experience explain some of the wage gap but not very much of it (about 12 percent). She also found that "gender differences in the opportunity to supervise and to perform certain tasks account for about 7 percent of the gender wage gap" (p. 8). Nonetheless, after looking at a large number of factors, her analysis was unable to account for a substantial amount of the gender wage gap.

Although it's useful to distinguish the three purposes of research, it bears repeating that most studies will have elements of all three. Suppose, for example, that you have set out to evaluate a new form of psychotherapy. Your study will have exploratory aspects, as you explore potentially relevant variables and map out the impacts of the therapy. You'll want to describe things like recovery rates, and you'll undoubtedly seek to explain why the therapy works better for some types of people (or problems) than for others.

You'll see these several purposes at work in the following discussions of other aspects of research design. Let's turn now to a consideration of whom or what you want to explore, describe, and explain.

Units of Analysis

In social scientific research, there is virtually no limit to what or whom can be studied, or the **units of analysis.** This topic is relevant to all forms of social research, although its implications are clearest in the case of nomothetic, quantitative studies.

The concept of unit of analysis may seem slippery at first because researchers, particularly those seeking nomothetic explanations, often study large collections of people or things, or aggregates. It's important to distinguish between units of analysis and the aggregates that we generalize about. For example, a researcher may study a class of people, such as professional hockey players, university undergraduates, aboriginal women under 30, or some other collection. But, if the researcher is interested in exploring, describing, or explaining how different groups of individuals behave *as individuals*, the unit of analysis is the individual, not the group. This is so even though the researcher then proceeds to generalize about aggregates of individuals, as in saying that more women than men favour gender equality. Think of it this way: Having an attitude about gender equality is something that can only be an attribute of an individual, not a group: that is, there is no one group "mind" that can have an attitude. So even when we generalize about women, we're generalizing about an attribute they possess as individuals.

However, we may sometimes want to study groups, considered as unitary "actors" or entities that have attributes *as groups*. For instance, we might want to compare the characteristics of different types of street gangs. In that case our unit of analysis would be gangs (not members of gangs), and we might proceed to make generalizations about different types of gangs.

Social scientists perhaps most typically choose individual people as their units of analysis. Researchers can note the characteristics of individual people: gender, age, region of birth, attitudes, and so forth. They can then combine these descriptions to provide a composite picture of the group the individuals represent, whether a street-corner gang or a whole society.

For example, you may note the age and gender of each student enrolled in Political Science 110 and then characterize the group of students descriptively as being 53 percent men and 47 percent women and as having a mean age of 18.6 years. Although the final description would be of the class as a whole, the description is based on characteristics that members of the class have as individuals. The individual characteristics are aggregated for purposes of describing some larger group.

The same distinction between units of analysis and aggregations occurs in explanatory studies. Suppose you wished to discover whether students with good study habits received better grades in Political Science 110 than did students with poor study habits. You would operationalize the variable study habits and measure it, perhaps in terms of hours of study per week. You might then aggregate students with good study habits and those with poor study habits and see which group received the best grades in the course. The purpose of the study would be to explain why some groups of students do better in the course than others, but the unit of analysis is still individual students.

Units of analysis in a study are often also the *units of observation.* Thus, to study success in a political science course, we would observe individual students. Sometimes, however, we "observe" our units of analysis indirectly. For example, suppose we want to find out whether disagreements about abortion rights tend to cause divorce. We might "observe" individual husbands and wives by asking them about their attitudes toward abortion, in order to distinguish couples that agree and disagree on this issue. In this case, our *units of observation* are individual wives and husbands, but our *units of analysis* (the things we want to study) are couples.

Some studies try to describe or explain more than one unit of analysis. In these cases, the researcher must anticipate what conclusions she or he wishes to draw with regard to which units of analysis. For example, we may want to discover what kinds of university students (individuals) are most successful in their careers; we may also want to learn what kinds universities (organizations) produce the most successful graduates.

Units of analysis, then, are those things we examine in order to create summary descriptions of all such units and to explain differences among them. In most research projects, the unit of analysis will probably be clear to you. When the unit of analysis is not so clear, however, it's essential to determine what it is; otherwise, you cannot determine what observations are to be made about whom or what.

To help make this discussion more concrete, let's consider several common social science units of analysis.

Individuals

As we've just mentioned, individual human beings are perhaps the most typical units of analysis for social scientific research. Researchers tend to describe and explain social groups and interac-

tions by aggregating and analyzing the descriptions of individuals.

Any type of individual may be the unit of analysis for social scientific research. This point is more important than it may seem at first reading. Since social science seeks to understand human behaviour in general, this suggests that scientific findings are most valuable when they apply to *all* kinds of people. In practice, however, social scientists seldom study all kinds of people. At the very least, their studies are typically limited to the people living in a single country, though some comparative studies stretch across national boundaries. Often, though, studies are quite circumscribed.

Examples of classes of individuals that might be chosen for study include university students, gays and lesbians, autoworkers, Canadian voters, single parents, and professional athletes. Notice that each of these terms implies some population of individual persons. Descriptive studies with individuals as their units of analysis typically aim to describe the population that comprises those individuals, whereas explanatory studies aim to discover the social dynamics operating within that population.

As the units of analysis, individuals may be characterized in terms of their membership in social groupings. Thus, an individual may be described as belonging to a rich family or to a poor one, or as having a university-educated mother or not. We might conduct a research project to examine whether people with university-educated mothers are more likely to attend university than those with non-university-educated mothers or whether high school graduates in rich families are more likely to attend university than those in poor families. In each case, the unit of analysis—the "thing" whose characteristics we are seeking to describe or explain—is the individual. We can then aggregate these individuals and make generalizations about the population they belong to.

Groups

Social groups can also be the units of analysis for social scientific research. That is, we may be interested in characteristics that belong to one group, considered as a single entity. If you were to study criminals by looking at members of a criminal gang, the individual (criminal) would be the unit of analysis. But, if you studied all the gangs in a city to learn the differences, say, between big gangs and small ones, between "uptown" and "downtown" gangs, and so forth, you would be interested in gangs rather than their individual members. In this case, the unit of analysis would be the *gang*, a social group.

Here's another example. Suppose your interest was in the question of access to computers in different parts of society. You might describe families in terms of total annual income and according to whether or not they had computers. You could then aggregate families and describe the mean income of families and the percentage of families who have computers. You would then be in a position to determine whether families with higher incomes were more likely to have computers than those with lower incomes. In this case, the unit of analysis would be families.

As with other units of analysis, we can derive the characteristics of social groups from those of their individual members. Thus, we might describe a family in terms of the age, race, or education of its head. In a descriptive study, we might find the percentage of all families that have a university-educated head of family. In an explanatory study, we might determine whether such families have, on the average, more or fewer children than families headed by people who have not graduated from university. In each of these examples, the *family* would be the unit of analysis. In contrast, had we asked whether university-educated *individuals* have more or fewer children than their less educated counterparts, then the individual person would have been the unit of analysis.

Social groups may be characterized in other ways, such as according to their environments or their membership in larger groupings. Families, for example, might be described in terms of their dwelling: We might want to determine whether rich families are more likely to reside in single-family houses (as opposed to, say, apartments) than poor families. It's worth noting that some attributes only apply to collectivities, just as some only apply to individuals. For instance, families or gangs can be characterized by "number of members"—this factor varies among families or gangs but does not characterize individuals.

Other units of analysis at the group level could be friendship cliques, married couples, cities, or geographic regions. As in the case of individuals, each of these terms also implies some population. Street gangs imply some population that includes all street gangs, perhaps in a given city. The population of street gangs could be described, say, in terms of its geographical distribution throughout a city. In an explanatory study of street gangs you might discover whether large gangs are more likely than small ones to engage in intergang warfare.

Organizations

Formal social organizations may also be the units of analysis in social scientific research. For example, a researcher might study corporations, by which he or she implies a population of all corporations. Individual corporations might be characterized in terms of their number of employees, net annual profits, gross assets, number of defence contracts, percentage of employees from racial or ethnic minority groups, and so forth. We might determine whether large corporations hire a larger or smaller percentage of minority group employees than small corporations. Other examples of formal social organizations suitable as units of analysis would be church congregations, universities, academic departments, and supermarkets.

Social Artifacts

Another unit of analysis is the *social artifact*, or any product of social beings or their bahaviour. One class of artifacts includes concrete objects such as books, poems, paintings, automobiles, buildings, songs, pottery, jokes, student excuses for missing exams, and scientific discoveries. For example, studying the depiction of coverage of aboriginals in the media, Grenier's (1994) units of analysis were daily newspapers. In order to examine how the English-Canadian press covered Native-Indian issues, he did a content analysis of all regular

Montreal Gazette daily newspapers prior to and during a major Native-Indian protest called the "Oka Crisis" (January 2 – July 31, 1990).

Just as individuals and social groups imply populations, each social object implies a set of all objects of the same class: all books, all novels, all biographies, all introductory sociology textbooks, all cookbooks. In a study using books as the units of analysis, a book might be characterized by its size, weight, length, price, content, number of pictures, number sold, or description of its author. Then the population of all books or of a particular kind of book could be analyzed for the purpose of description or explanation: what kinds of books sell best and why, for example.

Similarly, a social scientist could analyze whether paintings by Russian, Chinese, or Canadian artists showed the greatest degree of working-class consciousness, taking paintings as the units of analysis and describing each, in part, by the nationality of its creator. Or you might examine a local newspaper's editorials regarding a local university for the purpose of describing, or perhaps explaining, changes in the newspaper's editorial position on the university over time. In this example, individual editorials would be the units of analysis.

Social interactions form another class of social artifacts suitable for social scientific research. For example, we might characterize weddings as racially or religiously mixed or not, as religious or secular in ceremony, as resulting in divorce or not, or by descriptions of one or both of the marriage partners (such as, "previously married"). When a researcher reports that weddings between partners of different religions are more likely to be performed by secular authorities than those between partners of the same religion, weddings are the units of analysis, not the individuals involved.

Other social interactions that might be units of analysis include friendship choices, court cases, traffic accidents, divorces, fistfights, ship launchings, airline hijackings, race riots, and student demonstrations. The student demonstrations could be characterized by whether or not they occurred during an election campaign, whether the demonstration leaders were male or female, whether the leaders had been convicted of a felony or not, and so on. Notice that even if we characterized and compared the demonstrations in terms of the leaders, the demonstrations themselves, not the individual leaders, would be our units of analysis.

Figure 4-1 provides a graphic illustration of some different units of analysis and the statements that might be made about them.

Units of Analysis in Review

The examples in this section should suggest the nearly infinite variety of possible units of analysis for social scientific research. Although individual human beings are typical objects of study, many research questions can be answered more appropriately through the examination of other units of analysis. Social scientists can study just about anything that bears on social life.

Moreover, the types of units of analysis named in this section don't begin to exhaust the possibilities. Morris Rosenberg (1968:234–48), for example, speaks of individual, group, organizational, institutional, spatial, cultural, and societal units of analysis. John and Lyn Lofland (1995:103–13) speak of practices, episodes, encounters, roles, relationships, groups, organizations, settlements, social worlds, lifestyles, and subcultures as suitable units of study. What's important here is to grasp the logic of units of analysis.

Categorizing possible units of analysis may make the concept seem more complicated than it needs to be. What you call a given unit of analysis—a group, a formal organization, or a social artifact—is irrelevant. The key is to be clear about what your unit of analysis is. When you begin a research project, you must decide whether you are studying marriages or marriage partners, crimes or criminals, corporations or corporate executives. Otherwise, you run the risk of drawing invalid conclusions because your assertions about one unit of analysis are actually based on the examination of another. We'll see an example of this issue as we look at the ecological fallacy.

Figure 4-1
Illustrations of Units of Analysis

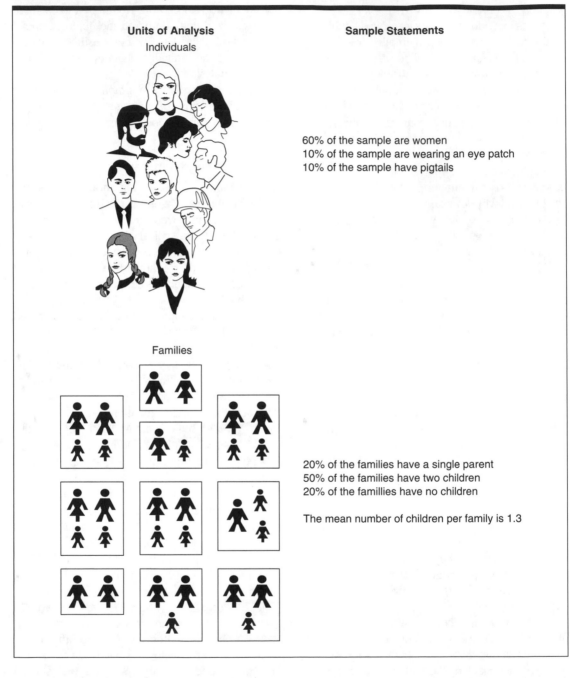

Units of Analysis
Individuals

Sample Statements

60% of the sample are women
10% of the sample are wearing an eye patch
10% of the sample have pigtails

Families

20% of the families have a single parent
50% of the families have two children
20% of the famillies have no children

The mean number of children per family is 1.3

Figure 4-1 (continued)
Illustrations of Units of Analysis

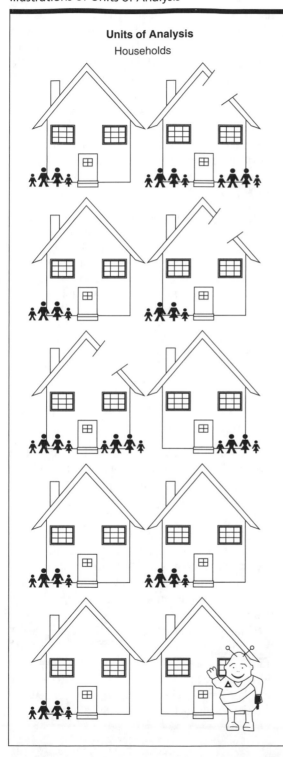

Units of Analysis
Households

Sample Statements

20% of the households are occupied
by more than one family

30% of the households have holes
in their roofs

10% of the households are occupied
by aliens

Notice also that 33% of the families live
in multiple-family households with family
as the unit of analysis

The Ecological Fallacy

A clear understanding of units of analysis will help you avoid committing the ecological fallacy. In this context, *ecological* refers to groups or sets or systems: something larger than individuals. The **ecological fallacy** is the assumption that something learned about an ecological unit says something about the individuals making up that unit. Let's consider a hypothetical illustration of this fallacy.

Suppose we're interested in learning something about the nature of electoral support received by a female political candidate in a recent citywide election. Let's assume we have the vote tally for each riding so we can tell which ridings gave her the greatest support and which the least. Assume also that we have census data describing some characteristics of these ridings. Our analysis of such data might show that ridings with relatively young voters gave the female candidate a greater proportion of their votes than did ridings with older voters. We might be tempted to conclude from these findings that young voters are more likely to vote for female candidates than older voters—in other words, that age affects support for women in politics. In reaching such a conclusion, we run the risk of committing the ecological fallacy because it may have been the older voters in those "young" ridings who voted for the woman. Our problem is that we have examined *ridings* as our units of analysis but wish to draw conclusions about *voters*.

The same problem would arise if we discovered that crime rates were higher in cities having large aboriginal populations than in those with few aboriginals. We would not know if the crimes were actually committed by aboriginals. Or if we found suicide rates higher in Protestant countries than in Catholic ones, we still could not know for sure that more Protestants than Catholics committed suicide.

Despite these hazards, social scientists very often have little choice but to address a particular research question through an ecological analysis. Perhaps the most appropriate data are simply not available. For example, the riding vote tallies and the riding characteristics mentioned in our initial example might be easy to obtain, but we may not have the resources to conduct a postelection survey of individual voters. In such cases, we may reach a tentative conclusion, recognizing and noting the risk of an ecological fallacy. This was the case for Werner Cohn, whose research concerning Jewish outmarriage and the east-west pattern of norm violations in Canada we discussed in Chapter 2. He was limited by the available data and therefore he was using group data in his analysis.

Cohn's unit of analysis was province. He spoke of percentages and rates of suicide, divorce, crime, intermarriage. These are all characteristics of the provinces (not of individuals). He was well aware of the limitations this placed on how he interpreted his findings. As he stated:

> A first difficulty lies in the fact that all the data concern provincial aggregates. While we know, for example, that the proportion of Jewish inmovers among the Jews of British Columbia is proportionately very high and while we also know that the rate of outmarriage among this group of Jews is proportionately high, we do not know whether or not it is the inmovers themselves who are responsible for the outmarriage: we have a firm basis only for saying that in the presence of a relatively high proportion of inmovers, a relatively high rate of outmarriage takes place.
>
> (1976:102)

There is no direct evidence from his data that the migrants themselves account for the increase in outmarriage, divorce, crimes and so forth, because he doesn't have individual level data. That is, he has no information on which of the individuals, migrants or those born in the province, are outmarrying, divorcing, etc. Therefore, all he can say is that in regions where the proportion of migrants is higher, so too is the rate of intermarriage and a vast number of other indicators of normative violation.

In taking care not to commit the ecological fallacy, don't let these warnings lead you into committing what we might call an *individualistic fallacy.* Some people approaching social research for the first time have trouble reconciling general patterns of attitudes and actions with individual exceptions.

As we noted in Chapter 2, generalizations and probabilistic statements are not invalidated by individual exceptions. Your knowing someone who has gotten rich without any formal education doesn't deny the general pattern of higher education relating to higher income.

The ecological fallacy deals with something else altogether—confusing units of analysis in such a way that we draw conclusions about individuals based solely on the observation of groups. Although the patterns observed between variables at the level of groups may be genuine, the danger lies in reasoning from the observed attributes of groups to the attributes of individuals who made up those groups when we have not actually observed individuals.

✗

The Time Dimension

So far in this chapter, we have regarded research design as a process for deciding *what aspects* we shall observe, *of whom,* and *for what purpose.* Now we must consider a set of time-related options that cuts across each of these earlier considerations. We can choose to make observations more or less at one time or over a long period.

Time plays many roles in the design and execution of research, quite aside from the time it takes to do research. We saw in Chapter 3 that time sequence of events and situations is critical to determining causation (a point we'll return to in Part 4). Time also affects the generalizability of research findings. Do the descriptions and explanations resulting from a particular study accurately represent the situation of 10 years ago, 10 years from now, or only the present? In dealing with the issue of time, researchers principally choose between cross-sectional and longitudinal study designs.

Cross-Sectional Studies

A **cross-sectional study** involves observations of a sample, or cross section, of a population of phenomenon at one point in time. Exploratory and descriptive studies are often cross-sectional. A single Canadian Census, for instance, is a study aimed at describing the Canadian population at a given time.

Many explanatory studies are also cross-sectional. A researcher conducting a large-scale national survey to examine the sources of racial and religious prejudice would, in all likelihood, be dealing with a single time frame, in essence, taking a "snapshot" of the sources of prejudice at a particular point in history.

Explanatory cross-sectional studies have an inherent problem. Though their conclusions are based on observations made at only one time, they typically aim at understanding causal processes that occur over time. This problem is somewhat akin to that of determining the speed of a moving object on the basis of a high-speed, still photograph that freezes the movement of the object.

Yanjie Bian, for example, conducted a survey of workers in Tianjin, China, for the purpose of studying stratification in contemporary, urban Chinese society. In undertaking the survey in 1988, however, he was conscious of the important changes brought about by a series of national campaigns, such as the Great Proletarian Cultural Revolution, dating from the 1949 Chinese Revolution (that brought the communists into power) and continuing into the present.

> These campaigns altered political atmospheres and affected people's work and nonwork activities. Because of these campaigns, it is difficult to draw conclusions from a cross-sectional social survey, such as the one presented in this book, about general patterns of Chinese workplaces and their effects on workers. Such conclusions may be limited to one period of time and are subject to further tests based on data collected at other times.
>
> (1994:19)

The problem of generalizations about social life from a snapshot in time is one this book addresses repeatedly. One solution is suggested by Bian's final comment about data collected "at other times." Social research often builds on the results of earlier research by revisiting phenomena.

Longitudinal Studies

Unlike cross-sectional studies, **longitudinal studies** are designed to permit observations of the same phenomena over an extended period. For example, a researcher can participate in and observe the activities of a radical political group from its inception to its demise. Other longitudinal studies use records or artifacts to study change over time. In analyses of newspaper editorials or Supreme Court decisions over time, for instance, the studies are longitudinal whether the researcher's actual observations and analyses are made at one time or over the course of the actual events under study.

Most field research projects, involving direct observation and perhaps in-depth interviews, are naturally longitudinal. For example, when Jacqueline Lewis (1998) studied the experiences of exotic dancers, her field observations and interviews in strip clubs in southern Ontario allowed her to examine the evolution of their occupational socialization over time—in other words, the process of becoming an exotic dancer.

In the classic study *When Prophecy Fails* (1956), Leon Festinger, Henry Reicker, and Stanley Schachter were specifically interested in learning what happened to a flying saucer cult when their predictions of an alien encounter failed to come true. Would the cult members close down the group or would they become all the more committed to their beliefs? A longitudinal study was required to provide an answer. (They redoubled their efforts to get new members.)

Longitudinal studies can be more difficult for quantitative studies such as large-scale surveys. Nonetheless, they are often the best way to study changes over time. There are three special types of longitudinal studies you should know about—trend, cohort, and panel studies.

Trend Studies

A researcher who examines changes within a population over time engages in a **trend study**. Simple examples include a comparison of Canadian Censuses over several decades, showing shifts in the makeup of the national population, and a series of Angus-Reid polls during the course of an election campaign, showing trends in the relative strengths and standing of different political parties.

Smart, Adlaf, and Walsh (1993) wanted to know whether drug use among Ontario youth was declining. To find out, they compared the results of surveys on alcohol and drug use conducted in 87 schools every two years from 1979 until 1991. A variety of the same questions tapping drug use were asked in each survey. Overall, the analysis showed that drug use was down (especially alcohol use). In 1979 about 77 percent of students reported using alcohol while in 1991 use was down to 59 percent. Over the same time period, reported marijuana use was down from about 32 percent to 12 percent and tobacco use down from about 35 percent to 22 percent.

Smart et al.'s larger goal was to determine whether there was an association between exposure to drug education and drug use. Questions on reported exposure to drug education in schools were also asked on these surveys. They found an overall increase in exposure, especially to education on alcohol. For example, in 1979 only 54 percent of students reported any education on alcohol compared to 78 percent in 1991. Data concerning marijuana education (available only from 1983), showed a slight increase from 42 percent to 49 percent in 1991. The largest change was for Grade 7 students (23 percent to 42 percent).

Ultimately, the researchers found a strong association between increased exposure to education on drugs and decreasing levels of drug use, especially alcohol. "In general, the strongest correlations were found for Grade 7 students. That is the grade which has been the focus of new drug education programs in Ontario, and they report the largest increases in exposure to all types of drug education" (1993:129).

Cohort Studies

When researchers examine specific subpopulations, or *cohorts*, as they change over time, they engage in a **cohort study**. Typically, a cohort is an age group, such as those people born during the 1950s, but it can also be based on some other time grouping, such as people born during World War II, people who got married in 2000, and so forth. An example of a cohort study would be a series of national surveys, conducted perhaps every 20 years, to study the economic attitudes of the cohort born during the Great Depression. A sample of people 15–20 years of age might be surveyed in 1950, another sample of those 35–40 years of age in 1970, another sample of those 55–60 years of age in 1990, and another of those 75–80 years old in 2010. Although the specific set of people studied in each survey would differ, each sample would represent the survivors of the cohort born between 1930 and 1935.

James Davis (1992) turned to a cohort analysis in an attempt to understand shifting political orientations during the 1970s and 1980s in the United States. Overall, he found a liberal trend on issues such as race, gender, religion, politics, crime, and free speech. But did this trend represent people in general getting a bit more liberal, or did it merely reflect more liberal younger generations replacing the conservative older ones?

To answer this question, Davis examined national surveys conducted in four time periods, five years apart. In each survey, he grouped the respondents into age groups, also five years apart. This strategy allowed him to compare different age groups at any given point in time, as well as follow the political development of each age group over time.

One of the questions he examined was whether a person who admitted to being a communist should be allowed to speak in the respondents' communities. Consistently, the younger respondents in each period of time were more willing to let the communist speak than were the older ones. Among those aged 20–40 in the first set of the survey, for example, 72 percent took this liberal position, contrasted with 27 percent among respondents 80 and older. What Davis found when he examined the youngest cohort over time is shown in Table 4-1.

This pattern of a slight, conservative shift in the 1970s, followed by a liberal rebound in the 1980s, typifies the several cohorts Davis analyzed (Davis 1992:269).

Table 4-1
Age and Political Liberalism

Survey Dates	1972 to 1974	1977 to 1980	1982 to 1984	1987 to 1989
Age of Cohort	20–24	25–29	30–34	35–39
Percent who would let the communist speak	72%	68%	73%	73%

Panel Studies

Though similar to trend and cohort studies, **panel studies** examine the same set of people each time. For example, we could interview the same sample of voters every month during an election campaign, asking for whom they intended to vote. Though such a study would allow us to analyze overall trends in voter preferences for different candidates, it would also show the precise patterns of persistence and change in intentions. For example, a trend study that showed that Candidates A and B each had exactly half of the voters on September 1 and on October 1 could indicate that none of the electorate had changed voting plans, that all of the voters had changed their intentions, or something in-between. A panel study would eliminate this confusion by showing what kinds of voters switched from A to B and what kinds switched from B to A, as well as other facts.

Recall the Sorensen and Krahn study concerning attitudes toward immigrants that we discussed in Chapter 1 to illustrate the relationship between education and prejudice and again in Chapter 3 as an example of nomothetic explanation. They used panel data obtained from Edmonton, Alberta high school graduates to determine if amount of education or scarce resources/group competition better explained attitudes of prejudice. The students in the study were followed for seven years (1985–92). They believed that studying the same students over time would allow them to better assess the "effects of education on attitudes, because we can compare their attitudes before and after acquiring postsecondary education. Furthermore, this age cohort might be most likely to be influenced by education" (1996:6–7). Previous research, they noted, indicated evidence of support for both of the explanations they were testing. However, they argued that the research designs used in the "previous studies limit the extent to which causal relationships can be determined" (p. 14).

> Some of these studies have relied on cross-sectional data that cannot directly measure changes in individual's attitudes. Rather, changes are inferred from attitudinal differences observed between individuals with different characteristics....For example, the liberalizing effects of education on attitudes are inferred from evidence that individuals with more education have more positive attitudes. However, it remains possible that people who pursue higher education already have more positive attitudes.
>
> (p. 14)

Therefore, they conclude that it's not possible to determine whether significant differences in attitudes are a result of obtaining more education or a result of prior selectivity.

Comparing their study to trend studies they say:

> Other studies have used trend analyses to demonstrate, for example, that a population's attitudes toward immigrants are less positive on average during times of high unemployment. Once again, conclusions about changes in individuals' attitudes must be inferred from evidence of aggregate differences. However, panel data allow researchers to demonstrate more conclusively the effects of different types of experiences (e.g. education, labor market difficulties) on attitude change and to identify causal relationships.
>
> (p. 14)

Using panel data they found, for example, that "young people who go on to higher education already express more positive attitudes toward immigrants before acquiring this additional education." However, they also find a further liberalizing effect on attitudes with exposure to postsecondary education. Those who on average didn't continue their education "became somewhat less accepting of immigrants between 1985 and 1992" (p. 14).

Comparison of the Three Types

To reinforce the distinctions among trend, cohort, and panel studies, let's contrast the three study designs in terms of the same variable: attitudes toward abortion. A trend study might look at shifts in attitudes of the general Canadian population, using polling data collected on a regular basis. A cohort study might follow shifts in attitudes among the "World War II generation," specifically, say, people who were between 20 and 30 in 1942. We could study a sample of people 30–40 years old in 1952, a new sample of people aged 40–50 in 1962, and so forth. A panel study could start with a sample of the whole population or of some special subset and study those specific individuals over time. Notice that only the panel study would give a full picture of the shifts in attitudes toward abortion—from "against" to "in favour," from "in favour" to "against" and other possible in-betweens, for example, "in favour only when the woman's life is at risk." Cohort and trend studies would uncover only net changes.

Longitudinal studies generally have an obvious advantage over cross-sectional ones in providing information describing processes over time. But this advantage often comes at a heavy cost in both time and money, especially in a large-scale survey. Observations may have to be made at the time events are occurring, and the method of observation may require many research workers.

Panel studies, which offer the most comprehensive data on changes over time, face a special problem: *panel attrition*. Some of the respondents studied in the first wave of the survey may not participate in later waves, whether by choice or circumstance. The danger is that those who drop out of the study may not be typical, thereby distorting the results of the study. For instance, Sorensen and Krahn looked for and found differences in the characteristics of those who remained in their panel study on attitudes toward immigrants—more females, academically-oriented respondents, and those from higher socioeconomic backgrounds—compared to study dropouts. These differences needed to be taken into account to avoid misleading conclusions in the interpretation of their results. For a further comparison of the three types of longitudinal studies, see the box entitled "The Time Dimension and Aging."

The Time Dimension and Aging

By Joseph J. Leon
Behavioral Science Department
California State Polytechnic University, Pomona

One way to identify the type of time dimension used in a study is to imagine a number of different research projects on growing older in Canadian society. If we studied a sample of individuals in 1990 and compared the different age groups, the design would be termed *cross-sectional*. If we drew another sample of individuals using the same study instrument in the year 2000 and compared the new data with the 1990 data, the design would be termed *trend*.

Suppose we wished to study only those individuals who were 51–60 in the year 2000 and compare them with the 1990 sample of 41–50-year-old persons (the 41–50 age cohort); this study design would be termed *cohort*. The comparison could be made for the 51–60 and 61–70 age cohorts as well. Now, if we desired to do a panel study on growing older in Canada, we would draw a sample in the year 1990 and, using the same sampled individuals in the year 2000, do the study again. Remember, there would be fewer people in the year 2000 study because some of the sampled individuals from 1990 would no longer be available to participate. For example, some would no longer be alive in the year 2000.

CROSS-SECTIONAL STUDY

1990

↑ 41– 50
↓ 51– 60
↕ 61– 70
↕ 71– 80

COHORT STUDY

1990	2000
41– 50	41– 50
51– 60	51– 60
61– 70	61– 70
71– 80	71– 80

TREND STUDY

1990	2000
41– 50 ⟷	41– 50
51– 60 ⟷	51– 60
61– 70 ⟷	61– 70
71– 80 ⟷	71– 80

PANEL STUDY

1990	2000
41– 50*	41– 50
51– 60*	51– 60*
61– 70*	61– 70*
71– 80*	71– 80*
	+81*

⟷ Denotes comparison
*Denotes same individuals

Approximating Longitudinal Studies

It's not always possible or practical to conduct longitudinal studies. However, researchers can often draw approximate conclusions about processes that take place over time, even when only cross-sectional data are available. Here are some ways to do that.

Sometimes, cross-sectional data imply processes over time on the basis of simple logic. For example, in a study of student drug use conducted at the University of Hawaii (Takeuchi 1974), students were asked to report whether they had ever tried each of several illegal drugs. The study found that some students had tried both marijuana and LSD, some had tried only one, and others had tried neither. Because these data were collected at one time, and because some students presumably would experiment with drugs later on, it would appear that such a study could not tell whether students were more likely to try marijuana or LSD first.

A closer examination of the data showed, however, that although some students reported having tried marijuana but not LSD, there were no students in the study who had tried only LSD. From this finding it was inferred, as common sense suggested, that marijuana use preceded LSD use. If the process of drug experimentation occurred in the opposite time order, then a study at a given time should have found some students who had tried LSD but not marijuana, and it should have found no students who had tried only marijuana.

Logical inferences may also be made whenever the time order of variables is clear. If we discover in a cross-sectional study of university students that those educated in private high schools received better university grades than those educated in public high schools, we would conclude that the type of high school attended affected university grades, not the other way around. Thus, even though our observations were made at only one time, we would feel justified in drawing conclusions about processes that took place across time.

Very often, age differences discovered in a cross-sectional study form the basis for inferring processes across time. Suppose you're interested in the pattern of worsening health over the course of the typical life cycle. You might study the results of annual checkups in a large hospital. You could group health records according to the ages of those examined and rate each age group in terms of several health conditions: sight, hearing, blood pressure, and so forth. By reading across the age-group ratings for each health condition, you would have something approximating the health history of individuals. Thus, you might conclude that the average person develops vision problems before hearing problems. You would need to be cautious in this assumption, however, because the differences might reflect society-wide trends. Perhaps improved hearing examinations instituted in the schools had affected only the young people in your study.

Asking people to *recall* their pasts is another common way of approximating observations over time. Researchers use that method when they ask people where they were born or when they graduated from high school or whom they voted for in 2000. Qualitative researchers often conduct in-depth "life history" interviews. Teppo Sintonen (1993) used this technique in a study concerning experiences of Canadian Finns who immigrated to Canada in the 1920s. Respondents were asked to reconstruct aspects of their life experiences, particularly those related to ethnicity. Answers to questions about experiences or events that happened a long time ago yield information that is sometimes called **retrospective** data.

The danger in this technique is evident. Sometimes people have faulty memories; sometimes they lie. When people are asked in postelection polls whom they voted for, the results inevitably show more people voting for the winner than actually did so on election day. As part of a series of in-depth interviews, such a report can be validated in the context of other reported details; however, results based on a single question in a survey must be regarded with caution.

These are some of the ways time figures into social research and some of the ways researchers confront the element of time in their studies. In designing any study, be sure to examine both the explicit and the implicit assumptions you're making about time. Are you interested in describing or explaining some process that occurs over time, or are you simply interested in what exists now? If you want to describe a process occurring over time, will you be able to make observations at different points in the process, or will you have to approximate such observations drawing logical inferences from what you can observe now? If you decide on a longitudinal design, which method best serves your research purposes?

How to Design a Research Project

You've just seen some of the options available to social researchers in designing projects. Now let's pull the parts together by looking at the actual process of designing a research project. Assume you were to undertake a research study. Where would you start? Then, where would you go?

Although research design occurs at the beginning of a research project, it involves all the steps of the subsequent project. This discussion, then, provides both guidance on how to start a research project and an overview of the topics that follow in later chapters of this book.

Figure 4-2 presents a schematic view of the social science research process. We present this view reluctantly, since it may suggest more of a step-by-step order to research than actual practice bears out. Nonetheless, this idealized overview of the process gives a context for the specific details of particular aspects of social research. It is another, more detailed picture of the scientific process presented in Chapter 2.

At the top of the diagram are interest, idea, and theory, the possible beginning points for a line of research. The letters (A, B, X, Y, and so forth) represent variables or concepts such as prejudice or alienation. Thus, you might have a general *interest* in finding out what causes some people to be more prejudiced than others, or you might want to know some of the consequences of alienation. Alternatively, your inquiry might begin with a specific *idea* about the way things are. For example, you might have the idea that working on an assembly line causes alienation. The question marks in the diagram indicate that you aren't sure things are the way you suspect they are. That's why you're conducting the research. Notice that a theory is represented as a set of complex relationships among several variables.

There is often a movement back and forth across these several possible beginnings—interest, idea, and theory—as the double-arrows suggest. An initial interest may lead to the formulation of an idea, which may be fit into a larger theory, and the theory may produce new ideas and create new interests.

Any or all of these three may suggest the need for empirical research. The purpose of such research can be to explore an interest, test a specific idea, or validate a complex theory. Whatever the purpose, the researcher needs to make a variety of decisions, as indicated in the remainder of the diagram.

To make this discussion more concrete, let's take a specific research example. Suppose you're concerned with the issue of abortion and have a special interest in learning why some university students support abortion rights and others oppose them. Going a step further, let's say you've formed the impression that students in the humanities and social sciences seem generally more inclined to support the idea of abortion rights than those in the natural sciences.

In terms of the options we've discussed earlier in this chapter, you probably have both descriptive and explanatory interests: What percentage of the student body supports a woman's right to an abortion (description), and what causes some to support it and others to oppose it (explanation)? The units of analysis are individuals: university students. Let's assume you'd be satisfied to learn something about the way things are now. You might then decide that a cross-sectional study would suit your purposes. Although this would provide you with no direct evidence of processes over time, you might be able to approximate some longitudinal analyses concerning changes in students' attitudes.

Getting Started

When you first begin your project, your interests would likely be exploratory. You might choose among several possible activities in pursuing your interest in student attitudes about abortion rights. At the start, you would want to read something about the issue. If you have a hunch that attitudes are somehow related to a university major, you might want to find out what other researchers may have written about that. In addition, you would probably talk to some people who support abortion rights and some who don't. You might attend meetings of abortion-related groups. All these activities could help prepare you to handle the various decisions of research design we're about to examine.

You must define the purpose of your project before you can design your study. Do you plan to

Figure 4-2
The Research Process

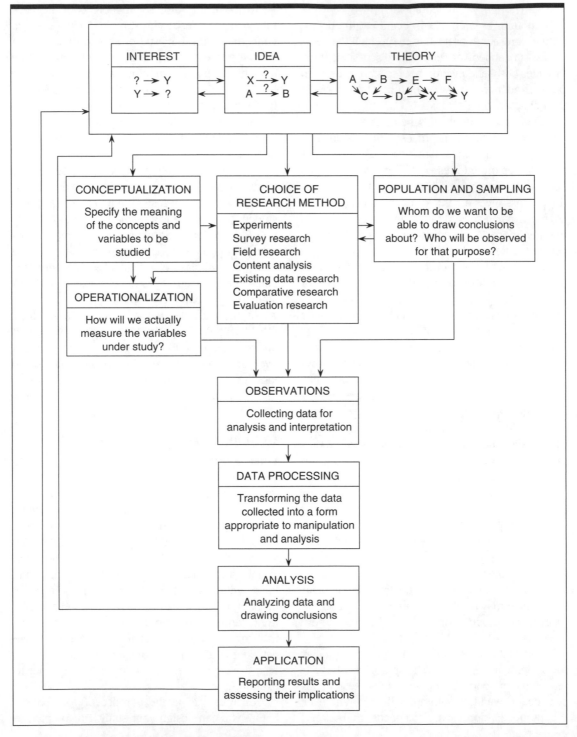

write a paper to satisfy a course or thesis requirement? Is your purpose to gain information that will support you in arguing for or against abortion rights? Do you want to write an article for the campus newspaper or for an academic journal? When reviewing the previous research literature regarding abortion rights, you should note the design decisions other researchers have made, always asking whether the same decisions would satisfy your purpose.

Usually, your purpose for undertaking research can be expressed in the form of a *report*. Appendix A of this book will help you organize a research report. We recommend outlining such a report as the first step in the design of your project. Although your final report may look quite different from your initial vision of it, this exercise can help you gauge the appropriateness of different research designs. During this step, clearly describe the kinds of statements you want to make when the research is complete. This will help guide your choices of appropriate research strategies. Here are some examples of such statements: "Students frequently mentioned abortion rights in the context of discussing social issues that concerned them personally." "*X* percent of Forest University students favour a woman's right to choose an abortion." "Engineers are (more/less) likely than sociologists to favour abortion rights."

Conceptualization

With a well-defined purpose and a clear description of the kinds of outcomes you want to achieve, you can move ahead to the step of conceptualization. We often talk pretty casually about social science concepts such as prejudice, alienation, religiosity, and liberalism, but it's necessary to clarify what we mean by these concepts in order to draw meaningful conclusions about them. Chapter 5 examines conceptualization in depth. For now, let's see what it might involve in our hypothetical example.

If you're going to study how university students feel about abortion and why, the first thing you'll have to specify is what you mean by "the right to an abortion." Support for abortion probably varies according to circumstances, so you'll want to pay attention to the different conditions under which people might approve or disapprove of abortion: for example, when the woman's life is in danger, in the case of rape or incest, or simply as a matter of personal choice. You'll also need to specify the exact meanings for all the other concepts you plan to study. If you want to study the possible effect of a university major on abortion opinions, you'll have to decide whether you want to consider only officially declared majors or include students' intentions as well. What will you do with those who have no major?

In surveys and experiments, such concepts need to be specified in advance. In less tightly structured research, such as open-ended interviews, an important part of the research may involve the discovery of different dimensions, aspects, or nuances of concepts. In this type of research, you may uncover aspects of social life that were not evident at the start of the project.

Choice of Research Method

As we discuss in Part 3, a variety of research methods serves the social scientist. Each method has its strengths and weaknesses, and certain concepts are more appropriately studied by some methods than by others. In our study of attitudes toward abortion rights, a survey might be the most appropriate method: either interviewing students or asking them to fill out a questionnaire. Surveys are particularly well suited to the study of public opinion. This is not to say that you couldn't make good use of the other methods presented in Part 3. For example, you might use the method of content analysis to examine letters to the editor and analyze the different images letter writers have of abortion. Field research would provide an avenue to understanding how people interact with one another regarding the issue of abortion, how they discuss it, and how they change their minds. In Part 3, you'll be introduced to other research methods as well that might be used in studying this topic. Usually, the best study design uses more than one research method, taking advantage of their different strengths.

Operationalization

Having specified the concepts to be studied and chosen a research method, the next step is operationalization—deciding on our measurement techniques (Chapters 5 and 6). As Chapter 3 discussed, the meaning of variables in a study is determined by how they are measured. One task is deciding how the desired data will be collected: direct observation, review of official documents, a questionnaire, or some other technique.

If you decided to use a survey to study attitudes toward abortion rights, part of operationalization is choosing the wording of questionnaire items. For instance, you might operationalize your main variable by asking respondents whether they would approve a woman's right to have an abortion under each of the conditions you've conceptualized: in the case of rape or incest, if her life were threatened by the pregnancy, and so forth. You'd design the questionnaire such that it asked respondents to express approval or disapproval for each situation. Similarly, you would specify exactly how respondents would indicate their university major and what choices to provide those who have not declared a major.

Ethics

Ethical decisions will come into play when making decisions about your choice of topic, concepts, measures, and research methods. The ethical issues of concern to a researcher depend in part on the issue under study and the research method chosen. When employing research methods involving direct interaction between researchers and study participants—such as interviews and surveys—the researcher must consider issues of voluntary participation and consent. In conducting a survey of university students, for example, you would need to obtain their consent to participate and insure that the students understood they were free to participate or not, as they choose. Statements informing participants about the goals of the study and consent forms would need to be prepared in advance. If any of the students happened to be minors, permission would need to be obtained from parents or legal guardians in order for them to participate.

Research participants also have the right to privacy, the maintenance of dignity, and protection against harm. Researchers must take these issues into account in their choice of methods and measures. Thus, a researcher must balance potential harm and undue inconvenience to participants with his or her desire to obtain the best information possible. In the case of a survey, for example, the questions asked must be thoughtfully considered to avoid topics that might cause undue stress or anxiety for some participants. Designing an efficient study, so that participants are not unduly burdened by long and confusing questionnaires or interviewers who are unprepared for their task, is another consideration.

A researcher must also consider how the confidentiality of the participants will be maintained. For example, a filing system might have to be developed so that respondents' answers could not be connected with respondents' names even if an unauthorized person were to gain access to the data. In designing a study, researchers must continually consider the impact of their choices on the study participants.

Population and Sampling

In addition to refining concepts and measurements, you must decide *whom* or *what* to study. The *population* for a study is that group (usually of people) about whom we want to draw conclusions. We're almost never able to study all the members of the population that interests us, however, and we can never make every possible observation of them. In every case, then, we select a *sample* from among the data that might be collected and studied. The sampling of information, of course, occurs in everyday life and often produces biased observations. (Recall the discussion of "selective observation" in Chapter 1.) Social researchers are more deliberate in their sampling of what will be observed.

Chapter 7 describes methods for selecting samples that adequately reflect the whole population that interests us. Notice in Figure 4-2 that decisions about population and sampling are related to decisions about the research method to be used. Whereas probability sampling techniques would be relevant to a large-scale survey or a content analysis, a field researcher might need to select only those informants who will yield a balanced picture of the situation under study, and an experimenter might assign subjects to experimental and control groups in a manner that creates comparability.

In your hypothetical study of abortion attitudes, the relevant population would be the student population of your university. As you'll discover in Chapter 7, however, selecting a sample will require you to get more specific than that. Will you include part-time as well as full-time students? Only degree candidates or everyone? International students as well as Canadian citizens? Undergraduates, graduate students, or both? There are many such questions, each of which must be answered in terms of your research purpose. For example, if your purpose is to predict how students would vote in a local referendum on abortion, you might want to limit your population to those eligible and likely to vote.

Observations

Having decided what to study, among whom, and by what method, you're now ready to make observations—to collect empirical data. The chapters of Part 3, which describe the various research methods, give the different observation techniques appropriate to each.

To conduct a survey on abortion, you might want to print questionnaires and mail them to a sample selected from the student body. Or, you could arrange to have a team of interviewers conduct the survey over the telephone. The relative advantages and disadvantages of these and other possibilities are discussed in Chapter 9.

Data Processing

Depending on the research method chosen, you'll have amassed a volume of observations in a form that probably isn't immediately interpretable. If you spend a month observing a street-corner gang firsthand, you'll have enough field notes to fill a book. In a historical study of ethnic diversity at your school, you could amass volumes of official documents, interviews with administrators and others, and so forth. Chapters 14 and 15 describe some of the ways social scientific data are processed or transformed for qualitative or quantitative analysis.

In the case of a survey, the "raw" observations are typically in the form of questionnaires with boxes checked, answers written in spaces, and the like. The data-processing phase of a survey typically involves the classification (*coding*) of written-in answers and the transfer of all the information to a computer.

Analysis

Once the collected data are in a suitable form, you're ready to interpret them for the purpose of drawing conclusions that reflect the interests, ideas, and theories that initiated the inquiry. Chapters 14 through 16 describe a few of the many options available to you in analyzing data. In Figure 4-2, notice that the results of your analyses feed back into your initial interests, ideas, and theories. Often this feedback represents the beginning of another cycle of inquiry.

In the survey of student attitudes about abortion rights, the analysis phase would pursue both descriptive and explanatory aims. You might begin by calculating the percentages of students who favoured or opposed each of the several different versions of abortion rights. Taken together, these several percentages would provide a good picture of student opinion on the issue.

Moving beyond simple description, you might describe the opinions of different subsets of the student body, like different university majors. If your design included gathering other information about your respondents, you could also look at first year students versus seniors; undergraduate versus graduate students; men versus women; or any other categories you included. The description of subgroups could then lead you into an explanatory analysis.

Application

The final stage of the research process involves the uses made of the research you've conducted and the conclusions you've reached. To start, you'll probably want to communicate your findings so that others will know what you've learned. It may be appropriate to prepare—and even publish—a written report. Perhaps you'll make oral presentations, such as papers delivered to professional and scientific meetings. Other students would also be interested in hearing what you've learned about them.

You may want to go beyond simply reporting what you've learned to discussing the implications of your findings. Do they say anything about actions that might be taken in support of policy goals? Both the proponents and the opponents of abortion rights would be interested.

Finally, you should consider what your research suggests in regard to further research on your subject. What mistakes should be corrected in future studies? What avenues, opened up slightly in your study, should be pursued further in later investigations?

Research Design in Review

As this overview shows, research design involves a set of decisions regarding *what topic* is to be studied among *which population* with *which research methods* for *what purpose*. Although you'll want to consider many ways of studying a subject and use your knowledge of a variety of methods, research design is the process of narrowing your choices and focusing your perspective for the purposes of a particular study.

If you're doing a research project for one of your courses, many aspects of research design may be specified for you in advance, including the method (such as an experiment) or the topic (as in a course on the subject of prejudice). The following summary assumes that you're free to choose your topic and research strategy.

In designing a research project, you'll find it useful to begin by assessing three things: your interests, abilities, and available resources. Each of these considerations will suggest a large number of possible studies.

Simulate the beginning of a somewhat conventional research project: Ask yourself what you're interested in understanding. Surely you have several questions about social behaviour and attitudes. Why are some people politically liberal and others politically conservative? Why are some people more religious than others? Why do people join militia groups? Do universities still discriminate against minority faculty members? Why would a woman stay in an abusive relationship? Spend some time thinking about the kinds of questions that interest and concern you.

Once you have a few questions you'd be interested in answering for yourself, think about the kind of information needed to answer them. What research units of analysis would provide the most relevant information: university students, young adult women, voters, corporations, cities, or neighbourhoods? This question will probably be inseparable in your thoughts from the question of research topics. Then ask which aspects of the units of analysis would provide the information you need to answer your research question. Keep in mind that you may not be able to study the population or units that would be most appropriate to your research interest using the methods and measures you deem most suitable. If you were interested in issues of child abuse, for example, ethical concerns might bar interviewing 6–12-year-olds because of the potential negative impact of raising such topics with victims of such abuse.

Once you have some ideas about the kind of information relevant to your purpose, ask yourself how you might go about getting that information. Are the relevant data likely to be already available somewhere (say, in a government publication), or would you have to collect them yourself? If you think you would have to collect the data, how would you go about doing it? Would you need to survey a large number of people or interview a few people in depth? Could you learn what you need to know by attending meetings of certain groups? Could you glean the data you need from books in the library?

As you answer these questions, you'll find yourself well into the process of research design. Keep in mind your own research abilities and the resources available to you. What's the point of designing a perfect study that you can't actually carry out? You may want to try a research method you have not used before so you can learn from it, but take care not to put yourself at too great a disadvantage.

Once you have a general idea of what you want to study and how, carefully review previous research in journals and books to see how other researchers have addressed the topic and what they have learned about it. Your review of the literature may lead you to revise your research design: Perhaps you'll decide to use a previous researcher's method or even *replicate* an earlier study. The independent replication of research projects is a standard procedure in the physical sciences, and it's just as important in the social sciences, although social scientists tend to overlook that. Or, you might want to go beyond replication and study some aspect of the topic that you feel previous researchers have overlooked.

Here's another approach you might take. Suppose a topic has been studied previously using field research methods. Can you design an experiment that would test the findings those earlier researchers produced? Or, can you think of existing statistics that could be used to test their conclusions? Did a mass survey yield results that you'd like to explore in greater detail through some on-the-spot observations and in-depth interviews? The use of several different research methods to test the same finding is sometimes called **triangulation**, and you should always keep it in mind as a valuable research strategy. Because each research method has particular strengths and weaknesses, there is always a danger that research findings will reflect, at least in part, the method of inquiry. In the best of all worlds, your own research design should bring more than one research method to bear on the topic.

The Research Proposal

Quite often, in the design of a research project, you'll have to lay out the details of your plan for someone else's review and/or approval. In the case of a course project, for example, your instructor might very well want to see a "proposal"

before you set off to work. Later in your career, if you wanted to undertake a major project, you might need to obtain funding from a foundation or governmental agency, who would most definitely want a detailed proposal that describes how you would spend their money.

This chapter concludes with a brief discussion of how you might prepare such a proposal. This will give you one more overview of the whole research process, which the rest of this book details.

Elements of a Research Proposal

Although some funding agencies (or your instructor, for that matter) may have specific requirements for the elements or structure of a research proposal, here are some basic elements you should include.

Problem or Objective

What exactly do you want to study? Why is it worth studying? Does the proposed study have practical significance? Does it contribute to the construction of social theories, for example?

Literature Review

What have others said about this topic? What theories address it and what do they say? What research has been done previously? Are there consistent findings, or do past studies disagree? Are there flaws in the body of existing research that you feel you can remedy?

Subjects for Study

Whom or what will you study in order to collect data? First, identify the subjects in general, theoretical terms; then in specific, more concrete terms, identify who is available for study and how you'll reach them. Will it be appropriate to select a sample? If so, how will you do that? If there is any possibility that your research will affect those you study, how will you insure that the research does not harm them?

Measurement

What are the key variables in your study? How will you define and measure them? Do your definitions and measurement methods duplicate or differ from those of previous research on this topic? If you have already developed your measurement device (a questionnaire, for example) or will be using something previously developed by others, it might be appropriate to include a copy in an appendix to your proposal.

Data-Collection Methods

How will you actually collect the data for your study? Will you conduct an experiment or a survey? Will you undertake field research or will you focus on the reanalysis of statistics already created by others? Perhaps you will use more than one method.

Ethical Approval

Once you've decided on your method of data collection, you'll have to determine whether you need to obtain ethical approval of your study. We'll discuss this process in Part 3 because ethical approval of data collection depends on the method of research you use. For instance, if you decided on an experiment or a survey, gaining ethical approval would be necessary. On the other hand, if you chose to analyze existing statistics or gather information from the archives, then gaining ethical approval wouldn't be required.

Analysis

Indicate the kind of analysis you plan to conduct. Spell out the purpose and logic of your analysis. Are you interested in precise description? Do you intend to explain why things are the way they are? Do you plan to account for variations in some quality: for example, why some students are more liberal than others? What possible explanatory variables will your analysis consider, and how will you know if you've explained variations adequately?

Schedule

It's often appropriate to provide a schedule for the various stages of research. Even if you don't do this for the proposal, do it for yourself. Unless you have a timeline for accomplishing the several stages of research and keeping track of how you're doing, you may end up in trouble.

Budget

When you ask someone to cover the costs of your research, you need to provide a specific budget. Large, expensive projects include budgetary categories such as personnel, equipment, supplies, telephones, and postage. Even for a project you'll pay for yourself, it's a good idea to spend some time anticipating expenses: office supplies, photocopying, computer disks, telephone calls, transportation, and so on.

As you can see, if you were interested in conducting a social science research project, it would be a good idea to prepare a research proposal for your own purposes, even if you weren't required to do so by your instructor or a funding agency. If you're going to invest your time and energy in such a project, you should do what you can to insure a return on that investment.

Now that you've had a broad overview of social research, let's move on to the remaining chapters in this book and learn exactly how to design and execute each specific step. If you've found a research topic that really interests you, you'll want to keep it in mind as you see how you might go about studying it.

Main Points

- Three major purposes of social research are exploration, description, and explanation. Research studies often combine more than one purpose.
- Exploration is the attempt to develop an initial, rough understanding of some phenomenon.
- Description is the precise reporting and/or measurement of the characteristics of some population or phenomenon under study.
- Explanation is the discovery and reporting of relationships among different aspects of the phenomenon under study. Whereas descriptive studies answer the question "What's so?" explanatory ones tend to answer the question "Why?"
- Units of analysis are the people or things whose characteristics social researchers observe,

describe, and explain. Typically, the unit of analysis in social research is the individual person, but it may also be a social group, a formal organization, a social artifact, or some other phenomenon such as lifestyles or social interactions.

- The ecological fallacy involves conclusions drawn from the analysis of the attributes of groups (e.g., cities) that are then assumed to apply to individuals (e.g., specific residents of different cities).

- Cross-sectional studies are based on observations made at one time. Although such studies are limited by this characteristic, researchers can sometimes make inferences about processes that occur over time.

- In longitudinal studies, observations are made at many times. Such observations may be made of samples drawn from general populations (trend studies), samples drawn from more specific subpopulations (cohort studies), or the same sample of people each time (panel studies).

- There are a number of ways to approximate longitudinal studies when such research studies are not feasible or practical.

- Research design begins with an initial interest, idea, or theoretical expectation and proceeds through interrelated steps to narrow the study's focus so that concepts, methods, and procedures are well defined.

- The researcher specifies the meaning of concepts or variables to be studied (conceptualization), chooses a research method or methods, specifies the population to be studied and, when applicable, how it will be sampled, and obtains ethical approval for the study when it's required.

- The researcher operationalizes the concepts to be studied by stating precisely how variables in the study will be measured. Research then proceeds through observation, processing the data, analysis, and application, such as reporting results and assessing their implications.

- Triangulation—using several different research methods to study a topic or test the same finding—is a valuable research strategy.

- A research proposal provides a preview of why a study will be undertaken and how it will be conducted. It may be required, but even if it's not, it's a useful device for planning.

Review Questions and Exercises

1. Here are some examples of real research topics. For each one, name the unit of analysis. (The answers are at the end of this chapter.)

   a. The present research is designed to test the hypothesis that the observed variation in provincial crime rates will be positively related to the amount of provincial geographic mobility (Hartnagel 1997:391).

   b. The sample was designed to represent the population of Canadian women between the ages of 18 and 65 who speak English or French....Nearly 77 percent of respondents reported more than one form of harassment and most women experienced more than one incident of each type (Lenton et al. 1999:523).

   c. This study describes the reaction of different Toronto newspapers to the possibility of Quebec separation in the period from September 12, 1994 to November 15, 1995.... Editorials form the basis of analysis since they represent the official views of the paper and so act as an indirect glimpse into the general stance taken on the Quebec issue by ethnic and mainstream communities (Bright et al. 1999:318).

   d. As a first step in our data analysis, we examined the socio-demographic characteristics of employees who use and do not use computers in the job they held at the time of the GSS [Canadian General Social Survey] (Hughes and Lowe 2000:36).

   e. Using a detailed 33-category occupational classification, and inspecting the proportion of workers in each occupation who use computers and their mean weekly hours of use, we were able to identify six discrete clusters for comparison. Three fell at the high end of the computer use scale, while the other three were at the low end (Hughes and Lowe 2000:37).

f. This analysis explores whether propositions and empirical findings of contemporary theories of organizations directly apply to both private product producing organizations (PPOs) and public human service organizations (PSOs) (Schiflett and Zey 1990:569).

g. The aim of this exploratory study was to identify among a range of sociodemographic, health, and lifestyle variables, those that differ significantly between adolescents who have had sexual intercourse and those who have not (Feldman et al. 1997:198).

2. Look through an academic research journal until you find examples of at least three different units of analysis. Identify each and present quotations from the journal to justify your conclusions.

3. Make up a research example—different from those discussed in the text—that illustrates a researcher falling into the trap of the ecological fallacy. Then modify the example to avoid this trap.

4. Using InfoTrac or the library, select a research report that illustrates a cross-sectional, trend, cohort, or panel study design. Justify your choice.

5. Suppose you wanted to undertake a survey to learn what students at your university regard as the most serious problems facing the world today. Prepare a research proposal you might submit for funding.

Continuity Project

Select one of the research techniques introduced in this chapter and describe how you might use that technique in the study of attitudes toward gender equality.

Additional Readings

Casley, D. J., and D. A. Lury. *Data Collection in Developing Countries.* Oxford: Clarendon Press, 1987. This book discusses the special problems of research in the developing world.

Cooper, Harris M. *Synthesizing Research: A Guide for Literature Reviews.* 3rd ed. Newbury Park, CA: Sage, 1998. The author leads you through each step in the literature review process.

Iversen, Gudmund R. *Contextual Analysis.* Newbury Park, CA: Sage, 1991. Contextual analysis examines the impact of socioenvironmental factors on individual bahaviour. Durkheim's study of suicide offers a good example of this, identifying social contexts that affect the likelihood of self-destruction.

Maxwell, Joseph A. *Qualitative Research Design: An Interactive Approach.* Thousand Oaks, CA: Sage Publications, 1996. Maxwell covers many of the same topics this chapter does but with attention devoted specifically to qualitative research projects.

Menard, Scott. *Longitudinal Research.* Newbury Park, CA: Sage, 1991. Beginning by explaining why we conduct longitudinal research, the author goes on to detail a variety of study designs as well as suggestions for the analysis of longitudinal data.

Miller, Delbert. *Handbook of Research Design and Social Measurement.* Newbury Park, CA: Sage, 1991. A useful reference book for introducing or reviewing numerous issues involved in design and measurement. In addition, the book contains a wealth of practical information relating to foundations, journals, and professional associations.

InfoTrac: You can find further relevant readings on the World Wide Web at

http://sociology.wadsworth.com

Answers to Review Questions and Exercises, Item 1

a. Province (groups)
b. Canadian women (individuals)
c. Editorials (artifacts)
d. Employees (individuals)
e. Occupations (groups)
f. Service and Production Organizations (formal organizations)
g. Adolescents (individuals)

Chapter 5

Conceptualization, Operationalization, and Measurement

The interrelated steps of conceptualization, operationalization, and measurement allow researchers to turn a general idea for a research topic into useful and valid measurements in the real world. An essential part of this process involves transforming the relatively vague terms of ordinary language into precise objects of study with well-defined and measurable meanings.

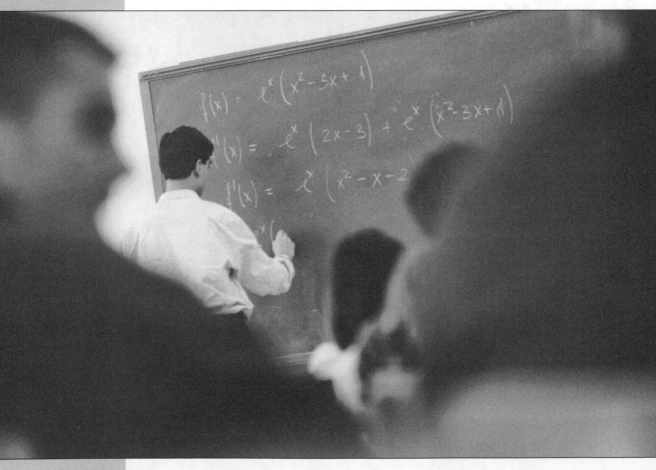

In this chapter . . .

Introduction

This chapter and the next deal with how researchers move from a general idea about what they want to study to effective and well-defined measurements in the real world. We discuss the interrelated processes of conceptualization, operationalization, and measurement. Chapter 6 builds on this to discuss more complex types of measurements.

We begin this chapter by confronting the hidden concern people sometimes have about whether it's possible to measure the stuff of life: love, hate, prejudice, radicalism, religiosity, alienation. The answer is yes, but it will take a few pages to see how. Once we establish that researchers can measure anything that exists, we'll turn to the steps involved in doing just that.

Measuring Anything That Exists

We said earlier in this book that one of the two pillars of science is observation. Because this word can suggest a casual, passive activity, scientists often use the term *measurement* instead, meaning careful, deliberate observations of the real world for the purpose of describing objects and events in terms of the attributes composing a variable.

You may have some reservations about the ability of science to measure the really important aspects of human social existence. If you've read research reports dealing with something like liberalism or religion or prejudice, you may have been dissatisfied with the way the researchers measured whatever they were studying. You may have felt they were too superficial, that they missed the aspects that really matter most. Maybe they measured *religiosity* as the number of times a person went to church, or maybe they measured *liberalism* by how people voted in a single election. Your dissatisfaction would surely have been increased if you found yourself being misclassified by the measurement system.

Your feeling of dissatisfaction reflects an important fact about social research: Most of the variables we want to study don't actually exist in the way that rocks exist. Indeed, they are created. Moreover, they seldom have a single, unambiguous meaning.

To illustrate this point, suppose we want to study *political party affiliation*. To measure this variable we might consult the list of party members to note whether the people we're studying are members of say the Liberal Party, the Progressive Conservatives, the Canadian Alliance, etc. In this fashion, we would have measured their political party affiliation. Or in an in-depth interview about political matters, we might simply ask someone what party they identify with and take their response as our measure. Notice that the two different measurement possibilities reflect somewhat different definitions of "political party affiliation." They would likely produce different results. Those who are not members of a party, when asked, may say they are affiliated with the party they feel the most kinship with. Others may be members of a political party at the time we consulted the member list, but for various reasons, perhaps due to an insensitive statement by its leader or a major event that occurred, decided to switch their party identification.

Similar points apply to *religious affiliation*. Sometimes this variable refers to official membership in a particular church; other times it simply means whatever religion, if any, you identify yourself with. Perhaps to you it means something else, such as church attendance.

The truth is that neither "party affiliation" nor "religious affiliation" has any *real* meaning, if by "real" we mean corresponding to some objective aspect of reality. These variables do not exist in nature. They are merely terms we have made up and assigned specific meanings to for some pur-

pose, such as doing social research (or communicating with others).

But, you might object, "political affiliation," "religious affiliation," and a host of other things social researchers are interested in, such as prejudice or compassion, have *some* reality. After all, we make statements about them, such as "In Happytown, 55 percent of adults affiliate with the Liberal party and 45 percent are Catholics. Overall, people in Happytown are low in prejudice and high in compassion." Even ordinary people, not just social researchers, have been known to make statements like that. If these things don't exist in reality, what is it that we're measuring and talking about?

What indeed? Let's take a closer look by considering a variable of interest to many social researchers (and many other people as well)—prejudice.

Conceptions, Concepts, and Reality

As we've wandered down the road of life, we've observed a lot of things and knew they were real through our observations, and we've heard reports from other people that seemed real. For example:

- We personally heard people say nasty things about minority groups.
- We have heard people say women are inferior to men.
- We read that women and minorities have earned less for the same work.
- We read about homosexuals and minorities being beaten and killed.
- We learned about "ethnic cleansing" and wars in which one ethnic group tried to eradicate another.

With additional experience, we noticed something more. People who participated in beatings and killings were also quite likely to call homosexuals and minorities ugly names. A lot of them, moreover, seem to want women to "stay in their place." Eventually, it dawned on us these several tendencies often appeared together and had something in common. At some point, someone had the bright idea: "Let's use the word *prejudiced* as a shorthand notation for people like that. We can use the term even if they don't do all those things, as long as they're pretty much like that."

Being basically agreeable and interested in efficiency, we agreed to go along with the system. That's where "prejudice" came from. We never observed it. We just agreed to use it as a shortcut, a name that represents a collection of apparently related phenomena that we've each observed in the course of life. In short, we made it up.

Here's another clue that prejudice isn't something that exists apart from our rough agreement to use the term in a certain way. Each of us develops our own mental image of what the set of real phenomena we've observed represents in general and what they have in common. When we say the word *prejudice,* it evokes a mental image in your mind, just as it evokes one in ours. It's as though file drawers in our minds contained thousands of sheets of paper, with each sheet of paper labelled in the upper right-hand corner. A sheet of paper in each of our minds has the term *prejudice* on it. On your sheet are all the things you were told about prejudice and everything you've observed that seemed to be an example of it. Someone else's sheet has what she was told about it plus all the things she has observed that seem to be examples of it—and her sheet isn't the same as yours.

The technical term for those mental images, those sheets of paper in our mental file drawers, is *conception.* That is, each of us has our own conception of prejudice. We can't communicate these mental images directly, so we use the terms written in the upper right-hand corner of our own mental sheets of paper as a way of communicating about our conceptions and the things we observe that are related to those conceptions. The terms make it possible for us to communicate and eventually agree on what we will specifically mean by those terms. In social research, the process of coming to an agreement about what terms mean is **conceptualization** and the result is called a **concept**.

Let's take another example of a conception. Suppose your mother is going to meet someone named Pat, whom you already know. She asks you what Pat is like. Now suppose you've seen Pat help lost children find their parents and put a tiny bird back in its nest. Pat got you to take turkeys to poor families on Thanksgiving and to visit a children's hospital on Christmas. You've seen Pat weep at a movie about a mother overcoming adversities to save and protect her child. As you search through your mental files, you may find all or most of those phenomena recorded on a single sheet labelled *compassionate.* You look over the other entries on the page, and you find they seem to provide an accurate description of Pat. So, you say, "Pat is compassionate."

Now your mother leafs through her own mental file drawer until she finds a sheet marked *compassionate.* She then looks over the things written on her sheet, and says, "Oh, that's nice." She now feels she knows what Pat is like, but her expectations in that regard reflect the entries on her file sheet, not yours. Later, when she meets Pat, she happens to find that her own experiences correspond to the entries she has on her *compassionate* file sheet, and she says that you sure were right. But say her observations of Pat contradict the things she has on her file sheet. She tells you that she doesn't think Pat is very compassionate, and you begin to compare notes.

You say, "I once saw Pat weep at a movie about a mother overcoming adversity to save and protect her child." She looks at her *compassionate* sheet and can't find anything like that. Looking elsewhere in her file, she locates that sort of phenomenon on a sheet labelled *sentimental.* She retorts, "That's not compassion. That's just sentimentality."

To further strengthen her case, she tells you that she saw Pat refuse to give money to an organization dedicated to saving the whales from extinction. "That represents a lack of compassion," she argues. You search through your files and find saving the whales on two sheets, *environmental activism* and *cross-species dating*, and you say so. Eventually, you set about comparing the entries you have on your respective sheets labelled *compassionate.* You then discover that you have many differing mental images corresponding to that term.

In the big picture, language and communication work only to the extent that we have considerable overlap in the kinds of entries we have on our corresponding mental file sheets. The similarities we have on those sheets represent the agreements existing in our society. As we grow up, we're told approximately the same thing when we're first introduced to a particular term. Dictionaries formalize the agreements our society has about such terms. Each of us, then, shapes his or her mental images to correspond with such agreements. But because all of us have different experiences and observations, no two people end up with exactly the same set of entries on any sheet in their file systems. If we want to measure "prejudice" or "compassion," we must first stipulate what, exactly, counts as prejudice or compassion for our purposes.

Returning to the assertion made at the outset of this chapter, we can measure anything that's real. We can measure, for example, whether Pat actually puts the little bird back in its nest, visits the hospital on Christmas, weeps at the movie, or refuses to contribute to saving the whales. All of those behaviours exist, so we can measure them. But is Pat really compassionate? We can't answer that question; we can't measure compassion in any objective sense, because compassion doesn't exist the way those things we just described exist. Compassion exists only in the form of the agreements we have about how to use the term in communicating about things that are real.

Concepts as Constructs

If you recall the discussions of postmodernism in Chapter 2, you'll recognize that some people would object to the degree of "reality" we've allowed in the preceding comments. Did Pat "really" visit the hospital on Christmas? Does the hospital "really" exist? Does Christmas? Though we're not going to be radically postmodern in this chapter, we think you'll recognize the importance of an intellectually tough view of what's real and what's not. (When the intellectual going gets tough, the tough become social scientists.)

In this context, Abraham Kaplan (1964) distinguishes three classes of things that scientists measure. The first class is *direct observables:* those things we can observe rather simply and directly, like the colour of an apple or the check mark made

in a questionnaire. The second class, *indirect observables,* require "relatively more subtle, complex, or indirect observations" (1964:55). We note a person's check mark beside *female* in a questionnaire and have indirectly observed that person's gender. History books or minutes of corporate board meetings provide indirect observations of past social actions. Finally, the third class of observables consists of *constructs*—theoretical creations that are based on observations but that cannot be observed directly or indirectly. Intelligence quotient, or IQ, is a good example. It is *constructed* mathematically from observations of the answers given to a large number of questions on an IQ test. No one can directly or indirectly observe IQ. It is no more a "real" characteristic of people than is compassion or prejudice.

Kaplan (1964:49) defines *concept* as a "family of conceptions." A concept is, as Kaplan notes, a construct, something we create. Concepts like compassion and prejudice are constructs created from your conception of them, our conception of them, and the conceptions of all those who have ever used these terms. They cannot be observed directly or indirectly, because they don't exist. We made them up.

To summarize, concepts are constructs derived by mutual agreement from mental images (conceptions). Our conceptions summarize collections of seemingly related observations and experiences. Although the observations and experiences are real, at least subjectively, conceptions, and the concepts derived from them, are only mental creations. The terms associated with concepts are merely devices created for the purposes of filing and communication. A term like *prejudice* is, objectively speaking, only a collection of letters. It has no intrinsic reality beyond that. It has only the meaning we agree to give it.

Usually, however, we fall into the trap of believing that terms for constructs do have intrinsic meaning—that they name real entities in the world. That danger seems to grow stronger when we begin to take terms seriously and attempt to use them precisely. Further, the danger is all the greater in the presence of experts who appear to know more than we do about what the terms really mean: It's very easy to yield to authority in such a situation.

Once we assume that terms like *prejudice* and *compassion* have real meanings, we begin the tortured task of discovering what those real meanings are and what constitutes a genuine measurement of them. Regarding concepts as real is called **reification.** The reification of concepts in day-to-day life is quite common. In science, we want to be quite clear about what it is we are actually measuring.

Does this discussion imply that compassion, prejudice, and similar constructs can't be measured? Interestingly, the answer is no. (And a good thing too, or a lot of us social researcher types would be out of work.) We've said that we can measure anything that's real. Constructs aren't real in the way that trees are real, but they do have another important virtue: They are useful. That is, they help us organize, communicate about, and understand things that *are* real. They help us make predictions about real things. Some of those predictions even turn out to be true. Constructs can work this way because, while not real or observable in themselves, they have a definite relationship to things that are real and observable. The bridge from direct and indirect observables to useful constructs is the process called conceptualization.

Conceptualization

As we've seen day-to-day communication usually occurs through a system of vague and general agreements about the use of terms. Although we don't agree completely about the use of the term *compassionate,* it's probably safe to assume that Pat won't pull the wings off flies. A wide range of misunderstandings and conflict, from the interpersonal to the international, is the price we pay for our imprecision, but somehow we muddle through. Science, however, aims at more than muddling; it cannot operate in a context of such imprecision.

The process through which we specify what we will mean when we use particular terms in research is called **conceptualization**. Suppose we want to find out, for example, whether women are more compassionate than men. We suspect many people assume this is the case, but it might be interesting to find out if it's really so. We can't meaningfully study the question, let alone agree on the answer, without some working agreements about the meaning of *compassion.* They are "working" agreements in the sense that they allow us to work on the question. We don't need to agree or even pretend to agree that a particular specification is ultimately the best one.

Conceptualization, then, produces a specific, agreed-upon meaning for a concept for the purposes of research. This process of specifying exact meaning involves describing the indicators we'll be using to measure our concept and the different aspects of the concept, called dimensions.

Indicators and Dimensions

Conceptualization gives definite meaning to a concept by specifying one or more indicators of what we have in mind. An **indicator** is a sign of the presence or absence of the concept we're studying. Here's an example.

We might agree that visiting children's hospitals during Christmas and Hanukkah is an indicator of compassion. Putting little birds back in their nests might be agreed on as another indicator, and so forth. If the unit of analysis for our study is the individual person, we can then observe the presence or absence of each indicator for each person under study. Going beyond that, we can add up the number of indicators of compassion observed for each individual. We might agree on 10 specific indicators, for example, and find six present in our study of Pat, three for John, nine for Mary, and so forth.

Returning to our original question about whether men or women are more compassionate, we might calculate that the women we studied displayed an average of 6.5 indicators of compassion, the men an average of 3.2. On the basis of our quantitative analysis of group difference, we might therefore conclude that women are, on the whole, more compassionate than men.

Usually, though, it's not that simple. Imagine you're interested in understanding a small fundamentalist religious cult, particularly their harsh views about various groups: gays, nonbelievers, feminists, and others. In fact, they suggest that anyone who refuses to join their group and abide by its teachings will "burn in hell." In the context of your continuing interest in compassion, they don't seem to have much. And yet, the group's literature often speaks of their compassion for others. You want to explore this seeming paradox.

To pursue this research interest, you might arrange to interact with cult members, getting to know them and learning more about their views. You could tell them you were a social researcher interested in learning about their group, or perhaps you'd just express an interest in learning more without saying why.

In the course of your conversations with group members and perhaps in attending religious services, you would put yourself in situations where you could come to understand what the cult members mean by *compassion*. You might learn, for example, that members of the group were so deeply concerned about sinners burning in hell that they were willing to be aggressive, even violent, to make people change their sinful ways. Within this paradigm, then, cult members would see beating up gays, prostitutes, and abortion doctors as an act of compassion.

Social researchers focus their attention on the meanings given to words and actions by the people under study. Doing so can often clarify the behaviours observed: At least now you understand how the cult can see violent acts as compassionate. On the other hand, paying attention to what words and actions mean to people under study almost always complicates the concepts researchers are interested in. (We'll return to this issue when we discuss the validity of measures, toward the end of this chapter.)

Whenever we take our concepts seriously and set about specifying what we mean by them, we discover disagreements and inconsistencies. Not only do we disagree, but each of us is likely to find a good deal of muddiness within our own mental images. If you take a moment to look at what you

mean by compassion, you'll probably find that your image contains several kinds of compassion. That is, the entries on your file sheet can be combined into groups and subgroups, say, compassion toward friends, humans, and birds. You may also find several different strategies for making the combinations. For example, you might group the entries into feelings and actions.

The technical term for such groupings is **dimension:** a specifiable aspect of a concept. For instance, we might speak of the feeling dimension of compassion and the action dimension of compassion. In a different grouping scheme, we might distinguish compassion for humans from compassion for animals. Or we might see compassion as helping people have what we want for them versus what they want for themselves. Still differently, we might distinguish compassion as forgiveness from compassion as pity.

Thus, we could subdivide *compassion* into several clearly defined dimensions. A complete conceptualization involves both specifying dimensions and identifying the various indicators for each.

Specifying the different dimensions of a concept often paves the way for a more sophisticated understanding of what we're studying. We might observe, for example, that women are more compassionate in terms of feelings, and men more so in terms of actions, or vice versa. Whichever turned out to be the case, we would not be able to say whether men or women are really more compassionate. Our research would have shown that there is no single answer to the question. That alone represents an advance in our understanding of reality.

The Interchangeability of Indicators

There is another way that the notion of indicators can help us in our attempts to understand reality by means of "unreal" constructs. Suppose, for the moment, that we have compiled a list of 100 indicators of compassion and its various dimensions. Suppose further that we disagree widely on which indicators give the clearest evidence of compassion or its absence. If we pretty much agree on some indicators, we could focus our attention on those, and we would probably agree on the answer they provided. We would then be able to say that some people are more compassionate than others in some dimension. But suppose we don't really agree on any of the possible indicators. Surprisingly, we can still reach an agreement on whether men or women are the more compassionate. How we do this has to do with the **interchangeability of indicators**.

The logic works like this. If we disagree totally on the value of the indicators, one solution would be to study all of them. Suppose that women turn out to be more compassionate than men on all 100 indicators—on all the indicators you favour and on all of ours. Then we would be able to agree that women are more compassionate than men even though we still disagree on exactly what compassion means in general.

The interchangeability of indicators means that if several different indicators all represent, to some degree, the same concept, then all of them will behave the same way that the concept would behave if it were real and could be observed. Thus, given a basic agreement about what "compassion" is, if women are generally more compassionate than men, we should be able to observe that difference by using any reasonable measure of compassion. If, on the other hand, women are more compassionate than men on some indicators but not on others, we should see if the two sets of indicators represent different dimensions of compassion.

You have now seen the fundamental logic of conceptualization and measurement. The discussions that follow are mainly refinements and extensions of what you've just read. Before turning to a technical elaboration of measurement, however, we need to fill out the picture of conceptualization by looking at some of the ways social researchers provide the meanings of terms with standards, consistency, and commonality.

Real, Nominal, and Operational Definitions

As we've seen, the design and execution of social research requires us to clear away the confusion over concepts and reality. To this end, logicians

and scientists have found it useful to distinguish three kinds of definitions: *real, nominal,* and *operational.*

The first of these reflects the reification of terms. As Carl Hempel (1952:6) has cautioned,

> A "real" definition, according to traditional logic, is not a stipulation determining the meaning of some expression but a statement of the "essential nature" or the "essential attributes" of some entity. The notion of essential nature, however, is so vague as to render this characterization useless for the purposes of rigorous inquiry.

In other words, trying to specify the "real" meaning of concepts only leads to a quagmire: It mistakes a construct for a real entity.

The specification of concepts in scientific inquiry depends instead on nominal and operational definitions. A **nominal definition** is one that is simply assigned to a term without any claim that the definition represents a "real" entity. Nominal definitions are arbitrary—we could define *compassion* as "plucking feathers off helpless birds" if we wanted to—but they can be more or less useful. For most purposes, especially communication, that last definition of compassion would be pretty useless. Most nominal definitions represent some consensus, or convention, about how a particular term is to be used.

An **operational definition**, as you may recall from an earlier chapter, specifies precisely how a concept will be measured—that is, the operations we will perform. An operational definition is nominal rather than real, but it has the advantage of achieving maximum clarity about what a concept means in the context of a given study. In the midst of disagreement and confusion over what a term "really" means, we can specify a working definition for the purposes of an inquiry. Wishing to examine socioeconomic status (SES) in a study, for example, we may simply specify that we're going to treat SES as a combination of income and educational attainment. In this decision, we rule out other possible aspects of SES: occupational status, money in the bank, property, lineage, lifestyle, and so forth. Our findings will then be interesting to the extent that our definition of SES is useful for our purpose.

Creating Conceptual Order

The clarification of concepts is a continuing process in social research. Catherine Marshall and Gretchen Rossman (1995:18) speak of a "conceptual funnel" through which a researcher's interest becomes increasingly focused. Thus, a general interest in social activism could narrow to "individuals who are committed to empowerment and social change" and further focus on discovering "what experiences shaped the development of fully committed social activists." This focusing process is inescapably linked to the language we use.

In some forms of qualitative research, the clarification of concepts is a key element in data collection. Suppose you were conducting interviews and observations in a radical political group devoted to combating oppression in Canadian society. Imagine how the meaning of oppression would shift as you delved more and more deeply into the members' experiences and worldviews. For example, you might start out thinking of oppression in physical and perhaps economic terms. The more you learned about the group, however, the more you might appreciate the possibility of psychological oppression.

The same point applies even to contexts where meanings might seem more fixed. In the analysis of textual materials, for example, social researchers sometimes speak of the "hermeneutic circle," a cyclical process of ever deeper understanding.

> The understanding of a text takes place through a process in which the meaning of the separate parts is determined by the global meaning of the text as it is anticipated. The closer determination of the meaning of the separate parts may eventually change the originally anticipated meaning of the totality, which again influences the meaning of the separate parts, and so on.
>
> (Kvale 1996:47)

Consider the concept "prejudice." Suppose you needed to write a definition of the term. You might start out thinking about racial/ethnic prejudice. At some point you would realize you should probably allow for gender prejudice, religious prejudice, anti-gay prejudice, and the like in your definition.

Examining each of these specific types of prejudice would affect your overall understanding of the general concept. As your general understanding changed, however, you would likely see each of the individual forms somewhat differently.

The continual refinement of concepts occurs in all social research methods. Often you'll find yourself refining the meaning of important concepts even as you write up your final report.

Although conceptualization is a continuing process, it's vital that you address it specifically at the beginning of any study design, especially rigorously structured research designs such as surveys and experiments. In a survey, for example, operationalization results in a commitment to a specific set of questionnaire items that will represent the concepts under study. Without that commitment, the study could not proceed further.

Even in less structured research methods, however, it's important to begin with an initial set of anticipated meanings that can be refined during data collection and interpretation. No one seriously believes we can observe life with no preconceptions; for this reason, scientific observers must be conscious of and explicit about these starting points.

Let's explore initial conceptualization the way it applies to structured inquiries such as surveys and experiments. Though specifying nominal definitions focuses our observational strategy, it does not allow us to observe. As a next step we must specify exactly what we are going to observe, how we will do it, and what interpretations we are going to place on various possible observations. All these further specifications make up the operational definition of the concept.

In the example of socioeconomic status, we might decide to ask survey respondents two questions, corresponding to the decision to measure SES in terms of income and educational attainment:

1. What was your total family income during the past 12 months?
2. What is the highest level of school you completed?

To organize our data, we would probably want to specify a system for categorizing the answers people give us. For income, we might use categories such as "under $10,000," "$10,000 to $20,000," and so on. Educational attainment might be similarly grouped in categories: less than high school, high school, college/university, graduate degree. Finally, we would specify the way a person's responses to these two questions would be combined in creating a measure of SES.

In this way we would create a working and workable definition of SES. Although others might disagree with our conceptualization and operationalization, the definition would have one essential scientific virtue: It would be absolutely specific and unambiguous. Even if someone disagreed with our definition, that person would have a good idea how to interpret our research results, because what we meant by SES—reflected in our analyses and conclusions—would be precise and clear.

Here's a diagram showing the progression of measurement steps from our vague sense of what a term means to specific measurements in a fully structured scientific study:

Conceptualization
↓

Nominal Definition
↓

Operational Definition
↓

Measurements in the Real World

An Example of Conceptualization: The Concept of Anomie

To bring this discussion of conceptualization in research together, let's look briefly at the history of a specific social scientific concept. Researchers studying urban riots are often interested in the part played by feelings of social dislocation. Social scientists sometimes use the word *anomie* in this context. (Recall that Cohn used this concept in his study of outmarriage and migration, discussed in Chapter 2.) This term was first introduced into social science by Emile Durkheim, the great French sociologist, in his classic 1897 study, *Suicide*.

Using only government publications on suicide rates in different regions and countries, Durkheim produced a work of analytical genius. To determine the effects of religion on suicide, he compared the suicide rates of predominantly Protestant countries with those of predominantly Catholic ones, Protestant regions of Catholic countries with Catholic regions of Protestant countries, and so forth. To determine the possible effects of the weather, he compared suicide rates in northern and southern countries and regions, and he examined the different suicide rates across the months and seasons of the year. Thus, he could draw conclusions about a supremely individualistic and personal act without having any data about the individuals engaging in it.

At a more general level, Durkheim suggested that suicide also reflected the extent to which a society's agreements were clear and stable. Noting that times of social upheaval and change often present individuals with grave uncertainties about what is expected of them, Durkheim suggested that such uncertainties cause confusion, anxiety, and even self-destruction. To describe this societal condition of normlessness, Durkheim chose the term *anomie*. Durkheim did not make this word up. Used in both German and French, it literally meant "without law." The English term *anomy* had been used for at least three centuries before Durkheim to mean disregard for divine law. However, Durkheim created the social scientific concept of anomie.

In the years that have followed the publication of *Suicide*, social scientists have found anomie a useful concept, and many have expanded on Durkheim's use. Robert Merton, in a classic article entitled "Social Structure and Anomie" (1938), concluded that anomie results from a disparity between the goals and means prescribed by a society. Monetary success, for example, is a widely shared goal in our society, yet not all individuals have the resources to achieve it through acceptable means. An emphasis on the goal itself, Merton suggested, produces normlessness, because those denied the traditional avenues to wealth go about getting it through illegitimate means. Merton's discussion, then, could be considered a further conceptualization of the concept of anomie.

Although Durkheim originally used the concept of anomie as a characteristic of societies, as did Merton after him, other social scientists have used it to describe individuals. To clarify this distinction, some scholars have chosen to use *anomie* in reference to its original, societal meaning and to use *anomia* in reference to the individual characteristic. In a given society, then, some individuals experience anomia, and others do not. Elwin Powell (1957:132), writing 20 years after Merton, provided the following conceptualization of anomia (though using the term *anomie*) as a characteristic of individuals:

> When the ends of action become contradictory, inaccessible or insignificant, a condition of anomie arises. Characterized by a general loss of orientation and accompanied by feelings of "emptiness" and apathy, anomie can be simply conceived as meaninglessness.

Powell went on to suggest there were two distinct kinds of anomia and to examine how the two rose out of different occupational experiences to result at times in suicide. In his study, however, Powell did not measure anomia per se; he studied the relationship between suicide and occupation, making inferences about the two kinds of anomia. Thus, the study did not provide an operational definition of anomia, only a further conceptualization.

Although many researchers have offered operational definitions of anomia, one name stands out over all. Two years before Powell's article appeared, Leo Srole (1956) published a set of questionnaire items that he said provided a good measure of anomia as experienced by individuals. It consists of five statements that subjects are asked to agree or disagree with.

1. In spite of what some people say, the lot of the average man is getting worse.

2. It's hardly fair to bring children into the world with the way things look for the future.

3. Nowadays a person has to live pretty much for today and let tomorrow take care of itself.

4. These days a person doesn't really know who he can count on.

5. There's little use writing to public officials because they aren't really interested in the problems of the average man.

(1956:713)

In the decades following its publication, the Srole scale has become a research staple for social scientists. You'll likely find this particular operationalization of anomia used in many of the research projects reported in academic journals. Srole touches on this in the accompanying box, "The Origins of Anomia," which he prepared for this book before his death.

This abbreviated history of anomie and anomia as social scientific concepts illustrates several points. First, it's a good example of the process through which general concepts become operationalized measurements. This is not to say that the issue of how to operationalize anomie/anomia has been resolved once and for all. Scholars will surely continue to reconceptualize and reoperationalize these concepts for years to come, continually seeking more useful measures.

The Srole scale illustrates another important point. Letting conceptualization and operationalization be open-ended does not necessarily produce anarchy and chaos, as you might expect. Order often emerges. For one thing, although we could define anomia any way we chose—in terms of, say, shoe size—we're likely to define it in ways not too different from other people's mental images. If you were to use a really offbeat definition, people would probably ignore you.

A second source of order is that as researchers discover the utility of a particular conceptualization and operationalization of a concept, they're likely to adopt it, which leads to standardized definitions of concepts. Besides the Srole scale, examples include IQ tests and a host of demographic and economic measures developed by Statistics Canada. Using such established measures has two advantages: They have been extensively pretested and debugged, and studies using the same scales can be compared. If two researchers do separate studies of two different groups and use the Srole scale, they can compare the two groups on the basis of anomia.

Social scientists, then, can measure anything that's real; through conceptualization and opera-

The Origins of Anomia

By Leo Srole
Center for Geriatrics and Gerontology,
Columbia University

My career-long fixation on anomie began with reading Durkheim's *Le Suicide* as a Harvard undergraduate. Later, as a graduate student at Chicago, I studied under two Durkheimian anthropologists: William Lloyd Warner and Alfred Radcliffe-Brown. Radcliffe-Brown had carried on a lively correspondence with Durkheim, making me a collateral "descendant" of the great French sociologist.

For me, the early impact of Durkheim's work on suicide was mixed but permanent. On the one hand, I had serious reservations about his strenuous, ingenious, and often awkward efforts to force the crude, bureaucratic records on suicide rates to fit with his unidirectional sociological determinism. On the other hand, I was moved by Durkheim's unswerving preoccupation with the moral force of the interpersonal ties that bind us to our time, place, and past, and also his insights about the lethal consequences that can follow from shrinkage and decay in those ties.

My interest in anomie received an eyewitness jolt at the finale of World War II, when I served with the United Nations Relief and Rehabilitation Administration, helping to rebuild a war-torn Europe. At the Nazi concentration camp of Dachau, I saw firsthand the depths of dehumanization that macrosocial forces, such as those that engaged Durkheim, could produce in individuals like Hitler, Eichmann, and the others serving their dictates at all levels in the Nazi death factories.

Returning from my UNRRA post, I felt most urgently that the time was long overdue to come to an understanding of the dynamics underlying disintegrated social bonds. We needed to work expeditiously, deemphasizing proliferation of macrolevel theory in favor of a direct exploratory encounter with individuals, using newly developed state-of-the-art survey research methodology. Such research, I also felt, should focus on a broader spectrum of behavioural pathologies than suicide.

My initial investigations were a diverse effort. In 1950, for example, I was able to interview a sample of 401 bus riders in Springfield, Massachusetts. Four years later, the Midtown Manhattan Mental Health Study provided a much larger population reach. These and other field projects gave me scope to expand and refine my measurements of that quality in individuals, which reflected the macrosocial quality Durkheim had called *anomie.*

While I began by using Durkheim's term in my own work, I soon decided that it was necessary to limit the use of that concept to its macrosocial meaning and to sharply segregate it from its individual manifestations. For the latter purpose, the cognate but hitherto obsolete Greek term, *anomia,* readily suggested itself.

I first published the anomia construct in a 1956 article in the *American Sociological Review,*[*] describing ways of operationalizing it, and presenting the results of its initial field application research. By 1982, the Science Citation Index and Social Science Citation Index had listed some 400 publications in political science, psychology, social work, and sociology journals here and abroad that had cited use of that article's instruments or findings, warranting the American Institute for Scientific Information to designate it a "citation classic."

[*]Leo Srole, "Social Integration and Certain Corollaries: An Exploratory Study," *American Sociological Review* 21 (1956): 709–16.

tionalization, they can even do a pretty good job of measuring things that aren't. Granting that such concepts as socioeconomic status, prejudice, compassion, and anomia aren't ultimately real, social scientists can create order in handling them. It is an order based on utility, however, not on ultimate truth.

Definitions in Descriptive and Explanatory Studies

As you recall from Chapter 4, two general purposes of research are *description* and *explanation*. The distinction between them has important implications for definition and measurement. If it seems that description is a simpler task than explanation, you may be surprised to learn that definitions are more problematic for descriptive research than for explanatory research. Before we turn to other aspects of measurement, you'll need a basic understanding of why this is so (we'll discuss this point more fully in Part 4).

It's easy to see the importance of clear and precise definitions for descriptive research. If we want to describe and report the unemployment rate in a city, our definition of *being unemployed* is critical. That definition will depend on our definition of another term: the *labour force*. If it seems patently absurd to regard a three-year-old child as being unemployed, it is because such a child is not considered a member of the labour force. Thus, we might follow Statistics Canada's convention for the census and exclude all people under 15 years of age from the labour force.

This convention alone, however, would not give us a satisfactory definition, because it would count as unemployed such people as high school students, the retired, the disabled, and homemakers. We might follow Statistics Canada's convention further by defining the labour force as "all persons 15 years of age and over, excluding institutional residents, who were either employed or unemployed during the week (Sunday to Saturday) prior to Census Day." Unemployed is further defined as those who were "without paid work and were available for work." If a student, homemaker, or retired person is not available for work, such a person would not be included in the labour force. Unemployed people, then, would be those members of the labour force, as defined, who are not employed.

But what does "available for work" mean? Would it be sufficient for a person to be open to an offer of employment or to desire work? Perhaps a person must go from door to door letting everyone know about his or her availability for employment? Or maybe a person must register with a government employment service. The census definition states clearly exactly what it means. Those considered unemployed had to not only be without paid work and available for work the week prior to the census, they also had to either: "(a) had actively looked for work in the past four weeks; or (b) were on temporary lay-off and expected to return to their job; or (c) had definite arrangements to start a new job in four weeks or less." (http://www.statcan.ca:80/english/census96/define.html July 27, 2001)

As you can see, the conclusion of a descriptive study about the unemployment rate depends directly on how each issue is resolved. Increasing the period of time during which people are counted as looking for work would have the effect of adding more unemployed people to the labour force as defined, thereby increasing the reported unemployment rate. On the other hand, decreasing the time period would decrease the reported unemployment rate.

Thus the descriptive statement that the unemployment rate in a city is 3 percent, or 9 percent, or whatever it might be, depends directly on the operational definitions used.

This example is relatively clear because there are several accepted conventions relating to the labour force and unemployment. Consider how difficult it would be to get agreement about the definitions you'd need in order to say, "Forty-five percent of the students at this institution are politically conservative." Like the unemployment rate, this percentage would depend directly on the definition of what is being measured, in this case political conservatism. A different definition might result in the conclusion, "Five percent of the student body are politically conservative."

Ironically, definitions are less problematic in the case of explanatory research. Let's suppose we're interested in explaining political conservatism. Why are some people conservative and others not? More specifically, let's suppose we're interested in whether conservatism increases with age. What if we have different operational definitions of *conservative,* and we can't agree on which definition is the best one? As we saw in the discussion of indicators, this is not necessarily an insurmountable obstacle. Suppose we found old people to be more conservative than young people in terms of *all 25 definitions!* Clearly, the exact definition would be of small consequence. Suppose we found old people more conservative than young people by every reasonable definition of conservatism we could think of. It wouldn't matter what our definition was. We would conclude that old people are generally more conservative than young people, even though we couldn't agree about exactly what *conservative* means.

In practice, explanatory research seldom results in findings quite as unambiguous as this example suggests; nonetheless, the general pattern is quite common in actual research. There *are* consistent patterns of relationships in human social life that result in consistent research findings. However, such consistency does not appear in a descriptive situation. Changing definitions almost inevitably result in different descriptive conclusions.

Operationalization Choices

In discussing conceptualization, we have frequently referred to operationalization because the two are intimately linked. To recap: Conceptualization is the refinement and specification of abstract concepts, and operationalization is the development of specific research procedures (operations) that will result in empirical observations representing those concepts in the real world.

As with the methods of data collection, social researchers have a variety of choices when operationalizing a concept. Although the several choices are intimately interconnected, we've separated them for the sake of discussion. Realize, though, that operationalization does not proceed through a systematic checklist.

Range of Variation

In operationalizing any concept, researchers must be clear about the range of variation that interests them in their research. The question is, to what extent are we willing to combine attributes in fairly gross categories?

Let's suppose you want to measure people's incomes in a study by collecting the information from either records or interviews. The highest annual incomes people receive run into the millions of dollars, but not many people get that much. Unless you're studying the very rich, it probably wouldn't add much to your study to keep track of extremely high categories. Depending on whom you study, you'll probably want to establish a highest income category with a much lower floor, maybe $100,000 or more. Although this decision will lead you to throw together people who earn a trillion dollars a year with paupers earning a mere $100,000, they'll survive it, and that mixing probably won't hurt your research any, either. The same decision faces you at the other end of the income spectrum. In studies of the general Canadian population, a cutoff of $10,000 or less would probably work just fine.

In studies of attitudes and orientations, the question of range of variation has another dimension. Unless you're careful, you may end up measuring only half an attitude without really meaning to. Here's an example of what we mean.

Suppose you're interested in people's attitudes toward the expanded use of nuclear power generators. You'd anticipate that some people consider it the greatest thing since the wheel, whereas other people have absolutely no interest in it. Given that anticipation, it would seem to make sense to ask people how much they favour expanding the use of nuclear energy and to give them answer categories ranging from "Favour it very much" to "Don't favour it at all."

This operationalization, however, conceals half the attitudinal spectrum regarding nuclear energy. Many people have feelings that go beyond simply not favouring it: They are, with greater or lesser degrees of intensity, actively opposed to it. In this instance, there is considerable variation on the left side of zero. Some oppose it a little, some quite a bit, and others a great deal. To measure the full range of variation, then, you'd want to operationalize attitudes toward nuclear energy with a range from favouring it very much, through no feelings one way or the other, to opposing it very much.

This consideration applies to many of the variables social scientists study. Virtually any public issue involves both support and opposition, each in varying degrees. Political orientations range from very liberal to very conservative, and depending on the people you're studying, you may want to allow for radicals on one or both ends. Similarly, people are not just more or less religious; some are positively antireligious.

The point is not that you must measure the full range of variation in every case. You should, however, consider whether you need to, given your particular research purpose. If the difference between not religious and antireligious isn't relevant to your research, forget it. Someone has defined pragmatism as "any difference that makes no difference is no difference." Be pragmatic.

Finally, decisions on the range of variation should be governed by the expected distribution of attributes among the subjects of the study. In a study of university professors' attitudes toward the value of higher education, you could probably stop at no value and not worry about those who might consider higher education dangerous to students' health. (If you were studying students, however....)

Variations between the Extremes

Degree of precision is a second consideration in operationalizing variables. What it boils down to is how fine you will make distinctions among the various possible attributes composing a given variable. Does it matter for your purposes whether a person is 17 or 18 years old, or could you conduct your inquiry by throwing them together in a group labelled 10 to 19 years old? Don't answer too quickly. If you wanted to study rates of voter registration and participation, you'd definitely want to know whether the people you studied were old enough to vote. In general, if you're going to measure age, you must look at the purpose and procedures of your study and decide whether fine or gross differences in age are important to you. In a survey, you'll need to make these decisions in order to design an appropriate questionnaire. In the case of in-depth interviews, these decisions will condition the extent to which you probe for details.

The same thing applies to other variables. If you measure religious affiliation, is it enough to know that a person is a Protestant, or do you need to know the denomination? Do you simply need to know whether or not a person is married, or will it make a difference to know if he or she has never married or is separated, widowed, or divorced?

There is, of course, no general answer to such questions. The answers come out of the purpose of a given study, or why we are making a particular measurement. We can give you a useful guideline, though. Whenever you're not sure how much detail to pursue in a measurement, get too much rather than too little. When a subject in an in-depth interview volunteers that she is 37 years old, record "37" in your notes, not "in her thirties." When you're analyzing the data, you can always combine precise attributes into more general categories, but you can never separate out any variations you lumped together during observation and measurement.

A Note on Dimensions

We've already discussed dimensions as a characteristic of concepts. When researchers get down to the business of creating operational measures of variables, they often discover—or worse, never notice—that they're not exactly clear about which dimensions of a variable they're really interested in. Here's an example.

Let's suppose you're studying people's attitudes toward government, and you want to include an examination of how people feel about corruption. Here are just a few of the dimensions you might examine:

- Do people think there is corruption in government?
- How much corruption do they think there is?
- How certain are they in their judgment of how much corruption there is?
- How do they feel about corruption in government as a problem in society?
- What do they think causes it?
- Do they think it's inevitable?
- What do they feel should be done about it?
- What are they willing to do personally to eliminate corruption in government?
- How certain are they that they would be willing to do what they say they would do?

The list could go on and on. How people feel about corruption in government has many dimensions. It's essential to be clear about which ones are important in your inquiry; otherwise, you may measure how people *feel* about corruption when you really wanted to know how much they think there is, or vice versa.

Once you've determined how you're going to collect your data (for example, survey, field research) and have decided on the relevant range of variation, the degree of precision needed between the extremes of variation, and the specific dimensions of the variables that interest you, you may have another choice: a mathematical-logical one. That is, you may need to decide what *level* of measurement to use. To discuss this point, we need to take another look at attributes and their relationship to variables.

Defining Variables and Attributes

An attribute, you'll recall, is a characteristic or quality of something. "Female" is an example. So is "old" or "student." Variables, on the other hand, are logical sets of attributes. Thus, *gender* is a variable composed of the attributes female and male.

The conceptualization and operationalization processes can be seen as the specification of variables and the attributes composing them. Thus, in the context of a study of unemployment, *employment status* is a variable having the attributes employed and unemployed; the list of attributes could also be expanded to include the other possibilities discussed earlier, such as homemaker.

Every variable must have two important qualities. First, the attributes composing it should be **exhaustive**. For the variable to have any utility in research, we must be able to classify every observation in terms of one of the attributes composing the variable. We'll run into trouble if we conceptualize the variable *political party affiliation* in terms of the attributes Liberals, Progressive Conservatives, and Canadian Alliance, because some of the people you set out to study will identify with the Bloc Québécois, the New Democratic Party or some other organization, and some (often a large percentage) will tell you they have no party affiliation. We could make the list of attributes exhaustive by adding "other" and "no affiliation." Whatever we do, we must be able to classify every observation.

At the same time, attributes composing a variable must be **mutually exclusive**. Every observation must be able to be classified in terms of one and only one attribute. For example, we need to define "employed" and "unemployed" in such a way that nobody can be both at the same time. That means being able to classify the person who is working at a job but is also looking for work. (We might run across a fully employed mud wrestler who is looking for the glamour and excitement of being a social researcher.) In this case, we might define the attributes so that employed takes precedence over unemployed, and anyone working at a job is employed regardless of whether he or she is looking for something better.

Levels of Measurement

Attributes operationalized as mutually exclusive and exhaustive may be related in other ways as well. For example, the attributes composing variables may represent different levels of measurement. In this section, we'll examine four levels of measurement: nominal, ordinal, interval, and ratio.

Nominal Measures   Variables whose attributes have only the characteristics of exhaustiveness and mutual exclusiveness are **nominal measures**. Examples include *gender, religious affiliation, political party affiliation, birthplace, university major,* and *hair colour.* Although the attributes composing each of these variables—as male and female compose the variable *gender*—are distinct from one another (and exhaust the possibilities of gender among people), they have no additional structures. Nominal measures merely offer names or labels for characteristics.

Imagine a group of people being characterized in terms of one such variable and physically grouped by the applicable attributes. For example, say we've asked a large gathering of people to stand together in groups according to the provinces in which they were born: all those born in British Columbia in one group, those born in Newfoundland in another, and so forth. The variable is *place of birth;* the attributes are "born in British Columbia," "born in Newfoundland," and so on. All the people standing in a given group have at least one thing in common and differ from the people in all other groups in that same regard. Where the individual groups form, how close they are to one another, or how the groups are arranged in the room would be irrelevant. All that matters is that all the members of a given group share the same province of birth and that each group has a different shared province of birth. All we can say about two people in terms of a nominal variable is that they are either the same or different.

Ordinal Measures   Variables with attributes we can logically rank-order are **ordinal measures**. The different attributes of ordinal variables represent relatively more or less of the variable. Variables of this type are *social class, conservatism, alienation, prejudice, intellectual sophistication,* and the like. In addition to saying that two people are the same or different in terms of an ordinal variable, you can also say one is "more" than the

other—that is, more conservative, more religious, more prejudiced, and so forth.

In the physical sciences, *hardness* is the most frequently cited example of an ordinal measure. We may say that one material (for example, diamond) is harder than another (say, glass) if the former can scratch the latter and not vice versa. By attempting to scratch various materials with other materials, we might eventually be able to arrange several materials in a row, ranging from the softest to the hardest. We could never say how hard a given material is in absolute terms; we could only say how hard in relative terms—which materials it is harder than and which softer than.

Let's pursue the earlier example of grouping the people at a social gathering. This time imagine that we asked all the people with a postsecondary degree to stand in one group, all those whose highest degree is a high school diploma to stand in another group, and all those who had not graduated from high school to stand in a third group. This manner of grouping people satisfies the requirements for exhaustiveness and mutual exclusiveness discussed earlier. In addition, however, we might logically arrange the three groups in terms of the relative amount of formal education (the shared attribute) each had. We might arrange the three groups in a row, ranging from most to least formal education. This arrangement would provide a physical representation of an ordinal measure. If we knew which groups two individuals were in, we could determine that one had more, less, or the same formal education as the other.

Notice in this example that it is irrelevant how close or far apart the educational groups are from one another. The postsecondary and high school groups might be five feet apart, and the less-than-high-school group 500 feet farther down the line. These actual distances don't have any meaning. The high school group, however, should be between the less-than-high-school group and the postsecondary group, or else the rank order would be incorrect.

Interval Measures   For the attributes composing some variables, the actual distance separating those attributes does have meaning. Such variables are **interval measures**. For these, the logical distance between attributes can be expressed in meaningful standard intervals.

For example, in the Celsius temperature scale, the difference, or distance, between 30 degrees and 40 degrees is the same as that between 10 degrees and 20 degrees. However, 40 degrees Celsius is not twice as hot as 20 degrees, because the zero points in the Celsius (and Fahrenheit) scales are arbitrary; zero degrees does not mean lack of heat. Similarly, minus 30 degrees on either scale doesn't represent 30 degrees less than no heat. (In contrast, the Kelvin scale is based on an absolute zero, which does mean a complete lack of heat.)

About the only interval measures commonly used in social scientific research are constructed measures such as standardized intelligence tests that have been more or less accepted. The interval separating IQ scores of 100 and 110 may be regarded as the same as the interval separating scores of 110 and 120 by virtue of the distribution of observed scores obtained by many thousands of people who have taken the tests over the years. But it would be incorrect to infer that someone with an IQ of 150 is 50 percent more intelligent than someone with an IQ of 100. (A person who received a score of 0 on a standard IQ test could not be regarded, strictly speaking, as having no intelligence, although we might feel he or she was unsuited to be a university professor or even a university student. But perhaps a dean . . . ?)

When comparing two people in terms of an interval variable, we can say they are different from one another (nominal), and that one is more than another (ordinal). In addition, we can say "how much" more.

Ratio Measures Most of the social scientific variables that meet the minimum requirements for interval measures also meet the requirements for ratio measures. In **ratio measures**, the attributes composing a variable, besides having all the structural characteristics mentioned previously, are based on a true zero point. The Kelvin temperature scale is one such measure. Examples from social

scientific research would include *age, income, length of residence in a given place, number of organizations belonged to, number of times married,* and *number of Arab friends.*

Returning to the illustration of methodological party games, we might ask a gathering of people to group themselves by age. All the one-year-olds would stand (or sit or lie) together, the two-year-olds together, the three-year-olds, and so forth. The fact that members of a single group share the same age and that each different group has a different shared age satisfies the minimum requirements for a nominal measure. Arranging the several groups in a line from youngest to oldest meets the additional requirements of an ordinal measure and lets us determine if one person is older than, younger than, or the same age as another. If we space the groups equally far apart, we satisfy the additional requirements of an interval measure and will be able to say *how much* older one person is than another. Finally, because one of the attributes included in age represents a true zero (babies carried by women about to give birth), the phalanx of hapless party goers also meets the requirements of a ratio measure, permitting us to say that one person is twice as old as another. Another example of a ratio measure is income, which extends from an absolute zero to approximately infinity, if you happen to be the founder of Microsoft.

Comparing two people in terms of a ratio variable, then allows us to conclude (1) they are different (or the same), (2) one is more than the other, (3) how much they differ, and (4) the ratio of one to another. Figure 5-1 summarizes this discussion by presenting a graphic illustration of the four levels of measurement.

Implications of Levels of Measurement Because it's unlikely you will undertake the physical grouping of people just described (try it once, and you won't be invited to many parties), we should draw your attention to some of the practical implications of the differences that have been distinguished. These implications primarily appear in the analysis of data (discussed in Part 4), but you need

Figure 5-1
Levels of Measurement

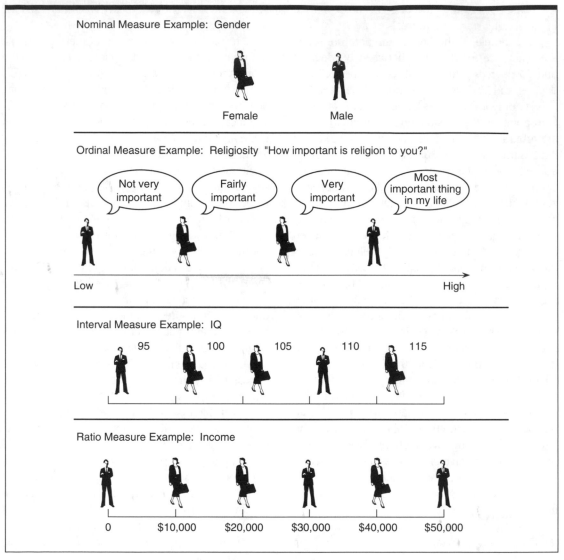

to anticipate such implications when you're structuring any research project.

Certain quantitative analysis techniques require variables that meet certain minimum levels of measurement. To the extent that the variables to be examined in a research project are limited to a particular level of measurement—say, ordinal—you should plan your analytical techniques accord-

ingly. More precisely, you should anticipate drawing research conclusions appropriate to the levels of measurement used in your variables. For example, you might reasonably plan to determine and report the mean age of a population under study (add up all the individual ages and divide by the number of people), but you should not plan to report the mean religious affiliation, because that is a nominal variable, and the mean requires ratio-level data. (You could report the modal—the most common—religious affiliation.)

At the same time, you can treat some variables as representing different levels of measurement. Ratio measures are the highest level, descending through interval and ordinal to nominal, the lowest level of measurement. A variable representing a higher level of measurement—say, ratio—may also be treated as representing a lower level of measurement—say, ordinal. Recall, for example, that age is a ratio measure. If you wished to examine only the relationship between age and some ordinal-level variable—say, self-perceived religiosity: high, medium, and low—you might choose to treat age as an ordinal-level variable as well. You might characterize the subjects of your study as being young, middle-aged, and old, specifying what age range composed each of these groupings. Finally, age might be used as a nominal-level variable for certain research purposes. People might be grouped as being born during World War II or not. Another nominal measurement, based on birth date rather than just age, would be the grouping of people by astrological signs.

The level of measurement you'll seek, then, is determined by the analytical uses you've planned for a given variable, keeping in mind that some variables are inherently limited to a certain level. If a variable is to be used in a variety of ways, requiring different levels of measurement, the study should be designed to achieve the highest level required. For example, if the subjects in a study are asked their exact ages, they can later be organized into ordinal or nominal groupings.

You need not necessarily measure variables at their highest level of measurement, however. If you're sure to have no need for ages of people at higher than the ordinal level of measurement, you may simply ask people to indicate their age range, such as 20 to 29, 30 to 39, and so forth. In a study of the wealth of corporations, rather than seek more precise information, you may use Dun & Bradstreet ratings to rank corporations. Whenever your research purposes are not altogether clear, however, seek the highest level of measurement

possible. Again, although ratio measures can later be reduced to ordinal ones, you cannot convert an ordinal measure to a ratio one. More generally, you cannot convert a lower-level measure to a higher-level one. This is a one-way street worth remembering.

Single or Multiple Indicators

With so many alternatives for operationalizing social scientific variables, you may find yourself worrying about making the right choices. To counter this feeling, let us add a momentary dash of certainty and stability.

Many social scientific variables have fairly obvious, straightforward measures. No matter how you cut it, gender usually turns out to be a matter of male or female: a nominal-level variable that can be measured by a single observation—either looking (well, not always) or asking a question (usually). In a study involving the size of families, you'll want to think about adopted and foster children, as well as blended families, but it's usually pretty easy to find out how many children a family has. For most research purposes, the resident population of a country is the resident population of that country. You can look it up in an almanac and know the answer. A great many variables, then, have obvious single indicators. If you can get one piece of information, you have what you need.

Sometimes, however, there is no single indicator that will give you the measure of a variable you really want. As discussed earlier in this chapter, many concepts are subject to varying interpretations, each with several possible indicators. In these cases, you'll want to make several observations for a given variable. You can then combine the several pieces of information you've collected to create a composite measurement of the variable in question. Chapter 6 is devoted to ways of doing that, so here let's just consider one simple illustration.

Consider the concept "university performance." All of us have noticed that some students perform well in university and others don't perform well. In studying these differences, we might ask what characteristics and experiences are related to high levels of performance; many researchers have done just that. How should we measure overall performance? Each grade in any single course is a potential indicator of university performance, but a single course grade may not typify the student's general performance. The solution to this problem is so firmly established that it is, of course, obvious: the *grade point average* (GPA). We assign numerical scores to each letter grade, total the points earned by a given student, and divide by the number of courses taken to obtain a composite measure. (If the courses vary in number of credits, we adjust the point values accordingly.) It's often appropriate to create such composite measures in social research.

Some Illustrations of Operationalization Choices

To bring together all the operationalization choices available to the social researcher and to show the potential in those possibilities, let's look at some of the distinct ways you might address various research problems. The alternative ways of operationalizing the variables in each case should demonstrate the opportunities that social research can present to our ingenuity and imaginations. To simplify matters, we have not attempted to describe all the research conditions that would make one alternative superior to the others, though in a given situation they would not all be equally appropriate.

Here are specific research questions, then, and some of the ways you could address them. We'll begin with an example discussed earlier in this chapter. It has the added advantage that one of the variables is straightforward to operationalize.

1. Are women more compassionate than men?
   a. Select a group of subjects for study, with equal numbers of men and women. Present them with hypothetical situations that involve someone being in trouble. Ask them what they would do if they were confronted with that situation. What would they do, for example, if they came across a small child who was lost and crying for his or her parents? Consider any answer that involves helping or comforting the child as an indicator of compassionate. See whether men or women are more likely to indicate they would be compassionate.
   b. Set up an experiment in which you pay a small child to pretend that he or she is lost. Put the child to work on a busy sidewalk, and observe whether men or women are more likely to offer assistance. Also, be sure to count the total number of men and women who walk by, because there may be more of one than the other. If that's the case, simply calculate the percentage of men and the percentage of women who help.
   c. Select a sample of people and do a survey in which you ask them what organizations they belong to. Calculate whether women or men are more likely to belong to those that seem to reflect compassionate feelings. To take account of men belonging to more organizations than women in general or vice versa, do this: For each person you study, calculate the percentage of his or her organizational memberships that reflect compassion. See if men or women have a higher average percentage.

2. Are sociology students or chemistry students better informed about world affairs?
   a. Prepare a short quiz on world affairs and arrange to administer it to the students in a sociology class and in a chemistry class at a comparable level. If you want to compare sociology and chemistry majors, be sure to ask students what they are majoring in.
   b. Get the instructor of a course in world affairs to give you the average grades of sociology and chemistry students in the course.
   c. Take a petition to sociology and chemistry classes that urges that "the United Nations headquarters be moved to New York City." Keep a count of how many in each class sign the petition and how many inform you that the UN headquarters is already located in New York City.

3. Who are the most popular instructors on your campus, those in the social sciences, the nat-

ural sciences, or the humanities?

a. If your school has a provision for student evaluation of instructors, review some recent results and compare the average ratings given the three groups.

b. Begin visiting the introductory courses given in each group of disciplines and measure the attendance rate of each class.

c. In December, select a group of faculty in each of the three divisions and ask them to keep a record of the numbers of holiday greeting cards and presents they receive from admiring students. See who wins.

The point of these examples is not necessarily to suggest respectable research projects but to illustrate the many ways variables can be operationalized.

Operationalization Goes On and On

Although we've discussed conceptualization and operationalization as activities that precede data collection and analysis—for example, you must design questionnaire items before you send out a questionnaire—these two processes continue throughout any research project, even if the data have been collected in a structured mass survey. As we've seen, in less-structured methods such as field research, the identification and specification of relevant concepts is inseparable from the ongoing process of observation.

As a researcher, always be open to reexamining your concepts and definitions. The ultimate purpose of social research is to clarify the nature of social life. The validity and utility of what you learn in this regard doesn't depend on when you first figured out how to look at things any more than it matters whether you got the idea from a learned textbook, a dream, or your brother-in-law.

Criteria for Measurement Quality

This chapter has come some distance. It began with the bald assertion that social scientists can measure anything that exists. Then we discovered that most of the things we might want to measure

and study don't really exist. Next we learned that it's possible to measure them anyway. Now we conclude the chapter with a discussion of some of the yardsticks against which we judge our relative success or failure in measuring things, even things that don't exist.

Precision and Accuracy

To begin, measurements can be made with varying degrees of precision. As we saw in the discussion of operationalization, precision concerns the fineness of distinctions made between attributes composing a variable. The description of a woman as "43 years old" is more precise than "in her forties." Saying a street-corner gang was formed in the summer of 1996 is more precise than saying "during the 1990s."

As a general rule, precise measurements are superior to imprecise ones, as common sense would dictate. There are no conditions under which imprecise measurements are intrinsically superior to precise ones. Even so, exact precision is not always necessary or desirable. If knowing that a woman is in her forties satisfies your research requirements, then any additional effort invested in learning her precise age is wasted. The operationalization of concepts, then, must be guided partly by an understanding of the degree of precision required. If your needs are not clear, be more precise rather than less.

Don't confuse precision with accuracy, however. Describing someone as "born in the Maritimes" is less precise than "born in New Brunswick"—but suppose the person in question was actually born in Prince Edward Island. The less precise description, in this instance, is more accurate, a better reflection of the real world.

Precision and accuracy are obviously important qualities in research measurement, and they probably need no further explanation. When social scientists construct and evaluate measurements, however, they pay special attention to two technical considerations: reliability and validity.

Reliability

In the abstract, **reliability** is a matter of whether a particular technique, applied repeatedly to the same object, yields the same result each time. Let's say you want to know how much your postal carrier weighs. (No, we don't know why.) As one technique, you might ask two different people to estimate his or her weight. If the first person estimated 55 kilograms and the other estimated 110, we have to conclude the technique of having people estimate your carrier's weight isn't very reliable.

Suppose, as an alternative, that you use a bathroom scale as your measurement technique. Your carrier steps on the scale twice, and you note the result each time. The scale reported the same weight both times, indicating that the scale provided a more reliable technique for measuring a person's weight than did asking people to estimate it.

Reliability, however, does not insure accuracy any more than precision does. Suppose your father set the bathroom scale to shave two kilograms off his weight just to make himself feel better. Although you would (reliably) report the same weight for your carrier each time, you would always be wrong. This new element, called *bias*, is discussed in Chapter 7. For now, just be warned that reliability does not insure accuracy.

Let's suppose we're interested in studying morale among factory workers in two different kinds of factories. In one set of factories, workers have specialized jobs, reflecting an extreme division of labour. Each worker contributes a tiny part to the overall process performed on a long assembly line. In the other set of factories, each worker performs many tasks, and small teams of workers complete the whole process.

How should we measure *morale*? Following one strategy, we could observe the workers in each factory, noticing such things as whether they joke with one another, whether they smile and laugh a lot, and so forth. We could ask them how they like their work and even ask them whether they think they would prefer their current arrangement or the other one being studied. By comparing what we observed in the different factories, we might reach a conclusion about which assembly process produced the higher morale.

Now let's look at some reliability problems inherent in this method. First, how we are feeling when we do the observing will likely colour what we see. We may misinterpret what we see. We may see workers kidding each other but think they're having an argument. We may catch them on an off day. If we were to observe the same group of workers several days in a row, we might arrive at different evaluations on each day. If several observers evaluated the same behaviour, on the other hand, they too might arrive at different conclusions about the workers' morale.

Here's another strategy for assessing morale. Suppose we check the company records to see how many grievances have been filed with the union during some fixed period of time. Presumably this would be an indicator of morale: the more grievances, the lower the morale. This measurement strategy would appear to be more reliable: Counting up the grievances over and over, we should keep arriving at the same number.

If you find yourself thinking that the number of grievances doesn't necessarily measure morale, you're worrying about validity, not reliability. We'll discuss validity in a moment. The point for now is that the last method is more like your bathroom scale—it gives consistent results.

In social research, reliability problems crop up in many forms. Reliability is a concern every time a single observer is the source of data, because we have no certain guard against the impact of that observer's subjectivity. We can't tell for sure how much of what's reported originated in the situation observed and how much in the observer.

Subjectivity is not only a problem with single observers, however. Survey researchers have known for a long time that different interviewers, because of their own attitudes and demeanors, get different answers from respondents. Or, if we were to conduct a study of newspapers' editorial positions on some public issue, we might create a team of coders to take on the job of reading hundreds of editorials and classifying them in terms of their position on the issue. Unfortunately, different coders will code the same editorial differently. Or, we might want to classify a few hundred specific occupations in terms of some standard coding scheme, say a set of categories created by Statistics Canada for the census. Working independently, we would not place all those occupations in the same categories.

Each of these examples illustrates problems of reliability. Similar problems arise whenever we ask people to give us information about themselves. Sometimes we ask questions that people don't know the answers to: How many times have you been to church? Sometimes we ask people about things they consider totally irrelevant: Are you satisfied with China's current relationship with Albania? In such cases, people will answer differently at different times because they're making up answers as they go. Sometimes we explore issues so complicated that a person who had a clear opinion in the matter might arrive at a different interpretation of the question when asked a second time.

So how do you create reliable measures? If your research design calls for asking people for information, you can be careful to ask only about things the respondents are likely to know the answer to. Ask about things relevant to them, and be clear in what you're asking. Of course, these techniques don't solve every possible reliability problem. Fortunately, social researchers have developed several techniques for cross-checking the reliability of the measures they devise.

Test-Retest Method   Sometimes it's appropriate to make the same measurement more than once, a technique called the test-retest method. If you do not expect the information sought to change, then you should expect the same response both times. If answers vary, the measurement method may, to the extent of that variation, be unreliable. Here's an illustration.

In their research on Health Hazard Appraisal (HHA), a part of preventive medicine, Jeffrey Sacks, W. Mark Krushat, and Jeffrey Newman (1980) wanted to determine the risks associated with various background and lifestyle factors, making it possible for physicians to counsel their patients appropriately. By knowing patients' life situations,

physicians could advise them on their potential for survival and on how to improve it. This purpose, of course, depended heavily on the accuracy of the information gathered about each subject in the study.

To test the reliability of their information, Sacks and his colleagues had all 207 subjects complete a baseline questionnaire that asked about their characteristics and behaviour. Three months later, a follow-up questionnaire asked the same subjects for the same information, and the results of the two surveys were compared. Overall, only 15 percent of the subjects reported the same information in both studies.

Sacks and his colleagues report (1980:730) the following:

> Almost 10 percent of subjects reported a different height at follow-up examination. Parental age was changed by over one in three subjects. One parent reportedly aged 20 chronologic years in three months. One in five ex-smokers and ex-drinkers have apparent difficulty in reliably recalling their previous consumption pattern.

Some subjects erased all trace of previously reported heart murmur, diabetes, emphysema, arrest record, and thoughts of suicide. One subject's mother, deceased in the first questionnaire, was apparently alive and well in time for the second. One subject had one ovary missing in the first study but present in the second. In another case, an ovary present in the first study was missing in the second study—and had been for 10 years! One subject was reportedly 55 years old in the first study and 50 years old three months later. (You have to wonder if the physician-counselors could ever have nearly the impact on their patients that their patients' memories did.) Thus, the test-retest revealed that this data-collection method was not especially reliable.

Split-Half Method   As a general rule, it's always good to make more than one measurement of any subtle or complex social concept, such as prejudice, alienation, or social class. This procedure lays the groundwork for another check on reliability.

Let's say you've created a questionnaire that contains 10 items you believe measure prejudice against women. Using the split-half technique, you would randomly assign those 10 items to two sets of five. As we saw in the discussion of "interchangeability of indicators," each set should provide a good measure of prejudice against women, and the two sets should classify respondents in the same way. If the two sets of items classify people differently, you likely have a problem of reliability in your measure of the variable.

Using Established Measures Another way to help insure reliability in getting information from people is to use measures that have proven their reliability in previous research. If you want to measure anomia, for example, you might want to follow Srole's lead.

The heavy use of measures, though, does not guarantee their reliability. For example, the Minnesota Multiphasic Personality Inventory (MMPI) has been accepted as a standard in the psychological assessment of individuals for decades. In recent years, though, it has needed fundamental overhauling to reflect changes in society.

Reliability of Research Workers As we've seen, it's possible for measurement unreliability to be generated by research workers: interviewers and coders, for example. There are several ways to check on reliability in such cases. To guard against interviewer unreliability, it is common practice in surveys to have a supervisor call a subsample of the respondents on the telephone and verify selected pieces of information.

Replication works in other situations also. If you're worried that newspaper editorials or occupations may not be classified reliably, you could have each independently coded by several coders. Those cases that are classified inconsistently can then be evaluated more carefully and resolved.

Finally, clarity, specificity, training, and practice can prevent a great deal of unreliability and grief. If you and your professor spent some time reaching a clear agreement on how to evaluate editorial positions on an issue—discussing various positions and reading through several together—you could probably do a good job of classifying them in the same way independently.

The reliability of measurements is a fundamental issue in social research, and we'll return to it more than once in the chapters ahead. For now, however, let's recall that even total reliability doesn't insure that our measures measure what we think they measure. Now let's plunge into the question of validity.

Validity

In conventional usage, the term *validity* refers to the extent to which an empirical measure adequately reflects the *real meaning* of the concept under consideration. Whoops! We're already committed to the view that concepts don't have real meanings. How can we ever say whether a particular measure adequately reflects the concept's meaning, then? Ultimately, of course, we can't. At the same time, as we've already seen, all of social life, including social research, operates on agreements about the terms we use and the concepts they represent. There are several criteria of success in making measurements that are appropriate to these agreed-upon meanings of concepts.

First, there's something called **face validity**. Particular empirical measures may or may not jibe with our common agreements and our individual mental images concerning a particular concept. For example, you might quarrel with us about the adequacy of measuring worker morale by counting the number of grievances filed with the union. Still, we'd surely agree that the number of grievances has *something* to do with morale. That is, the measure is valid "on its face," whether or not it's adequate. If we were to suggest that morale be measured by finding out how many books the workers took out of the library during their off-duty hours, you'd undoubtedly raise a more serious objection: That measure wouldn't have much face validity.

Second, we've already pointed to many of the more formally established agreements that define some concepts. Statistics Canada, for example, has created operational definitions of such concepts as family, household, and employment status that seem to have a workable validity in most studies using these concepts.

Three additional types of validity also specify particular ways of testing the validity of measures. The first, **criterion-related validity,** sometimes called *predictive validity,* is based on some external criterion. For example, many occupations have qualifying exams. The validity of the exam is shown in its ability to predict future evaluations of the individuals' job performances. The validity of a written driver's test is determined, in this sense, by the relationship between the scores people get on the test and their subsequent driving records. In these examples, job performance and driving record are the criteria.

To test your understanding of this concept, see if you can think of behaviours that might be used to validate each of the following attitudes:

Is very religious
Supports equality of men and women
Is concerned about the environment

Some possible validators would be, respectively, attends church, votes for women candidates, and belongs to the Sierra Club. Sometimes it's difficult to find behavioural criteria that can be taken to validate measures as directly as in such examples. In those instances, however, we can often approximate such criteria by applying a different test. We can consider how the variable in question ought, theoretically, to relate to other variables. **Construct validity** is based on the logical relationships among variables.

Let's suppose, for example, that you want to study the sources and consequences of marital satisfaction. As part of your research, you develop a measure of marital satisfaction, and you want to assess its validity.

In addition to developing your measure, you'll have developed certain theoretical expectations about the way the variable *marital satisfaction* relates to other variables. For example, you might reasonably conclude that satisfied husbands and wives will be less likely than dissatisfied ones to cheat on their spouses. If your measure relates to marital fidelity in the expected fashion, that constitutes evidence of your measure's construct validity. If satisfied marriage partners were as likely to cheat on their spouses as are the dissatisfied ones, however, that would challenge the validity of your measure.

Tests of construct validity, then, can offer a weight of evidence that your measure either does or doesn't tap the quality you want it to measure, without providing definitive proof. Although we have suggested that tests of construct validity are less compelling than those of criterion validity, there is room for disagreement over which kind of test a particular comparison variable (driving record, martial fidelity) represents in a given situation. It's less important to distinguish the two types of validity tests than to understand the logic of validation that they have in common: If we have been successful in measuring some variable, then our measures should relate in some logical fashion to other measures.

Finally, **content validity** refers to how much a measure covers the range of meanings included within the concept. For example, a test of mathematical ability cannot be limited to addition alone but also needs to cover subtraction, multiplication, division, and so forth. Or, if we are measuring prejudice, do our measurements reflect all types of prejudice, including prejudice against racial and ethnic groups, religious minorities, women, the elderly, and so on?

Who Decides What's Valid?

Our discussion of validity began with a reminder that we depend on agreements to determine what's real, and we've just seen some of the ways social scientists can agree among themselves that they have made valid measurements. There is yet another way of looking at validity.

Social researchers sometimes criticize themselves and each other for implicitly assuming they are somewhat superior to those they study. For instance, researchers often seek to uncover motivations that the social actors themselves are unaware of. You *think* you bought that new Burpo-Blasto because of its high performance and good looks, but *we know* you're really trying to achieve a higher social status.

This implicit sense of superiority would fit comfortably with a totally positivistic approach (the biologist feels superior to the frog on the lab table), but it clashes with the more humanistic and typically qualitative approach taken by many social scientists. This issue will be explored more deeply in Chapter 11.

In seeking to understand the way ordinary people make sense of their worlds, ethnomethodologists have urged all social scientists to pay more respect to these natural social processes of conceptualization and shared meaning. At the very least, behaviour that may seem irrational from the scientist's paradigm may make logical sense when viewed from the actor's paradigm.

Ultimately, social researchers should look both to their colleagues and to their subjects as sources of agreement on the most useful meanings and measurements of the concepts they study. Sometimes one source will be more useful, sometimes the other. But neither should be dismissed.

Tension between Reliability and Validity

Clearly we want our measures to be both reliable and valid. However, there is often a tension between the criteria of reliability and validity, forcing a trade-off between the two.

Recall the example of measuring morale in different factories. The strategy of immersing yourself in the day-to-day routine of the assembly line, observing what goes on, and talking to the workers would seem to provide a more valid measure of morale than counting grievances. It just seems obvious that we'd get a clearer sense of whether the morale was high or low using this first method.

As we pointed out earlier, however, the counting strategy would be more reliable. This situation reflects a more general strain in research measurement. Most of the really interesting concepts we want to study have many subtle nuances,

and it's hard to specify precisely what we mean by them. Researchers sometimes speak of such concepts as having a "richness of meaning." Although scores of books and articles have been written on the topic of anomie/anomia, for example, they still haven't exhausted its meaning.

Very often, then, specifying reliable operational definitions and measurements seems to rob concepts of their richness of meaning. Positive morale is much more than a lack of grievances filed with the union; anomie is much more than what's measured by the five items created by Leo Srole. Yet, the more variation and richness we allow for a concept, the more opportunity there is for disagreement on how it applies to a particular situation, thus reducing reliability.

To some extent, this dilemma explains the persistence of two quite different approaches to social research: quantitative, nomothetic, structured techniques such as surveys and experiments on the one hand, and qualitative, idiographic methods such as field research and historical studies on the other. In the simplest generalization, the former methods tend to be more reliable, the latter more valid.

By being forewarned, you'll be effectively forearmed against this persistent and inevitable dilemma. If there is no clear agreement on how to measure a concept, measure it several different ways. If the concept has several dimensions, measure them all. Above all, know that the concept does not have any meaning other than what we give it. The only justification for giving any concept a particular meaning is utility. Measure concepts in ways that help us understand the world around us.

Ethics and Measurement

When devising operational procedures, the measures researchers choose are limited by both practical and ethical considerations. As we noted, the researcher is continually searching for better measures of concepts, but there are tradeoffs that must be made between choosing the "better" measure and choosing the more ethical measure.

Suppose we were asked to study how women respond to sexual harassment. Some indicators of sexual harassment might be derogatory statements about women, misogynist jokes, unwanted touching, and stalking. Perhaps the best way for us to ensure exact uniformity across research subjects would be to supply a research assistant with a script and instructions to confront the research subjects. Subjecting women to such acts to determine their response would clearly be unethical. Therefore, the ethical researcher would devise other means of conducting such a study.

There are endless examples of tradeoffs that might be considered in designing an effective and ethical research study. Many issues of interest to social scientists involve topics that people are sensitive about or tap into events that people have experienced that caused them pain and trauma. Given that there are many ways that researchers can manipulate subjects, they must consider how much discomfort or harm a particular measure may cause a person? Could a measure put people at risk, such as tracking criminal activities that may get them in trouble with the law? How much deception is allowable for the sake of gathering more accurate data? Is it okay to lie to people or spy on them because the data collected will be better—a more accurate reflection of the concept or issue under study? If we want to learn how corporate executives make decisions, tapping their phones and bugging their boardrooms might supply the best information. Most would agree, however, that such strategies would be unethical (and probably illegal).

Many ethical concerns in measurement are more subtle, and there is often disagreement over what is or is not risky or harmful to the subjects of study. For example, let's reconsider one of the ways we discussed measuring "*compassion*." Recall that we suggested we might measure compassion by putting a child on the street and having her pretend to be lost so we could observe who comes to her aid and how. Some ethical concerns we might take into account are the potential stress to those who witness this, the major intrusion of such an event on people's lives, the lack of voluntary participation, the deception involved, and the risk to the

child actor. What impact might such an experience have on someone rushing by on her or his way to the hospital to attend to a family emergency? Has an unnecessary dilemma been posed for some people that may cause them anxiety or harm? And, what about the risk to the child actor who might be whisked off by some malevolent being?

How about creating studies where people might act in ways they might be ashamed of afterward—for example, provoking them to anger or pointing out their weakness in the face of authority? Demonstrating people's flaws and frailties in social experiments could cause them psychological harm or worse. Even in a questionnaire or an interview, some questions might be rude, insulting, or demeaning. Consideration of the research participants must be taken into account here as well.

How social scientists approach their research is therefore not guided merely by the quest for ever better measures. The validity and reliability of a measure must be weighed against the potential harm, inconvenience, and intrusion these measures might have on those whom they wish to study. Yet, there is often disagreement and debate over what actions are considered harmful and what topics are important enough to warrant some degree of potential risk or harm to subjects. Therefore, the determination of what is or is not ethical practice in research is now made collegially, as we shall see in Part 3.

Main Points

- Conceptions are mental images we use as summary devices for bringing together observations and experiences that seem to have something in common. We use terms or labels to reference these conceptions.

- Concepts are constructs; they represent the agreed-upon meanings we assign to terms. Our concepts do not exist in the real world, so they can't be measured directly, but it's possible to measure the things that our concepts summarize.

- Conceptualization is the process of specifying observations and measurements that give concepts definite meaning for the purposes of a research study.

- Conceptualization includes specifying the indicators of a concept and describing its dimensions. Operational definitions specify how variables relevant to a concept will be measured.
- Precise definitions are even more important in descriptive than in explanatory studies. The degree of precision needed varies with the type and purpose of a study.
- Operationalization is an extension of conceptualization that specifies the exact procedures that will be used to measure the attributes of variables.
- Operationalization involves a series of interrelated choices: specifying the range of variation that is appropriate for the purposes of a study, determining how precisely to measure variables, accounting for relevant dimensions of variables, clearly defining the attributes of variables and their relationships, and deciding on an appropriate level of measurement.
- Researchers must choose from four levels of measures that capture increasing amounts of information: nominal, ordinal, interval, and ratio. The most appropriate level depends on the purpose of the measurement.
- A given variable can sometimes be measured at different levels. When in doubt, researchers should use the highest level of measurement appropriate to that variable so they can capture the greatest amount of information.
- Operationalization begins in the design phase of a study and continues through all phases of the research project, including the analysis of data.
- Criteria of the quality of measures include precision, accuracy, reliability, and validity.
- Reliability means getting consistent results from the same measure. Validity refers to getting results that accurately reflect the concept being measured.
- Researchers can test or improve the reliability of measures through the test-retest method, the split-half method, the use of established measures, and the examination of work performed by research workers.
- The yardsticks for assessing a measure's validity include face validity, criterion-related validity, construct validity, and content validity.
- Creating specific, reliable measures often seems to diminish the richness of meaning our general concepts have. This problem is inevitable. The best solution is to use several different measures, tapping the different aspects of the concept.
- Ethical considerations are an important element of a researcher's choice of measures.

Review Questions and Exercises

1. Pick a social science concept such as liberalism or alienation, then specify that concept so that it could be studied in a research project. Be sure to specify the dimensions you wish to include and those you wish to exclude in your conceptualization.
2. What level of measurement—nominal, ordinal, interval, or ratio—describes each of the following variables:
   a. Race (White, Aboriginal, Asian, and so on)
   b. Order of finish in a race (first, second, third, and so on)
   c. Number of children in families
   d. Populations of nations
   e. Attitudes toward nuclear energy (strongly approve, approve, disapprove, strongly disapprove)
   f. Political orientation (very liberal, somewhat liberal, somewhat conservative, very conservative
3. In a newspaper or magazine, find an instance of invalid and/or unreliable measurement. Justify your choice.
4. Use the Web to locate a research report. Identify the key variable studied and describe how the variable was operationalized for measurement.

Continuity Project

There are many dimensions to the concept of gender equality/inequality. List at least five different dimensions and suggest how you might measure each. It's okay to use different research techniques for measuring the different dimensions.

Additional Readings

Atkinson, Tom. "The Stability and Validity of Quality of Life Measures." *Social Indicators Research*. 10:113-132, 1982. This article examines issues of reliability and validity in subjective social indicators (quality of life measures) using panel data of a sample of over 2,000 Canadians to determine the indicators' stability in unchanging situations and their sensitivity to dynamic circumstances.

Bohrnstedt, George W. "Measurement." Pp. 70-121 in *Handbook of Survey Research,* edited by Peter H. Rossi, James D. Wright, and Andy B. Anderson. New York: Academic Press, 1983. This essay offers the logical and statistical grounding of reliability and validity in measurement.

Lazarsfeld, Paul F., and Morris Rosenberg, eds. *The Language of Social Research.* New York: Free Press of Glencoe, 1955, Section I. An excellent and diverse classic collection of descriptions of specific measurements in past social research. These 14 articles present useful and readable accounts of actual measurement operations performed by social researchers as well as more conceptual discussions of measurement in general.

Miller, Delbert. *Handbook of Research Design and Social Measurement.* Newbury Park, CA: Sage, 1991. A powerful reference work. This book, especially Part 6, cites and describes a wide variety of operational measures used in earlier social research. In several cases, the questionnaire formats used are presented. Though the quality of these illustrations is uneven, they provide excellent examples of the variations possible.

Silverman, David. *Interpreting Qualitative Data: Methods for Analyzing Talk, Text, and Interaction.* 2nd e d. Thousand Oaks, CA: Sage, 2001, Chapter 8. This chapter deals with the issues of validity and reliability specifically in regard to qualitative research.

*Info*Trac: You can find further relevant readings on the World Wide Web at

http://sociology. wadsworth.com

Chapter 6

Indexes, Scales, and Typologies

Researchers often need to employ multiple indicators to measure a variable adequately and validly. Indexes, scales, and typologies are useful composite measures made up of several indicators of variables.

Introduction

As we saw in Chapter 5, many social scientific concepts have complex and varied meanings. Making measurements that capture such concepts can be a challenge. Recall our discussion of content validity, which concerns whether we've captured all the different dimensions of a concept.

To achieve broad coverage of the various dimensions of a concept, we usually need to make multiple observations pertaining to that concept. Thus, for example, Bruce Berg (2001:75) advises in-depth interviewers to prepare *essential questions,* which are "geared toward eliciting specific, desired information." In addition, the researcher should prepare extra questions: "questions roughly equivalent to certain essential ones, but worded slightly differently."

Multiple indicators are used with quantitative data as well. Suppose you're designing a survey. Although you can sometimes construct a single questionnaire item that captures the variable of interest—"Gender: ❏ Male ❏ Female" is a simple example—other variables are less straightforward and may require you to use several questionnaire items to measure them adequately.

Quantitative data analysts have developed specific techniques for combining indicators into a single measure. This chapter discusses the construction of two types of composite measures of variables: **indexes** and **scales**. Although these measures can be used in any form of social research, they are most common in survey research and other quantitative methods. A short section at the end of the chapter considers **typologies**, which are relevant to both qualitative and quantitative research.

Composite measures are frequently used in quantitative research, for several reasons. First, social scientists often wish to study variables that have no clear and unambiguous single indicators. Single indicators are sufficient for some variables, like age. We may determine a survey respondent's age by asking: "How old are you?" We may determine a newspaper's circulation by merely looking at the figure the newspaper reports. In the case of complex concepts, however, researchers can seldom develop single indicators before they actually do the research. This is especially true with regard to attitudes and orientations. Rarely can survey researchers, for example, devise single questionnaire items that adequately tap respondents' degrees of prejudice, religiosity, political orientations, alienation, and the like. More likely, they will devise several items, each of which provides some indication of the variables. Taken individually, each of these is likely to prove invalid or unreliable for many respondents. A composite measure, however, can overcome this problem.

Second, researchers may wish to employ a rather refined ordinal measure of a variable—alienation, say—for example, arranging cases in several ordinal categories from very low to very high. A single data item might not have enough categories to provide the desired range of variation, but an index or scale formed from several items can provide the desired range.

Finally, indexes and scales are efficient devices for data analysis. If considering a single data item gives us only a rough indication of a given variable, considering several data items may give us a more comprehensive and more accurate indication. For example, a single newspaper editorial may give us some indication of the political orientations of that newspaper. Examining several editorials would probably give us a better assessment, but the manipulation of several data items simultaneously could be very complicated. Indexes and scales (especially scales) are efficient *data-reduction devices:* They allow us to summarize several indicators in a single numerical score, while sometimes nearly maintaining the specific details of all the individual indicators.

Indexes versus Scales

The terms *index* and *scale* are typically used imprecisely and interchangeably in social research literature. Before considering the distinctions we'll make in this book between these two types of measures, let's see what they have in common.

Both scales and indexes are *ordinal* measures of variables. Both rank-order the units of analysis in terms of specific variables such as *religiosity, alienation, socioeconomic status, prejudice,* or *intellectual sophistication.* A person's score on either a scale or index of religiosity, for example, gives an indication of his or her relative religiosity vis-à-vis other people.

Further, both scales and indexes are *composite measures of variables*—that is, measurements based on more than one data item. Thus, a survey respondent's score on an index or scale of religiosity is determined by the responses given to several questionnaire items, each of which provides some indication of religiosity. Similarly, a person's IQ score is based on answers to a large number of test questions. The political orientation of a newspaper might be represented by an index or scale score reflecting the newspaper's editorial policy on various political issues.

Despite these shared characteristics, it's useful to distinguish between indexes and scales. In this book we'll distinguish them by the way scores are assigned in each. An **index** is constructed by simply accumulating scores assigned to individual attributes. We might measure prejudice, for example, by adding up the number of prejudiced statements each respondent agreed with. A **scale,** however, is constructed by assigning scores to *patterns* of responses, recognizing that some items reflect a relatively weak degree of the variable while others reflect something stronger. For example, agreeing that "Women are different from men" is, at best, weak evidence of sexism compared with agreeing that "Women should not be allowed to vote." A scale takes advantage of differences in intensity among the attributes of the same variable to identify distinct patterns of response.

Figure 6-1 provides a graphic illustration of the difference between indexes and scales. Let's assume we want to develop a measure of political activism, distinguishing those people who are very active in political affairs, those who don't participate much at all, and those who are somewhere in between.

The first part of Figure 6-1 illustrates the logic of indexes. The figure shows six different political actions. Although we might disagree on some specifics, we could probably agree that the six actions represent roughly the same degree of political activism. Using these six items, we could construct an index of political activism by giving each person 1 point for each of the actions he or she has taken. If you wrote to a public official and signed a petition, you'd get a total of 2 points. If your friend gave money to a candidate and persuaded someone to change his or her vote, she or he would get the same score as you. Using this approach, we'd conclude that you and your friend had the same degree of political activism, even though you had taken different actions.

The second part of Figure 6-1 describes the logic of scale construction. In this case, the actions clearly represent different degrees of political activism, ranging from simply voting to running for office. Moreover, it seems safe to assume a pattern of actions in this case. For example, all those who contributed money probably also voted. Those who worked on a campaign probably also gave some money and voted. This suggests that most people will fall into only one of five idealized action patterns, represented by the illustrations at the bottom of the figure. The discussion of scales, later in this chapter,

Figure 6-1
Indexes versus Scales

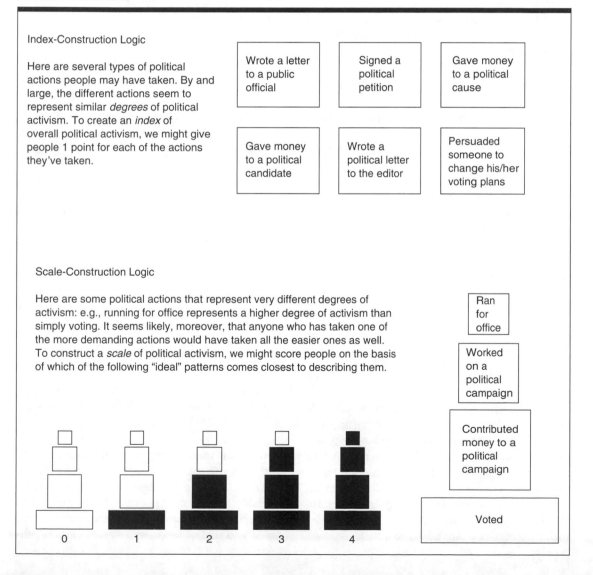

Index-Construction Logic

Here are several types of political actions people may have taken. By and large, the different actions seem to represent similar *degrees* of political activism. To create an *index* of overall political activism, we might give people 1 point for each of the actions they've taken.

| Wrote a letter to a public official | Signed a political petition | Gave money to a political cause |
| Gave money to a political candidate | Wrote a political letter to the editor | Persuaded someone to change his/her voting plans |

Scale-Construction Logic

Here are some political actions that represent very different degrees of activism: e.g., running for office represents a higher degree of activism than simply voting. It seems likely, moreover, that anyone who has taken one of the more demanding actions would have taken all the easier ones as well. To construct a *scale* of political activism, we might score people on the basis of which of the following "ideal" patterns comes closest to describing them.

Ran for office

Worked on a political campaign

Contributed money to a political campaign

Voted

0   1   2   3   4

describes ways of identifying people with the type they most closely represent.

Scales are generally superior to indexes, because scales take into consideration the intensity with which different items reflect the variable being measured. Also, as the example in Figure 6-1 shows, scale scores convey more information than index scores. Be aware, though, that the term *scale* is commonly misused to refer to measures that are only indexes. Merely calling a measure a scale instead of an index doesn't make it better.

There are two other misconceptions about scaling that you should know. First, whether the combination of several data items results in a scale almost always depends on the particular sample of observations under study. Certain items may form a scale within one sample but not within another. For this reason, do not assume that a given set of items is a scale simply because it turned out that way in an earlier study.

Second, the use of specific scaling techniques—such as Guttman scaling, to be discussed—does not ensure the creation of a scale. Rather, such techniques let us determine whether or not a set of items constitutes a scale.

An examination of actual social science research reports will show that researchers use indexes much more frequently than they do scales. Ironically, however, the methodological literature contains little if any discussion of index construction, while discussions of scale construction abound. There appear to be two reasons for this disparity. First, indexes may be used more frequently because scales are often difficult or impossible to construct from the data at hand. Second, methods of index construction seem so obvious and straightforward that they aren't discussed much.

Constructing indexes, however, is not a simple undertaking. The general failure to develop index construction techniques has resulted in many bad indexes in social research. With this in mind, we've devoted over half of this chapter to the methods of index construction. With a solid understanding of the logic of this activity, you'll be better equipped to try constructing scales. Indeed, a carefully constructed index may turn out to be a scale.

Index Construction

Let's look now at four main steps in the construction of an index: selecting possible items, examining their empirical relationships, scoring the index, and validating it. We'll conclude this discussion by examining the construction of an index that provided interesting findings about the status of women in different countries.

Item Selection

The first step in creating an index is selecting items for a composite index, which is created to measure some variable.

Face Validity The first criterion for selecting items to be included in the index is *face validity* (or logical validity). If you want to measure political conservatism, for example, each of your items should appear *on its face* to indicate conservatism (or its opposite, liberalism). Political party affiliation would be one such item. Another would be an item asking people to approve or disapprove of the views of a well-known conservative public figure. In constructing an index of religiosity, you might consider items such as church attendance, acceptance of certain religious beliefs, and frequency of prayer; each of these appears to offer some indication of religiosity.

Unidimensionality The methodological literature on conceptualization and measurement stresses the need for *unidimensionality* in scale and index construction. That is, a composite measure should represent only one dimension of a concept. Thus, items reflecting religiosity should not be included in a measure of political conservatism, even though the two variables might be empirically related to one another.

General or Specific Although measures should tap the same dimension, the general dimension you're attempting to measure may have many nuances. In the example of religiosity, the indicators mentioned previously—ritual participation, belief, and so on—represent different types of religiosity. If you wished to focus on ritual participation in religion, you should choose items specifically indicating this type of religiosity: church attendance, communion, confession, and the like. If you wished to measure religiosity in a more general way, you would include a balanced set of items, representing each of the different types of religiosity. Ultimately, the nature of the items you include will determine how specifically or generally the variable is measured.

Variance   In selecting items for an index, you must also be concerned with the amount of *variance* they provide. If an item is intended to indicate political conservatism, for example, you should note what proportion of respondents would be identified as conservatives by that item. If a given item identified no one as a conservative or everyone as a conservative—for example, if nobody indicated approval of a radical right political figure—that item would not be very useful in the construction of an index.

To guarantee variance, you have two options. First, you may select several items the responses to which divide people about equally in terms of the variable; for example, about half conservative and half liberal. Although no single response would justify the characterization of a person as very conservative, a person who responded as a conservative on all items might be so characterized.

The second option is to select items differing in variance. One item might identify about half the subjects as conservative, while another might identify few of the respondents as conservatives. Note that this second option is necessary for scaling, and it is reasonable for index construction as well.

Examination of Empirical Relationships

The second step in index construction is to examine the empirical relationships among the items being considered for inclusion. In this, we are anticipating a discussion that will be pursued more fully in Chapter 16. An empirical relationship is established when respondents' answers to one question—in a questionnaire, for example—help

us predict how they will answer other questions. If two items are empirically related to each other, we can reasonably argue that each reflects the same variable, and we may include them both in the same index. There are two types of possible relationships among items: bivariate and multivariate.

Bivariate Relationships   Simply put, a *bivariate relationship* is a relationship between two variables. Suppose we want to measure respondents' support for Canadian participation in the United Nations. One indicator of different levels of support might be the question "Do you feel that Canada's financial support of the UN is ❑ Too high ❑ About right ❑ Too low?"

A second indicator of support for the United Nations might be the question: "Should Canada contribute military personnel to UN peace-keeping actions? ❑ Strongly approve ❑ Mostly approve ❑ Mostly disapprove ❑ Strongly disapprove."

Both of these questions, on their face, seem to reflect different degrees of support for the United Nations. Nonetheless, some people might feel Canada should give more money but not provide troops. Others might favour sending troops but cutting back on financial support.

If the two items both reflect degrees of the same thing, however, we should expect responses to the two items to generally correspond with each other. Specifically, those who approve of military support should be more likely to favour financial support than would those who disapprove of military support. Conversely, those who favour financial support should be more likely to favour military support than would those disapproving of financial support. If these expectations are met, we say there is a *bivariate relationship* between the two items.

Here's another example. Suppose we want to determine the degree to which respondents feel women have the right to an abortion. We might ask (1) "Do you feel a woman should have the right to an abortion when her pregnancy was the result of rape?" and (2) "Do you feel a woman should have the right to an abortion if continuing her pregnancy would seriously threaten her life?"

Granted, some respondents might agree with item (1) and disagree with item (2); others will do just the reverse. However, if both items tap into some general opinion people have about the issue of abortion, then the responses to these two items should be related to each other. Those who support the right to an abortion in the case of rape should be more likely to support it if the woman's life is threatened than would those who disapproved of abortion in the case of rape. This would be another example of a bivariate relationship.

You should examine all the possible bivariate relationships among the several items being considered for inclusion in an index to determine the relative strengths of relationships among the several pairs of items. Percentage tables, correlation coefficients (see Chapter 16), or both may be used for this purpose. How we evaluate the strength of the relationships, however, can be rather subtle. The box entitled "'Cause' and 'Effect' Indicators" examines some of these subtleties.

Be wary of items that are not related to one another empirically: It's unlikely that they measure the same variable. You should probably drop any item that is not related to several other items.

At the same time, a very strong relationship between two items presents a different problem. If two items are perfectly related to each other, then only one is necessary for inclusion in the index, because it completely conveys the indications provided by the other—nothing more would be added by including the other item. (This problem will become even clearer in the next section.)

Here's an example to illustrate the testing of bivariate relationships in index construction. I (Babbie, 1970) once conducted a survey of medical school faculty members to find out about the consequences of a "scientific perspective" on the quality of patient care provided by physicians. The primary intent was to determine whether scientifically inclined doctors treated patients more impersonally than did other doctors.

The survey questionnaire offered several possible indicators of respondents' scientific perspectives. Of those, three items appeared to provide especially clear indications of whether the doctors were scientifically oriented:

1. As a medical school faculty member, in what capacity do you feel you can make your greatest teaching contribution: as a practicing physician or as a medical researcher?
2. As you continue to advance your own medical knowledge, would you say your ultimate medical interests lie primarily in the direction of total patient management or the understanding of basic mechanisms? [The purpose of this item was to distinguish those who were mostly interested in overall patient care from those mostly interested in biological processes.]
3. In the field of therapeutic research, are you generally more interested in articles reporting evaluations of the effectiveness of various treatments or articles exploring the basic rationale underlying the treatments? [Similarly, the goal was to distinguish those more interested in articles dealing with patient care from those more interested in biological processes.]

(1970:27–31)

For each of these items, we might conclude that those respondents who chose the second answer are more scientifically oriented than respondents who chose the first. Though this comparative conclusion is reasonable, we should not be misled into thinking that respondents who chose the second answer to a given item are scientists in any absolute sense. They are simply more scientifically oriented than those who chose the first answer to the item.

To see this point more clearly, let's examine the distribution of responses to each item. From the first item—greatest teaching contribution—only about one-third of the respondents appeared scientifically oriented. That is, approximately one-third said they could make their greatest teaching contribution as medical researchers. In response to the second item, ultimate medical interests, approximately two-thirds chose the scientific answer, saying they were more interested in learning about basic mechanisms than learning about total patient management. In response to the third item, reading preferences, about 80 percent chose the scientific answer.

These three questionnaire items can't tell us how many "scientists" there are in the sample, for none of them is related to a set of criteria for what constitutes being a scientist in any absolute sense.

Using the items for this purpose would present us with the problem of three quite different estimates of how many scientists there were in the sample.

However, these items do provide us with three independent indicators of respondents' relative inclinations toward science in medicine. Each item separates respondents into the more scientific and the less scientific. But each grouping of more or less scientific respondents will have a somewhat different membership from the others. Respondents who seem scientific in terms of one item will not seem scientific in terms of another. Nevertheless, to the extent that each item measures the same general dimension, we should find some correspon-

dence among the several groupings. Respondents who appear scientific in terms of one item should be more likely to appear scientific in their response to another item than those who appeared nonscientific in their response to the first. In other words, we should find an association or correlation between the responses given to two items.

Figure 6-2 shows the associations among the responses to the three items. Three bivariate tables are presented, showing the distribution of responses for each possible pairing of items. An examination of these three bivariate relationships supports the suggestion that the three items all measure the same variable: *scientific orientation*. To

Figure 6-2
Bivariate Relationships among Scientific Orientation Items

A.

| | | Greatest Teaching Contribution | |
		Physician	Researcher
Ultimate Medical Interest	Total patient management	49%	13%
	Basic mechanisms	51%	87%
		100% (268)	100% (159)

B.

| | | Reading Preferences | |
		Effectiveness	Rationale
Ultimate Medical Interest	Total patient management	68%	30%
	Basic mechanisms	32%	70%
		100% (78)	100% (349)

C.

| | | Reading Preferences | |
		Effectiveness	Rationale
Greatest Teaching Contribution	Physician	85%	64%
	Researcher	15%	36%
		100% (78)	100% (349)

see why this is so, let's begin by looking at the first bivariate relationship. The first table shows that faculty who responded that "researcher" was the role in which they could make their greatest teaching contribution were more likely to identify their ultimate medical interests as "basic mechanisms" (87 percent) than were those who answered "physician" (51 percent). The fact that the "physicians" are about evenly split in their ultimate medical interests is irrelevant for our purposes. It is only relevant that they are less scientific in their medical interests than the "researchers."

The strength of this relationship may be summarized as a 36 percentage point difference.

The same general conclusion applies to the other bivariate relationships. The strength of the relationship between reading preferences and ultimate medical interests may be summarized as a 38 percentage point difference, and the strength of the relationship between reading preferences and greatest contribution to teaching as a 21 percentage point difference. In summary, then, each single item produces a different grouping of "scientific" and "nonscientific" respondents. However,

"Cause" and "Effect" Indicators

by Kenneth Bollen
Department of Sociology,
University of North Carolina, Chapel Hill

While it often makes sense to expect indicators of the same variable to be positively related to one another, as discussed in the text, this is not always the case.

Indicators should be related to one another if they are essentially "effects" of a variable. For example, to measure self-esteem, we might ask a person to indicate whether he or she agrees or disagrees with the statements (1) "I am a good person" and (2) "I am happy with myself." A person with high self-esteem should agree with both statements while one with low self-esteem would probably disagree with both. Since each indicator depends on or "reflects" self-esteem, we expect them to be positively correlated. More generally, indicators that depend on the same variable should be associated with one another if they are valid measures.

But, this is not the case when the indicators are the "cause" rather than the "effect" of a variable. In this situation the indicators may correlate positively, negatively, or not at all. For example, we could use gender and race as indicators of the variable *exposure to discrimination*. Being non-

white or female increases the likelihood of experiencing discrimination, so both are good indicators of the variable. But we would not expect the race and gender of individuals to be strongly associated.

Or, we may measure *social interaction* with three indicators: time spent with friends, time spent with family, and time spent with coworkers. Though each indicator is valid, they need not be positively correlated. Time spent with friends, for instance, may be inversely related to time spent with family. Here, the three indicators "cause" the degree of social interaction.

As a final example, *exposure to stress* may be measured by whether a person recently experienced divorce, death of a spouse, or loss of a job. Though any of these events may indicate stress, they need not correlate with one another.

In short, we expect an association between indicators that depend on or "reflect" a variable, that is, if they are the "effects" of the variable. But if the variable depends on the indicators—if the indicators are the "causes"—those indicators may be either positively or negatively correlated, or even unrelated. Therefore, we should decide whether indicators are causes or effects of a variable before using their intercorrelations to assess their validity.

the responses given to each of the items correspond, to a greater or lesser degree, to the responses given to each of the other items.

Initially, the three items were selected on the basis of face validity. Each appeared to give some indication of faculty members' orientations to science. By examining the bivariate relationship between the pairs of items, we have found support for the expectation that they all measure basically the same thing. However, that support does not sufficiently justify including the items in a composite index. Before combining them in a single index, we need to examine the multivariate relationships among the several variables.

Multivariate Relationships among Items Whereas a bivariate relationship deals with two variables at a time, a *multivariate* one uses more than two variables. Recall that the primary purpose of index construction is to develop a method of classifying subjects in terms of some variable such as *political conservatism, religiosity, or scientific orientation*. An index of political conservatism should identify those who are very conservative, moderately conservative, not very conservative, and not at all conservative (or moderately liberal and very liberal, respectively, in place of the last two categories). The several gradations of the variable are provided by the combination of responses given to the several items included in the index. Thus, a respondent who appeared conservative on all items would be considered very conservative overall.

For an index to provide meaningful gradations in this sense, each item must add something to the evaluation of each respondent. Recall from the preceding section that two items perfectly related to one another should not be included in the same index. Once one item is included, the other adds nothing to our evaluation of respondents. The examination of multivariate relationships among the items is another way of eliminating deadwood. It also determines the overall power of the particular collection of items in measuring the variable under consideration.

We'll illustrate the purposes of this multivariate examination by returning to the earlier example of measuring scientific orientations among medical school faculty members. Figure 6-3 presents the trivariate relationships among the three items.

This figure categorizes the sample respondents into four groups according to (1) their greatest teaching contribution and (2) their reading preferences. The numbers in parentheses indicate the number of respondents in each group. Thus, 66 of the faculty members who said they could best teach as physicians also said they preferred articles dealing with the effectiveness of treatments. For each of the four groups, the figure presents the percentage of those who say they are ultimately more interested in basic mechanisms. So, for instance, of the 66 faculty mentioned, 27 percent are primarily interested in basic mechanisms.

The arrangement of the four groups is based on a previously drawn conclusion regarding scientific orientations. The group in the upper left corner of the table is presumably the least scientifically oriented, based on greatest teaching contribution and reading preference. The group in the lower right

Figure 6-3
Trivariate Relationships among Scientific Orientation Items

Percentage Interested in Basic Mechanisms		Greatest Teaching Contribution	
		Physician	Researcher
Reading Preferences	Effectiveness	27% (66)	58% (12)
	Rationale	58% (219)	89% (130)

corner is presumably the most scientifically oriented in terms of those items.

Recall that expressing a primary interest in basic mechanisms was also taken as an indication of scientific orientation. As we should expect, then, those in the lower right corner are the most likely to give this response (89 percent), and those in the upper left corner are the least likely (27 percent). The respondents who gave mixed responses in terms of teaching contributions and reading preferences have an intermediate rank in their concern for basic mechanisms (58 percent in both cases).

This table tells us many things. First, we may note that the original relationships between pairs of items are not significantly affected by the presence of a third item. Recall, for example, that the relationship between teaching contribution and ultimate medical interest was summarized as a 36 percentage point difference. Looking at Figure 6-3, we see that among only those respondents who are most interested in articles dealing with the effectiveness of treatments, the relationship between teaching contribution and ultimate medical interest is 31 percentage points (58 percent minus 27 percent: first row). The same is true among those most interested in articles dealing with the rationale for treatments (89 percent minus 58 percent: second row). The original relationship between teaching contribution and ultimate medical interest is essentially the same as in Figure 6-2, even among those respondents judged as scientific or nonscientific in terms of reading preferences.

We can draw the same conclusion from the columns in Figure 6-3. Recall that the original relationship between reading preferences and ultimate medical interests was summarized as a 38 percentage point difference. Looking only at the "physicians" in Figure 6-3, we see that the relationship between the other two items is now 31 percentage points. The same relationship is found among the "researchers" in the second column.

The importance of these observations becomes clearer when we consider what might have happened. In Figure 6-4, hypothetical data tell a much different story than do the actual data in Figure 6-3. As you can see, Figure 6-4 shows that the original relationship between teaching contribution and ultimate medical interest persists, even when reading preferences are introduced into the picture. In each row of the table the "researchers" are more likely to express an interest in basic mechanisms than the "physicians." Looking down the columns, however, we note that there is no relationship between reading preferences and ultimate medical interest. If we know whether a respondent feels he or she can make the greatest teaching contribution as a physician or as a researcher, knowing the respondent's reading preference adds nothing to our evaluation of his or her scientific orientation. If something like Figure 6-4 resulted from the actual data, we would conclude that reading preference should not be included in the same index as greatest teaching contribution, since it contributes nothing to the composite index.

Figure 6-4
Hypothetical Trivariate Relationship among Scientific Orientation Items

Percentage Interested in Basic Mechanisms		Greatest Teaching Contribution	
		Physician	Researcher
Reading Preferences	Effectiveness	51% (66)	87% (12)
	Rationale	51% (219)	87% (130)

This example used only three questionnaire items. If more were being considered, then more complex multivariate tables would be in order, constructed of four, five, or more variables. The purpose of this step in index construction, again, is to discover the simultaneous interaction of the items in order to determine which should be included in the same index.

Index Scoring

When you have chosen the best items for the index, you next assign scores for particular responses, thereby creating a single composite index out of the several items. There are two basic decisions to be made in this step.

First, you must decide the desirable range of the index scores. A primary advantage of an index over a single item is the range of gradations it offers in the measurement of a variable. As noted earlier, political conservatism might be measured from "very conservative" to "not at all conservative" or "very liberal". How far to the extremes, then, should the index extend?

In this decision, the question of variance enters once more. Almost always, as the possible extremes of an index are extended, fewer cases are to be found at each end. The researcher who wishes to measure political conservatism to its greatest extreme (somewhere to the right of Attila the Hun, as the saying goes) may find there is almost no one in that category. At some point, additional gradations don't add meaning to the results.

The first decision, then, concerns the conflicting desire for (1) a range of measurement in the index and (2) an adequate number of cases at each point in the index. You'll be forced to reach some kind of compromise between these conflicting desires.

The second decision concerns the actual assignment of scores for each particular response. Basically you must decide whether to give items in the index equal weight or different weights. Although there are no firm rules, we suggest—and practice tends to support this method—that items be weighted equally unless there are compelling reasons for differential weighting. That is, the burden of proof should be on differential weighting; equal weighting should be the norm.

Of course, this decision must be related to the earlier issue regarding the balance of items chosen. If the index is to represent the composite of slightly different aspects of a given variable, then you should give each aspect the same weight. In some instances, however, you may feel that, two items reflect essentially the same aspect, and the third reflects a different aspect. If you want to have both aspects equally represented by the index, you might give the different item a weight equal to the combination of the two similar ones. For example, you could assign a maximum score of 2 to the different item and a maximum score of 1 to each of the similar ones.

Although the rationale for scoring responses should take such concerns into account, typically researchers experiment with different scoring methods, examining the relative weights given to different aspects but at the same time worrying about the range and distribution of cases provided. Ultimately, the scoring method chosen will represent a compromise among these several demands. Of course, as in most research activities, such a decision is open to revision on the basis of later examinations. Validation of the index, to be discussed shortly, may lead the researcher to recycle his or her efforts toward constructing a completely different index.

In the example taken from the medical school faculty survey, the decision was to weight the items equally, since they were chosen, in part, because they represent slightly different aspects of the overall variable *scientific orientation*. On each of the items, the respondents were given a score of 1 for choosing the "scientific" response to the item and a score of 0 for choosing the "nonscientific" response. Each respondent, then, could receive a score of 0, 1, 2, or 3. This scoring method provided what was considered a useful range of variation— four index categories—and also provided enough cases for analysis in each category.

Here's another example of index scoring, with seven index categories, from a study by J. Rick Ponting (1988) on the Canadian public's knowledge about aboriginal affairs and familiarity with native events. Familiarity with native events/phenomena was measured by an index composed of seven events, organizations, or phenomena, which asked respondents how familiar they were with each one.

- Planned visit of the Pope to a Northwest Territories' Indian community in 1984
- The James Bay and Northern Quebec Agreement of 1975
- Aboriginal rights in the Canadian Constitution
- Last year's amendments to the Indian Act concerning sex discrimination
- The Lyell Island controversy on the Queen Charlotte Islands
- A Canadian organization called the Assembly of First Nations
- A constitutional conference involving the Prime Minister, provincial premiers, and Native leaders

The code for each of the items was: 1 = not at all familiar, 2 = slightly familiar, 3 = very familiar. "A respondent's score on the 1986 index was his/her average score over the seven items" (p. 11). In case you're interested, the national average was a score of 1.62.

Another index measuring Canadians' knowledge of Native affairs was constructed using "questions which tapped knowledge about certain rudimentary aspects of Native affairs" (p. 9), like the proportion of the total Canadian population that's Native, the percentage of Indians living on reserves, and knowledge about the existence of the *Indian Act*.

As you look through the social research literature, you'll find numerous similar examples of cumulative indexes being used to measure variables.

Handling Missing Data

Regardless of your data-collection method, you'll frequently face the problem of missing data (more on this in Chapter 16). In a content analysis of the political orientations of newspapers, for example, you may discover that a particular newspaper has never taken an editorial position on one of the issues being studied. In an experimental design involving several retests of subjects over time, some subjects may be unable to participate in some of the sessions. In virtually every survey, some respondents fail to answer some questions (or choose a "don't know" response). Although missing data present problems at all stages of analysis, they're especially troublesome in index construction. There are, however, several methods of dealing with these problems.

First, if there are relatively few cases with missing data, you may decide to exclude them from the construction of the index and the analysis. (This was done in the medical school faculty example.) The primary concerns in this instance are whether the numbers available for analysis will remain sufficient and whether the exclusion will result in an unrepresentative sample whenever the index, excluding some of the respondents, is used in the analysis. The latter possibility can be examined through a comparison, on other relevant variables, of those who would be included and excluded from the index.

Second, you may sometimes have grounds for treating missing data as one of the available responses. For example, if a questionnaire has asked respondents to indicate their participation in a number of activities by checking "yes" or "no" for each, many respondents may have checked some of the activities "yes" and left the remainder blank. In such a case, you might decide that a failure to answer meant "no," and score missing data in this case as though the respondents had checked the "no" space.

Third, a careful analysis of missing data may yield an interpretation of their meaning. In constructing a measure of political conservatism, for example, you may discover that respondents who failed to answer a given question were generally as conservative on other items as those who gave the conservative answer. In another example, a recent study measuring religious beliefs found that people who answered "don't know" about a given belief were almost identical to the "disbelievers" in their answers about other beliefs. (*Note:* You should not take these examples as empirical guides in your own studies, but only as suggestions of general ways to analyze your own data.) Whenever the analysis of missing data yields such interpretations, then, you may decide to score such cases accordingly.

There are many other ways of handling the problem of missing data. If an item has several possible values, you might assign the middle value to cases with missing data; for example, you could assign a 2 if the values are 0, 1, 2, 3, and 4. For a continuous variable such as *age,* you could similarly assign the mean to cases with missing data. Or, missing data can be supplied by assigning values at random. All of these are conservative solutions because they weaken the "purity" of your index and reduce the likelihood that it will relate to other variables in ways you may have hypothesized.

If you're creating an index out of a large number of items, you can sometimes handle missing data by using proportions based on what is observed. Suppose your index is composed of six indicators, and you only have four observations for a particular subject. If the subject has earned 4 points out of a possible 4, you might assign an index score of 6; if the subject has 2 points (half the possible score on four items), you could assign a score of 3 (half the possible score on six observations).

The choice of a particular method to be used depends so much on the research situation that we can't reasonably suggest a single "best" method or rank the several we have described. Excluding all cases with missing data can bias the representativeness of the findings, but including such cases by assigning scores to missing data can influence the nature of the findings. The safest and best method is to construct the index using more than one of these methods and see whether you reach the same conclusions using each of the indexes. Understanding your data is the final goal of analysis anyway.

Index Validation

Up to this point, we've discussed all the steps in the selection and scoring of items that result in an index purporting to measure some variable. If each of the preceding steps is carried out carefully, the likelihood of the index actually measuring the variable is enhanced. To demonstrate success, however, there must be *validation* of the index.

Following the basic logic of validation, we assume that the index provides a measure of some variable; that is, the scores on the index arrange cases in a rank order in terms of that variable. An index of political conservatism rank-orders people in terms of their relative conservatism. If the index does that successfully, then people scored as relatively conservative on the index should appear relatively conservative in all other indications of political orientation, such as their responses to other questionnaire items. There are several methods of validating an index.

Item Analysis   The first step in index validation is an *internal validation* called **item analysis**. In item analysis, you examine the extent to which the index is related to (or predicts responses to) the individual items it comprises. Here's an illustration of this step.

In the index of scientific orientations among medical school faculty, index scores ranged from 0 (most interested in patient care) to 3 (most interested in research). Now let's consider one of the items in the index: whether respondents wanted to advance their own knowledge more with regard to total patient management or more in the area of basic mechanisms. The latter were treated as being more scientifically oriented than the former. The following empty table shows how we would examine the relationship between the index and the individual item.

	Index of Scientific Orientations			
	0	1	2	3
Percentage who said they were more interested in basic mechanisms	??	??	??	??

If you take a minute to reflect on the table, you may see that we already know the numbers that go in two of the cells. To get a score of 3 on the index, respondents had to say "basic mechanisms" in response to this question and give the "scientific" answers to the other two items as well. Thus, 100 percent of the 3's on the index said "basic mechanisms." By the same token, all the 0's had to answer this item with "total patient management."

Thus, 0 percent of those respondents said "basic mechanisms." Here's how the table looks with the information we already know.

	Index of Scientific Orientations			
	0	1	2	3
Percentage who said they were more interested in basic mechanisms	0	??	??	100

If the individual item is a good refection of the overall index, we should expect the 1's and 2's to fill in a progression between 0 percent and 100 percent. More of the 2's should choose "basic mechanisms" than 1's. This result is not guaranteed by the way the index was constructed, however; it is an empirical question, one we answer in an item analysis. Here's how this particular item analysis turned out.

	Index of Scientific Orientations			
	0	1	2	3
Percentage who said they were more interested in basic mechanisms	0	16	91	100

As you can see, in accord with our assumption that the 2's are more scientifically oriented than the 1's, we find that a higher percentage of the 2's (91 percent) say "basic mechanisms" than the 1's (16 percent).

An item analysis of the other two components of the index yields similar results, as shown below.

	Index of Scientific Orientations			
	0	1	2	3
Percentage who said they could teach best as medical researchers	0	4	14	100
Percentage who said they preferred reading about rationales	0	80	97	100

Each of the items, then, seems an appropriate component in the index. Each seems to reflect the same quality that the index as a whole measures.

In a complex index containing many items, this step provides a convenient test of the independent contribution of each item to the index. If a given item is found to be poorly related to the index, it may be assumed that other items in the index cancel out the contribution of that item. If the item in question contributes nothing to the index's power, it should be excluded.

Although item analysis is an important first test of the index's validity, it is not a sufficient test. If the index adequately measures a given variable, it should successfully predict other indications of that variable. To test this, we must turn to items not included in the index.

External Validation People scored as politically conservative on an index should appear conservative by other measures as well, such as their responses to other items in the questionnaire. Of course, we're talking about relative conservatism, because we can't define "*conservatism*" in any absolute way. However, those respondents scored as the most conservative on the index should score as the most conservative in answering other questions. Those scored as the least conservative on the index should score as the least conservative on other items. Indeed, the ranking of groups of respondents on the index should predict the ranking of those groups in answering other questions dealing with political orientations.

In our example of the scientific orientation index, several questions in the questionnaire offered the possibility of such **external validation**. Table 6-1 presents some of these items, which provide several lessons regarding index validation. First, we note that the index strongly predicts the responses to the validating items in the sense that the rank order of scientific responses among the four groups is the same as the rank order provided by the index itself. That is, the percentages reflect greater scientific orientation as you read across the rows of the table. At the same time, each item gives a different description of scientific orientations overall. For example, the last validating item indicates that the great majority of *all* faculty were engaged in research during the preceding year. If this were the only indicator of scientific orientation, we would conclude that nearly all faculty were scientific. Nevertheless, those scored as more scientific on the index are more likely to have engaged in research than those who were scored as relatively less scientific. The third validating item provides a different descriptive picture: Only a minority of the faculty overall say they would prefer duties limited exclusively to research. Nevertheless, the relative percentages giving this answer correspond to the scores assigned on the index.

Bad Index versus Bad Validators Nearly every index constructor at some time must face the apparent failure of external items to validate the index. If the internal item analysis shows inconsistent relationships between the items included in the index and the index itself, something is wrong with the index. But if the index fails to predict strongly the external validation items, the conclusion to be drawn is more ambiguous. In this situation, we must choose between two possibilities: (1) the index does not adequately measure the variable in question, or (2) the validation items do not adequately measure the variable and thereby do not provide a sufficient test of the index.

Having worked long and conscientiously on the construction of an index, you'll likely find the second conclusion compelling. Typically, you will feel you have included the best indicators of the variable in the index; the validating items are, therefore, second-rate indicators. Nevertheless, you should recognize that the index is purportedly a very powerful measure of the variable; thus, it should be somewhat related to any item that taps the variable even poorly.

When external validation fails, you should reexamine the index before deciding that the validating items are insufficient. One way is to examine the relationships between the validating items and the individual items included in the index. If you discover that some of the index items relate to the validators and others do not, you'll have improved your understanding of the index as it was initially constituted.

There's no cookbook solution to this problem. It is an agony serious researchers must learn to survive. Ultimately, the wisdom of your decision to accept an index will be determined by the usefulness of that index in your later analyses. Perhaps you'll initially decide that the index is a good one and that the validators are defective, but you'll later find that the variable in question (as measured by the index) is not related to other variables in the ways you expected. Then you may have to compose a new index.

The Status of Women: An Illustration of Index Construction

For the most part, our discussion of index construction has focused on the specific context of survey research, but other types of research also lend themselves to this kind of composite measure.

Table 6-1
Validation of Scientific Orientation Index

| | Index of Scientific Orientation | | | |
| | Low | | | High |
	0	1	2	3
Percentage interested in attending scientific lectures at the medical school.............................	34	42	46	65
Percentage who say faculty members should have experience as medical researchers	43	60	65	89
Percentage who would prefer faculty duties involving research activities only	0	8	32	66
Percentage who engaged in research during the preceding academic year.............................	61	76	94	99

For example, when the United Nations (1995) set out to examine the status of women in the world, they chose to create two indexes, reflecting two different dimensions.

The Gender-related Development Index (GDI) compared women to men in terms of three indicators: life expectancy, education, and income. These indicators are commonly used in monitoring the status of women in the world. The Scandinavian countries of Norway, Sweden, Finland, and Denmark ranked highest on this measure.

The second index, the Gender Empowerment Measure (GEM), aimed more at power issues and comprised three different indicators:

- The proportion of parliamentary seats held by women
- The proportion of administrative, managerial, professional, and technical positions held by women
- A measure of access to jobs and wages

Once again, the Scandinavian countries ranked high but were joined by Canada, New Zealand, the Netherlands, the United States, and Austria. Having two different measures of gender equality rather than one allowed the researchers to make more sophisticated distinctions. For example, in several countries, most notably Greece, France, and Japan, women fared relatively well on the GDI but quite poorly on the GEM. Thus, while women were doing fairly well in terms of income, education, and life expectancy, they were still denied access to power. And while the GDI scores were higher in the wealthier nations than in the poorer ones, GEM scores showed that women's empowerment was less dependent on national wealth, with many poor, developing countries outpacing some rich, industrial ones in regard to such empowerment.

By examining several different dimensions of the variables involved in their study, the UN researchers also uncovered an aspect of women's earnings that generally goes unnoticed. Population Communications International (1996:1) has summarized the finding nicely:

> Every year, women make an invisible contribution of eleven trillion U.S. dollars to the global

economy, the UNDP [United Nations Development Programme] report says, counting both unpaid work and the underpayment of women's work at prevailing market prices. This "under evaluation" of women's work not only undermines their purchasing power, says the 1995 HDR [Human Development Report], but also reduces their already low social status and affects their ability to own property and use credit. Mahbub ul Haq, the principal author of the report, says that, "if women's work were accurately reflected in national statistics, it would shatter the myth that men are the main breadwinners of the world." The UNDP report finds that women work longer hours than men in almost every country, including both paid and unpaid duties. In developing countries, women do approximately 53% of all work and spend two-thirds of their work time on unremunerated activities. In industrialized countries, women do an average of 51% of the total work, and, like their counterparts in the developing world, perform about two-thirds of their total labor without pay. Men in industrialized countries are compensated for two-thirds of their work.

As you can see, indexes can be constructed from many different kinds of data for a variety of purposes. Now we'll turn our attention from the construction of indexes to an examination of scaling techniques.

Scale Construction

Good indexes provide an ordinal ranking of cases on a given variable. All indexes are based on this kind of assumption: A criminal court judge who sentences seven people in one year to a life sentence is considered more punitive than one who only sentences four people. What an index may fail to take into account, however, is that not all indicators of a variable are equally important or equally strong. The first judge might have sentenced seven first-degree murderers to life, whereas the second judge might have sentenced four repeat robbers. (No murderers may have appeared before the second judge for sentencing that year, while the first judge may have been more lenient to repeat robbers.)

Scales offer more assurance of ordinality by tapping the intensity structures among the indicators. The several items going into a composite measure may have different intensities in terms of the variable. Many methods of scaling are available. We'll look at four scaling procedures to illustrate the variety of techniques available, along with a technique called the semantic differential. Although these examples focus on questionnaires, the logic of scaling, like that of indexing, applies to other research methods as well.

Bogardus Social Distance Scale

Let's suppose you're interested in the extent to which Canadian citizens are willing to associate with, say, Albanians. You might ask the following questions:

1. Are you willing to permit Albanians to live in your country?
2. Are you willing to permit Albanians to live in your community?
3. Are you willing to permit Albanians to live in your neighbourhood?
4. Would you be willing to let an Albanian live next door to you?
5. Would you let your child marry an Albanian?

These questions increase in terms of the closeness of contact the respondents may or may not want with Albanians. Beginning with the original concern to measure willingness to associate with Albanians, you have developed several questions indicating differing degrees of intensity on this variable. The kinds of items presented constitute a **Bogardus social distance scale** (created by Emory Bogardus). This scale is a measurement technique for determining the willingness of people to participate in social relations—of varying degrees of closeness—with other kinds of people.

The clear differences of intensity suggest a structure among the items. Presumably if a person is willing to accept a given kind of association, he or she would be willing to accept all those preceding it in the list—those with lesser intensities. For example, the person who is willing to permit Albanians to live in the neighbourhood will surely accept them in the community and the nation but may or may not be willing to accept them as next-door neighbours or relatives. This, then, is the logical structure of intensity inherent among the items.

Empirically, one would expect to find the largest number of people accepting co-citizenship and the fewest accepting intermarriage. In this sense, we speak of "easy items" (for example, residence in Canada) and "hard items" (for example, intermarriage). More people agree to the easy items than to the hard ones. With some inevitable exceptions, logic demands that once a person has refused a relationship presented in the scale, he or she will also refuse all the harder ones that follow it.

The Bogardus social distance scale illustrates the important economy of scaling as a data-reduction device. By knowing *how many* relationships with Albanians a given respondent will accept, we know *which* relationships were accepted. Thus, a single number can accurately summarize five or six data items without a loss of information.

Thurstone Scales

Often the inherent structure of the Bogardus social distance scale is not appropriate to the variable being measured. Indeed, such a logical structure among several indicators is seldom apparent. **Thurstone scaling** (created by Louis Thurstone) is an attempt to develop a format for generating groups of indicators of a variable that have at least an empirical structure among them. A group of judges is given perhaps a hundred items thought to be indicators of a given variable. Each judge is then asked to estimate how strong an indicator of a variable each item is by assigning scores of perhaps 1 to 13. If the variable were *prejudice,* for example, the judges would be asked to assign the score of 1 to the very weakest indicators of prejudice, the score of 13 to the strongest indicators, and intermediate scores to those felt to be somewhere in between.

Once the judges have completed this task, the researcher examines the scores assigned to each item by all the judges to determine which items produced the greatest agreement among the judges. Those items on which the judges disagreed broadly would be rejected as ambiguous. Among those items producing general agreement in scoring, one or more would be selected to represent each scale score from 1 to 13.

The items selected in this manner might then be included in a survey questionnaire. Respondents who appeared prejudiced on those items representing a strength of 5 would then be expected to appear prejudiced on those having lesser strengths, and if some of those respondents did not appear prejudiced on the items with a strength of 6, it would be expected that they would also not appear prejudiced on those with greater strengths.

If the Thurstone scale items were adequately developed and scored, the economy and effectiveness of data reduction inherent in the Bogardus social distance scale would appear. A single score might be assigned to each respondent (the strength of the hardest item accepted), and that score would adequately represent the responses to several questionnaire items. And, as is true of the Bogardus scale, a respondent who scored 6 might be regarded as more prejudiced than one who scored 5 or less.

Thurstone scaling is not often used in research today, primarily because of the tremendous expenditure of energy and time required to have 10 to 15 judges score the items. Because the quality of their judgments would depend on their experience with the variable under consideration, professional researchers might be needed. Moreover, the meanings conveyed by the several items indicating a given variable tend to change over time. Thus an item having a given weight at one time might have quite a different weight later on. For a Thurstone scale to be effective, it would have to be periodically updated.

Likert Scaling

You may sometimes hear people refer to a questionnaire item containing response categories such as "strongly agree," "agree," "disagree," and "strongly disagree" as a Likert scale. This is technically a misnomer, although Rensis Likert (pronounced 'LICK-ert') did create this commonly used question format.

The particular value of this format is the unambiguous *ordinality* of response categories. If respondents were permitted to volunteer or select such answers as "sort of agree," "pretty much agree," "really agree," and so forth, the researcher would find it impossible to judge the relative strength of agreement intended by the various respondents. The Likert format resolves this problem.

Likert had something more in mind, however. He created a method by which this question format could be used to determine the relative intensity of different items. As a simple example, suppose we wished to measure prejudice against women. To do this, we create a set of 20 statements, each of which reflects that prejudice. One of the items might be "Women can't drive as well as men." Another might be "Women shouldn't be allowed to vote." Likert's scaling technique would demonstrate that difference in intensity between these items as well as pegging the intensity of the other 18 statements.

Let's suppose we ask a sample of people to agree or disagree with each of the 20 statements. Simply giving one point for each of the indicators of prejudice against women would yield the possibility of index scores ranging from 0 to 20. A **Likert scale** goes one step beyond that and calculates the *average index* score for those agreeing with each of the individual statements. Let's say that all those who agreed that women are poorer drivers than men had an average index score of 1.5 (out of a possible 20). Those who agreed that women should be denied the right to vote might have an average index score of, say, 19.5, indicating the greater degree of prejudice reflected in that response.

As a result of this item analysis, respondents could be rescored to form a scale: 1.5 points for agreeing that women are poorer drivers, 19.5 points for saying women shouldn't vote, and points for other responses reflecting how those items related to the initial, simple index. If those who disagreed with the statement, "I might vote for a woman for president," had an average index score of 15, then the scale would give 15 points to people disagreeing with that statement.

In practice, Likert scaling is seldom used today. It's unclear why; maybe it seems too complex. The item format devised by Likert, however, is one of the most commonly used in contemporary questionnaire design. Typically, it's now used in the creation of simple indexes. With, say, five response categories, scores of 0 to 4 or 1 to 5 might be assigned, taking the direction of the items into account (for example, assign a score of 5 to "strongly agree" for positive items and to "strongly disagree" for negative items). Each respondent would then be assigned an overall score representing the summation of the scores he or she received for responses to the individual items.

Semantic Differential

Like the Likert format, the **semantic differential** asks questionnaire respondents to choose between two opposite positions using qualifiers to bridge the gap between the two opposites. Here's how it works.

Suppose you're evaluating the effectiveness of a new music appreciation lecture on subjects' appreciation of music. As a part of your study, you want to play some musical selections and have the subjects report their feelings about them. A good way to tap those feelings would be to use a semantic differential format.

To begin, you must determine the dimensions along which subjects should judge each selection. Then you need to find two *opposite* terms, representing the polar extremes along each dimension. Let's suppose one dimension that interests you is simply whether subjects enjoyed the piece or not. Two opposite terms in this case could be "enjoyable" and "unenjoyable." Similarly, you might want to know whether they regarded the individual selections as "complex" or "simple," "harmonic" or "discordant," and so forth.

Once you have determined the relevant dimensions and have found terms to represent the extremes of each, you might prepare a rating sheet each subject would complete for each piece of music. Figure 6-5 shows what it might look like.

On each line of the rating sheet, the subject would indicate how he or she felt about the piece of music: whether it was enjoyable or unenjoyable, for example, and whether it was "somewhat" that way or "very much" so. To avoid creating a biased pattern of responses to such items, it's a good idea to vary the placement of terms that are likely to be related to each other. Notice, for example, that "discordant" and "traditional" are on the left side of the sheet, with "harmonic" and "modern" on the right. Most likely, those selections scored as "discordant" would also be scored as "modern" as opposed to "traditional."

Both the Likert and semantic differential formats have a greater rigour and structure than other question formats. As we've indicated earlier, these formats produce data suitable to both indexing and scaling.

Figure 6-5
Semantic Differential: Feelings about Musical Selections

	Very Much	Some-what	Neither	Some-what	Very Much	
Enjoyable	☐	☐	☐	☐	☐	Unenjoyable
Simple	☐	☐	☐	☐	☐	Complex
Discordant	☐	☐	☐	☐	☐	Harmonic
Traditional	☐	☐	☐	☐	☐	Modern
			etc.			

Guttman Scaling

Researchers today often use the scale developed by Louis Guttman. Like Bogardus, Thurstone, and Likert scaling, Guttman scaling is based on the fact that some items under consideration may prove to be more extreme indicators of the variable than others. One example should suffice to illustrate this pattern.

In the earlier example of measuring scientific orientation among medical school faculty members, you'll recall that a simple index was constructed. As it happens, however, the three items included in the index essentially form a **Guttman scale**.

The construction of a Guttman scale begins with some of the same steps that initiate index construction. You begin by examining the face validity of items available for analysis. Then, you would examine the bivariate and perhaps multivariate relations among those items. In scale construction, however, you also look for relatively "hard" and "easy" indicators of the variable being examined.

Earlier, when we talked about attitudes regarding a woman's right to have an abortion, we discussed several conditions that can affect people's opinions. Rita Simon (1998:131) reports the percentages for a sample of Canadians who supported a women's right to an abortion under various conditions—obtained from an international study conducted between 1991–94—for example, when a:

Woman's health is at risk	92.1%
Child will likely be born physically handicapped	64.0%
Woman is not married	32.3%

In this same study, the Canadian approval level was higher than the U.S. level, which was 86 percent, 54.1 percent, and 29.1 percent respectively (1998:192).

These differing conditions provide an excellent illustration of Guttman scaling. However, because the Canadian General Social Survey does not ask these questions, we'll turn to available U.S. data to illustrate. Here are the percentages of the people in a 1996 U.S. sample (General Social Survey) who supported a woman's right to an abortion, under three different conditions:

Woman's health is seriously endangered	92%
Pregnant as a result of rape	86%
Woman is not married	48%

The different percentages supporting abortion under the three conditions suggest something about the different levels of support that each item indicates. For example, if someone supports abor-

Table 6-2
Scaling Support for Choice of Abortion

	Women's Health	Result of Rape	Woman Unmarried	Number of Cases
Scale Types	+	+	+	612
	+	+	−	448
	+	−	−	92
	−	−	−	79
				Total = 1231
Mixed Types	−	+	−	15
	+	−	+	5
	−	−	+	2
	−	+	+	5
				Total = 27

+ = favours woman's right to choose; − = opposes woman's right to choose

tion when the mother's life is seriously endangered, that's not a very strong indicator of general support for abortion, because almost everyone agreed with that. Supporting abortion for unmarried women seems a much stronger indicator of support for abortion in general—fewer than half the sample took that position.

Guttman scaling is based on the notion that anyone who gives a strong indicator of some variable will also give the weaker indicators. In this case, we would assume that anyone who supported abortion for unmarried women would also support it in the case of rape or of the woman's health being threatened. Table 6-2 tests this assumption by presenting the number of respondents who gave each of the possible response patterns.

The first four response patterns in the table compose what we would call the *scale types:* those patterns that form a scalar structure. Following those respondents who supported abortion under all three conditions (line 1), we see (line 2) that those with only two pro-choice responses have

chosen the two easier ones; those with only one such response (line 3) chose the easiest of the three (the woman's health being endangered). And finally, there are some respondents who opposed abortion in all three circumstances (line 4).

The second part of the table presents those response patterns that violate the scalar structure of the items. The most radical departures from the scalar structure are the last two response patterns: those who accepted only the hardest item and those who rejected only the easiest one.

The final column in the table indicates the number of survey respondents who gave each of the response patterns. The great majority (1,231, or 98 percent) of the respondents fit into one of the scale types. The presence of mixed types, however, indicates that the items do not form a perfect Guttman scale.

Recall at this point that one of the chief functions of scaling is efficient data reduction. Scales provide a technique for presenting data in a summary form while maintaining as much of the original information as possible. When the scientific

Table 6-3
Index and Scale Scores

	Response Pattern	Number of Cases	Index Scores	Scale Scores*	Total Scale Errors
Scale Types	+ + +	612	3	3	0
	+ + −	448	2	2	0
	+ − −	92	1	1	0
	− − −	79	0	0	0
Mixed Types	− + −	15	1	2	15
	+ − +	5	2	3	5
	− − +	2	1	0	2
	− + +	5	2	3	5

Total Scale Errors = 27

$$\text{Coefficient of reproducibility} = 1 - \frac{\text{number of errors}}{\text{number of guesses}}$$

$$= 1 - \frac{27}{1258 \times 3} = \frac{27}{3774}$$

$$= .993 = 99.3\%$$

*This table presents one common method for scoring mixed types, but you should be advised that other methods are also used.

orientation items were formed into an index in our earlier discussion, respondents were given one point for each scientific response they gave. If these same three items were scored as a Guttman scale, some respondents would be assigned scale scores that would permit the most accurate reproduction of their original responses to all three items.

In the example of attitudes regarding abortion, respondents fitting into the scale types would receive the same scores as would be assigned in the construction of an index. Persons selecting all three pro-choice responses (+ + +) would still be scored 3, those who selected pro-choice responses to the two easier items and were opposed on the hardest item (+ + –) would be scored 2, and so on. For each of the four scale types we could predict accurately all the actual responses given by all the respondents based on their scores.

The mixed types in the table present a problem, however. The first mixed type (– + –) was scored 1 on the index to indicate only one pro-choice response. But, if 1 were assigned as a scale score, we would predict that the 15 respondents in this group had chosen only the easiest item (approving abortion when the woman's life was endangered), and we would be making two errors for each such respondent (+ – –), for a total of 30 errors. Scale scores are assigned, therefore, with the aim of minimizing the errors that would be made in reconstructing the original responses.

Table 6-3 illustrates the index and scale scores that would be assigned to each of the response patterns in our example. Note that one error is made for each respondent in the mixed types. This is the minimum we can hope for in a mixed type pattern. For example, in the first mixed type, using a scale score of two (+ + –), we would erroneously predict a pro-choice response to the easiest item for each of the 15 respondents in this group, making a total of 15 errors.

The extent to which a set of empirical responses form a Guttman scale is determined by the accuracy with which the original responses can be reconstructed from the scale scores. For each of the 1,258 respondents in this example, we will predict three questionnaire responses, for a total of 3,774 predictions. Table 6-3 indicates that we will make 27 errors using the scale scores assigned. The percentage of correct predictions is called the **coefficient of reproducibility**: the percentage of original responses that could be reproduced by knowing the scale scores used to summarize them. In the present example, the coefficient of reproducibility is 3,747/3,774 or 99.3 percent.

Except for the case of perfect (100 percent) reproducibility, there is no way of saying that a set of items does or does not form a Guttman scale in any absolute sense. Virtually all sets of such items approximate a scale. As a general guideline, however, coefficients of 90 or 95 percent are the commonly used standards. If the observed reproducibility exceeds the level you've set, you'll probably decide to score and use the items as a scale.

The decision concerning criteria in this regard is, of course, arbitrary. Moreover, a high degree of reproducibility does not insure that the scale constructed in fact measures the concept under consideration. What it does is increase confidence that all the component items measure *the same thing*. Also, you should realize that a high coefficient of reproducibility is most likely when few items are involved.

One concluding remark should be made with regard to Guttman scaling: It is based on the structure observed among the *actual data under examination*. This is an important point that is often misunderstood. It does not make sense to say that a set of questionnaire items (perhaps developed and used by a previous researcher) constitutes a Guttman scale. Rather, we can say only that they form a scale within a given body of data being analyzed. Scalability, then, is a sample-dependent, empirical matter. Although a set of items may form a Guttman scale among one sample of survey respondents, for example, there is no guarantee that this set will form such a scale among another sample. In this sense, then, a set of questionnaire items in and of themselves never forms a scale, but a set of empirical observations may.

In summary, like indexes, scales are composite measures of a variable, typically broadening the meaning of the variable beyond what a single indicator might capture. Both scales and indexes seek to measure variables at the ordinal level of measurement. Unlike indexes, however, scales take advantage of any intensity of structure that may be present among the individual indicators. To the extent that such an intensity structure is found and the data from the people or other units of analysis comply with the logic of that intensity structure, we can have confidence that we have created an ordinal measure.

Typologies

We'll conclude this chapter with a short discussion of one form of typology construction and analysis. Recall that indexes and scales are constructed to provide ordinal measures of given variables. We attempt to assign index or scale scores to cases in such a way as to indicate a rising degree of prejudice, religiosity, conservatism, and so forth. In such cases, we're dealing with single dimensions.

Often, however, the researcher wishes to summarize the intersection of two or more concepts or variables, thereby creating a set of categories or types—a nominal variable—called a **typology**. You may, for example, wish to examine the political orientations of newspapers separately in terms of domestic issues and foreign policy. The fourfold presentation in Table 6-4 describes such a typology.

Newspapers in cell A of the table are conservative on both foreign policy and domestic policy; those in cell D are liberal on both. Those in cells B and C are conservative on one and liberal on the other.

Table 6-4
A Political Typology of Newspapers

| | | Foreign Policy | |
		Conservative	Liberal
Domestic Policy	Conservative	A	B
	Liberal	C	D

You may arrive at a typology in the course of an attempt to construct an index or scale. The items that you felt represented a single variable appear to represent two. We might have been attempting to construct a single index of political orientations for newspapers but discovered, empirically, that foreign and domestic politics had to be kept separate.

In any event, you should be warned against a difficulty inherent in this form of typological analysis. Whenever such a typology is used as the independent variable, there will probably be no problem. In the preceding example, you might compute the percentages of newspapers in each cell that normally endorse Liberal candidates; you could then easily examine the effects of both foreign and domestic policies on political endorsements.

It is extremely difficult, however, to analyze this form of typology as a dependent variable. If you synthesize two or more unidimensional dependent variables into a typology because the evidence empirically warrants it, you cannot reverse ground and recover any inference about the separate dimensions that were combined. Thus, in this example, if you want to discover *why* newspapers fall into the different cells of typology, you're in trouble. That becomes apparent when we consider the ways you might construct and read your tables. Assume, for example, that you want to examine the effects of community size on political policies. With a single dimension, you could easily determine the percentages of rural and urban newspapers that were scored conservative and liberal on your index or scale.

Using this typology, however, you would have to present the distribution of the urban newspapers in your sample among types A, B, C, and D. Then you would repeat the procedure for the rural ones in the sample and compare the two distributions. Let's suppose that 80 percent of the rural newspapers are scored as type A (conservative on both dimensions) compared with 30 percent of the urban ones. Moreover, suppose that only 5 percent of the rural newspapers are scored as type B (conservative only on domestic issues) compared with 40 percent of the urban ones. It would be incorrect to conclude from an examination of type B that urban newspapers are more conservative on domestic issues than rural ones, since 85 percent of the rural newspapers, compared with 70 percent of the urban ones, have this characteristic. The relative sparsity of rural newspapers in type B is due to their concentration in type A. It should be apparent that an interpretation of such data would be very difficult for anything other than description.

In reality, you'd probably examine two such dimensions separately, especially if the dependent variable has more categories of responses than the example given.

Don't think that typologies should always be avoided in social research; often they provide the most appropriate device for understanding the data. To examine the "pro-life" orientation in depth, you might create a typology involving both abortion and capital punishment. Libertarianism could be seen in terms of both economic and social permissiveness. You've been warned, however, against the special difficulties involved in using typologies as dependent variables when they have been created based on the decision that the evidence empirically warranted a synthesis of two or more unidimensional variables.

This synthesis illustrates one possibility for the use of typology in research. Typologies, including other forms, are often used in qualitative analysis and theory building and will be further discussed in Chapter 14.

Main Points

- Single indicators of variables seldom capture all the dimensions of a concept, have sufficiently clear validity to warrant their use, or permit the desire range of variation to allow ordinal rankings. Composite measures, such as scales and indexes, solve these problems by including several indicators of a variable in one summary measure.
- Both scales and indexes are intended as ordinal measures of variables, although scales typically satisfy this goal better than indexes.

- Indexes are based on the simple cumulation of indicators of a variable.
- Scales take advantage of any logical or empirical intensity structures that exist among a variable's indicators.
- The principal steps in constructing an index include selecting items, examining their empirical relationships, scoring the index, and validating it.
- Criteria of item selection include face validity, unidimensionality, the degree of specificity with which a dimension is to be measured, and the amount of variance provided by the items.
- If different items are indeed indicators of the same variable, then they should be related empirically to one another. In constructing an index, the researcher needs to examine bivariate and multivariate relationships among the items.
- Index scoring involves deciding the desirable range of scores and determining whether items will have equal or different weights.
- There are various techniques that allow items to be used in an index in spite of missing data.
- A constructed index or scale must be validated. Item analysis is a type of internal validation based on the relationship between individual items in the composite measure and the measure itself. External validation refers to the relationships between the composite measure and other indicators of the variable—indicators not included in the measure.
- The Bogardus social distance scale is a device for measuring the varying degrees to which a person would be willing to associate with a given class of people. Thurstone scaling is a technique that uses judges to determine intensities of different indicators. Likert scaling is a measurement technique based on the use of standardized response categories. Guttman scaling is a method of discovering and using the empirical intensity structure among several indicators of a given variable. Guttman scaling is probably the most popular scaling technique in social research today.

- The semantic differential is a question format that asks respondents to make ratings that lie between two extremes, such as "very positive" and "very negative."
- A typology is a nominal composite measure often used in social research.

Review Questions and Exercises

1. In your own words, describe the difference between an index and a scale.
2. Name three data items that might be included in an index for rating the quality of universities.
3. Make up three questionnaire items that measure attitudes toward nuclear power and that would probably form a Guttman scale.
4. Find an example of a composite measure reported in the media: newspapers, magazines, television, or the Web. Detail the component elements in the measure.

Continuity Project

Create three indicators of attitudes toward gender equality that represent a scale of increasing intensity. Indicate which is the strongest indicator and which the weakest.

Additional Readings

Anderson, Andy B., Alexander Basilevsky, and Derek P. J. Hum. "Measurement: Theory and Techniques." Pp. 231–87 in *Handbook of Survey Research,* edited by Peter H. Rossi, James D. Wright, and Andy B. Anderson. New York: Academic Press, 1983. The logic of measurement is analyzed in the context of composite measures.

Indrayan, A., M. J. Wysocki, A. Chawla, R. Kumar, and Singh. 1999. "Three-Decade Trend in Human Development Index in India and Its Major States." *Social Indicators Research* 46 (1): 91–120. The authors use several human development indexes to compare the status of different states in India.

McIver, John P., and Edward G. Carmines. *Unidimensional Scaling.* Newbury Park, CA: Sage, 1981. Here's an excellent way to pursue Thurstone, Likert, and Guttman scaling in further depth.

Miller, Delbert. *Handbook of Research Design and Social Measurement.* Newbury Park, CA: Sage, 1991. An excellent compilation of frequently used and semistandardized scales. The many illustrations reported in Part 4 of the Miller book may be directly adaptable to studies or at least suggestive of modified measures. Studying the several different illustrations, moreover, may also give you a better understanding of the logic of composite measures in general.

InfoTrac: You can find further relevant readings on the World Wide Web at

http://sociology.wadsworth.com

Chapter 7

The Logic of Sampling

How can social scientists select a few people for discussion and make discoveries that apply to hundreds of millions they don't observe? The logic of sampling provides the answer.

In this chapter . . .

Introduction

In November 2000, the Liberal party won the popular vote in the Canadian federal election and Jean Chrétien kept his post as prime minister of Canada. The Liberal party (Lib) got 40.8 percent of the popular vote, Canadian Alliance (CA) received 25.5 percent, the Progressive Conservatives (PC) got 12.2 percent, the Bloc Québécois (BQ) 10.7 percent, and the New Democratic Party (NDP) 8.5 percent. The remaining 2.3 percent of the vote went to others. Prior to the election, the vast majority of political polls had predicted the Liberal party victory.

Here are the results of several national polls conducted before the election, from mid October to mid November (Table 7-1). The polls were reported with the "undecided" (those who didn't give a preference) distributed among the parties by the pollsters. This makes it easy for us to compare them.

Though the polls tended to overestimate the Liberal vote in 2000, many, as you can see, came within two or three percentage points of the actual vote.

Now, how many interviews do you suppose it took each of these pollsters to come within a couple of percentage points in estimating the behaviour of about 13 million voters? Fewer than 2,500! In fact most of the polls were under 2,000, ranging from 1,275 to 2,500. In this chapter, we're going to find out how social researchers can pull off such wizardry.

Political polling, like other forms of social research, rests on observations. But neither pollsters nor other social researchers can observe everything that might be relevant to their interests. A critical part of social research, then, is deciding what to observe and what not.

If you want to study voters, for example, which voters should you study?

Table 7-1
Polls Predicting Federal Election Outcomes

Dates	Agency	Percent of Votes for				
		Lib	CA	PC	BQ	NDP
10/17–26	Decima Research	44.3	24	9.5	8.5	9.9
10/27–11/1	Ipsos-Reid	42	29	8	10	9
11/9–10	Compas	43	24	8	12	8
11/10–11	Ipsos-Reid	40	28	9	11	9
11/8–14	Environics	46	23	10	11	9
11/11–14	Campas	44	25	10	10	8
11/11–15	EKOS Research	44.6	25.6	9.8	10	8.6
11/12–16	Leger Marketing	44	25	10	10	9
	Election Results	**40.8**	**25.5**	**12.2**	**10.7**	**8.5**

The total does not add up to 100 percent because 2.3 percent voted for other than these parties.

Source: CNEWS Decision 2000 Results
http://www.canoe.ca/CNEWSElection2000News/001027_flash2.html (January 27, 2001)

The process of selecting observations is called *sampling*. Although sampling can mean any procedure for selecting units of observation—for example, interviewing every tenth passerby on a busy street—the key to generalizing from a sample to a larger population is *probability sampling*, which involves the important idea of *random selection*.

Much of this chapter is devoted to the logic and skills of probability sampling. This topic is more rigorous and precise than some of the other topics in this book. Whereas social research as a whole is both art and science, sampling leans toward science. Although this subject is somewhat technical, the basic logic of sampling is not difficult to understand. In fact, the logical neatness of this topic can make it easier to comprehend than, say, conceptualization.

Although probability sampling is central to social research today, we'll take some time to examine a variety of nonprobability methods as well. These methods have their own logic and can provide useful samples for some social research purposes.

Before we discuss the two major types of sampling, we'll introduce you to some basic ideas by way of a brief history of sampling. As you'll see, the pollsters who correctly predicted the Liberal party's victory in the popular vote in 2000 did so in part because researchers had learned to avoid some pitfalls that earlier pollsters had not.

A Brief History of Sampling

Sampling in social research has developed hand in hand with political polling. This is the case, no doubt, because political polling is one of the few opportunities social researchers have to discover the accuracy of their estimates. On election day, they find out how well or how poorly they did. A brief look at the history of the successes and failures of political polling in the U.S. helps to illustrate some important lessons learned from them about sampling.

President Alf Landon

Was there a U.S. president named Alf Landon? No—but Alf Landon would have been president if a famous poll conducted by the *Literary Digest* had proved to be accurate. The *Literary Digest* was a popular news magazine published between 1890 and 1938 in the U.S. In 1920, *Digest* editors mailed postcards to people in six states, asking them whom they were planning to vote for in the presidential race between Warren Harding and James

Cox. Names were selected for the poll from telephone directories and automobile registration lists. Based on the postcards sent back, the *Digest* correctly predicted that Harding would be elected. In the elections that followed, the *Literary Digest* expanded the size of its poll and made correct predictions in 1924, 1928, and 1932.

In 1936, the *Digest* conducted its most ambitious poll: Ten million ballots were sent to people listed in telephone directories and on lists of automobile owners. Over two million people responded, giving the Republican contender, Alf Landon, a stunning 57 to 43 percent landslide over the incumbent, President Franklin Roosevelt. The editors modestly cautioned,

> We make no claim to infallibility. We did not coin the phrase "uncanny accuracy" which has been so freely applied to our Polls. We know only too well the limitations of every straw vote, however enormous the sample gathered, however scientific the method. It would be a miracle if every State of the forty-eight behaved on Election Day exactly as forecast by the Poll.
>
> (1936a:6)

Two weeks later, the *Digest* editors knew the limitations of straw polls even better: The voters gave Roosevelt a second term in office by the largest landslide in history, with 61 percent of the vote. Landon won only 8 electoral votes to Roosevelt's 523.

The editors were puzzled by their unfortunate turn of luck. How could their poll be so wrong? A part of the problem surely lay in the 22 percent return rate garnered by the poll. The editors asked,

> Why did only one in five voters in Chicago to whom the *Digest* sent ballots take the trouble to reply? And why was there a preponderance of Republicans in the one-fifth that did reply? . . . We were getting better cooperation in what we have always regarded as a public service from Republicans than we were getting from Democrats. Do Republicans live nearer to mailboxes? Do Democrats generally disapprove of straw polls?
>
> (1936b:7)

Actually, there was a better explanation—what is technically called the *sampling frame* used by the *Digest*. In this case the sampling frame consisted of telephone subscribers and automobile owners. In the context of 1936, this design selected a disproportionately wealthy sample of the voting population, especially coming on the tail end of the worst economic depression in the nation's history. The sample effectively excluded poor people, and the poor voted predominantly for Roosevelt's New Deal recovery program. The *Digest*'s poll may or may not have correctly represented the voting intentions of telephone subscribers and automobile owners. Unfortunately for the editors, it decidedly did not represent the voting intentions of the population as a whole.

President Thomas E. Dewey

The 1936 election also saw the emergence of a young pollster whose name would become synonymous with public opinion. In contrast to the *Literary Digest*, George Gallup correctly predicted that Roosevelt would beat Landon. Gallup's success in 1936 hinged on his use of *quota sampling*, which we'll look at more closely later in the chapter. For now, it's enough to know that quota sampling is based on a knowledge of the characteristics of the population being sampled: what proportion are men, what proportion are women, what proportions are of various incomes, ages, and so on. Quota sampling selects people to match a set of these characteristics: the right number of poor, white, rural men; the right number of rich, black, urban women; and so on. The quotas are based on those variables most relevant to the study. In the case of Gallup's poll, the sample selection was based on levels of income; the sample procedure ensured the right proportion of respondents at each income level.

Gallup and his American Institute of Public Opinion used quota sampling to good effect in 1936, 1940, and 1944 correctly picking the presidential winner each of those years. Then, in 1948, Gallup and most political pollsters suffered the embarrassment of predicting that Governor Thomas Dewey of New York would win the election over the incumbent, President Harry Truman. The pollsters' embarrassing miscue continued right up to election night. A famous photograph shows a jubilant Truman—whose followers' battle cry was "Give 'em hell, Harry!"—holding aloft a newspaper with the banner headline, "Dewey Defeats Truman."

Several factors accounted for the pollsters' failure in 1948. First, most pollsters stopped polling in early October despite a steady trend toward Truman during the campaign. In addition, many voters were undecided throughout the campaign, and they went disproportionately for Truman when they stepped in the voting booth.

More important, Gallup's failure rested on the unrepresentativeness of his samples. Quota sampling, which had been effective in earlier years, was Gallup's undoing in 1948. This technique requires that the researcher know something about the total population—in this case, the population of voters. For national political polls, such information came primarily from census data. By 1948, however, World War II had produced a massive movement from the country to cities, radically changing the character of the U.S. population from what the 1940 census showed, and Gallup relied on 1940 census data. City dwellers, moreover, tended to vote Democratic; hence the overrepresentation of rural voters in his poll had the effect of underestimating the number of Democratic votes. As you'll see below, quota sampling and straw polls (discussed above) are both nonprobability samples.

Polling In Canada

In Claire Hoy's book "on the use and abuse and history of polling and pollsters" in Canada, he notes that the origins of polling in Canada can be traced to the World War II period. Just so you don't think he is totally critical of polls, he also states that "…polls, properly conducted and carefully reported, can be a useful tool for journalists, politicians, and the public" (1989:v). Thus, understanding what underlies polls—issues of samples and sampling—will help you in assessing whether a poll is properly conducted and accurately reported. But, before we move ahead with our dis-

cussion of sampling, let's take a brief look at the introduction of polling in Canada.

Political polling, and polling people for their views on many other issues, has become more sophisticated and quite accepted as a prominent feature in North American society. However, this has not always been so. Polling has its dark side as well. As Hoy notes, when the Gallop organization first arrived in Canada in 1941, then Prime Minister Mackenzie King was not keen on having them. The prime minister was worried about the potential effect reporting opinions of the Canadian population might have, like making the French-English divide more visible and possibly revealing information that could be embarrassing, like showing how many Canadians were really against conscription in WWII. He was also concerned about the potential misuse of information, like the number of Canadians who thought Hitler was a great man, by such people as Nazi propagandists. Although Prime Minister King publicly claimed a disdain for polls, those close to him were advocating the commission of secret polls. Even in the 1970s, then Prime Minister Trudeau publicly claimed no interest in polls, although in reality he avidly used them for political advantage and as a guide in styling himself.

Polls provide us with much useful information, but there has always been concern expressed about who conducts them, how they are conducted, and their potential impact and misuse, among other things. Thus polls and polling are often the subjects of debate. Nonetheless, they are the means by which we may obtain useful information. Learning about sampling and other issues raised in this chapter will help you in your assessment of the information reported by polls as well as other forms of information you read and hear about.

Two Types of Sampling Methods

By 1948, some academic researchers had been experimenting with a form of sampling based on probability theory. This technique involves the selection of a "random sample" from a list containing the names of everyone in the population under study being sampled. By and large, the probability sampling methods used in 1948 were far more accurate than quota sampling techniques.

Today, probability sampling remains the primary method for selecting large, representative samples for social science research, including national political polls. At the same time, many research situations make probability sampling impossible or inappropriate. Therefore, before turning to the logic and techniques of probability sampling, we'll first look at nonprobability sampling techniques and how they're used in social research.

Nonprobability Sampling

Social research is often conducted in situations that don't permit the kinds of probability samples used in large-scale social surveys. Suppose you wanted to study homelessness: There is no list of all homeless individuals, nor are you likely to create such a list. Moreover, as you'll see, there are times when probability sampling wouldn't be appropriate even if it were possible. Many such situations call for *nonprobability sampling*. We'll examine four types in this section: reliance on available subjects, purposive or judgmental sampling, snowball sampling, and quota sampling. We'll conclude with a brief discussion of the use of informants as a technique for gathering information about social groups.

Reliance on Available Subjects

Relying on available subjects, such as stopping people at a street corner or some other location, is an extremely risky sampling method, yet it's used all too frequently. Such a method doesn't allow control over the representativeness of a sample. It's justified only if the researcher wants to study the characteristics of people passing the sampling point at specified times or if less risky sampling methods are not feasible. Even when use of this method is justified on grounds of feasibility,

researchers must exercise great caution in generalizing from their data. Also, they should alert readers to the risks associated with this method.

University researchers frequently conduct surveys among the students enrolled in large lecture classes. The ease and inexpense of such a method explains its popularity, but it seldom produces data of any general value. It may be useful for pretesting a questionnaire, but such a sampling method should not be used for a study purportedly describing students as a whole.

Consider this report on the sampling design of a research study:

> Participants were recruited for a study of sexual thoughts and experiences by way of sign-up sheets, class announcements and advertisements in university residences.
>
> (Renaud and Byers 1999:20)

After all is said and done, what will the results of this study represent? The study consisted of 292 volunteer undergraduate students. They do not provide a meaningful representation of students in Canada or even in their university. Is there anything different about students who are willing to volunteer for studies? We can guess that these students were probably more comfortable with issues of sex than were other students, but we can't say for sure. While such studies can be the source of useful insights, we must take care not to overgeneralize from them. The authors of this study do address the lack of generalizability to the general population, concluding that further research should be conducted using nonstudent samples.

Purposive or Judgmental Sampling

Sometimes it's appropriate for you to select your sample on the basis of your own knowledge of the population and the purpose of the study. This type of sampling is called *purposive* or *judgmental sampling*. In the initial design of a questionnaire, you might wish to select the widest variety of respondents to test the broad applicability of questions. Although the study findings would not represent any meaningful population, the test run might effectively uncover any peculiar defects in your questionnaire. This situation would be considered a pretest, however, rather than a final study.

In some instances, you may wish to study a small subset of a larger population in which many members of the subset are easily identified, but the enumeration of all of them would be nearly impossible. For example, you might want to study the leadership of a student protest movement; many of the leaders are easily visible, but it would not be feasible to define and sample *all* leaders. In studying all or a sample of the most visible leaders, you may collect data sufficient for your purposes.

Or let's say you want to compare left-wing and right-wing students. Because you may not be able to enumerate and sample from all such students, you might decide to sample the memberships of left and right-leaning groups, such as campus organizations of the New Democratic Party and the Conservative Party. Although such a sample design would not provide a good description of either left-wing or right-wing students as a whole, it might suffice for general comparative purposes.

Selecting deviant cases for study is another example of purposive sampling. Field researchers are often particularly interested in studying *deviant cases*—cases that don't fit into the fairly regular patterns, for instance, of attitudes and behaviours—in order to improve their understanding of the more regular pattern. For example, you might gain important insights into the nature of school spirit as exhibited at a pep rally by interviewing people who did not appear to be caught up in the emotions of the crowd or by interviewing students who did not attend the rally at all.

Snowball Sampling

Another nonprobability sampling technique, which some consider to be a form of accidental sampling, is called **snowball sampling**. This procedure is appropriate when the members of a special population are difficult to locate, such as homeless individuals, prostitutes, or undocumented immigrants. In snowball sampling researchers collect data on the few members of the target population they can locate, and then ask those individuals to provide the information needed to locate other members of that population whom they happen to know. *Snowball* refers to the process of accumulation as each located subject suggests other subjects. Because this procedure also results in samples with questionable representativeness, it's used primarily for exploratory purposes.

Suppose you want to learn the pattern of recruitment to a community organization over time, you might begin by interviewing fairly recent recruits, asking them who introduced them to the group. You might then interview the people named, asking them who introduced *them* to the group. You might then interview those people named, asking, in part, who introduced *them*. In studying a loosely structured political group, you might ask one of the participants who he or she believes to be the most influential members of the group. You might interview those people and, in the course of the interviews, ask who *they* believe to be the most influential. In each of these examples, your sample would "snowball" as each of your interviewees suggested others to interview.

Quota Sampling

Quota sampling is the method that helped George Gallup avoid disaster in 1936 but set up the polling disaster of 1948. Like probability sampling, **quota sampling** addresses the issue of representativeness, although the two methods approach the issue quite differently.

Quota sampling begins with a matrix, or table, describing the characteristics of the target population. Depending on your research purposes, you need to know what proportion of the population is male and what proportion female, as well as what proportions of each gender fall into various age categories, educational levels, ethnic groups, and so forth. In establishing a national quota sample, you would need to know what proportion of the national population is urban, eastern, male, under 25, white, working class, and the like, and all the other possible combinations of these attributes.

Once such a matrix is created and a relative proportion assigned to each cell in the matrix, you proceed to collect data from people having all the characteristics of a given cell. You then assign a weight to all the people in a given cell that is appropriate to their portion of the total population. When all the sample elements are so weighted, the overall data should provide a reasonable representation of the total population.

Quota sampling has several inherent problems. First, the *quota frame* (the proportions that different cells represent) must be accurate, and it is often difficult to get up-to-date information for this purpose. The Gallup polling failure in 1948 was partly due to this problem. Second, the selection of sample elements within a given cell may be biased even though its proportion of the population is accurately estimated. Instructed to interview five people who meet a complex set of characteristics, an interviewer might introduce bias in a sample by avoiding people who have particularly run-down homes or who own vicious dogs.

In recent years, attempts have been made to combine probability and quota sampling methods, but the effectiveness of this effort remains to be seen. At present, you would be advised to treat quota sampling warily if your purpose is statistical description.

At the same time, the logic of quota sampling can sometimes be applied usefully to a field research project. In the study of a formal group, for example, you might wish to interview both leaders and nonleaders. In studying a student organization, you might want to interview radical, moderate, and conservative members of that group. You may be able to achieve sufficient representativeness in such cases by using quota sampling to ensure that you interview both men and women, both younger and older people, and so forth.

Selecting Informants

When field research involves the researcher's attempt to understand some social setting—a juvenile gang or local neighbourhood, for example— much of that understanding comes from collaboration with some members of the group being studied. Whereas social researchers speak of *respondents* as people who provide information about themselves, allowing the researcher to construct a composite picture of the group those respondents represent, an ***informant*** is a member of the group who can talk directly about the group.

Especially important to anthropologists, informants can be very helpful to other social researchers as well. If you wanted to learn about informal social networks in a local public housing project, for example, you would do well to locate individuals who could understand what you were looking for and help you find it.

When Young and Craig (1997:179) did a study on Canadian skinhead subculture they discussed the important role of informants in their research.

> Ongoing contact with the group and smooth relations in the field were facilitated through the assistance of three key informants, two of whom were current members, and one who maintained frequent contact with SHARP and neo-Nazi skinheads through his work with an anti-racist organization. All key informants tirelessly addressed our questions and requests for interviews, and provided additional sources of data such as skinhead newspapers, books, magazines and musical tapes.

Usually, you'll want to select informants somewhat typical of the groups you're studying. Otherwise, their observations and opinions may be misleading. Interviewing only physicians will not give you a well-rounded view of how a community medical clinic is working, for example. Along the same lines, an anthropologist who interviews only men in a society where women are sheltered from outsiders will get a biased view.

Simply because they're the ones willing to work with outside investigators, informants will sometimes be somewhat "marginal" or atypical within their group. At times this is obvious. Other times, however, you'll learn about their marginality only in the course of your research. Informants' marginality may not only bias the view you get, but their marginal status may also limit their access (and hence yours) to the different sectors of the community you wish to study.

These comments should give you some sense of the concerns involved in nonprobability sampling. We'll conclude with the following injunction (Lofland and Lofland 1995:16):

> Your overall goal is to collect the *richest possible data*. Rich data mean, ideally, a wide and diverse range of information collected over a relatively

prolonged period of time. Again, ideally, you achieve this through direct, face-to-face contact with, and prolonged immersion in, some social location or circumstance.

Thus, nonprobability samples can be very useful, particularly in qualitative research studies. But care must be taken to acknowledge the limitations of nonprobability sampling, particularly regarding accurate representations of populations. This point will become clearer as we discuss the logic and techniques of probability sampling.

The Theory and Logic of Probability Sampling

While appropriate to some research purposes, nonprobability sampling methods cannot guarantee that the sample we observed is representative of the whole population. When researchers want precise, statistical descriptions of large populations—for example, the percentage of the population who are unemployed, plan to vote for Candidate X, or feel a rape victim should have the right to an abortion—they turn to **probability sampling**. Large-scale surveys, therefore, use probability sampling methods.

The basic logic of probability sampling is not hard to understand even though the application of probability sampling involves some sophisticated use of statistics. If all members of a population were identical in all respects—all demographic characteristics, attitudes, experiences, behaviours, and so on—there would be no need for careful sampling procedures. In this extreme case of homogeneity, in fact, any single case would suffice as a sample to study characteristics of the whole population.

In fact, of course, the human beings who compose real populations are quite heterogeneous, varying in many ways. Figure 7-1 offers a simplified illustration of a heterogeneous population: The 100 members of this small population differ by gender and race. We'll use this hypothetical micropopulation to illustrate various aspects of sampling.

To provide useful descriptions of the total population, a sample of individuals from a population must contain essentially the same variations that exist in the population. This isn't as simple as it might seem, however. Let's take a minute to look at some of the ways researchers might go astray. Then we'll see how probability sampling provides an efficient method for selecting a sample that should adequately reflect variations that exist in the population.

Conscious and Unconscious Sampling Bias

At first glance, it may look as though sampling is pretty straightforward. To select a sample of 100 university students, you might simply interview the first 100 students you find walking around campus. Untrained researchers often use this kind of sampling method, but the risk is very high that biases will be introduced into the samples. *Bias* in connection with sampling simply means that those selected are not typical or representative of the larger populations they have been chosen from—and such bias need not be intentional. This kind of bias is virtually inevitable when you pick people by the seat of your pants.

Figure 7-2 illustrates what can happen when you simply select people who are convenient for study. Although women are only 50 percent of our micropopulation, the group closest to the researcher (in the upper-right corner) happens to be 70 percent women; and although the hypothetical population is 12 percent Aboriginal Canadian, none were selected into the sample.

Beyond the risks inherent in simply studying people who are convenient, other problems can arise. To begin with, researchers' personal leanings may affect the sample to the point where it does not truly represent the target population. Suppose you're a little intimidated by students who look like they might ridicule your research effort. You might consciously or unconsciously avoid interviewing such people. Or, you might feel that the attitudes of "super-straight-looking" students would be irrelevant to your research purposes, and so avoid interviewing them.

Figure 7-1
A Population of 100 Folks

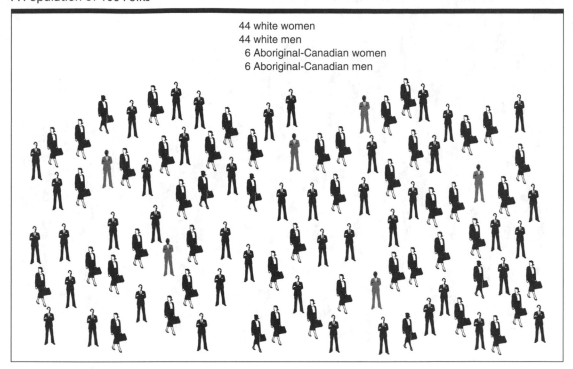

44 white women
44 white men
  6 Aboriginal-Canadian women
  6 Aboriginal-Canadian men

Even if you sought to interview a "balanced" group of students, you wouldn't know the exact proportions of different types of students making up such a balance, and you wouldn't always be able to identify the different types just by watching them walk by. Even if you made a conscientious effort to interview every tenth student entering the university library, for example, you could not be sure of a *representative* sample, because different types of students visit the library with different frequencies. Your sample would overrepresent students who visit the library most often.

Similarly, the "public-opinion call-in polls," in which radio stations or newspapers ask people to call specified telephone numbers to register their opinions, cannot be trusted to represent general populations. At the very least, not everyone in the population will even be aware of the poll. This problem also invalidates polls by magazines and newspapers that publish coupons for readers to complete and mail in. Even among those who are aware of such polls, not all will express an opinion, especially if doing so will cost them a stamp, an envelope, or a telephone charge.

Ironically, the failure of such polls to represent all opinions equally was inadvertently acknowledged by Philip Perinelli (1986), a staff manager of AT&T Communications' DIAL-IT 900 Service, which offers a call-in poll facility to organizations. Perinelli attempted to counter criticisms by saying, "The 50-cent charge assures that only interested parties respond and helps assure also that no individual 'stuffs' the ballot box." But researchers cannot determine general public opinion while considering "only interested parties." This excludes those who don't care 50-cents' worth, as well as those who recognize that such polls are not valid. Both types of people may have opinions and may even vote on election day. Additionally, Perinelli's assertion that the 50-cent charge will prevent ballot stuffing actually means that only those that can afford it will engage in ballot stuffing.

Figure 7-2
A Sample of Convenience: Easy, but Not Representative

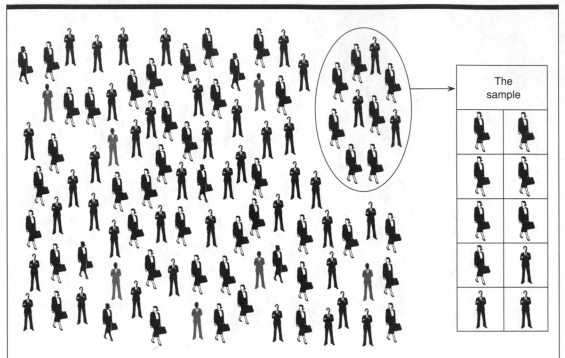

The possibilities for inadvertent sampling bias are endless and not always obvious. Fortunately there are techniques that help us avoid bias.

Representativeness and Probability of Selection

Although the term **representativeness** has no precise, scientific meaning, it carries a common sense meaning that makes it useful here. For our purpose, a sample will be representative of the population from which it is selected if the aggregate characteristics of the sample closely approximate those same aggregate characteristics in the population. For example, if the population contains 50 percent women, then a sample must contain "close to" 50 percent women to be representative. Later, we'll discuss "how close" in detail. Note that samples need not be representative in all respects; representativeness is limited to those characteristics relevant to the substantive interests of the study, however you may not know in advance which are relevant.

A basic principle of probability sampling is that a sample will be representative of the population from which it is selected if all members of the population have an equal chance of being selected in the sample. (We'll see shortly that the size of the sample selected also affects the degree of representativeness.) Samples that have this quality are often labelled **EPSEM** samples (equal probability of selection method). Later we'll discuss variations of this principle, which forms the basis of probability sampling.

Moving beyond this basic principle, we must realize that samples, even carefully selected EPSEM samples, seldom if ever perfectly represent the populations from which they're drawn. Nevertheless, probability sampling offers two special advantages.

First, probability samples, although never perfectly representative, are typically more representative than other types of samples, because the biases previously discussed are avoided. In practice, a probability sample is more likely to be representative of the population from which it is drawn than a nonprobability sample.

Second, and more important, probability theory permits us to estimate the accuracy or representativeness of samples. Conceivably, an uninformed researcher might, through wholly haphazard means, select a sample that nearly perfectly represents the larger population. The odds are against doing so, however, and we would be unable to estimate the likelihood that he or she has achieved representativeness. The probability sampler, on the other hand, can provide an accurate estimate of the probability of how close he or she will come. We'll discuss shortly how to achieve this estimate.

Probability sampling ensures that samples are representative of the population we desire to study, as we've said. Probability sampling is based on the use of a random selection procedure, as you'll see in a moment. To develop this idea, however, we must give more precise meaning to two important terms: element and population.

An **element** is that unit about which information is collected and that provides the basis of analysis. Typically, in survey research, elements are people or certain types of people. However, other kinds of units can constitute the elements for social research: Families, social clubs, or corporations might be the elements of a study. In a given study, elements are often the same as units of analysis, but the former are used in sample selection and the latter in data analysis.

So far we've used the term population to mean the group or collection that we're interested in generalizing about. More technically, a **population** is the theoretically specified aggregation of the elements in a study. Whereas the vague term Canadians might be the target for a study, the delineation of the population would include the definition of the element Canadians (for example, citizenship, residence) and the time referent for the study (Canadians as of when?). Translating the abstract adult Torontonians into a workable population would require a specification of the age defining adult and the boundaries of Toronto. Specifying the term university student would include a consideration of full- and part-time students, degree candidates and nondegree candidates, undergraduate and graduate students, and so forth.

A **study population** is that aggregation of elements from which the sample is actually selected. As a practical matter, researchers are seldom in a position to guarantee that every element meeting the theoretical definitions laid down actually has a chance of being selected in the sample. Even when lists of elements exist for sampling purposes, the lists are usually somewhat incomplete. Some students are always inadvertently omitted from student rosters. Some telephone subscribers request that their names and numbers be unlisted.

Often, researchers decide to limit their study populations more severely than indicated in the preceding examples. National polling firms and other organizations may limit their national samples to the 10 provinces, omitting the Territories for practical reasons. This is done, for example, by Statistics Canada in conducting the General Social Survey. A researcher wishing to sample psychology professors may limit the study population to those in psychology departments, omitting those in other departments. Such redefinitions of the population under examination must be made clear to readers.

Random Selection

The ultimate purpose of sampling is to select a set of elements from a population in such a way that descriptions of those elements (statistics) accurately portray the parameters of the total population from which the elements are selected. Probability sampling enhances the likelihood of accomplishing this aim and also provides methods for estimating the degree of probable success.

Random selection is the key to this process. In random selection, each element has an equal chance of selection independent of any other event in the selection process. Flipping a perfect coin (one that doesn't have a bias in terms of coming up heads or tails) is the most frequently cited example: The "selection" of a head or a tail is independent of previous selections of heads or tails. It doesn't matter how many tails turn up in a row, the chance that the next flip will produce "tails" is exactly 50-50. Rolling a perfect set of dice is another example. Such images of random selection are useful but seldom apply directly to sampling methods in social research. Social researchers more typically use tables of random numbers or computer programs that provide a random selection of sampling units. A *sampling unit* is that element or set of elements considered for selection in some stage of sampling.

In Chapter 9 on survey research, we'll see how computers are used to select random telephone numbers for interviewing called *random-digit dialling*.

The reasons for using random selection methods are twofold. First, this procedure serves as a check on conscious or unconscious bias on the part of the researcher. The researcher who selects cases on an intuitive basis might very well select cases that would support his or her research expectations or hypotheses. Random selection erases this danger. More important, random selection offers access to the body of probability theory, which provides the basis for estimating the characteristics of the population as well as estimates of the accuracy of samples. Let's now examine probability theory in greater detail.

Probability Theory, Sampling Distributions, and Estimates of Sampling Error

Probability theory is a branch of mathematics that provides the tools researchers need to devise sampling techniques that produce representative samples and to statistically analyze results derived from such samples. More formally, probability theory provides the basis for estimating the parameters of a population. A *parameter* is the summary description of a given variable in a population. The mean income of all families in a city is a parameter; so is the age distribution of the city's population. When researchers generalize from a sample, they're using sample observations to estimate population parameters. Probability theory enables them to both make these estimates and to judge how likely the estimates will accurately represent the actual parameters in the population. So, for example, probability theory allows researchers to infer from a sample of 2,000 voters how a population of 30 million voters is likely to vote, and to specify exactly the probable margin of error in the estimates.

Probability theory accomplishes this by way of the concept of sampling distributions. A single sample selected from a population will give an estimate of the population parameter. Other samples would give the same or slightly different estimates. Probability theory tells us about the distribution of estimates that would be produced by a large number of such samples.

Let's look at two examples of sampling distributions to see how this works.

The Sampling Distribution of 10 Cases We'll begin with a simple example of a population of only 10 cases.[1] Suppose there are 10 people in a group, and each has a certain amount of money in his or her pocket. To simplify, let's assume that one person has no money, another has $1, another has $2, and so forth up to the person with $9. Figure 7-3 presents the population of 10 people.

Our task is to determine the average amount of money in this population: specifically, the mean number of dollars. If you simply add up the money shown in Figure 7-3, you'll find that the total is $45, so the true mean is $4.50. Our purpose in the rest of this exercise is to estimate that mean without actually observing all 10 individuals. We'll do that by selecting random samples from the population and using the means of those samples to estimate the mean of the whole population.

To start, suppose we were to select—at random—a sample of only *one* person from the 10. Our 10 possible samples thus consist of the 10 cases

1 We thank Hanan Selvin for suggesting this method of introducing probability sampling.

Figure 7-3
A Population of 10 People with $0–$9

shown in Figure 7-3. The 10 dots shown on the graph in Figure 7-4 represent these 10 samples. Since we're taking samples of only one, they also represent the "means" we would get as estimates of the population. The distribution of the dots on the graph is called the *sampling distribution.* Clearly, depending on which person we select, we'll estimate the group's mean as anywhere from $0 to $9. Obviously, it isn't a very good idea to select a sample of only one, since we'll stand a very good chance of missing the true mean of $4.50 by quite a bit.

But what if we take samples of two? As Figure 7-5 shows, increasing the sample size improves our estimations. There are now 45 possible samples: [$0 $1], [$0 $2], . . . [$7 $8], [$8 $9]. Moreover, some of those samples produce the same means. For example, [$0 $6], [$1 $5], and [$2 $4] all produce means of $3. In Figure 7-5, the three dots shown above the $3 mean represent those three samples.

In addition, the 45 sample means are not evenly distributed, as they were when the sample size was one. Rather, they are somewhat clustered around the true value of $4.50. Only two possible samples deviate by as much as $4 from the true value ([$0

$1] and [$8 $9]), whereas five of the samples would give the true estimate of $4.50; another eight samples miss the mark by only 50 cents (plus or minus).

Now suppose we select even larger samples. What do you suppose that will do to our estimates of the mean? Figure 7-6 presents the sampling distributions of samples of 3, 4, 5, and 6. The progression of sampling distributions is clear. Every increase in sample size improves the distribution of estimates of the mean. The limiting case in this example, of course, is to select a sample of 10. There would be only one possible sample (everyone) and it would give us the true mean of $4.50.

Sampling Distributions and Estimates of Sampling Error Let's turn now to a more realistic sampling situation and see how the notion of sampling distribution applies. Assume we want to study the student population of Noname University (NU) to determine approval or disapproval of a student conduct code proposed by the administration. The study population will be that aggregation of, say, 20,000 students contained in a student roster. The elements will be the individual students at NU.

Figure 7-4
The Sampling Distribution of Samples of 1

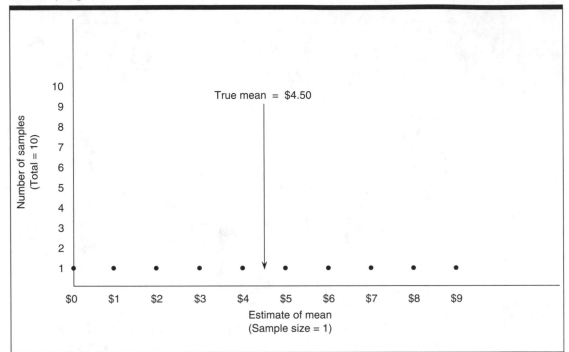

Figure 7-5
The Sampling Distribution of Samples of 2

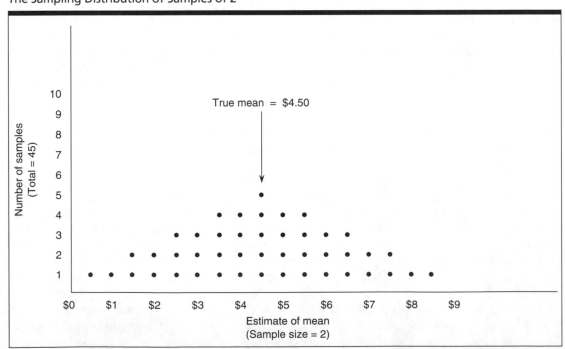

Figure 7-6
The Sampling Distribution of Samples of 3, 4, 5, and 6

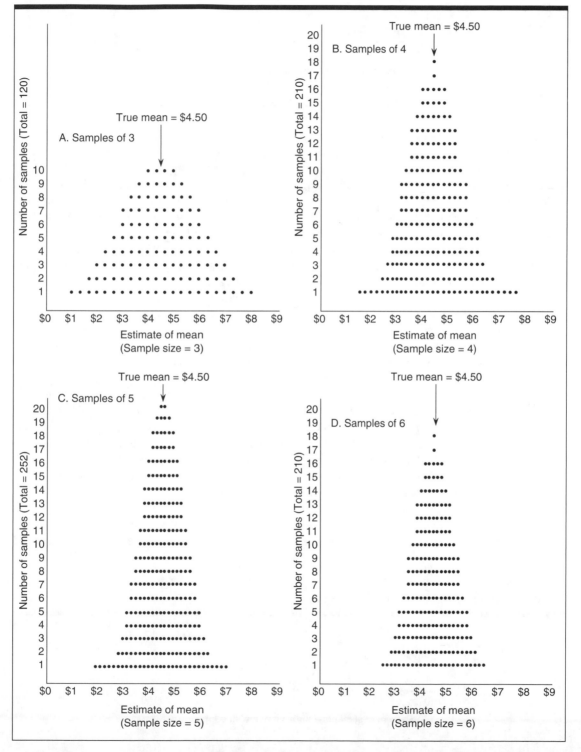

Figure 7-7
Range of Possible Sample Study Results

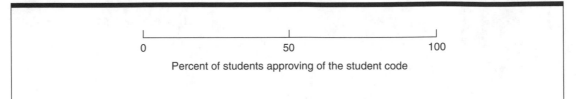

Percent of students approving of the student code

We'll select a random sample of, say, 100 students for the purposes of estimating the entire student body. The variable under consideration will be *attitudes toward the code,* a binomial (or dichotomous) variable—that is, a variable composed of two attributes: *approve* and *disapprove.* The logic of probability sampling applies to the examination of other types of variables, such as mean income, but the computations are somewhat more complicated. Consequently, this introduction focuses on binomials.

The horizontal axis of Figure 7-7 presents all *possible* values of the parameter we want to estimate in the population, from 0 percent to 100 percent approval. The midpoint of the axis, 50 percent, represents half the students approving of the code and the other half disapproving.

To choose our sample, we give each student on the student roster a number and select 100 random numbers from a table of random numbers. Then we interview the 100 students whose numbers have been selected and ask for their attitudes toward the student code: whether they approve or disapprove. Suppose this operation gives us 48 students who approve of the code and 52 who disapprove. This summary description of a variable in a sample is called a **statistic**. We present this statistic by placing a dot on the *x* axis at the point representing 48 percent.

Now let's suppose we select another sample of 100 students in exactly the same fashion and measure their approval or disapproval of the student code. Perhaps 51 students in the second sample approve of the code. We place another dot in the appropriate place on the *x* axis. Repeating this process once more, we may discover that 52 students in the third sample approve of the code.

Figure 7-8 presents the three different sample statistics representing the percentages of students in each of the three random samples who approved of the student code. The basic rule of random sampling is that such samples drawn from a population give estimates of the parameter that exists in the total population. Each of the random samples, then, gives us an estimate of the percentage of students in the total student body who approve of the student code. Unhappily, however, we have selected three samples and now have three separate estimates.

To retrieve ourselves from this problem, let's draw more and more samples of 100 students each, question each of the samples concerning

Figure 7-8
Results Produced by Three Hypothetical Studies

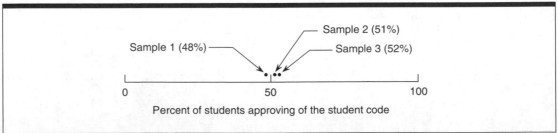

Percent of students approving of the student code

Figure 7-9
The Sampling Distribution

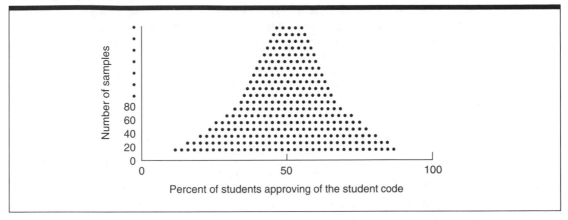

their approval or disapproval of the code, and plot the new sample statistics on our summary graph. In drawing many such samples, we discover that some of the new samples provide duplicate estimates, as in the illustration of 10 cases. Figure 7-9 shows the sampling distribution of, say, hundreds of samples. This U-shaped distribution is often referred to as a *normal curve*.

Note that by increasing the number of samples selected and interviewed, we have also increased the range of estimates provided by the sampling operation. In one sense we have increased our dilemma in attempting to guess the parameter in the population. Probability theory, however, provides certain important rules regarding the sampling distribution presented in Figure 7-9.

First, if many independent random samples are selected from a population, the sample statistics provided by those samples will be *distributed around the population parameter* in a known way. Thus, although Figure 7-9 shows a wide range of estimates, more of them are in the vicinity of 50 percent than elsewhere in the graph. Probability theory tells us, then, that the true value is in the vicinity of 50 percent.

Second, probability theory gives us a formula for estimating *how closely* the sample statistics are clustered around the true value. In other words, probability theory enables us to estimate the **sampling error**—the degree of error to be expected for a given sample design. This formula contains three

factors: the parameter, the sample size, and the *standard error* (a measure of sampling error):

$$s = \sqrt{\frac{P \times Q}{n}}$$

The symbols P and Q in the formula equal the population parameters for the binomial: If 60 percent of the student body approve of the code and 40 percent disapprove, P and Q are 60 percent and 40 percent, respectively, or .6 and .4. Note that $Q = 1 - P$ and $P = 1 - Q$. The symbol n equals the number of cases in each sample, and s is the standard error.

Let's assume that the actual population parameter is 50 percent approving of the code and 50 percent disapproving. Recall that we've been selecting samples of 100 cases each. When these numbers are put into the formula, we find that the standard error equals .05, or 5 percent.

In probability theory, the standard error is a valuable piece of information because it indicates how tightly the sample estimates will be distributed around the population parameter. If you are familiar with the *standard deviation* in statistics, you may recognize that the standard error, in this case, is the standard deviation of the sampling distribution.

Specifically, probability theory indicates that certain proportions of the sample estimates will fall within specified increments—each equal to one standard error—from the population parameter.

Approximately 34 percent (.3413) of the sample estimates will fall within one standard error increment above the population parameter, and another 34 percent will fall within one standard error below the parameter. In our example, the standard error increment is 5 percent, so we know that 34 percent of our samples will give estimates of student approval between 50 percent (the parameter) and 55 percent (one standard error above); another 34 percent of the samples will give estimates between 50 percent and 45 percent (one standard error below the parameter). Taken together, then, we know that roughly two-thirds (68 percent) of the samples will give estimates within plus or minus 5 percent of the parameter.

Moreover, probability theory dictates that roughly 95 percent of the samples will fall within plus or minus two standard errors of the true value, and 99.9 percent of the samples will fall within plus or minus three standard errors. In our present example, then, we know that only one sample out of a thousand would give an estimate lower than 35 percent approval or higher than 65 percent.

The proportion of samples falling within one, two, or three standard errors of the parameter is constant for any random sampling procedure such as the one just described. The size of the standard error in any given case, however, is a function of the population parameter and the sample size. If we return to the formula for a moment, we note that the standard error will increase as a function of an increase in the quantity P times Q. Note further that this quantity reaches its maximum in the situation of an even split in the population. If $P = .5$, $PQ = .25$; if $P = .6$, $PQ = .24$; if $P = .8$, $PQ = .16$; if $P = .99$, $PQ = .0099$. By extension, if P is either 0.0 or 1.0 (either 0 percent or 100 percent approve of the student code), the standard error will be 0. That is, if everyone in the population has the same attitude (no variation), then every sample will give exactly that estimate.

The standard error is also a function of the sample size—an *inverse* function. As the sample size increases, the standard error decreases. In other words, as the sample size increases, the several samples will be clustered nearer to the true value. Another general guideline is evident in the formula: Because of the square root, the standard error is reduced by half if the sample size is *quadrupled*. In our present example, samples of 100 produce a standard error of 5 percent; to reduce the standard error to 2.5 percent, we must increase the sample size to 400.

All of this information is provided by established probability theory in reference to the selection of large numbers of random samples. (If you've taken a statistics course, you may know this as the "Central Limit Theorem.") If the population parameter is known and many random samples are selected, we can predict how many of the samples will fall within specified intervals from the parameter. Recognize that this discussion only illustrates the *logic* of probability sampling; it does not describe the way research is actually conducted. Usually, we don't know the parameter: The reason we conduct a sample survey is to estimate that value. Moreover, we don't actually select large numbers of samples: We select only one sample. Nevertheless, the preceding discussion of probability theory provides the basis for inferences about the typical social research situation. Knowing what it would be like to select thousands of samples allows us to make assumptions about the one sample we do select and study.

Confidence Levels and Confidence Intervals
Whereas probability theory specifies that 68 percent of that fictitious large number of samples would produce estimates falling within one standard error of the parameter, we can turn the logic around and infer that any single random sample has a 68-percent chance of falling within that range. This observation leads us to the two key components of sampling error estimates, **confidence level** and **confidence interval**. We express the accuracy of our sample statistics in terms of a *level of confidence* that the statistics fall within a specified interval from the parameter. For example, we may say we are confident that in 95 percent of samples, sample statistics (such as 50 percent favour the new student code) are within plus or minus two standard errors of the population parameter. As the confidence interval is expanded for a given statistic, the confidence level increases.

For example, we may say we are confident that in 99.9 percent of samples, estimates from samples (i.e., statistics) will fall within plus or minus three standard errors of the true value.

Although we may use confidence intervals to express the ranges of accuracy for the parameter, we've already noted that we seldom know what the parameter actually is. But, the formula for estimating sampling error requires that we specify some value for the parameter. To resolve this problem in the case of the binomial, we substitute our sample estimate for the parameter in the formula; that is, lacking the true value, we substitute the best available guess.

The result of these inferences and estimations is that we can estimate a population parameter and also the expected degree of error on the basis of one sample drawn from a population. Beginning with the question, "What percentage of the student body approves of the student code?" you could select a random sample of 100 students and interview them. You might then report that your best estimate is that 50 percent of the student body approves of the code and that the theory of random samples assures us that the range of 40 percent to 60 percent (plus or minus two standard errors) would contain the true value in 95 percent of samples. The range from 40 to 60 percent is the *confidence interval.* (At the 68 percent confidence level, the confidence interval would be 45 to 55 percent.)

The logic of confidence levels and confidence intervals also provides the basis for determining the appropriate sample size for a study. Once you've decided on the degree of sampling error you can tolerate, you'll be able to calculate the number of cases needed in your sample. For example, to achieve an accuracy of plus or minus 5 percent, with confidence of 95 percent, you should select a sample of at least 400. (Appendix E is a convenient guide in this regard.)

This then is the basic logic of probability sampling. Random selection permits the researcher to link findings from a sample to the body of probability theory so as to estimate the accuracy of those findings. All statements of accuracy in sampling must specify both a confidence level and a confidence interval.

Here's what *The Globe and Mail* (2001:1) had to say about a poll concerning Canadian support for the death penalty ("Support for death penalty plunges") conducted by Ipsos-Reid:

> The poll of 1,000 randomly selected adults was conducted Jan. 22–25. The results are considered accurate within 3.1 percentage points, 19 times out of 20.

And here is what *Maclean's* magazine (Dec. 25, 2000–Jan. 1, 2001:52) had to say about their 17th year-end poll conducted by The Strategic Counsel:

> The results are drawn from telephone interviews with 1,400 adult Canadians between Nov. 7 and 12, in the midst of the federal election campaign. Respondents were selected randomly from all 10 provinces, including a disproportionate number from the smaller ones to bring the minimum sample from each up to a statistically meaningful level. National results are considered accurate to within 3.1 percentage points, 19 times out of 20. Accuracy ranges are wider for results from individual provinces, regions or other subgroups.

The *New York Times* presented a seven paragraph description "How Poll Was Done" (1999:A14) when reporting on the American public's perceptions of the U.S. Senate. They tell the reader that it was a telephone interview survey, when it was conducted, how many people were interviewed, what the sampling frame was, how the sample was selected, how the sample was weighted to account for household size, number of residence phone lines, and to adjust for other variations in the sample such as geographic region, sex, race, and education. They then state that

> In theory, in 19 cases out of 20 the results based on such samples will differ by no more than three percentage points in either direction from what would have been obtained by seeking out all American adults.

They go on to report: "For smaller sub-groups the margin of sampling error is larger. For example, for self-identified Republicans it is plus or minus six percentage points." They even inform the reader about potential sources of error other than sampling error: "Variations in the wording and order of questions, for example, may lead to somewhat different results."

Frequently the media is somewhat casual in providing the details about how the polls they are reporting on were conducted. This has been changing somewhat in the recent past as the *New York Times'* example illustrates. It is essential to report results of polls such that readers are provided with enough information to evaluate the findings presented. In addition, technically the reported confidence in the statistics presented is "In theory...for such samples," or "For samples of this size" and this should somehow be indicated.

When you read statements about polls in the popular media, be warned that such statements are sometimes made when they are not warranted. Be especially wary of survey or poll results that fail to indicate confidence levels and confidence intervals. Without these specifications, the "findings" are of dubious value. Overall, the more information communicated about how the study was conducted, the better able you are to determine if the claims made are warranted.

Before we conclude this discussion, there are two more cautionary notes. First, the survey uses of probability theory as discussed in this section are technically not wholly justified. The theory of sampling distribution makes assumptions that almost never apply in survey conditions. The exact proportions of samples contained within specified increments of standard errors, for example, mathematically assumes an infinitely large population, an infinite number of samples, and sampling with replacement (that is, every sampling unit selected is then put back such that it could be selected again). Second, the inferential jump from the distribution of several samples to the probable characteristics of one sample has been oversimplified in our discussion.

These cautions are offered to give you perspective on the uses of probability theory in sampling. Social researchers often appear to overestimate the precision of estimates produced by using probability theory. As we'll mention elsewhere in this chapter and throughout the book, variations in sampling techniques and nonsampling factors may

further reduce the legitimacy of such estimates. For instance, those selected in a sample who do not participate further detract from the sample's representativeness. Nevertheless, the calculations discussed in this section can be extremely valuable to you in understanding and evaluating your data. Although the calculations do not provide estimates as precisely as some researchers might assume, they can be quite valid for practical purposes. They are unquestionably more valid than less rigorously derived estimates based on less rigorous sampling methods. Most important, being familiar with the basic *logic* underlying the calculations can help you react sensibly to your own data and to those reported by others.

Populations and Sampling Frames

The preceding section has introduced the theoretical model for social research sampling. Although as research consumers, students, and researchers we need to understand that theory, it is no less important to appreciate the less-than-perfect conditions that exist in the field. The present section discusses one aspect of field conditions that requires a compromise with idealized theoretical conditions and assumptions; the congruence of, or disparity between, populations and sampling frames.

Simply put, a **sampling frame** is the list or quasi list of elements from which a probability sample is selected. If a sample of students is selected from a student roster, the roster is the sampling frame. If the primary sampling unit for a complex population sample is the census block, the list of census blocks composes the sampling frame—in the form of a printed booklet, a magnetic tape file, or some other computerized record. Here are some reports of sampling frames appearing in research journals, with the actual sampling frames italicized in each:

The sample used in that study was drawn from the *Directory of the Korean Society of Toronto*.... First a simple random sample of households was drawn and then one adult from each household was randomly selected.

(Noh and Avison 1996:196)

A random cluster sample was chosen by grade and home room from *class lists submitted by the principals of the three [Ontario] high schools.*

(Feldman et al. 1997:199)

The sampling frame for the survey was the municipal assessment lists maintained, largely for property taxation purposes, by the various regional governments within the Grand River watershed. The sampling involved clustered selections of households....

(Warriner et al. 1996:547)

Properly drawn samples provide information appropriate for describing the population of elements composing the sampling frame—nothing more. We emphasize this point in view of the all-too-common tendency for researchers to select samples from a given sampling frame and then make assertions about a population that is similar but not identical to, the population defined by the sampling frame.

For example, take a look at this report, which discusses the drugs most frequently prescribed by U.S. physicians:

Information on prescription drug sales is not easy to obtain. But Rinaldo V. DeNuzzo, a professor of pharmacy at the Albany College of Pharmacy, Union University, Albany, NY, has been tracking prescription drug sales for 25 years by polling nearby drugstores. He publishes the results in an industry trade magazine, *MM&M.*

DeNuzzo's latest survey, covering 1980, is based on reports from 66 pharmacies in 48 communities in New York and New Jersey. Unless there is something peculiar about that part of the country, his findings can be taken as representative of what happens across the country.

(Moskowitz 1981:33)

What's striking in the excerpt is the casual comment about whether there is anything peculiar about New York and New Jersey. There is. The lifestyle in these two states hardly typifies the other 48. We cannot assume that residents in these large, urbanized, Eastern seaboard states necessarily have the same drug-use patterns as residents of Mississippi or Nebraska.

Does the survey even represent prescription patterns in New York and New Jersey? To determine that, we would have to know something about the way the 48 communities and the 66 pharmacies were selected. We should be wary in this regard, in view of the reference to "polling nearby drugstores." As we'll see, there are several methods for selecting samples that ensure representativeness, and unless they're used, we shouldn't generalize from the study findings.

A sampling frame, then, must be consonant with the population we wish to study. In the simplest design, the sampling frame is a list of the elements composing the study population. In practice, though, existing sampling frames often define the study population rather than the other way around. That is, we often begin with a population in mind for our study; then we search for possible sampling frames. The frames available for our use are examined and evaluated, and we decide which frame presents a study population most appropriate to our needs.

Studies of organizations are often the simplest from a sampling standpoint because organizations typically have membership lists. In such cases, the list of members constitutes an excellent sampling frame. If a random sample is selected from a membership list, the data collected from that sample may be taken as representative of all members—if all members are included in the list.

Populations that can be sampled from good organizational lists include elementary school, high school, and university students and faculty; factory workers; fraternity or sorority members; members of social, service, or political clubs; and members of professional associations.

The preceding comments apply primarily to local organizations. Often province-wide or national organizations do not have a single membership list. There is, for example, no single list of high school students. However, a slightly more complex sample design could take advantage of local high school student lists by first sampling high schools and then subsampling the student lists of those schools selected. (More about that later.)

Other lists of individuals can be relevant to the research needs of a particular study. Government agencies maintain lists of registered voters, for example, that might be used to conduct a preelection poll or an in-depth examination of voting behaviour, but the researcher would have to be satisfied that the list is up-to-date. Similar lists contain the names of automobile owners, welfare recipients, taxpayers, business permit holders, licensed professionals, and so forth. Although it may be difficult to gain access to some of these lists, they provide excellent sampling frames for specialized research purposes.

Realizing that the sampling elements in a study need not be individual persons, we may note that the lists of other types of elements also exist: universities, businesses of various types, cities, academic journals, newspapers, unions, professional associations, and so forth.

Telephone directories are frequently used for "quick and dirty" public opinion polls. Undeniably they're easy and inexpensive to use—no doubt the reason for their popularity. And, if you want to make assertions about telephone subscribers, the directory is a fairly good sampling frame. (Realize, of course, that a given directory will not include new subscribers or those who have requested unlisted numbers. Sampling is further complicated by the directories' inclusion of nonresidential listings.) Unfortunately, telephone directories are all too often used as a listing of a city's population. Of the many defects in this reasoning, the chief one involves a social-class bias. Poor people are less likely to have telephones; rich people may have more than one line. A telephone directory sample, therefore, is likely to have a middle- or upper-class bias.

Street directories and tax maps are often used for easy samples of households, but they may also suffer from incompleteness and possible bias. For example, in strictly zoned urban regions, illegal housing units are unlikely to appear on official records. As a result, such units could not be selected, and sample findings could not be representative of those units, which are often poorer and more overcrowded than the average.

Though most of these comments apply to Canada and the United States, the situation is different in some other countries. In Japan, for example, the government maintains quite accurate population registration lists. Moreover, citizens are required by law to keep their information up-to-date, such as changes in residence or births and deaths in the household. As a consequence, you can select simple random samples of the Japanese population more easily.

Types of Sampling Designs

Up to this point, we've focused on simple random sampling (SRS). And, indeed, the body of statistics typically used by social researchers assumes such a sample. As you'll see shortly, however, researchers have several options in choosing a sampling method, and they seldom if ever choose simple random sampling. There are two reasons for this. First, with all but the simplest sampling frame, simple random sampling is not feasible. Second, and probably surprisingly, simple random sampling may not be the most accurate method available. Let's turn now to a discussion of simple random sampling and the other options available.

Simple Random Sampling

As noted, **simple random sampling** is the basic sampling method assumed in the statistical computations of social research. Because the mathematics of random sampling are especially complex, we'll detour around them in favour of describing the ways of employing this method in the field.

Once a sampling frame has been properly established, to use simple random sampling the researcher assigns a single number to each element in the list, not skipping any number in the process. A table of random numbers (Appendix B) is then used to select elements for the sample. The box entitled "Using a Table of Random Numbers" explains its use.

If your sampling frame is in a machine-readable form, such as computer disk or magnetic tape, a simple random sample can be selected automatically by computer. (In effect, the computer program numbers the elements in the sampling frame, generates its own series of random numbers, and prints out the list of elements selected.)

Figure 7-10 offers a graphic illustration of simple random sampling. Note that the members of our hypothetical micropopulation have been numbered from 1 to 100. Moving to Appendix B, we decide to use the last two digits of the first column and to begin with the third number from the top. This yields person number 30 as the first

one selected into the sample. Number 67 is next, and so forth. (Person 100 would have been selected if "00" had come up in the list.)

Systematic Sampling

Simple random sampling is seldom used in practice. As you'll see, it's not usually the most efficient method, and it can be labourious if done manually. SRS typically requires a list of elements. When such a list is available, researchers often employ systematic sampling instead.

Figure 7-10
A Simple Random Sample

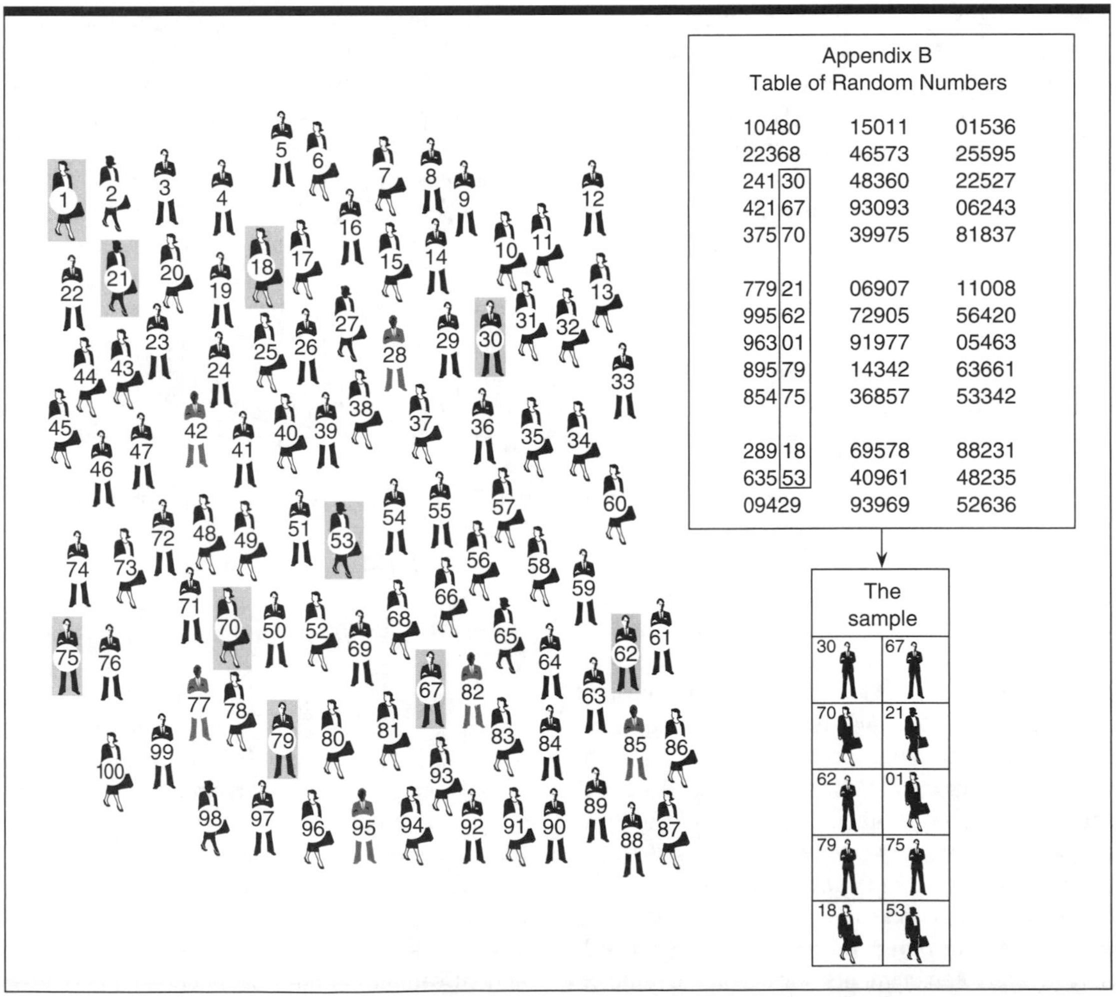

Appendix B Table of Random Numbers		
10480	15011	01536
22368	46573	25595
241[30]	48360	22527
421[67]	93093	06243
375[70]	39975	81837
779[21]	06907	11008
995[62]	72905	56420
963[01]	91977	05463
895[79]	14342	63661
854[75]	36857	53342
289[18]	69578	88231
635[53]	40961	48235
09429	93969	52636

The sample: 30, 67, 70, 21, 62, 01, 79, 75, 18, 53

Using a Table of Random Numbers

In social research, it's often appropriate to select a set of random numbers from a table such as the one in Appendix B. Here's how to do it.

Suppose you want to select a simple random sample of 100 people (or other units) out of a population totalling 980.

1. To begin, number the members of the population: in this case, from 1 to 980. Now the problem is to select 100 random numbers. Once you've done that, your sample will consist of the people having the numbers you've selected. (Note: It's not essential to actually number them, as long as you're sure of the total. If you have them in a list, for example, you can always count through the list after you've selected the numbers.)
2. The next step is to determine the number of digits you'll need in the random numbers you select. In our example, there are 980 members of the population, so you'll need three-digit numbers to give everyone a chance of selection. (If there were 11,825 members of the population, you'd need to select five-digit

numbers.) Thus, we want to select 100 random numbers in the range from 001 to 980.
3. Now turn to the first page of Appendix B. Notice there are several rows and columns of five-digit numbers, and there are several pages. The table represents a series of random numbers in the range from 00001 to 99999. To use the table for your hypothetical sample, you have to answer these questions:
    a   How will you create three-digit numbers out of five-digit numbers?
    b. What pattern will you follow in moving through the table to select your numbers?
    c. Where will you start?
    Each of these questions has several satisfactory answers. The key is to create a plan and follow it. Here's an example.
4. To create three-digit numbers from five-digit numbers, let's agree to select five-digit numbers from the table but consider only the leftmost three digits in each case. If we picked the first number on the first page, 10480, we would only consider the 104. (We could agree to take the digits furthest to the right, 480, or the middle three digits, 048, and any of these plans

In **systematic sampling,** every kth element in the total list is chosen (systematically) for inclusion in the sample. If the list contains 10,000 elements and you want a sample of 1,000, you select every tenth element for your sample. To ensure against any possible human bias in using this method, you should select the first element at random. Thus, in the preceding example, you would begin by selecting a random number between 1 and 10. The element having that number is included in the sample, plus every tenth element following it. This method is technically referred to as a *systematic sample with a random start.* Two terms are frequently used in connection with systematic sampling. The **sampling interval** is the standard distance between elements selected in the sample:

10 in the preceding sample. The **sampling ratio** is the proportion of elements in the population that are selected: 1/10 in the example.

$$\text{sampling interval} = \frac{\text{population size}}{\text{sample size}}$$

$$\text{sampling ratio} = \frac{\text{sample size}}{\text{population size}}$$

In practice, systematic sampling is virtually identical to simple random sampling. If the list of elements is indeed randomized before sampling, one might argue that a systematic sample drawn from that list is in fact a simple random sample. By now, debates over the relative merits of simple random sampling and systematic sampling have would work.) The key is to make a plan and stick with it. For convenience, let's use the leftmost three digits.

5. We can also choose to progress through the tables any way we want: down the columns, up them, across to the right or to the left, or diagonally. Again, any of these plans will work just fine as long as we stick to it. For convenience, let's agree to move down the columns. When we get to the bottom of one column, we'll go to the top of the next; when we exhaust a given page, we'll start at the top of the first column of the next page.

6. Now, where do we start? You can close your eyes and stick a pencil into the table and start wherever the pencil point lands. (We know it doesn't sound scientific, but it works.) Or, if you're afraid you'll hurt the book or miss it altogether, close your eyes and make up a column number and a row number. ("We'll pick the number in the fifth row of column 2.") Start with that number.

7. Let's suppose we decide to start with the fifth number in column 2. If you look on the first page of Appendix B, you'll see that the starting number is 39975. We've selected 399 as our first random number, and we have 99 more to go. Moving down the second column, we select 069, 729, 919, 143, 368, 695, 409, 939, and so forth. At the bottom of column 2, we select number 104 and continue to the top of column 3: 015, 255, and so on.

8. See how easy it is? But trouble lies ahead. When we reach column 5, we're speeding along, selecting 816, 309, 763, 078, 061, 277, 988 . . . Wait a minute! There are only 980 students in the senior class. How can we pick number 988? The solution is simple: Ignore it. Any time you come across a number that lies outside your range, skip it and continue on your way: 188, 174, and so forth. The same solution applies if the same number comes up more than once. If you select 399 again, for example, just ignore it the second time.

9. That's it. You keep up the procedure until you've selected 100 random numbers. Returning to your list, your sample consists of person number 399, person number 69, person number 729, and so forth.

been resolved largely in favour of the latter, simpler method. Empirically, the results are virtually identical. And, as you'll see in a later section, systematic sampling, in some instances, is slightly more accurate than simple random sampling.

There is one danger involved in systematic sampling. The arrangement of elements in the list can make systematic sampling unwise. Such an arrangement is usually called *periodicity.* If the list of elements is arranged in a cyclical pattern that coincides with the sampling interval, a grossly biased sample may be drawn. For example, suppose we select a sample of apartments in an apartment building. If the sample is drawn from a list of apartments arranged in numerical order (for example, 101, 102, 103, 104, 201, 202, and so on), there is a danger of the sampling interval coinciding with the number of apartments on a floor or some multiple thereof. Then the samples might include only northwest-corner apartments or only apartments near the elevator. If these types of apartments have some other particular characteristic in common (for example, higher rent), the sample will be biased. The same danger would appear in a systematic sample of houses in a subdivision arranged with the same number of houses on a block.

In considering a systematic sample from a list, then, you should carefully examine the nature of that list. If the elements are arranged in any particular order, you should figure out whether that order will bias the sample to be selected and take steps to counteract any possible bias (for example, take a simple random sample from cyclical portions).

Usually, however, systematic sampling is superior to simple random sampling, in convenience if nothing else. Problems in the ordering of elements in the sampling frame can usually be remedied quite easily.

Stratified Sampling

We have so far discussed two methods of sample selection from a list: random and systematic. **Stratification** is not an alternative to these methods; rather, it represents a possible modification in their use.

Simple random sampling and systematic sampling both insure a degree of representativeness and permit an estimate of the error present. Stratified sampling is a method for obtaining a greater degree of representativeness—decreasing the probable sampling error. To understand this method, we must return briefly to the basic theory of sampling distribution.

Recall that sampling error is reduced by two factors in the sample design. First, a large sample produces a smaller sampling error than a small sample. Second, a homogeneous population produces samples with smaller sampling errors than does a heterogeneous population. If 99 percent of the population agrees with a certain statement, it's extremely unlikely that any probability sample will greatly misrepresent the extent of agreement. If the population is split 50-50 on the statement, then the sampling error will be much greater.

Stratified sampling is based on this second factor in sampling theory. Rather than selecting a sample from the total population at large, the researcher ensures that appropriate numbers of elements are drawn from homogeneous subsets of that population. To get a stratified sample of university students, for example, you would first organize your population by university class and then draw appropriate numbers of first-, second-, third-, and fourth-year students. In a nonstratified sample, representation by class would be subjected to the same sampling error as other variables. In a sample stratified by class, the sampling error on this variable is reduced to zero.

More complex stratification methods are possible. In addition to stratifying by class, you might also stratify by gender, by grade point average (GPA), and so forth. In this fashion you might be able to ensure that your sample will contain the proper numbers of second-year male students with a 3.0 average, second-year female students with a 4.0 average, and so forth.

The ultimate function of stratification, then, is to organize the population into homogeneous subsets (with heterogeneity between subsets) and to select the appropriate number of elements from each. To the extent that the subsets are homogeneous on the stratification variables, they may be homogeneous on other variables as well. Because *age* is related to *university class,* a sample stratified by class will be more representative in terms of age as well. To the extent that occupational aspirations are still related to gender, a sample stratified by gender will be more representative in terms of occupational aspirations.

The choice of stratification variables typically depends on what variables are available. Gender can often be determined in a list of names. University lists are typically arranged by class. Lists of faculty members may indicate their departmental affiliation. Government agency files may be arranged by geographical region.

In selecting stratification variables from among those available, however, you should be concerned primarily with those that are presumably related to variables you want to represent accurately. Because gender is related to many variables and is often available for stratification, it is often used. Education is related to many variables, but it is often not available for stratification. Geographical location within a city, province, or nation is related to many things. Within a city, stratification by geographical location usually increases representativeness in social class, ethnic group, and so forth. Within a nation, it increases representativeness in a broad range of attitudes as well as in social class and ethnicity.

When you're working with a simple list of all elements in the population, two methods of stratification predominate. In one method, you sort the population elements into discrete groups based on whatever stratification variables are being used.

Figure 7-11
A Stratified, Systematic Sample with a Random Start

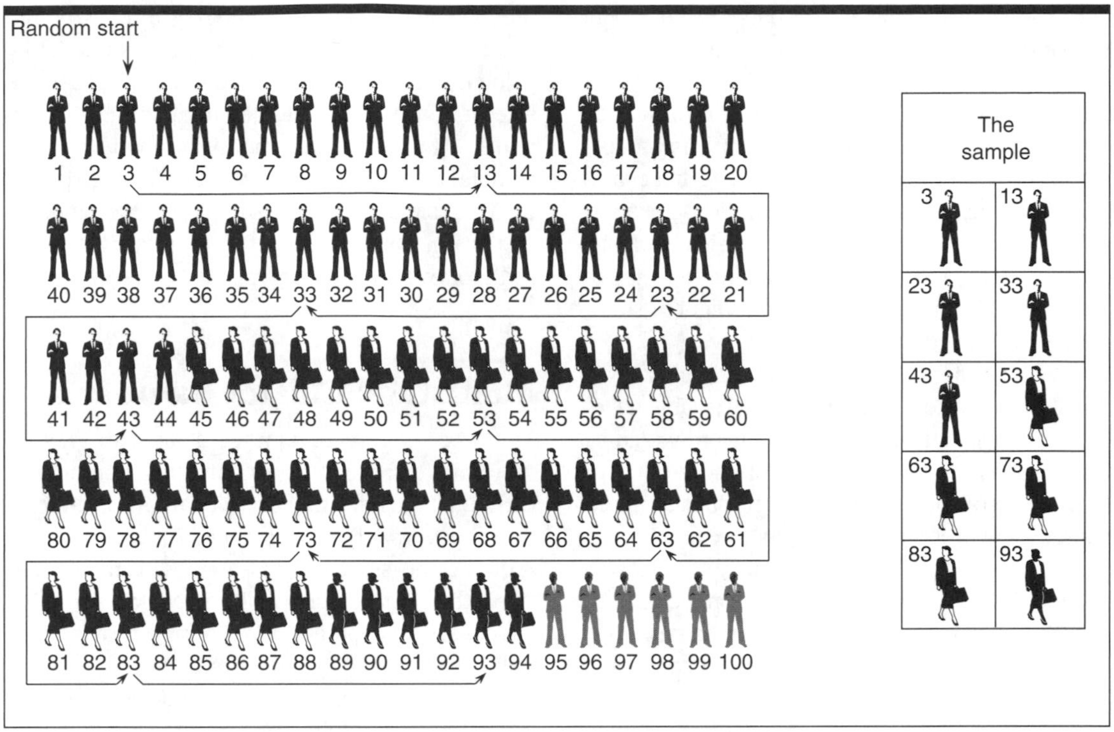

On the basis of the relative proportion of the population represented by a given group, you select—randomly or systematically—several elements from that group constituting the same proportion of your desired sample size. For example, if second-year female students with a 4.0 average compose 1 percent of the student population and you desire a sample of 1,000 students, you would select 10 second-year female students with a 4.0 average.

The other method is to group students as described and then put those groups together in a continuous list, beginning with all first-year female students with a 4.0 average and ending with all fourth-year male students with a 1.0 or below. You would then select a systematic sample, with a random start, from the entire list. Given the arrangement of the list, a systematic sample would select proper numbers (within an error range of 1 or 2) from each subgroup. (*Note:* A simple random sample drawn from such a composite list would cancel out the stratification.)

Figure 7-11 offers a graphic illustration of stratified, systematic sampling. As you can see, the micropopulation has been lined up according to gender and race. Then, beginning with a random start of "3," every tenth person thereafter is selected: 3, 13, 23, . . . , 93.

Stratified sampling ensures the proper representation of the stratification variables. This, in turn, enhances representation of other variables related to them. Taken as a whole, then, a stratified sample is likely to be more representative on several variables than a simple random sample. Although the simple random sample is still regarded as somewhat sacred, it should now be clear that you can often do better.

Hypothetical Illustration: Sampling University Students

Let's put these principles into practice by looking at a hypothetical sampling design used to select a sample of university students. Suppose we want to survey a representative cross section of students attending the main campus of Noname University. The following sections will describe the steps and decisions involved in selecting that sample.

Study Population and Sampling Frame An obvious sampling frame for use in this sample selection would be the computerized file maintained by the university administration. Let's say we have access to it. The tape contains students' names, local and permanent addresses, and a variety of other information such as field of study, class, age, and gender.

The computer database, however, contains files on all people who could, by any conceivable definition, be called students, many of whom would be inappropriate to the purposes of the study (for example, students registered for special, non-degree night programs). As a result, we must define the *study population* in a somewhat more restricted fashion. In this case, the final definition includes all 15,000 full-time degree program candidates registered for the fall semester on the main campus of the university, including all departments, both undergraduate and graduate students, and both Canadian and foreign students. The computer program we are using for sampling, therefore, will limit consideration to students fitting this definition.

Stratification The sampling program also permits stratification of students before sample selection. For our purposes, stratification by university class is sufficient, although the students could be further stratified within class, if desired, by gender, major, and so forth.

Sample Selection Once the students have been arranged by class, we select a systematic sample across the entire rearranged list. We'll set the sample size for the study at 1,000. To achieve this sample, we set the sampling program for a 1/15 **sampling ratio**. The program will generate a random number between 1 and 15; the student having that number and every fifteenth student thereafter will be selected in the sample.

Note that alternatively we could have chosen to take a simple random sample from each class pro-

portionate to its size and achieve the same effect. For example, if one class had 3,600 students, another 3,000 students, and so forth, we could obtain our stratified sample of 1,000 students by using our 1/15 sampling ratio to obtain a sample size for each of the classes totaling 15,000 students. Thus, we could choose a simple random sample of 240 students (3600/15) from the class of 3,600, a simple random sample of 200 students (3000/15) from the class of 3,000 students, and so forth for each of the classes.

Multistage Cluster Sampling

The preceding sections have dealt with reasonably simple procedures for sampling from lists of elements. Such a situation is ideal. Unfortunately, however, much interesting social research requires the selection of samples from populations that cannot be easily listed for sampling purposes: the population of a city, province, or nation; all university students in Canada; and so forth. In such cases, the sample design must be much more complex. Such a design typically involves a multistage approach, with an initial sampling of groups of elements—*clusters*—followed by the selection of elements within each of the selected clusters.

Cluster sampling may be used when it's either impossible or impractical to compile an exhaustive list of the elements composing the target population, such as all church members in Canada. Often, however, the population elements are already grouped into subpopulations, and a list of those subpopulations either exists or can be created practically. In our example, church members in Canada belong to discrete churches, which are either listed or could be. Following a cluster sample format, then, researchers could sample the list of churches in some manner (for example, a stratified, systematic sample). Next, they would obtain lists of members from each of the selected churches. Each of the lists would then be sampled, to provide samples of church members for study.

Another typical situation concerns sampling among population areas such as a city. Although there is no single list of a city's population, citizens reside on discrete city blocks. You can, therefore, select a sample of blocks initially, create a list of persons living on each of the selected blocks, and subsample persons on each block.

In a more complex design, you might sample blocks, list the households on each selected block, sample the households, list the persons residing in each household, and, finally, sample persons within each selected household. This multistage sample design ultimately leads to a selection of a sample of individuals but does not require the initial listing of all individuals in the city's population.

Multistage cluster sampling, then, involves repeating two basic steps: listing and sampling. The list of primary sampling units (churches, blocks) is compiled and, perhaps, stratified for sampling. Then a sample of those units is selected. The selected primary sampling units are then listed and perhaps stratified. The list of secondary sampling units is then sampled, and so forth.

Although cluster sampling is highly efficient, the price of that efficiency is a less accurate sample. A simple random sample drawn from a population list is subject to a single sampling error, but a two-stage cluster sample is subject to two sampling errors. First, the initial sample of clusters represents the population of clusters only within a range of sampling error. Second, the sample of elements selected within a given cluster represents all the elements in that cluster only within a range of sampling error. Thus, for example, a researcher runs the risk of selecting a sample of disproportionately wealthy city blocks, plus a sample of disproportionately wealthy households within those blocks. The best solution to this problem lies in the number of clusters selected initially and the number of elements selected within each cluster.

Typically, researchers are restricted to some total sample size, for example, a limit of 2,000 interviews in a city. Given this broad limitation, however, there are several options in designing a cluster sample. At the extremes you might choose one cluster and select 2,000 elements within that cluster, or you could select 2,000 clusters with one element selected within each. Of course, neither approach is advisable, but a broad range of choices

lies between them. Fortunately, the logic of sampling distributions provides a general guideline for this task.

Recall that sampling error is reduced by two factors: an increase in the sample size and increased homogeneity of the elements being sampled. These factors operate at each level of a multistage sample design. A sample of clusters will best represent all clusters if a large number are selected and if all clusters are very much alike. A sample of elements will best represent all elements in a given cluster if a large number are selected from the cluster and if all the elements in the cluster are very much alike.

With a given total sample size, however, if the number of clusters is increased, the number of elements within a cluster must be decreased. In this respect, the representativeness of the clusters is increased at the expense of more poorly representing the elements composing each cluster, or vice versa. Fortunately, the factor of homogeneity can be used to ease this dilemma.

Typically, the elements composing a given natural cluster within a population are more homogeneous than are all elements composing the total population. The members of a given church are more alike than are all church members; the residents of a given city block are more alike than are the residents of a whole city. As a result, relatively few elements may be needed to represent a given natural cluster adequately, although a larger number of clusters may be needed to adequately represent the diversity found among the clusters. This fact is most clearly seen in the extreme case of very different clusters composed of identical elements within each. In such a situation, a large number of clusters would adequately represent all its members. Although this extreme situation never exists in reality, it's closer to the truth in most cases than its opposite: identical clusters composed of grossly divergent elements.

The general guideline for cluster design, then, is to maximize the number of clusters selected while decreasing the number of elements within each cluster. However, this scientific guideline must be balanced against an administrative constraint. The efficiency of cluster sampling is based on the ability to minimize the listing of population elements. By initially selecting clusters, you need only list the elements composing the selected clusters, not all elements in the entire population. Increasing the number of clusters, however, works directly against this efficiency factor. A small number of clusters may be listed more quickly and more cheaply than a large number. (Remember that all the elements in a selected cluster must be listed even if only a few are to be chosen in the sample.)

The final sample design will reflect these two constraints. In effect, you'll probably select as many clusters as you can afford. Lest this issue be left too open-ended, here's one general guideline. Population researchers conventionally aim at the selection of five households per city block. If a total of 2,000 households are to be interviewed, you would aim at 400 blocks with five household interviews on each. Figure 7-12 presents a graphic overview of this process.

Before turning to other, more detailed procedures available to cluster sampling, we'll repeat that this method almost inevitably involves a loss of accuracy. The manner in which this appears, however, is somewhat complex. First, as noted earlier, a multistage sample design is subject to a sampling error at each stage. Because the sample size is necessarily smaller at each stage than the total sample size, the sampling error at each stage will be greater than would be the case for a single-stage random sample of elements. Second, sampling error is estimated on the basis of observed variance among the sample elements. When those elements are drawn from among relatively homogeneous clusters, the estimated sampling error will be too optimistic and must be corrected in the light of the cluster sample design.

Multistage Cluster Sampling with Stratification

Thus far, we've looked at cluster sampling as though a simple random sample were selected at each stage of the design. In fact, stratification techniques can be used to refine and improve the sample being selected.

The basic options here are essentially the same as those in single-stage sampling from a list. In selecting a national sample of churches, for example, you might initially stratify your list of churches by denomination, geographical region, size, rural or urban location, and perhaps by some measure of social class.

Once the primary sampling units (churches, blocks) have been grouped according to the relevant, available stratification variables, either simple random or systematic sampling techniques can be used to select the sample. You might select a specified number of units from each group, or *stratum,* or you might arrange the stratified clusters in a continuous list and systematically sample that list.

To the extent that clusters are combined into homogeneous strata, the sampling error at this stage will be reduced. The primary goal of stratification, as before, is homogeneity.

There's no reason why stratification couldn't take place at each level of sampling. The elements listed within a selected cluster might be stratified before the next stage of sampling. Typically, however, this is not done. (Recall the assumption of relative homogeneity within clusters.)

Probability Proportionate to Size (PPS) Sampling

This section introduces a more sophisticated form of cluster sampling, often used in large-scale survey sampling projects. In the preceding discussion, we talked about selecting a random or systematic sample of clusters and then a random or systematic sample of elements within each cluster selected. Notice that this procedure produces an overall sampling scheme in which every element in the whole population has the same probability of selection.

Let's say we're selecting households within a city. If there are 1,000 city blocks and we initially select a sample of 100, that means that each block has a 100/1,000 or .1 chance of being selected. If we next select 1 household in 10 from those residing on the selected blocks, each household

Figure 7-12
Multistage Cluster Sampling

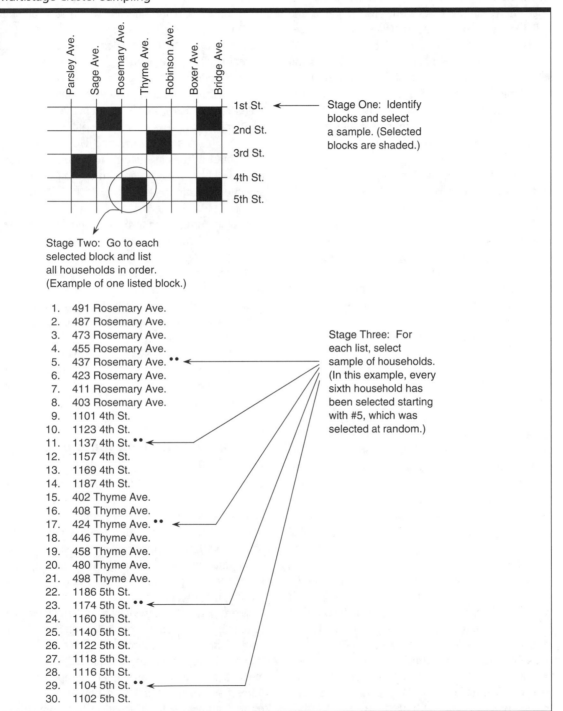

Stage One: Identify blocks and select a sample. (Selected blocks are shaded.)

Stage Two: Go to each selected block and list all households in order. (Example of one listed block.)

1.   491 Rosemary Ave.
2.   487 Rosemary Ave.
3.   473 Rosemary Ave.
4.   455 Rosemary Ave.
5.   437 Rosemary Ave. ••
6.   423 Rosemary Ave.
7.   411 Rosemary Ave.
8.   403 Rosemary Ave.
9.   1101 4th St.
10. 1123 4th St.
11. 1137 4th St. ••
12. 1157 4th St.
13. 1169 4th St.
14. 1187 4th St.
15. 402 Thyme Ave.
16. 408 Thyme Ave.
17. 424 Thyme Ave. ••
18. 446 Thyme Ave.
19. 458 Thyme Ave.
20. 480 Thyme Ave.
21. 498 Thyme Ave.
22. 1186 5th St.
23. 1174 5th St. ••
24. 1160 5th St.
25. 1140 5th St.
26. 1122 5th St.
27. 1118 5th St.
28. 1116 5th St.
29. 1104 5th St. ••
30. 1102 5th St.

Stage Three: For each list, select sample of households. (In this example, every sixth household has been selected starting with #5, which was selected at random.)

has a .1 chance of selection within its block. To calculate the overall probability of a household being selected, we simply multiply the probabilities at the individual steps in sampling. That is, each household has a 1/10 chance of its block being selected and a 1/10 chance of that specific household being selected if the block is one of those chosen. Each household, in this case, has a $1/10 \times 1/10 = 1/100$ chance of selection overall. Because each household would have the same chance of selection, the sample so selected should be representative of all households in the city.

There are dangers in this procedure, however. In particular, the variation in the size of blocks (measured in numbers of households) presents a problem. Let's suppose that half the city's population resides in 10 densely packed blocks filled with high-rise apartment buildings, and suppose that the rest of the population lives in single-family dwellings spread out over the remaining 900 blocks. When we first select our sample of 1/10 of the blocks, it's quite possible that we'll miss all of the 10 densely packed high-rise blocks. No matter what happens in the second stage of sampling, our final sample of households will be grossly unrepresentative of the city, comprising only single-family dwellings.

Whenever the clusters sampled are of greatly differing sizes, it's appropriate to use a modified sampling design called **probability proportionate to size (PPS)**. This design guards against the problem just described and still produces a final sample in which each element has the same chance of selection.

As the name suggests, each cluster is given a chance of selection proportionate to its size. Thus, a city block with 200 households has twice the chance of selection as one with only 100 households. (We'll look at how this is done in the context of a hypothetical study of prison inmates shortly.) Within each cluster, however, a fixed *number* of elements is selected, say, five households per block. Notice how this procedure results in each household having the same probability of selection overall.

Let's look at households of two different city blocks. Block A has 100 households, Block B has only 10. In PPS sampling, we would give Block A 10 times as good a chance of being selected as Block B. So if, in the overall sample design, Block A has a 1/20 chance of being selected, that means Block B would only have a 1/200 chance. Notice that this means that all the households on Block A would have a 1/20 chance of having their block selected; Block B households have only a 1/200 chance.

If Block A is selected and we're taking 5 households from each selected block, then the households on Block A have a 5/100 chance of being selected into the block's sample. Since we can multiply probabilities in a case like this, we see that every household on Block A had an overall chance of selection equal to $1/20 \times 5/100 = 5/2000 = 1/400$.

If Block B happens to be selected, on the other hand, its households stand a much better chance of being among the 5 chosen there: 5/10. When this is combined with their relatively poorer chance of having their block selected in the first place, however, they end up with the same chance of selection as those on Block A: $1/200 \times 5/10 = 5/2000 = 1/400$.

Further refinements to this design make it a very efficient and effective method for selecting large cluster samples. For now, however, it's enough for you to understand the basic logic involved.

Disproportionate Sampling and Weighting

Ultimately, a probability sample is representative of a population if all elements in the population have an equal chance of selection in that sample. Thus, in each of the preceding discussions, we've noted that the various sampling procedures result in an equal chance of selection—even though the ultimate selection probability is the product of several partial probabilities.

More generally, however, a probability sample is one in which each population element has a *known nonzero* probability of selection—even though different elements may have different probabilities. If controlled probability sampling procedures have been used, any such sample may be representative of the population from which it is drawn if each sample element is assigned a weight equal to the inverse of its probability of selection. Thus, where all sample elements have had the same chance of selection, each is given the same weight: 1. This is called a *self-weighting sample.*

It's sometimes appropriate to give some cases more weight than others, a process called **weighting**. Disproportionate sampling and weighting come into play in two basic ways. First, you may sample subpopulations disproportionately to insure sufficient numbers of cases from each for analysis. For example, when Fiona Kay was interested in examining causal factors that "push" lawyers out of law firm practice as well as those that "pull" them toward other options, she used "A disproportionately stratified random sample of lawyers...selected from the membership lists of the Law Society of Upper Canada" (1997:309). Given her interest in gender issues, she stratified the sample by gender and oversampled women so she would have equal numbers of women and men.

In another example, a given city may have a suburban area containing one-fourth of its total population. Yet you might be especially interested in a detailed analysis of households in that area and may feel that one-fourth of this total sample size would be too few. As a result, you might decide to select the same number of households from the suburban area as from the remainder of the city. Households in the suburban area, then, are given a disproportionately better chance of selection than those located elsewhere in the city.

As long as you analyze the two area samples separately or comparatively, you need not worry about the differential sampling. If you want to combine the two samples to create a composite picture of the entire city, however, you must take the disproportionate sampling into account. If n is the number of households selected from each area, then the households in the suburban area had a chance of selection equal to n divided by one-fourth of the total city population. Because the total city population and the sample size are the same for both areas, the suburban households should be given a weight of $1/4n$, and the remaining households should be given a weight of $3/4n$. This weighting procedure could be simplified by merely giving a weight of 3 to each of the households selected outside the suburban area. (This procedure gives a proportionate representation to each sample element. The population figure would have to be included in the weighting if population estimates were desired.)

Here's an example of the problems that can be created when disproportionate sampling is not accompanied by a weighting scheme. When the *Harvard Business Review* decided to survey its subscribers on the issue of sexual harassment at work, for example, it seemed appropriate to oversample women. Here's how G. C. Collins and Timothy Blodgett explained the matter:

> We also skewed the sample another way: to insure a representative response from women, we mailed a questionnaire to virtually every female subscriber, for a male/female ratio of 68% to 32%. This bias resulted in a response of 52% male and 44% female (and 4% who gave no indication of gender) compared to HBR's U.S. subscriber proportion of 93% male and 7% female.
>
> (1981:78)

Notice a couple of things in this quotation. First, it would be nice to know a little more about what "virtually every female" means. Evidently, they didn't send questionnaires to all female subscribers, but there's no indication of who was omitted and why. Second, they didn't use the term *representative* in its normal social science usage. What they mean, of course, is that they want to get a substantial or "large enough" response from women, and oversampling is a perfectly acceptable way of accomplishing that.

By sampling more women than a straightforward probability sample would have produced, they were able to get enough women (812) to compare with the men (960). Thus, when the authors report, for example, that 32 percent of the women and 66 percent of the men agree that "the amount of sexual harassment at work is greatly exaggerated," we know that the female response is based on a substantial number of cases. That's good. There are problems, however.

To begin, subscriber surveys are always problematic. In this case, the best the researchers can hope to talk about is "what subscribers to *Harvard Business Review* think." In a loose way, it might make sense to think of that population as representing the more sophisticated portion of corporate management. Unfortunately, the overall response rate was 25 percent. Although that's quite good for subscriber surveys, it's a low response rate in terms of generalizing from probability samples.

Beyond that, however, the disproportionate sample design creates a further problem. When the authors state that 73 percent of respondents favour company policies against harassment (Collins and Blodgett, 1981:78), that figure is undoubtedly too high, since the sample contains a disproportionately high percentage of women, who are more likely to favour such policies. And, when the researchers report that top managers are more likely to feel that claims of sexual harassment are exaggerated than are middle- and lower-level managers (1981:81), that finding is also suspect. As the researchers report, women are disproportionately represented in lower management. That alone might account for the apparent differences in different levels of management. In short, the failure to take account of the oversampling of women confounds all survey results that don't separate findings by gender. The solution to this problem would have been to weight the responses by gender, as described earlier in this section.

Hypothetical Illustration: Sampling Prison Inmates

Let's complete the discussion of cluster sampling with a hypothetical research example. The example that follows is not as complex as the area probability samples employed in studies of geographic areas such as cities, provinces, or the nation. Nonetheless, it should illustrate the various principles of cluster sampling.

The purpose of this study will be to examine the attitudes toward punishment and justice of inmates held in Canadian federal penitentiaries for men. A representative sample of all male inmates in the federal system is desired. Because we are not able to obtain a single list of all such inmates, we'll

create a multistage sample design. In the initial stage of sampling, we will use PPS to select the prisons and then inmates from each prison.

Selecting the Prisons The federal government provides a list of all penitentiaries for men on the Web, approximately 45, and the number of inmates in each. This listing constitutes the sampling frame for the first stage of sampling.

A total of approximately 525 respondents is desired for the study. We decide to select 15 prisons with probability proportionate to size and take 35 inmates from each of those selected. To accomplish this, the list of prisons is arranged geographically, and then a table is created similar to the partial listing shown in Table 7-2.

Next to each prison in the table, we enter the number of inmates. We then use these figures to compute the cumulative total running through the list. Let's say the final total comes to approximately 9,000. The object at this point is to select a sample of 15 prisons in such a way that each would have a chance of selection proportionate to the number of its inmates. To accomplish this, the cumulative totals are used to create ranges of numbers for each prison equalling the number of inmates in that prison. Prison A in the table is assigned the numbers 1 through 200; Prison B is assigned 201 through 600; Prison C is assigned 601 through 700; and so forth.

By selecting 15 numbers ranging between 1 and 9,000, it is possible to select 15 prisons for the study. We'll select the 15 numbers in a systematic sample as follows. The sampling interval is set at 600 (9,000/15), and a random start is selected between 1 and 600. Let's say the random number is 332. Because that number falls within the range of numbers assigned to Prison B (201–600), Prison B is selected.

Increments of 600 (the sampling interval) are then added to the random start, and every prison within whose range one of the resultant numbers appears is selected into the sample of prisons. It should be apparent that in this fashion, each prison has a chance of selection directly proportionate to its inmate size. A prison with 400 inmates has twice the chance of selection as a prison of 200 and eight times the chance of selection as one with only 50 inmates.

Table 7-2
Form Used in Listing of Prisons

Prison	Inmates	Cumulative Inmates
Prison A	200	200
Prison B	400	600
Prison C	100	700

Selecting the Inmates Once the sample of prisons is selected, we make arrangements to get lists of the inmates in each (having previously gained permission to access this information). As the list arrives from a selected prison, a sampling interval for that prison is computed on the basis of the number of inmates and the number desired (35). If a prison has 425 inmates, the sample interval is set at 12 (425/35). To select the sample of inmates from that prison, we select a random number between 1 and 12 and increment it by the sampling interval. This procedure is repeated for each prison, yielding the final sample of inmates.

Sampling can be much more complicated than the examples we've presented here. Some populations are extremely difficult to determine. Clever sampling designs are often a major component of a research project. For example, Bill Reimer (2001) and colleagues are involved in a long-term project concerning research and education in Canadian rural communities. In 1995 he proposed a systematic design for rural research: a national sample frame of 32 selected rural sites that allow researchers to compare important dimensions.

Part of the research project is the ongoing evaluation of this national sample frame and its refinement. The basis for the site selections was the census subdivisions (CSD) in the 1991 Canadian census, which provided an exhaustive set of possible locations. Although this research design is too intricate to briefly describe here, we mention it as an illustration of the time and skill involved in developing useful sampling frames for extensive research on important topics.

Probability Sampling in Review

Much of this chapter has been devoted to the key sampling method used in controlled survey research: probability sampling. In each of the variations examined, we've seen that elements are chosen for study from a population on a basis of random selection with known nonzero probabilities.

Depending on the field situation, probability sampling can be either very simple or very difficult, time consuming, and expensive. Whatever the situation, however, it remains the most effective method for the selection of study elements. There are two reasons for this.

First, probability sampling avoids researchers' conscious or unconscious biases in element selection. If all elements in the population have an equal (or unequal and subsequently weighted) chance of selection, there is an excellent chance that the sample so selected will closely represent the population of all elements.

Second, probability sampling permits estimates of sampling error. Although no probability sample will be perfectly representative in all respects, controlled selection methods permit the researcher to estimate the degree of expected error.

In this lengthy chapter, we've taken on a basic issue in much social research: selecting observations that will tell us something more general than the specifics we've actually observed. This issue confronts field researchers, who face more action and more actors than they can observe and fully record, as well as political pollsters who want to predict an election but can't interview all voters. As we continue through the book, we'll see in greater detail how social researchers have found ways to deal with this issue.

Main Points

- Social researchers must select observations that will allow them to generalize to people and events not observed. Often, this involves a selection of people to observe—sampling.

- Social researchers have developed several sampling techniques appropriate to different research situations. Sometimes you can and should select probability samples using precise statistical techniques, but other times nonprobability techniques are more appropriate.
- Nonprobability sampling techniques include relying on available subjects, purposive or judgmental sampling, and snowball sampling.
- Quota sampling is another nonprobability sampling method. You begin with a detailed description of the characteristics of the total population (quota matrix) and then select your sample members so that they include different composite profiles that exist in the population. The representativeness of a quota sampling depends in large part on how accurately the quota matrix reflects the characteristics of the population.
- Researchers may also make use of informants. Informants should be selected such that they provide a broad, diverse view of the group under study.
- Nonprobability techniques are useful, but none of them ensures that the resulting sample is representative of the population being sampled.
- Probability sampling methods provide an excellent way of selecting representative samples from large, known populations. The chief principle of probability sampling is that every member of the total population must have some known nonzero probability of being selected into the sample. The key to probability sampling is random selection.
- The most carefully selected sample will never provide a perfect representation of the population from which it was selected. There will always be some degree of sampling error.
- Probability sampling methods make it possible to estimate the amount of sampling error expected in a given sample by predicting the distribution of samples with respect to the target parameter. The expected error in a sample is expressed in terms of confidence levels and confidence intervals.

- A sampling frame is a list or quasi list of the members of a population. It is the resource used in the selection of a sample. A sample's representativeness depends directly on the extent to which a sampling frame contains all the members of the total population that the sample is intended to represent.
- Simple random sampling is logically the most fundamental technique in probability sampling, although it's seldom used in practice.
- Systematic sampling involves the selection of every kth member from a sampling frame. This method is more practical than simple random sampling, and, with a few exceptions; it's functionally equivalent.
- Stratification is the process of grouping the members of a population into relatively homogeneous strata before sampling. This practice improves the representativeness of a sample by reducing the degree of sampling error.
- Multistage cluster sampling is a relatively complex sampling technique frequently used when a list of all the members of a population does not exist. Researchers typically must balance the number of clusters and the size of each cluster to achieve a given sample size.
- Probability proportionate to size (PPS) is an efficient method for multistage cluster sampling.
- If the members of a population have unequal probabilities of selection into the sample, researchers must assign weights to the different observations made, in order to provide a representative picture of the total population. Basically, the weight assigned to a particular sample member should be the inverse of its probability of selection.

Review Questions and Exercises

1. Using Appendix B of this book, select a simple random sample of 10 numbers in the range from 1 to 9,876. Describe each step in the process.

2. In a paragraph or two, describe the steps involved in selecting a multistage cluster

sample of students taking first-year English in the nation's universities.

3. The Canadian General Social Survey employs careful sampling methods. Use the World Wide Web to find out the sizes of the original samples for the two most recent surveys and the number of completed interviews ("completed cases") achieved in each survey. Start at the Statistics Canada homepage (http://www.statcan.ca/english/) and then go to Statistic Canada's Index of Surveys.

4. Using the Web, find two Canadian newspaper articles that report the results of national surveys. For each, write down what the article reports about how the survey was conducted. Then critique the description in terms of the survey results reported in the article and the information provided the reader about the way the survey was conducted. Were you given enough information to assess the worth of the study and the accuracy of the claims?

Continuity Project

Describe the method by which you might select a sample of your university's student body to study attitudes toward gender equality. Be sure to stratify on variables relevant to the topic and to defend your choices.

Additional Readings

Kalton, Graham. *Introduction to Survey Sampling.* Newbury Park, CA: Sage, 1983. Kalton goes into more of the mathematical details of sampling than the present chapter without attempting to be as definitive as Kish, described next.

Kish, Leslie. *Survey Sampling.* New York: Wiley, 1965. Unquestionably the definitive work on sampling in social research. Kish's coverage ranges from the simplest matters to the most complex and mathematical, both highly theoretical and downright practical. Easily readable and difficult passages intermingle as Kish exhausts everything you could want or need to know about each aspect of sampling.

Sudman, Seymour. "Applied Sampling." Pp. 145–94 in *Handbook of Survey Research,* edited by Peter H. Rossi, James D. Wright, and Andy B. Anderson. New York: Academic Press, 1983. An excellent, practical guide to survey sampling.

InfoTrac: You can find further relevant readings on the World Wide Web at

http://sociology.wadsworth.com

Part 3
Modes of Observation and Ethical Considerations:
Quantitative and Qualitative Approaches

Introduction

Modes of Observation and Ethical Considerations

INTRODUCTION

Having explored the structuring of inquiry in some depth, we're now ready to dive into the various observational techniques available to social scientists. We'll cover both quantitative and qualitative techniques and interactive and unobtrusive (non-reactive) methods of observing. It is, of course, possible to gather both qualitative and quantitative data using most modes of observation. However, as you'll see, some methods are more suited to a qualitative approach to research and others to a quantitative one. Therefore, Chapters 8 and 9 focus on methods well suited to producing quantitative data and Chapters 11 and 12 cover methods that are highly suited to generating qualitative data.

Many methods of observations, such as experiments, surveys, and many forms of field research, are interactive. They necessarily involve intrusion of varying degrees on whatever is under study. In the case of an interactive technique, the method of observing has the potential to change or affect what is being studied. There are modes of observing, however, where the method does not affect what is being studied. Discussion of such unobtrusive methods is concentrated in Chapter 10. Many nonreactive methods are equally suited to a qualitative or quantitative approach to research.

As we'll discuss, each method of research has its strengths and weaknesses, so it's often best to think of the various alternatives as complementary. In the end, the ideal method is that which best fits the research problem at hand.

Experiments are usually thought of in connection with the physical sciences. In Chapter 8 we'll see how social scientists use experiments. This is the most rigorously controllable of the methods we'll examine. Understanding experiments is also a useful way to enhance your understanding of the general logic of social scientific research.

Chapter 9 will describe survey research, one of the most popular of methods in social science. This type of research involves collecting data by asking people questions, either in self-administered questionnaires or through interviews, which, in turn, can be conducted face-to-face or over the telephone.

Chapter 10 discusses three forms of unobtrusive data collection that take advantage of some of the data available all around us. The analysis of existing statistics offers a way of studying people without having to talk to them. Governments and a variety of private organizations regularly compile great masses of data, which you often can use with little or no modification to answer properly posed questions. Content analysis is a method of collecting social data through carefully specifying a coding scheme and applying it to social artifacts such as books, songs, speeches, and paintings. Without making any personal contact with people, you can use this method to examine a wide variety of social phenomena. Finally, historical documents are another valuable resource for social scientific analysis.

Chapter 11, on qualitative field research, examines perhaps the most natural form of data collection used by social scientists: the direct observation of social phenomena in natural settings. As you'll see, some researchers go beyond mere observation to participate in what they're studying, because they want a more intimate view and fuller understanding.

Chapter 12 looks at different forms and goals of qualitative interviewing. It begins with a general discussion of in-depth interviews and moves to a group interview format known as focus groups. It ends with a discussion of oral history, a method of gathering data about the past through in-depth interviewing of informants.

Chapter 13, on evaluation research, looks at a rapidly growing subfield in social science, involving the application of experimental and quasi-experimental models to the testing of social interventions in real life. You might use evaluation research, for example, to test the effectiveness of a drug rehabilitation program or the efficiency of a new school cafeteria. In the same chapter, we'll look briefly at social indicators as a way of assessing broader social processes.

When reading these chapters, you'll probably discover that you've been using these scientific methods casually in your daily life for as long as you can remember. You use some form of field research every day. You employ a crude form of content analysis every time you judge an author's motivation or orientation from his or her writings. You engage in at least casual experiments frequently. The chapters in Part 3 will show you how to improve your use of these methods so as to avoid the pitfalls of casual, uncontrolled observation.

None of the data-collection methods described in the following chapters is appropriate to all research topics and situations. We have tried to give you some ideas, early in each chapter, of when a given method might be appropriate. Still, we could never anticipate all the possible research topics that may one day interest you. As a general guideline, you should always use a variety of techniques in the study of any topic. Because each method has its weaknesses, the use of several methods can help fill in any gaps. If the different, independent approaches to the topic all yield the same conclusion, you've achieved a form of replication.

Before we turn to the descriptions of the several methods, there is an important issue we should revisit, the ethical dimension of social research. No research study should be designed and implemented without careful thought to who might be affected and how.

THE ETHICAL DIMENSION OF SOCIAL RESEARCH

In order to communicate the various elements that go into a research study, it's necessary to discuss the process as a series of steps or phases. In practice, however, the steps involved in conducting research are interdependent. Researchers must understand the various modes of observation available when considering the operationalization of concepts, for example. Knowledge of the variety of techniques for data analysis is important at the stage of data gathering. In short, the phases of social research are highly interconnected. Ethical considerations, therefore, must be attended to during all phases of the research process. We have waited to discuss ethical issues in more depth at this point in the book for the practical reason that this section focuses specifically on ways of gathering data, and it is in this phase of research where human subjects are directly encountered. Therefore, many ethical issues of concern in research are more salient and readily illustrated in the context of this section.

Let's briefly consider the following. Imagine yourself working with a team of researchers trying to design a study to observe how individuals initially respond to hearing stressful news. News of the death of a loved one is considered to be highly stressful. So is hearing that you've just lost your job. Someone on your research team suggests that you draw a random sample of individuals in a community and inform each in turn that a member of their immediate family has just died—of course, insuring that the family member is someplace else at the time—so you can watch their reactions when they hear the news. Likely upon hearing this suggestion, it would strike you as highly unethical. How about working with an organization that is willing to randomly choose people in their employ and inform them that they have been fired, because the organization's managers want to learn more about how to cope with people's responses under such circumstances? We imagine that this approach to researching the topic would strike you

as unethical also. Perhaps someone then suggests that instead of creating a false stressful experience, the research team should try to gain access to a hospital where they could observe real life situations of people being informed about the death of a loved one. Would it be ethical to observe them at that moment in their lives, ask them questions or hand them a questionnaire? How about gaining access to a company that is about to layoff thousands of workers? What kind of observation and inquiry might be ethical to engage in then?

Just as certain procedures are too impractical to use, others are either ethically prohibitive or politically difficult or impossible. The problem with ethical considerations, however, is that they are not always self-evident. While some situations may appear to be black and white, there are also many shades of gray. Here's a story to show you what we mean.

Several years ago, one of us was invited to sit in on a planning session to design a study of legal education in California. The joint project was to be conducted by a university research centre and the state bar association. The purpose of the project was to improve legal education by learning which aspects of the law school experience were related to success on the bar exam. Essentially, the plan was to prepare a questionnaire that would get detailed information about the law school experiences of individuals. People would be required to answer the questionnaire when they took the bar exam. By analyzing how people with different kinds of law school experiences did on the bar exam, we could find out what sorts of things worked and what didn't. The findings of the research could be made available to law schools, and ultimately legal education could be improved.

The exciting thing about collaborating with the bar association was that all the normally irritating logistical hassles would be handled. There would be no problem getting permission to administer questionnaires in conjunction with the exam, for example, and the problem of nonresponse could be eliminated altogether.

I (Babbie) left the meeting excited about the prospects for the study. When I told a colleague about it, I glowed about the absolute handling of the nonresponse problem. Her immediate comment turned everything around completely. "That's unethical. There's no law requiring the questionnaire, and participation in research has to be voluntary." The study wasn't done. In retelling this story, it is obvious to me that requiring participation would have been inappropriate. You may have seen that before you read my colleague's comment. I still feel a little embarrassed over the matter. However, there is a specific purpose in the telling of this story.

All of us consider ourselves ethical; not perfect perhaps, but more ethical than most of humanity. The problem in social research, and probably in life, is that ethical considerations are not always apparent to us. As a result, we often plunge into things without seeing ethical issues that may be apparent to others and may even be obvious to us when pointed out.

Any of us can immediately see that a study that requires the torturing of small children is unethical. You'd no doubt speak out immediately if we suggested you interview people about their sex lives and then publish what they said in the local newspaper. But, as ethical as you are, you'd totally miss the ethical issue in some other situations not because you're bad, but because we all do that.

Concern with ethical standards and guidelines in research gained momentum in North America in the second half of the 20th century. Much of the impetus for greater attention to research ethics had to do with medical experimentation on human subjects. Horrifying stories of tortures in Nazi Germany were conducted, in the name of medical experimentation, on Jews and others in concentration camps. North America, however, is not exempt from horrifying tales of research conducted in the name of science.

The Tuskegee Syphilis Study (*Bad Blood*) is an infamous example. The study began in the U.S. around 1930. It examined the long-term consequences of untreated syphilis. Although no treatment was available for syphilis at the time the study began, it was allowed to run until 1972, well after a cure for the disease was available, so the study would not be ruined. The sample was comprised entirely of black males. It was public pressure that forced the termination of the study once it was exposed by the news media.

Canada has its share of scandalous medical research stories also. At the Allan Memorial Institute in Montreal, Dr. Evan Cameron oversaw LSD experiments (sponsored by the U.S. Central Intelligence Agency, CIA) conducted on unwitting psychiatric patients in the 1960s. These patients were subjected to mind altering drugs—for government experiments concerning such issues as brainwashing—without their knowledge or consent and indeed were not even told that this had been done to them. Not only did the experiments have no relationship to their illnesses—hence were devoid of even potential therapeutic value—but some subjects experienced severe, sometimes life long, psychological impairment as a result of the drugs administered. Experimentation on Canadian prisoners provides another illustration. Much of this research, for example drug testing, tests to determine the toxicity of food additives, and sensory deprivation studies, was conducted between 1955 and 1975 (Osborne 1999). This research gained attention following allegations by Dorothy Proctor (a former inmate) in the mid-1990s and a series of stories on the use of prisoners in experimental research in the *Ottawa Citizen* in 1998. As a result, Correctional Service Canada commissioned an ethics report on the topic from McGill University and an independent researcher to review how extensive such inmate research was in Canada (Osborne 1999). Other cases have involved issues of falsification of data, as well as informed consent and potential harm to subjects. The breast cancer research scandal in the 1990s is an example. This scandal concerned Dr. Poisson and clinical trials he was conducting in Montreal from the 1970s through 1990. The case gained Canadian public attention in 1994 (although the fraud was detected in 1990).

Social scientific research also has the potential to harm research subjects. The possibility of psychological harm and stress is one major concern. Milgram's famous obedience to authority experiment (discussed in Chapter 8) is often used to illustrate such concerns. But physical harm, while much more rare, is a possibility that must be guarded against as well. The Zimbardo prison experiment is a good illustration of this concern (discussed in Chapter 8). There is the potential of putting subjects into legal jeopardy, particularly when one is researching underground or deviant activities. (We'll discuss the Ogden case shortly). In addition to placing subjects at legal risk, there are other major forms of risk to the research subject that must be attended to, such as loss of job, destruction of family life, and even blackmail. Humphreys' *Tearoom Trade* study will be discussed in Chapter 11 to illustrate the need to guard against such possibilities.

Ethical Codes, REBS, and the Tri-Council Policy Statement

To guard against the variety of potential harms that can come to human subjects, codes of ethics and other guidelines for moral conduct in research became prevalent during the second half of the 20th century. Most professions and disciplines have their own ethical guidelines, as do many organizations, institutions, and granting agencies. Nonetheless, with the passing of each decade, greater attention has been given to ethical reviews of research. In Canada, for example, a national set of ethical guidelines has recently been established for institutions that receive federal funding. These guidelines are applicable across disciplines to all types of research concerning human subjects.

In 1994, the three major granting agencies in Canada, the Medical Research Council (MRC) (recently renamed the Canadian Institutes of Health Research [CIHR]), the Natural Science & Engineering Research Council (NSERC), and the Social Sciences & Humanities Research Council (SSHRC), formed the Tri-Council Working Group to create a joint policy concerning ethical standards for research involving humans. The goal was to create a standard of ethical norms that transcended disciplinary boundaries. In 1998, after several draft reports, they issued the Tri-Council Policy Statement: Ethical Conduct for Research Involving Humans (TCPS), which articulates their standards. A condition of their funding is that researchers and their institutions must follow the principles and policies laid out in the statement.

Because ethical issues in research are both important and ambiguous, formal codes of conduct describing what is considered acceptable and unacceptable professional behaviour are by themselves not adequate. Gaining ethical approval of proposed research projects by an ethics or human subjects committee has been required by many institutions and granting agencies for decades. The organization and composition of such ethical review boards, however, have varied greatly. The TCPS has laid out rules for the standardization of the ethics review process. Research Ethics Boards (REBs) now have common procedures and follow the same ethical guidelines. The minimum five persons REB must include a member from the community and a person knowledgeable in ethics. Universities establish their own REBs according to the standards laid out and mandate these REBs to review all research that involves human subjects to ensure they meet the minimum ethical standards of the Policy. The REB has the right to approve, reject, or request modifications to research involving human subjects that is proposed or ongoing. Ethical review is required of all research involving human subjects, including research conducted by undergraduate students. The researchers' job in designing a study is to carefully consider ethical issues and to explain the goals and methods of their proposed research clearly so the review board can make an informed decision in their particular case.

Figure P3-1 contains a section of the TCPS, Guiding Ethical Principles, which provides a good summary of the common standards and values that have been adopted. The full policy statement may be obtained from a number of Web sites, for example: http://www.nserc.ca/programs/ethics/english/index.htm

Figure P3-1
Tri-Council Policy Statement: Ethical Conduct for Research Involving Humans

CONTEXT OF AN ETHICS FRAMEWORK

C. Guiding Ethical Principles

The approach taken in this framework is to guide and evoke thoughtful actions based on principles. The principles that follow are based on the guidelines of the Councils over the last decades, on more recent statements by other Canadian agencies, and on statements from the international community. The principles have been widely adopted by diverse research disciplines. As such, they express common standards, values and aspirations of the research community.

Respect for Human Dignity: The cardinal principle of modern research ethics, as discussed above, is respect for human dignity. This principle aspires to protecting the multiple and interdependent interests of the person—from bodily to psychological to cultural integrity. This principle forms the basis of the ethical obligations in research that are listed below.

In certain situations, conflicts may arise from application of these principles in isolation from one other. Researchers and REBs must carefully weigh all the principles and circumstances involved to reach a reasoned and defensible conclusion.

Respect for Free and Informed Consent: Individuals are generally presumed to have the capacity and right to make free and informed decisions. Respect for persons thus means respecting the exercise of individual consent. In practical terms within the ethics review process, the principle of respect for persons translates into the dialogue, process, rights, duties and requirements for free and informed consent by the research subject.

Respect for Vulnerable Persons: Respect for human dignity entails high ethical obligations towards vulnerable persons — to those whose diminished competence and/or decision-making capacity make them vulnerable. Children, institutionalized persons or others who are vulnerable are entitled, on grounds of human dignity, caring, solidarity and fairness, to special protection against abuse, exploitation or discrimination. Ethical obligations to vulnerable individuals in the research enterprise will often translate into special procedures to protect their interests.

Respect for Privacy and Confidentiality: Respect for human dignity also implies the principles of respect for privacy and confidentiality. In many cultures, privacy and confidentiality are considered fundamental to human dignity. Thus, standards of privacy and confidentiality protect the access, control and dissemination of personal information. In doing so, such standards help to protect mental or psychological integrity. They are thus consonant with values underlying privacy, confidentiality and anonymity respected.

Respect for Justice and Inclusiveness: Justice connotes fairness and equity. Procedural justice requires that the ethics review process have fair methods, standards and procedures for reviewing research protocols, and that the process be effectively independent. Justice also concerns the distribution of benefits and burdens of research. On the one hand, distributive justice means that no segment of the population should be unfairly burdened with the harms of research. It thus imposes particular obligations toward individuals who are vulnerable and unable to protect their own interests in order to ensure that they are not exploited for the advancement of knowledge. History has many chapters of such exploitation. On the other hand, distributive justice also imposes duties neither to neglect nor discriminate against individuals and groups who may benefit from advances in research.

Balancing Harms and Benefits: The analysis, balance, and distribution of harms and benefits are critical to the ethics of human research. Modern research ethics, for instance, require a favourable harms-benefit balance — that is, that the foreseeable harms should not outweigh anticipated benefits. Harms-benefits analysis thus affects the welfare and rights of research subjects, the informed assumption of harms and benefits, and the ethical justifications for competing research paths. Because research involves advancing the frontiers of knowledge, its undertaking often involves uncertainty about the precise magnitude and kind of benefits or harms that attend proposed research. These realities and the principle of respect for human dignity impose ethical obligations on the prerequisites, scientific validity, design and conduct of research. These concerns are particularly evident in biomedical and health research; in research they need to be tempered in areas such as political science, economics or modern history (including biographies), areas in which research may ethically result in the harming of the reputations of organizations or individuals in public life.

Minimizing Harm: A principle directly related to harms-benefits analysis is non-maleficence, or the duty to avoid, prevent or minimize harms to others. Research subjects must not be subjected to unnecessary risks of harm, and their participation in research must be essential to achieving scientifically and societally important aims that cannot be realized without the participation of human subjects. In addition, it should be kept in mind that the principle of minimizing harm requires that the research involve the smallest number of human subjects and the smallest number of tests on these subjects that will ensure scientifically valid data.

Maximizing Benefit: Another principle related to the harms and benefits of research is beneficence. The principle of beneficence imposes a duty to benefit others and, in research ethics, a duty to maximize net benefits. The principle has particular relevance for researchers in professions such as social work, education, health care and applied psychology. As noted earlier, human research is intended to produce benefits for subjects themselves, for other individuals or society as a whole, or for the advancement of knowledge. In most research, the primary benefits produced are for society and for the advancement of knowledge.

Adapted from the Tri-Council Policy Statement: Ethical Conduct for Research Involving (footnotes 2-5 not included), Medical Research Council, Natural Sciences and Engineering Research Council, Social Sciences and Humanities Research Council (1998).

Source: http://www.nserc.ca/programs/ethics/english/intro03.htm#C, May 15, 2001.

ETHICAL ISSUES IN SOCIAL RESEARCH

As the councils themselves acknowledge, ethical considerations concerning "human subjects are complex and continually evolving." We, therefore, cannot possibly cover all of the ethical issues that might arise or provide standard solutions to those we do highlight. First, there's not always agreement on what is or is not ethical. Second, any given research situation may present researchers with new, challenging ethical dilemmas. Our goal here, therefore, is to *sensitize* you to the ethical component in research so that you'll look for it whenever you plan a study. Even when the ethical aspects of a situation are debatable, you should know there's something to argue about. Toward this end, we'll discuss some of the broadly agreed-upon norms describing what's ethical and what's not.

In most dictionaries and in common usage, **ethics** is typically associated with morality, and both deal with matters of right and wrong. But what is right and what is wrong? What is the source of the distinction? For individuals the sources vary. They may be religions, political ideologies, or the pragmatic observation of what seems to work and what doesn't.

Webster's New World Dictionary is typical among dictionaries in defining *ethical* as "conforming to the standards of conduct of a given profession or group." Although the idea may frustrate those in search of moral absolutes, what we regard as morality and ethics in day-to-day life is a matter of agreement among members of a group. And, not surprisingly, different groups have agreed on different codes of conduct. Part of living successfully in a particular society is knowing what that society considers ethical and unethical. The same holds true for the social research community.

Anyone involved in social scientific research, then, needs to be aware of the general agreements shared by researchers about what's proper and improper in the conduct of scientific inquiry. This section summarizes some of the most important ethical agreements that prevail in social research.

Voluntary Participation

Social research often, though not always, represents an intrusion into people's lives. The interviewer's knock on the door or the arrival of a questionnaire in the mail signals the beginning of an activity that the respondent has not requested and one that may require a significant portion of his or her time and energy. Participation in a social experiment disrupts the subject's regular activities.

Social research, moreover, often requires that people reveal personal information about themselves—information that may be unknown to their friends and associates. And social research often requires that such information be revealed to strangers. Other professionals, such as physicians and lawyers, also require such information. Their requests may be justified, however, because the information is required for them to serve the personal interests of the individual. Social researchers can seldom make this claim. Like medical scientists, they can only argue that the research effort may ultimately help all humanity.

A major tenet of medical research ethics is that experimental participation must be *voluntary*. The same norm applies to social research. No one should be forced to participate. This norm is far easier to accept in theory than to apply in practice, however.

Again, medical research provides a useful parallel. Many experimental drugs have been tested on prisoners. In the most rigorously ethical cases, the prisoners were told the nature and the possible dangers of the experiment; they were told that participation is completely voluntary; and they were further instructed that they could expect no special rewards, such as early parole, for participation. Even under these conditions, it's often clear that volunteers are motivated by the belief that they will personally benefit from their cooperation.

When the instructor in an introductory sociology class asks students to fill out a questionnaire that he or she hopes to analyze and publish, students should always be told that their participation in the survey is completely voluntary. Even so, most students will fear that nonparticipation will somehow affect their grade. The instructor should therefore be especially sensitive to the implied sanctions and make special provisions to obviate them. For example, the instructor could leave the room while the questionnaires are being completed. Or, students could be asked to return the questionnaires by mail or to drop them in a box near the door just before the next course meeting.

This norm of voluntary participation, though, goes directly against a number of scientific concerns. In the most general terms, the scientific goal of *generalizability* is threatened if experimental subjects or survey respondents are only the kinds of people who willingly participate in such things. Because this orientation probably reflects more general personality traits, the results of the research might not be generalizable to all kinds of people. Most clearly, in the case of a descriptive survey, a researcher cannot generalize the sample survey findings to an entire population unless a substantial majority of the scientifically selected sample actually participates—the willing respondents and the somewhat unwilling.

Field research has its own ethical dilemmas in this regard (see Chapter 11). Very often, the researcher cannot even reveal that a study is being done, for fear that that revelation might significantly affect the social processes being studied. Clearly, the subjects of study in such cases are not given the opportunity to volunteer or refuse to participate.

Though the norm of voluntary participation is important, it's often impossible to follow it. In cases where you feel ultimately justified in violating it, it's all the more important that you observe the other ethical norms of scientific research, such as bringing no harm to the people under study.

No Harm to the Participants

Social research should never injure the people being studied, regardless of whether they volunteer for the study. Perhaps the clearest instance of this norm in practice concerns the revealing of information that would embarrass them or endanger their home life, friendships, jobs, and so forth. This aspect of the norm is discussed more fully in a moment.

Because subjects can be harmed psychologically in the course of a study, the researcher must look for the subtlest dangers and guard against them. Quite often, research subjects are asked to reveal deviant behaviour, attitudes they feel are unpopular, or personal characteristics that may seem demeaning, such as low income, the receipt of welfare payments, and the like. Revealing such information usually makes them feel at least uncomfortable.

Social research projects may also force participants to face aspects of themselves they don't normally consider. This can happen even when the information is not revealed directly to the researcher. In retrospect, a certain past behaviour may appear unjust or immoral. The project, then, can be the source of a continuing, personal agony for the subject. If the study concerns codes of ethical conduct, for example, the subject may begin questioning his or her own morality, and that personal concern may last long after the research has been completed and reported. For instance, probing questions can injure a fragile self-esteem.

It should be apparent from these observations that just about any research you might conduct runs the risk of injuring other people somehow. It's not possible to insure against all these potential injuries, however, some study designs make such injuries more likely than others. If a particular research procedure seems likely to produce unpleasant effects for subjects—asking survey respondents to report deviant behaviour, for example—the researcher should have the firmest of scientific grounds for doing it. If the research design is essential and also likely to be unpleasant for subjects, you'll find yourself in an ethical netherworld and may go through some personal agonizing. Although agonizing has little value in itself, it may be a healthy sign that you've become sensitive to the problem.

Increasingly, the ethical norms of voluntary participation and no harm to participants have become formalized in the concept of **informed consent**. This means that voluntary participation must be decided on the basis of a full understanding of the risks involved. For example, prospective subjects of a medical experiment will be presented with a discussion of the experiment and all the possible risks to themselves. They'll be required to sign a statement indicating that they are aware of the risks and choose to participate anyway. While the value of such a procedure is obvious when subjects will be injected with drugs designed to produce physical effects, for example, it's hardly appropriate when a participant observer rushes to the scene of urban rioting to study deviant behaviour. While the researcher in this latter case is not excused from the norm of not bringing harm to those observed, gaining informed consent is not the means to achieving that end.

Although the fact often goes unrecognized, subjects can be harmed by the analysis and reporting of data. Every now and then, research subjects read the books published about the studies they participated in. Reasonably sophisticated subjects can locate themselves in the various indexes and tables. Having done so, they may find themselves characterized, though not identified by name, as bigoted, unpatriotic, irreligious, and so forth. At the very least, such characterizations are likely to trouble them and threaten their self-images. Yet the whole purpose of the research project may be to explain why some people are prejudiced and others are not.

Like voluntary participation, avoiding harm to people is easy in theory but often difficult in practice. Sensitivity to the issue and experience with its applications, however, should improve the researcher's tact in delicate areas of research.

In recent years, social researchers have been getting greater support for abiding by this norm. The requirement of independent evaluation of the treatment of human subjects for research proposals by review committees, such as the REBs we just discussed, serves this function. Although sometimes troublesome and inappropriately applied, such requirements not only guard against unethical research but can also reveal ethical issues overlooked by the most scrupulous of researchers.

Anonymity and Confidentiality

The clearest concern in the protection of the subjects' interests and well-being is the protection of their identity. Two techniques, *anonymity* and *confidentiality*, assist researchers in this regard, although the two are often confused.

Anonymity A subject may be guaranteed anonymity only when both the researcher and the people who read about the research cannot identify a given response with a given subject. This means an interview survey respondent, for example, can never be considered anonymous, since an interviewer collects the information from an identifiable individual. (We assume here that standard sampling methods are followed.) An example of anonymity would be the mail survey in which no identification numbers are put on the questionnaires before their return to the research office (see Chapter 9).

Assuring anonymity makes it difficult to keep track of who has or hasn't returned the questionnaires. Despite this problem, there are some situations in which you may be advised to pay the necessary price. In studies seeking information on sensitive topics or illegal behaviour such as sexual practices or drug use, some researchers feel that honestly assuring anonymity would increase the likelihood and accuracy of responses. In addition, the researcher may not want to be in the position of being asked by authorities for the names of the respondents when illegal behaviour is the topic of study.

Confidentiality A respondent is guaranteed confidentiality when the researcher can identify a given person's responses but essentially promises not to do so publicly. In an interview survey, for example, the researcher would be in a position to make public the income reported by a given respondent, but the respondent is assured that this will not be done.

Whenever a research study is confidential rather than anonymous, it's the researcher's responsibility to make that fact clear to the subject. Moreover, researchers should never use the term *anonymous* to mean *confidential.*

With few exceptions (such as surveys of public figures who agree to have their responses published), the information research participants give must at least be kept confidential. This is not always an easy norm to follow, since the courts (at least until recently in Canada), have not recognized social research data as constituting the kind of "privileged communication" accepted in the case of priests and attorneys.

This unprotected guarantee of confidentiality was challenged in Canada in 1994 in the case of Russel Ogden. Ogden was a graduate student at Simon Fraser University (SFU) in the early 1990s conducting research for his Masters thesis on assisted death among people with HIV/AIDs. Investigating underground practices such as these necessarily involves gaining knowledge of illegal activities. The ethical rules he followed were to protect his subjects from harm. In order to do this, he had to maintain strict confidentiality, a promise he made to those who volunteered to participate in his study. He obtained ethical approval of his proposed research from the university Ethics Committee—a proposal that stated his commitment to complete confidentiality.

When he completed his thesis in 1994, his research received a great deal of attention. This attention brought with it a subpoena issued in a coroner's inquest. He was asked to report his knowledge of practices of assisted death and provide names. Refusing to comply, he faced contempt of court charges. He sought support and assistance from the university administration but was denied it.

Ogden chose to maintain his ethical responsibilities and fight for the right of privileged communication between the researcher and subject, bearing the risks and the legal costs himself. He was successful in defending the confidentiality of his research participants and thus established a common law precedent in Canada concerning academic privilege.

This case brought to light not only the responsibilities of and risks to researchers in maintaining ethical standards, but those of universities to protect the rights and interests of research participants and the rights of academic freedom and research. Although Ogden ultimately succeeded, he was left to defend the ethical principle of confidentiality on his own. The university gave him $2,000 on "compassionate" grounds to assist in his legal expenses, but refused to become involved in the case on any level. Ogden sued the university and lost. Nonetheless, from the remarks made by the judge in his suit to those made in the internal review of SFU's decision, the university's actions were duly criticized.

Two SFU professors, Nicholas Blomley and Steven Davis, conducted the review of the university's decision in the Ogden case. Their 1998 report is a well-argued presentation of the key issues. Although too long to justly summarize here, they concluded that the university had made "the wrong decision." Among other things, the decision put at risk the rights and interests of Ogden's research participants. The president of SFU accepted the recommendations they made. The report of their decision review is worth reading (http://www.sfu.ca/~palys/ogden.htm). Ted Palys and John Lowman have written a number of papers on ethics in research and on the Ogden case itself (see http://www.sfu.ca/~palys/ Conf&Law.html).

Here is another case illustrating the seriousness of this issue. Rik Scarce was a graduate student at Washington State University when he undertook participant observation among animal rights activists. In 1990, he published a book based on his research: *Ecowarriors: Understanding the Radical Environmental Movement.* In 1993, Scarce was called before a grand jury and asked to identify the activists he had studied. In keeping with the norm of confidentiality, the young researcher refused to answer the grand jury's questions and spent 159 days in the Spokane county jail.

You can use several techniques to guard against such dangers and insure better performance on the guarantee of confidentiality. To begin, interviewers and others with access to respondent identifications should be trained in their ethical responsibilities. Another fundamental technique is to remove all identifying information as soon as it's no longer necessary. In surveys, for instance, names and addresses should be removed from questionnaires and replaced by identification numbers. An identification file should be created that links numbers to names to permit the later correction of missing or contradictory information, but this file should not be available except for legitimate purposes.

The same technique holds for interviews. You may need to identify survey respondents initially so you can recontact them to verify that the interview was conducted and perhaps to get information that was missing in the original interview. As soon as you've verified an interview and assured yourself that you don't need any further information from the respondent, however, you can safely remove all identifying information from the interview booklet. Often, interview booklets are printed so that the first page contains all the identifiers. It can be torn off once the respondent's identification is no longer needed. This technique is no less true for data gathered in field research. Using codes for people and places instead of real identifying information when typing up your notes and organizing your data is an excellent precaution. Keep in mind, however, that even without the identifying information, if someone has access to all of your data, however it is gathered, it may still be possible to identify an individual, especially if the information has been gathered from a small, defined population of people.

In cases where you intended to remove the identifying information, but haven't done so yet, what do you do when the police or a court orders you to provide the responses given by your

research subjects? This is a real issue for practicing social researchers, even though they sometimes disagree about how to protect subjects. Harry O'Neill, the vice chair of The Roper Organization, for example, suggested the best solution is to avoid altogether the ability to identify respondents with their responses:

> So how is this accomplished? Quite simply by not having any respondent-identifiable information available for the court to request. In my initial contact with a lawyer-client, I make it unmistakably clear that, once the survey is completed and validated, all respondent-identifiable information will be removed and destroyed immediately. Everything else connected with the survey—completed questionnaires, data tapes, methodology, names of interviewers and supervisors—of course will be made available.
>
> (O'Neill 1992:4)

Board Chairman Burns Roper (1992:5) disagrees, saying that such procedures might raise questions about the validity of the research methods. Instead, Roper says that he feels he must be prepared to go to jail if necessary. (He notes that Vice Chair O'Neill has promised to visit him in that event.)

In the case of some types of surveys, O'Neill's strategy may be enough to protect confidentiality, but it may not suffice for data gathered in field research or through interviews, where observation and communication with research participants is face to face. In some instances, Roper's strategy may be the only way to guarantee participants' confidentiality. As in the cases of Ogden and Scarce, there are times when participants have to rely on the researcher's silence, on his or her ethical word to protect their confidences.

Deception

We've seen that the handling of subjects' identities is an important ethical consideration. Handling your own identity as a researcher can be tricky also. Sometimes it's useful and even necessary to identify yourself as a researcher to those you want to study. You'd have to be a master con artist to get people to participate in a laboratory experiment or complete a lengthy questionnaire without letting on that you were conducting research.

Even when you must conceal your research identity, you need to consider the following. Because deceiving people is unethical, deception within social research needs to be justified by compelling scientific or administrative concerns. Even then, the justification will be arguable.

Sometimes researchers admit that they're doing research but fudge about why they're doing it or for whom. Suppose you've been asked by a public welfare agency to conduct a study of living standards among aid recipients. Even if the agency is looking for ways of improving conditions, the recipient-subjects are likely to fear a witch-hunt for "cheaters." They might be tempted, therefore, to give answers making them seem more destitute than they really are. Unless they provide truthful answers, however, the study will not produce accurate data that will contribute to an effective improvement of living conditions. What do you do? One solution would be to tell subjects that you're conducting the study as part of a university research program, concealing your affiliation with the welfare agency. Doing that improves the scientific quality of the study, but it raises a serious ethical issue.

Lying about research purposes is common in laboratory experiments. Although it's difficult to conceal the fact you're conducting research, it's usually simple, and sometimes appropriate, to conceal your purpose. Many experiments in social psychology, for example, test the extent to which subjects will abandon the evidence of their own observations in favour of the views expressed by others. Recall our discussion in Chapter 2 of the classic Asch experiment—frequently replicated by psychology classes—in which subjects are shown three lines of differing lengths (A, B, and C) and asked to compare them with a fourth line (D). Subjects are then asked, "Which of the first three lines is the same length as the fourth?"

As you saw, you'd probably find it a fairly simple task to identify B as the correct answer. Your job, of course would be complicated by the fact that several other "subjects" sitting beside you (who in reality are all confederates of the researcher, told to agree on the wrong answer) all agree that A is the same length as D! The experiment's purpose is to see whether you'd give up your own judgment in favour of the group agreement. We think you can see that conformity is a useful phenomenon to study and understand, and it couldn't be studied experimentally without deceiving the subjects. We'll examine a similar situation in the discussion of the Milgram experiment in Chapter 8.

If deception is necessary for the experiment to work, how do we deal with the ethical issue of deceit? One solution researchers have found appropriate is to debrief subjects following the experiment. **Debriefing** involves interviewing the subjects to determine if the research experience generated any problems and then attempting to correct such problems. Even though subjects can't be told the true purpose of the study prior to their participation in it, there's usually no reason they can't know afterward. Telling them the truth afterward may make up for having to lie to them at the outset. This must be done with care, however, making sure the subjects aren't left with bad feelings or doubts about themselves based on their performance in the experiment. If this seems complicated, it's simply the price we pay for using other people's lives as the subject matter for our research.

Analysis and Reporting

Researchers have ethical obligations to their colleagues in the scientific community in addition to their ethical obligations to their subjects. These obligations concern the analysis of data and the way results are reported.

In any rigorous study, the researcher should be more familiar than anyone else with the technical shortcomings and failures of the study. Researchers have an obligation to make such shortcomings known to their readers, even if admitting mistakes and qualifications makes them feel foolish.

Negative findings, for example, should be reported if they're at all related to the analysis. There is an unfortunate myth in scientific reporting that only positive discoveries are worth reporting (journal editors are sometimes guilty of believing this as well). In science, however, it is often as important to know that two variables are **not** related as to know that they are.

Similarly, researchers must avoid the temptation to save face by describing their findings as the product of a carefully preplanned analytical strategy when that's not the case. Many findings arrive unexpectedly, even though they may seem obvious in retrospect. So an interesting relationship is uncovered by accident. So what? Embroidering such situations with descriptions of fictitious hypotheses is dishonest. It also does a disservice to less experienced researchers. It misleads them into thinking that all scientific inquiry is rigorously preplanned and organized.

In general, science progresses through honesty and openness; ego-defenses and deception retard it. Researchers can best serve their peers, and scientific discovery as a whole, by telling the truth about all the pitfalls and problems they've experienced in a particular line of inquiry. Perhaps they'll save others from the same problems.

Some topics of research provoke more attention to ethical concerns than do others. For example, given the highly sensitive nature of research on human sexuality, it is quite noticeable that articles reporting such research often explicitly address concerns the readers might have about the ethical precautions the researchers have taken and the impact such precautions may have on their findings. This is often true of research concerning vulnerable populations such as children, prisoners, mental patients, and the homeless as well. When a research study happens to combine such topics and populations, these concerns are even greater. Two examples will help to illustrate.

Stephen Baron researched homeless Canadian skinheads youths. Here's what he said about the consideration of ethical issues when designing his study and the impact of his choices. "[O]nly male youths were approached, so that ethical concerns surrounding questions directed at respondents' sexual and physical victimization were minimized" (1997:131). He described the thinking that surrounded this choice in a footnote.

[T]he female population created a number of ethical dilemmas in designing the research. In research of this nature, a number of questions necessarily tap into delicate areas of the respondent's lives. For example, areas of the interview required details concerning physical and sexual victimization in childhood histories. It also included questions concerning various types of victimization outside the home (sexual assault), as well as probed for participation in illegal activities, including prostitution. These questions are sensitive in character, and the fact that the primary researcher was male would likely have made them even more so for female respondents.

(1997:131)

Baron concluded, "along with the ethics board," that it wasn't proper for a male researcher to ask such questions of females. He acknowledged that while these questions could have been removed, past research indicated such factors to be important in explaining street youths' behaviour. Because the author felt the questions were essential to his research, he chose to limit his study to males.

Baron further communicated how he obtained contact and informed consent, his appearance in the field, and the fact that respondents were given $10 in food coupons for their participation. For example, such a population is likely to have problems with illiteracy. Recognizing this, Baron offered to help the participants read the consent forms and questioned them about their understanding of the forms after they had reviewed them.

Shelley Young (1997) addressed the care taken in her study on the sexual exploitation of children. She gathered data from case-files concerning child sexual assault at a Victim-Witness Assistance Programme. She reported, for example, that she had "to swear an oath of confidentiality" concerning the information to which she was given access. In addition she discussed her strategy for protecting the identities of those involved in potentially identifiable cases. "Although highly unusual or unique cases were included in the sample, they were not presented in totality; only elements of these cases which fit with other scenarios were used in the final presentation. Data were presented as profiles or aggregate scenarios to prevent the identification of any particular case or individual involved." (1997:288) Ethical approval of the project from the University of Windsor Department of Sociology and Anthropology Ethics Committee was noted as well.

DISCUSSION EXAMPLES

Research ethics, then, is an important though ambiguous topic. The difficulty of resolving ethical issues should not be an excuse for ignoring them. To sensitize you further to the ethical component in social research, below is a prepared list of real and hypothetical research situations. See if you can find the ethical component in each. How do you feel about it? Do you feel the procedures described are ultimately acceptable or unacceptable? It would be useful to discuss some of these with others in your methods course.

1. After a field study of deviant behaviour during a riot, law enforcement officials demand that the researcher identify those people who were observed looting. Rather than risk arrest as an accomplice after the fact, the researcher complies.

2. After completing the final draft of a book reporting a research project, the researcher-author discovers that 25 of the 2,000 survey interviews were falsified by interviewers but chooses to ignore that fact and publish the book anyway.

3. Researchers obtain a list of right-wing radicals they wish to study. They contact the radicals with the explanation that each has been selected "at random" from among the general population to take a sampling of "public opinion."

4. A university instructor who wants to test the effect of unfair berating administers an hour exam to both sections of a specific course. The overall performance of the two sections is essentially the same. The grades of one section are artificially lowered, however, and the instructor berates them for performing so badly. The instructor then administers the same final exam to both sections and discovers that the performance of the unfairly berated section is worse. The hypothesis is confirmed, and the research report is published.

5. A researcher studying dorm life on campus discovers that 60 percent of the residents regularly violate restrictions on alcohol consumption. Publication of this finding would probably create a furor in the campus community. Because no extensive analysis of alcohol use is planned, the researcher decides to ignore the finding and keep it quiet.

6. To test the extent to which people may try to save face by expressing attitudes on matters they are wholly uninformed about, the researcher asks for their attitudes regarding a fictitious issue.

7. A research questionnaire is circulated among students as part of their university registration packet. Although students are not told they must complete the questionnaire, the hope is that they will believe they must thus ensuring a higher completion rate.

8. A participant-observer pretends to join a radical political group in order to study it and is successfully accepted as a member of the inner planning circle. What should the researcher do if the group makes plans for the following?
   a. A peaceful, though illegal, demonstration
   b. The bombing of a public building during a time it is sure to be unoccupied
   c. The assassination of a public official

With these issues in mind, you can evaluate some of the research examples presented in the following chapters in terms of the ethical considerations raised above. It's worth stressing that the decision to elaborate on ethical concerns in Part 3 in no way indicates that such matters need only be considered during the data gathering phase of research. Ethical considerations are prominent in research design from its inception, and they remain prominent throughout every phase of the process, down to the reporting of the research and application of findings.

Chapter 8

Experiments

An experiment is a mode of observation that enables researchers to probe causal relationships. Many experiments in social research are conducted under the controlled conditions of a laboratory, but experiments can also take advantage of natural occurrences to study the effects of events in the social world.

In this chapter . . .

Introduction

This chapter addresses the research method probably most frequently associated with structured science in general—the experiment. Here we'll focus on the experiment as a mode of scientific observation in social research. At base, experiments involve (1) taking action and (2) observing the consequences of that action. Social scientific researchers typically select a group of subjects, do something to them, and observe the effect of what was done. In this chapter, we'll examine the logic and some of the techniques of social scientific experiments.

It's worth noting at the outset that we often use experiments in nonscientific inquiry. In preparing a stew, for example, we add salt, taste, add more salt, and taste again. In defusing a bomb, we clip the red wire, observe whether the bomb explodes, clip another, and . . . .

We also experiment copiously in our attempts to develop generalized understandings about the world we live in. All skills are learned through experimentation: eating, walking, riding a bicycle, and so forth. Through experimentation, students discover how much studying is required for aca-

demic success. Through experimentation, professors learn how much preparation is required for successful lectures. This chapter discusses how social researchers use experiments to develop generalized understandings. We'll see that, like other methods available to the social researcher, experimenting has its special strengths and weaknesses.

Topics Appropriate to Experiments

Experiments are more appropriate for some topics and research purposes than others. Experiments are especially well suited to research projects involving relatively limited and well-defined concepts and propositions. In terms of the traditional image of science, discussed earlier in this book, the experimental model is especially appropriate for hypothesis testing. Because experiments focus on determining causes, they're also better suited to explanatory than to descriptive purposes.

Let's assume, for example, we want to study prejudice against Aboriginal Canadians. We hypothesize that learning about the contribution of

Aboriginal Canadians to Canadian history will reduce prejudice, and we decide to test this hypothesis experimentally. To begin, we might test a group of experimental subjects to determine their levels of prejudice against Aboriginal Canadians. Next, we might show them a documentary film depicting the many important ways Aboriginal Canadians have contributed to the scientific, literary, political, and social development of the nation. Finally, we measure our subjects' levels of prejudice against Aboriginal Canadians to determine whether the film has actually reduced prejudice.

Experimentation has also been successful in the study of small group interaction. Thus, we might bring together a small group of experimental subjects and assign them a task, such as making recommendations for popularizing car pools. We observe, then, how the group organizes itself and deals with the problem. Over the course of several such experiments, we might systematically vary the nature of the task or the rewards for handling the task successfully. By observing differences in the way groups organize themselves and operate under these varying conditions, we can learn a great deal about the nature of small group interaction and the factors that influence it.

We typically think of experiments as being conducted in laboratories. Indeed, most of the examples in this chapter will involve such a setting. This need not be the case, however. Social researchers often study what are called *natural experiments:* "experiments" that occur in the regular course of social events. The latter portion of this chapter will deal with such research.

The Classical Experiment

In both the natural and the social sciences, the most conventional type of experiment involves three major pairs of components: (1) independent and dependent variables, (2) pretesting and posttesting, and (3) experimental and control groups. This section looks at each of these components and the way they're put together in the execution of the experiment.

Independent and Dependent Variables

Essentially, an experiment examines the effect of an independent variable on a dependent variable. Typically, the independent variable takes the form of an experimental stimulus, which is either present or absent. That is, the stimulus is a **dichotomous variable**, having two attributes, present or not present. In this typical model, the experimenter compares what happens when the stimulus is present to what happens when it is not.

In the example concerning prejudice against Aboriginal Canadians, *prejudice* is the dependent variable and *exposure to Aboriginal Canadian history* is the independent variable. The researcher's hypothesis suggests that prejudice depends, in part, on a lack of knowledge of Aboriginal Canadian history. The purpose of the experiment is to test the validity of this hypothesis by presenting some subjects with an appropriate stimulus, such as a documentary film. In other terms, the independent variable is the cause and the dependent variable is the effect. Thus, we might say that watching the film caused a change in prejudice or that reduced prejudice was an effect of watching the film.

The independent and dependent variables appropriate to experimentation are nearly limitless. Moreover, a given variable might serve as an independent variable in one experiment and as a dependent variable in another. For example, *prejudice* is the dependent variable in our example, but it might be the independent variable in an experiment examining the effect of prejudice on voting behaviour.

To be used in an experiment, both independent and dependent variables must be operationally defined. Such operational definitions might involve a variety of observation methods. Responses to a questionnaire, for example, might be the basis for defining prejudice. Speaking to or ignoring Aboriginal Canadians, or agreeing or disagreeing with them in conversation, might be elements in the operational definition of interaction with Aboriginal Canadians in a small group setting.

Conventionally, in the experimental model, dependent and independent variables must be operationally defined before the experiment begins. However, as you'll see in connection with survey research and other methods, it's sometimes appropriate to make a wide variety of observations during data collection and then determine the most useful operational definitions of variables during later analyses. Ultimately, however, experimentation, like other quantitative methods, requires specific and standardized measurements and observations.

Pretesting and Posttesting

In the simplest experimental design, subjects are measured in terms of a dependent variable (**pretesting**), exposed to a stimulus representing an independent variable, and then remeasured in terms of the dependent variable (**posttesting**). Any differences between the first and last measurements on the dependent variable are then attributed to the independent variable.

In the example of prejudice and exposure to Aboriginal Canadian history, we'd begin by pretesting the extent of prejudice among our experimental subjects. Using a questionnaire asking about attitudes toward Aboriginal Canadians, for example, we could measure both the extent of prejudice exhibited by each individual subject and the average prejudice level of the whole group. After exposing the subjects to the Aboriginal Canadian history film, we could administer the same questionnaire again. Responses given in this posttest would permit us to measure the later extent of prejudice for each subject and the average prejudice level of the group as a whole. If we discovered a lower level of prejudice during the second administration of the questionnaire, we might conclude that the film had indeed reduced prejudice.

In the experimental examination of attitudes such as prejudice, we face a special practical problem relating to validity. As you may already have imagined, the subjects might respond differently to the questionnaires the second time even if their attitudes remained unchanged. During the first administration of the questionnaire, the sub-

jects may be unaware of its purpose. By the time of the second measurement, they may have figured out that we are interested in measuring their prejudice. Because no one wishes to seem prejudiced, the subjects may "clean up" their answers the second time around. Thus, the film will seem to have reduced prejudice although, in fact, it had not.

This is an example of a more general problem that plagues many forms of social research. The very act of studying something may change it. The techniques for dealing with this problem in the context of experimentation will be discussed in various places throughout the chapter. The first technique involves the use of control groups.

Experimental and Control Groups

Laboratory experiments seldom, if ever, involve only the observation of an **experimental group** to which a stimulus has been administered. In addition, the researchers also observe a **control group**, which does not receive the experimental stimulus.

In the example of prejudice and Aboriginal Canadian history, we might examine two groups of subjects. To begin, we give each group a questionnaire designed to measure their prejudice against Aboriginal Canadians. Then, the experimental group is shown the film. Later, the researcher administers a posttest of prejudice to *both* groups. Figure 8-1 illustrates this basic experimental design.

Using a control group allows the researcher to detect any effects of the experiment itself. If the posttest shows that the overall level of prejudice exhibited by the control group has dropped as much as that of the experimental group, then the apparent reduction in prejudice must be a function of the experiment or of some external factor rather than a function of the film. If, on the other hand, prejudice were reduced *only* in the experimental group, such reduction would seem to be a consequence of exposure to the film, because that's the only difference between the two groups. Alternatively, if prejudice were reduced *more* in the experimental group than in the control group, that, too, would be grounds for assuming that the film reduced prejudice.

The need for control groups in social research became clear in connection with a series of studies of employee satisfaction conducted by F. J. Roeth-lisberger and W. J. Dickson (1939) in the late 1920s and early 1930s. These two researchers studied working conditions in the telephone "bank wiring room" of the Western Electric Works in the Chicago suburb of Hawthorne, Illinois. They were interested in discovering what changes in working conditions would improve employee satisfaction and productivity.

To the researchers' great satisfaction, they discovered that making working conditions better consistently increased satisfaction and productivity. As the workroom was brightened up through better lighting, for example, productivity went up. When lighting was further improved, productivity went up again. To further substantiate their scientific conclusion, the researchers then *dimmed* the lights: *Productivity again improved!*

It became evident then that the wiring room workers were responding more to the attention given them by the researchers than to improved working conditions. As a result of this phenomenon, often called the **Hawthorne effect,** social researchers have become more sensitive to and cautious about the possible effects of experiments themselves. The use of a proper control group in the wiring room study—one that was studied intensively without any other changes in the working conditions—would have pointed to the existence of this effect.

The need for control groups in experimentation has been nowhere more evident than in medical research. Time and again, patients who participate in medical experiments have appeared to improve, and it has been unclear how much of the improvement has come from the experimental treatment and how much from the experiment. In testing the effects of new drugs, then, medical researchers frequently administer a **placebo**—a "drug" that actually should have no effect, like sugar pills—to a control group. Thus, the control group patients believe they, like the experimental group, are receiving an experimental drug. Often, they improve. If the new drug is effective, however, those receiving the actual drug will improve more than those receiving the placebo.

In social scientific experiments, control groups guard against not only the effects of the experiments themselves but also the effects of any events outside the laboratory during the experiments. In the example of the study of prejudice, suppose that a popular leader of an Aboriginal Canadian com-

Figure 8-1
Diagram of Basic Experimental Design

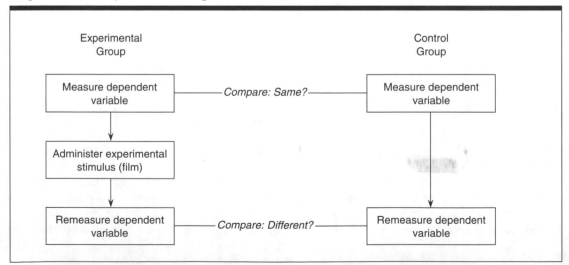

munity was beaten by the police in the middle of, say, a week-long experiment. Such an event might very well horrify the experimental subjects, requiring them to examine their own attitudes toward Aboriginal Canadians, with the result of reduced prejudice. Because such an effect should happen about equally for members of the control and experimental groups, a *greater* reduction of prejudice among the experimental group would, again, point to the impact of the experimental stimulus: the documentary film.

Sometimes an experimental design requires more than one experimental or control group. In the case of the documentary film, for example, we might also want to examine the impact of reading a book on Aboriginal Canadian history. In that case, we might have one group see the film and read the book; another group only see the movie; still another group only read the book; and the control group do neither. With this kind of design, we could determine the impact of each stimulus separately, as well as their combined effect.

The Double-Blind Experiment

Like patients who improve when they merely *think* they're receiving a new drug, sometimes experimenters tend to prejudge results. In medical research, the experimenters may be more likely to "observe" improvements among patients receiving the experimental drug than among those receiving the placebo. (This would be most likely, perhaps, for the researcher who developed the drug.) A **double-blind experiment** eliminates this possibility, because neither the subjects nor the experimenters know which is the experimental group and which the control. In the medical case, those researchers responsible for administering the drug and for noting improvements would not be told which subjects were receiving the drug and which the placebo. Conversely, the researcher who knew which subjects were in which group would not administer the experiment.

In social scientific experiments, as in medical experiments, the danger of experimenter bias is further reduced to the extent that the operational definitions of the dependent variables are clear and precise. Thus, medical researchers would be less

likely to bias unconsciously their reading of a patient's temperature than they would to bias their assessment of how lethargic the patient was. For the same reason, the small group researcher would be less likely to misperceive which subject spoke, or to whom he or she spoke, than whether the subject's comments sounded cooperative or competitive.

As we've indicated several times, seldom can we devise operational definitions and measurements that are wholly precise and unambiguous. This is another reason it may sometimes be appropriate to employ a double-blind design in social research experiments.

Selecting Subjects

The logic of sampling was discussed in Chapter 7. We talked at length about selecting samples that are representative of some population. Many social scientific laboratory experiments are conducted with university undergraduates as subjects because a large number of social researchers work in universities. Typically, the experimenter asks students enrolled in his or her classes to participate in experiments or advertises for subjects in a university newspaper. Subjects may or may not be paid for participating in such experiments.

In relation to the norm of *generalizability* in science, this tendency clearly represents a potential defect in social scientific research. Simply put, university undergraduates do not typify the public at large. There is a danger, therefore, that we may learn much about the attitudes and actions of university undergraduates but not about social attitudes and actions in general.

However, this potential defect is less significant in explanatory research than in descriptive research. True, having noted the level of prejudice among a group of university undergraduates in our pretesting, we would have little confidence that the same level existed among the public at large. On the other hand, if we found that a documentary film reduced the level of prejudice that existed among those undergraduates, we would have more confidence—without being certain—that it would have a comparable effect in the community at large.

Social processes and patterns of causal relationships appear to be more generalizable and more stable than specific characteristics like an individual's prejudice level.

Aside from the question of generalizability, the cardinal rule of subject selection and experimentation concerns the comparability of experimental and control groups. Ideally, the control group represents what the experimental group would be like if it had **not** been exposed to the experimental stimulus. Therefore, the logic of experiments requires that experimental and control groups be as similar as possible. There are several ways to accomplish this.

Probability Sampling

The discussions in Chapter 7 of the logic and techniques of probability sampling provide one method for selecting two groups of people similar to each other. Beginning with a sampling frame composed of all the people in the population under study, the researcher might select two probability samples. If these samples each resemble the total population from which they're selected, they'll also resemble each other.

Recall also, however, that the degree of resemblance (representativeness) achieved by probability sampling is largely a function of the sample size. As a general guideline, probability samples of less than 100 are not likely to be terribly representative, and social scientific experiments seldom involve that many subjects in either experimental or control groups. As a result, then, probability sampling is seldom used in experiments to select subjects from a larger population. Researchers in assigning subjects to groups, however, use the logic of random selection.

Randomization

Having recruited, by whatever means, a total group of subjects, the experimenter may randomly assign those subjects to either the experimental or the control group. Such **randomization** may be accomplished by numbering all of the subjects serially and selecting numbers by means of a random number table. Alternatively, the experimenter might assign the odd-numbered subjects to the experimental group and the even-numbered subjects to the control group.

Let's return again to the basic concept of probability sampling. If we recruit 40 subjects altogether in response to a newspaper advertisement, there's no reason to believe that the 40 subjects represent the entire population from which they've been drawn. Nor can we assume that the 20 subjects randomly assigned to the experimental group represent that larger population. We may have greater confidence, however, that the 20 subjects randomly assigned to the experimental group will be reasonably similar to the 20 assigned to the control group.

Following the logic of our earlier discussions of sampling, we can view the 40 subjects as a population from which we select two probability samples, each consisting of half the population. Because each sample reflects the characteristics of the total population, the two samples will mirror each other. As we saw in Chapter 7, our assumption of similarity in the two groups depends in part on the number of subjects involved. In the extreme case, if we recruited only two subjects and assigned, by the flip of a coin, one as the experimental subject and one as the control, there would be no reason to assume that the two subjects are similar to each other. With larger numbers of subjects, however, randomization makes good sense.

Although the logic of random selection underlies the process of randomization, randomization should not be confused with a probability sample such as the simple random sample. The probability sample ensures that the subjects from whom actual data is gathered will be as representative as possible of some larger population. Randomization ensures that the subjects exposed to the test factor (experimental group) are as comparable as possible to those exposed to the control factor (control group). All equal, randomization is an excellent step even when the subjects for the experiment are not randomly selected from a population (for example, are volunteers).

Matching

Another way to achieve comparability between experimental and control groups is through **matching.** This process is similar to the quota sampling methods discussed in Chapter 7. If 12 of our subjects are young white men, we might assign six of those at random to the experimental group and the other six to the control group. If 14 are middle-aged Aboriginal Canadian women, we might assign seven to each group. The overall matching process could be most efficiently achieved through the creation of a *quota matrix* constructed of all the most relevant characteristics. Figure 8-2 provides a simplified illustration of such a matrix. The experimenter in this example decided that age, race, and gender are the relevant characteristics. Ideally, the quota matrix is constructed to result in an even number of subjects in each cell of the matrix. Then, half the subjects in each cell would go into the experimental group and half into the control group.

Alternatively, we might recruit more subjects than our experimental design requires. We might then examine many characteristics of the large ini-

tial group of subjects. Whenever we discover a pair of quite similar subjects, we would assign one to the experimental group and the other to the control group. Potential subjects who are unlike anyone else in the initial group would be left out of the experiment altogether.

Whatever method we employ, the desired result is the same. The overall average description of the experimental group should be the same as that of the control group. For example, on average each group should have about the same ages, the same gender composition, the same racial composition, and so forth. This same test of comparability should be used whether the two groups are created through probability sampling or through randomization.

Thus far, we've referred to the "relevant" variables without saying clearly what those variables are. Of course, these variables can't be specified in any definite way, any more than we could specify in Chapter 7 which variables should be used in stratified sampling. Which variables are relevant ultimately depends on the nature and purpose of an experiment. As a general rule, however, the exper-

Figure 8-2
Quota Matrix Illustration

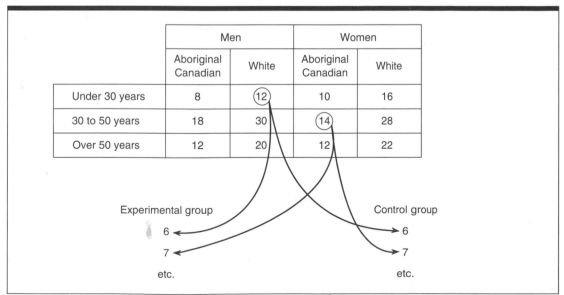

imental and control groups should be comparable in terms of those variables most likely to be related to the dependent variable under study. In a study of prejudice, for example, the two groups should be alike in terms of education, ethnicity, and age, among other factors. In some cases, moreover, we may delay assigning subjects to experimental and control groups until we have initially measured the dependent variable. Thus, for example, we might administer a questionnaire measuring subjects' prejudice and then match the experimental and control groups on this variable to assure ourselves that the two groups exhibit the same overall level of prejudice.

When assigning subjects to the experimental and control groups, you should be aware of two arguments in favour of randomization over matching. First, you may not be in a position to know in advance which variables are relevant for the matching process. Second, most of the statistics used to analyze the results of experiments assume randomization. Failure to design your experiment that way, then, makes your later use of those statistics less meaningful.

Sometimes researchers combine matching and randomization. When conducting an experiment on the educational enrichment of young adolescents, Yinger and his colleagues (1977) needed to assign a large number of students, ages 13 and 14, to several different experimental and control groups to ensure the comparability of students composing each of the groups. They achieved this goal by the following method.

Beginning with a pool of subjects, the researchers first created strata of students nearly identical to one another in terms of some 15 variables. From each of the strata, students were randomly assigned to the different experimental and control groups. In this fashion, the researchers actually improved on conventional randomization. Essentially, they used a stratified sampling procedure (Chapter 7), except that they employed far more stratification variables than are typically used in, say, survey sampling.

Thus far we've described the classical experiment—the experimental design that best represents the logic of causal analysis in the laboratory. In practice, however, social researchers use a great variety of experimental designs. Let's look at some now.

Variations on Experimental Design

Donald Campbell and Julian Stanley (1963), in a classic book on research design, describe some 16 different experimental and quasi-experimental designs. This section describes some of these variations to better show the potential for experimentation in social research.

To begin, Campbell and Stanley discuss three "preexperimental" designs—not to recommend them but because they're frequently used in less-than-professional research. In the first such design, the *one-shot case study*, a single group of subjects is measured on a dependent variable following the administration of some experimental stimulus. Suppose, for example, that we show the Aboriginal Canadian history film mentioned earlier to a group of people and then administer a questionnaire that seems to measure prejudice against Aboriginal Canadians. Suppose further that the answers given to the questionnaire seem to represent a low level of prejudice. We might be tempted to conclude that the film reduced prejudice. Lacking a pretest, however, we can't be sure. Perhaps the questionnaire doesn't really represent a very sensitive measure of prejudice, or perhaps the group we're studying was low in prejudice to begin with. In either case, the film might have made no difference, though our experimental results might have misled us into thinking it did.

The second preexperimental design discussed by Campbell and Stanley adds a pretest for the experimental group but lacks a control group. This design, which the authors call the *one-group pretest-posttest design*, suffers from the possibility that some factor other than the independent variable might cause a change between the pretest and posttest results, such as the beating of a respected Aboriginal Canadian leader by the police. Thus, although we can see that prejudice has been reduced, we can't be sure the film caused that reduction.

To round out the possibilities for preexperimental designs, Campbell and Stanley point out that some research is based on experimental and control groups but has no pretests. They call this design the *static-group comparison.* For instance, we might show the Aboriginal Canadian history film to one group and not to another and then measure prejudice in both groups. If the experimental group had less prejudice at the conclusion of the experiment, we might assume the film was responsible. But unless we had randomized our subjects, we would have no way of knowing that the two groups had the same degree of prejudice initially; perhaps the experimental group started out with less.

Figure 8-3 graphically illustrates these three preexperimental research designs using a different research question: *Does exercise cause weight reduction?* To make the several designs clearer, the figure shows individuals rather than groups, but the same logic pertains to group comparisons. Let's review the three preexperimental designs in this new example.

The one-shot case study represents a common form of logical reasoning. Asked whether exercise causes weight reduction, we may bring to mind an example that would seem to support the proposition: someone who exercises and is thin. There are problems with this reasoning, however. Perhaps the person was thin long before beginning to exercise. Or, perhaps he became thin for some other reason, like eating less or getting sick. The observations shown in the diagram do not guard against these other possibilities. Moreover, the observation that the man in the diagram is in trim shape depends on our intuitive idea of what constitutes trim and overweight body shapes. All told, this is very weak evidence for testing the relationship between exercise and weight loss.

The one-group pretest-posttest design offers somewhat better evidence that exercise produces weight loss. Specifically, we've ruled out the possibility that the man was thin before beginning to exercise. However, we still have no assurance that it was his exercising that caused him to lose weight.

Finally, the static-group comparison eliminates the problem of our questionable definition of what constitutes trim or overweight body shapes. In this case, we can compare the shapes of the man who exercises and the one who does not. This design, however, reopens the possibility that the man who exercises was thin to begin with.

Validity Issues In Experimental Research

At this point we want to present in a more systematic way the factors that affect the validity of experimental research. We'll first look at what Campbell and Stanley call *the sources of internal invalidity,* reviewed and expanded in a follow-up book by Thomas Cook and Donald Campbell (1979). Then we'll discuss the problem of generalizing experimental results to the "real" world, referred to as *external invalidity.* Having examined these, we'll be in a position to appreciate the advantages of some of the more sophisticated experimental and quasi-experimental designs social science researchers sometimes use.

Sources of Internal Invalidity The problem of **internal invalidity** refers to the possibility that the conclusions drawn from experimental results may not accurately reflect what has gone on in the experiment itself. The threat of internal invalidity is present whenever anything other than the experimental stimulus can affect the dependent variable. Campbell and Stanley (1963:5–6) and Cook and Campbell (1979:51–55) point to several sources of internal invalidity. Here are twelve:

1. *History.* During the course of the experiment, historical events may occur that will confound the experimental results. The beating by police of an Aboriginal Canadian leader during the course of an experiment on reducing anti-Aboriginal Canadian prejudice would be an example.
2. *Maturation.* People are continually growing and changing, and such changes affect the

Figure 8-3
Three Preexperimental Research Designs

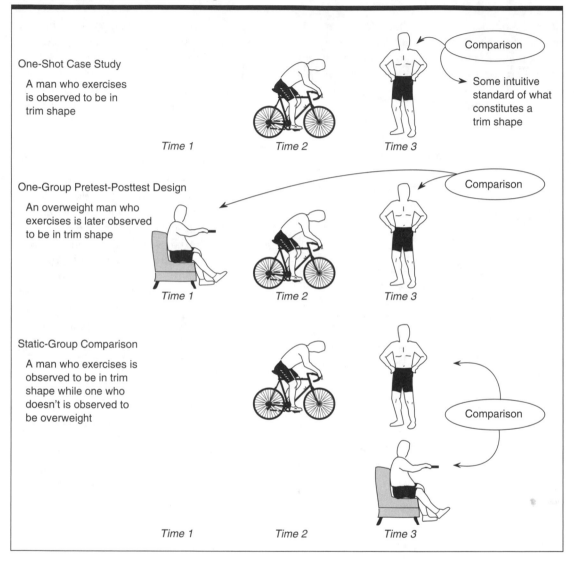

results of the experiment. In a long-term experiment, the fact that the subjects grow older (and wiser?) may have an effect. In shorter experiments, they may grow tired, sleepy, bored, or hungry, or change in other ways that may affect their behaviour in the experiment.

3. *Testing.* Often the process of testing and retesting will influence people's behaviour,

thereby confounding the experimental results. Suppose we administer a questionnaire to a group as a way of measuring their prejudice. Then we administer an experimental stimulus and remeasure their prejudice. By the time we conduct the posttest, the subjects will probably have gotten more sensitive to the issue of prejudice and will be more thoughtful in their answers. In fact, they may have figured out that we're trying to find out how prejudiced they are, and, because few people like to appear prejudiced, they may give answers that they think we want or that will make them look good.

4. *Instrumentation.* The process of measurement in pretesting and posttesting brings to light some of the issues of conceptualization and operationalization discussed earlier in the book. If we use different measures of the dependent variable in the pretest and posttest (say, different questionnaires about prejudice), how can we be sure they're comparable to one another? Perhaps prejudice will seem to have decreased simply because the pretest measure was more sensitive than the posttest measure. Or if the experimenters are making the measurements, their standards or their abilities may change over the course of the experiment.

5. *Statistical regression.* Sometimes it's appropriate to conduct experiments on subjects who start out with extreme scores on the dependent variable. If you were testing a new method for teaching math to hardcore failures in math, you'd want to conduct your experiment on people who previously have done extremely poorly in math. But consider for a minute what's likely to happen to the math achievement of such people over time without any experimental interference. They're starting out so low that they can only stay at the bottom or improve: They can't get worse. Even without any experimental stimulus, then, the group as a whole is likely to show some improvement over time. Referring to a *regression to the mean,* statisticians often point out that extremely tall people as a group are likely to have children shorter than themselves, and extremely short people as a group are likely to have children taller than themselves. There's a danger, then, that changes occurring by virtue of subjects starting out in extreme positions will be attributed erroneously to the effects of the experimental stimulus.

6. *Selection biases.* We discussed bias in selection earlier when we examined different ways of selecting subjects for experiments and assigning them to experimental and control groups. Comparisons don't have any meaning unless the groups are *comparable.*

7. *Experimental mortality.* Although some social experiments could, we suppose, kill subjects, *experimental mortality* refers to a more general and less extreme problem. Often, experimental subjects will drop out of the experiment before it's completed, which can affect statistical comparisons and conclusions. In the classical experiment involving an experimental and a control group, each with a pretest and posttest, suppose that the bigots in the experimental group are so offended by the Aboriginal Canadian history film that they leave before it's over. Those subjects sticking around for the posttest will have been less prejudiced to start with, so the group results will reflect a substantial "decrease" in prejudice.

8. *Causal time-order.* Though rare in social research, ambiguity about the time order of the experimental stimulus and the dependent variable can arise. Whenever this occurs, the research conclusion that the stimulus caused the dependent variable can be challenged with the explanation that the "dependent" variable actually caused changes in the stimulus (see Chapter 3).

9. *Diffusion or imitation of treatments.* When experimental and control-group subjects can communicate with each other, experimental subjects could pass on some elements of the experimental stimulus to the control group. If, for example, there is a time lapse between the showing of the Aboriginal Canadian history film and the administration of the posttest, members of the experimental group might tell control-group subjects about the film. In that case, the control group becomes affected by the stimulus and is not a real control. Sometimes we speak of the control group as having been "contaminated."

10. *Compensation.* As you'll see in Chapter 13, in experiments in real-life situations, such as a special educational program, subjects in the

control group are often deprived of something considered to be of value. In such cases, there may be pressures to offer some form of compensation. For example, hospital staff might feel sorry for control group patients and give them extra "tender loving care." In such a situation, the control group is no longer a genuine control group.

11. *Compensatory rivalry.* In real-life experiments, the subjects deprived of the experimental stimulus may try to compensate for the missing stimulus by working harder. Suppose an experimental math program is the experimental stimulus; the control group may work harder than before on their math in the attempt to beat the "special" experimental subjects.

12. *Demoralization.* On the other hand, feelings of deprivation within the control group may result in their giving up. In educational experiments, demoralized control group subjects may stop studying, act up, or get angry.

These, then, are some of the sources of internal invalidity in experiments. Aware of these, experimenters have devised designs aimed at handling them. The classical experiment, if coupled with proper subject selection and assignment, addresses each of these problems. Let's look again at that study design, presented graphically in Figure 8-4.

If we use the experimental design shown in Figure 8-4 in our study of prejudice against Aboriginal Canadians, we should expect two findings. For the experimental group, the level of prejudice measured in their posttest should be less than was found in their pretest. In addition, when the two posttests are compared, less prejudice should be found in the experimental group than in the control.

This design also guards against the problem of history in that anything occurring outside the experiment that might affect the experimental group should also affect the control group. Therefore, there should still be a difference in the two posttest results. The same comparison guards against problems of maturation as long as the subjects have been randomly assigned to the two groups. Testing and instrumentation can't be problems, since both the experimental and control groups are subject to the same tests and experimenter effects. If the subjects have been assigned to the two groups randomly, statistical regression should affect both equally, even if people with extreme scores on prejudice (or whatever the dependent variable is) are being studied. Selection bias is ruled out by the random assignment of subjects. Experimental mortality is more complicated to handle, but the data provided in this study design offer several ways to deal with it. Slight modifications to the design—administering a placebo (such as a film having nothing to do with Aboriginal Canadians) to the control group, for example—can make the problem even easier to manage.

The remaining five problems of internal invalidity are avoided through the careful administration of a controlled experimental design. The experimental design we've been discussing facili-

Figure 8-4
Another Look at the Classical Experiment

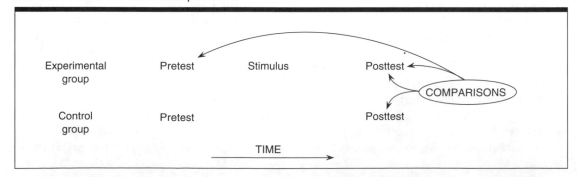

tates the clear specification of independent and dependent variables. Experimental and control subjects can be kept separate, reducing the possibility of diffusion or imitation of treatments. Administrative controls can avoid compensations given to the control group, and compensatory rivalry can be watched for and taken into account in evaluating the results of the experiment, as can the problem of demoralization.

Sources of External Invalidity Internal invalidity accounts for only some of the complications faced by experimenters. In addition, there are problems of what Campbell and Stanley call **external invalidity**, which relates to the *generalizability* of experimental findings to the "real" world. Even if the results of an experiment are an accurate gauge of what happened during that experiment, do they really tell us anything about life in the wilds of society?

Campbell and Stanley describe four forms of this problem; We'll present one as an illustration. The generalizability of experimental findings is jeopardized, as the authors point out, if there is an interaction between the testing situation and the experimental stimulus (1963:18). Here's an example of what they mean.

Staying with the study of prejudice and the Aboriginal Canadian history film, let's suppose that our experimental group in the classical experiment has less prejudice in its posttest than in its pretest and that its posttest shows less prejudice than that of the control group. We can be confident that the film actually reduced prejudice among our experimental subjects. But would it have the same effect if the film were shown in theatres or on television? We can't be sure, since the film might only be effective when people have been sensitized to the issue of prejudice, as the subjects may have been in taking the pretest. This is an example of interaction between the testing and the stimulus. The classical experimental design cannot control for that possibility. Fortunately, experimenters have devised other designs that can.

The *Solomon four-group design* (Campbell and Stanley 1963:24–25) addresses the problem of testing interaction with the stimulus. As the name suggests, it involves four groups of subjects,

assigned randomly from a pool. Figure 8-5 presents this design graphically.

Notice that Groups 1 and 2 in Figure 8-5 compose the classical experiment. Group 3 is administered the experimental stimulus without a pretest, and Group 4 is only posttested. This latest experimental design permits four meaningful comparisons. If the Aboriginal Canadian history film really reduces prejudice—unaccounted for by the problem of internal validity and unaccounted for by an interaction between the testing and the stimulus—we should expect four findings:

1. In Group 1, posttest prejudice should be less than pretest prejudice.
2. There should be less prejudice evident in the Group 1 posttest than in the Group 2 posttest.
3. The Group 3 posttest should show less prejudice than the Group 2 pretest.
4. The Group 3 posttest should show less prejudice than the Group 4 posttest.

Notice that findings (3) and (4) rule out any interaction between the testing and the stimulus. And remember that these comparisons are meaningful only if subjects have been assigned randomly to the different groups, thereby providing groups of equal prejudice initially, even though their preexperiment prejudice is only measured in Groups 1 and 2.

There is a side benefit to this research design, as the authors point out. Not only does the Solomon four-group design rule out interactions between testing and the stimulus, it also provides data for comparisons that will reveal the amount of such interaction that occurs in the classical experimental design. This knowledge allows a researcher to review and evaluate the value of any prior research that used the simpler design.

The last experimental design we'll mention is what Campbell and Stanley (1963:25–26) call the *posttest-only control group design;* it consists of the second half (Groups 3 and 4) of the Solomon design. As the authors argue persuasively, with proper randomization, only Groups 3 and 4 are needed for a true experiment that controls for the problems of internal invalidity as well as for the interaction between testing and stimulus. With

Figure 8-5
The Solomon Four-Group Design

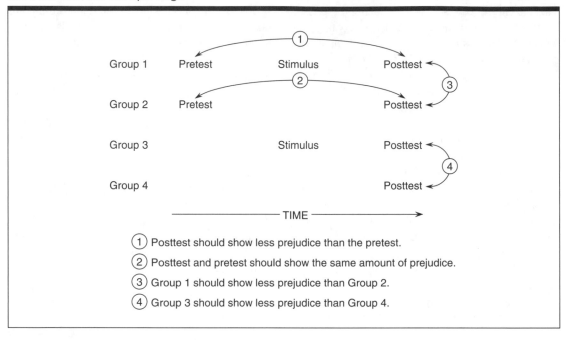

(1) Posttest should show less prejudice than the pretest.

(2) Posttest and pretest should show the same amount of prejudice.

(3) Group 1 should show less prejudice than Group 2.

(4) Group 3 should show less prejudice than Group 4.

randomized assignment to experimental and control groups (which distinguishes this design from the static-group comparison discussed earlier), the subjects will be initially comparable on the dependent variable—comparable enough to satisfy the conventional statistical tests used to evaluate the results—so it's not necessary to measure them. Indeed, Campbell and Stanley suggest that the only justification for pretesting in this situation is tradition. Experimenters have simply grown accustomed to pretesting and feel more secure with research designs that include it. Be clear, however, that this point applies only to experiments in which subjects have been assigned to experimental and control groups *randomly*, because that's what justifies the assumption that the groups are equivalent—without actually measuring them to find out.

This discussion has introduced the intricacies of experimental design, its problems, and some solutions. There are, of course, a great many other possible experimental designs in use. Some involve more than one stimulus and combinations of stimuli. Others involve several tests of the dependent variable over time and the administration of the stimulus at different times for different groups. If you're interested in pursuing this topic, you might look at the Campbell and Stanley book.

An Illustration of Experimentation

Experiments have been used to study a wide variety of topics in the social sciences. Some experiments have been conducted within laboratory situations; others occur in the "real world." The following discussion provides a glimpse of both.

In George Bernard Shaw's well-loved play, *Pygmalion*, the basis for the musical *My Fair Lady*, Eliza Doolittle speaks of the powers others have in determining our social identity. Here's how she distinguishes the way she's treated by her tutor, Professor Higgins, and by Higgins' friend, Colonel Pickering:

You see, really and truly, apart from the things anyone can pick up (the dressing and the proper way of speaking, and so on), the difference between a lady and a flower girl is not how she behaves, but how she's treated. I shall always be a flower girl to Professor Higgins, because he always treats me as a flower girl, and always will, but I know I can be a lady to you, because you always treat me as a lady, and always will.

(Act V)

The sentiment Eliza expresses here is basic social science, addressed more formally by sociologists such as Charles Horton Cooley ("Looking-glass self") and George Herbert Mead ("the generalized other"). The basic point is that who we think we are—our *self-concept*—and how we behave are largely a function of how others see and treat us. Related to this, the way others perceive us is largely conditioned by expectations they have in advance. If they've been told we're stupid, for example, they're likely to see us that way, and we may come to see ourselves that way and actually act stupidly.

This topic has generally been called the *Pygmalion effect* and is nicely suited to controlled experiments. In one of the best-known experiments on this topic, Robert Rosenthal and Lenore Jacobson (1968) administered what they called a "Harvard Test of Inflected Acquisition" to students in a West Coast school in the U.S. Subsequently, they met with the students' teachers to present the results of the test. In particular, Rosenthal and Jacobson identified certain students as very likely to exhibit a sudden spurt in academic abilities during the coming year, based on the results of the test.

When IQ test scores were compared later, the researchers' predictions proved accurate. The students identified as "spurters" far exceeded their classmates during the following year, suggesting that the predictive test was a powerful one. In fact, the test was a hoax! The researchers had made their predictions randomly among both good and poor students. What they told the teachers did not really reflect students' test scores at all. The progress made by the "spurters" was simply a result of the teachers expecting the improvement and paying more attention to those students, encouraging them, and rewarding them for achievements. (Notice the similarity between this situation and the Hawthorne effect, mentioned earlier.)

The Rosenthal-Jacobson study attracted a great deal of popular as well as scientific attention. Subsequent experiments have focused on specific aspects of what has become known as the *attribution process,* or the *expectations communication model.* This research, largely conducted by psychologists, parallels research primarily by sociologists, which takes a slightly different focus and is often gathered under the label *expectations-states theory.* The psychological studies focus on situations in which the expectations of a dominant individual affect the performance of subordinates, as in the case of a teacher and students, or a boss and employees. The sociological research has tended to focus more on the role of expectations among equals in small, task-oriented groups. In a jury, for example, how do jurors initially evaluate each other, and how do those initial assessments affect later interactions?

Here's the case of an experiment conducted to examine the way our perceptions of our abilities and those of others affect our willingness to accept the other person's ideas. Martha Foschi, G. Keith Warriner, and Stephen Hart (1985) were particularly interested in the role "standards" played in that respect.

In general terms, by "standards" we mean how well or how poorly a person has to perform in order for an ability to be attributed or denied him/her. In our view, standards are a key variable affecting how evaluations are processed and what expectations result. For example, depending on the standards used, the same level of success may be interpreted as a major accomplishment or dismissed as unimportant.

(1985:108–109)

To begin examining the role of standards, the researchers designed an experiment involving four experimental groups and a control. Subjects were told the experiment involved something called "pattern recognition ability," which was an innate ability some people had and others didn't. The researchers said subjects would be working in pairs on pattern recognition problems. Of course, there's no such thing as pattern recognition ability. The goal of the experiment was to determine how information about this supposed ability affected subjects' subsequent behaviour.

The first stage of the experiment was to "test" each subject's abilities at pattern recognition. If you had been a subject in the experiment, you would have been shown a geometrical pattern for eight seconds, followed by two more patterns, each of which was similar to but not the same as the first one. Your task would be to choose which of the subsequent set had a pattern closest to the first one you saw. You would be asked to do this 20 times, and a computer would print out your "score." Half the subjects would be told they had gotten 14 correct and the other half told they had only gotten 6 correct, regardless of which patterns they matched with which. Depending on the luck of the draw, you would think you had done either quite well or quite badly. Notice, however, that you wouldn't really have any standard for judging your performance—since 4 correct might be considered a great performance.

At the same time you were given your score, however, you would also be given your "partner's score," although both the "partners" and their "scores" were also computerized fictions. (Subjects were told they would be communicating with their partners via computer terminals but would not be allowed to see each other.) If you were assigned a score of 14, you'd be told your partner had a score of 6; if you were assigned 6, you'd be told your partner had 14.

This procedure meant that you would enter the teamwork phase of the experiment believing either (1) you had done better than your partner or (2) you had done worse than your partner. This information constituted part of the "standard" you would be operating under in the experiment. In addition, half of each group was told that a score of between 12 and 20 meant the subject *definitely* had pattern recognition ability; the other subjects were told that a score of 14 wasn't really high enough to prove anything definite. Thus, you would emerge from this with one of the following beliefs:

1. You are *definitely better* at pattern recognition than your partner.
2. You are *possibly better* than your partner.
3. You are *possibly worse* than your partner.
4. You are *definitely worse* than your partner.

The control group for this experiment was told nothing about their own abilities or their partners'. In other words, they had no expectations.

The final step in the experiment was to set the "teams" to work. As before, you and your partner would be given an initial pattern, followed by a comparison pair to choose from. When you entered your choice in this round, however, you would be told what your partner had answered; then you would be asked to choose again. In your final choice, you could either stick with your original choice or switch. The "partner's" choice was, of course, created by the computer, and as you can guess, there were often disagreements in the team: 16 out of 20 times, in fact.

The dependent variable in this experiment was the extent to which subjects would switch their choices to match those of their partners. The researchers hypothesized that the *definitely better* group would switch least often, followed by the *probably better* group, followed by the *control group,* followed by the *probably worse* group, followed by the *definitely worse* group, who would switch most often.

The number of times subjects in the five groups switched their answers follows. Realize that each had 16 opportunities to do so. These data indicate that each of the researchers' expectations was correct—with the exception of the comparison between the *possibly worse/definitely worse* groups. Although the latter group was in fact the more likely to switch, the difference is too small to be taken as a confirmation of the hypothesis.

Group	Mean Number of Switches
Definitely better	5.05
Possibly better	6.23
Control Group	7.95
Possibly worse	9.23
Definitely worse	9.28

More detailed analyses found that the same basic pattern held for both men and women, though it was somewhat clearer for women than for men. Here are the actual data:

	Mean Number of Switches	
	Women	Men
Definitely better	4.50	5.66
Possibly better	6.34	6.10
Control Group	7.68	8.34
Possibly worse	9.36	9.09
Definitely worse	10.00	8.70

Because specific research efforts like this one sometimes seem extremely focused in their scope, you might wonder about their relevance to anything. As part of a larger research effort, however, studies like this one add concrete pieces to our understanding of more general social processes.

It's worth taking a minute or so to consider some of the life situations where "expectation states" might have important consequences. We've mentioned the case of jury deliberations. How about all forms of prejudice and discrimination? Or, consider how expectation states figure into job interviews or meeting your heartthrob's parents. If you think about it, you'll no doubt see other situations where these laboratory concepts apply in real life.

"Natural" Experiments

Although we tend to equate the terms *experiment* and *laboratory experiment,* many important social scientific experiments occur outside controlled settings, often in the course of normal social events. Sometimes nature designs and executes experi-ments that we can observe and analyze; some-times social and political decision makers serve this natural function.

Imagine, for example, that a hurricane has struck a particular town. Some residents of the town suffer severe financial damages while others escape relatively lightly. What, we might ask, are the behavioural consequences of suffering a natural disaster? Are those who suffer most more likely to take precautions against future disasters than those who suffer least? To answer these questions, we might interview residents of the town some time after the hurricane. We might question them regarding their precautions before the hurricane and the ones they're currently taking, comparing the people who suffered greatly from the hurricane with those who suffered relatively little. In this fashion, we might take advantage of a *natural experiment,* which we could not have arranged even if we'd been perversely willing to do so.

A similar example comes from the annals of social research concerning World War II. After the war ended, social researchers undertook retrospective surveys of wartime morale among civilians in several German cities. Among other things, they wanted to determine the effect of mass bombing on the morale of civilians. They compared the reports of wartime morale of residents in heavily bombed cities with reports from cities that received relatively little bombing. (Bombing did not reduce morale.)

Because the researcher must take things pretty much as they occur, natural experiments raise many of the validity problems discussed earlier. Thus, taking special care in the study design is an important step.

Coldevin (1976) was able to take advantage of a unique opportunity to study the impact of the introduction of television into a Canadian Eskimo community. In 1972 the CBC initiated a four-hour a day Frontier Coverage Package into Frobisher Bay community on lower Baffin Island. The study was conducted in 1973 during a break in the programming, prior to the introduction of full service television in the community.

The initial survey was intended as both an evaluation of the impact of the Frontier Service and as baseline data toward monitoring the developmental effects of full service television.

(1976:34)

The goal of the study was to assess whether such television exposure increased the level of national and international information among the community members and to evaluate the effect of television exposure on socio-economic aspirations, desire for life-style change, and preference to travel to further destinations, among other things. The foundation of the study was open-ended interview questionnaires administered in the regional dialect.

Since the community had access to television for nearly a year, how could any changes due to the effects of television be determined? Coldevin found a control community, Fort Chimo, in northern Quebec to which he could make comparisons. Fort Chimo was a non-television community and it was predominately Eskimo like Frobisher Bay. In addition, its access to direct outside information was limited.

Coldevin's study design was necessarily based on the idea that the two communities were equivalent to each other except for the existence of television. Since he could not, of course, randomly assign his subjects to the experimental and control groups, he could not assume this. Instead, he compared characteristics of the two communities to see whether they were equivalent. He concluded that "the two samples closely parallel each other on a variety of demographic dimensions and accordingly were considered as highly satisfactory for comparison of the primary variables under consideration" (p. 36).

There were other problems that Coldevin had to deal with in trying to control factors in this natural setting. For example, his sample was selected from heads of households on the following basis:

[T]hey represent the existing link between the traditional, nomadic hunting and fishing culture and the present day relatively stationary community and for the most part have not been exposed to the information resources of the school currently available to their children. It was therefore assumed that the thrust from a relatively information poor to information rich home environment would primarily accrue to the adult segment of the family.

(p. 35)

His analysis also had to take into account the potential impact of the introduction, one month before his survey began, of a weekly bilingual newspaper (Eskimo and English) in the television community but not the nontelevision community.

This example points both to the special problems involved in natural experiments and to the possibility of taking those problems into account. Social research generally requires ingenuity and insight; natural experiments call for a little more than the average.

For those of you who are curious about the outcome, Coldevin found, among other things, that the first year of the Frontier television "had little effect on information levels...but did affect socio-economic aspirations" (p. 34). The adults interviewed showed increased aspirations for their children's employment but not for themselves. These increased aspirations were "particularly prominent for daughters" (p. 38).

This example anticipates the subject of Chapter 13, *evaluation research*, which can be seen as a special type of natural experiment. As you'll see, evaluation research involves taking the logic of experimentation into the field to observe and evaluate the effects of stimuli in real life. Because this is an increasingly important form of social research, we devote an entire chapter to it.

Ethical Considerations

In the introduction to Part 3, we provided illustrations of ethical concerns arising from experiments. Potential for harm in some research methods is higher than in others. Experiments are particularly vulnerable to ethical breaches due to the degree of manipulation of subjects by researchers. We'll briefly discuss the Milgram experiment here because of the controversy it provoked and the role many believe it played in heightening ethical concerns in social research.

Stanley Milgram's laboratory experiment in the early 1960s generated debate about ethical practices in research soon after he completed it. Stimulated by the atrocities committed during World War II, his research concerned how willing people were to obey authority even when they were told to engage in wrongful or immoral behaviour, including the potential of killing someone.

Milgram advertised for men to participate in a study concerning memory and learning. The research participant (experimental subject) was cast in the role of "teacher." As "teacher," he was asked to test the "learner's" memory of word lists and administer electric shocks of increasing intensity to him each time he gave an incorrect answer. The "learner" (believed by the research subject to be a study participant as well) was placed in an adjacent room. He was not visible to the "teacher," but he was audible. As the shock levels increased, the "learner's" indication of discomfort increased from noises of pain and discomfort to screaming, begging that the experiment be stopped, kicking the wall, and ultimately silence.

Milgram reported his findings in his book *Obedience to Authority* (1969). When the research subjects indicated concern about the learner and a desire to stop administering shocks, the researcher would tell him that he must continue and most did. All of the first 40 men in Milgram's experiment continued to administer the shocks until the learner began to kick the wall, and the majority of the subjects continued the shocks to their highest level—clearly marked as highly dangerous. Nonetheless, many of them experienced a great deal of stress when doing so, exhibited by sweating, groaning, and pressing their fingernails into their skin; some had uncontrollable seizures.

The "learner" was a confederate, and the shocks being administered by the "teacher" were not real, although he didn't know this of course. Ironically, in trying to determine the conditions under which people will obey authority even in situations regarded as immoral, the study, while praised by many as one of the most important pieces of social psychological research conducted in its time, was also condemned by others on grounds of unethical practices.

The criticism focused on the effects of the experiment on the human subjects. Is it right to (deceptively) subject research participants to this degree of psychological stress and pain? In weighing the human costs and benefits of this research, many believe that the research was worthwhile—what was learned about human behaviour was important. Others believe the risk to the human subjects crossed the ethical line.

In defense of the research, Milgram wrote that despite the unexpected degree of stress experienced by many of the subjects during the experiment, they themselves reported overwhelmingly that they were glad they participated. After his participation, each subject was debriefed. They were immediately informed that no one was actually harmed in the experiment. Once the experiment was complete, the subjects received a report detailing the procedures and the results. After receiving the report, they were sent a follow-up questionnaire concerning participation. As Milgram (1969:195) reported: "In its quantitative aspect...84 percent of the subjects stated they were glad to have been in the experiment; 15 percent indicated neutral feelings; and 1.3 percent indicated negative feelings." While acknowledging the need to interpret such information with caution, he noted that such data should not be ignored either. He further reported that 80 percent believed that further experiments of this nature should be conducted, and nearly three-quarters said "that they had learned something of personal importance as a result of being in the study."

This raises interesting questions as well. The vast majority of the subjects were not condemning of the research. Do we protect people from what they themselves may want to know more about and better understand? Perhaps there was a different research design that could have been used to investigate obedience?

The Milgram experiment illustrates the ambiguity that surrounds ethical issues in research. None of the issues raised has an easy solution, but they certainly warrant much consideration and debate.

Almost a decade later Zimbardo led what is called the Stanford Prison Experiment. This experiment too raised many ethical concerns. An experiment regarding the psychology of imprisonment was supposed to last for two weeks. Student volunteers, chosen for their "normal" scores on personality tests, were assigned the roles of guards and prisoners in a mock prison. The researchers stopped the experiment after six days due to the risk of long-term psychological harm and immediate physical harm to the research subjects. A 50-minute documentary, *Quiet Rage* (Zimbardo and Musen 1992), illustrates the transformation of the research subjects over the six days through edited clips of the experiment, presents follow-up interviews with some of the subjects, and explores the ethical dimension of the study. It's a good documentary that is worth watching and discussing.

Finally, consider the experiments used as illustrations in this chapter. Did any ethical concerns cross your mind when you were reading about them? For example, what did you think when you read about Rosenthal and Jacobson's study? It's likely that you thought about the effect of such a study on the students. Did you stop to weigh the importance of their findings against the impact of their hoax on the subjects? If you were sitting on a Review Ethics Board, what might your response be to the proposal of such a study?

Strengths and Weaknesses of the Experimental Method

The chief advantage of a controlled experiment lies in the isolation of the experimental variable and its impact over time. This is seen most clearly in terms of the basic experimental model. A group of experimental subjects are found, at the outset of the experiment, to have a certain characteristic; following the administration of an experimental stimulus, they're found to have a different characteristic. To the extent that subjects have experienced no other stimuli, we may conclude that the change of characteristics is attributable to the experimental stimulus.

Further, since individual experiments are often rather limited in scope, requiring relatively little time and money and relatively few subjects, we can often replicate a given experiment several times using several different groups of subjects. (This isn't always the case, of course, but it's usually easier to repeat experiments than, say, surveys.) As in all other forms of scientific research, replication of research findings strengthens our confidence in the validity and generalizability of those findings.

The greatest weakness of laboratory experiments lies in their artificiality. Social processes that occur in a laboratory setting might not necessarily occur in more natural social settings. For example, an Aboriginal Canadian history film might genuinely reduce prejudice among a group of experimental subjects. This would not necessarily mean, however, that the same film shown in neighbourhood movie theatres throughout the country would reduce prejudice among the general public. Artificiality is not as much of a problem, of course, for natural experiments as for those conducted in the laboratory.

In discussing several of the sources of internal and external invalidity mentioned by Campbell, Stanley, and Cook, we saw that we can create experimental designs that logically control such problems. This possibility points to one of the great advantages of experiments: They lend themselves to a logical rigor that is often much more difficult to achieve in other modes of observation. Thus, experiments are a primary tool for studying causal relationships.

Main Points

- Experiments are an excellent vehicle for the controlled testing of causal processes.
- The classical experiment tests the effect of an experimental stimulus (the independent vari-

able) on a dependent variable through the pretesting and posttesting of experimental and control groups.

- It's generally less important that a group of experimental subjects be representative of some larger population than that experimental and control groups be similar to each other. Probability sampling, randomization, and matching are all methods of achieving comparability in the experimental and control groups. Randomization is the generally preferred method. In some designs, it can be combined with matching.
- Campbell and Stanley describe three forms of preexperiments: the one-shot case study, the one-group pretest-posttest design, and the static-group comparison. None of these designs contain all the controls available in a true experiment.
- Campbell and Stanley list 12 sources of internal invalidity in experimental design. The classical experiment with random assignment of subjects guards against each of these 12 sources of internal invalidity.
- Experiments also face problems of external invalidity: Experimental findings may not reflect real life.
- The interaction of testing with the stimulus is an example of external invalidity that the classical experiment does not guard against.
- The Solomon four-group design and other variations on the classical experiment can safeguard against external invalidity
- Campbell and Stanley suggest that, given proper randomization in the assignment of subjects to the experimental and control groups, there is no need for pretesting in experiments.
- Natural experiments often occur in the course of social life in the real world, and social researchers can implement them in somewhat the same way they would design and conduct laboratory experiments.
- Experiments are particularly vulnerable to ethical breaches due to the degree of manipulation of subjects by researchers.

Review Questions and Exercises

1. Pick 6 of the 12 sources of internal invalidity discussed in the book and make up examples (not discussed in the book) to illustrate each.
2. Think of a recent natural disaster you've witnessed or read about. Frame a research question that might be studied by treating that disaster as a natural experiment. In two or three paragraphs, outline how the study might be done.
3. In this chapter, we looked briefly at the problem of "placebo effects." On the Web, find a study in which the placebo effect figured importantly. Write a brief report on the study, including the source of your information. (*Hint:* you might want to do an Internet search of *placebo.*)

Continuity Project

Think of an experimental stimulus that might affect students' attitudes toward gender equality. Describe an experiment that would test that stimulus.

Additional Readings

Campbell, Donald, and Julian Stanley. *Experimental and Quasi-Experimental Designs for Research.* Chicago: Rand McNally, 1963. An excellent analysis of the logic and methods of experimentation in social research. This book is especially useful in its application of the logic of experiments to other social research methods. Though fairly old, this book has attained the status of a classic and is still frequently cited.

Cook, Thomas D., and Donald T. Campbell. *Quasi-Experimentation: Design and Analysis Issues for Field Settings.* Chicago: Rand McNally, 1979. An expanded and updated version of Campbell and Stanley.

Jones, Stephen R. G. "Worker Independence and Output: The Hawthorne Studies Reevaluated." *American Sociological Review* 55, 1990:176–90. This article reviews these classical studies and questions the traditional interpretation (which was presented in this chapter).

Martin, David W. *Doing Psychology Experiments.* 4th ed. Monterey, CA: Brooks/Cole, 1996. Thorough explanations of the logic behind research methods, often in a humourous style. The book emphasizes ideas of particular importance to the beginning researcher, such as getting an idea for an experiment or reviewing the literature.

*Info*Trac: You can find further relevant readings on the World Wide Web at

http://sociology.wadsworth.com

Chapter 9

Survey Research

Researchers have many methods for collecting data through surveys, from mail questionnaires to personal interviews to online surveys conducted over the Internet. Social researchers should know how to select an appropriate method and how to implement it effectively.

In this chapter . . .

Introduction

Survey research is a very old research technique. In the Old Testament, for example, we find the following:

> After the plague the Lord said to Moses and to Eleazar the son of Aaron, the priest, "Take a census of all the congregation of the people of Israel, from twenty old and upward. . . ."
> (Numbers 26:1–2)

Ancient Egyptian rulers conducted censuses to help them administer their domains. Jesus was born away from home because Joseph and Mary were journeying to Joseph's ancestral home for a Roman census.

A little-known survey was attempted among French workers in 1880. A German political sociologist mailed some 25,000 questionnaires to workers to determine the extent of their exploitation by employers. The rather lengthy questionnaire included items such as these:

> Does your employer or his representative resort to trickery in order to defraud you of a part of your earnings?
> If you are paid piece rates, is the quality of the article made a pretext for fraudulent deductions from your wages?

The survey researcher in this case was not George Gallup but Karl Marx ([1880] 1956: 208). Though 25,000 questionnaires were mailed out, there is no record of any being returned.

Today, survey research is a frequently used mode of observation in the social sciences. In a typical survey, the researcher selects a sample of respondents and administers a standardized questionnaire to them. Chapter 7 discussed sampling techniques in detail. This chapter discusses how to prepare a questionnaire and describes the various options for administering it so that respondents answer your questions adequately.

The chapter concludes with a short discussion of *secondary analysis*, the analysis of survey data collected by someone else. This use of survey results has become an important aspect of survey research in recent years, and it's especially useful for students and others with scarce research funds.

Let's begin by looking at the kinds of topics that researchers can appropriately study using survey research.

Topics Appropriate to Survey Research

Surveys may be used for descriptive, explanatory, and exploratory purposes. They are chiefly used in studies that have individual people as the units of analysis. Although this method can be used for other units of analysis, such as groups or interactions, some individual persons must serve as **respondents** or informants. Thus, we could undertake a survey in which divorces were the unit of analysis, but we would need to administer the survey questionnaire to the participants in the divorces (or to some other informants).

Survey research is probably the best method available to the social scientist interested in collecting original data for describing a population too large to observe directly. Careful probability sampling provides a group of respondents whose characteristics may be taken to reflect those of the larger population, and carefully constructed standardized questionnaires provide data in the same form from all respondents.

Surveys are also excellent vehicles for measuring attitudes and orientations in a large population. Public opinion polls—for example, Gallup, Angus Reid, Decima, and Environics—are well-known examples of this use. Indeed, polls have become so prevalent that at times the public seems unsure what to think of them. Pollsters are criticized by those who don't think (or want to believe) that polls are accurate (candidates who are "losing" in polls often tell voters not to trust the polls). But polls are also criticized for being *too* accurate—for example when exit polls on election day are used to predict a winner before the actual voting is complete.

The general attitude toward public opinion research is further complicated by scientifically unsound "surveys" that nonetheless capture people's attention because of the topics they cover and/or their "findings." A good example may be found in the "Hite Reports" on human sexuality. While enjoying considerable attention in the popular press, the writer Shere Hite was roundly criticized by the research community for her data-collection methods. For example, a 1987 Hite report was based on questionnaires completed by women around the U.S.—but *which* women? Hite reported that she distributed some 100,000 questionnaires through various organizations, and around 4,500 were returned. Now 4,500 and 100,000 are large numbers in the context of survey sampling. However, given Hite's research methods, her 4,500 respondents didn't necessarily represent U.S. women any more than the *Literary Digest*'s enormous 1936 sample represented the U.S. electorate when their two million sample ballots indicated Landon would bury Roosevelt in a landslide.

Sometimes, people use the pretense of survey research for quite different purposes. For example, you may have received a telephone call indicating you've been selected for a survey, only to find the first question was "How would you like to make thousands of dollars a week right there in your own home?" Or you may have been told you could win a prize if you could name the person whose picture is on the penny. (Tell them it's Elvis.) Unfortunately, a few unscrupulous telemarketers do try to prey on the general cooperation people have given to survey researchers.

By the same token, political parties and charitable organizations have begun conducting phony "surveys." Often under the guise of collecting public opinion about some issue, callers ultimately ask respondents for a monetary contribution.

Recent political campaigns have produced another form of bogus survey, called the "push poll." Here's what the American Association for Public Opinion Polling says in condemning this practice:

> A "push poll" is a telemarketing technique in which telephone calls are used to canvass potential voters, feeding them false or misleading "information" about a candidate under the pretense of taking a poll to see how this "information" affects voter preferences. In fact, the intent is not to measure public opinion but to manipulate it to "push" voters away from one candidate and toward the opposing candidate. Such polls defame selected candidates by spreading false or misleading information about them. The intent is to disseminate campaign propaganda under the guise of conducting a legitimate public opinion poll.
>
> (Bednarz 1996)

In short, the labels "survey" and "poll" are sometimes misused. When done properly, however, survey research is one of the most valuable tools of social inquiry. For example, there are countless survey studies conducted concerning issues such as public attitudes toward crime and justice, abortion, and government. Large surveys are conducted to determine the amount of victimization in a society, the degree of violence against women, the use of public services, perceptions of satisfaction and happiness, engagement in cultural activities, and participation in sports, for example. They are also conducted to collect information on issues of employment, income, job benefits, heath care experiences, the use of alcohol, smoking, support networks, division of household work, occupational and emotional health, and so forth. Statistics Canada conducts a large number of national surveys, some annually, concerning the above issues and much more. Designing useful (and trust-

worthy) survey research begins with clearly identified topics of interest and well-defined concepts as discussed in Chapter 5. The survey makes use of questions as a means of operationalizing such concepts. Therefore, the formulation of good questions is essential to developing a useful survey. Let's turn to that topic now.

Guidelines for Asking Questions

In social research, variables are often operationalized when researchers ask people questions as a way of getting data for analysis and interpretation. Sometimes the questions are asked by an interviewer; sometimes they are written down and given to respondents for completion. In other cases, several general guidelines can help you frame and ask questions that serve as excellent operationalizations of variables while avoiding pitfalls that can result in useless or even misleading information.

Surveys include the use of a **questionnaire**—an instrument specifically designed to elicit information that will be useful for analysis. While some of the specific points to follow are more appropriate to structured questionnaires than to the more open-ended questionnaires used in qualitative, in-depth interviewing, the underlying logic is valuable whenever we ask people questions in order to gather data.

Choose Appropriate Question Forms

Let's begin with some of the options available to you in creating questionnaires. These options include using questions or statements and choosing open-ended or closed-ended questions.

Questions and Statements Although the term *questionnaire* suggests a collection of questions, an examination of a typical questionnaire will probably reveal as many statements as questions. This is not without reason. Often, the researcher is interested in determining the extent to which respondents hold a particular attitude or perspective. If you can summarize the attitude in a fairly brief statement, you can present that statement and ask respondents whether they agree or disagree with it. As you may remember, Rensis Likert greatly formalized this procedure through the creation of the Likert scale (Chapter 6), a format in which respondents are asked to strongly agree, agree, disagree, or strongly disagree, or perhaps strongly approve, approve, and so forth.

Both questions and statements may be used profitably. Using both in a given questionnaire gives you more flexibility in the design of items and can make the questionnaire more interesting as well.

Open-Ended and Closed-Ended Questions

In asking questions, researchers have two options. They may ask **open-ended questions**, in which case the respondent is asked to provide his or her own answer to the question. For example, the respondent may be asked, "What do you feel is the most important issue facing Canada today?" and be provided with a space to write in the answer (or be asked to report it verbally to an interviewer). As we'll see in Chapter 12, in-depth, qualitative interviewing relies almost exclusively on open-ended questions. However, they are also used in survey research.

In the case of **closed-ended questions**, the respondent is asked to select an answer from among a list provided by the researcher. Closed-ended questions are very popular in survey research because they provide a greater uniformity of responses and are more easily processed.

Open-ended responses must be coded before they can be processed for computer analysis, as will be discussed in Chapter 15. This coding process often requires that the researcher interpret the meaning of responses, opening the possibility of misunderstanding and researcher bias. There is also a danger that some respondents will give answers that are essentially irrelevant to the researcher's intent. Closed-ended responses, on the other hand, can often be transferred directly into a computer format.

The chief shortcoming of closed-ended questions lies in the researcher's structuring of responses. When the relevant answers to a given question are relatively clear, there should be no problem. In other cases, however, the researcher's structuring of responses may overlook some important responses. In asking about "the most important issue facing Canada," for example, his or her checklist of issues might omit certain issues that respondents would have said were important.

The construction of closed-ended questions should be guided by the two structural requirements. First, the response categories provided should be exhaustive: They should include all the possible responses that might be expected. Often, researchers ensure this by adding a category such as "Other (Please specify: _____)." Second, the answer categories must be mutually exclusive: The respondent should not feel compelled to select more than one. (In some cases, you may wish to solicit multiple answers, but these may create difficulties in data processing and analysis later on.) To ensure that your categories are mutually exclusive, carefully consider each combination of categories, asking yourself whether a person could reasonably choose more than one answer. In addition, it's useful to add an instruction to the question asking the respondent to select the one best answer, but such an instruction should not be used as a substitute for a carefully constructed set of responses.

Make Items Clear

It should go without saying that questionnaire items should be clear and unambiguous, but the broad proliferation of unclear and ambiguous questions in surveys makes the point worth emphasizing. Often we can become so deeply involved in the topic under examination that opinions and perspectives are clear to us but not to our respondents, many of whom have paid little or no attention to the topic. Or, if we have only a superficial understanding of the topic, we may fail to specify the intent of a question sufficiently. The question "What do you think about the proposed peace plan?" may evoke in the respondent a counterquestion: "Which proposed peace plan?" Questionnaire items should be precise so that the respondent knows exactly what the researcher is asking.

The possibilities for misunderstanding are endless and no researcher is immune (Polivka and Rothgeb 1993). For example, a study to determine the accuracy of a survey conducted by the U.S. Census Bureau found that some questions used to determine the nation's employment patterns were ambiguous. When the Census Bureau asked questions about activities during the "last week" they meant Sunday through Saturday. Yet, more than half the respondents took "last week" to include only Monday through Friday. By the same token, whereas they define "working full-time" as 35 or more hours a week, the same evaluation studies showed respondents using the more traditional definition of 40 hours per week. These findings resulted in modification of the questions to specify the Bureau's definitions. A look at the Canadian Census Dictionary shows that many employment questions concern information about a respondent's activities during the "last week," which Statistics Canada also defines as Sunday through Saturday. When inquiring about full versus part-time employment, however, a full-time week is defined by Statistics Canada as 30 or more hours.

Avoid Double-Barrelled Questions

Frequently, researchers ask respondents for a single answer to a question that actually has multiple parts. That seems to happen most often when the researcher has personally identified with a complex question. For example, you might ask respondents to agree or disagree with the statement "Canada should spend less money on welfare programs and more money on education." Although many people would unequivocally agree with the statement and others would unequivocally disagree, still others would be unable to answer. For example, some would want to cut welfare spending and use the money to reduce taxes. Others would want to continue spending the same amount on welfare programs and spend more money on edu-

cation. These latter respondents could neither agree nor disagree without misleading you.

As a general rule, whenever the word *and* appears in a question or questionnaire statement, check whether you're asking a double-barrelled question.

Respondents Must Be Competent to Answer

In asking respondents to provide information, you should continually ask yourself whether they are able to do so reliably. In a study of child rearing, you might ask respondents to report the age at which they first talked back to their parents. Quite aside from the problem of defining *talking back to parents*, it's doubtful that most respondents would remember with any degree of accuracy.

As another example, student government leaders occasionally ask their constituents to indicate how students' fees ought to be spent. Typically, respondents are asked to indicate the percentage of available funds that should be devoted to a long list of activities. Without a fairly good knowledge of the activities and their costs, the respondents cannot provide meaningful answers.

One group of researchers examining the driving experience of teenagers insisted on asking an open-ended question concerning the number of miles driven since receiving a licence. Although consultants argued that few drivers would be able to estimate such information with any accuracy, the question was asked nonetheless. In response, some teenagers reported driving hundreds of thousands of miles.

Respondents Must Be Willing to Answer

Often, we would like to learn things from people that they are unwilling to share with us. For example, Yanjie Bian indicates that it has often been difficult to get candid answers from people in China,

> [Here] people are generally careful about what they say on nonprivate occasions in order to

survive under authoritarianism. During the Cultural Revolution between 1966 and 1976, for example, because of the radical political agenda and political intensity throughout the country, it was almost impossible to use survey techniques to collect valid and reliable data inside China about the Chinese people's life experiences, characteristics, and attitudes towards the Communist regime.

(1994:19–20)

Sometimes, North American respondents may say they are undecided when, in fact, they have an opinion but think they are in a minority. Under that condition, they may be reluctant to tell a stranger (the interviewer) what that opinion is. Given this problem, the Gallup Organization, for example, has used a "secret ballot" format, which simulates actual election conditions, in that the "voter" enjoys complete anonymity. In an analysis of the Gallup Poll election data from 1944 to 1988, Andrew Smith and G. F. Bishop (1992) have found that this technique substantially reduced the percentage saying they were undecided about how they would vote.

Questions Should Be Relevant

Similarly, questions asked in a questionnaire should be relevant to most respondents. When attitudes are requested on a topic that few respondents have thought about or really care about, the results are not likely to be very useful. Of course, because the respondents may express attitudes even though they've never given any thought to the issue, you run the risk of being misled.

This point is illustrated occasionally when researchers ask for responses relating to fictitious people and issues. In one political poll I (Babbie) conducted, respondents were asked whether they were familiar with each of 15 political figures in the community. As a methodological exercise, I made up a name: Tom Sakumoto. In response, 9 percent of the respondents said they were familiar with him. About half of the respondents reporting familiarity with him also reported seeing him on television and reading about him in the newspapers.

When you obtain responses to fictitious issues, you can disregard those responses. But when the

issue is real, you may have no way of telling which responses genuinely reflect attitudes and which reflect meaningless answers to an irrelevant question.

Ideally, we would like respondents to simply report that they don't know, have no opinion, or are undecided in instances where that is the case. Unfortunately, however, they often make up answers.

Short Items Are Best

In the interests of being unambiguous and precise and pointing to the relevance of an issue, researchers tend to create long and complicated items. This should be avoided. Respondents are often unwilling to study an item in order to understand it. The respondent should be able to read an item quickly, understand its intent, and select or provide an answer without difficulty. In general, assume that respondents will read items quickly and give quick answers. Accordingly, provide clear, short items that will not be misinterpreted under those conditions.

Avoid Negative Items

The appearance of a negation in a questionnaire item paves the way for easy misinterpretation. Asked to agree or disagree with the statement "Canada should not support United Nations peacekeeping missions," a sizeable portion of the respondents will read over the word *not* and answer on that basis. Thus, some will agree with the statement when they're in favour of support, and others will agree when they oppose it. And you may never know which is which.

Similar considerations apply to other "negative" words. In a study of civil liberties support, respondents were asked whether they felt "the following kinds of people should be *prohibited* from teaching in public schools," and were presented with a list including such items as a Communist, a Ku-Klux-Klansman, and so forth. The response categories "yes" and "no" were given beside each entry. A comparison of the responses to this item with other items reflecting support for civil liberties strongly suggested that many respondents gave the answer "yes" to indicate willingness for such a person to teach, rather than to indicate that such a person should be prohibited from teaching. (A later study in the series giving as answer categories "permit" and "prohibit" produced much clearer results.)

Avoid Biased Items and Terms

Recall from our discussion of conceptualization and operationalization in Chapter 5 that there are no ultimately true meanings for any of the concepts we typically study in social science. *Prejudice* has no ultimately correct definition; whether a given person is prejudiced depends on our definition of that term. This same general principle applies to the responses we get from people completing a questionnaire.

The meaning of someone's response to a question depends in large part on its wording. This is true of every question and answer. Some questions seem to encourage particular responses more than do other questions. In the context of questionnaires, **bias** refers to any property of questions that encourages respondents to answer in a particular way. Questions that contain bias are also referred to as "loaded questions" or "leading questions."

Most researchers recognize the likely effect of a question that begins, "Don't you agree with the prime minister of Canada that . . ." and no reputable researcher would use such an item. Unhappily, the biasing effect of items and terms is far subtler than this example suggests.

The mere identification of an attitude or position with a prestigious person or agency can bias responses. The item "Do you agree or disagree with the recent Supreme Court decision that . . ." would have a similar effect. Such wording may not produce consensus or even a majority in support of the position identified with the prestigious person or agency, but it will likely increase the level of support over what would have been obtained without such identification.

Sometimes the impact of different forms of question wording is relatively subtle. For example the use of certain words or terms can affect the outcome of responses. As a result, different ways of asking questions are often tested and evaluated. There have been several demonstrations, for instance, that people are less likely to indicate support for "welfare" programs and more likely to indicate support for social programs that are intended to assist the "poor" or reduce "poverty."

Statistics Canada illustrates how the wording of a question can impact the results as follows:

In your opinion, should Sunday shopping be allowed in Ontario; that is, should stores that want to stay open on Sunday be allowed to stay open on Sundays if they want to?

Results:

73%	In favour of Sunday shopping
25%	Opposed to Sunday shopping
2%	No opinion

In your opinion, should a Sunday pause day be adopted in Ontario; that is, should the government make Sunday the one uniform day a week when most people do not have to work?

Results:

50%	Opposed to a Sunday pause day
44%	In favour of a Sunday pause day
6%	No opinion

(Toronto Area Survey 1991, an annual survey conducted by the Institute for Social Research at York University. Statistics Canada's Internet site at http://www.statcan.ca/english/edu/prototype/data_collection/dpart4.htm May 4, 2001.)

Questions are often tested to determine the quality of data obtained from them. Statistics Canada has published numerous reports detailing the outcome of their research on potential questions for use in the Canadian census and other surveys they conduct. Reading through such reports provides valuable insights into the kinds of issues that must be considered in developing useful questions. For example, in 1993 a series of questions directed at measuring the impact on labour market participation of giving and getting unpaid care were tested in the Survey of Labour and Income Dynamics (SLID) interview. The researchers were concerned with both the respondent's reactions to and understanding of the questions. The research report, therefore, discussed issues such as the following:

Respondents did not like to say how many hours they helped others who needed help and could not understand why we asked. They didn't like to call it "unpaid help" and did not want anyone to think that they would have wanted to work rather than help those in need.

(Yves Saint-Pierre, 1993. Statistics Canada's Internet site at http://www.statcan.ca/english/IPS/Data/75F0002MIE93013.htm May 4, 2001.)

In this context, be wary of what researchers call the *social desirability* of questions and answers. Whenever you ask people for information, they answer through a filter of what will make them look good. This is especially true if they're interviewed face-to-face. Thus, for example, a particular man may feel that things would be a lot better if women were kept in the kitchen, not allowed to vote, forced to be quiet in public, and so forth. Asked whether he supports equal rights for women, however, he may want to avoid looking like a chauvinist. Recognizing that his views are out of step with current thinking, he may choose to say "yes."

The best way to guard against this problem is to imagine how you would feel giving each of the answers you intend to offer to respondents. If you would feel embarrassed, perverted, inhumane, stupid, irresponsible, or otherwise socially disadvantaged by any particular response, give serious thought to how willing others will be to give those answers.

The biasing effect of particular wording is often difficult to anticipate. In both surveys and experiments, it's sometimes useful to ask respondents to consider hypothetical situations and say how they think they would behave in such situations. Because those situations often involve other people, the names used can affect responses. For example, researchers have long known that male names for the hypothetical people may produce different responses than do female names. Research by Joseph Kasof (1993) points to the importance of what the specific names are: whether they generally evoke positive or negative images in terms of attractiveness, age, intelligence,

and so forth. Kasof's review of past research suggests there has been a tendency to use more positively valued names for men than for women.

As in all other research, carefully examine the purpose of your inquiry and construct items that will be most useful to it. You should never be misled into thinking there are ultimately "right" and "wrong" ways of asking the questions. When in doubt about the best question to ask, moreover, remember that you should ask more than one.

These, then, are some general guidelines for writing questions to elicit data for analysis and interpretation. Before we turn to how to construct questionnaires, a bit of caution is advised. Writing good questions is important, but interpreting responses, even when a clear, straightforward question is asked, requires logic and thought. For example, when asked whether Canada should be a leader in peacekeeping efforts around the world, 82 percent of Canadians agreed, according to the *Maclean's* 2000 year-end poll. Does this translate into support for greater military spending? Well, as *Maclean's* points out, not necessarily. In the same poll when the public was asked to choose between putting more money into strengthening and updating the military versus investing in housing for Canada's homeless population, 75 percent chose housing for the homeless over the military. (*Maclean's* Dec. 25, 2000–Jan.1, 2001: 30).

Questionnaire Construction

Questionnaires are used in connection with many modes of observation in social research. Although structured questionnaires are essential to and most directly associated with survey research, they're also widely used in experiments, field research, and other data-collection activities. For this reason, questionnaire construction can be an important practical skill for researchers. As we discuss the established techniques for constructing questionnaires, let's begin with some issues of questionnaire format.

General Questionnaire Format

The format of a questionnaire is just as important as the nature and wording of the questions asked. An improperly laid out questionnaire can lead respondents to miss questions, confuse them about the nature of the data desired, and even lead them to throw the questionnaire away.

As a general rule, the questionnaire should be spread out and uncluttered. Inexperienced researchers tend to fear that their questionnaire will look too long; as a result, they squeeze several questions onto a single line, abbreviate questions, and try to use as few pages as possible. These efforts are ill-advised and even dangerous. Putting more than one question on a line will cause some respondents to miss the second question altogether. More generally, respondents who find they have spent considerable time on the first page of what seemed a short questionnaire will be more demoralized than respondents who quickly complete the first several pages of what initially seemed a rather long form. Moreover, the latter will have made fewer errors and will not have been forced to reread confusing, abbreviated questions. Nor will they have been forced to write a long answer in a tiny space.

The desirability of spreading out questions in the questionnaire cannot be overemphasized. Squeezed-together questionnaires are disastrous, whether completed by the respondents themselves or administered by trained interviewers. And the processing of such questionnaires is another nightmare. We'll have more to say about that in Chapter 15.

Formats for Respondents

In one of the most common types of questionnaire items, the respondent is expected to check one response from a series. For this purpose boxes adequately spaced apart seem to be the best format. Modern word processing makes the use of boxes a practical technique these days; setting boxes in type can also be accomplished easily and neatly. You can approximate boxes by using

brackets: [ ], but if you're creating a questionnaire on a computer, you should take the few extra minutes to use genuine boxes that will give your questionnaire a more professional look. Here are some easy examples:

☐   ◯   ⬚

Rather than providing boxes to be checked, you might print a code number beside each response and ask the respondent to circle the appropriate number (see Figure 9-1). This method has the added advantage of specifying the code number to be entered later in the processing stage. If numbers are to be circled, however, you should provide clear and prominent instructions to the respondent, because many will be tempted to cross out the appropriate number, which makes data-processing even more difficult. (Note that the technique can be used more safely when interviewers administer the questionnaires, for they can specially instruct and supervise the respondents.)

Figure 9-1
Circling the Answer

```
    1. Yes

   (2.) No

    3. Don't know
```

Contingency Questions

Quite often in questionnaires, certain questions will be relevant to some of the respondents and irrelevant to others. In a study of birth control methods, for instance, you would probably not want to ask men if they take birth control pills.

This sort of situation often arises when researchers wish to ask a series of questions about a certain topic. You may want to ask whether your respondents belong to a particular organization and, if so, how often they attend meetings, whether they have held office in the organization, and so forth. Or, you might want to ask whether respondents have heard anything about a certain political issue and then learn the attitudes of those who have heard of it.

Each subsequent question in series such as these is called a **contingency question:** Whether it is to be asked and answered is contingent on responses to the first question in the series. The proper use of contingency questions can facilitate the respondents' task in completing the questionnaire, because they are not faced with trying to answer questions irrelevant to them.

There are several formats for contingency questions. The one shown in Figure 9-2 is probably the clearest and most effective. Note two key elements in this format. First, the contingency question is isolated from the other questions by being set off to the side and enclosed in a box. Second, an arrow connects the contingency question to the answer on which it is contingent. In the illustration, only those respondents answering yes are expected to answer the contingency question. The rest of the respondents should simply skip it.

Note that the questions shown in Figure 9-2 could have been dealt with in a single question. The question might have read, "How many times, if any, have you smoked marijuana?" The response categories, then, might have read: "Never," "Once," "2 to 5 times," and so forth. This single question would apply to all respondents, and each would

find an appropriate answer category. Such a question, however, might put some pressure on respondents to report having smoked marijuana, because the main question asks how many times they have smoked it, even though it allows for those *exceptional* cases *who have never smoked marijuana even once.* (The emphases used in the previous sentence give a fair indication of how respondents might read the question.) The contingency question format illustrated in Figure 9-2 should reduce the subtle pressure on respondents to report having smoked marijuana.

Used properly, even rather complex sets of contingency questions can be constructed without confusing the respondent. Figure 9-3 illustrates a more complicated example.

Sometimes a set of contingency questions is long enough to extend over several pages. Suppose you're studying political activities of university students, and you wish to ask a large number of questions of those students who had voted in a federal, provincial, or local election. You could separate out the relevant respondents with an initial question such as "Have you ever voted in a federal, provincial, or local election?" but it would be confusing to place the contingency questions in a box stretching over several pages. It would make more sense to enter instructions in parentheses after each answer telling respondents to answer or skip the contingency questions. Figure 9-4 provides an illustration of this method.

Figure 9-2
Contingency Question Format

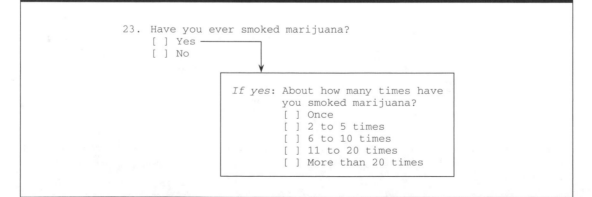

Figure 9-3
Complex Contingency Question

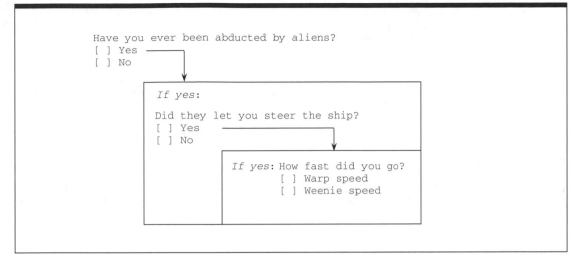

Figure 9-4
Instructions to Skip

```
13. Have you ever voted in a federal, provincial, or local election?
    [ ] Yes (Please answer questions 14-25.)
    [ ] No  (Please skip questions 14-25. Go directly to question 26 on page 8.)
```

Figure 9-5
Matrix Question Format

```
17. Beside
 of the statements presented below, please indicate whether you Strongly Agree (SA),
Agree (A), Disagree (D), Strongly Disagree (SD), or are Undecided (U).
```

	SA	A	D	SD	U
a. What this country needs is more law and order......	[ ]	[ ]	[ ]	[ ]	[ ]
b. The police should be disarmed in Canada.........	[ ]	[ ]	[ ]	[ ]	[ ]
c. The death penalty should be made legal in Canada....	[ ]	[ ]	[ ]	[ ]	[ ]

In addition to these instructions, it's worthwhile to place an instruction at the top of each page containing only the contingency questions. For example, you might say, "This page is only for respondents who have voted in a federal, provincial, or local election." Clear instructions such as these spare respondents the frustration of reading and puzzling over questions that are irrelevant to them and increase the likelihood of responses from those for whom the questions are relevant.

Matrix Questions

Quite often, you'll want to ask several questions that have the same set of answer categories. This is typically the case whenever the Likert response categories are used. In such cases, it's often possible to construct a matrix of items and answers as illustrated in Figure 9-5.

This format offers several advantages over other formats. First, it uses space efficiently. Second, respondents will probably find it faster to complete a set of questions presented in this fashion. In addition, this format may increase the comparability of responses given to different questions for the respondent as well as for the researcher. Because respondents can quickly review their answers to earlier items in the set, they might choose between, say, "strongly agree" and "agree" on a given statement by comparing the strength of their agreement with their earlier responses in the set.

There are some dangers inherent in using this format, however. Its advantages may encourage you to structure an item so that the responses fit into the matrix format when a different, more idiosyncratic set of responses might be more appropriate. Also, the matrix question format can foster a *response-set* among some respondents: They may develop a pattern of, say, agreeing with all the statements. This would be especially likely if the set of statements began with several that indicated a particular orientation (for example, a liberal political perspective) with only a few later ones representing the opposite orientation. Respondents might assume that all the statements represented the same orientation and, reading quickly, misread

some of them, thereby giving the wrong answers. This problem can be reduced somewhat by alternating statements representing different orientations and by making all statements short and clear.

Ordering Items in a Questionnaire

The order in which questionnaire items are presented can also affect responses. First, the appearance of one question can affect the answers given to later ones. For example, if several questions have been asked about the dangers of crime in Canada and then a question asks respondents to volunteer (open-ended) what they believe to be the most severe social problems facing Canada, crime will receive more citations than would otherwise be the case. In this situation, it is preferable to ask the open-ended question first.

Similarly, if respondents are asked to assess their overall religiosity ("How important is your religion to you in general?"), their responses to later questions concerning specific aspects of religiosity will be aimed at consistency with the prior assessment. The converse is true as well. If respondents are first asked specific questions about different aspects of their religiosity, their subsequent overall assessment will reflect the earlier answers.

The impact of item order is not uniform. When J. Edwin Benton and John Daly (1991) conducted a local government survey, they found that the less educated respondents were more influenced by the order of questionnaire items than were those with more education.

Some researchers attempt to overcome this effect by randomizing the order of items. This effort is usually futile. In the first place, a randomized set of items will probably strike respondents as chaotic and worthless. The random order also makes it more difficult for respondents to answer because they must continually switch their attention from one topic to another. Finally, even a randomized ordering of items will have the effect discussed previously—except that you'll have no control over the effect.

The safest solution is sensitivity to the problem. Although you cannot avoid the effect of item order, try to estimate what that effect will be so you can interpret results meaningfully. If the order of items seems especially important in a given study, you might construct more than one version of the questionnaire with different orderings of the items. You will then be able to determine its effects by comparing responses to the various versions. At the very least, you should pretest your questionnaire in the different forms. (We'll discuss pretesting in a moment.)

The desired ordering of items differs between interviews and self-administered questionnaires. In the latter, it's usually best to begin the questionnaire with the most interesting set of items. The potential respondents who glance casually over the first few items should want to answer them. Perhaps the items will ask for attitudes they're aching to express. At the same time, however, the initial items should not be threatening. (It might be a bad idea to begin with items about sexual behaviour or drug use.) Requests for duller, demographic data (age, gender, and the like) should generally be placed at the end of a self-administered questionnaire. Placing these items at the beginning, as many inexperienced researchers are tempted to do, gives the questionnaire the initial appearance of a routine form, and the person receiving it may not be motivated to complete it.

Just the opposite is generally true for interview surveys. When the potential respondent's door first opens, the interviewer must begin gaining rapport quickly. After a short introduction to the study, the interviewer can best begin by enumerating the members of the household, getting demographic data about each. Such items are easily answered and generally nonthreatening. Once the initial rapport has been established, the interviewer can then move into the area of attitudes and more sensitive matters. An interview that began with the question "Do you believe in witchcraft?" would probably end rather quickly.

Questionnaire Instructions

Every questionnaire, whether it is to be completed by respondents or administered by interviewers, should contain clear instructions and introductory comments where appropriate. (We'll further dis-

cuss information that should be included in an introduction to respondents, written or oral, in the section on Ethical Considerations later in this chapter.)

It's useful to begin every self-administered questionnaire with basic instructions for completing it. Although many people have experience with forms and questionnaires, begin by telling them exactly what you want: that they are to indicate their answers to certain questions by placing a check mark or an X in the box beside the appropriate answer or by writing in their answer when asked to do so. If many open-ended questions are used, respondents should be given some guidelines about whether brief or lengthy answers are expected. If you wish to encourage your respondents to elaborate on their responses to closed-ended questions, that should be noted.

If a questionnaire has subsections—political attitudes, religious attitudes, background data—introduce each section with a short statement concerning its content and purpose. For example, "In this section, we'd like to know what people consider the most important community problems." Demographic items at the end of a self-administered questionnaire might be introduced thus: "Finally, we would like to know just a little about you so we can see how different types of people feel about the issues we have been examining."

Short introductions such as these help the respondent make sense of the questionnaire. They make the questionnaire seem less chaotic, especially when it taps a variety of data. And they help put the respondent in the proper frame of mind for answering the questions.

Some questions may require special instructions to facilitate proper answering. This is especially true if a given question varies from the general instructions pertaining to the whole questionnaire. Some specific examples will illustrate this situation.

Despite attempts to provide mutually exclusive answer categories in closed-ended questions, often more than one answer will apply for respondents. If you want a single answer, you should make this perfectly clear in the question. An example would be "From the list below, please check the primary reason for your decision to attend university." Often the main question can be followed by a parenthetical note: "Please check the one best answer." If, on the other hand, you want the respondent to check as many answers as apply, you should make this clear.

When a set of answer categories are to be rank-ordered by the respondent, the instructions should indicate this, and a different type of answer format should be used (for example, blanks instead of boxes). These instructions should indicate how many answers are to be ranked (for example, all, only the first and second, only the first and last, the most important and least important). These instructions should also spell out the order of ranking (for example, "Place a 1 beside the most important, a 2 beside the next important, and so forth"). Rank-ordering of responses is often difficult for respondents, however, because they may have to read and reread the list several times, so this technique should only be used in those situations where no other method will produce the desired result.

Pretesting the Questionnaire

No matter how carefully researchers design a data-collection instrument such as a questionnaire, there is always the possibility—indeed the certainty—of error. They will always make some mistake: an ambiguous question, one that people cannot answer, or some other violation of the rules just discussed.

The surest protection against such errors is to pretest the questionnaire in full or in part. Give the questionnaire to a diverse set of 10 people, for example. It's not usually essential that the pretest subjects comprise a representative sample, although you should use people to whom the questionnaire is at least relevant.

By and large, it's better to ask people to complete the questionnaire rather than to read through it looking for errors. All too often, a question seems to make sense on a first reading, but it proves to be impossible to answer. Stanley Presser and Johnny Blair (1994) describe several different pretesting strategies and report on the effectiveness of each technique. There are more tips and guidelines for questionnaire construction, but covering them all would take a book in itself. We'll complete this discussion with an illustration of a real questionnaire, showing how some of these comments find substance in practice.

Before turning to the illustration, however, we want to mention a critical aspect of questionnaire design that we discuss in Chapter 15: precoding. Because the information collected by questionnaires is typically transformed into some type of computer format, it's usually appropriate to include data-processing instructions on the questionnaire itself. These instructions indicate where specific pieces of information will be stored in the machine-readable data files. In Chapter 15, we'll discuss the nature of such storage and point out appropriate questionnaire notations. As a preview, however, notice that the following illustration has been precoded with the mysterious numbers that appear near questions and answer categories. While such precoding makes data entry easier and often more accurate, care should be taken that the data-processing instructions not interfere with the respondent's ability to understand and easily respond to the questions on the questionnaire. After all, it would be of little value to more easily and accurately enter data that is flawed due the inclusion of such data-processing instructions.

A Composite Illustration

Figure 9-6 is part of a questionnaire used by Statistics Canada in the 1996 Agriculture Census. The questionnaire deals with information about the organization, operation, and ownership of farms in Canada and is designed to be self-administered.

Self-Administered Questionnaires

So far we've discussed how to formulate questions and how to design effective questionnaires. As important as these tasks are, the labour will be wasted unless the questionnaire produces useful data—which means that respondents actually complete the questionnaire. We turn now to the major methods for getting responses to questionnaires.

Figure 9-6
A Sample Questionnaire

> **Please answer the following questions about the operating arrangements of this operation in 1996.**
>
> **STEP 1**
>
> 1. Print the farm name *(if applicable)*.
>
> 2. Is this operation **legally incorporated**?
>
>   ₁ ◯ No   ₂ ◯ Yes ▶ **If Yes**, indicate:
>
>   (a) In what year did the operation become
>   **legally incorporated**? . . . . | 1 | 9 | |
>
>   (b) Is this a **family-held** corporation?   ₃ ◯ No   ₄ ◯ Yes
>
>   (c) Print the corporation name
>   *(if different from the farm name)*.
>
> 3. Is this operation a **partnership**?
>
>   ₅ ◯ No   ₆ ◯ Yes ▶ **If Yes**, does this partnership have a written agreement?
>
>   ₇ ◯ No   ₈ ◯ Yes
>
> 4. Is this operation a **sole proprietorship**?
>
>   ₁ ◯ No   ₂ ◯ Yes
>
> 5. Indicate if this operation is one of the following other types:
>
>   − An institution (e.g. research station, university farm, prison farm, etc.) . . . .   ₃ ◯
>
>   − A community pasture, co-operative grazing association or grazing reserve . . . .   ₄ ◯
>
>   − Other (e.g. Hutterite colony, trust or estate, etc.) . . . .   ₅ ◯
>   *Specify:* _____
>
> If STEP 1 does not completely describe the operating arrangements of this operation, please explain in the COMMENTS space below. One questionnaire should be completed for **each** agricultural operation. If additional questionnaires are required or for help completing this form, please call toll-free 1-800-216-2299.
>
> | **COMMENTS** | 036 |
> |---|---|
> | | |
> | | |
> | | |
> | | |
> | | |
> | | |
> | | |
> | | |
>
> Page 2

Figure 9-6 cont'd

A Sample Questionnaire

STEP 2

Please answer the following questions about each of the operators of this agricultural operation as of May 14, 1996.
- The operators are those persons **responsible for the day-to-day management decisions** made in the operation of this agricultural operation.
- If there are more than 3 operators, please provide names and addresses in the COMMENTS section on page 2 or attach a separate sheet.

Operator 1

6. Surname or Family Name *(Print)*

Given Name and Initial(s) *(Print)*

Date of Birth | Day | Month | 1 | Year   Sex   1 ◯ Male   2 ◯ Female

R.R. No.   P.O. Box No.   Number and Name of Road or Street

Village, Town or City   Province

Postal Code   Area Code   Telephone No.

7. Did this person live on this agricultural operation at any time during the last 12 months?

01 ◯ No   02 ◯ Yes

8. **In 1995**, what was this person's time contribution to the operation of this agricultural operation? *(Mark one circle only.)*

03 ◯ On average, more than 40 hours per week

04 ◯ On average, 20 to 40 hours per week

05 ◯ On average, less than 20 hours per week

9. **In 1995**, did this person do any custom work (e.g. planting, harvesting, trucking, snowplowing, etc.)?

06 ◯ No   07 ◯ Yes

10. **In 1995**, did this person receive any wage or salary from other employment not involved with this agricultural operation? *(Do not include custom work.)*

08 ◯ No   09 ◯ Yes ▶ **If Yes**, indicate the amount of work done. *(Mark one circle only.)*

10 ◯ On average, more than 40 hours per week

11 ◯ On average, 20 to 40 hours per week

12 ◯ On average, less than 20 hours per week

11. **In 1995**, did this person **operate** another business (other than farming)?

13 ◯ No   14 ◯ Yes ▶ **If Yes**, indicate the type(s) of business: *(Mark all applicable circles.)*

15 ◯ Sales (e.g. real estate, consumer products, etc.)

16 ◯ Services (e.g. machinery repair, accounting, bed and breakfast, etc.)

17 ◯ Construction

18 ◯ Manufacturing

19 ◯ Other *(Specify)* _____

12. **In 1995**, did this person suffer any injuries that required medical attention from a health professional (e.g. broken limbs, cuts requiring stitches, concussions, etc.) caused by activities related to the operation of this agricultural operation?

20 ◯ No   21 ◯ Yes ▶ **If Yes**, *specify the injury or injuries:*

_____

Page 3

Source: Statistics Canada, 1996 Form 6 Agriculture Questionnaire, 1996 Census.

We've referred several times in this chapter to interviews versus self-administered questionnaires. Actually, there are three main methods of administering survey questionnaires to a sample of respondents: self-administered questionnaires, in which respondents are asked to complete the questionnaires themselves; surveys administered by interviewers in face-to-face encounters; and surveys conducted by telephone. This section and the next two discuss each of these methods in turn.

The most common form of self-administered questionnaire is the mail survey. However, there are several other techniques that are often used as well. At times, it may be appropriate to administer the questionnaire to a group of respondents gathered at the same place at the same time. A survey of students taking introductory psychology might be conducted in this manner during class. High school students might be surveyed during homeroom period.

Some recent experimentation has been conducted with regard to the home delivery of questionnaires. A research worker delivers the questionnaire to the home of sample respondents and explains the study. Then the questionnaire is left for the respondent to complete, and the researcher picks it up later.

Home delivery and the mail can also be used in combination. Questionnaires are mailed to families, and then research workers visit homes to pick up the questionnaires and check them for completeness. Just the opposite technique is to have questionnaires hand delivered by research workers with a request that the respondents mail the completed questionnaires to the research office. On the whole, when a research worker either delivers the questionnaire, picks it up, or both, the completion rate seems higher than for straightforward mail surveys. The remainder of this section, however, is devoted specifically to the mail survey, which is still the typical form of self-administered questionnaire.

Mail Distribution and Return

The basic method for collecting data through the mail has been to send a questionnaire accompanied by a letter of explanation and a self-addressed, stamped envelope for returning the questionnaire. The respondent is expected to complete the questionnaire, put it in the envelope, and return it. If, by any chance, you've received such a questionnaire and failed to return it, it would be valuable to recall the reasons you had for not returning it and keep them in mind any time you plan to send questionnaires to others.

A common reason for not returning questionnaires is that it's too much trouble. To overcome this problem, researchers have developed several ways to make returning them easier. For instance, a self-mailing questionnaire requires no return envelope: When the questionnaire is folded a particular way, the return address appears on the outside. The respondent doesn't have to worry about losing the envelope.

More elaborate designs are available also. For example, a questionnaire may be bound in a booklet with a special, two-panel back cover. Once the questionnaire is completed, the respondent need only to fold out the extra panel, wrap it around the booklet, and seal the whole thing with the adhesive strip running along the edge of the panel. The foldout panel contains the return address and postage. This design could be further modified such that both the front and back covers have foldout panels: one for sending the questionnaire out and the other for getting it back—thus avoiding the use of envelopes altogether.

The point here is that anything you can do to make the job of completing and returning the questionnaire easier will improve your study. Imagine receiving a questionnaire that made no provisions for its return to the researcher. Suppose you had to (1) find an envelope, (2) write the address on it, (3) figure out how much postage it required, and (4) put the stamps on it. How likely is it that you would return the questionnaire?

A few brief comments on postal options are in order. You have options for mailing questionnaires out and for getting them returned. On outgoing mail, your choices are essentially between first-class postage and bulk rate. First class is more certain, but bulk rate is far cheaper. (Check your local post office for rates and procedures.) On return mail, your choice is between postage stamps and business-reply permits. Here, the cost differential is more complicated. If you use stamps, you pay for them whether people return their questionnaires or not. With the business-reply permit, you pay for only those that are used, but you pay an additional surcharge of about a nickel. This means that stamps are cheaper if many questionnaires are returned, but business-reply permits are cheaper if fewer are returned (and you won't know in advance how many will be returned).

There are many other considerations involved in choosing among the several postal options. Some researchers, for example, feel that the use of postage stamps communicates more "humanness" and sincerity than bulk rate and business-reply permits. Others worry that respondents will peel off the stamps and use them for some purpose other than returning the questionnaires. Because both bulk rate and business-reply permits require establishing accounts at the post office, you'll probably find stamps much easier in small surveys.

Monitoring Returns

The mailing of questionnaires sets up a new research question that may prove valuable to a study. Researchers shouldn't sit back idly as questionnaires are returned; instead, they should undertake a careful recording of the varying rates of return among respondents.

An invaluable tool in this activity will be a return rate graph. The day on which questionnaires were mailed is labelled Day 1 on the graph, and every day thereafter the number of returned questionnaires should be logged on the graph. It's usually best to compile two graphs. One shows the number returned each day—rising, then dropping. The second reports the cumulative number or percentage. It's the researcher's guide to how the data collection is going. If follow-up mailings are planned, the graph provides a clue about when such mailings should be launched. (The dates of subsequent mailings should be noted on the graph.)

As completed questionnaires are returned, each should be opened, scanned, and assigned an iden-

tification number. These numbers should be assigned serially as the questionnaires are returned, even if other identification (ID) numbers have already been assigned. Two examples should illustrate the important advantages of this procedure.

Let's assume you're studying attitudes toward a political figure. In the middle of the data collection, the media break the story that the politician is having extramarital affairs. By knowing the date of that public disclosure and the dates when questionnaires were received, you'll be in a position to determine the effects of the disclosure. (Recall the discussion in Chapter 8 of history in connection with experiments.)

In a less sensational way, serialized ID numbers can be valuable in estimating nonresponse biases in the survey. Barring more direct tests of bias, you may wish to assume that those who failed to answer the questionnaire will be more like respondents who delayed answering than like those who answered right away. An analysis of questionnaires received at different points in the data collection might then be used for estimates of sampling bias. For example, if the grade point averages (GPAs) reported by student respondents decrease steadily through the data collection, with those replying right away having higher GPAs and those replying later having lower GPAs, then you might tentatively conclude that those who failed to answer at all have lower GPAs yet. Although it would not be advisable to make statistical estimates of bias in this fashion, you could take advantage of approximate estimates based on the patterns you've observed.

If respondents have been identified for purposes of follow-up mailing, then preparations for those mailings should be made as the questionnaires are returned.

Follow-up Mailings

Follow-up mailings may be administered in several ways. In the simplest, nonrespondents are sent a letter of additional encouragement to participate. A better method, however, is to send a new copy of the survey questionnaire with the follow-up letter.

If potential respondents have not returned their questionnaires after two or three weeks, the questionnaires have probably been lost or misplaced. Receiving a follow-up letter might encourage them to look for the original questionnaire, but if they can't find it easily, the letter may go for naught.

In general, the longer a potential respondent delays replying, the less likely he or she is to do so at all. The methodological literature strongly suggests that properly timed follow-up mailings provide an effective method for increasing return rates in mail surveys.

The effects of follow-up mailings will be seen in the response rate curves recorded during data collection. The initial mailings will be followed by a rise and subsequent subsiding of returns; the follow-up mailings will spur a resurgence of returns; and more follow-ups will do the same. In practice, three mailings (an original and two follow-ups) seem the most efficient.

The timing of follow-up mailings is also important. Here the methodological literature offers less precise guides. Two or three weeks is a reasonable space between mailings. (This period might be increased by a few days if the mailing time—out and in—is more than two or three days.)

When researchers conduct several surveys of the same population over time, they can develop more specific guidelines in this regard. The Survey Research Office at the University of Hawaii conducts frequent student surveys and has been able to refine the mailing and remailing procedure considerably. Indeed, they have found a consistent pattern of returns that appears to transcend differences of survey content, quality of instrument, and so forth. Within two weeks of the first mailing, approximately 40 percent of the questionnaires are returned; within two weeks of the first follow-up, an additional 20 percent are received; and within two weeks of the final follow-up, an additional 10 percent are received. (These response rates reflect the sending of additional questionnaires, not just letters.) Your results may vary, but this illustration should indicate the value of carefully tabulating return rates for every survey conducted.

If the individuals in the survey sample are not identified on the questionnaires, it may not be possible to remail only to nonrespondents. In such a case, send your follow-up mailing to all members of the sample, thanking those who may have already participated and encouraging those who have not to do so.

To reduce the follow-up mailing costs in anonymous surveys, the postcard method may be used, enabling the researcher to send follow-up mailings only to nonrespondents while still maintaining the anonymity of respondents. Each respondent would be mailed a questionnaire that had no identifying marks, plus a stamped postcard addressed to the research office, with the respondent's mailing label affixed to the reverse side of the card. The introductory letter would ask the respondent to complete and return the questionnaire, assuring anonymity. The postcard method would be explained, and the respondents would be asked to return the postcard separately but simultaneously with the survey. Receiving the postcard would tell the researcher—without indicating which questionnaire it was—that the respondent had returned the questionnaire. This procedure would then facilitate follow-up mailings to only those who had yet to return their surveys.

Acceptable Response Rates

A question that new survey researchers frequently ask concerns the percentage return rate, or **response rate**, that should be achieved in a mail survey. The body of inferential statistics used in connection with survey analysis assumes that all members of the initial sample complete and return their questionnaires. Because this almost never happens, response bias becomes a concern, with the researcher testing (and hoping) for the possibility that the respondents look essentially like a random sample of the initial sample, and thus a somewhat smaller random sample of the total population. (For more detailed discussions of response bias, you might want to read Donald [1960], Brownlee [1975], and Goyder [1987].)

Nevertheless, overall response rate is one guide to the representativeness of the sample respondents. If a high response rate is achieved, there's less chance of significant response bias than in a low rate. Conversely, a low response rate is a danger signal, because the nonrespondents are likely to differ from the respondents in ways other than just their willingness to participate in your survey. Richard Bolstein (1991), for example, found that those who did not respond to a preelection political poll were less likely to vote than those who did participate. Estimating the turnout rate from the survey respondents, then, would have overestimated the number who would show up at the polls.

But what is a high or low response rate. A quick review of the survey literature will uncover a wide range of response rates. Even so, it's possible to state some rules of thumb about return rates. We feel that a response rate of 50 percent is *adequate* for analysis and reporting. A response of 60 percent is *good;* a response rate of 70 percent is *very good.* Bear in mind, however, that these are only rough guides; they have no statistical basis, and a demonstrated lack of response bias is far more important than a high response rate. If you want to pursue this matter further, Delbert Miller (1991:145–55) has reviewed several specific surveys to offer a better sense of the variability of response rates.

As you can imagine, one of the more persistent discussions among survey researchers concerns ways of increasing response rates. You'll recall that this was a chief concern in the earlier discussion of options for mailing out and receiving questionnaires. Survey researchers have developed many ingenious techniques addressing this problem. Some have experimented with novel formats. Others have tried paying respondents to participate. The problem with paying, of course, is that it's expensive to make meaningfully high payments to hundreds or thousands of respondents, but some imaginative alternatives have been used. Some researchers have said, "We want to get your two-cents' worth on some issues, and we're willing to pay" enclosing two pennies. Another enclosed a quarter, suggesting that the respondent make some little child happy. Still others have enclosed paper money.

Warriner et al. (1996) used an experimental design in a mail survey study in Ontario to assess the impact of various types of incentives on response rates. They found that prepaid cash incentives were effective in increasing the response rate while charity donations and lotteries were not. Survey response rate was increased by larger cash incentives: $10 producing a higher response rate than $5, and $5 greater than $2. However, added improvement in response rate using the $10 incentive was small and thus not a cost-effective strategy when compared to the $5 incentive.

Don Dillman (1978; 1991) provides excellent reviews of the various techniques survey researchers have used to increase return rates on mail surveys, and he evaluates the impact of each. More important, Dillman stresses the necessity of paying attention to *all* aspects of the study—what he calls the "Total Design Method" rather than one or two special gimmicks.

John Goyder (1982; 1985; 1987) has also written extensively on survey response rates, assessing factors affecting response rates, net difference in response rates between types of surveys, and non-response bias.

Let's turn now to the second principal method of conducting surveys, in-person interviews.

Interview Surveys

The **interview** is an alternative method of collecting survey data. Rather than asking respondents to read questionnaires and enter their own answers, researchers send interviewers to ask the questions orally and record respondents' answers. Interviewing is typically done in a face-to-face encounter, but telephone interviewing, discussed in the next section, follows most of the same guidelines.

Most interview surveys require more than one interviewer, although you might undertake a small-scale interview survey yourself. Portions of this section will discuss methods for training and supervising a staff of interviewers assisting you with a survey.

This section deals specifically with survey interviewing. Chapter 12 discusses the less structured, in-depth interviews often conducted in qualitative field research.

The Role of the Survey Interviewer

There are several advantages to having a questionnaire administered by an interviewer rather than the respondent. To begin with, interview surveys typically attain higher response rates than mail surveys. A properly designed and executed interview survey ought to achieve a completion rate of at least 80 to 85 percent. Respondents seem more reluctant to turn down an interviewer standing on their doorstep than to throw away a mailed questionnaire.

The presence of an interviewer also generally decreases the number of "don't knows" and "no answers." If minimizing such responses is important to the study, the interviewer can be instructed to probe for answers ("If you had to pick one of the answers, which do you think would come closest to your feelings?").

Interviewers can also serve as a guard against confusing questionnaire items. If the respondent clearly misunderstands the intent of a question or indicates that he or she does not understand, the interviewer can clarify matters, thereby obtaining relevant responses. (As we'll discuss shortly, such clarifications must be strictly controlled through formal specifications.)

Finally, the interviewer can observe respondents as well as ask questions. For example, the interviewer can note the quality of the dwelling, the presence of various possessions, the respondent's general reactions to the study, and so forth. In one survey of students, respondents were given a short, self-administered questionnaire concerning sexual attitudes and behaviour to complete during the course of the interview. While a student completed the questionnaire, the interviewer made detailed notes regarding the dress and grooming of the respondent.

This procedure raises an ethical issue. Some researchers have objected that such practices violate the spirit of the agreement by which the respondent has allowed the interview. If the respondent is not aware that such information is being collected, then he or she has not been fully informed about the study. This puts into question whether the respondent has truly been given the choice of voluntarily participation. Although ethical issues are seldom clear-cut in social research, it's important to be sensitive to them.

Survey research is of necessity based on an unrealistic stimulus-response theory of cognition and behaviour. Researchers must assume that a questionnaire item will mean the same thing to every respondent, and every given response must mean the same when given by different respondents. Although this is an impossible goal, survey questions are drafted to approximate the ideal as closely as possible.

The interviewer must also fit into this ideal situation. The interviewer's presence should not affect a respondent's perception of a question or the answer given. In other words, the interviewer should be a neutral medium through which questions and answers are transmitted.

As such, different interviewers should obtain exactly the same responses from a given respondent. (Recall earlier discussions of reliability.) This neutrality has a special importance in area samples. To save time and money, a given interviewer is typically assigned to complete all the interviews in a particular geographical area such as a city block or a group of nearby blocks. If the interviewer does anything to affect the responses obtained, the bias thus interjected might be interpreted as a characteristic of that area.

Let's suppose that a survey is being done to determine attitudes toward low-cost housing to help in the selection of a site for a new government-sponsored development. An interviewer assigned to a given neighbourhood might, through word or gesture, communicate his or her own distaste for low-cost housing developments. Respondents might therefore tend to give responses in general agreement with the interviewer's own position. The results of the survey would indicate that the neighbourhood in question strongly resists construction of the development in its area when in fact their apparent resistance simply reflects the interviewer's attitudes.

General Rules for Survey Interviewing

The manner in which interviews ought to be conducted will vary somewhat by survey population and will be affected to some degree by the nature of the survey content. Nevertheless, some general guidelines apply to most if not all interviewing situations.

Appearance and Demeanor As a rule, interviewers should dress in a fashion similar to that of the people they'll be interviewing. A richly dressed interviewer will probably have difficulty getting good cooperation and responses from poorer respondents; a poorly dressed interviewer will have similar difficulties with richer respondents. To the extent that the interviewer's dress and grooming differ from those of the respondents, it should be in the direction of cleanliness and neatness in modest apparel. Although middle-class neatness and cleanliness may not be accepted by all sectors of Canadian society, they remain the primary norm and are the most likely to be acceptable to the largest number of respondents.

Dress and grooming are typically regarded as signs of a person's attitudes and orientations. At the time this is being written, torn jeans, green hair, and razor-blade earrings may communicate—correctly or incorrectly—that the interviewer is politically radical, sexually permissive, favourable to drug use, and so forth. Any of these impressions could bias responses or affect the willingness of people to be interviewed.

In demeanor, interviewers should be pleasant if nothing else. Because they'll be prying into a respondent's personal life and attitudes, they must communicate a genuine interest in getting to know the respondent without appearing to spy. They must be relaxed and friendly without being too casual or clinging. Good interviewers also have the ability to determine very quickly the kind of person the respondent will feel most comfortable with, the kind of person the respondent would most enjoy talking to. Clearly, the interview will be more successful if the interviewer can become the kind of person the respondent is comfortable with. Further, because respondents are asked to volunteer a portion of their time and to divulge personal information, they deserve the most enjoyable experience the researcher and interviewer can provide.

Familiarity with Questionnaire If an interviewer is unfamiliar with the questionnaire, the study suffers and an unfair burden is placed on the respondent. The interview is likely to take more time than necessary and be unpleasant. Moreover, the interviewer cannot acquire familiarity by skimming through the questionnaire two or three times. He or she must study it carefully, question by question, and must practice reading it aloud.

Ultimately, the interviewer must be able to read the questionnaire items to respondents without error, without stumbling over words and phrases. A good model is the actor reading lines in a play or movie. The lines must be read as though they constituted a natural conversation, but that conversation must follow exactly the language set down in the questionnaire.

By the same token, the interviewer must be familiar with the specifications prepared in conjunction with the questionnaire. Inevitably some questions will not exactly fit a given respondent's situation, and the interviewer must determine how the question should be interpreted in that situation. The specifications provided to the interviewer should give adequate guidance in such cases, but the interviewer must know the organization and contents of the specifications well enough to refer to them efficiently. It would be better for the interviewer to leave a given question unanswered than to spend five minutes searching through the specifications for clarification or trying to interpret the relevant instructions.

Following Question Wording Exactly The first part of this chapter discussed the significance of question wording for the responses obtained. A slight change in the wording of a given question may lead a respondent to answer "yes" rather than "no." Therefore, interviewers must be instructed to follow the wording of questions exactly. Otherwise all the effort that the developers have put into carefully phrasing the questionnaire items to obtain the information they need and to insure that respondents will interpret items precisely as intended will be wasted.

Recording Responses Exactly Whenever the questionnaire contains open-ended questions, those soliciting the respondent's own answer, the interviewer must record that answer exactly as given. No attempt should be made to summarize, paraphrase, or correct bad grammar.

This exactness is especially important because the interviewer will not know how the responses are to be coded. Indeed, the researchers may not know the coding until they've read a hundred or so responses. For example, the questionnaire might ask respondents how they feel about the traffic situation in their community. One respondent might answer that there are too many cars on the roads and that something should be done to limit their numbers. Another might say that more roads are needed. If the interviewer recorded these two responses with the same summary—"congested traffic"—the researchers would not be able to take advantage of the important differences in the original responses.

Sometimes, verbal responses are too inarticulate or ambiguous to permit interpretation. However, the interviewer may be able to understand the intent of the response through the respondent's gestures or tone. In such a situation, the interviewer should still record the exact verbal response but also add marginal comments giving both the interpretation and the reasons for arriving at it.

More generally, researchers can use any marginal comments explaining aspects of the response not conveyed in the verbal recording, such as the respondent's apparent anger, embarrassment, uncertainty in answering, and so forth. In each case, however, the exact verbal response should also be recorded.

Probing for Responses Sometimes respondents in an interview will give an inappropriate or incomplete answer. In such cases a **probe**, or request for an elaboration, can be useful. For example, a closed-ended question may present an attitudinal statement and ask the respondent to strongly agree, agree somewhat, disagree somewhat, or strongly disagree. The respondent, however, may reply: "I think that's true." The interviewer should follow this reply with: "Would you say you strongly agree or agree somewhat?" If necessary, interviewers can explain that they must check one or the other of the categories provided. If the respondent adamantly refuses to choose, the interviewer should write in the exact response given by the respondent.

Probes are more frequently required in eliciting responses to open-ended questions. For example, in response to a question about traffic conditions, the respondent might simply reply, "Pretty bad." The interviewer could obtain an elaboration on this response through a variety of probes. Sometimes the best probe is silence; if the interviewer sits quietly with pencil poised, the respondent will probably fill the pause with additional comments. (This technique is used effectively by newspaper reporters.) Appropriate verbal probes might be "How is that?" or "In what ways?" Perhaps the most generally useful probe is "Anything else?"

Often, interviewers need to probe for answers that will be sufficiently informative for analytical purposes. In every case, however, such probes *must* be completely neutral; they must not in any way affect the nature of the subsequent response. Whenever you anticipate that a given question may require probing for appropriate responses, you should provide one or more useful probes next to the question in the questionnaire. This practice has two important advantages. First, you'll have more time to devise the best, most neutral probes. Second, all interviewers will use the same probes whenever they're needed. Thus, even if the probe isn't perfectly neutral, all respondents will be presented with the same stimulus. This is the same logical guideline discussed for question wording. Although a question should not be loaded or biased, it's essential that every respondent be presented with the same question, even if it's biased.

Coordination and Control

Most interview surveys require the assistance of several interviewers. In large-scale surveys, interviewers are hired and paid for their work. Student researchers might find themselves recruiting friends to help them interview. Whenever more than one interviewer is involved in a survey, their efforts must be carefully controlled. This control has two aspects: training interviewers and supervising them after they begin work.

The interviewers' training session should begin with the description of what the study is about. Even though the interviewers may be involved only in the data-collection phase of the project, it will be useful to them to understand what will be done with the interviews they conduct and what purpose will be served. Morale and motivation are usually lower when interviewers don't know what's going on.

The training on how to interview should begin with a discussion of general guidelines and procedures, such as those discussed earlier in this section. Then the whole group should go through the questionnaire together, question by question. Don't simply ask if anyone has any questions about the first page of the questionnaire. Read the first question aloud, explain the purpose of the question, and then entertain any questions or comments the interviewers may have. Once all their questions and comments have been handled, go on to the next question in the questionnaire.

It's always a good idea to prepare specifications to accompany an interview questionnaire. *Specifications* are explanatory and clarifying comments about handling difficult or confusing situations that may occur with regard to particular questions in the questionnaire. When drafting the questionnaire, try to think of all the problem cases that might arise—the bizarre circumstances that might make a question difficult to answer. The survey specifications should provide detailed guidelines on how to handle such situations. For example, even as simple a matter as age might present problems. Suppose a respondent says he or she will be 25 next week. The interviewer might not be sure whether to take the respondent's current age or the nearest one. The specifications for that question should explain what should be done. (Probably, you would specify that the age as of last birthday should be recorded in all cases.)

Once you've gone through the whole questionnaire, you should conduct one or two demonstration interviews in front of everyone. Preferably, you should interview someone other than one of the interviewers, as a model interview for those you're training. Thus, the demonstration interview should be done as realistically as possible. Do not pause during the demonstration to point out how you've handled a complicated situation: Handle it, and then explain later. After the demonstration interviews, pair off your interviewers and have them practice on each other. Interviewing is the best training for interviewing. Once the practice is completed, the whole group should discuss their experiences and ask any other questions they may have.

The final stage of the training for interviewers should involve some "real" interviews. Have them conduct some interviews under the actual conditions that will pertain to the final survey. You may want to assign them people to interview or allow them to pick people themselves. Do not have them practice on people you've selected in your sample, however. After each interviewer has completed three to five interviews, have him or her check back with you. Look over the completed questionnaires for any evidence of misunderstanding. Once you're convinced that a given interviewer knows what to do, assign some actual interviews using the sample you've selected for the study.

It's essential to continue supervising the work of interviewers over the course of the study. You might assign 20 interviews and have the interviewer give you those questionnaires when they're completed. Once you have checked them over, you can assign another 20 or so. Although this may seem overly cautious, you must continually protect yourself against misunderstandings that may not be evident early in the study.

If you're the only interviewer in your study, these comments may not seem relevant. However, it would be wise, for example, to prepare specifications for potentially troublesome questions in your questionnaire. Otherwise, you run the risk of making *ad hoc* decisions during the course of the study that you'll later regret or forget. Also, the emphasis on practice applies equally to the one-person project and to the complex funded survey with a large interviewing staff.

Telephone Surveys

For years telephone surveys had a rather bad reputation among professional researchers. Telephone surveys are limited by definition to people who have telephones. Years ago, this method produced a substantial social-class bias by excluding poor people from the surveys. This was vividly demonstrated by the *Literary Digest* fiasco of 1936. Recall that even though voters were contacted by mail, the sample was partially selected from telephone subscribers, who were hardly typical in a nation just recovering from the Great Depression. Over time, however, the telephone has become a standard fixture in almost all Canadian homes. "[O]nly about 2 percent of Canadian households have no telephones" (Gray and Guppy 1999:147), so the earlier form of class bias has been substantially reduced.

A related sampling problem involved unlisted numbers. A survey sample selected from the pages of a local telephone directory would totally omit all those people, typically richer, who requested that their numbers not be published. This potential bias has been erased through a technique that has advanced telephone sampling substantially: random-digit dialing.

Telephone surveys have many advantages that underlie the growing popularity of this method. Probably the greatest advantages are money and time, in that order. In a face-to-face, household interview, you may drive several miles to a respondent's home, find no one there, return to the research office, and drive back the next day, possibly finding no one there again. It's cheaper and quicker to let your fingers make the trips.

Interviewing by telephone, you can dress any way you please without affecting the answers respondents give. And sometimes respondents will be more honest in giving socially disapproved answers if they don't have to look you in the eye. Similarly, it may be possible to probe into more sensitive areas, though this isn't necessarily the case. People are, to some extent, more suspicious when they can't see the person asking them questions—perhaps a consequence of "surveys" aimed at selling magazine subscriptions and time-share condominiums.

Interviewers can communicate a lot about themselves over the phone, however, even though they can't be seen. For example, researchers worry about the impact of an interviewer's name (particularly if ethnicity is relevant to the study) and debate the ethics of having all interviewers use bland "stage names" such as Smith or Jones. (Female interviewers sometimes ask permission to do this, to avoid subsequent harassment from men they interview.)

Telephone surveys can allow greater control over data collection if several interviewers are engaged in the project. If all the interviewers are calling from the research office, they can get clarification from the person in charge whenever problems occur, as they inevitably do. Alone in the boondocks, an interviewer may have to wing it between weekly visits with the interviewing supervisor.

Finally, another important factor involved in the growing use of telephone surveys has to do with personal safety. Concerns for safety work two ways to hamper face-to-face interviews. Potential respondents may refuse to be interviewed, fearing the stranger–interviewer. And the interviewers themselves may incur some risks. All this is made even worse by the possibility of the researchers being sued for huge sums if anything goes wrong.

There are still problems involved in telephone interviewing, however. As we've already mentioned, the method is hampered by the proliferation of bogus "surveys," that are actually sales campaigns disguised as research. If you have any questions about any such call you receive, by the way, ask the interviewer directly whether you've been selected for a survey only or if a sales "opportunity" is involved. It's also a good idea, if you have any doubts, to get the interviewer's name, phone number, and company. Hang up if the caller refuses to provide any of these.

For the researcher, the ease with which people can hang up is another shortcoming of telephone surveys. Once you've been let inside someone's home for an interview, the respondent is unlikely to order you out of the house in mid-interview. It's much easier to terminate a telephone interview abruptly, saying something like, "Whoops! Someone's at the door. I gotta go." or "OMIGOD! The pigs are eating my Volvo!" (That sort of thing is much harder to fake when the interviewer is sitting in your living room.)

While anecdotal, the following experience conveys spontaneous views on telephone surveys by a member of the public. The views reflect some of the issues we have cautioned about that survey researchers should consider when deciding what to ask and how to ask it. I (Benaquisto) was working on this chapter when a technician was at my home repairing something. The phone rang, and I noted that it was a computer call, recognizable by the delay before hearing any sound on the other end. Once I hung up, the technician began talking about how annoying many such phone calls can be. He noted one occasion when he got a phone call asking if he'd answer some questions. He said, "They started asking me things like how much I drink when I'm at a party and at other times. I'm not going to answer that – it's an invasion of privacy." Once he got going, he started giving his opinion on other kinds of questions people are asked. For instance, he said, "I don't believe those surveys that report that say 80 percent of people believe in God. If someone calls and asks you if you believe in God, most people are going to say yes. Most people wouldn't be willing to admit they don't believe in God. That kind of question gets thrown at you and what are you going to say–what would people think if you said no. Maybe one in five people would be willing to tell a stranger they didn't believe in God, most wouldn't." (Note that he'd clearly thought about it because he had his percentages right.) "So, I think that kind of number isn't true." Luckily I had a file folder and pencil in hand when I answered the phone, so I was able to jot down what he was saying as he worked. There are many issues and trade-offs that researchers must consider when selecting the best method of collecting survey data

for their particular studies. While people are often more willing to report their views about sensitive issues over the telephone, there are those for which the opposite might be true. There are no certain guidelines for how best to ask personal questions and get honest responses, or for that matter, any response.

Another potential problem for telephone interviewing is the prevalence of answering machines. A study conducted by Walker Research (1988) found that half of the owners of answering machines acknowledged using their machines to "screen" calls at least some of the time. Research by Peter Tuckel and Barry Feinberg (1991:201), however, showed that answering machines have not yet had a significant effect on the ability of telephone researchers to contact prospective respondents. Nevertheless, the researchers concluded that as answering machines continue to proliferate, "the sociodemographic characteristics of owners will change." This fact makes it likely that "different behaviour patterns associated with the utilization of the answering machine" could emerge (1991:216).

Computer Assisted Telephone Interviewing (CATI)

In Part 4, we'll be looking at some of the ways computers have influenced the conduct of social research, particularly data processing and analysis. Computers are also changing the nature of telephone interviewing. One innovation is computer-assisted telephone interviewing (CATI). Academic, government, and commercial survey researchers increasingly use this method. Though there are variations in practice, here's what CATI can look like.

Imagine an interviewer wearing a telephone headset, sitting in front of a computer terminal and its video screen. The central computer has been programmed to select a telephone number at random and dials it. (Random digit dialing avoids the problem of unlisted telephone numbers.) On the video screen is an introduction ("Hello, my name is . . .") and the first question to be asked

("Could you tell me how many people live at this address?").

When the respondent answers the phone, the interviewer says hello, introduces the study, and asks the first question displayed on the screen. When the respondent answers the question, the interviewer types that answer into the computer terminal—either the verbatim response to an open-ended question or the code category for the appropriate answer to a closed-ended question.

The answer is immediately stored in the central computer. The second question appears on the video screen, is asked, and the answer is entered into the computer. Thus, the interview continues.

In addition to the obvious advantages in terms of data collection, CATI automatically prepares the data for analysis; in fact, the researcher can begin analyzing the data before the interviewing is complete, thereby gaining an advanced view of how the analysis will turn out.

Voice Capture™

by James E. Dannemiller
SMS Research, Honolulu

The development of various CATI techniques has been a boon to survey and marketing research, though mostly it has supported the collection, coding, and analysis of "data as usual." The Voice Capture™ technique developed by Survey Systems, however, offers quite unusual possibilities, which we are only beginning to explore.

In the course of a CATI-based telephone interview, the interviewer can trigger the computer to begin digitally recording the conversation with the respondent. Having determined that the respondent has recently changed his or her favorite TV news show, for example, the interviewer can ask, "Why did you change?" and begin recording the verbatim response. (Early in the interview, the interviewer has asked permission to record parts of the interview.)

Later on, coders can play back the responses and code them, much as they would do with the interviewer's typescript of the responses. This offers an easier and more accurate way of accomplishing a conventional task. But that's a tame use of the new capability.

It's also possible to incorporate such oral data as parts of a cross-tabulation during analysis. We may create a table of gender by age by reasons for switching TV news shows. Thus, we can hear, in turn, the responses of the young men, young women, middle-aged men, and so forth. In one such study we found the younger and older men tending to watch one TV news show, while the middle-aged men watched something else. Listening to the responses of the middle-aged men, one after another, we heard a common comment: "Well, now that I'm older...." This kind of aside might have been lost in the notes hastily typed by interviewers, but such comments stood out dramatically in the oral data. The middle-aged men seemed to be telling us they felt "maturity" required them to watch a particular show, while more years under their belts let them drift back to what they liked in the first place.

These kinds of data are especially compelling to clients, particularly in customer satisfaction studies. Rather than summarize what we feel a client's customers like and don't like, we can let the respondents speak directly to the client in their own words. It's like a focus group on demand. Going one step further, we have found that letting line employees (bank tellers, for example) listen to the responses has more impact than having their supervisors tell them what they are doing right or wrong.

As exciting as these experiences are, I have the strong feeling that we have scarcely begun to tap into the possibilities for such unconventional forms of data.

Still another innovation that computer technology makes possible is described in the box entitled "Voice Capture™."

New Technologies and Survey Research

As we have already seen in the case of CATI, many of the new technologies affecting people's lives also open new possibilities for survey research. For example, recent innovations in self-administered questionnaires make use of the computer. Among the techniques being used are (Nicholls, Baker, and Martin 1997):

CAPI (computer assisted personal interviewing): Similar to CATI but used in face-to-face interviews rather than over the phone.

CASI (computer assisted self-interviewing): A research worker brings a computer to the respondent's home, and the respondent reads questions on the computer screen and enters his or her own answers.

CSAQ (computerized self-administered questionnaire): The respondent receives the questionnaire via floppy disk, bulletin board, or other means and runs the software, which asks questions and accepts the respondent's answers. Then the respondent returns the data file.

TDE (touchtone data entry): The respondent initiates the process by calling a number at the research organization. This prompts a series of computerized questions, which the respondent answers by pressing keys on the telephone keypad.

VR (voice recognition): Instead of asking the respondent to use the telephone keypad, as in TDE, this system accepts spoken responses.

Nicholls et al. report that such techniques are more efficient than conventional techniques, and they do not appear to result in a reduction of data quality.

Jeffery Walker (1994) has explored the possibility of conducting surveys by fax machine. Questionnaires are faxed to respondents, who are asked to fax their answers back. Of course, such surveys can only represent that part of the population that has fax machines. Walker reports that fax surveys don't achieve as high a response rate as face-to-face interviews, but because of the perceived urgency, they do produce higher response rates than mail or telephone surveys. In one test case, all those who had ignored a mail questionnaire were sent a fax follow-up, and 83 percent responded.

The new technology of survey research includes the use of the Internet and the World Wide Web. Some researchers feel that the Internet can be used to conduct meaningful survey research. An immediate objection that many social researchers make to online surveys, however, concerns representativeness: Will the people who can be surveyed online be representative of meaningful populations, such as all Canadian adults, all voters, and so on? This is the criticism raised with regard to surveys via fax and, earlier, with regard to telephone surveys.

There are, of course, some populations highly suited to online surveys—research geared toward gathering information from particular Web site users, for example. But how about general population surveys? The survey research community has already begun to debate this topic. There are advocates who, while noting the need for caution, strongly favour online polling. Critics warn that a more sound, theoretical basis on which to ground the new technique is needed. It is a debate that should be followed by any who desire to conduct online surveys.

Whether online surveys will gain the respect and extensive use enjoyed by telephone surveys today remains to be seen. Students who consider using this technique should do so in full recognition of its potential shortcomings.

Comparison of the Different Survey Methods

Now that we've seen several ways to collect survey data, let's take a moment to compare them directly.

Self-administered questionnaires are generally cheaper and quicker than face-to-face interview surveys. These considerations are likely to be important for an unfunded student wishing to undertake a survey for a term paper or thesis. Moreover, if you use the self-administered mail format, it costs no more to conduct a national survey than a local one of the same sample size. In contrast, a national interview survey (either face-to-face or by telephone) would cost far more than a local one. Also, mail surveys typically require a small staff: One person can conduct a reasonable mail survey alone, although you shouldn't underestimate the work involved. Further, respondents are sometimes reluctant to report controversial or deviant attitudes or behaviours in interviews but are willing to respond to an anonymous self-administered questionnaire.

Interview surveys also offer many advantages. For example, they generally produce fewer incomplete questionnaires. Although respondents may skip questions in a self-administered questionnaire, interviewers are trained not to do so. In CATI surveys, the computer offers a further check on this. Interview surveys, moreover, have typically achieved higher completion rates than self-administered questionnaires.

Although self-administered questionnaires may be more effective for sensitive issues, interview surveys are definitely more effective for complicated ones. Prime examples include the enumeration of household members and the determination of whether a given address corresponds to more than one housing unit. Although the concept of housing unit has been refined and standardized by those responsible for the census and interviewers can be trained to deal with the concept, it's extremely difficult to communicate in a self-administered questionnaire. This advantage of interview surveys pertains generally to all complicated contingency questions.

With interviewers, you can conduct a survey based on a sample of addresses or phone numbers rather than on names. An interviewer can arrive at an assigned address, or call the assigned number, introduce the survey, and even, following instructions, choose the appropriate person at that address to respond to the survey. In contrast, self-administered questionnaires addressed to "occupant" receive a notoriously low response.

Finally, as we've seen, interviewers questioning respondents face-to-face can make important observations aside from responses to questions asked in the interview. In a household interview, they may note the characteristics of the neighbourhood, the dwelling unit, and so forth. They may also note characteristics of the respondents or the quality of their interaction with the respondents: whether the respondent had difficulty communicating, was hostile, and so forth.

The chief advantages of telephone surveys over those conducted face-to-face center primarily on time and money. Telephone interviews are much cheaper and can be mounted and executed quickly. Also, interviewers are safer when interviewing in high-crime areas. Moreover, the impact of the interviewers on responses is somewhat lessened when they can't be seen by the respondents.

Online surveys have many of the strengths and weaknesses of mail surveys. Once the available software has been further developed, they are likely to be substantially cheaper. An important weakness, however, lies in the difficulty of assuring that respondents to an online survey will be representative of some more general population.

Clearly, each survey method has its place in social research. Ultimately, you must balance the advantages and disadvantages of the different methods in relation to your research needs and your resources.

Strengths and Weaknesses of Survey Research

Regardless of the specific method used, surveys, like other modes of observation in social scientific research, have special strengths and weaknesses. You should keep these in mind when determining whether the survey is appropriate for your research goals.

Surveys are particularly useful in describing the characteristics of a large population. A carefully selected probability sample in combination with a standardized questionnaire offers the possibility of making refined descriptive assertions about a student body, a city, a nation, or any other large population. Surveys determine unemployment rates, voting intentions, and the like with uncanny accuracy. Although the examination of official documents such as marriage, birth, or death records can provide equal accuracy for a few topics, no other method of observation can provide this general capability.

Surveys, especially self-administered ones, make large samples feasible. Surveys of 2,000 respondents are not unusual. A large number of cases is important for both descriptive and explanatory analyses, especially wherever several variables are to be analyzed simultaneously.

In one sense, surveys are flexible. Many questions may be asked on a given topic, giving you considerable flexibility in your analyses. Whereas an experimental design may require you to commit yourself in advance to a particular operational definition of a concept, surveys let you develop operational definitions from actual observations.

Finally, standardized questionnaires have an important strength in regard to measurement generally. Earlier chapters have discussed the ambiguous nature of most concepts: They have no ultimately real meanings. One person's religiosity is quite different from another's. Although you must be able to define concepts in those ways most relevant to your research goals, you may not find it easy to apply the same definitions uniformly to all subjects. The survey researcher is bound to this requirement by having to ask exactly the same questions of all subjects and having to impute the same intent to all respondents giving a particular response.

Survey research also has several weaknesses. First, the requirement for standardization often seems to result in the fitting of round pegs into square holes. Standardized questionnaire items often represent the least common denominator in assessing people's attitudes, orientations, circumstances, and experiences. By designing questions that will be at least minimally appropriate to all respondents, you may miss what is most appropriate to many respondents. In this sense, surveys often appear superficial in their coverage of complex topics. Although this problem can be partly offset by sophisticated analyses, it is inherent in survey research.

Similarly, survey research can seldom deal with the context of social life. Although questionnaires can provide information in this area, the survey researcher rarely develops the feel for the total life situation in which respondents are thinking and acting that, say, the participant observer can (see Chapter 11).

In many ways, surveys are inflexible. Studies involving direct observation can be modified as field conditions warrant, but surveys typically require that an initial study design remain unchanged throughout. As a field researcher, for example, you can become aware of an important new variable operating in the phenomenon you're studying and begin making careful observations of it. The survey researcher would probably be unaware of the new variable's importance and could do nothing about it in any event.

Finally, surveys are subject to the artificiality mentioned earlier in connection with experiments. Finding out that a person gives conservative answers to a questionnaire does not necessarily mean the person is conservative; finding out that a person gives prejudiced answers to a questionnaire does not necessarily mean the person is prejudiced. This shortcoming is especially salient in the realm of action. Surveys cannot measure social action; they can only collect self-reports of recalled past action or of prospective or hypothetical action.

The problem of artificiality has two aspects. First, the topic of study may not be amenable to measurement through questionnaires. Second, the act of studying that topic—an attitude, for example—may affect it. A survey respondent may have given no thought to whether a Member of Parliament should resign until asked for his or her opinion by an interviewer. He or she may, at that point, form an opinion on the matter.

Survey research is generally weak on validity and strong on reliability. In comparison with field research, for example, the artificiality of the survey format puts a strain on validity. As an illustration, people's opinions on issues seldom take the form of strongly agreeing, agreeing, disagreeing, or strongly disagreeing with a specific statement. Their survey responses in such cases must be regarded as approximate indicators of what the researchers had in mind when they framed the questions. This comment, however, needs to be held in the context of earlier discussions of the ambiguity of validity itself. To say something is a valid or an invalid measure assumes the existence of a "real" definition of what's being measured, and many scholars now reject that assumption.

Reliability is a clearer matter. By presenting all subjects with a standardized stimulus, survey research goes a long way toward eliminating unreliability in observations made by the researcher. Moreover, careful wording of the questions can also significantly reduce the subject's own unreliability.

As with all methods of observation, a full awareness of the inherent or probable weaknesses of survey research can partially resolve them in some cases. Ultimately, though, researchers are on the safest ground when they can employ several research methods in studying a given topic.

Ethical Considerations

The ethical issues discussed in the introduction to Part 3 apply to survey research as they do to all forms of research. We've mentioned several ethical considerations in the course of this chapter as well. Whether a survey is conducted face-to-face, over the telephone, or through the mail, the researcher must provide for voluntary, informed consent from each participant. Participants should be told the purposes of the study through an introductory letter, or orally when it's a telephone or face-to-face interview survey. In the case of a mail survey, whether the responses will be anonymous or confidential, should be clearly indicated. In the case of interview surveys, assurances of confidentiality should be indicated, if that is the intent. If such assurances are not intended, that too should be clearly indicated. If a researcher plans to tape an interview, over the phone or in person, the respondent must be made aware of this and their permis-

sion must be sought. Information about how the respondents were selected for the study, the auspices under which the study is being conducted, and contact information should be provided for those who might want more information about the study. In the case of a mail survey, information about the mechanisms of how to return the questionnaire is also often included in the letter.

When seeking ethical approval for a survey research project, the letter or speech of introduction must be submitted to the review board. As you can see, such introductions may vary, depending on the study's design and purpose. An illustration of a short telephone introduction used in the 2000 General Social Survey follows:

> Hello I'm...from Statistics Canada. We are calling you for a study on new technology. The purpose of the study is to better understand people's use of technology and how it has affected their daily lives.
>
> All information we collect in this voluntary survey will be kept strictly confidential. Your participation is essential if the survey results are to be accurate.
>
> Optional:
> My supervisor is working with me today and may listen to the interview to evaluate the survey.
>
> (Statistics Canada, June, 2001:B2)

Some of the ethical responsibilities of the survey researcher are initially rather subtle. When research is conducted from afar, as in mail surveys for example, the impact of the research on the respondent may not be as salient. The absence of face-to-face interaction may make the researcher less sensitive to respondents' needs and concerns. We want to emphasize, therefore, the researchers' moral and ethical responsibility to be considerate of respondents—of their time, their interests, their feelings, and their experience with the survey— when conducting any type of survey. In interview surveys, the interviewers should be familiar with the questionnaire so that the interview runs smoothly. In mail surveys, the questionnaires should be easy to understand and fill out.

As Gray and Guppy (1999) note—in a chapter in their book on surveys devoted to ethical concerns—researchers must show respect for respondents and be sure to accurately represent the information they are provided by them. The potential risks of a study to participants must be thoughtfully considered, and a plan should be made concerning how confidentiality or anonymity will be maintained. Survey researchers must carefully consider ethical issues when designing, implementing, and reporting their research.

Secondary Analysis

As a mode of observation, survey research involves the following steps: (1) questionnaire construction, (2) sample selection, and (3) data collection, through either interviewing or self-administered questionnaires. As you've gathered, surveys are usually major undertakings. It's not unusual for a large-scale survey to take several months or even more than a year to progress from conceptualization to data in hand. (Smaller-scale surveys can, of course, be done more quickly.) Through a method called *secondary analysis,* however, researchers can pursue their particular social research interests—analyzing survey data from, say, a national sample of 2,000 respondents—while avoiding the enormous expenditure of time and money such a survey entails.

Secondary analysis is a form of research in which the data collected and processed by one researcher are reanalyzed—often for a different purpose—by another. Beginning in the 1960s, survey researchers became aware of the potential value that lay in archiving survey data for analysis by scholars who had nothing to do with the survey design and data collection. Even when one researcher had conducted a survey and analyzed the data, others with slightly different interests could further analyze those same data. Thus, if you were interested in the relationship between political attitudes and attitudes toward gender equality, you could examine that research question through the analysis of any dataset that happened to contain questions relating to those two variables. Data archives, therefore, contain datasets available to others for secondary analysis. There are now a large number of them containing a wide range of datasets. These datasets are usually available on computer disks, CD-ROMs, or online servers. Once you have obtained such data from the archive it's yours to keep and use again and again if you desire.

Statistics Canada has conducted the General Social Survey (GSS) on an annual basis since 1985 (with two exceptions, 1987 and 1997), gathering national information on a wide range of topics. (We discuss Statistics Canada at length in the next chapter, including how to obtain data from them.) It also conducts special surveys on various issues. The information generated from these surveys is a great source of secondary data for social researchers. For example, Rosemary Gartner and Ross Macmillan (2000) used Statistics Canada's Violence Against Women (VAW) survey to investigate whether the relationship between the offender and female victim has an impact on the reporting of violence against women to the police. They noted that the VAW survey was "the most comprehensive survey data set" on the topic currently available (p. 128). There are great advantages to having such data at hand, as noted above. There are also some limitations, however, when using existing studies to investigate research questions for which they are not specifically designed. The exact information desired may not have been gathered. As Gartner and Macmillan stated, "Ideally, we should control for characteristics of the victim and offender that might be associated with the likelihood of the police learning of the victimization" (2000:132). However, due to lack of this information in the VAW survey, with the exception of age, such controls were not possible in their analyses. Despite these data limitations, they were able to conduct valuable analyses and report important findings, for example, all violence against women is underreported to police, but "violence by known offenders is much less likely to come to the attention of authorities than is violence by strangers" (2000:135).

Other examples of surveys conducted by Statistics Canada are the National Population Health survey, National Longitudinal Survey of Children and Youth (NLSCY), Workplace and Employee survey, and the Survey of Labour and Income Dynamics (SLID).

Survey data for secondary analysis may be obtained in a number of places. The Inter-University Consortium for Political and Social Research (ICPSR) at the University of Michigan, for example, has an excellent data archive (http://www.icpsr. umich.edu/). Researchers can gain access to a number of surveys, including the U.S. General Social Survey, a major survey of American residents (funded by the U.S. federal government) that gathers numerous social science variables. Many Canadian universities are ICPSR member institutions. If you desire a list of public opinion polls in Canada by such groups as Canada Gallup and Angus Reid, for example, you can search the Roper Center for Public Opinion Research Web site (http://www.ropercenter.uconn.edu/) at the University of Connecticut, which contains this and much more.

If you are interested in finding available data sources for a particular research question or for a given country, a Web search may prove very useful. There are a number of international archives available to social researchers. In addition, many universities have data librarians who are highly knowledgeable about sources of archived data available to scholars at little or no cost. (Chapter 10 discusses the Data Liberation Initiative (DLI) that makes a large amount of Statistics Canada data available to members of subscribing colleges and universities.)

The advantages of secondary analysis are obvious and enormous: It's cheaper and faster than doing original surveys, and, depending on who did the original survey, you may benefit from the work of topflight professionals. The key problem with secondary analysis involves the recurrent question of validity. When one researcher collects data for one particular purpose, you have no assurance that those data will be appropriate for your research interests. Typically, you'll find that the original researcher asked a question that "comes close" to measuring what you're interested in, but you'll wish the question had been asked just a little differently or that another related question had also been asked. Your question, then, is whether the question that was asked provides a valid measure of the variable you want to analyze. (Chapter 10 contains further discussion of the limitations of using existing data.) Nonetheless, secondary analysis can be very useful. While no single method unlocks all puzzles, there is no limit to the ways you can find out about things. And when you zero in on an issue from several independent directions, you gain that much more expertise.

Main Points

- Survey research, a popular social research method, is the administration of questionnaires to a sample of respondents selected from some population.

- Survey research is especially appropriate for making descriptive studies of large populations; survey data may be used for explanatory purposes as well.

- Questionnaires provide a method of collecting data by (1) asking people questions or (2) asking them to agree or disagree with statements representing different points of view.

- Questions may be open-ended (respondents supply their own answers) or closed-ended (they select from a list of provided answers).

- Questionnaire items should be clear. They should ask about a single thing (avoiding double-barrelled questions). Short items are usually best. Questions should be directed toward respondents competent to answer, and they should be relevant to the respondent. Respondents must be willing to answer. Items should avoid negative terms because they may confuse respondents. Items should be worded to avoid biasing responses, i.e., encouraging respondents to answer in a particular way or to support a particular point of view.

- Questionnaire formats can influence the quality of data collected.
- Contingency questions require a clear format to ensure that respondents answer all questions intended for them.
- The matrix question is an efficient format for presenting several items sharing the same response categories.
- The order of items in a questionnaire can influence the responses given.
- Clear instructions are important for getting appropriate responses in a questionnaire.
- Questionnaires should be pretested before being administered to the study population.
- Questionnaires may be administered in three basic ways: self-administered questionnaires, face-to-face encounters, or telephone surveys.
- It's generally best to plan follow-up mailings in the case of self-administered questionnaires, sending new questionnaires to those respondents who fail to respond to the initial appeal. Properly monitoring questionnaire returns will provide a good guide to when a follow-up mailing is appropriate.
- The essential characteristic of interviewers is that they be neutral; their presence in the data-collection process must not have any effect on the responses given to questionnaire items.
- Interviewers must be carefully trained to be familiar with the questionnaire, to follow the question wording and question order exactly, and to record responses exactly as they are given.
- Probes can be used to elicit an elaboration on an incomplete or ambiguous response. Ideally, all interviewers should use the same probes and the probes should be neutral.
- Telephone surveys are often cheaper, more efficient, and safer for the interviewer than face to face interviews. Telephone surveys may also have less effect on the interview itself. Computer-assisted telephone interviewing (CATI) techniques are especially promising and can permit greater control over data collection.
- Surveys are now being conducted via fax and over the Internet. These two methods, however, must be used with caution because respondents may not be representative of the intended population.
- The advantages of a self-administered questionnaire over an interview survey are economy, speed, lack of interviewer bias, and the possibility of anonymity and privacy to encourage candid responses on sensitive issues.
- The advantages of an interview survey over a self-administered questionnaire are fewer incomplete questionnaires and fewer misunderstood questions, generally higher return rates, and greater flexibility in terms of sampling and special observations.
- Survey research in general offers advantages in terms of economy, the amount of data that can be collected, and the chance to sample a large population. The standardization of the data collected represents another special strength of survey research.
- Survey research has the weaknesses of being somewhat artificial, potentially superficial, and relatively inflexible. It's difficult to use surveys to gain a full sense of social processes in their natural settings. In general, survey research is comparatively weak on validity and strong on reliability.
- Secondary analysis is advantageous because it provides researchers with access to data collected by other researchers, saving time and money. A disadvantage is the potential problem of validity.

Review Questions and Exercises

1. For each of the following open-ended questions, construct a closed-ended question that could be used in a questionnaire.
   a. What was your family's total income last year?
   b. How important is religion in your life?
   c. What was your main reason for attending university?

d. What do you feel is the biggest problem facing your community?

2. Construct a set of contingency questions for use in a self-administered questionnaire that would solicit the following information:
   a. Is the respondent employed?
   b. If unemployed, is the respondent looking for work?
   c. If the unemployed respondent is not looking for work, is he or she retired, a student, or a homemaker?
   d. If the respondent is looking for work, how long has he or she been looking?

3. Find a questionnaire printed in a magazine or newspaper (for a reader survey, for example). Consider at least five of the questions in it and critique each one either positively or negatively.

4. Locate a survey being conducted on the Web. Briefly describe the survey and discuss its strengths and weaknesses.

Continuity Project

Write 10 questionnaire items that would tap attitudes toward gender equality. Format the questions as they would appear in a questionnaire, using any of the formats illustrated in this chapter. Then discuss the relative advantages and disadvantages of using self-administered questionnaires, face-to-face interviews, and telephone interviews as survey methods in a study of gender equality. In particular, think about any impact interviewers might have in such a study.

Additional Readings

Babbie, Earl. *Survey Research Methods.* Belmont, CA: Wadsworth, 1990. A comprehensive overview of survey methods. (You thought maybe we'd say it was lousy?) This textbook, although overlapping the present one somewhat, covers aspects of survey techniques omitted here.

Bradburn, Norman M., and Seymour Sudman. *Polls and Surveys: Understanding What They Tell Us.* San Francisco: Jossey-Bass, 1988. These veteran survey researchers answer questions about their craft the general public commonly ask.

Dillman, Don A. *Mail and Telephone Surveys: The Total Design Method.* New York: Wiley, 1978. An excellent review of the methodological literature on mail and telephone surveys. Dillman makes many good suggestions for improving response rates.

Feick, Lawrence F. "Latent Class Analysis of Survey Questions That Include Don't Know Responses." *Public Opinion Quarterly* 53, no. 4 (Winter 1989): 525–47. *Don't know* can mean a variety of things, as this analysis indicates.

Fowler, Floyd J., Jr. *Improving Survey Questions: Design and Evaluation.* Thousand Oaks, CA: Sage, 1995. A comprehensive discussion of questionnaire construction, including a number of suggestions for pretesting questions. This book discusses the logic of obtaining information through survey questions and gives numerous guidelines for being effective. It also offers several examples of questions you might use.

Gray, George and Neil Guppy. *Successful Surveys: Research Methods and Practice.* Second Edition. Toronto: Harcourt Brace Canada, 1999. The book is a useful source for beginners in survey methods. The ethical considerations they raise in Chapter 3 deserve particular attention and provide a good backdrop for an extended discussion.

Groves, Robert M. "Theories and Methods of Telephone Surveys." Pp. 221–40 in *Annual Review of Sociology,* Vol. 16, edited by W. Richard Scott and Judith Blake. Palo Alto, CA: Annual Reviews, 1990. An attempt to place telephone surveys in the context of sociological and psychological theories and to address the various kinds of errors common to this research method.

Sheatsley, Paul F. "Questionnaire Construction and Item Writing." Pp. 195–230 in *Handbook of*

Survey Research, edited by Peter H. Rossi, James D. Wright, and Andy B. Anderson. New York: Academic Press, 1983. An excellent examination of the topic by an expert in the field.

Smith, Eric R. A. N., and Peverill Squire, "The Effects of Prestige Names in Question Wording." *Public Opinion Quarterly* 54 (Spring 1990): 97–116. Not only do prestigious names affect the overall responses given to survey questionnaires, they also affect such things as the correlation between education and the number of don't know answers.

Tourangeau, Roger, et al. "Carryover Effects in Attitude Surveys." *Public Opinion Quarterly* 53 (Winter 1989): 495–524. The authors asked six target questions in a telephone survey of 1,100 respondents, varying the questions immediately preceding the target questions. They found substantial differences

***Info*Trac:** You can find further relevant readings on the World Wide Web at

http://sociology.wadsworth.com

Chapter 10

Unobtrusive Research

*This chapter will present overviews of three unob-
trusive research methods: the analysis of existing
statistics, content analysis, and historical/compara-
tive analysis. Each of these methods allows
researchers to study social life from afar, without
influencing it in the process.*

Introduction

The modes of observation discussed so far require the researcher to intrude to some degree on whatever he or she is studying. This is most obvious in the case of experiments, followed closely by survey research. Even the field researcher, as we'll see, can change things in the process of studying them.

At least one previous example in this book, however, was totally exempt from that danger. Durkheim's analysis of suicide did nothing to affect suicides one way or the other (see Chapter 5). His study is an example of **unobtrusive research,** or methods of studying social behaviour without affecting it. As you'll see, unobstrusive measures can be qualitative or quantitative.

This chapter examines three types of unobstrusive research methods: analysis of existing statistics, content analysis, and historical/comparative analysis. The Durkheim study is an example of the *analysis of existing statistics.* As you'll see, there are great masses of data all around you, awaiting your use in the understanding of social life. In *content analysis,* researchers examine a class of social artifacts that are usually written documents such as newspaper editorials. Finally, *historical/comparative analysis,* a form of research with a venerable history in the social sciences is currently enjoying a resurgence of popularity. Historical/comparative analysis is for many a qualitative method, one in which the main resources for observation and analysis are historical records. There are also, however, a number of historical/comparative analysts who use quantitative techniques. The method's name often includes the word *comparative* because social scientists—in contrast to historians who may simply describe a particular set of events—seek to discover common patterns that recur in different times and places.

To set the stage for our examination of these three research methods, we want to draw your attention to an excellent book that should sharpen your senses about the potential for unobtrusive measures in general. It is, among other things, the book from which we take the term *unobtrusive measures.*

In 1966, Eugene Webb and three colleagues published an ingenious little book on social research (revised in 2000) that has become a classic. It focuses on the idea of unobtrusive or nonreactive research. Webb and his colleagues have played freely with the task of learning about human behaviour by observing what people inadvertently leave behind them. Do you want to know what exhibits are the most popular at a museum? You could conduct a poll, but people might tell you what they thought you wanted to hear or what might make them look more intellectual and serious. You could stand by different exhibits and count the viewers that came by, but people might come over to see what you were doing. Webb and his colleagues suggest you check the wear and tear on the floor in front of various exhibits. Those where the tiles have been worn down the most are probably the most popular. Want to know which exhibits are popular with little kids? Look for mucus on the glass cases. To get a sense of the most popular radio stations, you could arrange with an auto mechanic to check the radio dial settings for cars brought in for repair.

The possibilities are limitless. Like a detective investigating a crime, the social researcher looks for clues. If you stop to notice, you'll find that clues of social behaviour are all around you. In a sense, everything you see represents the answer to some important social scientific question. All you have to do is think of the question.

Although problems of validity and reliability crop up in unobtrusive measures, a little ingenuity can either handle them or put them in perspective. We encourage you to look at Webb's book. It's enjoyable reading, and it can be a source of stimulation and insight for social inquiry through data that already exist. For now, let's turn our attention to three unobtrusive methods often employed by social scientists.

Analyzing Existing Statistics

Frequently, you can or must undertake social scientific inquiry through the use of official or quasi-official statistics. In this section we're going to look at ways of drawing on data analyses reported by others, such as government agencies. This differs from secondary analysis, in which you obtain a copy of someone else's data and undertake your own statistical analysis. Nonetheless, there is a great deal of overlap between secondary analysis and the use of existing statistics. Many of the data problems and limitations that apply to the use of existing statistics also apply to secondary analysis. For example, the researcher must often face the

limitations and constraints of available measures, and sound judgment often requires knowledge of exactly how the measures were devised, collected, and coded—and thus what they incorporate. There are other similarities as well, for example, ethical approval is almost never required when using existing statistics or conducting a secondary analysis. However, the data available to you may at times be constrained because of promises of confidentiality in the initial data collections.

The method of using existing statistics is particularly significant because such statistics should always be considered at least a supplemental source of data. If you were planning a survey of political attitudes, for example, you would do well to examine and present your findings within a context of voting patterns, rates of voter turnout, or similar statistics relevant to your research interest. Or, if you were doing evaluation research on an experimental morale-building program on an assembly line, statistics on absenteeism, sick leave, and so on would probably be interesting and revealing in connection with the data your own research would generate. Existing statistics, then, can often provide a historical or conceptual context within which to locate your original research. For example, Sosteric (1996) did a participant observation study in a nightclub in a small Canadian city. In support of his claim that the club's workers made above average incomes, he reported data from Statistics Canada on industry averages for full and part-time waitresses and bartenders.

Existing statistics can also provide the main data for a social scientific inquiry. An excellent example is the classic study mentioned at the beginning of this chapter, Emile Durkheim's *Suicide* ([1897] 1951). Let's take a closer look at Durkheim's work before considering some of the special problems this method presents.

Studying Suicide

Why do people kill themselves? Undoubtedly every suicide case has a unique history and explanation, yet all such cases could no doubt be grouped according to certain common causes: financial failure, trouble in love, disgrace, and other kinds of personal problems. The French sociologist Emile Durkheim had a slightly different question in mind when he addressed the matter of suicide, however. He wanted to discover the environmental conditions that encouraged or discouraged it, especially social conditions.

The more Durkheim examined the available records, the more patterns of differences became apparent to him. One of the first things to attract his attention was the relative *stability* of suicide rates. Looking at several countries, he found suicide rates to be about the same year after year. He also discovered that a disproportionate number of suicides occurred in summer, leading him to hypothesize that temperature might have something to do with suicide. If this were the case, suicide rates should be higher in the southern European countries than in the temperate ones. However, Durkheim discovered that the highest rates were found in countries in the central latitudes, so temperature couldn't be the answer.

He explored the role of age (35 was the most common suicide age), gender (men outnumbered women around four to one), and numerous other factors. Eventually, a general pattern emerged from different sources.

In terms of the stability of suicide rates over time, for instance, Durkheim found the pattern was not totally stable. He found spurts in the rates during times of political turmoil, which occurred in several European countries around 1848. This observation led him to hypothesize that suicide might have something to do with "breaches in social equilibrium." Put differently, social stability and integration seemed to be a protection against suicide.

This general hypothesis was substantiated and specified through Durkheim's analysis of a different set of data. The different countries of Europe had radically different suicide rates. The rate in Saxony, for example, was about 10 times that of Italy, and the relative ranking of various countries persisted over time. As Durkheim considered other differences among the various countries, he eventually noticed a striking pattern: Predominantly Protestant countries had consistently higher suicide rates

than Catholic ones. The predominantly Protestant countries had 190 suicides per million population; mixed Protestant–Catholic countries, 96; and predominantly Catholic countries, 58 (Durkheim [1897] 1951:152).

Although suicide rates therefore seemed to be related to religion, Durkheim reasoned that some other factor, such as level of economic and cultural development, might explain the observed differences. If religion had a genuine effect on suicide, then the religious difference would have to be found *within* given countries as well. To test this idea, Durkheim first noted that the German state of Bavaria had both the most Catholics and the lowest suicide rates in that country, whereas heavily Protestant Prussia had a much higher suicide rate. Not content to stop there, however, Durkheim examined the provinces composing each of those states.

Table 10-1 shows what he found. As you can see, in both Bavaria and Prussia, provinces with the highest proportion of Protestants also had the highest suicide rates. Increasingly, Durkheim became confident that religion played a significant role in the matter of suicide.

Returning eventually to a more general theoretical level, Durkheim combined the religious findings with the earlier observation about increased suicide rates during times of political turmoil. Put most simply, Durkheim suggested many suicides are a product of *anomie,* "normlessness," or a general sense of social instability and disintegration. During times of political strife, people may feel that the old ways of society are collapsing. They become demoralized and depressed, and suicide is one answer to the severe discomfort. Seen from the other direction, social integration and solidarity—reflected in personal feelings of being part of a coherent, enduring social whole—offer protection against depression and suicide. That was where the religious difference fit in. Catholicism, as a far more structured and integrated religious system, gave people a greater sense of coherence and stability than did the more loosely structured Protestantism.

From these theories, Durkheim created the concept of *anomic suicide.* More important, as you

Table 10-1

Suicide Rates in Various German Provinces, Arranged in Terms of Religious Affiliation

Religious Character of Province	Suicides per Million Inhabitants
Bavarian Provinces (1867–1875)*	
Less than 50% Catholic	
Rhenish Palatinate	167
Central Franconia	207
Upper Franconia	204
Average	192
50% to 90% Catholic	
Lower Franconia	157
Swabia	118
Average	135
More than 90% Catholic	
Upper Palatinate	64
Upper Bavaria	114
Lower Bavaria	19
Average	75
Prussian Provinces (1883–1890)	
More than 90% Protestant	
Saxony	309.4
Schleswig	312.9
Pomerania	171.5
Average	264.6
68% to 89% Protestant	
Hanover	212.3
Hesse	200.3
Brandenburg and Berlin	296.3
East Prussia	171.3
Average	220.0
40% to 50% Protestant	
West Prussia	123.9
Silesia	260.2
Westphalia	107.5
Average	163.6
28% to 32% Protestant	
Posen	96.4
Rhineland	100.3
Hohenzollern	90.1
Average	95.6

*Note: The population below 15 years has been omitted.

Source: Adapted with the permission of The Free Press, a Division of Simon & Schuster, Inc., from SUICIDE: A Study in Sociology by Emile Durkheim, translated by J.A. Spaulding and George Simpson. Edited by George Simpson. Copyright © 1951, copyright renewed 1979 by The Free Press.

know, he added the concept of *anomie* to the lexicon of the social sciences.

This account of Durkheim's classic study is greatly simplified, of course. Anyone studying social research would profit from studying the original. For our purposes, though, Durkheim's approach provides a good illustration of the possibilities for research contained in the masses of data regularly gathered and reported by government agencies and other organizations.

Units of Analysis

The unit of analysis involved in the analysis of existing statistics is often *not* the individual. Durkheim, for example, was required to work with political–geographical units: countries, regions, states, and cities. The same situation would probably appear if you were to undertake a study of crime rates, accident rates, or disease. By their nature, most existing statistics are aggregated: They describe groups.

The aggregate nature of existing statistics can present a problem, though not an insurmountable one. As we saw, for example, Durkheim wanted to determine whether Protestants or Catholics were more likely to commit suicide. The difficulty was that none of the records available to him indicated the religion of those people who committed suicide. Ultimately, then, it was not possible for him to say whether Protestants committed suicide more often than Catholics, though he inferred as much. Because Protestant countries, regions, and states had higher suicides than Catholic countries, regions, and states, he drew the obvious conclusion.

There's danger in drawing this kind of conclusion, however. It's always possible that patterns of behaviour at a group level may not reflect corresponding patterns on an individual level. Such errors are said to be due to an ecological fallacy, which was discussed in Chapter 4. In the case of Durkheim's study, it was altogether possible, for example, that it was Catholics who committed suicide in the predominantly Protestant areas. Perhaps Catholics in predominantly Protestant areas were so badly persecuted that they were led into despair and suicide. In that case it would be possible for Protestant countries to have high suicide rates without any Protestants committing suicide.

Durkheim avoided the danger of ecological fallacy in two ways. First, his general conclusions were based as much on rigorous theoretical deductions as on the empirical facts. The correspondence between theory and fact made a counterexplanation, such as the one we just made up, less likely. Second, by extensively retesting his conclusions in a variety of ways, Durkheim further strengthened the likelihood that they were correct. Suicide rates were higher in Protestant countries than in Catholic ones; higher in Protestant regions of Catholic countries than in Catholic regions of Protestant countries; and so forth. The replication of findings added to the weight of evidence in support of his conclusions.

Problems of Validity

Whenever we base our research on an analysis of data that already exist, we're obviously limited to what exists. Often, the existing data do not cover exactly what we're interested in, and our measurements may not be altogether valid representations of the variables and concepts we want to draw conclusions about.

Two characteristics of science are used to handle the problem of validity in analysis of existing statistics: *logical reasoning* and *replication*. Durkheim's strategy provides an example of logical reasoning. Although he could not determine the religion of people who committed suicide, he reasoned that most of the suicides in a predominantly Protestant region would be Protestants.

Replication can be a general solution to problems of validity in social research. Recall the earlier discussion of the interchangeability of indicators (Chapter 5). Crying in sad movies isn't necessarily a valid measure of compassion; nor is putting little birds back in their nests or giving money to charity. None of these things, taken alone, would prove that one group (women, say) was more compassionate than another (men). But if women appeared more compassionate than men by all these measures, that would create a weight of evidence in support of the conclusion. In the analysis of existing statistics, a little ingenuity and reasoning can usually turn up several independent tests of a given hypothesis. If all the tests seem to support the hypothesis, then the weight of evidence supports the validity of the measure.

Problems of Reliability

The analysis of existing statistics depends heavily on the quality of the statistics themselves: Are they accurate reports of what they claim to report? This can be a substantial problem sometimes, because the weighty tables of government statistics are sometimes grossly inaccurate.

Consider research into crime. Because a great deal of the research into crime depends on official crime statistics, this body of data has come under critical evaluation. The results have not been too encouraging. As an illustration, suppose you were interested in tracing the long-term trends in violence against women in Canada since the late 1960s, specifically the crime of rape. Official statistics on the numbers of people arrested for rape or attempted rape would seem to be a reasonable measure of use. Right? Not necessarily.

To begin, you face a hefty problem of validity. The first thing you would become aware of in attempting to gather official statistics is that there is no longer a legally defined crime of "rape" in Canada. Laws can change and therefore so too do the definitions of what constitutes a given criminal act. "The sections of the *Criminal Code* dealing with rape were repealed and replaced in a process begun in 1980, partly as a result of the modern feminist movement" (Silverman et al. 2000:8). Since the legal reform of 1983, sexually aggressive acts are covered under three levels of seriousness of sexual assault (sections 271–273 of the *Criminal Code*). As Roberts and Gebotys (1992:558–59) state, prior to 1983 the offense of rape "had a degree of conceptual clarity that is absent from the sexual assault offenses. If a victim reported a coerced sexual act involving penetration, the incident was by definition rape and not indecent assault. Sexual Assault is undefined in the current *Criminal Code* of Canada, leaving the courts free to resolve the question of what kinds of behaviours are included in the offense." Thus, "there is no direct, one-to-one correspondence between the prereform and postreform offenses (i.e. rape does not correspond exclusively to any particular level of sexual assault)" (p. 560).

Because there is no direct correspondence between the old and new offenses, you would not be able get a valid measure of rape in Canada from the 1960s to the present using official crime statistics. But even if you limited your study to the period prior to the change in law, for example, you would still have problems of reliability, stemming from the nature of law enforcement and crime record keeping. As Kong (2000:63) warns, "...many factors could influence official crime statistics. These include reporting by the public to the police; reporting by police to the CCJS [Canadian Centre

for Justice Statistics]; and the impact of new initiatives such as changes in legislation, policies or enforcement practices."

Law enforcement, for example, is subject to various pressures. A public outcry against the poor handling of rape cases and the negative treatment of rape victims by the criminal justice system could affect reporting and the processing of cases by the police, for example increasing the number of cases the police find credible and hence in which charges are laid. A sensational story in the press can have a similar effect. In addition, the volume of overall business facing the police can affect the handling of offenses more generally.

As analyses of victimization surveys and data concerning police processing of cases demonstrate, the official records present a far less accurate history of the occurrence of rape and other forms of sexual assaults than actually exist in our society. Most sexual assaults are not reported to the police and a high percentage of reported incidents are classified as unfounded, indicating the police investigation declared the crime did not occur (Roberts and Gebotys 1992). On a different level of analysis, Donald Black (1970) and others have analyzed the factors influencing whether an offender is actually arrested by police or let off with a warning. Ultimately, official crime statistics are influenced by whether specific offenders are well or poorly dressed, whether they are polite or abusive to police officers, and so forth. When we consider unreported crimes in general, sometimes estimated to be as much as ten times the number of crimes known to police, the reliability of crime statistics gets even shakier.

Finally, the process of record keeping affects the data available to researchers. Whenever a law enforcement unit improves its record-keeping system—computerizes it, for example—the apparent crime rates always increase dramatically. This can happen even if the number of crimes committed, reported, and investigated does not increase.

Researchers' first protection against the problems of reliability in the analysis of existing statistics is knowing that the problem may exist. Investigating the nature of the data collection and tabulation may enable you to assess the nature and degree of unreliability so you can judge its potential impact on your research interest. If you also use logical reasoning and replication, you can usually cope with the problem.

Sources of Existing Statistics

It would take a whole book just to list the sources of data available for analysis. We want to mention a few sources and point you in the direction of finding others relevant to your research interest.

One of the most valuable sources of data for Canada is *Statistics Canada*, the statistics bureau of the federal government. As their Web site states, their programs are "organized into three broad subject matter areas: demographic and social, socio-economic, and economic. Under the Statistics Act, *Statistics Canada* is required to collect, compile, analyse, abstract and publish statistical information on virtually every aspect of the nation's society and economy" (http://www. statcan.ca/english/about/info.htm).

Statistics Canada develops and conducts statistical surveys and other types of studies (discussed in Chapter 9). It is responsible for the Canadian census, labour statistics, and statistics on health and welfare, finance, agriculture, and industry. It is also responsible for the collection and reporting of official crime statistics in Canada. "Since 1962, all criminal incidents are reported by police agencies to the Uniform Crime Reporting Survey [UCR] at the Canadian Centre for Justice Statistics" (CCJS) located within Statistics Canada (CCJS 1999:vi). Thus, Statistics Canada is responsible for providing population information, economic data, data on crime and justice, and indicators such as the unemployment rate and the consumer price index. The list of information that is gathered and reported by Statistics Canada is nearly endless.

Statistics Canada publishes numerous analytic periodicals and series of reports such as *Canadian Social Trends, Canadian Economic Observer, Perspectives on Labour and Income, Juristat, Health Reports,* and *Focus on Culture,* that present statistics and analyses on a wide range of topics. It has also made available an electronic edition of *Historical Statistics of Canada* (second edition), jointly produced with the Social Science Federation of Canada, that can be viewed online or downloaded from their Internet site without charge. "This volume contains about 1,088 statistical tables on the social, economic, and institutional conditions of Canada from the start of the Confederation in 1867 to the mid-1970s" (http://www. statcan. ca/english/freepub/11-516-XIE/sectiona/toc.htm). It's located on their Education Resources Web page, along with information about their Data Liberation Initiative (DLI), which provides affordable access to a wide range of Statistics Canada data for research and teaching. A large number of Canadian universities subscribe to it. You can check their Web page to see if yours subscribes and then obtain the DLI contact information for your university as well—or you can check with the data librarian at your university.

The only way to truly gain a sense of the information available to you from Statistics Canada is to explore their Web site at http://www.statcan.ca/.

A vast majority of governments have highly developed institutions for gathering statistics and most produce annual volumes reporting a wide range of information about their countries. For example, there is the annual *Statistical Abstract of the United States; Annuaire Statistique de la France; Annuario Statistico Italiano;* and the *Japan Statistical Yearbook* (published in English). Collection of data—official statistics—by governments provides some of the best sources of available data.

The Statistics Canada Web site has links to many useful Web sites that provide statistics for countries all over the world. We suggest you also take a quick look and explore some of these sites as well (http://www.statcan.ca/english/reference/servrs.htm). You'll find, for example, links to such sites as the Australian Bureau of Statistics (http://www.abs.gov.au/).

Government agencies at all levels publish countless data series. World statistics are available through the United Nations. Its *Demographic Yearbook* presents annual vital statistics (births, deaths, and other data relevant to population) for the individual nations of the world. Other publications report a variety of other kinds of data. To find out what's available, go to your library, find the government documents section, and spend a few hours browsing through the shelves. In addition, search the Web. The World Wide Web is the latest

Suffering Around the World

In 1992, the Population Crisis Committee, a nonprofit organization committed to combating the population explosion, undertook to analyze the relative degree of suffering in nations around the world. Every country with a population of one million or more was evaluated in terms of the following ten indicators with a score of 10 on any indicator representing the highest level of adversity:

Life expectancy

Daily per capita calorie supply

Percentage of the population with access to clean drinking water

Proportion of infant immunization

Rate of secondary school enrolment

Gross national product

Inflation

Number of telephones per 1,000 people

Political freedom

Civil rights

Here's how the world's nations ranked in terms of these indicators. Remember, high scores are signs of overall suffering.

Extreme Human Suffering:

93–Mozambique
92–Somalia
89–Afghanistan, Haiti, Sudan
88–Zaire
87–Laos
86–Guinea, Angola
85–Ethiopia, Uganda
84–Cambodia, Sierra Leone
82–Chad, Guinea-Bissau
81–Ghana, Burma
79–Malawi
77–Cameroon, Mauritania
76–Rwanda, Vietnam, Liberia
75–Burundi, Kenya, Madagascar, Yemen

High Human Suffering:

74–Ivory Coast
73–Bhutan, Burkina Faso, Central African Republic
71–Tanzania, Togo
70–Lesotho, Mali, Niger, Nigeria

development in access to existing statistics. Here are just a few Web sites to illustrate the richness of this new resource:

Government of Canada
    http://canada.gc.ca
Correctional Service Canada
    http://www.csc-scc.gc.ca/
National Library of Canada
    http://www.nlc-bnc.ca/
City of Toronto Drug Prevention Centre
    http://www.city.toronto.on.ca/drugcentre/
Canadian Institute for Health Information
    http://www.cihi.ca/
The World Bank
    http://www.worldbank.org/

The amount of data provided by nongovernmental agencies is as staggering as the amount your taxes buy. Chambers of commerce often publish data reports on business, as do private con-

sumer groups. Non-profit organizations such as the Canadian Council on Social Development (http://www.ccsd.ca) provide free access to statistics concerning poverty, welfare, and income, for example. Ralph Nader has information on automobile safety. George Gallup publishes reference volumes on public opinion as tapped by Gallup Polls since 1935. Statistical and other types of data can be found in such places as the genealogy Web site for Prince Edward Island (http://www. island register.com/) as well.

Organizations such as the Population Reference Bureau (http://www.prb.org/) publish a variety of international demographic data that a researcher could use. Their *World Population Data Sheet* and *Population Bulletin* are resources heavily used by social scientists.

The sources listed here are only a tiny fraction of the thousands that are available. With so much data already collected, the lack of funds to support

69–Guatemala, Nepal
68–Bangladesh, Bolivia, Zambia
67–Pakistan
66–Nicaragua, Papua-New Guinea, Senegal, Swaziland,
    Zimbabwe
65–Iraq
64–Gambia, Congo, El Salvador, Indonesia, Syria
63–Comores, India, Paraguay, Peru
62–Benin, Honduras
61–Lebanon, China, Guyana, South Africa
59–Egypt, Morocco
58–Ecuador, Sri Lanka
57–Botswana
56–Iran
55–Suriname
54–Algeria, Thailand
53–Dominican Republic, Mexico, Tunisia, Turkey
51–Libya, Colombia, Venezuela
50–Brazil, Oman, Philippines

Moderate Human Suffering:

49–Solomon Islands
47–Albania
45–Vanuatu
44–Jamaica, Romania, Saudi Arabia, Seychelles, Yugoslavia
    (former)
43–Mongolia

41–Jordan
40–Malaysia, Mauritius
39–Argentina
38–Cuba, Panama
37–Chile, Uruguay, North Korea
34–Costa Rica, South Korea, United Arab Emirates
33–Poland
32–Bulgaria, Hungary, Qatar
31–Soviet Union (former)
29–Bahrain, Hong Kong, Trinidad and Tobago
28–Kuwait, Singapore
25–Czechoslovakia, Portugal, Taiwan

Minimal Human Suffering:

21–Israel
19–Greece
16–United Kingdom
12–Italy
11–Barbados, Ireland, Spain, Sweden
 8–Finland, New Zealand
 7–France, Iceland, Japan, Luxembourg
 6–Austria, Germany
 5–United States
 4–Australia, Norway
 3–Canada, Switzerland
 2–Belgium, Netherlands
 1–Denmark

expensive data collection is no reason for not doing good and useful social research.

The availability of existing statistics also makes it possible to create some fairly sophisticated measures. The accompanying box, "Suffering Around the World," describes an analysis published by the Population Crisis Committee based on the kinds of data available in government practice.

Let's move from the analysis of existing statistics now and turn to a related research method: content analysis. Although communications rather than numbers are the substance analyzed in this case, we think you'll see some similarity to the analysis of existing statistics.

Content Analysis

As we mentioned in the chapter introduction, **content analysis** is the study of recorded human com-

munications. Among the forms suitable for study are books, Web pages, magazines, poems, newspapers, songs, paintings, speeches, letters, e-mail messages, laws, and constitutions, as well as any components or collections thereof. Shulamit Reinharz (1992: 146–47) points out that feminist researchers have used content analysis to study "children's books, fairy tales, billboards, feminist nonfiction and fiction books, children's art work, fashion, fat-letter postcards, Girl Scout handbooks, works of fine art, newspaper rhetoric, clinical records, research publications, introductory sociology textbooks, and citations, to mention only a few."

Topics Appropriate to Content Analysis

Content analysis is particularly well suited to the study of communications and to answering the classic question of communications research: "Who says what, to whom, why, how, and with what effect?" Are popular French novels more concerned with love than Canadian ones? Was the popular British music of the 1960s more politically cynical than the popular German music during that period? Do political candidates who primarily address "bread and butter" issues get elected more often than those who address issues of high principle? Each of these questions addresses a social scientific research topic: The first might address national character, the second political orientations, and the third political process. Although such topics might be studied by observing individual people, content analysis provides another approach.

Tremblay used content analysis to examine the legislative behaviour of female and male members of the Canadian Parliament. Her goal was to determine if female members of the House of Commons have an impact on politics and, in particular, whether they are more likely than male MPs to represent women by promoting women's issues. In addition to a survey, a "content analysis was conducted specifically on the Index of the Debates in the House of Commons [Hansard Index] during the first session of the 35th Parliament. This Index covered over 17,700 pages of debate. Both MPs (who spoke on women's issues) and themes (which women's issues were raised) were analyzed" (1998:444). What Tremblay found was that a higher percentage of the female MPs addressed women's issues than did the male MPs, but that MPs of both genders acted to support women's issues— although such issues were a relatively minor area of interest for both.

Bright et al. conducted a content analysis of newspaper editorials in Toronto, Ontario. They were interested in the accessibility of public discourse in a multicultural society; for example, whether "the voices of a variety of ethnic communities are heard on issues of general interest" (1999:317). They assessed the views expressed on Quebec independence in both mainstream and "marginal 'ethnic'" newspaper editorials in the year preceding the 1995 Quebec referendum. (Interviews with editorialists were also conducted to determine what factors influenced editorial opinion.) From their qualitative content analysis, they concluded:

Editorials in both the mainstream and marginal presses are steadfastly anti-separatist, a stance evident both in the predictions of economic doom in the event of Quebec independence and the focus on and vilification of the sovereignist forces. At the same time, the ethnic presses demonstrate a measure of autonomy in their discourse, emphasizing the cultural aspects of the Quebec issue and focussing on the reaction of minority communities.

(1999:319)

Some topics are more appropriately addressed by content analysis than by any other method of inquiry. Suppose that you're interested in violence on television. Maybe you suspect that the manufacturers of men's products are more likely to sponsor violent TV shows than are other kinds of sponsors. Content analysis would be the best way of finding out.

Briefly, here's what you would do. First, you'd develop operational definitions of the two key variables in your inquiry: *men's products* and *violence*. The section on coding, later in this chapter, will discuss some of the ways you could do that. Ultimately, you'd need a plan that would allow you to watch TV, classify sponsors, and rate the degree of violence on particular shows.

Next, you'd have to decide what to watch. Probably you'd decide (1) what stations to watch, (2) for what period, and (3) at what hours. Then, you'd stock up on beer and potato chips and start watching, classifying, and recording. Once you had completed your observations, you'd be able to analyze the data you collected and determine whether men's product manufacturers sponsored more blood and gore than did other sponsors.

As a mode of observation, content analysis requires a thoughtful handling of the "what" that is being communicated. The analysis of data collected in this mode, as in others, addresses the "why" and "with what effect."

Sampling in Content Analysis

In the study of communications, as in the study of people, you often can't observe directly all you would like to explore. In your study of TV violence and sponsorship, we'd advise against attempting to watch everything that's broadcast. It wouldn't be possible, and your brain would probably short-circuit before you came close to discovering that for yourself. Usually, then, it's appropriate to sample. Let's begin by revisiting the idea of units of analysis. We'll then review some of the sampling techniques that might be applied to them in content analysis.

Units of Analysis   As we discussed in Chapter 4, determining appropriate units of analysis—the individual units that we make descriptive and explanatory statements about—can be a complicated task. For example, if we wished to compute the average family income, the individual family would be the unit of analysis. But we'll have to ask individual members of families how much money they make. Thus, individuals will be the units of *observation*, even though the individual family remains the unit of analysis. Similarly, we may wish to compare crime rates of different cities in terms of their sizes, geographical region, racial composition, and other differences. Even though the characteristics of these cities are partly a function of the behaviours and characteristics of their individual residents, the cities would ultimately be the units of analysis.

The complexity of this issue is often more apparent in content analysis than in other research methods, especially when the units of observation differ from the units of analysis. A few examples should clarify this distinction.

Let's suppose we want to find out whether television news programs differ in presenting men versus women as sources of professionally qualified opinion ("talking heads"). In this instance, the individual television news programs would be both the units of observation and the units of analysis. We might select a sample of news programs on television in Canada and then categorize each program in terms of the percentage of male versus female "talking heads" they use per news program.

Somewhat differently, we might wish to determine whether television stations are more likely to differ in their use of men versus women as sources of professionally qualified opinion in news pro-

grams. Although the examination of this question would also involve the coding of individual television news programs, the unit of analysis in this case is the individual television station, not the news program.

Or, changing topics radically, let's suppose we're interested in representationalism in painting. If we wish to compare the relative popularity of representational and nonrepresentational paintings, the individual paintings will be our units of analysis. If, on the other hand, we wish to discover whether representationalism in painting is more characteristic of wealthy or impoverished painters, of educated or uneducated painters, of capitalist or socialist painters, the individual painters will be our units of analysis.

It's essential that this issue be clear, because sample selection depends largely on what the unit of analysis is. If individual writers are the units of analysis, the sample design should select all or a sample of the writers appropriate to the research question. If books are the units of analysis, we should select a sample of books, regardless of their authors. Bruce Berg (2001:246–47) points out that even if you plan to analyze some body of textual materials, the units of analysis might be words, themes, characters, paragraphs, items (such as a book or letter), concepts, semantics, or combinations of these.

We're not suggesting that sampling should be based solely on the units of analysis. Indeed, we may often *subsample*—select samples of subcategories—for each individual unit of analysis. Thus, if writers are the units of analysis, we might (1) select a sample of writers from the total population of writers, (2) select a sample of books written by each writer selected, and (3) select portions of each selected book for observation and coding.

Finally, let's look at a trickier example: the study of TV violence and sponsors. What's the unit of analysis for the research question "Are the manufacturers of men's products more likely to sponsor violent shows than other sponsors?" Is it the TV show? The sponsor? The instance of violence?

In the simplest study design, it would be none of these. Though you might structure your inquiry in various ways, the most straightforward design would be based on the commercial as the unit of analysis. You would use two kinds of observational units: the commercial and the program (the show that gets squeezed in between commercials). You'd want to observe both units. You would classify commercials by whether they advertised men's products and the programs by their violence. The program classifcations would be transferred to the commercials occurring near them. Figure 10-1 provides an example of the kind of record you might keep.

Notice that in the research design illustrated in Figure 10-1, all the commercials occurring in the same program break are bracketed and get the same scores. Also, the number of violent instances recorded as following one commercial break is the same as the number preceding the next break. This simple design allows us to classify each commercial by its sponsorship and the degree of violence associated with it. Thus, for example, the first Grunt Aftershave commercial is coded as being a men's product and as having 10 instances of violence associated with it. The Buttercup Bra commercial is coded as not being a men's product and as having no violent instances associated with it.

In the illustration, we have four men's product commercials with an average of 7.5 violent instances each. The four commercials classifed as definitely not men's products have an average of 1.75, and the two that might or might not be considered men's products have an average of one violent instance each. If this pattern of differences persisted across a much larger number of observations, we'd probably conclude that manufacturers of men's products are more likely to sponsor TV violence than other sponsors.

The point of this illustration is to demonstrate how units of analysis figure into the data collection and analysis. You need to be clear about your unit of analysis before planning your sampling strategy, but in this case you can't simply sample commercials. Unless you have access to the stations' broadcasting logs, you won't know when the commercials are going to occur. Moreover, you need to observe the programming as well as the commercials. As a result, you must set up a sampling design that will include everything you need in order to observe.

In designing the sample, you would need to establish the universe to be sampled from. In this case, what TV stations will you observe? What will be the period of the study—number of days? And during which hours of each day will you observe? Then, how many commercials do you want to observe and code for analysis? Watch television for a while and find out how many commercials occur each hour; then you can figure out how many hours of observation you'll need (and can stand).

Now you're ready to design the sample selection. As a practical matter, you wouldn't have to sample among the different stations if you had assistants. Each of you could watch a different channel during the same time period. But let's suppose you're working alone. Your final sampling frame, from which a sample will be selected and watched, might look something like this:

Jan. 7, Channel 2, 7–9 p.m.
Jan. 7, Channel 4, 7–9 p.m.
Jan. 7, Channel 9, 7–9 p.m.
Jan. 7, Channel 2, 9–11 p.m.
Jan. 7, Channel 4, 9–11 p.m.
Jan. 7, Channel 9, 9–11 p.m.
Jan. 8, Channel 2, 7–9 p.m.
Jan. 8, Channel 4, 7–9 p.m.
Jan. 8, Channel 9, 7–9 p.m.
Jan. 8, Channel 2, 9–11 p.m.
Jan. 8, Channel 4, 9–11 p.m.
Jan. 8, Channel 9, 9–11 p.m.
Jan. 9, Channel 2, 7–9 p.m.
Jan. 9, Channel 4, 7–9 p.m.
etc.

Notice that we've made several decisions for you in the illustration. First, we've assumed that channels 2, 4, and 9 are the ones appropriate to your study. We've assumed that you found the 7–11 p.m. prime-time hours to be the most relevant and that two-hour periods would do the job. We picked January 7 out of the hat for a starting date. In practice, of course, all these decisions should be based on your careful consideration of what would be appropriate to your particular study.

Once you have become clear about your units of analysis and the observations best suited to those

Figure 10-1
Example of Recording Sheet for TV Violence

Sponsor	Men's Product?			Number of Instances of Violence	
	Yes	No	?	Before	After
Grunt Aftershave	✓			6	4
Brute Jock Straps	✓			6	4
Roperot Cigars	✓			4	3
Grunt Aftershave	✓			3	0
Snowflake Toothpaste		✓		3	0
Godliness Cleanser		✓		3	0
Big Thumb Hammers			✓	0	1
Snowflake Toothpaste		✓		1	0
Big Thumb Hammers			✓	1	0
Buttercup Bras		✓		0	0

units and have created a sampling frame like the one we've illustrated, sampling is simple and straightforward. The alternative procedures available to you are the same ones described in Chapter 7: random, systematic, stratified, and so on.

Sampling Techniques   As we've seen, in the content analysis of written prose, sampling may occur at any or all of several levels, including the contexts relevant to the works. Other forms of communication may also be sampled at any of the conceptual levels appropriate to them.

In content analysis, we could employ any of the conventional sampling techniques discussed in Chapter 7. We might select a random or systematic sample of French and Canadian novelists, of laws passed in the province of Alberta, or of Shakespearean soliloquies. We might select (with a random start) every 23rd paragraph in Tolstoy's *War and Peace*. Or we might number all of the songs recorded by the Beatles and select a random sample of 25.

Stratified sampling is also appropriate to content analysis. To analyze the editorial policies of Canadian newspapers, for example, we might first group all newspapers by region of the country or size of the community in which they are published, frequency of publication, or average circulation. We might then select a stratified random or systematic sample of newspapers for analysis. Having done so, we might select a sample of editorials from each selected newspaper, perhaps stratified chronologically.

Cluster sampling is equally appropriate to content analysis. Indeed, if individual editorials are our units of analysis, then the selection of newspapers at the first stage of sampling would be a cluster sample. In an analysis of political speeches, we might begin by selecting a sample of politicians; each politician would represent a cluster of political speeches. In the TV commercial study described previously, the initial sample of TV stations would be a cluster sample.

It should be repeated that sampling need not end when we reach the unit of analysis. If novels are the unit of analysis in a study, we might select a sample of novelists, subsamples of novels written by each selected author, and a subsample of paragraphs within each novel. We would then analyze the content of the paragraphs for the purpose of describing the novels themselves. (*Note*: Researchers speak of samples within samples as "subsamples.")

Let's turn now to the coding or classifcation of material being observed. Part 4 discusses the manipulation of such classifcations to draw descriptive and explanatory conclusions.

Coding in Content Analysis

Content analysis is essentially a **coding** operation. *Coding* is the process of transforming raw data into a standardized form. In content analysis, communications—oral, written, or other—are coded or classified according to some conceptual framework. Thus, for example, TV shows may be coded as violent or nonviolent. Novels may be coded as romantic or not, paintings as representational or not, and political speeches as containing character assassinations or not. Recall that terms such as these are subject to many interpretations, and the researcher must specify definitions clearly.

Coding in content analysis involves the logic of conceptualization and operationalization as discussed in Chapter 5. As in other research methods, you must refine your conceptual framework and

develop specific methods for observing in relation to that framework.

Manifest and Latent Content In field research (Chapter 11), the researcher faces a fundamental choice between depth and specificity of understanding. Often, this represents a choice between validity and reliability, respectively. Typically, field researchers opt for depth, preferring to base their judgments on a broad range of observations and information, even at the risk that another observer might reach a different judgment of the same situation. Through the use of standardized questionnaires, survey research represents the other extreme: total specificity, even though the specific measures of variables may not be adequately valid reflections of those variables. The content analyst has some choice in this matter, however.

Coding the **manifest content**—the visible, surface content—of a communication is analogous to using a standardized questionnaire. To determine, for example, how erotic certain novels are, you might simply count the number of times the word *love* appears in each novel or the average number of appearances per page. Or, you might use a list of words, such as *love, kiss, hug,* and *caress,* each of which might serve as an indicator of the erotic nature of the novel. This method would have the advantage of ease and reliability in coding and of letting the reader of the research report know precisely how eroticism was measured. It would have a disadvantage, on the other hand, in terms of validity. Surely the phrase *erotic novel* conveys a richer and deeper meaning than the number of times the word *love* is used.

Alternatively, you may code the **latent content** of the communication: its underlying meaning. In the present example, you might read an entire novel or a sample of paragraphs or pages and make an overall assessment of how erotic the novel was. Although your total assessment might very well be influenced by the appearance of words such as *love* and *kiss,* it would not depend fully on their frequency.

Clearly, this second method seems better designed for tapping the underlying meaning of communications, but its advantage comes at a cost of reliability and specifcity. Especially if more than one person is coding the novel, somewhat different definitions or standards may be employed. A passage that one coder regards as erotic may not seem erotic to another. Even if you do all the coding yourself, there's no guarantee that your definitions and standards will remain constant throughout the enterprise. Moreover, the reader of your research report will likely be uncertain about the definitions you've employed.

Wherever possible, the best solution to this dilemma is to use both methods. For example, Carol Auster was interested in changes in the socialization of young women in the Girl Scouts. To explore this, she undertook a content analysis of the Girl Scout manuals as revised over time. In particular, Auster was interested in the view that women should be limited to homemaking. Her analysis of the manifest content suggested a change: "I found that while 23 percent of the badges in 1913 centered on home life, this was true of only 13 percent of the badges in 1963 and 7 percent of the badges in 1980" (1985:361).

An analysis of the latent content also pointed to an emancipation of the Girl Scouts, similar to that occurring in North American society at large. The change of uniform was one indicator: "The shift from skirts to pants may reflect an acknowledgement of the more physically active role of women as well as the variety of physical images available to modern women" (Auster 1985:362). Supporting evidence was found in the appearance of badges such as "Science Sleuth," "Aerospace," and "Ms. Fix-It."

Conceptualization and the Creation of Code Categories   For all research methods, conceptualization and operationalization typically involve the interaction of theoretical concerns and empirical observations. If, for example, you believe some newspaper editorials to be liberal and others to be conservative, ask yourself why you think so. Read some editorials and try to pick out the cues or details that are prompting you to categorize some as liberal and others as conservative. Was the

political orientation of a particular editorial most clearly indicated by its manifest content or by its tone? Was your decision based on the use of certain terms (for example, *leftist, fascist,* and so on) or on the support or opposition given to a particular issue or political personality?

Both inductive and deductive methods should be used in this activity. If you're testing theoretical propositions, your theories should suggest empirical indicators of concepts. If you begin with specific empirical observations, you should attempt to derive general principles relating to them and then apply those principles to the other empirical observations.

Bruce Berg (2001:245) places code development in the context of grounded theory and likens it to solving a puzzle:

> Coding and other fundamental procedures associated with grounded theory development are certainly hard work and must be taken seriously, but just as many people enjoy finishing a complicated jigsaw puzzle, many researchers find great satisfaction in coding and analysis. As researchers . . . begin to see the puzzle pieces come together to form a more complete picture, the process can be downright thrilling.

Throughout this activity, remember that the operational definition of any variable is composed of the attributes included in it. Such attributes, moreover, should be mutually exclusive and exhaustive. A newspaper editorial, for example, should not be described as both liberal and conservative, though you should probably allow for some to be middle-of-the-road. It may be sufficient for your purposes to code novels as erotic or nonerotic, but you may also want to consider that some could be anti-erotic. Paintings might be classified as representational or not, if that satisfied your research purpose, or you might wish to classify them as impressionistic, abstract, allegorical, and so forth.

Realize further that different levels of measurement may be used in content analysis. You may, for example, use the nominal categories of liberal and conservative for characterizing newspaper editorials, or you might wish to use a more refined ordinal ranking, ranging from extremely liberal to extremely conservative. Bear in mind, however, that the level of measurement implicit in your coding methods—nominal, ordinal, interval, or ratio—does not necessarily carry over to the interpretation of the variables that are your ultimate interest. If the word *love* appeared 100 times in Novel A and 50 times in Novel B, you would be justified in saying that the word *love* appeared twice as often in Novel A, but not that Novel A was twice as erotic as Novel B. Similarly, agreeing with twice as many anti-Semitic statements in a questionnaire does not necessarily make one twice as anti-Semitic.

Counting and Record Keeping If you plan to evaluate your content analysis data quantitatively, your coding operation must be amenable to data processing. This means, first, that the end product of your coding must be numerical. If you're counting the frequency of certain words, phrases, or other manifest content, the coding is necessarily numerical. But even if you're coding latent content on the basis of overall judgments, it will be necessary to represent your coding decision numerically: 1 = very liberal, 2 = moderately liberal, 3 = moderately conservative, and so on.

Second, your record keeping must clearly distinguish between units of analysis and units of observation, especially if these two are different. The initial coding, of course, must relate to the units of observation. If novelists are the units of analysis, for example, and you wish to characterize them through a content analysis of their novels, your primary records will represent novels as the units of observation. You may then combine your scoring of individual novels to characterize each novelist, the unit of analysis.

Third, while you're counting, it will normally be important to record the base from which the counting is done. It would tell us little that the word *love* appeared 87 times in a novel if we didn't know about how many words there were in the entire novel. Similarly, it would probably be useless to know the number of realistic paintings produced by a given painter without knowing the total number of all paintings he or she has done; the painter would be regarded as a realistic painter if a high percentage of his or her total output of paintings were of that genre. The issue of observational base is most easily resolved if every observation is coded in terms of one of the attributes making up a variable. Rather than simply counting the number of liberal editorials in a given collection, for example, code each editorial by its political orientation, even if it must be coded "no apparent orientation."

Let's suppose we want to describe and explain the editorial policies of different newspapers. Figure 10-2 presents part of a tally sheet that might result from the coding of newspaper editorials. Note that newspapers are the units of analysis. Each newspaper has been assigned an identification number to facilitate mechanized processing. The second column has a space for the number of editorials coded for each newspaper. This will be an important piece of information, since we want to be able to say, for example, "Of all the editorials, 22 percent were pro-United Nations," not just "There were eight pro-United Nations editorials."

One column in Figure 10-2 is for assigning a subjective overall assessment of the newspapers' editorial policies. (Such assignments might later be compared with the several objective measures.) Other columns provide space for recording numbers of editorials reflecting specific editorial positions. In a real content analysis, there would be spaces for recording other editorial positions plus noneditorial information about each newspaper, such as the region in which it is published, its circulation, and so forth.

Qualitative Data Analysis Not all content analysis results in counting. Sometimes a qualitative assessment of the materials is most appropriate, as in Carol Auster's examination of changes in Girl Scout uniforms and handbook language.

Bruce Berg (2001:256–58) discusses "negative case testing" as a technique for qualitative hypothesis testing. First, in the grounded theory tradition, you begin with an examination of the data, which may yield a general hypothesis. Let's say that

Figure 10-2
Sample Tally Sheet (Partial)

Newspaper ID	Number of editorials evaluated	SUBJECTIVE EVALUATION 1. Very liberal 2. Moderately liberal 3. Middle-of-road 4. Moderately conservative 5. Very conservative	Number of "anticommunist" editorials	Number of "pro-UN" editorials	Number of "anti-UN" editorials
001	37	2	0	8	0
002	26	5	10	0	6
003	44	4	2	1	2
004	22	3	1	2	3
005	30	1	0	6	0

you're examining the leadership of a new community association by reviewing the minutes of meetings to see who made motions that were subsequently passed. Your initial examination of the data suggests that the wealthier members are the most likely to assume this leadership role.

The second stage in the analysis is to search your data to find all the cases that would contradict the initial hypothesis. In this instance, you would look for poorer members who made successful motions and wealthy members who never did. Third, you must review each of the disconfirming cases and either (1) give up the hypothesis or (2) see how it needs to be fine-tuned.

Let's say that in your analysis of disconfirming cases, you notice that each of the unwealthy leaders has a graduate degree, while each of the wealthy nonleaders has very little formal educa-

tion. You may revise your hypothesis to consider both education and wealth as routes to leadership in the association. Perhaps you'll discover some threshold for leadership (a white-collar job, a level of income, and a university degree) beyond which those with the most money, education, or both are the most active leaders.

This process is an example of what Barney Glaser and Anselm Strauss (1967) call *analytic induction*. It is inductive in that it primarily begins with observations, and it is analytic because it goes beyond description to find patterns and relationships among variables.

There are, of course, dangers in this form of analysis, as in all others. The chief risk is misclassifying observations so as to support an emerging hypothesis. For example, you may erroneously conclude that a nonleader didn't graduate from university or you may decide that the job of factory foreman is "close enough" to being white-collar.

Berg (2001:257) offers techniques for avoiding these errors: (1) If there are sufficient cases, select some at random from each category in order to avoid merely picking those that best support the hypothesis. (2) Give at least three examples in support of every assertion you make about the data. (3) Have your analytic interpretations carefully reviewed by others uninvolved in the research project to see whether they agree. (4) Report whatever inconsistencies you do discover—any cases that simply do not fit your hypotheses. Realize that few social patterns are 100 percent consistent, so you may have discovered something important even if it doesn't apply to absolutely all of social life. However, you should be honest with your readers in that regard.

An Illustration of Content Analysis

Several studies have indicated that women are stereotyped in traditional roles on television. R. Stephen Craig (1992) took this line of inquiry one step further to examine the portrayal of both men and women during different periods of television programming.

To study gender stereotyping in television commercials, Craig selected a sample of 2,209 network commercials during several periods between January 6 and 14, 1990.

> The weekday day part (in this sample, Monday–Friday, 2–4 p.m.) consisted exclusively of soap operas and was chosen for its high percentage of women viewers. The weekend day part (two consecutive Saturday and Sunday afternoons during sports telecasts) was selected for its high percentage of men viewers. Evening "prime time" (Monday–Friday, 9–11 p.m.) was chosen as a basis for comparison with past studies and the other day parts.
>
> (1992:199)

Each of the commercials was coded in several ways. "Characters" were coded as:

All male adults
All female adults
All adults, mixed gender
Male adults with children or teens (no women)
Female adults with children or teens (no men)
Mixture of ages and genders

In addition, Craig's coders noted which character was on the screen longest during the commercial—the "primary visual character"—as well as the roles played by the characters (such as spouse, celebrity, parent), the type of product advertised (such as body product, alcohol), the setting (such as kitchen, school, business), and the voice-over narrator.

Table 10-2 indicates the differences in the times when men and women appeared in commercials. Women appeared most during the daytime (with its soap operas), men predominated during the weekend commercials (with its sports programming), and men and women were equally represented during evening prime time.

Craig found other differences in the ways men and women were portrayed.

> Further analysis indicated that male primary characters were proportionately more likely than females to be portrayed as celebrities and professionals in every day part, while women were proportionately more likely to be portrayed as interviewer/demonstrators, parent/spouses, or sex object/models in every day part. . . . Women were proportionately more likely to appear as sex objects/models during the weekend than during the day.
>
> (1992:204)

The research also showed that different products were advertised during different time periods. As you might have imagined, almost all the daytime commercials dealt with body, food, or home products. These products accounted for only one in three on the weekends. Instead, weekend commercials stressed automotive products (29 percent), business products or services (27 percent), or alcohol (10 percent). There were virtually no alcohol ads during evenings and daytime.

As you might suspect, women were most likely to be portrayed in home settings, men most likely to be shown away from home. Other findings

Table 10-2

Percentages of Adult Primary Visual Characters by Gender Appearing in Commercials in Three Day Parts

	Daytime	Evening	Weekend
Adult male	40	52	80
Adult female	60	48	20

Source: R. Stephen Craig, "The Effect of Television Day Part on Gender Portrayals in Television Commercials: A Content Analysis," *Sex Roles* 26, nos. 5/6 (1992): 204.

dealt with the different roles played by men and women.

> The women who appeared in weekend ads were almost never portrayed without men and seldom as the commercial's primary character. They were generally seen in roles subservient to men (e.g., hotel receptionist, secretary, or stewardess), or as sex objects or models in which their only function seemed to be to lend an aspect of eroticism to the ad.
>
> (1992:208)

Although some of Craig's findings may seem unsurprising, remember that "common knowledge" does not always correspond with reality. It's always worthwhile to check out widely held assumptions. And even when we think we know about a given situation, it's often useful to know more specific details such as those provided by a content analysis like this one.

Strengths and Weaknesses of Content Analysis

Probably the greatest advantage of content analysis is its economy in terms of both time and money. A single university student might undertake a content analysis, whereas undertaking a survey, for example, might not be feasible. There is no requirement for a large research staff; no special equipment is required. As long as you have access to the material to be coded, you can undertake content analysis.

Safety is another advantage of content analysis. If you discover you've botched up a survey or an experiment, you may be forced to repeat the whole research project with all its attendant costs in time and money. If you botch up your field research, it may be impossible to redo the project; the event under study may no longer exist. In content analysis, it's usually easier to repeat a portion of the study than it is in other research methods. You might be required, moreover, to recode only a portion of your data rather than all of it.

A third advantage of content analysis is that it permits the study of processes occurring over a long time. You might focus on the imagery of women conveyed in Canadian magazines from 1960 to 1970, for example, or you might examine changing imagery from 1960 to the present.

Finally, content analysis has the advantage of all unobtrusive measures, namely, that the content analyst seldom has any effect on the subject being studied. Because the novels have already been written, the paintings already painted, the speeches already presented, content analyses can have no effect on them.

Content analysis has disadvantages as well. For one thing, it's limited to the examination of *recorded* communications. Such communications may be oral, written, or graphic, but they must be recorded in some fashion to permit analysis.

As we've seen, content analysis has both advantages and disadvantages in terms of validity and reliability. For example, the concreteness of materials studied in content analysis strengthens the likelihood of reliability. You can always code and recode and even recode again if you want, making certain that the coding is consistent. In field research, by contrast, there's probably nothing you can do after the fact to insure greater reliability in observation and categorization.

Historical/Comparative Analysis

Historical/comparative research differs substantially from the methods discussed so far, though it overlaps somewhat with content analysis and the analysis of existing statistics. It involves the use of historical methods by sociologists, political scientists, and other social scientists.

The discussion of longitudinal research designs in Chapter 4 notwithstanding, our examination of research methods so far has focused primarily on studies anchored in one point in time and in one locale, whether a particular small group or a nation. Although accurately portraying the main thrust of contemporary social scientific research, this focus conceals the fact that social scientists are also interested in tracing the development of social forms over time and comparing those developmental processes across cultures. After describing some prominent examples of historical and comparative research, this section discusses the key elements of this method.

Examples of Historical/Comparative Analysis

August Comte, who coined the term *sociologie,* saw that new discipline as the final stage in a historical development of ideas. With his broadest brush, he painted an evolutionary picture that took humans from a reliance on religion to metaphysics to science. With a finer brush, he portrayed science as evolving from the development of biology and the other natural sciences to the development of psychology and, finally, to the development of scientific sociology.

A great many later social scientists have also turned their attention to broad historical processes. Several have examined the historical progression of social forms from the simple to the complex, from rural–agrarian to urban–industrial societies. The anthropologist, Robert Redfield, for example, wrote about a shift from "folk society" to "urban society" (1941). Emile Durkheim saw social evolution largely as a process of ever-greater division of labour ([1893] 1964). In a more specific analysis, Karl Marx examined economic systems progressing historically from primitive to feudal to capitalistic forms ([1867] 1967). All history, he wrote in this context, was a history of class struggle: the "haves" struggling to maintain their advantages and the "have-nots" struggling for a better lot in life. Looking beyond capitalism, Marx saw the development of socialism and finally communism.

Not all historical studies in the social sciences have had this evolutionary flavour, however. Some

social scientific readings of the historical record, in fact, point to grand cycles rather than to linear progressions. No scholar better represents this view than Pitirim A. Sorokin. A participant in the Russian Revolution of 1917, Sorokin served as secretary to Prime Minister Kerensky. Both Kerensky and Sorokin fell from favour, however, and Sorokin began his second career as an American sociologist.

Whereas Comte read history as a progression from religion to science, Sorokin (1937–1940) suggested that societies alternate cyclically between two points of view, which he called "ideational" and "sensate." Sorokin's sensate point of view defines reality in terms of sense experiences. The ideational, by contrast, places a greater emphasis on spiritual and religious factors. Sorokin's reading of the historical record further indicated that the passage between the ideational and sensate was through a third point of view, which he called the "idealistic." This third view combined elements of the sensate and ideational in an integrated, rational view of the world.

These examples indicate some of the topics historical/comparative researchers have examined. To get a better sense of what historical/comparative research entails, let's look at a few examples in somewhat more detail.

Weber and the Role of Ideas   In his analysis of economic history, Karl Marx put forward a view of economic determinism. That is, he felt that economic factors determined the nature of all other aspects of society. For example, Marx's analysis showed that a function of European churches was to justify and support the capitalist status quo. Religion was a tool of the powerful in maintaining their dominance over the powerless. "Religion is the sigh of the oppressed creature," Marx wrote in a famous passage, "the sentiment of a heartless world, and the soul of soulless conditions. It is the opium of the people" (Bottomore and Rubel [1843] 1956:27).

Max Weber, a German sociologist, disagreed. Without denying that economic factors could and did affect other aspects of society, Weber argued that economic determinism did not explain everything. Indeed, Weber said, economic forms could come from noneconomic ideas. In his research in the sociology of religion, Weber examined the extent to which religious institutions were the source of social behaviour rather than mere reflections of economic conditions. His most noted statement of this side of the issue is found in *The Protestant Ethic and the Spirit of Capitalism* ([1905] 1958). Here's a brief overview of Weber's thesis.

John Calvin (1509–1564), a French-born Swiss theologian, was an important figure in the Protestant reformation of Christianity. Calvin taught that the ultimate salvation or damnation of every individual had already been decided by God; this idea is called *predestination*. Calvin also suggested that God communicated his decisions to people by making them either successful or unsuccessful during their earthly existence. God gave each person an earthly "calling"—an occupation or profession—and manifested their success or failure through that medium. Ironically, this point of view led Calvin's followers to seek proof of their coming salvation by working hard, saving their money, and generally striving for economic success.

In Weber's analysis, Calvinism provided an important stimulus for the development of capitalism. Rather than "wasting" their money on worldly comforts, the Calvinists reinvested it in their economic enterprises, thus providing the capital necessary for the development of capitalism. In arriving at this interpretation of the origins of capitalism, Weber researched the official doctrines of the early Protestant churches, studied the preachings of Calvin and other church leaders, and examined other relevant historical documents.

In three other studies, Weber conducted detailed historical analyses of Judaism ([1934] 1952) and the religions of China ([1934] 1951) and India ([1934] 1958). Among other things, Weber wanted to know why capitalism had not developed in the ancient societies of China, India, and Israel. In none of the three religions did he find any teaching that would have supported the accumulation and reinvestment of capital, thus strengthening his conclusion about the role of Protestantism in that regard.

Japanese Religion and Capitalism Weber's thesis regarding Protestantism and capitalism has become a classic in the social sciences. Not surprisingly, other scholars have attempted to test it in other historical situations. Robert Bellah examined the growth of capitalism in Japan during the late 19th and early 20th centuries, *Tokugawa Religion* (1957).

As both an undergraduate and a graduate student, Bellah had developed interests in Weber and in Japanese society. Thus, in 1951, he first conceived his Ph.D. thesis topic as "nothing less than an 'Essay on the Economic Ethic of Japan' to be a companion to Weber's studies of China, India, and Judaism: *The Economic Ethic of the World Religions*" (recalled in Bellah 1967:168). Originally, Bellah sketched his research design as follows:

> Problems would have to be specific and limited—no general history would be attempted—since time span is several centuries. Field work in Japan on the actual economic ethic practiced by persons in various situations, with, if possible, controlled matched samples from the U.S. (questionnaires, interviews, etc.).
>
> (1967:168)

Bellah's original plan, then, called for surveys of contemporary Japanese and Americans. However, he did not receive the financial support necessary for the study as originally envisioned. So instead, he immersed himself in the historical records of Japanese religion, seeking the roots of the rise of capitalism in Japan.

In the course of several years' research, Bellah uncovered numerous leads. In 1952, he felt he had found the answer in the samurai code of Bushido and in the Confucianism practiced by the samurai class:

> Here I think we find a real development of this worldly asceticism, at least equaling anything found in Europe. Further, in this class the idea of duty in occupation involved achievement without traditionalistic limits, but to the limits of one's capacities, whether in the role of bureaucrat, doctor, teacher, scholar, or other role open to the Samurai.
>
> (quoted in Bellah 1967:171)

The samurai, however, made up only a portion of Japanese society. So Bellah kept looking at the religions among Japanese generally. His understanding of the Japanese language was not yet very good, but he wanted to read religious texts in the original. Under these constraints and experiencing increased time pressure, Bellah decided to concentrate his attention on a single group: Shingaku, a religious movement among merchants in the 18th and 19th centuries. He found that Shingaku had two infuences on the development of capitalism. It offered an attitude toward work similar to the Calvinist notion of a "calling," and it had the effect of making business a more acceptable calling for Japanese. Previously, commerce had had a very low standing in Japan.

In other aspects of his analysis, Bellah examined the religious and political roles of the Emperor and the economic impact of periodically appearing emperor cults. Ultimately, Bellah's researches pointed to the variety of religious and philosophical factors that laid the groundwork for capitalism in Japan. It seems unlikely that he would have achieved anything approaching that depth of understanding if he had been able to pursue his original plan to interview matched samples of U.S. and Japanese citizens.

These examples of historical/comparative research should have given you some sense of the potential power in the method. Let's turn now to an examination of the sources and techniques used in this method.

Sources of Historical/Comparative Data

As we saw in the case of existing statistics, there is no end of data available for analysis in historical research. To begin, historians may have already reported on whatever it is you want to examine, and their analyses can give you an initial grounding in the subject, a jumping-off point for more in-depth research.

Most likely, you'll want to go beyond others' conclusions and examine some "raw data" to draw your own conclusions. These data vary, of course, according to the topic under study. In Bellah's study of Tokugawa religion, raw data included the sermons of Shingaku teachers. When W. I. Thomas and Florian Znaniecki (1918) studied the adjust-

ment process for Polish peasants who went to the United States in the early 20th century, they examined letters written by the immigrants to their families in Poland. (They obtained the letters through newspaper advertisements.) Other researchers have analyzed old diaries. Such personal documents only scratch the surface, however. In discussing procedures for studying the experience of women in the settlement of Canada's western prairie region, Sandra Rollings-Magnusson (2000:228) lists the following sources:

> In analyzing the work done and contributions made by women in the process of prairie development, contemporaneous historical sources were utilized. Newspapers, government publications and brochures, advertisements printed by private companies, and women settlers' autobiographies, writings, diaries, letters and other materials held in the Saskatchewan Archives in Regina, were reviewed. The most informative material was discovered in letters, poems and articles written by prairie women and submitted to newspapers for publication. Weekly issues of *The Grain Grower's Guide* and *The Nor'-West Farmer*, cumulatively covering a period extending from 1888 to 1913, were examined for comments relating to the farm experience of women. While most of these sources are anecdotal forms of self-reporting and thus potentially biased, advice columns proved to be a key source of candid information. Women, many writing under pseudonyms, sent in questions and comments on topics ranging from earning their own money, to baking tips, child rearing, property rights and complaints of hardship on the farm. It is recognized that these source materials provide information on a subset of the female rural population, as only those individuals with the education to read and write English and the financial ability to purchase newspapers and pay for correspondence would be included. As such, the information contained in this article cannot be taken as representative of the experiences of all women settlers.

Organizations generally document themselves, so if you're studying the development of some organization as Bellah studied Shingaku, for example you should examine its official documents: charters, policy statements, speeches by leaders, and so on.

Often, official government documents provide the data needed for analysis. Howlett (1986) examined legal–historical records to illustrate their importance in interpreting the intentions of governments in policy-making decisions in a federal state. He points to conflicting interpretations in the literature concerning whether policy decisions made by the Canadian federal government at the turn of the 20th century had "the objective of creating and fostering the development of a national capitalist market economy" (p. 366). In trying to establish what, if any, the financial policies of the Canadian government were, he argues that one cannot simply look at federal legislation where the government took action (acts of commission). To establish intentionality, the researcher must establish that an alternative course of action was a possibility that was actively considered but was rejected by the government (acts of omission). In a federal system, legislative policies can be proposed at different levels of government. When there is disagreement over such policies, this may result in conflict over who has the jurisdictional authority to act. Constitutional arbitration is often used to settle the matter, leaving behind some legal record of the policy issues over which there was conflict. Thus, for example, when the provincial government initiates policies that are overturned by the federal government, such information is likely to be contained in the legal–historical record, positively demonstrating "acts of omission." Howlett concludes that: "By pointing out the existence of a fiscal and monetary act of omission, the legal–historical evidence tends to support Naylor's argument that the federal government pursued a financial policy with direct and foreseeable consequences in terms of favouring certain interests over others" (p. 370).

The sources of data for historical analysis are too extensive to cover even in outline here, though the few examples we've looked at should suggest some ideas. Whatever resources you use, however, a couple of cautions are in order.

As you saw in the case of existing statistics, you can't trust the accuracy of records, official or unofficial, primary or secondary. Your protection lies in replication. In the case of historical research, that means corroboration. If several sources point to the same set of "facts," your confidence in them might reasonably increase.

At the same time, you need always be wary of bias in your data sources. If all your data on the development of a political movement are taken from the movement itself, you're unlikely to gain a well-rounded view of it. The diaries of well-to-do gentry of the Middle Ages may not give you an accurate view of life in general during those times. Note the recognition of possible bias by Rollings-Magnusson in the above example when discussing her data sources. Where possible, obtain data from a variety of sources, representing different points of view. Here's what Bellah (1967:179) said regarding his analysis of Shingaku:

> One could argue that there would be a bias in what was selected for notice by Western scholars. However, the fact that there was material from Western scholars with varied interests from a number of countries and over a period of nearly a century reduced the probability of bias.

The issues raised by Bellah are important ones. As Ron Aminzade and Barbara Laslett indicate in the box "Reading and Evaluating Documents," there's an art in knowing how to regard such documents and what to make of them. Incidentally, the critical review that they urge for the reading of historical documents is useful in many areas of your life.

Analytical Techniques

The analysis of historical/comparative data is another large subject that we can't cover exhaustively here. Moreover, because historical/comparative research is frequently approached qualitatively, there are no easily listed steps to follow in the analysis of historical data. Nevertheless, a few comments are in order.

Max Weber used the German term *verstehen*—"understanding"—in reference to an essential quality of social research. He meant that the researcher must be able to take on, mentally, the circumstances, views, and feelings of those being studied, so that the researcher can interpret their actions appropriately.

The historical/comparative researcher must find patterns among the voluminous details describing the subject matter of study. Often, this takes the form of what Weber called *ideal types:* conceptual models composed of the essential characteristics of social phenomena. Thus, for example, Weber himself did considerable research on bureaucracy. Having observed numerous actual bureaucracies, Weber ([1925] 1946) detailed those qualities essential to bureaucracies in general: jurisdictional areas, hierarchically structured authority, written files, and so on. Weber did not merely list those characteristics common to all the actual bureaucracies he observed. Rather, to create a theoretical model of the "perfect" (ideal type) bureaucracy, he needed to understand fully the essentials of bureaucratic operation.

Often, historical/comparative research is informed by a particular theoretical paradigm. Thus Marxist scholars may undertake historical analyses of particular situations such as the history of black minorities in Canada to determine whether they can be understood in terms of the Marxist version of conflict theory. Sometimes, historical/comparative researchers attempt to replicate prior studies in new situations—for example, Bellah's study of Tokugawa religion in the context of Weber's studies of religion and economics.

While historical/comparative research is often regarded as a qualitative rather than quantitative technique, this is by no means necessary. Historical analysts sometimes use *time-series* data to monitor changing conditions over time, such as data on population, crime rates, unemployment, infant mortality rates, and so forth. The analysis of such data sometimes requires sophistication, however.

A. R. Gillis has done extensive research on France between 1852 and 1914. His work provides good examples of the combination of historical and quantitative research skills. He has grappled with key issues and factors related to historical changes in rates of crime. He has examined the impact of various forms of social control, such as the amount of state policing, and other factors

believed to impact on the rates of both major and minor crimes and crimes of violence versus property crimes (1989). His research and analyses on 19th century France have brought to light novel findings on the relationships between literacy and violence (1994) and marital dissolution and domestic violence (1996). His tests of key hypotheses derived from the literature have shown that expectations were not always borne out in reality and that potentially more subtle relationships are worthy of attention.

To provide an illustration, Gillis (1994) analysed time series data to examine the impact of literacy on major crimes of violence. He showed that, although major crimes of violence and "passion-inspired homicide" decreased as literacy increased, there's more to the story if one delves a little deeper. His analysis shows that while rates of passionate violence against others declined, violence against self, as indicated by rates of suicide, greatly increased. As he states, "In fact between 1852 and 1914, the increase in rates of suicide in France was almost eight times greater than the decline in homicide, suggesting that literacy transformed rather than depressed death by violence" (p. 371).

Many historical analysts combine methods in addressing research questions. Mosher and Hagan's (1994:613) "study combines qualitative and qualitative data in an examination of historical patterns in the sentencing of narcotics offenders in five Upper Canadian cities for the years 1908 to 1953." They use jail records as their quantitative data source and daily police court reports in the local newspapers as their primary source of qualitative historical data. Using the jail records to obtain offender names and court appearance dates, they then searched local newspapers for reports on individual cases. In this way, they gathered qualitative information on almost 1,000 cases and included the data in their statistical analysis. In addition, they systematically examined a vast amount of qualitative historical data concerning police courts from sources such as annual police department reports, parliamentary debates, local newspapers, and popular magazines to gain local knowledge of the legal culture over this extended

Reading and Evaluating Documents

By Ron Aminzade and Barbara Laslett
University of Minnesota

The purpose of the following comments is to give you some sense of the kind of interpretive work historians do and the critical approach they take toward their sources. It should help you to appreciate some of the skills historians develop in their efforts to reconstruct the past from residues, to assess the evidentiary status of different types of documents, and to determine the range of permissible inferences and interpretations. Here are some of the questions historians ask about documents:

1. Who composed the documents? Why were they written? Why have they survived all these years? What methods were used to acquire the information contained in the documents?

2. What are some of the biases in the documents and how might you go about checking or correcting them? How inclusive or representative is the sample of individuals, events, and so on, contained in the document? What were the institutional constraints and the general organizational routines under which the document was prepared? To what extent does the document pro-

vide more of an index of institutional activity than of the phenomenon being studied? What is the time lapse between the observation of the events documented and the witnesses' documentation of them? How confidential or public was the document meant to be? What role did etiquette, convention, and custom play in the presentation of the material contained within the document? If you relied solely upon the evidence contained in these documents, how might your vision of the past be distorted? What other kinds of documents might you look at for evidence on the same issues?

3. What are the key categories and concepts used by the writer of the document to organize the information presented? What selectivities or silences result from these categories of thought?

4. What sorts of theoretical issues and debates do these documents cast light on? What kinds of historical and/or sociological questions do they help to answer? What sorts of valid inferences can one make from the information contained in these documents? What sorts of generalizations can one make on the basis of the information contained in these documents?

---

period. As they note, understanding the contemporary context of the actors who generated the data is necessary to more accurately interpret patterns. One key finding they report is that despite changes in judicial decision-making patterns, "sensitivity" to class remained constant in the sentencing of narcotics offenders over this period. The brunt of harsh treatment was experienced by the working class while the upper-class offenders received "disproportionately lenient treatment" by mid-century.

I (Benaquisto 1991) have combined quantitative and qualitative sources of data in my research on the historical use of punishment to investigate alternative hypotheses concerning the amount of

imprisonment in France, Italy, Spain, and Japan, over approximately a 100 year period, I gathered annual totals of incarceration from existing statistics and used variations on time series analysis to identify and rank order the upsurges in imprisonment in terms of intensity. Historical accounts were used to assess the countries' political climates during each of the identified periods of upsurge in imprisonment. The common denominator across political climates was identified as unusually high levels of political tension and regime instability. Constitutional regime changes, civil wars, and nonconstitutional regime changes coincided with the most intense outbursts of imprisonment and less intense upsurges in imprisonment were generally accompanied by somewhat less striking indications of acute political crisis such as major uprisings, declared states of emergency, and political assassinations. Ultimately a strong correlation between regime instability and outbursts of incarceration was established.

In another study that focused on the French Criminal Justice System in the 19th century, analysis of official documents were supplemented by judicial statistics to gain insights into the use of state repression in the transition from the authoritarian regime of Napoleon III's Second Empire to France's Third Republic (Benaquisto and Couton, 2001). It might be expected that state repression would decline in the onset of a liberal regime. However, examination of official documents such as circulars, pamphlets, letters, reports, and official bulletins of the Ministries of Justice and Interior, and laws and legislative debates, helped to demonstrate that, if anything, state repression was enhanced in the establishment of the Third Republic.

As you can see, unobtrusive research methods can be used to gather and assess both qualitative and quantitative data. Like all methods, some are more suitable to generating one type of data as opposed to another. In the next two chapters we'll turn our attention once again to interactive modes of observation and focus on methods that are particularly suited to a qualitative approach to research.

- Existing statistics often have problems of reliability, so they must be used with caution.
- Content analysis is a social research method appropriate for studying human communications through social artifacts. Researchers can use it to study not only communication processes, but other aspects of social behaviour as well.
- Common units of analysis in content analysis include elements of communication: words, paragraphs, books, and so forth. Standard probability sampling techniques are sometimes appropriate in content analysis.
- Content analysis involves coding—transforming raw data into categories based on some conceptual scheme. Coding may attend to both manifest and latent content. The determination of latent content requires judgments on the part of the researcher.
- Both quantitative and qualitative techniques are appropriate for interpreting content analysis data.
- The advantages of content analysis include economy, safety, and the ability to study processes occurring over a long time. Its disadvantages are that it is limited to recorded communications and can raise issues of reliability and validity.
- Social scientists use historical/comparative methods to discover patterns in the histories of different cultures.
- Although often regarded as a qualitative method, historical/comparative research can make use of quantitative techniques.

Main Points

- Unobtrusive measures are ways of studying social behaviour without affecting it in the process.
- A variety of governmental and nongovernmental agencies provide aggregate statistical data for studying aspects of social life.
- Problems of validity in the analysis of existing statistics can often be handled through logical reasoning and replication.

Review Questions and Exercises

1. Using the World Wide Web, find out how many countries have a higher "life expectancy" than Canada. (You might want to try the Population Reference Bureau at http://www.prb.org/.)
2. In two or three paragraphs, outline a content analysis design to determine whether the Liberal or the Canadian Alliance party is the more

supportive of free speech. Be sure to specify units of analysis and sampling methods.

3. Describe a coding scheme that you could use for the content analysis in item 2.

4. Locate pictures from three non-Canadian social settings on the Web. What social features do the different locations share in common? How do they differ? Include the pictures with your report, either on paper or as Web addresses (URLs).

Continuity Project

Locate existing statistics that reflect on the realities of gender equality/inequality over time. Present those data and interpret what they tell us about trends in this phenomenon.

Additional Readings

Berg, Bruce L. *Qualitative Research Methods for the Social Sciences.* 4th ed. Boston: Allyn and Bacon, 2001. Contains excellent materials on unobtrusive measures, including a chapter on content analysis. While focusing on qualitative research, Berg shows the logical links between qualitative and quantitative approaches.

Øyen, Else, ed. *Comparative Methodology: Theory and Practice in International Social Research.* Newbury Park, CA: Sage, 1990. Here are a variety of viewpoints on different aspects of comparative research. Appropriately, the contributors are from many different countries.

Webb, Eugene J., Donald T. Campbell, Richard D. Schwartz, and Lee Sechrest. 2000 (1966). *Unobtrusive Measures* (Revised Edition). Thousand Oaks, CA: Sage Publications. A compendium of unobtrusive measures. Includes physical traces, a variety of archival sources, and observation. Good discussion of the ethics involved and the limitations of such measures.

Weber, Robert Philip. *Basic Content Analysis.* Newbury Park, CA: Sage, 1990. Here's an excellent beginner's book for the design and execution of content analysis. Both general issues and specific techniques are presented.

*Info***Trac:** You can find further relevant readings on the World Wide Web at

http://sociology.wadsworth.com

Chapter 11

Qualitative Field Research

Qualitative field research allows researchers to observe social life in its natural habitat: to go where the action is and watch. The observational techniques used in this type of research enable the properly skilled researcher to collect rich, detailed data.

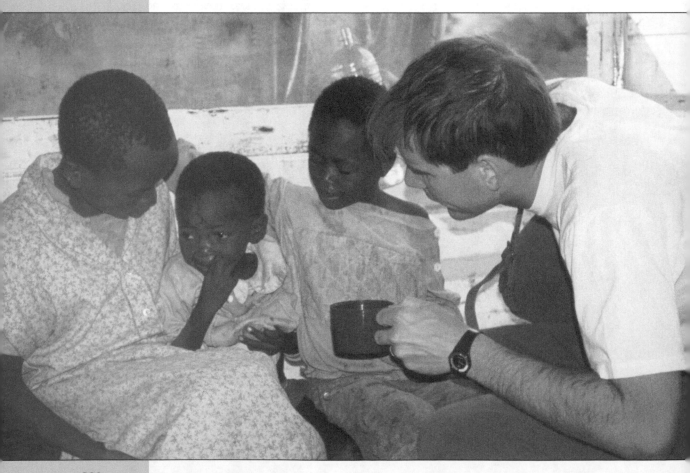

In this chapter . . .

Introduction

Several chapters ago, we suggested that you've been doing social research all your life. This notion should become even clearer as we turn now to what probably seems like the most obvious method of making observations: qualitative field research. In a sense, we do field research whenever we observe or participate in social behaviour and try to understand it, whether in a university classroom, a doctor's waiting room, or an airplane. Whenever we report our observations to others, we're reporting our field research efforts.

Field research is at once very old and very new in social science. Social researchers have used many of the techniques discussed in this chapter for centuries. Within the social sciences, anthropologists are especially associated with this method and have contributed to its development as a scientific technique. Moreover, many people who might not, strictly speaking, be regarded as social science researchers employ something similar to this

method. Newspaper reporters are one example; welfare department caseworkers are another.

While these are "natural" activities, you'll see that they're also skills to be learned and honed. Qualitative research demands a number of strong skills. The accumulation of empirical evidence is a deliberate and demanding task, requiring extensive documentation, skill at observation and interviewing, sensitivity to situations, and the capacity to organize vast amounts of material. In addition, the researcher requires creativity and good writing skills. Themes and patterns must be recognized and developed and then communicated to a larger audience. Many of these skills will be detailed in this chapter while others will be discussed in Chapters 12 and 14. Here we will examine some of the major approaches to field research and describe some of the specific techniques that make scientific field research more useful than the casual observation we all engage in.

We use the term qualitative field research to distinguish this type of observation method from methods designed to produce data appropriate for quantitative (statistical) analysis. Surveys provide data from which to calculate the percentage unemployed in a population, mean incomes, and so forth. Field research more typically yields *qualitative* data: observations not easily reduced to numbers. Thus, for example, a field researcher may note the "paternalistic demeanour" of leaders at a political rally or the "defensive evasions" of a public official at a public hearing without trying to express either the paternalism or the defensiveness as numerical quantities or degrees. Although field research is typically qualitative, it can be used to collect quantitative data such as noting the number of interactions of various specified types within a field setting. David Aliaga, for example, reported "[a] descriptive analysis of socioeconomic data, gathered through interviews and participant observation of Italian male immigrants in Calgary, Canada" (1994:141). His analysis included data on occupational and leisure activities, number of children per family, age at time of arrival in Calgary, and language most used at home.

Field observation also differs from some other models of observation in that it's not just a data-collecting activity. Frequently, perhaps typically, it's a theory-generating activity as well. As a field researcher, you'll seldom approach your task with precisely defined hypotheses to be tested. More typically, you'll attempt to make sense out of an ongoing process that can't be predicted in advance—making initial observations, developing tentative general conclusions that suggest particular types of further observations, making those observations and thereby revising your conclusions, and so forth. The alternation of induction and deduction discussed in Part 1 of this book is perhaps nowhere more evident and essential than in good field research. Although in qualitative research data collection, theory, and analysis are tightly intertwined, for expository purposes this chapter focuses primarily on some of the theoretical foundations of field research and on techniques of data collection. The analysis of qualitative data will be discussed in Chapter 14.

Topics Appropriate to Field Research

One of the key strengths of field research is the comprehensiveness of perspective it gives researchers. By going directly to the social phenomenon under study and observing it as completely as possible, researchers can develop a deeper and fuller understanding of it. Therefore, this mode of observation is especially, though not exclusively, appropriate to research topics and social studies that appear to defy simple quantification. Field researchers may recognize several nuances of attitude and behaviour that might escape researchers using other methods.

Field research is especially appropriate to the study of those attitudes and behaviours best understood within their natural setting, as opposed to the somewhat artificial settings of experiments and surveys. For example, field research provides a superior method for studying the dynamics of religious conversion at a revival meeting, just as a statistical analysis of membership rolls would be a better way of discovering whether men or women were more likely to convert.

Finally, field research is well suited to the study of social processes over time. Thus, the field researcher might be in a position to examine the rumblings and final explosion of a riot as events actually occur rather than afterward in a reconstruction of the events.

Other good places to apply field research methods include campus demonstrations, courtroom proceedings, labour negotiations, public hearings, or similar events taking place within a relatively limited area and time. In general, several observations of a given event, form of interaction, or place under study are made over time and must be combined to achieve a more comprehensive examination.

In *Analyzing Social Settings* (1995:101–13), John and Lyn Lofland discuss several elements of social life appropriate to field research.

1. *Practices.* Various kinds of behaviour such as talking.

2. *Episodes.* A variety of events such as divorce, crime, and illness.

3. *Encounters.* Two or more people meeting and interacting in immediate proximity with one another.

4. *Roles.* The analysis of the positions people occupy and the behaviour associated with those positions: occupations, family roles, ethnic groups.

5. *Relationships.* Behaviour appropriate to pairs or sets of roles: mother–son relationships, friendships, and the like.

6. *Groups.* Small groups, such as friendship cliques, athletic teams, and work groups.

7. *Organizations.* Formal organizations, such as hospitals or schools.

8. *Settlements.* It's difficult to study large societies such as nations, but field researchers often study smaller-scale "societies" such as villages, ghettos, and neighbourhoods.

9. *Social Worlds.* Ambiguous social entities with vague boundaries and populations such as "the sports world" and "Wall Street."

10. *Lifestyles or Subcultures.* How large numbers of people adjust to life in groups such as a "ruling class" or an "urban underclass."

In all these social settings, field research can reveal things that would not otherwise be apparent.

Field research offers the advantage of probing social life in its natural habitat. Although some things can be studied adequately in questionnaires or in the laboratory, others cannot. And direct observation in the field lets you observe subtle communications and other events that might not be anticipated or measured otherwise.

Methodological Terms In Field Research

If you read much of the literature on qualitative inquiry—either reports of qualitative research or texts on how to do it—you're likely to encounter a "terminological jungle" (Lofland and Lofland 1995:6). In this jungle, authors often use different labels for research approaches that can seem confusingly similar.

Field research incorporates a number of data gathering techniques and variations in perspectives concerning what questions should be asked and how they should be answered—what we'll call puzzle solving—that are communicated through terms such as grounded theory, interpretivisim, ethnomethodology, phenomenology, social constructionism, institutional ethnography, extended case-study method, and participatory action research. For example, phenomenology is a term associated with the idea that reality is socially constructed. This perspective is prominent in qualitative research and emphasizes attention to the worldview of the people being observed and/or interviewed. A major aim is to discover subjects' experiences and how subjects make sense of them.

Data gathering techniques in field research tend to cut across these various perspectives. We'll therefore first talk about general aspects of field research and labels used to signify common data gathering techniques. We'll then talk about some of the issues that field researchers must consider when preparing for and engaging in fieldwork. After presenting an illustration of a field research study, we'll discuss a few of the alternative frameworks to puzzle solving in qualitative field research mentioned above. We'll then look at some specific ideas and guidelines for conducting field research.

Ethnography and Participant Observation

When you read accounts of qualitative research, you'll see that many field researchers refer to their research method as **ethnography** or **participant observation**. Some use these terms synonymously while others distinguish them in relation to their history, disciplinary association, and research orientation. Both research methods are rooted in the tradition of **naturalism.** As Schatzman and Strauss' book title—*Field Research: Strategies for a Natural Sociology*—indicates, ethnography and participant observation have in common the natural setting. When they speak of "observations of actual situations," they refer "directly to what is known as the field method—a generic term for observing events in a natural situation. The activities of the naturalist in sociology and anthropology have distinct similarities to those of naturalists in zoology, archeology and geology" (1973:13–14).

Thus, some see ethnography and participant observation as a way of studying any group, phenomenon, and so forth in its natural environment. For others ethnography is viewed as somewhat distinctive, referring to naturalistic observations and holistic understandings of cultures or subcultures. Still others use the term ethnography to refer more broadly to the set of activities engaged in while in the field, and participant observation is included within this set.

Ethnography is historically associated with anthropology while participant observation has often been linked to sociology. The more traditional ethnography is associated with travel to a foreign land by anthropological researchers who immerse themselves in a different culture and report their investigations in a richly descriptive manner, providing readers with an intimate feel for the way of life they observed (for example, the works of Bronislaw Malinowski, Maragret Mead, and E. Evans-Pritchard). Nonetheless, for many, contemporary ethnography has come to refer to any research conducted in the field. Finally, in addition to referring to a method of research, ethnography also refers to the written report of the research produced from the field.

Both ethnography and participant observation typically combine a variety of techniques for gathering data. As Reinharz (1992:46) states, "Contemporary ethnography or fieldwork is multimethod research. It usually includes observation, participation, archival analysis, and interviewing...." Others speak of participant observation in the same manner. Both terms connote researchers immersing themselves in a social setting and gathering data that lends itself to interpretation.

In summary, the techniques of ethnography and participant observation are terms that refer to multi-method modes of data gathering in a natural setting (the field) and are employed by researchers with differing orientations to qualitative social sci-

entific puzzle solving. Another term you will frequently run across in your readings is case study.

Case Study Design

A **case study** is conducted when the social researcher focuses attention on a single instance of some social phenomenon like a town, an industry, a community, an organization, or a person. An immediate variation is to study more than one such instance (case), usually a limited number like two, three, or four. Some use the term "case" when referring to a study that focuses on a particular process or period of time as well. As indicated in Reinharz (1992:164), a case may refer to any unit of social life.

Although many researchers refer to the case study as a method, it is not a technique for gathering data such as observation, in-depth interviews, or self-administered questionnaires. It more appropriately refers to the design of a research study. It concerns what unit the researcher will focus upon—not how the data will be gathered.

We introduce the case study in this chapter because it is prominent in qualitative research studies and thus often associated with qualitative research. Nonetheless, a case study design may be used in both qualitative and quantitative research. It may be combined with any number of methods of collecting data. For example, one can gather data on a single organization through the use of a self-administered questionnaire, in-depth interviews, or participant observation (or a combination of modes of gathering data as you'll see in the examples mentioned below).

The chief purpose of a case study is to focus on the specificities of the case, providing rich, detailed data. The greater time and energy that may be directed to the study of a single instance permits this more intensive investigation. This is an advantage of the case study approach, particularly when the case is a complex, multi-person social phenomenon such as an organization—for instance a social problems agency like a welfare office or a private drug rehabilitation centre. The trade-off, of course, is between depth and breadth of cases— much more information on one instance as opposed to lesser information on a range of instances.

Sometimes a case study is used as a preliminary to a more elaborate study of many instances—in other words, it is exploratory. The goal of a case study is often descriptive as well; for example, an idiographic account of a particular street gang or an anthropologist's detailed depiction of a specific, nonliterate tribe. While case studies are often exploratory or descriptive, researchers whose goals are explanatory insight also use the design. This is often accomplished through comparison of several cases, but it is also attempted through the use of a single case considered to be typical of a set of cases of a given type. Below we discuss the extended case method, a qualitative research approach using a case study design for nomothetic theorizing.

Classic illustrations of case studies are community studies such as the Lynds' study of Middletown (1929; 1937), Gan's study of a Boston West End working class Italian community (*Urban Villagers*, 1962), and Gan's The *Lcvittowncrs* (1967).

Recent examples of the case study design include David Aliaga's (1994) study mentioned above. He conducted a case study of a single Italian immigrant community in Calgary in an effort to describe the economic integration and success of the immigrants as well as the maintenance of old world values. His method of gathering data was interviews with and participant observation of Italian male immigrants. He found, for example, that the immigrants had substantially improved their economic position and had maintained their desire to have large families. Gomme and Hall (1995) studied Crown prosecutors in an eastern Canadian province. They were interested in examining the social organization of Crown prosecutors' work. As they note, "the research that forms the basis of this analysis is an exploratory case study of a professional group, Crown prosecutors, working in a bureaucratic organizational context in a Canadian province." In short they studied a single professional group in a single province. Their goal was to study the impact of role overload on prosecutors and the consequent role strain to which it contributes. They conducted "in-depth

semistructured interviews with all Crown attorneys working full time with the Department of Justice in the province" (p. 192). Participant observation was conducted over a five-month period, and data were gathered from documents and reports, including official statistics.

Micucci (1998) conducted field research on the private security force of one Canadian educational institution. His goal was to provide a descriptive account that might be useful in the development of policy by organizations that employ private security forces. He developed a typology of three competing work styles from the data he gathered via "participant observation, intensive open-ended interviews, and the analysis of secondary documents" (1998:41). As he said, "The typology emerges from a case study...of an in-house unionized security force comprised of thirty-six officers servicing a university located in central Canada" (p. 42). The three work styles of the private security officers that emerged from his data—crime fighters, guards, and bureaucratic cops—were distinguished on the basis of criteria that he laid out. He organized the typology "along four underlying conceptual dimensions" (p. 42). The four dimensions that shaped each of the types were (1) background characteristics such as age, education, prior experience; (2) differences in orientation to policing functions such as the crime control function and the service function; (3) relationships with and attitudes toward colleagues and public; and (4) sources and levels of job satisfaction.

As Mullins' (1988) title suggests "The Organizational Dilemmas of Ethnic Churches: A Case Study of Japanese Buddhism in Canada," he chose one religious body as a means of examining the internal tensions that develop within ethnic religious organizations—due, for instance, to problems that arise when such organizations' memberships are highly assimilated but the religious leadership is drawn primarily from the country of origin. He conducted field research over a four-year period. His multi-method data collection strategy included participant observation, interviews, and questionnaires.

Although the term case study may be difficult to grasp at times because it is used in a variety of ways by researchers, the limitation of attention to a particular instance of something is the essential characteristic of the case study. As the above examples illustrate, in each study the researchers focused on a single unit of a larger possible set, spending long periods of time becoming intimately familiar with the details and nuances of their case. These examples should also give you some sense of the various contexts in which case studies are conducted and the variety of data gathering techniques used in a case study design.

Considerations in Qualitative Field Research

When you use field research methods, there are decisions that you'll need to make about the role you'll play as an observer and your relations with the people you're observing. Here we'll examine some of the issues involved in these decisions.

The Various Roles of the Observer

Observers in field research can play a variety of roles, including participating in what they want to observe. Even when the term *participant observation* is used by researchers to describe their method, it need not mean that they actively participated in what they studied, though it typically does indicate that they studied it directly at the scene of the action. As Catherine Marshall and Gretchen Rossman (1995:60) point out:

> The researcher may plan a role that entails varying degrees of "participantness" that is, the degree of actual participation in daily life. At one extreme is the full participant, who goes about ordinary life in a role or set of roles constructed in the setting. At the other extreme is the complete observer, who engages not at all in social interaction and may even shun involvement in the world being studied. And, of course, all possible complementary mixes along the continuum are available to the researcher.

The *complete participant*, in this sense, may be a genuine participant in what he or she is studying

(for example, a participant in a campus demonstration) or may pretend to be a genuine participant. In any event, if acting as the complete participant, you let people see you *only* as a participant, not as a researcher. For instance, if you're studying a group made up of uneducated and inarticulate people, it wouldn't be appropriate for you to talk and act like a university professor or student.

This type of research introduces an ethical issue, one on which social researchers themselves are divided. Is it ethical to deceive the people you're studying in the hope that they will confide in you as they will not confide in an identified researcher? Do the potential benefits to be gained by the research offset such considerations? Although many professional associations have addressed this issue, the norms to be followed remain somewhat ambiguous when applied to specific situations.

Related to this ethical consideration is a scientific one. No researcher deceives his or her subjects solely for the purpose of deception. Rather, it's done in the belief that the data will be more valid and reliable, that the subjects will be more natural and honest if they don't know the researcher is doing a research project. If the people being studied know they're being studied, they might modify their behaviour in a variety of ways. First, they might expel the researcher. Second, they might modify their speech and behaviour to appear more "respectable" than would otherwise be the case. Third, the social process itself might be radically changed. Students making plans to burn down the university administration building, for example, might give up the plan altogether once they learn that one of their group is a social scientist conducting a research project.

On the other side of the coin, if you're a complete participant, you may affect what you're studying. To play the role of participant, you must participate. Yet, your participation may importantly affect the social process you're studying. Suppose, for example, that you're asked for your ideas about what the group should do next. No matter what you say, you will affect the process in some fashion. If the group follows your suggestion, your influence on the process is obvious. If the group decides not to follow your suggestion, the process whereby the suggestion is rejected may affect what happens next. Finally, if you indicate that you just don't know what should be done next, you may be adding to a general feeling of uncertainty and indecisiveness in the group.

Ultimately, anything the participant–observer does or does not do will have some effect on what is being observed; it's simply inevitable. More seriously, what you do or do not do may have an important effect on what happens. There is no complete protection against this effect, though sensitivity to the issue may provide a partial protection. (This influence, the Hawthorne effect, was discussed in Chapter 8.)

Because of these several considerations, ethical and scientific, the field researcher frequently chooses a different role from that of complete participant. You could participate fully with the group under study but make it clear that you were also undertaking research. As a member of the volleyball team, for example, you might use your position to launch a study in the sociology of sports, letting your teammates know what you're doing. There are dangers in this role also, however. The people being studied may shift much of their attention to the research project rather than focus on the natural social process, making the process being observed no longer typical. Or, conversely, you yourself may come to identify too much with the interests and viewpoints of the participants. You may begin to "go native" and lose much of your scientific detachment.

At the other extreme, the *complete observer* studies a social process without becoming a part of it in any way. Quite possibly, because of the researcher's unobtrusiveness, the subjects of study might not realize they're being studied. Sitting at a bus stop to observe jaywalking at a nearby intersection would be an example. Although the complete observer is less likely to affect what's being studied and less likely to "go native" than the complete participant, she or he is also less likely to develop a full appreciation of what's being studied. Observations may be more sketchy and transitory.

Fred Davis (1973) characterizes the extreme roles that observers might play as "the Martian" and "the Convert." The latter involves delving deeper and deeper into the phenomenon under study, running the risk of "going native." We'll examine this further in the next section.

To better appreciate the "Martian" approach, imagine that you were sent to observe some new-found life on Mars. Probably you would feel yourself inescapably separate from the Martians. Some social scientists adopt this degree of separation when observing cultures or social classes different from their own.

Marshall and Rossman (1995:60–61) also note that the researcher can vary the amount of time spent in the setting being observed: You can be a full-time presence on the scene or just show up now and then. Moreover, you can focus your attention on a limited aspect of the social setting or seek to observe all of it—framing an appropriate role to match your aims.

Different situations ultimately require different roles for the researcher. Unfortunately, there are no clear guidelines for making this choice. You must rely on your understanding of the situation and your own good judgment. In making your decision, however, you must be guided by both methodological and ethical considerations. Because these often conflict, your decision will frequently be difficult, and you may find sometimes that your role limits your study.

Relations to Subjects

Having introduced the different roles field researchers might play in connection with their observations, we're now going to focus more specifically on how researchers may relate to the subjects of their study and to the subjects' points of view. We will discuss techniques for conducting field research, for example, gaining access, preparing for the field, and recording observations, later in the chapter.

We've already mentioned the possibility of pretending to occupy social statuses we don't really occupy. Now consider how you would think and feel in such a situation.

Suppose you've decided to study a religious cult that has enrolled many people in your neighbourhood. You might study the group by joining it or pretending to join it. Take a moment to ask yourself what the difference is between "really" joining and "pretending" to join. The main difference is whether or not you actually take on the beliefs, attitudes, and other points of view shared by the "real" members. If the cult members believe that Jesus will come next Thursday night to destroy the world and save the members of the cult, do you believe it or do you simply pretend to believe it?

Traditionally, social scientists have tended to emphasize the importance of "objectivity" in such matters. In this example, that injunction would be to avoid getting swept up in the beliefs of the group. Without denying the advantages associated with such objectivity, social scientists today also recognize the benefits gained by immersing themselves in the points of view they're studying, what Lofland and Lofland (1995:61) refer to as "insider understanding." Ultimately, you won't be able to fully understand the thoughts and actions of the cult members unless you can adopt their points of view as true, at least temporarily. To fully appreciate the phenomenon you've set out to study, you need to *believe* that Jesus is coming Thursday night.

Adopting an alien point of view is an uncomfortable prospect for most people. It's often difficult enough simply to learn about views that seem strange to you; you at times may find it hard just to tolerate certain views. But to take them on as your own is ten times worse. Robert Bellah (1970, 1974) has offered the term *symbolic realism* to indicate the need for social researchers to treat the beliefs they study as worthy of respect rather than as objects of ridicule. If you seriously entertain this prospect, you may appreciate why William Shaffir and Robert Stebbins (1991:1) concluded that "field-work must certainly rank with the more disagreeable activities that humanity has fashioned for itself."

There is, of course, a danger in adopting the points of view of the people that you're studying. When you abandon your objectivity in favour of adopting such views, you lose the possibility of seeing and understanding the phenomenon within frames of reference unavailable to your subjects.

On the one hand, accepting the belief that the world will end Thursday night allows you to appreciate aspects of that belief available only to believers; stepping outside that view, however, makes it possible for you to consider some reasons why people might adopt such a view. You may discover that some did so as a consequence of personal trauma (such as unemployment or divorce) while others were brought into the fold through their participation in particular social networks (for example, their whole bowling team joined the cult). Notice that the cult members might disagree with those "objective" explanations, and you might not come up with them to the extent that you had operated legitimately within the group's views.

The apparent dilemma here is that both of these postures offer important advantages but seem to be mutually exclusive. In fact, it is possible to assume both postures. Sometimes you can simply shift viewpoints at will. When appropriate, you can fully assume the beliefs of the cult; later, you can step outside those beliefs (more accurately, you step inside the viewpoints associated with social science). As you become more adept at this kind of research, you may come to hold contradictory viewpoints simultaneously, rather than switch back and forth. Allowing yourself to remain open to various possibilities helps in this regard. For example, as a researcher with the cult you might try to suspend your beliefs while in that realm; neither believing that the world will end on Thursday night to be genuine (like most of the other participants) nor disbelieving it (like most scientists).

The problem we've just been discussing could be seen as psychological, occurring mostly inside the researcher's head. There is a corresponding problem at a social level, however. When you become deeply involved in the lives of the people you're studying, you're likely to be moved by their personal problems and crises. Imagine, for example, that one of the cult members becomes ill and needs a ride to the hospital. Should you provide transportation? Sure. Suppose someone wants to borrow money to buy a stereo. Should you loan it? Probably not. Suppose they need the money for food?

There are no black-and-white rules for resolving situations such as these, however, you should realize that you'll need to deal with them regardless of whether or not you reveal yourself as a researcher. Such problems do not tend to arise in other types of research—surveys and experiments, for example—but they are part and parcel of field research.

An Illustration of Qualitative Field Research

Books on qualitative methodology often refer to qualitative inquiry as a craft or a mindset and suggest that the best way to learn about the variety of ways of going about it is to become involved in several differing qualitative studies. Short of that, let's now examine an illustration of a field research study to give you a better sense of the diverse and creative ways such research has been conducted. The following example helps to demonstrate the flexibility, adaptability, and dynamism of this method as well as the types of problems and issues the field researcher confronts when observing and participating with research subjects in their natural habitat.

Observing Outlaw Bikers

Daniel Wolf (1990) was a graduate student in Alberta, Canada, when he decided to engage in field research among an outlaw motorcycle club. He understood how the bikers were perceived by the general society, but he wanted to learn about their own worldview: How did they see themselves and how did they collectively create their subculture?

Though he bought an appropriate motorcycle and biker clothing, Wolf found it particularly difficult to gain access to a club.

> In Calgary, I met several members of the Kings Crew MC in a motorcycle show and expressed an interest in "hanging around." But I lacked patience and pushed the situation by asking too many questions. I found out quickly that outsiders, even bikers, do not rush into a club, and that anyone who doesn't show the proper restraint will be shut out.
>
> (Wolf 1991:213)

Notice that while his attempt to join up with the Kings Crew was unsuccessful, Wolf learned something about biker clubs nonetheless. His rapport with the club was not helped, however, when he got into a barroom fight with a club member days later.

> He flattened my nose and began choking me. Unable to get air down my throat and breathing only blood through my nostrils, I managed a body punch that luckily found his solar plexus and loosened his grip. I then grabbed one of his hands and pulled back on the thumb until I heard the joint break. Mistake number two. It was time to move on.
>
> (Wolf 1991:213)

Eventually, Wolf made a successful contact with the Rebels, beginning with a casual conversation about motorcycles with a gang member. He was invited to drink with the club, then to ride with them. Gradually, he became a friend with more and more club members, and his participation increased steadily.

For three years, Wolf became more involved with the Rebels and came to grasp their worldview more fully. He experienced his friendship with club members as genuine; they became more his brothers than research subjects.

> Brotherhood, I came to learn, is the foundation of the outlaw club community. It establishes among members a sense of moral, emotional, and material interdependence and commitment. The enduring emotion of brotherhood is comradeship. To a patch holder, brotherhood means being there when needed; its most dramatic expression occurs when brothers defend each other from outside threats.
>
> (Wolf 1991:216)

As he felt himself more and more a full participant in the Rebels, his role as researcher became increasingly problematic. Doing secret research was a blatant betrayal of the men he now regarded as his friends. Moreover, Wolf knew that three police officers who had attempted to infiltrate the club previously had been murdered. He wanted to tell the club members about his research but was afraid to do so.

Then one day, he got a lucky break. Club members knew that Wolf was an anthropology graduate student, and one asked if he had ever considered doing research on the club. Wolf said he would be interested in doing that and now had an excuse for making a proposal to the club leadership and members. After some heated disagreements, the club agreed, and Wolf could conduct his research openly.

Wolf eventually completed his thesis and gave a copy to the club. His desire to publish his thesis as a book, however, raised more disagreements among club members. Ultimately, he worked with club members to create fictional names that would protect them as individuals. The club itself was well known, however, and Wolf made no attempt to disguise it.

While Wolf continued to feel a personal friendship with members of the Rebels, his emergence as a researcher steadily eroded that relationship.

> I continued to ride with the Rebels for another year and a half, during which time I carried out formal data procedures—structured interviews. As my role as an ethnographer became more evident, my role as a biker became more contrived and I began to be excluded from the brotherhood. My contact with members became less frequent and less intense. As an ethnographer, my relationship with the club lost its substance and meaning and I lost touch with the innermost core of Rebel reality; I simply faded away.
>
> (Wolf 1991:222)

Various Frameworks for Field Research: Posing and Solving Puzzles

Although we've described field research as going where the action is and observing it, there are actu-

ally many different approaches to this research method. These alternatives concern the framework of the study: what puzzles (research questions) should be posed and how to solve them. While there are many such variations, this section looks at only a few of these alternative approaches to field research—grounded theory, the extended case method, institutional ethnography, and participatory action research—to give you a sense of the possibilities. The distinctions between the numerous approaches are sometimes subtle for those newly exposed to field methods. However, the more qualitative research you read, the more variety of approaches you will run across, and the clearer the distinctions among these approaches will become.

Before we turn to our examination of some of these alternative frameworks in field research, let's briefly revisit our discussion of the relationship between the researcher and subject. In the conventional view of science, there are implicit differences of power and status separating the researcher from the subjects of research. For example, when talking about experimental designs, it's clear that the experimenter is in charge. It is the experimenter who organizes things and tells the subjects what to do. Many times the experimenter is the only one who knows what the research is truly about. Something similar might be said about survey research. The person running the survey designs the questions, decides who will be selected for questioning, and is responsible for making sense out of the data collected.

Sociologists often look at these kinds of relationships as power or status relationships. In experimental and survey designs, the researcher clearly has more power and a higher status than do the people being studied. The researchers have a special knowledge that the subjects don't enjoy. They're not so crude as to say they're superior to the subjects, but there's a sense in which that's implicitly assumed. This sense of superiority, however, does not necessarily translate into greater power and status in all social settings. For example, it would rarely apply in the study of elites. Thus, power and status differences must be evaluated as a variable possibility, taking the particularity of the research setting into account.

Nonetheless, implicit assumptions of researcher superiority can be problematic in field research. When the early European anthropologists set out to study what were originally called "primitive" societies, there was no question but that the anthropologists thought they knew best. Whereas the natives "believed" in witchcraft, for example, the anthropologists "knew" it wasn't really true. While the natives said some of their rituals would appease the gods, the anthropologists explained that the "real" functions of these rituals were the creation of social identity, the establishment of group solidarity, and so on. They never thought to question the intrinsic superiority of the European culture that they took for granted as a standpoint.

The more social researchers have gone into the field to study their fellow humans face-to-face, however, the more they have become conscious of these implicit assumptions about researcher superiority, and the more they have considered alternatives. As we now turn to the various approaches to field research, we'll see some of the ways in which that ongoing concern has worked itself out.

Grounded Theory

Grounded theory originated from the collaboration of Barney Glaser and Anselm Strauss. This approach has evolved and developed since the first major presentation of it in their book *The Discovery of Grounded Theory* (1967). It has many facets; therefore, our goal here is simply to present some of the key ideas associated with that approach.

Grounded theory is the attempt to derive theory from an analysis of the patterns, themes, and common categories discovered in observational data. According to Strauss and Corbin, "A researcher does not begin a project with a preconceived theory in mind (unless his or her purpose is to elaborate and extend existing theory). Rather, the researcher begins with an area of study and allows the theory to emerge from the data" (1998:12). Grounded theory can be described as an attempt to combine a naturalist approach with an explicit concern for a "systematic set of procedures" in doing qualitative research.

Strauss and Corbin speak of qualitative data analysis as both science and art. As they state, "It is

science in the sense of maintaining a certain degree of rigor and by grounding analysis in data. Creativity manifests itself in the ability of researchers to aptly name categories, ask stimulating questions, make comparisons, and extract an innovative, integrated, realistic scheme from masses of unorganized raw data" (1998:13). The researcher can be both scientific and creative in the development of grounded theory as long as procedures of data collection and analysis are followed. Coding procedures are analytic tools to assist the researcher in both systematically and creatively identifying, developing, and relating concepts. Systematic coding is important for achieving validity and reliability in the analysis of the data.

Although an essential element of this approach to research is the standardization and rigor these procedures lend to the process of data analysis and ultimately theory construction, this rigour is not achieved by lock-step adherence to a rigid set of rules. It is achieved through the deep understanding of the logic that lies behind the coding procedures (discussed further in Chapter 14). The logic of these research procedures is the backbone to grounded theory. The procedures guide the alternating process of data collection and analysis that is central to this approach. Analysis begins at the very outset of interviewing and observation and therefore propels the collection of data.

The researcher becomes intimately connected with her or his data in this process, which raises the issue of "how one can immerse oneself in the data and still maintain a balance between objectivity and sensitivity" (Strauss and Corbin, 1998:42). Maintaining such a balance in scientific discovery is the key to making this process work. Strauss and Corbin (1998:42–46) outline numerous techniques that help the researcher guard against bias creeping into analysis while maintaining sensitivity to what the data says. Thinking comparatively, gaining multiple points of view of an event, gathering data on the same phenomenon in various ways, checking out assumptions and hypotheses with respondents on occasion, and periodically stopping to ask "'What is going on here?' and 'Does what I think I see fit the reality of the data?' The data themselves do not lie," are all potential ways of dealing with the problem of objectivity. Another technique is to "maintain an attitude of skepticism. All theoretical explanations, categories, hypotheses, and questions about the data arrived at through analysis should be regarded as provisional. These should be validated against data in subsequent interviews or observations." Finally they stress that one's ability to be scientific and objective while also being creative and sensitive to the data requires following the research procedures.

> Although researchers may pick and choose among some of the analytic techniques that we offer, the <u>procedures of making comparisons, asking questions, and sampling based on evolving theoretical concepts</u> are essential features of the methodology. They differentiate it from other methods and provide the means for developing theory....Coding cannot be done haphazardly or at the whim of the analyst. There is a reason for alternating data collection with analysis. Not only does this allow for sampling on the basis of emerging concepts, but it also enables validation of concepts and hypotheses as these are being developed. Those found not to 'fit' can then be discarded, revised, or modified during the research process.
>
> (1998:46)

When reading the literature it is clear that some researchers make a claim to using a grounded theory approach when they are merely trying to indicate that they have grounded their theory in data. The grounded theory approach is much more than this as you can see. If you are to engage in grounded theory, reading several books on the topic before you begin is highly recommended.

The following example will illustrate some aspects of the grounded theory approach in qualitative research.

Clifton F. Conrad's (1978) study of academic change in universities is an early example of the grounded theory approach. Conrad hoped to uncover the major sources of changes in academic curricula and at the same time understand the process of change. Using the grounded theory idea of *theoretical sampling*, whereby groups or institutions are selected on the basis of their theoretical relevance, Conrad chose four universities for the

purpose of his study. In two, the main vehicle of change was the formal curriculum committee; in the other two, the vehicle of change was an ad hoc group.

Conrad explained, step by step the advantage of using the grounded theory approach in building his theory of academic change. He described the process of systematically coding data in order to create categories that must "emerge" from the data and then assessing the fitness of these categories with each other. Going continuously from data to theory and theory to data allowed him to reassess the validity of his initial conclusions about academic change.

For instance, it first seemed that academic change was mainly caused by an administrator who was pushing for it. By reexamining the data and looking for more plausible explanations, Conrad found the pressure of interest groups a more convincing source of change. The emergence of these interest groups actually allowed the administrator to become an agent of change.

Assessing how data from each of the two types of universities fit with the other helped refine theory building. Conrad's conclusion was that changes in university curricula are based on the following process: Conflict and interest groups emerge because of internal and external social structural forces; they push for administrative intervention and recommendation to make changes in the current academic program; these changes are then made by the most powerful decision-making body.

Extended Case Method

As previously discussed, the case study design may be used by researchers for the purpose of generating in-depth description or explanatory insights. Thus, case study researchers may seek only an idiographic understanding of a particular case or they may use case studies as the basis for the development of more general, nomothetic theories—for example, using the grounded theory approach.

Michael Burawoy and colleagues (1991) have suggested a somewhat different relationship between case studies and theory. For them, the

extended case method has the purpose of discovering flaws in, and then modifying, existing social theories.

While in the grounded theory approach researchers attempt to enter the field without preconceived theory in mind, Burawoy suggests the opposite approach: to try "to lay out as coherently as possible what we expect to find in our site *before* entry" (Burawoy et al. 1991:9). He sees the extended case method as a way to rebuild or improve theory instead of approving or rejecting it. The goal is to look for all the ways in which observations conflict with existing theories and for what Burawoy calls "theoretical gaps and silences" (1991:10). In this orientation to field research becoming deeply familiar with the literature before entering the field appears to be essential, whereas grounded theorists, in their goal of generating knowledge, feel that being too deeply entrenched in the literature beforehand might block creativity and constrain theory development.

Here's an example of a study by one of Burawoy's students to illustrate the extended case method. Katherine Fox (1991) set out to study an agency whose goal was to fight the AIDS epidemic by bringing condoms and bleach for cleaning needles to intravenous drug users. It's a good example of finding the limitations of well-used models of theoretical explanation in the realm of understanding deviance—specifically, the "treatment model" that predicted that drug users would come to the clinic and ask for treatment. Fox's interactions with outreach workers, most of whom were part of the community of drug addicts or former prostitutes, contradicted that model.

To begin, it was necessary to understand the drug users' subculture and use that knowledge to devise more realistic policies and programs. The target users had to be convinced, for example, that the program workers could be trusted, that they were really interested only in providing bleach and condoms. The target users needed to be sure they were not going to be arrested.

Fox's field research didn't stop with an examination of the drug users. She also studied the agency workers, discovering that the outreach program meant different things to the research directors and the outreach workers. Some of the volunteers who were actually providing the bleach and condoms were frustrated about the minor changes they felt they could make. Many thought the program was just a bandage on the AIDS and drug abuse problems. Some resented having to take field notes. Directors, on the other hand, needed reports and field notes so that they could validate their research in the eyes of the government agencies that financed the project. Fox's study showed how the AIDS research project developed the bureaucratic inertia typical of established organizations. Its goal became that of sustaining itself.

This study illustrates how the extended case method can operate. The researcher enters the field with full knowledge of existing theories but aims to uncover contradictions that require the modification of those theories.

Institutional Ethnography

Conducting research from the "standpoint of women" (and more recently other subordinated groups) is key to the **institutional ethnography** approach originally developed by Dorothy Smith (1987). Challenging conventional methodological approaches, Smith argued that closer attention to women's voices and experiences would open the door to greater understanding of how these experiences are organized and determined.

Smith and other social scientists believe that if researchers ask women or other oppressed people about "how things work," they can discover the institutional practices that shape their realities. Although the individuals' experiences are essential to the research approach, the individuals themselves are not the focus of inquiry. The institutional ethnographer starts with the personal experiences of the oppressed or "ruled" but proceeds to uncover the institutional power relations that structure and govern those experiences—the social organization of ruling relations. The goal of such inquiry is to uncover forms of oppression that are often overlooked by more traditional types of research.

As Marie Campbell (1998:57) states:

Institutional ethnography, like other forms of ethnography, relies on interviewing, observation and documents as data. Institutional ethnography departs from other ethnographic approaches by treating those data not as the topic or object of interest, but as 'entry' into the social relations of the setting. The idea is to tap into people's expertise....The conceptual framing of everyday experiences heard or read about, or observed, constitutes one of the distinctive features of an institutional ethnography, another is its political nature.

Campbell applied this framework in her study of the impact of a new management strategy called the "Service Quality Initiative," implemented in a long-term care hospital in Victoria, Canada. One major aim of her work was to investigate how this management strategy reorganized the values and practices of the caregivers to take into account fiscal concerns. The entry point of her investigation was the nursing assistants' experiences. Following the institutional ethnography approach, her initial goal was to learn how the setting worked by listening to what these subordinates or "ruled" had to say. Developing an understanding of the social relations from the perspective of the ruled, she then inquired into the effects of specific ruling practices on the nursing assistants—those whose work lives were structured by them.

Another key point of Campbell's article concerned methodology and her desire to illustrate the central importance of people's experience in gaining a "trustworthy analysis." In describing her investigation into what was actually going on in the research setting, she stated: "I was not entering it as a naïve observer working in a naturalist mode, nor was I looking for theory to arise out of data, as a grounded theorist might. As an institutional ethnographer, I was informed by prior analysis of the Canadian health care system and its increasingly rationalist stance towards management. I was also informed by a social organization of knowledge approach" (1998:58).

Beginning from the viewpoint of the nursing assistants, she followed the structure of social relations to gain insight into the way they shaped the nurses' thoughts and actions. The trustworthiness of the data, according to Campbell, concerns the extent to which it accounts for their experiences. She, therefore, illuminated how the discourse of management structured the nursing assistants' work lives. The principles of the new initiative, attention to bottom line budgets among other things, influenced the organization of social relations and hence the nurses' experiences. She discovered that the emphasis on market concerns came to overshadow the concerns of care in the day-to-day decisions of the health care workers.

Another illustration of institutional ethnography is taken from Didi Khayatt's (1995) study of the institutionalization of compulsory heterosexuality in schools and its effects on lesbian students. In 1990, Khayatt began her research by interviewing 12 Toronto lesbians, 15 to 24 years of age. Beginning with the young women's viewpoint, she then expanded her inquiry to other students, teachers, guidance counsellors, and administrators.

Khayatt found that the school's administrative practices generated a *compulsory heterosexuality*, which produced a sense of marginality and vulnerability among lesbian students. For example, the school didn't punish harassment and name-calling against gay students. The issue of homosexuality was excluded from the curriculum lest it appear to students as an alternative to heterosexuality.

Khayatt's inquiry began with the women's standpoint: lesbian students. However, instead of emphasizing the subjects' viewpoints, her analysis focused on the power relations that shaped these women's experiences and reality.

Participatory Action Research

The role of the researcher in **participatory action research** (PAR) is to serve as a resource to those being studied—typically, disadvantaged groups—as an opportunity for them to act effectively in their own interest. In this approach the researcher's attempt to provide alternatives to the conventional view of the status and power differences between researchers and subjects is quite clear. The disadvantaged subjects define their problems, define the remedies desired, and take the lead in designing the research that will help them realize their aims.

The approach comes from a critique of classical social science research. From the perspective of PAR, traditional research is seen as an "elitist model" (Whyte, Greenwood, and Lazes 1991) that reduces the "subjects" of research to "objects" of research. Many who advocate this perspective believe the distinction between the researcher and the researched should disappear. They argue that the subjects who will be affected by research should also be responsible for its design.

The approach began in Third World research but quickly spread to Europe and North America. Implicit in this approach is the belief that research functions not only as a means of knowledge production but also as a "tool for the education and development of consciousness as well as mobilization for action" (Gaventa 1991:121–22). Advocates of participatory action research equate access to information with power and argue that this power has been kept in the hands of the dominant class, sex, ethnicity, or nation. Once people see themselves as researchers, they automatically regain power over knowledge. Therefore, in this approach both researchers and participant–subjects contribute to the research project collaboratively. A major goal of the research is to produce results that are beneficial to the participant–subjects of the research. The focus of research attention is usually local, specific problems and the researcher contributes to the development of specific plans to help solve the problems with the knowledge obtained through the cooperative research. Examples of this approach include community power structure research, corporate research, and "right-to-know" movements (Whyte et al. 1991). Here's an example of community power structure research from applied anthropology.

A research project took place at the initiative of the Dene Cultural Institute and the Dogrib community of Lac La Martre, N.W.T.; the Dogrib is one of several tribal groups within the Dene Nation. Their goal was to document Dene traditional justice among the Dogrib in order to assess whether their system of justice could be usefully revived and sustained if the non-Dene justice system that overlay

it was removed. Joan Ryan (1995) was asked to assist them in gaining research funding and coordinating the project. Her objective was to ensure that the Lac La Martre community's interests were being met by the research project. Thus, she adopted a participatory action research approach.

In the course of documenting traditional Dene justice, the research revealed some of the inconsistencies between traditional rules and values and those imposed on the community by the non-Native institutions. The Dene had their own oral tradition of a rigid system of rules that guided behaviour and group harmony was at its core—harmony among group members and of the group with its environment. The non-Dene justice system that was imposed on the Dene people, however, emphasized individual rights which were secondary to group harmony in Dene tradition. The adversarial, individualistic nature of non-Dene justice ran counter to the acknowledgement of responsibility and restoration of group harmony central to Dene traditional values.

The elders of the community indicated a lack of desire to adapt to the new legal system. Their preference was to regain control of their community and institutions. Maintaining a focus on producing results—knowledge and plans of action—that contribute to positive changes in the lives of the participant–subjects, Ryan led the investigation toward an exploration of traditional values that might help the community regain "personal and social control." Key to reclaiming these traditional values was to first overcome the widespread alcohol abuse problem the community faced. This recognition led to the recommendation that the community call in a treatment team and hold healing circles as a means of confronting and helping to resolve the problem. Four other major recommendations were made as well, including the formation of a Dogrib justice committee and the establishment of a pilot project to test the effectiveness of rules, both old and new, in dealing with community social problems. The aim of these recommendations was to help the Dogrib people reclaim responsibility for administering Dogrib justice and to retake control of other key elements in their community in an effort to revitalize their own institutions and cultural systems.

In reporting the research, Ryan discussed many of the problems and challenges the PAR project faced as well as its successes. For example, the community advisory committee unexpectedly hired the Native interviewers without consultation with Ryan, who was the principle investigator (PI), or the project director (PD). There were gender and other issues as well that the PI and PD had to contend with as strangers in the community, causing both of them some stress. Other difficulties included how the project prematurely set off community action. Midway though the project a major problem that severely destabilized it was the loss of three out of the four Native research team members: one dismissed due to an assault conviction and two because of alcohol related absences. Nonetheless, two other Native members were hired to replace them and the research was able to continue.

This project was a combination of an ethnographic description of traditional Dene justice and participatory action research. The members of the community instigated, and were actively involved in, the research. Ryan served as a resource to the participant–subjects and maintained a focus on the practical, political considerations that motivated the research. The field research uncovered the feelings shared by the Dogrib elders and some of the problems that required resolution. Steps for action were then recommended for how the community and other Dene people might reestablish control.

As you can see, the seemingly simple process of observing social action as it occurs has subtle though important variations. Thus, there are a variety of approaches to puzzle posing and solving in qualitative field research that have been developed to enrich the observation of social life.

Conducting Qualitative Field Research

We've so far discussed topics appropriate to field research, common terms and issues, special considerations in doing this kind of research, and sev-

eral different approaches to field research that direct different types of research efforts.

Throughout the chapter we've presented some examples that illustrate field research in action. It's now time to turn to specific ideas and techniques for conducting field research, starting with how researchers prepare for fieldwork.

Preparing for the Field

Suppose for the moment that you've decided to undertake field research on a campus political organization. Let's assume further that you're not a member of that group, that you do not know a great deal about it, and that you will identify yourself to the participants as a researcher. This section will discuss some of the ways you might prepare yourself before undertaking direct observations.

As is true of all research methods, you would be well advised to begin with a search of the relevant literature, filling in your knowledge of the subject and learning what others have said about it.

In the next phase of your research, you might wish to discuss the student political group with others who have already studied it or with anyone else likely to be familiar with it. In particular, you might find it useful to discuss the group with one or more informants (discussed in Chapter 7). Perhaps you have a friend who is a member, or you can meet someone who is. This aspect of your preparation is likely to be more effective if your relationship with the informant extends beyond your research role. In dealing with members of the group as informants, you should take care that your initial discussions do not compromise or limit later aspects of your research. Keep in mind that the impression you make on the informant, the role you establish for yourself, may carry over into your later effort. For example, creating the initial impression that you may be an undercover government agent is unlikely to facilitate later observations of the group.

You should also be wary about the information you get from informants. Although they may have more direct, personal knowledge of the subject under study than you do, what they "know" is probably a mixture of fact and point of view. Members of the political group in our example would be unlikely to give you completely unbiased information (as would members of opposing political groups). Before making your first contact with the student group, then, you should already be quite familiar with it, and you should understand its general philosophical context.

There are a variety of ways to establish your initial contact with the people you plan to study. How you do it will depend, in part, on the role you intend to play. Especially if you decide to take on the role of complete participant, you must find a way to develop an identity with the people to be studied. If you wish to study dishwashers in a restaurant, the most direct method would be to get a job as a dishwasher. In the case of the student political group, you might simply join the group.

Many of the social processes appropriate to field research are open enough to make your contact with the people to be studied rather simple and straightforward. If you wish to observe a mass demonstration, just be there. If you wish to observe patterns in jaywalking, hang around busy streets.

Whenever you wish to make more formal contact with the people, identifying yourself as a researcher, you must establish a certain rapport with them. You might contact a participant with whom you feel comfortable and gain that person's assistance. In studying a formal group, you might approach the group's leader. Or you may find that one of your informants can introduce you.

While you'll probably have many options in making your initial contact with the group, realize that your choice can influence your subsequent observations. Suppose, for example, that you're studying a university and begin with high-level administrators. Important consequences might result from this choice. First, your initial impressions of the university are going to be shaped to some degree by the administrators' views, which will be quite different from those of students or faculty. This initial impression may influence the way you observe and interpret events subsequently, particularly if you're unaware of the influence.

Second, if the administrators approve of your research project and encourage students and faculty to cooperate with you, the latter groups will probably look on you as somehow aligned with the administration, which can affect what they say to you. Faculty might be reluctant to tell you about plans to organize through the teamsters' union.

In making a direct, formal contact with the people you want to study, you'll be required to give them some explanation of the purpose of your study. Here again, you face an ethical dilemma. Telling them the complete purpose of your research might eliminate their cooperation altogether or importantly affect their behaviour. On the other hand, giving only what you believe would be an acceptable explanation may involve outright deception. Your decisions in this and other matters will probably be largely determined by the purpose of your study, the nature of what you're studying, the observations you wish to use, and similar factors, but ethical concerns must be considered as well.

Previous field research offers no fixed rule—methodological or ethical—to follow in this regard. Your appearance as a researcher, regardless of your stated purpose, may result in a warm welcome from people who are flattered that a scientist finds them important enough to study. Or, it may result in your being totally ostracized or worse. For example, it likely wouldn't be a good idea to burst into a meeting of an organized crime syndicate and announce that you're writing a term paper on organized crime.

Another important issue to consider when trying to develop an identity with the people you desire to study concerns the statuses or roles they may attribute to you. These may be independent of, or even contrary to, those you attempt to establish. The statuses, roles, and/or resources that are attributed to researchers often play a part in how people react to them and what kinds of information they are willing to share. It is frequently the case that contrasts such as gender, race, and class must be taken into account. Such ascribed roles may limit or assist researchers in establishing identities and connections with those under study. They can affect the experiences and information available to them. Being alert to possible role attributions by those in the field environment can help you to sort out the information you are gathering and the interpretations you place on that information. Sometimes field workers are surprised when they learn of particular interpretations that study participants have been making about their identities. Such discoveries can lead to fruitful reconsiderations of observations collected earlier.

In part, field research is a matter of going where the action is and simply watching and listening. You can learn a lot merely by paying attention to what's going on. At the same time, as we've already indicated, field research can involve more active inquiry. Sometimes it's appropriate to ask people questions and record their answers. Your on-the-spot observations of a full-blown riot will lack something if you don't know why people are rioting. Ask somebody.

Because various methodological techniques involve **qualitative interviewing**, Chapter 12 is devoted to this topic. As you'll see, much of what we discussed in Chapter 9 on interviewing applies to qualitative interviewing, however, the interviewing you'll do in connection with field observation is different enough to demand a separate treatment. Although discussed in the next chapter, keep in mind that interviewing is frequently combined with observational techniques in field research.

Recording Observations

The greatest advantage of the field research method is the presence of an observing, thinking researcher on the scene of the action. Even tape recorders and cameras cannot capture all the relevant aspects of social processes. Thus, in both direct observation and interviewing, it's vital to make full and accurate notes of what goes on. If possible, you should take notes on your observations *as you observe.* When that's not feasible, write down your notes as soon as possible afterward.

Your notes should include both your empirical observations and your interpretations of them. In other words, record what you "know" has happened and what you "think" has happened. Be sure to identify these different kinds of notes for what they are. For example, you might note that Person X spoke out in opposition to a proposal made by a group leader (an observation), that you *think* this represents an attempt by Person X to take over leadership of the group (an interpretation), and that you *think* you heard the leader comment to that effect in response to the opposition (a tentative observation).

Just as you cannot hope to observe everything, neither can you record everything you do observe. Therefore, your observations will represent a sample of all possible observations. Likewise, your notes will represent a sample of your observations. The goal, of course, is to record the most relevant ones.

Some of the most important observations can be anticipated before you begin the study; others will become apparent as your observations progress. Sometimes you can make note taking easier by preparing standardized recording forms in advance. In a study of jaywalking, for example, you might anticipate the characteristics of pedestrians that are most likely to be useful for analysis—age, gender, social class, ethnicity, and so forth—and prepare a form in which observations of these factors can be recorded easily. Or, you might develop a symbolic shorthand in advance to speed up recording. For studying audience participation at a mass meeting, you might want to construct a numbered grid representing the different sections of the meeting room; then you could record the location of participants easily, quickly, and accurately.

None of this advance preparation should limit your recording of unanticipated events and aspects of the situation. Quite the contrary, speedy handling of anticipated observations can give you more freedom to observe the unanticipated.

You're already familiar with the process of taking notes, just as you already have at least informal experience with field research in general. Like good field research, however, good note taking requires careful and deliberate attention and involves some specific skills. Some guidelines follow. (You can learn more from John and Lyn Lofland's *Analyzing Social Settings* [1995:91–96].)

First, don't trust your memory any more than you have to; it's untrustworthy. To illustrate this point, try this experiment. Recall the last four movies you saw that you really liked. Now, name five of the actors or actresses. Who had the longest hair? Who was the most likely to start conversations? Who was the most likely to make suggestions that others followed? Now, if you didn't have any trouble answering any of these questions, how *sure* are you of your answers? Would you be willing to bet a hundred dollars that a panel of impartial judges would observe what you recall?

Even if you pride yourself on having a photographic memory, it's a good idea to take notes either during the observation or as soon afterward as possible. Be sure to include the place, time, and date in your notes, and as many details about the circumstances and people present as possible. If you take notes during observation, do it unobtrusively, because people are likely to behave differently if they see you taking down everything they say or do.

Second, it's usually a good idea to take notes in stages. In the first stage, you may need to take sketchy notes (words and phrases) in order to keep abreast of what's happening. Then go off by yourself and rewrite your notes in more detail. If you do this soon after the events you've observed, the sketchy notes should allow you to recall most of the details. The longer you delay, the less likely you'll be able to recall things accurately and fully.

We know this method sounds logical, but it takes self-discipline to put it into practice. Careful observation and note taking can be tiring, especially if it involves excitement or tension and if it extends over a long period. If you've just spent eight hours observing and making notes on how people have been coping with a disastrous flood, your first desire afterward will likely be to get some sleep, dry clothes, or a drink. You may need to take some inspiration from newspaper reporters who undergo the same sorts of hardships, then write their stories to meet their deadlines.

Third, you'll inevitably wonder *how much* you should record. Is it really worth the effort to write out all the details you can recall right after the observation session? The general guideline here is *yes*. Generally, in field research you can't be really sure of what's important and what's unimportant until you've had a chance to review and analyze a great volume of information, so you should even record things that don't seem important at the outset. They may turn out to be significant after all. Also, the act of recording the details of something "unimportant" may jog your memory of something that is important.

Realize that most of your field notes will not be reflected in your final report on the project. Put more harshly, most of the notes you take will be "wasted." But take heart: Even the richest gold ore yields only about 30 grams of gold per metric tonne, meaning that 99.997 percent of the ore is wasted. Yet, that 30 grams of gold can be hammered out to cover an area two metres square—the equivalent of about 685 book pages. So take a tonne of notes, and plan to select and use only the gold.

Like other aspects of field research (and all research for that matter), proficiency comes with practice. The nice thing about field research is you can begin practicing now and can continue practicing in almost any situation. You don't have to be engaged in an organized research project to practice observation and recording. You might start by volunteering to take the minutes at committee meetings, for example. Or you might sit in a coffee shop window and observe and record particular characteristics of those who pass by. Observing and recording are worthwhile, professional skills that improve with practice.

Research Ethics in Field Research

As we've repeatedly said, all forms of social research raise ethical issues. By bringing researchers into direct and often intimate contact with their subjects, field research raises these concerns in a particularly dramatic way. Before we discuss the ethical particularities of a specific field research study, here are some of the issues mentioned by John and Lyn Lofland (1995:63):

- Is it ethical to talk to people when they do not know you will be recording their words?
- Is it ethical to get information for your own purposes from people you hate?

- Is it ethical to see a severe need for help and not respond to it directly?
- Is it ethical to be in a setting or situation but not commit yourself wholeheartedly to it?
- Is it ethical to develop a calculated stance toward other humans, that is, to be strategic in your relations?
- Is it ethical to take sides or to avoid taking sides in a factionalized situation?
- Is it ethical to "pay" people with trade-offs for access to their lives and minds?
- Is it ethical to "use" people as allies or informants in order to gain entree to other people or to elusive understandings?

Humphreys' *Tearoom Trade* (1970) study is often used to illustrate some key ethical concerns in field research. Humphrey's was interested in male homosexual acts between strangers who met in public restrooms in parks, referred to as "tearooms" by participants. He was able to study the sexual encounters between these men because they usually included a third person. He, therefore, pretended to participate as the voyeur/lookout, known as the "watchqueen," whenever possible— a perfect opportunity to make field observations.

In order to find out more about these men and the lives they led, he secretly took down their licence plate numbers and used the police registers to obtain their names and addresses. In disguise, Humphreys then went to these men's homes on the pretense that he was conducting a health survey in order to gather further information about them.

This controversial study has provoked a great deal of argument and debate over what is or is not acceptable, ethical behaviour in field research. Some of the key issues this study raised concern invasion of privacy, deceit, lack of consent, and risk of harm to the research subjects. There were those who argued that the study of behaviour engaged in publicly was not unethical, that he was careful to protect the men's identities, and that his research did not result in any personal harm to the men. Arguments in support of the research also noted that the research revealed previously unknown information that dispelled some prior beliefs about men who engaged in these casual, homosexual encounters. For instance, the tearoom participants

were otherwise living rather conventional family lives and were respected community members.

While some praised his research as worthwhile, many others disapproved of the deceit and invasion of privacy the study entailed, particularly the follow-up survey. Others expressed concern that the information had the potential to seriously harm the subjects in any number of ways, including the risk of criminal charges since such acts were at that time and place illegal. This study continues to provoke debate over what research practices, under what circumstances, are ethical.

Strengths and Weaknesses of Field Research

Qualitative field research, like all research methods, has its strengths and weaknesses. As we've already indicated, field research is especially effective for studying the subtle nuances in attitudes and behaviours and for examining social processes over time. As such, the chief strength of this method lies in the depth of understanding it permits. Although other research methods may be challenged as "superficial," this charge is seldom lodged against field research.

Flexibility is another advantage of field research. As illustrated and discussed earlier, you may modify your field research design at any time. Moreover, you're always prepared to engage in field research, whenever the occasion should arise, whereas you could not as easily initiate a survey or an experiment.

Field research can be relatively inexpensive as well. Other social scientific research methods may require expensive equipment or an expensive research staff, but field research can typically be undertaken by one researcher with a notebook and a pencil. This is not to say that field research is never expensive. The nature of the research project, for example, may require a large number of trained observers. Expensive recording equipment may be needed. Or you may wish to undertake participant observation of interactions in expensive Paris nightclubs.

Field research has a number of weaknesses as well. First, being qualitative rather than quantitative, it's not an appropriate means for arriving at statistical descriptions of a large population. Observing casual political discussions in laundromats, for example, would not yield trustworthy estimates of the future voting behaviour of the total electorate. Such a study would lack representativeness; therefore, the findings would not be generalizable. Nevertheless, the study could provide important insights into how political attitudes are formed.

To assess field research further, let's focus on the issues of validity and reliability. Recall that validity and reliability are both qualities of measurements. Validity concerns whether measurements actually measure what they're supposed to rather than measuring something else. Reliability, on the other hand, is a matter of dependability: If you made the same measurement again and again, would you get the same result? Let's see how field research stacks up in these respects.

Validity

Field research seems to provide more valid measures than survey and experimental measurements, which are often criticized as superficial and not really valid. Let's review a couple of field research examples to see why this is so.

"Being there" is a powerful technique for gaining insights into the rich and complex nature of human affairs. Listen, for example, to what this nurse reports about the impediments to patients' coping with cancer:

Common fears that may impede the coping process for the person with cancer can include the following:
  —Fear of death—for the patient, and the implications his or her death will have for significant others.
  —Fear of incapacitation—because cancer can be a chronic disease with acute episodes that may result in periodic stressful periods, the variability of the person's ability to cope and constantly adjust may require a dependency upon others for activities of daily living and may consequently become a burden.
  —Fear of alienation—from significant others and health care givers, thereby creating helplessness and hopelessness.

  —Fear of contagion—that cancer is transmissible and/or inherited.
  —Fear of losing one's dignity—losing control of all bodily functions and being totally vulnerable.

(Garant 1980:2167)

Observations and conceptualizations such as these are valuable in their own right. In addition, they can provide the basis for further research, both qualitative and quantitative.

Now listen to what Joseph Howell has to say about "toughness" as a fundamental ingredient of life on Clay Street, a white, working-class neighbourhood in Washington, D.C.

Most of the people on Clay Street saw themselves as fighters in both the figurative and literal sense. They considered themselves strong, independent people who would not let themselves be pushed around. For Bobbi, being a fighter meant battling the welfare department and cussing out social workers and doctors upon occasion. It meant spiking Barry's beer with sleeping pills and bashing him over the head with a broom. For Barry it meant telling off his boss and refusing to hang the door, an act that led to his being fired. It meant going through the ritual of a duel with Al. It meant pushing Bubba around and at times getting rough with Bobbi.

June and Sam had less to fight about, though if pressed they both hinted that they, too, would fight. Being a fighter led Ted into near conflict with Peg's brothers, Les into conflict with Lonnie, Arlene into conflict with Phyllis at the bowling alley, etc.

(1973:292)

Even without having heard the episodes Howell refers to in this passage, you have the distinct impression that Clay Street is a tough place to live in. That "toughness" comes through far more powerfully through these field observations than it would in a set of statistics on the median number of fistfights occurring during a specified period.

These examples point to the superior validity of field research, as compared with surveys and experiments. The kinds of comprehensive measurements available to the field researcher tap a depth of meaning in concepts such as common fears of cancer patients and "toughness" (or such as liberal and conservative) that are generally unavailable to surveys and experiments. Instead of specifying concepts, field researchers commonly give detailed illustrations.

Reliability

Field research has, however, a potential problem with reliability. Suppose you were to characterize your best friend's political orientations based on everything you know about him or her. Your assessment of your friend's politics would appear to have much validity; it's certainly unlikely to be superficial. We couldn't be sure, however, that someone else would characterize your friend's politics the same way you did, even with the same amount of observation.

Although in-depth, field research measurements are also often very personal. How another judges your friend's political orientation depends very much on his or her own, just as your judgment depends on your political orientation. Conceivably, then, you could describe your friend as middle-of-the-road, although one of us might feel that we've been observing a fire-breathing radical.

As we've suggested earlier, researchers who use qualitative techniques are conscious of this issue and take pains to address it. Individual researchers often sort out their own biases and points of view, and the communal nature of science means that their colleagues will help them in that regard. Nonetheless, it's wise to be wary of purely descriptive measurements in field research, whether it's your own or someone else's. If a researcher reports that the members of a club are somewhat conservative, such a judgment is unavoidably linked to the researcher's own politics. You can be more trusting of *comparative evaluations*: identifying who is more conservative than whom, for example. Even if you and a friend had different political orientations, you would probably agree pretty much in ranking the relative conservatism of the members of a group.

As we've seen, field research is a potentially powerful tool for social scientists, one that pro-

vides a useful balance to the strengths and weaknesses of experiments and surveys.

Main Points

- Field research involves the direct observation of social phenomena in their natural settings. Field research is typically qualitative rather than quantitative.
- Field research is particularly appropriate to topics and processes that are not easily quantified, that are best understood in their natural settings, or that change over time. Topics include the study of practices, episodes, encounters, roles, relationships, groups, organizations, settlements, social worlds, and lifestyles or subcultures.
- In field research, observation, data processing, and analysis are interwoven and cyclical processes.
- Field research is typically multi-method, including observation, interviews, and examination of documents. Two terms commonly used by field researchers in describing their research methods are ethnography and participant observation.
- A case study design is frequently used in qualitative research, although it is used by quantitative researchers as well. It refers to the focus of the study, not to how the data will be gathered. The limitation of attention to a particular instance of something is the essential characteristic of the case study.
- Among the considerations involved in field research are the various possible roles of the observer and the researcher's relations with subjects. As a field researcher, you must decide whether to observe as an outsider or as a participant, whether or not to identify yourself as a researcher, and how to negotiate your relationships with subjects.
- Grounded theory, extended case study, institutional ethnography, and participatory action research are examples of different approaches to field research. They communicate variation

in researchers' perspectives on what puzzles should be posed and how they should be solved.

- Preparing for the field involves doing background research, determining how to make contact with subjects, and resolving issues of what your relationship to your subjects will be.
- Keeping a full and accurate record of what you see and hear in the field is vital. Whenever possible, field observations should be recorded as they're made; otherwise, they should be recorded as soon afterward as possible.
- Responsible field research involves consideration of ethical issues that arise from the researcher's direct contact with subjects.
- Among the advantages of field research are its flexibility and the depth of understanding it can provide. Many field research studies can also be relatively inexpensive.
- Compared with surveys and experiments, field research measurements generally have more validity but less reliability.

Review Questions and Exercises

1. Imagine that you've been asked to investigate allegations that local automobile dealerships treat men more seriously than women as potential buyers. Describe how you might go about studying this question through direct observation, using field research techniques.

2. Think of some group or activity you participate in or are very familiar with. In two or three paragraphs, describe how an outsider might effectively go about studying that group or activity. What should he or she read, what contacts should be made, and so on? List at least four ethical issues you can imagine this person confronting if the study was conducted.

3. Using the Web, find a research article using the grounded theory method. Summarize the study design and main findings. Do the same for a research article using either the extended case method or institutional ethnography.

4. To better appreciate the strengths and weaknesses of experiments, surveys, and field research, choose a research topic such as crime, worker satisfaction, sexual orientation, or prejudice and write brief descriptions of studies that could be conducted on that topic using each of these methods. For each description, discuss why the method chosen is the most appropriate for the study you propose.

Continuity Project

Undertake some participant observation on your campus and identify some possible indicators of gender equality/inequality. You might pay special attention to how people interact with one another and how gender affects those interactions.

Additional Readings

Gubrium, Jaber F. and James A. Holstein. *The New Language of Qualitative Method.* New York: Oxford University Press, 1997. This book provides the necessary foundations for understanding some of the main approaches in qualitative field research.

Johnson, Jeffrey C. *Selecting Ethnographic Informants.* Newbury Park, CA: Sage, 1990. The author discusses the various strategies that apply to the task of sampling in field research.

Lofland, John and Lyn Lofland. *Analyzing Social Settings,* 3rd ed. Belmont, CA: Wadsworth, 1995. An unexcelled presentation of field research methods from beginning to end. This eminently readable book manages successfully to draw the links between the logic of scientific inquiry and the nitty-gritty practicalities of observing, communicating, recording, filing, reporting, and everything else involved in field research. In addition, the book contains a wealth of references to field research illustrations.

Shaffir, William B. and Robert A. Stebbins, eds. *Experiencing Fieldwork: An Inside View of*

Qualitative Research. Newbury Park, CA: Sage, 1991. Several field research practitioners discuss the nature of the craft and recall experiences in the field. Here's an opportunity to gain a "feel" for the method as well as learn some techniques.

Silverman, David. *Doing Qualitative Research: A Practical Handbook.* Thousand Oaks, CA: Sage, 1999. This book focuses on the process of collecting and interpreting qualitative data.

Strauss, Anselm and Juliet Corbin. Basics of Qualitative Research: Techniques and Procedures for Developing Grounded Theory. 2nd ed. Newbury Park, CA: Sage, 1998. An essential read prior to beginning data collection and during data analysis if you plan to undertake a grounded theory approach.

*Info*Trac: You can find further relevant readings on the World Wide Web at

http://sociology.wadsworth.com

Chapter 12

Qualitative Interviewing

This chapter discusses some of the guidelines for qualitative interviewing and focuses on three interview-based methods of research: in-depth interview studies, focus group interviews, and oral history.

In this chapter . . .

Introduction

In Chapter 9, we discussed the techniques of survey interviewing. In this chapter we'll examine a different type of interviewing, one that is less structured and gives the subject of the interview more freedom to direct the flow of conversation. Such interviews provide the researcher the opportunity to explore topics, particularly unanticipated issues that may arise in the course of an interview. Unlike survey interviews, where standardized questions are asked of each respondent, **qualitative interviews** allow the researcher to pursue issues and topics in greater depth.

Qualitative interviews stand alone as a method of gathering data, however, they are frequently used in conjunction with other research methods as well. They are a mainstay of field research used both by participant observers and by researchers who make no pretense of being a part of what is being studied. Qualitative interview studies are sometimes combined with quantitative techniques like survey research as a means of gaining deeper insights into the topic under study.

Like many of the techniques we've already discussed, you'll see that (1) you already engage in qualitative interviews in your daily life and (2) there are special techniques that move this activity from

a casual form of interaction to a powerful scientific tool.

In this chapter we will first review issues related to qualitative interviewing more generally and offer some guidelines for conducting such interviews. We then turn to three research methods centred on qualitative interviewing: in-depth interview studies, focus group interviews, and oral history. The term *in-depth interview studies* will be used to signify research designs where qualitative interviewing is the primary means of data gathering. The *focus group interview* method is when a number of people are brought together in a laboratory type setting to be interviewed together, as a group. The *oral history* method of qualitative interviewing concerns in-depth interviews that focus on recollections of the past.

Qualitative Depth Interviewing: Definitions and Guidelines

As Patton (1987:108) says:

Depth interviewing involves asking open-ended questions, listening to and recording the answers, and then following up with additional relevant questions. On the surface this appears to require no more than knowing how to talk and listen. Beneath the surface, however, interviewing becomes an art and science requiring skill, sensitivity, concentration, interpersonal understanding, insight, mental acuity, and discipline.

As we've noted, in Chapter 9 on survey research, interviewing has already been discussed. In qualitative interviewing, however, unlike surveys where questionnaires are rigidly structured, the interviews are less structured or unstructured. Herbert and Riene Rubin (1995:43) make this distinction: "Qualitative interviewing design is flexible, iterative, and continuous, rather than prepared in advance and locked in stone." They further state:

> Design in qualitative interviewing is iterative. That means that each time you repeat the basic process of gathering information, analyzing it, winnowing it, and testing it, you come closer to a clear and convincing model of the phenomenon you are studying. . . .
>   The continuous nature of qualitative interviewing means that the questioning is redesigned throughout the project.
>
> (Rubin and Rubin 1995:46, 47)

A *qualitative interview* is an interaction between an interviewer and a respondent in which the interviewer has a general plan of inquiry but not a rigid set of questions that must be asked in particular words and in a particular order. It is essentially a conversation in which the interviewer establishes a general direction for the conversation and pursues specific topics raised by the respondent. The degree of direction supplied by the interviewer varies from a general set of questions or topics that the researcher wishes to cover in each interview to a very unstructured conversation guided by the interviewer, depending on the researcher and the topic under study. Ideally, the respondent does most of the talking.

Steinar Kvale (1996:3–5) offers two metaphors for interviewing: the interviewer is a "miner" or a "traveller." The first model assumes that the subject possesses specific information and that the interviewer's job is to dig it out. By contrast, in the second model, the interviewer

wanders through the landscape and enters into conversations with the people encountered. The traveler explores the many domains of the country, as unknown territory or with maps, roaming freely around the territory. . . . The interviewer wanders along with the local inhabitants, asks questions that lead the subjects to tell their own stories of their lived world.

Asking questions and noting answers is a natural process, and it seems simple enough to add it to your bag of tricks as a field researcher. Be a little cautious, however. Wording questions is a tricky business. All too often, the way we ask questions subtly biases the answers we get. Sometimes we put our respondent under pressure to look good. Sometimes we ask a question in a particular context such that the most relevant answers are not provided.

Suppose you want to find out why a group of students is rioting and pillaging on campus. You might be tempted to focus your questions on how students feel about the dean's recent ruling that requires students to always carry *The Basics of Social Research* with them on campus. (Makes sense to us.) Although you may collect a great deal of information about students' attitudes toward the infamous ruling, they may be rioting for some other reason. Perhaps most are simply joining in for the excitement. It would be better, therefore, to ask them what prompted them to take part in the events that are occurring. Thus, properly done, qualitative interviewing would enable you to find out.

Although you may set out to conduct interviews with a pretty clear idea of what you want to ask, one of the special strengths of qualitative interviewing is its flexibility. The answers evoked by your initial questions should shape your subsequent ones. It doesn't work merely to ask preestablished questions and record the answers. Instead, you need to ask a question, listen carefully to the answer, interpret its meaning for your general inquiry, frame another question either to dig into the earlier answer or to redirect the person's attention to an area more relevant to your inquiry. In short, you need to be able to listen, think, and talk almost at the same time.

The discussion of probes in Chapter 9 provides a useful guide to getting answers in more depth without biasing later answers. Learn the skills of being a good listener. Be more interested than interesting. Learn to say things like "How is that?" "In what ways?" "How do you mean that?" "What would be an example of that?" Learn to look and listen expectantly, and let the person you're interviewing fill in the silence.

At the same time, you can't afford to be a totally passive receiver in the interaction. You should go into your interviews with some general (or specific) questions you want answered and some topics you want addressed. At times you'll have to learn the skills of subtly directing the flow of conversation.

We can learn something in this regard from the martial arts. The aikido master never resists an opponent's blow but instead accepts it, joins with it, and then subtly redirects it in a more appropriate direction. Qualitative interviewing requires a similar type of skill. It's best not to try to halt your respondent's line of discussion. Instead, learn to take what he or she has just said and branch that comment back in the direction appropriate to your purposes. Most people love to talk to anyone who's really interested. Stopping their line of conversation tells them you aren't interested; asking them to elaborate in a particular direction tells them you are. Consider this hypothetical example in which you're interested in why university students chose their majors.

You: What are you majoring in?
Resp: Engineering.
You: I see. How did you come to choose engineering?
Resp: I have an uncle who was voted the best engineer in Alberta in 1981.
You: Gee, that's great.
Resp: Yeah. He was the engineer in charge of developing the new civic centre in Edmonton. It was written up in most of the engineering journals.
You: I see. Did you talk to him about your becoming an engineer?
Resp: Yeah. He said that he got into engineering by accident. He needed a job when he graduated from high school, so he went to work as a labourer on a construction job. He spent eight years

working his way up from the bottom, until he decided to go to university and come back nearer the top.
You: So is your main interest civil engineering, like your uncle, or are you more interested in some other branch of engineering?
Resp: Actually, I'm leaning more toward electrical engineering, computers, in particular. I started messing around with computers when I was in high school, and my long-term plan is. . . .

Notice how the interview first begins to wander off into a story about the respondent's uncle. The first attempt to focus things back on the student's own choice of major failed—"Did you talk to your uncle....?" The second attempt, the query about the student's "main interest," succeeded. Now the student is providing the kind of information you're looking for. It's important for you to develop the ability to "control" conversations in this fashion.

Herbert and Riene Rubin offer several ways to control a "guided conversation," such as the following:

> If you can limit the number of main topics, it is easier to maintain a conversational flow from one topic to another. Transitions should be smooth and logical. "We have been talking about mothers, now let's talk about fathers," sounds abrupt. A smoother transition might be, "You mentioned your mother did not care how you performed in school—was your father more involved?" The more abrupt the transition, the more it sounds like the interviewer has an agenda that he or she wants to get through, rather than wanting to hear what the interviewee has to say.
>
> (1995:123)

Because qualitative interviewing is so much like normal conversation, you must keep reminding yourself that you are not having a normal conversation. In normal conversations, each of us wants to come across as an interesting, worthwhile person. If you watch yourself the next time you chat with someone you don't know too well, you'll probably find that much of your attention is spent on thinking up interesting things to say—contributions to the conversation that will make a good impression. Often, we don't really hear each other, because we're too busy thinking of what we'll say next. As an interviewer, the desire to appear interesting is counterproductive. The interviewer needs to make the other person seem interesting, by being interested. This can often be accomplished by listening more than talking. (Do this in ordinary conversations, and people will actually regard you as a great conversationalist.)

John and Lyn Lofland (1995:56–57) suggest that investigators adopt the role of the "socially acceptable incompetent" when interviewing. That is, offer yourself as someone who does not understand the situation you find yourself in, someone who must be helped to grasp even the most basic and obvious aspects of that situation. As Lofland and Lofland (1995:56) state:

> A naturalistic investigator, almost by definition, is one who does not understand. She or he is "ignorant" and needs to be "taught." This role of watcher and asker of questions is the quintessential *student* role.

You may recall that we stressed the need to review your notes every night when conducting field research—making sense out of what you've observed, getting a clearer feel for the situation you're studying, and finding out what you should pay more attention to in further observations. In this same fashion, you need to review your notes on interviews, or listen to the interviews if you taped them, recording especially effective questions and detecting all those questions you should have asked but didn't. Start asking such questions the next time you interview. In addition, pay attention to the wording you used when asking questions, your responses to what was said, remarks that you let slip by without further probing, statements where you assumed meaning when you should have asked the person what he or she intended to convey by the remark, and times when you let the interview get away from you. Think about ways you might more effectively deal with such issues in your future interviews.

Steinar Kvale (1996:88) details seven stages in a complete interviewing process:

1. *Thematizing:* clarifying the purpose of the interviews and the concepts to be explored.
2. *Designing:* laying out the process through which you'll accomplish your purpose, including a consideration of the ethical dimension.
3. *Interviewing:* doing the actual interviews.
4. *Transcribing:* creating a written text of the interviews.
5. *Analyzing:* determining the meaning of gathered materials in relation to the purpose of the study.
6. *Verifying:* checking the reliability and validity of the materials.
7. *Reporting:* telling others what you've learned.

Interviewing, like many things, improves with practice. Fortunately, it's something you can practice any time you want. Practice on your friends.

In-Depth Interview Studies

When speaking of qualitative interviews, researchers will variously refer to them as in-depth interviews, depth interviews, open-ended interviews, unstructured interviews, semi-structured interviews, and even structured "conversations," among other terms. We use the term *in-depth interview study* here to signify the method of using the qualitative interview as the primary means by which the researcher gathers data for his or her study.

In the feminist literature, methodology that allows the researcher to listen to women's voices is prominent. The many forms of qualitative interviewing provide methods that allow such voices to be heard. In a study concerning experiences of mature women students in the United Kingdom, Janet Parr conducted in-depth interviews with 49 mature women students about the barriers they faced when returning to education. Here's what she had to say about why she chose this methodology:

I was looking more for explanations and processes rather than 'numbers of women who....' I realized over the months that if my real interest was in explanations and perceptions, then it was greater depth rather than breadth which was required in the research data. One of the ways of achieving this depth in terms of explanations and perceptions was by listening to, and hearing, what the women themselves had to say. During this period, I was also reading more of the literature on feminist methodology, where the emphasis is on understanding the social and cultural context of events as well as the events themselves.

(Parr 1998:89)

She then adopted a grounded theory approach to the analysis of her data (discussed in Chapter 14).

In illustrating interview studies that include some ethnographic component, Reinharz (1992:281) discusses Kaufman's study concerning "newly orthodox Jewish women." Kaufman described how she used "loosely structured interviews"—what she terms "structured conversations"—in order to learn from the women what issues they viewed as significant in their lives. She wanted to gain an understanding of their theology and their family and community relationships. She also spent weeks in each community interacting with its members and engaging in a variety of familial and social activities. She wanted to be able to put in context the experiences that the women she was interviewing were describing to her. Nonetheless, as she said, "Although this is neither an ethnographic nor participant observation study, I borrowed many of the techniques both kinds of researchers use." Thus, as Reinharz (1992:281) states, "Ethnographic studies frequently include interviewing components, and interview studies frequently include ethnographic components."

While ethnographic or participant observation studies typically involve a small number of people, several times as many could be included in an in-depth interview study for the same or even lesser investment of time. One trade-off of interview studies versus field observation is that interviews impose a somewhat artificial setting of questions and answers. Nonetheless, the semi-structured to unstructured form, and the length of time invested in each interview, often allows issues and perceptions to emerge that would not emerge in more structured, briefer interviews used for surveys. The in-depth interview format, however, requires a great deal of cooperation from the subjects of study. Each interview is time consuming and often hard to obtain. Thus, small, nonprobability samples are generally used, such as purposive or snowball samples. A potential drawback of this is that such studies may produce idiosyncratic findings. The standardization of questions, the use of probability samples, and the larger sample sizes used in survey interviews make generalizations much more feasible. The in-depth interview, however, provides researchers with the flexibility to pursue issues they may not have anticipated. The exciting potential of confronting serious challenges to your own assumptions when conducting an in-depth interview study must be weighed against the representativeness that large-scale surveys offer.

Let's turn to another qualitative interviewing technique, one in which a number of individuals are interviewed at the same time.

Focus Groups

Focus groups are often viewed as special forms of interviews because the researcher discusses an issue with a small group of people rather than a single individual. According to David Morgan (1997:2), "The hallmark of focus groups is their explicit use of group interaction to produce data and insights that would be less accessible without the interaction found in a group." The type of data that results is typically qualitative in nature. Focus groups are a good tool for exploratory research and social scientists often use them to help them interpret results obtained from quantitative analysis. I (Benaquisto) was speaking to a friend who does a great deal of survey research in Russia but also conducts numerous focus groups. I asked her what role focus groups play in her studies. She told me that she uses them to help her flesh out the meaning of unexpected and sometimes seemingly paradoxical findings she gets when she analyzes her survey data. The deeper meaning behind the answers given on the surveys, and insights into potential interpretations of unforeseen relationships revealed in the data analysis, may be gained in group interviews. These sessions can be very informative, especially when we are conducting studies in cultures different from our own.

This type of qualitative interviewing that brings people together in one place for discussion and observation is particularly popular in marketing research. Let's suppose that you've invented a new computer that not only does word processing, spreadsheets, data analysis, and the like, but also contains a fax machine, AM/FM/TV tuner, CD player, dual-cassette unit, microwave oven, denture cleaner, and coffee-maker. To highlight its computing and coffee-making features, you're thinking of calling it *The Compulator.* You figure the new computer will sell for about $28,000, and you want to know whether people are likely to buy it. Your prospects might be well served by focus groups.

In a focus group, typically six to 10 people are brought together in a room to engage in a discussion, guided by a *moderator*, of some topic, in this case, the acceptability and saleability of *The Compulator.* The subjects are selected on the basis of relevance to the topic under study. Given the likely cost of *The Compulator,* your focus group participants would probably be limited to upper-income groups, for example. Other, similar considerations might figure into the selection. Focus group participants are not likely to be chosen through rigorous, probability sampling methods. This means that participants do not statistically represent any meaningful population. However, the purpose of the study is to explore rather than to describe or explain in any definitive sense. Nonetheless, typically, more than one focus group is convened in a given study, because there is a serious danger that a single group of six to 10 people would be too atypical to offer any generalizable insights.

In a similar vein, focus groups are often used to gauge viewer response to movies (testing two dif-ferent endings, for example), new television shows, and other forms of media entertainment (for example, how might people respond to a talking dog as a show's host?). They are also used by the news media near election time to gain a sense of voters' preferences for political parties and candidates, especially the undecided voters, and to gather their views on the issues. Political actors and organizations use focus groups to test public response to issues, potential policy positions, and particular political figures (not unlike product marketing).

Using Focus Groups in Social Scientific Research

Focus group interviews have been a widely used method in market research for quite some time. It is more recently, however, that this method has gained wider usage in social scientific research. Sometimes called group interviewing, the technique gained in popularity in the 1980s. As an example of a precursor to the current focus group method, the following illustration shows how the techniques of market research were blended into an experimental design to study something of social scientific importance.

Gamson, Fireman, and Rytina (1982) conducted a social psychology experiment that was an extension of Milgram's research on obedience to authority. It was an experiment that made use of group discussion interviews in order to study *Encounters with Unjust Authority* (the book's title). In the guise of conducting marketing research, they advertised for research participants in the newspaper. (It should be noted that in the preliminary telephone screening, the participants were asked if they were willing to participate in a number of different kinds of research, including "research in which you were misled about the purpose until afterward" (p. 42).) Participants were assembled into different experimental groups. They were read a summary of a legal case said to be before the courts. A coordinator (moderator) was present to give instructions and to videotape (with the knowledge of the participants) the group's responses to a series of questions concerning the case, which turned on issues of "standards communities have about what kinds of behavior may be morally wrong" (p. 43). But the case was designed so that nearly all subjects' true opinions would be highly unfavourable to the (fictive) oil company that subjects had been led to believe was paying for the research. The goal was to see how the subjects would react when the coordinator requested, and ultimately insisted, that the subjects give false opinions (favourable to the sponsoring oil company) for the videotape being made for a potential legal proceeding. Thus the groups of subjects were confronted with an unjust exercise of authority and the dilemma of complying or resisting.

The study provides insights into the conditions under which rebellion against unjust authority occurs, that is, what it takes to rebel. As they conclude "Much of what has been written on obedience to authority emphasizes the willingness of people to comply, even when such compliance involves serious injury to others. ...Perhaps the most hopeful message in our account is the frequency with which ordinary people...were able to join together in actively resisting an unjust authority...." (p. 155).

Using the guise of a marketing research setting, Gamson, Fireman, and Rytina conducted a social scientific experiment to investigate whether and how groups of individuals might rebel against demands of unjust authority. The group interview context allowed them to explore how people negotiate agreement and disagreement—shared meaning and understanding—and potential joint action. Although the groups they used in the experiment were not called focus groups at the time, their group discussion format was clearly an early form of this method of research.

In a recent example, Harlton, Keating, and Fast (1998) used focus groups to determine perspectives on eldercare for the purposes of policymaking and practice. The idea of "partnership" in the care of the elderly has become prominent in Canadian heath policy. It stems from the belief that informal care is better and less expensive than formal care. The researchers wanted to know if those involved in eldercare shared this view. They identified seven key stakeholders in eldercare: (1) older adults, (2) family members, (3) neighbours and friends, (4) volunteers, (5) direct service providers, (6) local and provincial policymakers and (7) federal policymakers. The researchers sought to find out the stakeholders' views on what defined eldercare, the tasks and services that comprise it, and who they thought should be responsible for supplying these services. They were also concerned with their views on the criteria that should be used to determine who requires the services.

In order to gather such perspectives, they used the method of focus group interviews. They conducted a focus group with members of each of the seven stakeholders using purposive sampling to select participants. One of the bases for selection was experience with eldercare. They noted that, "Although members of each group needed to be homogeneous in their structural relationship to eldercare, attempts were made to ensure sufficient variation among participants to allow for contrasting opinions" (1998:283). Yet due to time and funding constraints, and the desire to interview all stakeholder groups, they were only able to hold one focus group per stakeholder category, though they would have preferred to conduct multiple focus groups per category "to allow for saturation of responses."

Given their focus on stakeholder perspectives, the researchers felt the focus group method was particularly suited to this study because it facilitates the gathering of "in-depth, qualitative data about individuals' definitions of problems, opinions and feelings, and meanings associated with various phenomenon" (p. 283). The focus group interviews were recorded. Following each session, the researchers met with each other to discuss themes that emerged and other issues that arose from the focus group interviews. They taped these meetings as well.

Using techniques of analysis for developing grounded theory, the researchers were able to identify the main criteria for what constitutes eldercare. The idea of elder independence and choice concerning their care was stressed across groups. A wide range of tasks and services were identified as supporting such independence, yet there were key differences over what these services should entail, some of which stemmed from the group members relationship to the care and to the elder recipient of care. As Harlton et al. (1998:287) state, "Perhaps the most important finding from this study on stakeholder perspectives is that those with most influence on public policy have a very different interpretation of the new policy paradigm than those whose lives will be most affected by eldercare policy."

Focus groups are also a valuable means of testing questions to be used in surveys. Statistics Canada, for example, used focus groups as part of their research on redesigning their short form census questionnaire for 2001. In particular, they were concerned with respondents' reactions to alternative questions on aboriginal identity and marital status and the data quality gained from these questions. "Ten focus groups (a total of 81 persons) and 10 interviews (individual or in groups of two persons) were conducted in Ottawa, Montréal, Toronto, Winnipeg, and Saskatoon to get feedback about respondents' opinion and reactions." (Source: Statistics Canada's Internet site, http://www.statcan.ca/english/IPS/Data/92F009 6XIE.htm, May 4, 2001.)

Topics Appropriate to Focus Group Interviews

As we've seen from the above examples, there are several reasons why a researcher may choose focus groups over individual interviews. With multiple people presenting their views, what others have to say often stimulates qualifications and modifications of viewpoints—points that may not be readily elicited in a one-on-one interview. In many situations, the interviewees are likely to talk more candidly to each other. When groups are created on the basis of similar characteristics (such as age, education, occupation) or shared experiences (such as physical attacks by family members or strangers, illness or disease, loss of employment), the discussants may have more access to what each other is thinking and thus spark a more realistic presentation of views. In the group interview setting, subjects may challenge each other's statements. This added element may provide a different

vantage point on people's perspective. On a practical level, focus groups may be appropriate when there are a large number of people to interview but only a short period of time to do so.

The focus group setting also allows the researcher to examine how people make sense of issues in a collective manner. The process of expressing views in the context of others, potentially meeting challenges, and having ideas or positions sparked or elicited by what others around them say, makes the focus group context somewhat more reflective of how opinions and perspectives are articulated and molded in day-to-day life. Additionally, focus groups are a useful technique when the topic of study concerns psychological issues or deeply embedded attitudes—topics not readily accessed with mere observation. Thus, the dynamism of the group forum often brings to light issues that an individual interviewer or participant observer may be unable to access.

Conducting Focus Groups

There are a number of practical considerations to keep in mind when conducting focus group interviews. As we noted, the group size varies but is typically less than a dozen people. The number of people in a group depends on the topic under study and the success of recruiting people who will show up at the scheduled time. If the topic is complex and requires coverage of a large number of issues, a smaller size group is advised. A smaller group is also advisable when an issue is emotionally charged or controversial and thus likely to evoke much discussion.

The number of focus groups varies considerably from one study to another. The best guide is a theoretical one; that is, continue conducting focus groups until the number of new issues arising has diminished to a point where little new information is gathered. In essence, when the moderator is able to anticipate with some degree of accuracy the issues and viewpoints that those in the next group will express—*saturation of responses*—then it is likely that a sufficient number of groups have been conducted. Of course, issues of time and expense play a role in the number of groups conducted, as does the topic of study and the number of factors of concern to the researchers. As a rule of thumb, a range of 10 to 15 groups is rather common in focus group studies. However, if you expect a wide variety of perspectives on a topic, then a larger number of groups would be necessary. For example, if you anticipate that views on your study topic are likely to vary with age, ethnicity, gender, occupation, and other socio-demographic factors, you would likely stratify your groups in terms of such variables (recall our discussion of stratified samples in Chapter 7). When examining a large number of factors, a larger number of focus groups would be needed. Such decisions will also affect decisions about who is selected to participate in the groups. Selection of participants will depend on the issue under study and characteristics the researcher anticipates may contribute to variation in views on the topic. Researchers typically select participants for whom the topic is relevant.

A focus group is often lead by a trained moderator who helps to facilitate the discussion. The degree of guidance provided by the moderator varies. Some discussions are relatively unguided, while others may have a set of open-ended questions or issues that the researcher desires to have covered over the course of the session. Typically, the goal is to ensure that everyone has an opportunity to speak. The role of the moderator in many focus groups is to both keep the discussion on track and to ensure that no one person dominates the conversation, while interfering as little as possible.

If there are a specified set of questions that the researchers desire to have answered, then the moderator will play a larger role, making sure that each line of questioning is covered in the session. Keep in mind, however, that too much interference may stifle a line of conversation that could prove worthwhile. Allowing the participants some freedom to pursue topics may reveal issues of importance. The setting of the focus group interview is typically one of informality. The participants usually address remarks to each other. As we've noted, in this context, issues and arguments often arise that the researcher in a one-on-one interview would not have thought to address. Practice in guiding group discussions helps in this regard.

If you plan to moderate a focus group yourself, preparation of a guide is advised. You need to introduce the group to the topic and goals of the study. You also need to tell the subjects the basic guidelines for discussion: what to expect in the focus group session and the procedures you will follow. Your introductory remarks should provide you with the opportunity to develop a rapport with the subjects. Allowing the subjects to get to know each other a bit is also useful at the start of the session. For example, you might have them introduce themselves and give a brief statement about who they are in terms of occupation and interests. If a list of questions is to be used to prompt a series of discussions covering certain topics, these should be written down so you can follow them. As in individual interviews, preparing a set of probes in advance may be useful should probes be necessary to keep the conversation moving.

If possible, as in individual interviews, taping the focus group interview is best. When there are several people talking over a period of one to two hours, it's very difficult to recall who said what and in which order. People often talk quickly, interrupt each other, and talk over each other. Who speaks more and whose statements may have the greatest impact on others is something the researcher may want to address. Also, attending to how people express themselves may be as important as the exact words they use. Often the goal of focus group interviews is to examine the dynamic process of people collectively constructing meaning. Taping and transcribing the sessions makes this task much more feasible. However, as one colleague recently noted when talking about her first experiences with focus group interviews, taping and transcribing the sessions are not foolproof. Distinguishing voices on a tape can be difficult, especially if someone who was not present in the focus group transcribes the tape. After reviewing the transcript of their initial focus group, she and her colleague realized that it would be necessary to take notes in each focus group session as well as taping it. In their subsequent groups, they noted each person as he or she spoke and the first few words that were said so the transcripts could be corrected for accuracy.

Advantages and Disadvantages of Focus Groups

Richard Krueger (1988:47) points to five advantages of focus groups:

1. The technique is a socially oriented research method capturing real-life data in a social environment;
2. It has flexibility;
3. It has high face validity;
4. It has speedy results; and
5. It is low in cost.

In addition to these advantages, group dynamics that occur in focus groups frequently bring out aspects of the topic that would not have been anticipated by the researcher and would not have emerged from interviews with individuals. In a side conversation, for example, a couple of the participants might start joking about the risk of leaving out one letter from a product's name. This realization might save the manufacturer from great embarrassment later on. The same type of conversation might lead to insights into question wording, policy issues, attitudes, opinions, social problem solutions, or any number of issues of interest to researchers.

Krueger (1988:44–45) also notes some disadvantages of the focus group method:

1. Focus groups afford the researcher less control than individual interviews;
2. Data are difficult to analyze;
3. Moderators require special skills;
4. Difference between groups can be troublesome;
5. Groups are difficult to assemble; and
6. The discussion must be conducted in a conducive environment.

Nonetheless, focus group research is a qualitative in-depth interviewing method that allows the researcher to set in motion a free flow of conversation in response to a given question or topic, where issues can emerge and evolve through the dynamics of group interaction. The flexibility of the format also allows the researcher to seek guided responses when such are desired. The focus group interview not only gives researchers the chance to hear people's attitudes, opinions, insights, and so forth, but also provides them with the opportunity to observe the interactions among the group participants to see how such ideas and issues emerge and unfold. In addition, as David Morgan (1993) suggests, focus groups are an excellent device for generating questionnaire items for a subsequent survey.

We'll now turn to another variant of qualitative interviewing, one that focuses on the past by gathering data through recollections or memory. This method can be used in the study of a single individual or a sample of individuals.

Oral History

Oral history is a form of historical research that uses depth interviewing to gather data. Instead of looking in the archives, the researcher delves into the minds and memories of individuals—learning about their lives, culture, and community. Like in-depth interviewing, it seeks to gather detailed information on a given topic or about a given individual, however, the focus is historical; it concerns the past.

Li (1985:68) summarizes the technique as follows:

> The basic approach of oral history as a research method is straightforward. A researcher speaks to respondents who previously have been exposed to a set of experiences, and asks them to describe the experiences and their feelings about those experiences as they recall them. The information being sought may pertain to an event, a place, a tradition, or a biography. For example, the history of a community, memories of a war, and life stories of individuals are among the many suitable projects of oral history. The objective is to record the recollections of the respondents, which later can be transcribed to written documents. Frequently, the respondents are ordinary people whose verbal accounts represent a folk version of events, as

opposed to an official version contained in institutional records.

In the third edition of his book, *The Voice of the Past: Oral History*, Paul Thompson (2000:xi) quotes the *New Shorter Oxford English Dictionary* definition of oral history as "tape-recorded historical information drawn from the speaker's personal knowledge; the use or interpretation of this as an academic subject." Thompson notes that historians have made use of oral history as a primary data-gathering technique for decades. Anthropologists have used oral history in this way as well. Nonetheless, the use of oral history has gained momentum recently in the social sciences. One reason is the growing interest in incorporating the voice of the people into our understanding of past events, particularly the voices of underprivileged members of society.

Orals histories can provide a counter to writings derived from official documents and other works written from the perspective of white, male, dominant members of society. Thompson (2000:vi) believes that

> the richest possibilities for oral history lie within the development of a more socially conscious and democratic history. Of course, a telling case could equally be made, from a conservative position, for the use of oral history in preserving the full richness and value of tradition The merit of oral history is not that it entails this or that political stance, but that it leads historians to an awareness that their activity is inevitably pursued within a social context and with political implications.

This method has, therefore, become prominent among feminist researchers as a means of allowing women's voices to be heard. It is also advocated as a valuable technique for those studying minority racial and ethnic groups, and it is an advantageous technique in the study of nonliterate populations. Anthropologists, for example, have long employed this method to document societies with limited to no written histories. None of this, of course, precludes the use of oral history in the study of the privileged elite.

Researchers who employ the oral history method have used a variety of labels to refer to this technique for gathering data. This creates the potential for confusion. Reinharz found that among feminist researchers "oral history" was used interchangeably with terms such as "case studies, in-depth life history interviews, biographical interviews, life histories, and personal narratives" (1992: 129).

While some researchers are trying to convey slight differences with the use of these varied terms, there is clearly overlap and commonalities among these methods. For example, life histories focus on the memories and experiences of a particular, typically elderly, individual's life. Other materials supplement the retrospective information gathered orally. Oral histories may also focus on the lives of individual people, but the method signifies the potential for gathering information that goes beyond their particular life stories.

In oral histories, researchers use in-depth interviews to ask people about past events and generate information about an individual's personal life, the life of someone else, or any number of topics. In addition to gathering biographical information about a person, social patterns can be abstracted from the stories gathered from a sample of people. Subjects are usually asked to focus on specific events or periods of time such as what it was like living through World War II or being a minority female in the 1960s. For example, Li mentions the study by Marlatt (1975) of a Japanese–Canadian fishing town. Martlatt used oral histories to describe the process and impact of urban development from the perspective of this racial minority group living near Vancouver.

The Use of Oral History: Some Illustrations and Methodological Considerations

Studs Terkel's account of life during the Great Depression of the 1930s (*Hard Times*, 1970) is a classic illustration of the use of oral history. He interviewed countless people to gain their view of what life entailed during that period. He wrote about the past from the perspective of the people who lived it.

More recently, Peter S. Li collected detailed life histories of 55 elderly Chinese in Saskatchewan. Writing in 1985, he lamented that "social scientists in general have not paid sufficient attention to oral history as a research method" (p. 67). The goal of his paper was to illustrate the value and use of this method. He detailed how he applied the oral history method to the study of Chinese–Canadians and addressed issues of the validity, reliability, and interpretation of the data he collected.

Among the advantages of the oral history method in studying social history, Li notes its potential for helping to fill in the gaps in our knowledge gained from official documents and statistical overviews. For instance, the census indicates a major increase in occupations related to the restaurant business among Chinese–Canadians from the late 19th century to the 1930s, but these numbers tell us little about why this increase occurred and its effects. Obtaining oral histories, Li was able to gain insights into racism's impact on Chinese–Canadians' economic opportunities and how they coped with and understood the racial conflict they experienced.

Li (1985:69) directly addresses "two major methodological issues" of concern when using the oral history method. Are the respondents' stories "reliable or truthful?" Is developing a "valid framework for organizing the case histories" possible and if so, how might the researcher assess the framework's validity? Noting that it's hard to assess the reliability and validity of oral history, he offers several ways to consider these issues. For instance, because selective memory concerning past events and experiences is inevitable on the part of the informant, he suggests the researcher engage the inevitable. Narrowing the focus of the interview to certain aspects of the informant's past can be helpful in this regard. In his study, for example, they focused on job histories. Helping people with their recollections can also be accomplished by a series of probes and specific questions on a particular topic.

Another issue he addresses is that of subjectivity. The respondent's subjectivity "does not necessarily reduce the reliability of their stories, but rather, it is a part of oral history that enriches it" (1985:71). In examining reliability in the context of oral history, the concept of truth concerns the relationship between the story and what happened in reality. To determine what happened, one often uses other information sources like official reports, records, and news stories. But, there are problems with "accuracy" of information in such sources as well. To illustrate this, Li points to a number of subjective distortions contained in official reports on Chinese immigration.

How, then, do researchers make sense of inconsistencies between the subjects' stories and official reports? Looking more closely at interpretation in oral history, Li notes that there are a variety of ways to interpret a story's reliability or unreliability by taking into account the different levels of reality when interpreting the data—in short, he is referring to the aspect of the information researchers focus on and the interpretations or conclusions they draw from that information.

When researchers suspect incorrect recall of facts due to inconsistencies between what the informants tell them and information reported in official documents, this might spark a deeper investigation. In the case of the Chinese–Canadian study, upon further investigation the researchers determined that the official records were incorrect, not the informants. The official documents left out cases that were not part of the bureaucratic rules. For example, when those interviewed claimed entrance into Canada between 1923 and 1947, this contradicted the Chinese Immigration Act of 1923, which excluded Chinese immigrants during this period. For instance, one informant who reported immigrating in 1936 told how "his father, who was in Canada at the time, bought him a birth certificate with which he could claim to be native-born in Canada" (1985:72). Such stories led them to research practices of illegal immigration and other means by which some Chinese came to Canada to stay during a period in which the official documents indicated they could not, thus verifying the practices through other informants.

Another issue Li raised that speaks to issues of reliability and validity in the use of the oral history method concerns the relationship between what informants believe to be true and what is true in reality. There are times when the distinction is not relevant to the interpretation of the data. For example, a number of the informants were asked to compare the situation of Chinese–Canadians pre and post World War II. A large number of them felt that things had greatly improved and discrimination had decreased considerably after the war. In this case, whether or not discrimination had decreased considerably is not the point. What's important is their belief. As Li stated (1985:73), "As long as the participants believed that there was no discrimination, their behavior would reflect this belief." Li (1985:73) further states:

> From the point of view of a researcher, the key question is not so much to find out whether the respondent is stating the facts as they took place, but rather, to sort out the different levels of perception and interpretation which are present in oral history. From the point of view of an interviewer, the task is to assist the respondent to reconstruct the past in the way the respondent sees it.

The issues of reliability and validity in oral history are not always straightforward. Some concerns regarding the information gathered using this method are relevant only in relation to the questions and issues being addressed and the interpretation being offered.

The oral history method is often combined with other modes of gathering data. Kwok Chan studied aging and self-identify among elderly Chinese women in Canada by administering a close-ended survey and conducting intensive, unstructured interviews with 26 elderly women. The goal of the interviews were "to collect their personal oral histories, with a focus on their histories of work, relationships with spouse, children, grandchildren, and sons- and daughters-in law, and feelings about living in Chinatown" (1983:38). He also conducted unstructured interviews with community workers from social agencies in Chinatown. In this way, Chan was able to gather a variety of data to probe the social world of elderly Chinese women, gathering evidence that helped to debunk both positive and negative myths concerning elderly ethnic minorities in general and elderly Chinese in particular. The oral history component of his study, which focused "on the women's own definition of the situation," enabled him to gain insights into

how these women managed their identifies and their efforts at maintaining a feeling of self worth.

Turner, Kaara, and Brownhill (1997) used oral histories in conjunction with secondary materials in their study concerning the process of "gendered class struggle." They examined this process by focusing on two groups of landless women in Kenya between 1985 and 1996 who struggled to gain control over their labour in agricultural production. Use of the oral history method helped the researchers to gain insights into these women's strategies in the context of the situation that they faced. Paying particular attention to relationships, the researchers' goals were "to examine the historical roots of the changing relationships represented in the conflict in question" and to gain insights into "the self-expression of participants with respect to their experiences, conceptions and demands" (214–15). Oral histories were central to their study because they approached their research from the perspective of "standpoint theories which 'show how to move from including others' lives and thoughts in research and scholarly projects to starting from their lives to ask research questions' (Harding, 1991)" (1997:215).

The researchers were able to describe how the exploited women farmers fought against agriculture for export. They told how the women gained control over their own labour power by resisting the exploitation and control of their often violent husbands, by going against state policies, and by resisting the demands of private firms (capital) to incorporate them into global markets. The women's struggles have helped to expand sustenance agriculture, which is a more sound and sustainable strategy for them.

Greater accessibility of oral history sources has contributed to the wider use of this method in recent years. The oral history technique can be expensive and time consuming when the researcher seeks to investigate issues that require interviews with people who live in diverse and far away places. A number of oral history archives have been available in countries all over the world for quite some time, yet gaining access to the archived data could be costly due to the expense of travelling to another place to make use of the sources. The Internet, however, has now placed a wide range of oral history archives at the researcher's fingertips. The following are examples of some well designed Web sites that contain transcribed interviews, audio files, or both.

Ontario Black History Society Archives: http://collections.ic.gc.ca/obho/

Holocaust Survivor Oral Histories: http://holocaust.umd.umich.edu/

Rutgers Oral History Archives of World War II: http://fas-history.rutgers.edu/oralhistory/orlhorn.htm

USM Oral History Civil Rights Documentation Project: http://www-dept.usm.edu/~mcrohb/

Suffragists Oral History Project: http://www.lib. berkeley.edu/BANC/ROHO/ohonline/suffragists.html

Strengths and Weaknesses of Oral History

The strengths and weaknesses of the oral history method are similar to those of qualitative interviews more generally. The technique is flexible and issues may be pursued in-depth, reinforcing the validity of the information obtained. Reliability, however, is relatively weak and difficult to determine. Some argue that relying on people's memories or stories means that the researcher is not necessarily gaining facts. Others argue that it is the memories and perspectives of those who lived the history that are important to understand, and it is this that makes the method a valuable one. As we noted above, the issue of reliability in oral history is complex. Problems of reliability often depend on the issue under study and the interpretation being offered.

Generalizability is often a problem when using the oral history method because the individuals interviewed are seldom selected on the basis of probability sampling. For some researchers using this technique, generalizability is not at issue—they are documenting a single individual's life story.

Finally, qualitative interviewing is interactive, and like all forms of interactive research, the researcher has the potential to affect the outcome of the data gathered. This affect is readily apparent in the context of all interviewing methods.

Although in-depth interviewing allows the voice of the individual to be heard, what is heard and how it is heard may be coloured by the person to whom the individual is speaking.

Main Points

- A qualitative interview is an interaction between an interviewer and a respondent. The researcher typically has a general plan of inquiry but not a set of questions that must be rigidly followed. Respondents' answers to initial questions shape a researcher's subsequent questions.
- Qualitative interviews allow the researcher to pursue issues in depth and give respondents more freedom to direct the flow of conversation.
- Effective interviewing involves skills of active listening and the ability to direct conversations unobtrusively.
- Qualitative interviews are often used in combination with other research methods, such as field research; however, they may also be used as the primary means of gathering data.
- The flexibility of in-depth interviews allows respondents to raise novel issues and provides the latitude for researchers to follow these up. Pursuing issues in greater depth reinforces the validity of the information obtained. However, practical considerations usually limit in-depth interview studies to small, nonprobability samples, making generalizations problematic.
- To create a focus group, researchers bring subjects together for an interview and observe their interactions as they explore a specific topic.
- Focus group interviews stimulate viewpoints from respondents that may not be readily elicited in an individual interview. They also allow researchers to examine how people make sense of issues in a collective manner.
- A focus group is lead by a moderator who helps to facilitate discussion and ensure that no person dominates the conversation, while interfering as little as possible.
- The best guide to the number of groups to conduct is theoretical, that is, when the moderator

is able to anticipate with some accuracy the issues that will be expressed in the next group, enough groups have likely been conducted.

- It is best to both tape focus group interviews and take notes during each session.
- Oral history is a method that uses in-depth interviews as a means of gathering data about the past from individuals' recollections, typically focusing on specific events or periods of time.
- Oral histories enable researchers to incorporate the voice of the people into the understanding of past events, particularly those of women, members of ethnic minorities, and other under-privileged members of society.
- The use of oral histories allows the researcher to examine issues in-depth, which makes the method strong on validity. The issue of relia-bility in oral history is complex and often depends on the topic under study and the inter-pretations of data being offered.

Review Questions and Exercises

1. Conduct a taped, in-depth interview with a friend concerning his or her future occupa-tional aspirations. Transcribe the taped inter-view. Evaluate your interview technique and the questions you asked in terms of the guide-lines for question wording discussed in Chapter 9 and the guidelines for qualitative inter-viewing discussed in this chapter.
2. Let's assume you've been asked to do research to determine the acceptability of a new, hand-held computer. Plan a focus-group session that might yield useful information for this purpose.
3. Use the Web to search for several oral history archives. Design a research question that you could examine using a number of the archived interviews that you have located.

Continuity Project

Conduct an interview with an elderly female rela-tive or neighbour. Obtain detailed information about her life experiences, focusing on gender equality/inequality. Immediately following the interview, review your notes or listen to the tape, keeping in mind the guidelines for qualitative inter-viewing. Record particularly effective questions and note places where you should have asked questions but didn't.

Additional Readings

Kvale, Steinar. *InterViews: An Introduction to Qual-itative Research Interviewing.* Thousand Oaks, CA: Sage, 1996. An in-depth presentation on in-depth interviewing. Besides presenting tech-niques, Kvale places interviewing in the con-text of postmodernism and other philosophical systems.

Peter S. Li. "The Use of Oral History in Studying Elderly Chinese–Canadians." *Canadian Ethnic Studies*, 17: 67–77, 1985. This short article does a nice job of summarizing the method of oral history and topics appropriate for study using this method. It's easy to read and makes many good methodological points that are illustrated by examples drawn from his study of elderly Chinese–Canadians.

Morgan, David L. *Focus Groups as Qualitative Research* (2nd edition). Thousand Oaks, CA: Sage Publications, 1997. A clearly written and concise 80 page guide to focus groups.

Morgan, David L., ed. *Successful Focus Groups: Advancing the State of the Art.* Newbury Park, CA: Sage, 1993. This collection of articles on the uses of focus groups points to many aspects not normally considered.

Thompson, Paul. *The Voice of the Past: Oral History.* 3rd Ed. Oxford: Oxford University Press, 2000. Written from the perspective of an historian, this book covers all aspects of the method of oral history.

*Info*Trac: You can find further relevant readings on the World Wide Web at

http://sociology.wadsworth.com

Chapter 13

Evaluation Research

Now you're going to see one of the most rapidly growing uses of social research: the evaluation of social interventions. You'll come away from this chapter able to judge whether social programs have succeeded or failed.

In this chapter . . .

Introduction

You may not be familiar with *Twende na Wakati* ("Let's Go with the Times"), but it's the most popular radio show in Tanzania. It's a soap opera. The main character, Mkwaju, is a truck driver with some pretty traditional ideas about gender roles and sex. By contrast, Fundi Mitindo, a tailor, and his wife, Mama Waridi, have more modern ideas regarding the roles of men and women, particularly on issues of overpopulation and family planning.

Twende na Wakati was the creation of Population Communications International (PCI) and other organizations working in conjunction with the Tanzanian government in response to two problems facing that country today: (1) a population growth rate over twice that of the rest of the world and (2) an AIDS epidemic particularly heavy along the international truck route, where more than a fourth of the truck drivers and over half the commercial sex workers were found to be HIV positive in 1991. The prevalence of contraceptive use was 11 percent (Rogers et al. 1996:5–6).

The purpose of the soap opera was to bring about a change in knowledge, attitudes, and prac-

tices (KAP) relating to contraception and family planning. Rather than instituting a conventional educational campaign, PCI felt it would be more effective to illustrate the message through entertainment.

Between 1993 and 1995, 108 episodes of *Twende na Wakati* were aired, aiming at the 67 percent of Tanzanians who listen to the radio. Eighty-four percent of the radio listeners reported listening to the PCI soap opera, making it the most popular show in the country. Ninety percent of the show's listeners recognized Mkwaju, the sexist truck driver, and only three percent regarded him as a positive role model. Over two-thirds identified Mama Wardi, a businesswoman, and her tailor husband as positive role models.

Surveys conducted to measure the impact of the show indicated it had affected knowledge, attitudes, and behaviour. For example, 49 percent of the married women who listened to the show said they now practiced family planning, compared with only 19 percent of the nonlisteners. There were other impacts:

> Some 72 percent of the listeners in 1994 said that they adopted an HIV/AIDS prevention

behavior because of listening to "Twende na Wakati," and this percentage increased to 82 percent in our 1995 survey. Seventy-seven percent of these individuals adopted monogamy, 16 percent began using condoms, and 6 percent stopped sharing razors and/or needles.

(Rogers et al. 1996:21)

We can judge the effectiveness of the soap opera because of a particular form of social science. *Evaluation research*—sometimes called *program evaluation*—refers to a research purpose rather than a specific research method. This purpose is to evaluate the impact of social interventions such as new teaching methods, innovations in parole, and a wide variety of such programs. Many methods—surveys, experiments, and so on—can be used in evaluation research.

Evaluation research is probably as old as general social research itself. Whenever people have instituted a social reform for a specific purpose, they've paid attention to its actual consequences, even if they haven't always done so in a conscious, deliberate, or sophisticated fashion. In recent years, however, the field of evaluation research has become an increasingly popular and active research specialty, as reflected in textbooks, courses, and projects. Moreover, the growth of evaluation research indicates a more general trend in the social sciences. As a researcher, you'll likely be asked to conduct evaluations.

In part, the growth of evaluation research reflects social scientists' increasing desire to make a difference in the world. At the same time, we can't discount the influence of (1) an increase in government requirements that program evaluations must accompany the implementation of new programs and (2) the availability of research funds to fulfill those requirements. In any event, it seems clear that social scientists will be bringing their skills into the real world more than ever before.

This chapter looks at some of the key elements in this form of social research. After considering the kinds of topics commonly subjected to evaluation, we'll move through some of its main operational aspects: measurement, study design, and execution. As you'll see, formulating questions is as important as answering them. Because it occurs

within real life, evaluation research has its own problems, some of which we'll examine. Besides logistical problems, special ethical issues arise from evaluation research generally and from its specific, technical procedures. As you review reports of program evaluations, you should be especially sensitive to these problems.

Evaluation is a form of *applied* research; that is, it's intended to have some real-world effect. It will be useful, therefore, to consider whether and how it's actually applied. As you'll see, the obvious implications of an evaluation research project do not necessarily affect real life. They may become the focus of ideological, rather than scientific, debates. They may simply be denied out of hand, for political or other reasons. Perhaps most typically, they are simply ignored and forgotten, left to collect dust in bookcases across the land.

The chapter concludes with a look at a particular resource for large-scale evaluation: *social indicators research*. This type of research is also a rapidly growing specialty. Essentially it involves the creation of aggregated indicators of the "health" of society, similar to the economic indicators that give diagnoses and prognoses of economies.

Topics Appropriate to Evaluation Research

Evaluation research is appropriate whenever some social intervention occurs or is planned. A *social intervention* is an action taken within a social context for the purpose of producing some intended result. In its simplest sense, **evaluation research** is a process of determining whether a social intervention has produced the intended result.

Topics appropriate to evaluation research are limitless. When the federal government adopted the Youth Offenders Act (YOA) in Canada in 1984, researchers soon after began to evaluate its impact. Any number of policies and programs are the target of evaluation research. How effective is Vancouver, BC's needle exchange program in reducing the prevalence of HIV? Do school drug use prevention programs actually reduce student drug use? Is the money spent on no smoking campaigns a worthwhile expenditure? Are programs to limit teen smoking effective? Do community-based sex offender management programs reduce the likelihood of their reoffending? What's the impact of tougher drunk driving policies on morbidity and mortality due to automobile accidents?

Some years ago Potvin et al. (1988) conducted an evaluation of the impact of a new law instituted in 1983 by the Quebec government that made driver training courses mandatory for all newly licensed drivers in an effort to increase road safety. The researchers set out to determine whether the new policy was warranted in Quebec even though nearly 20 years of research evidence had shown that driver education programs didn't have the beneficial effects of making the roads safer as many people believed. A key advantage to their study was that it could be undertaken on nonvolunteer subjects. Previous researchers in North America had to contend with the confounding factor that those who took driver's training were volunteers, which created a self-selection problem.

Was the policy effective in Quebec, justifying the quite substantial extra expense to newly licensed drivers? Not according to Potvin et al. Their results were consistent with most other major studies conducted. Driver training programs did not appear to improve road safety by reducing the number of accidents or the rate of death or serious injury per accident among new drivers.

In fact, what they did show was that following the new policy there was greater risk of accidents for those aged 16 and 17. Prior to the new law, mandatory driver training for newly licensed drivers was required only for those under 18 years old. All the new law may have done is contribute to an increased number of newly licensed drivers aged 16 and 17 by taking away their financial incentive to wait until they were 18 before obtaining their license. Since they would have to pay for driver education in any event, it was no longer an advantage to wait the extra year or two.

Nonetheless, public opinion in Quebec indicated that the vast majority believed driver training made people better drivers and helped reduce accidents. Policies of government and other institutions reflected this same opinion. Thus, the mandatory driver training requirement was not removed until 1997. Even today, those who have taken driver training courses reap some advantage; they only have to have a learner's permit for eight months instead of 12 and insurance companies often take driver education programs into account in their insurance rates.

Here's a very different example of evaluation research. Rudolf Andorka, a Hungarian sociologist, has been particularly interested in his country's shift to a market economy. Even before the dramatic events in Eastern Europe in 1989, Andorka and his colleagues had been monitoring the nation's "second economy"—jobs pursued outside the socialist economy. Their surveys followed the rise and fall of such jobs and examined their impact within Hungarian society. One conclusion was that "the second economy, which earlier probably tended to diminish income inequalities or at least improved the standard of living of the poorest part of the population, in the 1980s increasingly contributed to the growth of inequalities" (Andorka 1990:111).

As you can see, the questions appropriate to evaluation research are of great practical significance: jobs, programs, and investments as well as beliefs and values are at stake. Let's now examine how these questions are answered—how evaluations are conducted.

Formulating the Problem: Measurement Issues

Several years ago, I (Babbie) headed an institutional research office that conducted research of direct relevance to the operation of the university. Often, we were asked to evaluate new programs in the curriculum. The following description shows the problem that arose in that context, and it points to one of the key barriers to good evaluation research.

Faculty members would appear at my office to say they'd been told by the university administration to arrange for an evaluation of the new program they had permission to try. This points to a common problem: Often the people whose programs are being evaluated aren't thrilled at the prospect. For them, an independent evaluation threatens the survival of the program and perhaps even their jobs.

The main problem we want to introduce, however, has to do with the purpose of the intervention to be evaluated. The question "What is the intended result of the new program?" often produced a rather vague response; for example, "Students will get an in-depth and genuine understanding of mathematics, instead of simply memorizing methods of calculations." Fabulous! And how could we measure that "in-depth and genuine understanding?" Often, they reported that the program aimed at producing something that could not be measured by conventional aptitude and achievement tests. No problem there; that's to be expected when we're innovating and being unconventional. What would be an unconventional measure of the intended result? Sometimes this discussion came down to an assertion that the effects of the program would be "unmeasurable."

There's the common rub in evaluation research: measuring the "unmeasurable." Evaluation research is a matter of finding out whether something is there or not there, whether something happened or didn't happen. To conduct evaluation research, we must be able to operationalize, observe, and recognize the presence or absence of what is under study.

Often, desired outcomes are derived from published program documents or agency goals. In 1996 the Ministry for Children and Families was created in British Columbia. In order to evaluate their performance success a year later, they began with the statement of their four broad goals:

> to promote the healthy development of children, youth and families;
> to protect children and youth from abuse, neglect and harm;
> to support adults with developmental disabilities to live successfully and participate in the community; and
> public safety (from youth crime).

> (http://www.mcf.gov.bc.ca/publications/measure_success/msbackground.htm, May 28, 2001)

These goals contained within them the information concerning desired outcomes for the various population groups. The next step was to create operational measures appropriate to each of the goals. They created 16 specific outcome objectives and over 100 indicators.

While "official" purposes of interventions are often the key to designing an evaluation, this may not always be sufficient. Anna-Marie Madison (1992), for example, warns that programs designed to help disadvantaged minorities do not always reflect what the targets of the aid may need and desire.

> The cultural biases inherent in how middle-class white researchers interpret the experiences of low-income minorities may lead to erroneous assumptions and faulty propositions concerning causal relationships, to invalid social theory, and consequently to invalid program theory. Descriptive theories derived from faulty premises, which have been legitimized in the literature as existing knowledge, may have negative consequences for program participants.
>
> (1992:38)

In setting up an evaluation, then, researchers must pay careful attention to issues of measurement. Let's take a closer look at the types of measurements that evaluation researchers must deal with.

Specifying Outcomes

As we've suggested, a key variable for evaluation researchers to measure is the outcome or what is called the response variable. If a social program is intended to accomplish something, we must be able to measure that something. If we want to reduce prejudice, we need to be able to measure prejudice. If we want to increase marital harmony, we need to be able to measure that.

It's essential to achieve agreements on definitions in advance:

> The most difficult situation arises when there is disagreement as to standards. For example, many parties may disagree as to what defines serious drug abuse—is it defined best as 15% or

more of students using drugs weekly, 5% or more using hard drugs such as cocaine or PCP monthly, students beginning to use drugs as young as seventh grade, or some combination of the dimensions of rate of use, nature of use, and age of user? . . . Applied researchers should, to the degree possible, attempt to achieve consensus from research consumers in advance of the study (e.g., through advisory groups) or at least ensure that their studies are able to produce data relevant to the standards posited by all potentially interested parties.

(Hedrick, Bickman, and Rog 1993:27)

In the case of the BC Ministry evaluation study above, the outcome objectives were determined by examining the existing evaluation and research literature, consulting with community and professional stakeholders, and examining what had been done in other jurisdictions. Thus,

The four goals are translated into a series of outcome objectives. Each outcome objective is accompanied by a set of indicators. An indicator can be considered an operationalization of an outcome. Indicators are used to measure the existence and direction of change and to assess whether observed changes are consistent with the achievement of desired outcomes and goals.

(http://www.mcf.gov.bc.ca/publications/ measure_success/msbackground.htm, May 28, 2001)

For instance, the goal of promoting the healthy development of children, youth and families, was translated into nine outcome objectives. These included the reduction of teen pregnancy, reducing suicide by children and youth, and reducing substance abuse by children and youth. Then indicators—ways of measuring these objectives—had to be determined. For example, to measure whether the desired objective of reducing suicide by children and youth is being met, the official rates of suicide for specific age groups of children and youth would be examined over time to determine whether they have decreased.

Sometimes the definitions of a problem and a sufficient solution are defined by law or by agency regulations; if so, you must be aware of such specifications and accommodate them. Moreover, whatever the agreed-on definitions, you must also achieve agreement on how the measurements will be made. Because there are different possible methods for estimating the percentage of students "using drugs weekly," for example, you'd have to be sure that all the parties involved understood and accepted the method(s) you've chosen.

In the case of the Tanzanian soap opera, there were several outcome measures. In part, the purpose of the program was to improve knowledge about both family planning and AIDS. Thus, for example, one show debunked the belief that the AIDS virus was spread by mosquitoes and could be avoided by the use of insect repellant. Studies of listeners showed a reduction in that belief (Rogers et al. 1996:21).

PCI also wanted to change Tanzanian attitudes toward family size, gender roles, HIV/AIDS, and other related topics; the research indicated that the show had affected these as well. Finally, the program aimed at affecting behaviour. We've already seen that radio listeners reported changing their behaviour with regard to AIDS prevention. They reported a greater use of family planning as well. However, because there's always the possibility of a gap between what people say they do and what they actually do, the researchers sought independent data to confirm their conclusions.

Tanzania's national AIDS-control program had been offering condoms free of charge to citizens. In the areas covered by the soap opera, the number of condoms given out increased sixfold between 1992 and 1994. This far exceeded the increase of 1.4 times in the control area, where broadcasters did not carry the soap opera.

Measuring Experimental Contexts

Measuring the dependent variables directly involved in the experimental program is only a beginning. As Henry Riecken and Robert Boruch (1974:120–21) point out, it's often appropriate and important to measure aspects of the context of an experiment. Though external to the experiment itself, some variables may affect it.

Consider, for example, an evaluation of a program aimed at training unskilled people for employment. The primary outcome measure would be their success at gaining employment after completing the program. You would, of course, observe and calculate the subjects' employment rate, but you should also determine what has happened to the employment/unemployment rates of society at large during the evaluation. A general slump in the job market should be taken into account in assessing what might otherwise seem a relatively low employment rate for subjects. Or, if all the experimental subjects get jobs following the program, you should consider whether there has been any general increase in available jobs. Combining complementary measures with proper control group designs should allow you to pinpoint the effects of the program you're evaluating.

Specifying Interventions

Besides making measurements relevant to the outcomes of a program, researchers must measure the program intervention—the experimental stimulus. In part, this measurement will be handled by the assignment of subjects to experimental and control groups, if that's the research design. Assigning a person to the experimental group is the same as scoring that person yes on the stimulus, and assignment to the control group represents a score of no. In practice, however, it's seldom that simple.

Let's stick with the job-training example. Some people will participate in the program; others will not. But imagine for a moment what job-training programs are probably like. Some subjects will participate fully; others will miss a lot of sessions or fool around when they are present. So you may need measures of the extent or quality of participation in the program. If the program is effective, you should find that those who participated fully have higher employment rates than do those who participated less.

Other factors may further confound the administration of the experimental stimulus. Suppose we're evaluating a new form of psychotherapy designed to cure sexual impotence. Several therapists administer it to subjects composing an experimental group. We plan to compare the recovery rate of the experimental group with that of a control group, which receives some other therapy or none at all. It may be useful to include the names of the therapists treating specific subjects in the experimental group, because some may be more effective than others. If this turns out to be the case, we must find out why the treatment worked better for some therapists than for others. What we learn will further develop our understanding of the therapy itself.

Specifying the Population

When evaluating a program, it's important to define the population of possible subjects for whom the program is appropriate. Ideally, all or a sample of appropriate subjects will then be assigned to experimental and control groups as warranted by the study design. Defining the population, however, can itself involve specifying measurements. If we're evaluating a new form of psychotherapy, it's probably appropriate for people with mental problems, but how will "mental problems" be defined and measured? The job-training program mentioned previously is probably intended for people who are having trouble finding work, but what counts as "having trouble"?

Beyond defining the relevant population, then, the researcher should make fairly precise measurements on the variables considered in the definition. For example, even though the randomization of subjects in the psychotherapy study would insure an equal distribution of those with mild and severe mental problems in the experimental and control groups, we'd need to keep track of the relative severity of different subjects' problems in case the therapy turns out to be effective only for those with mild disorders. Similarly, we should measure such demographic variables as gender, age, race, and so forth in case the therapy works only for women, the elderly, or some other group.

New versus Existing Measures

In providing for the measurement of these different kinds of variables, the researcher must continually choose whether to create new measures or to use ones already devised by other researchers. If a study addresses something that's never been measured before, the choice is easy. If it addresses something that others have tried to measure, the researcher will have to evaluate the relative worth of various existing measurement devices in terms of his or her specific research situations and purpose. Recall that this is a general issue in social research that applies well beyond evaluation research. Let's examine briefly the advantages of creating new measures versus using existing ones.

Creating measurements specifically for a study can offer greater relevance and validity than using existing ones. If the psychotherapy we're evaluating aims at a specific aspect of recovery, we can create measures that pinpoint that aspect. We might not be able to find any standardized psychological measures that hit that aspect right on the head. However, creating our own measure will cost us the advantages to be gained from using preexisting measures. Creating good measures takes time and energy, both of which could be saved by adopting an existing technique. Of greater scientific significance, measures that have been used frequently by other researchers carry a body of possible comparisons that might be important to our evaluation. If the experimental therapy raises scores by an average of 10 points on a standardized test, we'll be in a position to compare that therapy with others that had been evaluated using the same measure. Finally, measures with a long history of use usually have known degrees of validity and reliability, but newly created measures will require pretesting or will be used with considerable uncertainty.

Operationalizing Success/Failure

Potentially, one of the most taxing aspects of evaluation research is determining whether the program under review succeeded or failed. The purpose of a foreign language program may be to help students better learn the language, but how much better is enough? The purpose of the conjugal visit program at a prison may be to raise morale, but how high does morale need to be raised to justify the program?

As you may anticipate, there are almost never clear-cut answers to questions like these. This dilemma has surely been the source of what is generally called *cost–benefit analysis.* How much does the program cost in relation to what it returns in benefits? If the benefits outweigh the cost, keep the program going. If the reverse, junk it. That's simple enough, and it seems to apply in straightforward economic situations: If it cost you $20 to produce something and you can sell it for only $18, there's no way you can make up the difference in volume.

Unfortunately, the situations usually faced by evaluation researchers are seldom amenable to straightforward economic accounting. The foreign language program may cost the school district $100 per student, and it may raise students' performances on tests by an average of 15 points. Because the test scores can't be converted into dollars, there's no obvious ground for weighing the costs and benefits.

Sometimes, as a practical matter, the criteria of success and failure can be handled through competition among programs. If a different foreign language program costs only $50 per student and produces an increase of 20 points in test scores, it would undoubtedly be considered more successful than the first program—assuming that test scores were seen as an appropriate measure of the purpose of both programs and the less expensive program had no negative unintended consequences.

Ultimately, the criteria of success and failure are often a matter of agreement. The people responsible for the program may commit themselves in advance to a particular outcome that will be regarded as an indication of success. If that's the case, all you need to do is make absolutely certain that the research design will measure the specified outcome. We mention this obvious requirement simply because researchers sometimes fail to meet it, and there's little or nothing more embarrassing than that.

Thus, researchers must take measurement quite seriously in evaluation research, carefully determining all the variables to be measured and getting appropriate measures for each. As we've implied, however, such decisions are typically not purely scientific ones. Evaluation researchers often must work out their measurement strategy with the people responsible for the program being evaluated. It usually doesn't make sense to determine whether a program achieves Outcome X when its purpose is to achieve Outcome Y. (Realize, however, that evaluation designs sometimes have the purpose of testing for unintended consequences.)

There's a political aspect to these choices, also. Because evaluation research often affects other people's professional interest—their pet program may be halted, or they may be fired or lose professional standing—the results of evaluation research are often argued about.

Let's turn now to some of the evaluation designs commonly employed by researchers.

Evaluation Research Designs

We noted at the beginning of this chapter that evaluation research is not itself a method but rather one application of social research methods. Therefore, it can involve any of several research designs. In this section we'll consider three main types of research design appropriate for evaluations: experimental designs, quasi-experimental designs, and qualitative evaluations.

Experimental Designs

Many of the experimental designs discussed in Chapter 8 can be used in evaluation research. By way of illustration, let's see how the classical experimental model might be applied to our evaluation of the new psychotherapy treatment for sexual impotence.

We should begin by identifying a population of patients relevant to the therapy. Researchers experimenting with the new therapy might make this identification. Let's say we're dealing with a clinic that already has 100 patients being treated for sexual impotence. We might take that group and the clinic's definition of sexual impotence as a starting point, and we should maintain any existing assessments of the severity of the problem for each specific patient.

For purposes of the evaluation research, however, we would need to develop a more specific measure of impotence. Maybe it would involve whether patients have sexual intercourse at all within a specified time, how often they have intercourse, or whether and how often they reach orgasm. Alternatively, the outcome measure might be based on the assessments of independent therapists not involved in the therapy who interview the patients later. In any event, we'd need to agree on the measures to be used.

In the simplest design, we would assign the 100 patients randomly to experimental and control groups; the former would receive the new therapy, and the latter would be taken out of therapy altogether during the experiment. Because ethical practice would probably prevent withdrawing therapy altogether from the control group, however, it's more likely that the control group would continue to receive their conventional therapy.

Having assigned subjects to the experimental and control groups, we would need to agree on the length of the experiment. Perhaps the designers of the new therapy feel it ought to be effective within two months, and an agreement could be reached. The duration of the study doesn't need to be rigid, however. One purpose of the experiment and evaluation might be to determine how long it actually takes for the new therapy to be effective. Conceivably, then, an agreement could be struck to measure recovery rates weekly, say, and let the ultimate length of the experiment rest on a continual review of the results.

Let's suppose the new therapy involves showing pornographic movies to patients. We'd need to specify that stimulus. How often would patients see the movies, and how long would each session be? Would they see the movies in private or in groups? Should therapists be present? Perhaps we should observe the patients while the movies are being shown and include our observations among the measurements of the experimental stimulus. Do some patients watch the movies eagerly but others look away from the screen? We'd have to ask these kinds of questions and create specific measurements to address them.

Having thus designed the study, all we have to do is "roll 'em." The study is set in motion, the observations are made and recorded, and the mass of data is accumulated for analysis. Once the study has run its course, we can determine whether the new therapy had its intended—or perhaps some unintended—consequences. We can tell whether the movies were most effective for mild problems or severe ones, whether they worked for young subjects but not older ones, and so forth.

This simple illustration should show you how the standard experimental designs presented in Chapter 8 can be used in evaluation research. Stevahn, et al. (1997) used this design to evaluate the effectiveness of conflict resolution training on high school students in Ontario, Canada. Forty students in two ninth-grade classes participated in the study. Each class contained 20 students with varied academic backgrounds: each class had both gifted and special-needs students. The researchers randomly assigned the students from both classes to an experimental group and a control group. The experimental condition was one "in which conflict-resolution training was integrated into the study of the required literature curriculum." The control condition was one "in which the identical required literature curriculum was taught without the integration of conflict-resolution training" (p. 304). Many, perhaps most, of the evaluations reported in the research literature, however, don't look exactly like these illustrations. Because it's nested in real life, evaluation research often calls for quasi-experimental designs. Let's see what this means.

Quasi-Experimental Designs

Quasi experiments are distinguished from "true" experiments primarily by the lack of random assignment of subjects to an experimental and a control group. In evaluation research, it's often impossible to achieve such an assignment of subjects. Rather than forgo evaluation altogether, researchers sometimes create designs that give some evaluation of the program in question. This section describes some of these designs.

Time-Series Designs   To illustrate the *time-series design*—studies that involve measurements taken over time—we'll begin by asking you to assess the meaning of some hypothetical data. Suppose we come to you with what we claim is an effective technique for getting students to participate in

classroom sessions of a course we're teaching. To prove our assertion, we tell you that on Monday, only four students asked questions or made a comment in class; on Wednesday we devoted the class time to an open discussion of a controversial issue raging on campus; and on Friday, when we returned to the subject matter of the course, eight students asked questions or made comments. In other words, we contend, the discussion of a controversial issue on Wednesday has doubled classroom participation. This simple set of data is presented graphically in Figure 13-1.

Have we persuaded you that the open discussion on Wednesday has had the consequence we say it has? Probably you'd object that our data do not prove the case. Two observations (Monday and Friday) aren't really enough to prove anything. Ideally we should have had two classes, with students assigned randomly to each, held an open discussion in only one, and then compared the two on Friday. But we don't have two classes with random assignment of students. Instead, we've been keeping a record of class participation throughout the semester for the one class. This record allows you to conduct a time-series evaluation.

Figure 13-2 presents three possible patterns of class participation over time—both before and after the open discussion on Wednesday. Which of these patterns would give you some confidence that the discussion had the impact we contend it had?

Figure 13-1

Two Observations of Class Participation: Before and After an Open Discussion

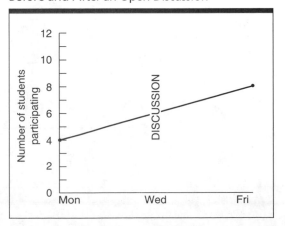

If the time-series results looked like the first pattern in Figure 13-2, you'd probably conclude that the process of greater class participation had begun on the Wednesday before the discussion and had continued, unaffected, after the day devoted to the discussion. The long-term data suggest that the trend would have occurred even without the discussion on Wednesday. The first pattern, then, contradicts our assertion that the special discussion increased class participation.

The second pattern contradicts our assertion by indicating that class participation has been bouncing up and down in a regular pattern throughout the semester. Sometimes it increases from one class to the next, and sometimes it decreases; the open discussion on that Wednesday simply came at a time when the level of participation was about to increase. More to the point, we note that class participation decreased again at the class following the alleged postdiscussion increase.

Only the third pattern in Figure 13-2 supports our contention that the open discussion mattered. As the figure depicts, the level of discussion before that Wednesday had been a steady four students per class. Not only did the level of participation double following the day of discussion, but it continued to increase further afterward. Although

Figure 13-2

Three Patterns of Class Participation in a Longer Historical Period

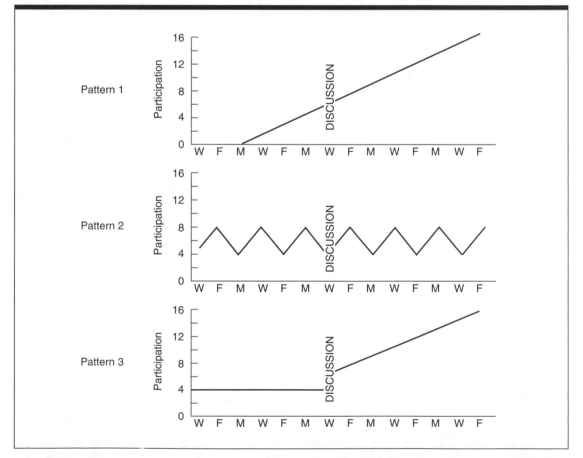

these data do not protect us against the possible influence of some extraneous factor (we might also have mentioned that participation would figure into students' grades), they do exclude the possibility that the increase results from a process of maturation (indicated in the first pattern) or from regular fluctuations (indicated in the second).

Nonequivalent Control Groups The time-series design just described involves only an "experimental" group; it doesn't provide the value that would be gained from having a control group. Sometimes, when researchers can't create experimental and control groups by random assignment from a common pool, they can find an existing "control" group that appears similar to the experimental group. Such a group is called a *nonequivalent control group*. If an innovative foreign language program is being tried in one class in a large high school, for example, you may be able to find another foreign language class in the same school that has a very similar student population: one that has about the same composition in terms of grade in school, gender, ethnicity, IQ, and so forth. The second class, then, could provide a point of comparison. At the end of the semester, both classes could be given the same foreign language test, and you could compare performances.

In our discussion of natural experiments in Chapter 9, we mentioned the study of the effects of the CBC Frontier Television Service in an Eskimo community. You may recall the researcher had to accept the real life circumstances of the study. The community under study had not been randomly assigned to groups where half had TV access and half did not. Thus, there was no official control group. Therefore, Coldevin (1976) searched for a nonequivalent control group – a community that came as close in composition as possible to the community under study. This "control group," although not formally part of the CBC Frontier TV service area, provided him with a non-television, Eskimo community against which he could compare the outcomes in the TV community.

Finding any control or comparison group can be difficult in some evaluation studies. It can be par-

ticularly difficult in programs concerning criminal or deviant activities and behaviours. As Wilson et al. (2000:186) reported in their assessment of a community-based sex offender management protocol:

> This study, like many others in the recidivism literature, suffers from the lack of a comparison group. Numerous attempts were made in the context of this study to identify a comparison group; however, it is particularly difficult to find sexual offenders who are not being offered community-based treatment intervention in a comparable environment (i.e., urban Canadian setting). Indeed, there are ethical concerns associated with not offering offenders appropriate community treatment and supervision.

In their case, they discussed their results in light of outcomes that other treatment sites reported and compared them to general offenders' rates of recidivism in Canada. However, they readily acknowledged that while they found a low rate of sexual reoffending in their evaluation, lacking a control group, it wasn't possible for them to "claim that the results are primarily attributable to effective treatment or even the collaboration of treatment and parole supervisory personnel, as advocated in the relapse prevention model" (p. 186).

Multiple Time-Series Designs Sometimes the evaluation of processes occurring outside of "pure" experimental controls can be made easier by the use of more than one time-series analysis. This design is an improved version of the nonequivalent control group design just described. Carol Weiss has presented a useful example of this design:

> An interesting example of multiple time series was the evaluation of the Connecticut crackdown on highway speeding. Evaluators collected reports of traffic fatalities for several periods before and after the new program went into effect. They found that fatalities went down after the crackdown, but since the series had had an unstable up-and-down pattern for many years, it was not certain that the drop was due to the program. They then compared the statistics with

time-series data from four neighboring states where there had been no changes in traffic enforcement. Those states registered no equivalent drop in fatalities. The comparison lent credence to the conclusion that the crackdown had had some effect.

(1972:69)

Although this study design is not as good as one in which subjects are assigned randomly, it's nonetheless an improvement over assessing the experimental group's performance without any comparison. That's what makes these designs quasi experiments instead of just fooling around. The key in assessing this aspect of evaluation studies is *comparability,* as the following example illustrates.

A growing concern in the poor countries of the world, rural development has captured the attention and support of many rich countries. Through national foreign assistance programs and through international agencies such as the World Bank, the developed countries are in the process of sharing their technological knowledge and skills with the developing countries. Such programs have had mixed results, however. Often, modern techniques do not produce the intended results when applied in traditional societies.

Rajesh Tandon and L. Dave Brown (1981) undertook an experiment in which technological training would be accompanied by instruction in village organization. They felt it was important for poor farmers to learn how to organize and exert collective influence within their villages—getting needed action from government officials, for example. Only then would their new technological skills bear fruit.

Both intervention and evaluation were attached to an ongoing program in which 25 villages had been selected for technological training. Two poor farmers from each village had been trained in new agricultural technologies. Then they had been sent home to share their new knowledge with their village and to organize other farmers into "peer groups" who would assist in spreading that knowledge. Two years later, the authors randomly selected two of the 25 villages (subsequently called

Group A and Group B) for special training and 11 other untrained groups as controls. A careful comparison of demographic characteristics showed the experimental and control groups to be strikingly similar, suggesting they were sufficiently comparable for the study.

The peer groups from the two experimental villages were brought together for special training in organization building. The participants were given some information about organizing and making demands on the government; they were also given opportunities to act out dramas similar to the situations they faced at home. The training took three days.

The outcome variables considered by the evaluation all had to do with the extent to which members of the peer groups initiated group activities designed to improve their situation. Six types were studied. "Active initiative," for example, was defined as "active effort to influence persons or events affecting group members versus passive response or withdrawal" (Tandon and Brown 1981:180). The data for evaluation came from the journals that the peer group leaders had been keeping since their initial technological training. The researchers read through the journals and counted the number of initiatives taken by members of the peer groups. Two researchers coded the journals independently and compared their work to test the reliability of the coding process.

Figure 13-3 compares the number of active initiatives by members of the two experimental groups with those coming from the control groups. Similar results were found for the other outcome measures.

Notice two things about the graph. First, there's a dramatic difference in the number of initiatives by the two experimental groups as compared with the eleven controls. This seems to confirm the effectiveness of the special training program. Second, notice that the number of initiatives also increased among the control groups. The researchers explain this latter pattern as a result of contagion. Because all the villages were near each other, the lessons learned by peer group members in the experimental groups were communicated in part to members of the control villages.

This example illustrates the strengths of multiple time-series designs in situations where true experiments are inappropriate to the program being evaluated.

Qualitative Evaluations

While we've laid out the steps involved in tightly structured, mostly quantitative evaluation research, evaluations can also be less structured

Figure 13-3
Active Initiatives over Time

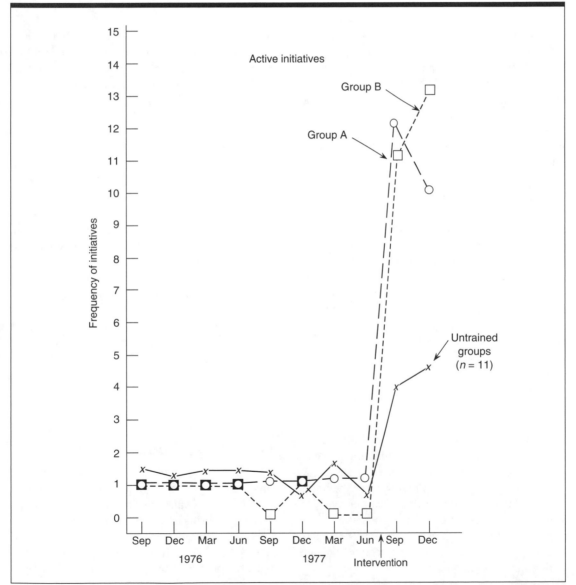

Source: Rajesh Tandon and L. Dave Brown, "Organization-Building for Rural Development: An Experiment in India," *Journal of Applied Behavior Science,* April–June 1981, p. 182.

and more qualitative. For example, Pauline Bart and Patricia O'Brien (1985) wanted to evaluate different ways to stop rape, so they undertook in-depth interviews with both rape victims and women who had successfully fended off rape attempts.

As an illustration of the focus group method in Chapter 12, we mentioned the qualitative evaluation research conducted by Harlton, Keating, and Fast (1998). You may recall that they were interested in evaluating stakeholders' perspectives on the idea of "partnership" in Canadian heath care policy concerning the elderly. They conducted separate focus group interviews with seven key stakeholder groups identified in eldercare. Their analysis revealed that very different understandings of the new "partnership" policy were held by those stakeholders who had the most influence on eldercare policy and those whose lives would be most affected by the policy.

Bucharski, Brockman, and Lambert (1999) used focus groups and informant interviews in a project to develop a prenatal care model that would be culturally appropriate for aboriginal women. Reports indicated a disproportionate number of infants with HIV in Alberta were born to aboriginal women who had not had prenatal care. The researchers' goal was to develop new strategies to reach aboriginal women in an effort to reduce the passing of HIV from mothers to their infants. Two of their major project objectives were to develop a prenatal care model that would support HIV screening and "to identify site(s) and develop resources for the implementation of the prevention model for the target risk group" (1999:151). The target group profile was developed through interviews with HIV health care providers in northern Alberta. Involving the target group in the process, focus groups consisting of female aboriginal leaders were conducted. A main goal of the informant interviews with aboriginal women was to help the researchers better understand the dynamics of the relationship between the clients and service providers in order to create relevant and worthwhile programming.

Sometimes even structured, quantitative evaluations can yield unexpected qualitative results. Paul Steel is a social researcher specializing in the evaluation of programs aimed at pregnant drug users. One program he evaluated involved counselling by public health nurses, who warned pregnant drug users that continued drug use would likely result in underweight babies whose skulls would be an average of 10 percent smaller than normal. In his in-depth interviews with program participants, however, he discovered that the program omitted one important piece of information: that undersized babies were a bad thing. Many of the young women Steel interviewed thought that smaller babies would mean easier deliveries (personal communication, November 22, 1993).

The most effective evaluation research is one that combines qualitative and quantitative components. While making statistical comparisons is useful, so is gaining an in-depth understanding of the processes producing the observed results—or preventing the expected results from appearing.

The evaluation of the Tanzanian soap opera, presented earlier in this chapter, employed several research techniques. We've already mentioned the listener surveys and data obtained from clinics. In addition, the researchers conducted numerous focus groups to probe more deeply into the impact the shows had on listeners. Also, content analyses were done on the soap opera episodes themselves and on the many letters received from listeners. Both quantitative and qualitative analyses were undertaken (Swalehe et al. 1995).

The Social Context

Many of the comments in previous sections have hinted at the possibility of problems in the actual execution of evaluation research projects. Of course, all forms of research can run into problems, but evaluation research has a special propensity for it. This section looks at some of the logistical problems and special ethical issues in evaluation research. It concludes with some observations about using evaluation research results.

Logistical Problems

In a military context, *logistics* refers to moving supplies around—making sure people have food, guns, and tent pegs when they need them. Here, we use it to refer to getting subjects to do what they're supposed to do, getting research instruments distributed and returned, and other seemingly unchallenging tasks. These tasks are more challenging than you might guess!

Coordinating Service When a team of researchers sets out to evaluate a new program aimed at improving coordination of activities among mental health service providers (Forster, Evans, and Fisher, 1990), they found out just how many problems can occur. The purpose of the research was to evaluate the implementation of a six-month pilot project to help coordinate services among eight agencies in a small city in western Canada. A previous study of service providers from agencies throughout the city identified problems and concerns related to lack of service coordination that they felt hindered client care. Thus the pilot project had four specific goals:

1. increased quality and efficiency of direct mental health services to specified clients
2. reduced redundancy in delivery of mental health services to specified clients
3. reduced use of unnecessary mental health services by specified clients
4. increased consumer provider satisfaction with the range and type of services the client is receiving

(1990:617)

These goals would be accomplished by means such as opening up communication among the agencies and increasing joint treatment planning. The expected impact of the project was to reduce the time spent on a specific client's care while improving satisfaction and service.

Service providers from the agencies designed the project. The evaluators were consulted in the design, and the design included the evaluation components. The project was implemented only after all staff were informed about it and instructed on the procedures required for the project. They were asked to participate and encouraged to give feedback and make suggestions. The committee that oversaw the project consisted of the head administrator from each agency involved. This arrangement might sound promising for evaluation researchers. But, even under these circumstances, the problems of execution in evaluation research can be extensive.

In reality not all agencies were committed to the project, and it was not properly implemented. Although the researchers had an elaborate and well-planned evaluation design that included baseline questionnaires, service provider daily record sheets, client profile forms, case conference meetings with minutes, case conference questionnaires, and postproject questionnaires, there were problems from the very start.

Fourteen clients were selected in total for both the experimental and control groups, but only seven were chosen in the appropriate time frame. Therefore not all clients were part of the project for the full six months. This affected the client improvement measures. And, of the 14 chosen, only half were chosen using criteria consistent with the project. For example, some were chosen because they requested to participate and others because they required more help than they were getting. Case conferences weren't properly implemented: regular meetings were not always held and even when they were held not all agencies participated.

Commitment to the project was said to be "at least" moderate for five of the eight agencies, which meant that three were not committed. A number of service providers didn't fill out the questionnaires at all, some didn't fill them out completely, and others filled out the wrong questionnaires, contributing to unusable data and a smaller sample size. In addition, the sizes of the treatment and control groups were unequal.

Fourteen potential clients were identified, but only 8 completed the pretest and 10 the posttest questionnaires. Only 2 of the final 10 respondents were in the control group. Questionnaires were completed by service providers from only six of the eight originally involved agencies.

(1990:623)

With due cautions, the researchers presented results in terms of the pilot project objectives. The authors concluded that the program was neither implemented as intended nor successful. There was "no substantial effects on improving service coordination in any of the five intended areas" (1990:628). Nonetheless, there was much to be learned from the evaluation that might help in the implementation of future service coordination projects.

The special, logistical problems of evaluation research grow out of the fact that it occurs within the context of real life. Although evaluation research is modelled after the experiment—which suggests that the researchers have control over what happens—it takes place within frequently uncontrollable daily life. Of course, the participant–observer in field research doesn't have control over what's observed either, but that method doesn't strive for control. Given the objectives of evaluation research, lack of control can create real dilemmas for the researcher.

Administrative Control As suggested in the previous example, the logistical details of an evaluation project often fall to program administrators. Let's suppose you're evaluating a "conjugal visit" program on the morale of married prisoners. The program allows inmates periodic visits from their spouses during which they can have sexual relations. On the fourth day of the program, a male prisoner dresses up in his wife's clothes and escapes. Although you might be tempted to assume that his morale was greatly improved by escaping, that turn of events would complicate your study design in many ways. Perhaps the warden will terminate the program altogether, and where's your evaluation then? Or, if the warden is brave, he or she may review the files of all those

prisoners you selected randomly for the experimental group and veto the "bad risks." There goes the comparability of your experimental and control groups. As an alternative, stricter security measures may be introduced to prevent further escapes, and the security measures may have a dampening effect on morale. So the experimental stimulus has changed in the middle of your research project. Some of the data will reflect the original stimulus; other data will reflect the modification. Although you'll probably be able to sort it all out, your carefully designed study has become a logistical snake pit.

Or suppose you've been engaged to evaluate the effect of gender relations lectures on sexual harassment in the military. You've carefully studied the soldiers available to you for study, and you've randomly assigned some to attend the lectures and others to stay away. The rosters have been circulated weeks in advance, and at the appointed day and hour, the lectures begin. Everything seems to be going smoothly until you begin processing the files: The names don't match. Checking around, you discover that military field exercises, KP duty, and a variety of emergencies required some of the experimental subjects to be elsewhere at the time of the lectures. That's bad enough, but then you learn that helpful commanding officers sent others to fill in for the missing soldiers. And whom do you suppose they picked to fill in? Soldiers who didn't have anything else to do or who couldn't be trusted to do anything important. You might learn this bit of information a week or so before the deadline for submitting your final report on the impact of the gender relations lectures.

These are some of the logistical problems confronting evaluation researchers. You need to be familiar with the problems to understand why some research procedures may not measure up to the design of the classical experiment. As you read reports of evaluation research, however, you'll find that—our earlier comments notwithstanding—it is possible to carry out controlled social research in conjunction with real-life experiments.

The accompanying box, "Testing Soap Operas in Tanzania," describes some of the logistical problems involved in the research discussed at the outset of this chapter.

Just as evaluation research has special logistical problems, it also raises special ethical concerns. Because ethical problems can affect the scientific quality of the research, we should look at them briefly.

Ethical Concerns

Ethics and evaluation are intertwined in many ways. Sometimes the social interventions being evaluated raise ethical issues. Evaluating the impact of busing school children to achieve educational integration will throw the researchers directly into the political, ideological, and ethical issues of busing itself. It's not possible to evaluate a sex education program in elementary schools without becoming involved in the heated issues surrounding sex education itself, and the researcher will find it difficult to remain impartial. The evaluation study design will *require* that some children receive sex education—in fact, you may very well be the one who decides which children do. (From a scientific standpoint, you *should* be in charge of selection.) This means that when parents become outraged that their child is being taught about sex, you'll be directly responsible.

Now let's look on the "bright" side. Maybe the experimental program is of great value to those participating in it. Let's say that the new industrial safety program being evaluated reduces injuries dramatically. But then, what about the control group members who were deprived of the program by the research design? The evaluators' actions could be an important part of the reason that a

Testing Soap Operas in Tanzania

By William N. Ryerson
Executive Vice-President

Population Communications International

*T*wende na Wakati ("Let's Go With the Times") has been broadcast on Radio Tanzania since mid-1993 with support from the United Nations Population Fund. The program was designed to encourage family planning use and AIDS prevention measures.

There were many different elements to the research. One was a nationwide, random-sample survey given prior to the first airing of the soap opera in June 1993 and then annually after that. Many interviewers faced particularly interesting challenges. For example, one interviewer, Fridolan Banzi, had never been in or on water in his life and couldn't swim. He arranged for a small boat to take him through the rough waters of Lake Victoria so he could carry out his interviews at a village that had no access by road. He repeated this nerve-wracking trip each year afterward in order to measure the change in that village.

Another interviewer, Mr. Tende, was invited to participate in a village feast that the villagers held to welcome him and to indicate their enthusiasm about having been selected for the study. They served him barbequed rats. Though they weren't part of his normal diet, he ate them anyway to be polite and to ensure that the research interviews could be carried out in that village.

Still another interviewer, Mrs. Masanja, was working in a village in the Pwani region along the coast of the Indian Ocean when cholera broke out in that village. She wisely chose to abandon the interviews there, which reduced the 1993 sample size by one ward.

The unsung heroes of this research, the Tanzanian interviewers, deserve a great deal of credit for carrying out this important work under difficult circumstances.

control group subject suffered an injury. Ironically, when a program is effective, it may be ethically dubious to deprive a control group of its benefits.

As we noted earlier in this book, most research studies require ethical review and approval; however, we also noted that many ethical determinations are debatable and some may be inaccurate. For example, in their article, "Myths and misconceptions about sex offenders," Fedoroff and Moran (1997:266) noted that a proposal to study the effects of masturbation on sex offenders was presented for ethical review. The design of the research called for subjects "to either a) masturbate at their usual frequency; b) cease masturbation...or c) masturbate at twice their usual frequency" for a period of one month.

> The human subjects ethical review body objected to condition c) on the basis of the belief that encouraging sex offenders to masturbate more frequently was unethical due to the possibility that they might "lose control" and re-offend.

> The study was conducted following the revisions imposed by the ethics committee. The results, however,

> while preliminary, suggest that the ethics committee had actually recommended dropping the wrong arm of the study since, at least in the case of sex offenders, abstinence from masturbation appears to be more dangerous than continuing to masturbate at their habitual frequency. Fortunately, since it is clearly important to determine whether or not sex offenders are more dangerous when they masturbate more than they would normally, a second study including all three conditions has now been approved and is currently being conducted.
>
> (1997:266)

Issues of responsibility to subjects, informed consent, voluntary participation, and deception are ever present in evaluation research. Researchers must carefully weigh the risks and benefits to both the human subjects and the larger community.

You may recall that in the introduction to Part 3 we mentioned the Tuskegee Syphilis Study, which began in Alabama in the early 1930s. The program claimed to provide free treatment for syphilis to poor, black men suffering from the disease. Over the years that followed, several hundred men participated in the program. What they didn't know was that they were not actually receiving any treatment at all; the physicians conducting the study merely wanted to observe the natural progress of the disease. Even after penicillin was found to be an effective cure, the researchers still withheld the treatment. While there is no doubt unanimous agreement today as to the unethical nature of the study, this was not the case at the time. Even when the study began being reported in research publications, the researchers refused to acknowledge they had done anything wrong. When professional complaints were finally lodged with the U.S. Center for Disease Control in 1965, there was no reply (J. Jones 1981). This study had a clear absence of informed consent. The subjects were deceived and put at grave risk—the researchers withheld a known and effective treatment.

Research designs that would yield the most scientifically decisive evidence are not always ethical. It is essential to evaluate a research design in terms of whether the subjects are being treated fairly, whether they are being denied assistance or benefits as a result of the study, and whether they have been clearly informed about the potential risks involved in the research. It is the responsibility of the researcher to ensure that participation is voluntary and that participants may withdraw at any time. In our earlier example of the evaluation of the new psychotherapy treatment for sexual impotence, recall that we said it would likely be unethical to withdraw therapy altogether from the control group. Despite the compromise of ideal design, it would be ethically warranted to allow their conventional therapy to continue. In this same study, it would be our ethical responsibility to honestly inform the subjects of all known risks and the potential for unanticipated consequences. Moreover, it would be unethical to give subjects false hopes of positive treatment outcomes as a means of obtaining their voluntary participation.

Use of Research Results

One more facts-of-life aspect of evaluation research concerns how evaluations are used.

Because the purpose of evaluation research is to determine the success or failure of social interventions, you might think it reasonable that a program would automatically be continued or terminated based on the results of the research.

Reality isn't that simple and reasonable, however. Other factors intrude on the assessment of evaluation research results, sometimes blatantly and sometimes subtly. Research indicating that boot camps are ineffective as a means of controlling youth crime was becoming prevalent in the literature in the late 20th century. The policy of getting tough with youth and scaring them into good bahaviour proved counterproductive. Researchers found that those exposed to the boot camp experience were more likely—not less likely—to reoffend. None of this evidence stopped Premier Mike Harris and his Ontario Conservative government in the 1990s from calling for a get-tough policy on young offenders—more specifically, for putting violent young offenders into boot camps as a means of securing a safer society.

Why are such policies often proposed and at times even implemented? Some argue that it has much to do with politics—it's what the public wants to hear. Promoting such policies can help to win elections and voter support, independent of the fact that they may be poorly designed for addressing the issues at hand. There are times, however, when those in charge simply believe, along with others, that the research evidence is wrong. In either case, the research contradicts some deep seeded understanding that is widely held about what *should* work, independent of what the evidence indicates. The research results therefore may be ignored or set aside.

A good example of the neglect of research in the creation of policy can be found in an article by Patricia Erickson (1998). Her abstract nicely summarizes the specific policy her article examines, the creation of a new Canadian drug law.

> After four years, two governments, and three Parliamentary committees, the Controlled Drugs and Substances Act was proclaimed in May 1997. Despite a rich legacy of empirical research pointing drug policy in a new direction, away from aggressive criminalization, the new law reaffirms both the seriously deviant status of illicit drug users and the primacy of the criminal justice model over public health and social justice alternatives.
>
> (1998:263)

Erickson is talking about 25 years of drug policy debate in the Canadian social science research literature; research evidence that was "often presented directly to the policy makers" yet was ultimately rejected.

Less dramatic examples of the failure to follow the implications of evaluation research could be listed endlessly. Undoubtedly every evaluation researcher can point to studies he or she conducted—studies providing clear research results and obvious policy implications—that were ignored.

There are three important reasons why the implications of the evaluation research results are not always put into practice. First, the implications may not always be presented in a way that the nonresearchers can understand. Second, evaluation results sometimes contradict deeply held beliefs as noted above. That's often the case, for example, when it comes to research and evaluation of policies toward crime and punishment. If *everybody knows* that harsh punishment deters criminal bahaviour and reduces crime, then it's likely that research results to the contrary will have little immediate impact. By the same token, people thought Copernicus was crazy when he said the earth revolved around the sun. Anybody could tell the earth was standing still. The third barrier to the use of evaluation results is vested interests. Imagine that you've devised a new rehabilitation program that you're convinced will keep ex-convicts from returning to prison, and that people have taken to calling it "the ____Plan," (fill in your name). How do you think you're going to feel when our evaluation suggests the program doesn't work? You might apologize for misleading people, fold up your tent, and go into another line of work. But more likely, you'd call our research worthless and begin intense lobbying with the appropriate authorities to have your program continue.

By its nature, evaluation research takes place in the midst of real life, affecting it and being affected by it. Here's another example, well known to social researchers.

Rape Reform Legislation   For years, many social scientists, advocacy groups, and other observers have noted certain problems with the prosecution of rape cases. The victims of sexual assault were seen as poorly treated when attempting to seek criminal justice. The rate of charges laid was low and when the offender was brought to trial, all too often, it was felt, the victim ended up suffering almost as much on the witness stand as in the rape itself. Frequently, she had to withstand personal attacks about her shady moral character and accusations of encouraging the sex act, attacks aimed at deflecting responsibility from the accused rapist. This negative treatment of sexual assault victims by the criminal justice system and the low level of charges contributed to the high rate of underreporting of such crimes. Criticisms such as these resulted in major changes to the *Criminal Code* of Canada that reformed the rape laws in 1983 (discussed in Chapter 10).

Julian Roberts and Robert Gebotys (1992:557) tracked the impact of this legislative reform aimed at increasing "the number of reports made to the police" and improving "the processing of cases of sexual aggression by the police and the courts." It was generally expected that the new legislation would encourage women to report acts of sexual aggression while at the same time encouraging a decrease in the number of offences reported as unfounded and an increase in the number of charges laid. (If the investigating officers decide that a crime was not attempted or did not occur, it is reported as unfounded.) To examine these expected outcomes, the researchers used existing statistics from the Canadian Uniform Crime Reports (UCR) and focused on the period from 1979 to 1988.

You may recall from our discussion in Chapter 10 that because the offences of rape and indecent assault were altered significantly in the new Canadian sexual assault law, a comparable valid measure of rape following the legal reform is not directly available in the UCR statistics. Rape and other sexual assaults were incorporated into three

levels of seriousness of sexual assault, so there is no direct correspondence of offences pre and post reform. Nonetheless, the researchers were able to establish a valid, comparable measure for the pre and post reform periods by combining the pre reform offences of rape and indecent assault and then combining the three levels of sexual assault for the post reform period, since "the new offences capture all the incidents previously classified as one of the pre reform offences." They also analyzed the data on all nonsexual assaults over the same time period for the purpose of comparative analysis. In this way they could examine whether there was a change in reporting for assault charges in general or whether change was particular to sexual assaults.

Roberts and Gebotys, therefore, were able to present

> national data on the effects of the 1983 reforms on four critical statistics relating to sexual assault: (a) reports made to the police, (b) classification by the police of those reports among the three levels of sexual assault, (c) the founding rate, and (d) the charging rate. These statistics concern the "front-end" of the criminal justice system, and are only part of the story. Rape reform legislation also addresses deep-end issues such as conviction rates and sentencing trends. However, national statistics on conviction rates and sentencing are not published in Canada (see Roberts, 1990a).
>
> (1992:556)

Using time-series analyses to analyze the data, they found that the legislation was successful in meeting one of its goals.

> Ironically, its success has been in attracting more victims into the system, rather than in changing the way that the system functions. The reforms have had no significant effect upon the decision as to whether a particular case is founded and as to whether a charge is laid in the case.
>
> (1992:581)

Finally, since their evaluation study indicated that the reform legislation failed to have an impact on the processing of sexual assault cases by the police, they were able to direct attention to where greater research and intervention is needed. It is the police who determine if a report is classified as an offence and if, and at what level, a charge is laid. Their actions have "consequences for all subsequent stages of the criminal justice process" (p. 572). Therefore, attention must be directed to reforming police practices.

This study demonstrates the importance of following up on social interventions to determine whether, in what ways, and to what degree they accomplish their intended results, and where greater research and intervention may be needed to accomplish them.

By now, you've seen various scientific and nonscientific aspects of evaluation research that affect how its results are used. But, this "messiness" is balanced by the potential contributions that evaluation research can make toward the betterment of human life.

Social Indicators Research

We'd like to conclude this chapter with a type of research that combines what you've learned about evaluation research and the analysis of existing data. A rapidly growing field in social research involves the development and monitoring of *social indicators,* aggregated statistics that reflect the social condition of a society or social subgroup. Researchers use social indicators to monitor aspects of social life in much the same way that economists use indexes such as gross national product (GNP) per capita as an indicator of a nation's economic development.

Suppose we wanted to compare the relative health conditions in different societies. One strategy would be to compare their death rates (number of deaths per 1,000 population). Or, more specifically, we could look at infant mortality: the number of infants who die during their first year of life among every 1,000 births. Depending on the particular aspect of health conditions we were interested in, we could devise any number of other measures: physicians per capita, hospital beds per capita, days of hospitalization per capita, and so

forth. Notice that intersocietal comparisons are facilitated by calculating per capita rates (dividing by the size of the population).

Before we go further, recall from Chapter 10 the problems involved in using existing statistics. In a word, they're often unreliable, reflecting their modes of collection, storage, and calculation. With this in mind, we'll look at some of the ways we can use social indicators for evaluation research on a large scale.

The Death Penalty and Deterrence

Maclean's magazine reported in its year end poll conducted in 2000 that 55 percent of Canadians feel that Canada should have the death penalty for first degree murder (January 1, 2001:30).

Does the death penalty deter capital crimes such as murder? This question is hotly debated every time a government considers eliminating or reinstating capital punishment and every time someone is executed in the U.S. Those supporting capital punishment often argue that the threat of execution will keep potential murderers from killing people. Opponents of capital punishment often argue that it has no effect in that regard. Social indicators can help shed some light on the question.

Research conducted on the use of the death penalty in the United States, a country where the death penalty exists in some states but not others, provides a good illustration. If capital punishment actually deters people from committing murder, then we should expect to find lower murder rates in those states that have the death penalty than in those that do not. The relevant comparisons in this instance are not only possible, they've been compiled and published. Table 13-1 presents data compiled by William Bailey (1975) that directly contradict the view that the death penalty deters murderers. In both 1967 and 1968, those states with capital punishment had dramatically *higher* murder rates than those without capital punishment. Some people criticized the interpretation of Bailey's data, saying that most states had not used the death penalty in recent years, even when they had it on the books. That could explain why it didn't seem to work as a deterrent. Further analysis, however, contradicts this explanation. When Bailey compared those states that hadn't used the death penalty with those that had, he found no real difference in murder rates.

Another counterexplanation is possible, however. It could be the case that the interpretation given Bailey's data was *backward.* Maybe the existence of the death penalty as an option was a consequence of high murder rates: Those states with high rates instituted it; those with low rates didn't institute it or repealed it if they had it on the books. It could be the case, then, that instituting the death penalty would bring murder rates down, and repealing it would increase murders and still produce—in a broad aggregate—the data presented in Table 13-1. Not so, however. Analyses over time do not show an increase in murder rates when a state repeals the death penalty or a decrease in murders when one is instituted. A more recent examination by Bailey and Ruth D. Peterson (1994) confirmed the earlier findings and also indicated that law enforcement officials doubted the deterrent effect.

Notice from the preceding discussion that it's possible to use social indicators data either for comparison across groups either at one time or across some period of time. Often, doing both sheds the most light on the subject.

At present, work on the use of social indicators is proceeding on two fronts. On the one hand, researchers are developing ever more refined indicators—finding which indicators of a general variable are the most useful in monitoring social life. At the same time, research is being devoted to discovering the relationships among variables within whole societies.

Computer Simulation

One of the most exciting prospects for social indicators research lies in the area of *computer simulation.* As researchers begin compiling mathematical equations describing the relationships that link social variables to one another (for example, the relationship between growth in population and the number of automobiles), those equations can be stored and linked to one another in a computer.

Table 13-1
Average Rate per 100,000 Population of First- and Second-Degree Murders for Capital-Punishment and Non-Capital-Punishment States, 1967 and 1968

	Non-Capital-Punishment States		Capital-Punishment States	
	1967	1968	1967	1968
First-degree murder	.18	.21	.47	.58
Second-degree murder	.30	.43	.92	1.03
Total murders	.48	.64	1.38	1.59

Source: "Murder and Capital Punishment," Walter C. Bailey and William J. Chambliss, ed, *Criminal Law in Action,* Copyright © 1975, Bailey. Reprinted by permission of John Wiley & Sons, Inc.

With a sufficient number of adequately accurate equations on tap, researchers one day will be able to test the implications of specific social changes by computer rather than in real life.

Suppose a province contemplated doubling the size of its tourism industry, for example. We could enter that proposal into a computer simulation model and receive in seconds or minutes a description of all the direct and indirect consequences of the increase in tourism. We could know what new public facilities would be required, which public agencies such as police and fire departments would have to be increased and by how much, what the labour force would look like, what kind of training would be required to provide it, how much new income and tax revenue would be produced, and so forth, through all the intended and unintended consequences of the action. Depending on the results, the public planners might say, "Suppose we increased the industry only by half," and have a new printout of consequences immediately.

An excellent illustration of computer simulation linking social and physical variables is to be found in the research of Donella and Dennis Meadows and their colleagues at Dartmouth and Massachusetts Institute of Technology. They've taken as input data known and estimated reserves of various nonreplaceable natural resources (for example, oil, coal, iron), past patterns of population and economic growth, and the relationships between growth and use of resources. Using a complex computer simulation model, they've been able to project, among other things, the probable number of years various resources will last in the face of alternative usage patterns in the future. Going beyond the initially gloomy projections, such models also make it possible to chart out less gloomy futures, specifying the actions required to achieve them. Clearly, the value of computer simulation is not limited to evaluation research, though it can serve an important function in that regard.

This potentiality points to the special value of evaluation research in general. Throughout human history, we've been tinkering with our social arrangements, seeking better results. Evaluation research provides a means for us to learn right away whether a particular tinkering really makes things better. Social indicators allow us to make that determination on a broad scale; coupling them with computer simulation opens up the possibility of knowing how much we would like a particular intervention without having to experience its risks.

Main Points

- Evaluation research is a form of applied research that studies the effects of social interventions.
- A careful formulation of the problem, including relevant measurements and criteria of success or failure, is essential in evaluation research. Key steps in measurement include specifying outcomes—what the intervention is intended to accomplish, measuring experimental contexts, specifying the intervention under study and the target population of the intervention, and deciding whether to create new measures or use existing ones.
- Evaluation researchers typically use experimental or quasi-experimental designs. Examples of quasi-experimental designs include time-series studies and the use of nonequivalent control groups.
- Evaluation researchers can also use qualitative methods of data collection. Both quantitative

and qualitative data analyses can be appropriate in evaluation research, sometimes in the same study.
- Evaluation research entails special logistical and ethical problems because it's embedded in the day-to-day events of real life.
- The implications of evaluation research won't necessarily be put into practice, especially if they conflict with official points of view.
- Social indicators are aggregated descriptions of populations such as societies or social subgroups. They can provide an understanding of broad social processes.
- Computer simulation models offer the potential of assessing the possible results of social interventions without having to experience those results in real life.

Review Questions and Exercises

1. Use the Web or the library to locate a report of evaluation research that was conducted to monitor the implementation of a policy or program for which a federal, provincial, or local government agency is responsible. Write a short summary of the study design and the findings.

2. Suppose a community created a teen clubhouse with a game room, organized sports, and other activities and entertainment in an effort to keep youths off the streets and thus reduce youth crime. Describe how you might go about evaluating the effectiveness of the centre. Indicate whether your design would be experimental, quasi-experimental, or qualitative (or some combination of these).

3. Take a minute to think of the many ways your society has changed during your own lifetime. Specify three social indicators that could be used in monitoring the effects of at least one of those changes on the quality of life in your society.

4. Conduct a search on the Web to locate any of the social indicators that you specified in question (3). If you cannot, discuss how two or

three social indicators that you are able to find might be used to monitor the quality of life in your society.

Continuity Project

On the Web or in other media, find some intervention that has been suggested as a way of changing attitudes toward gender equality. Describe an evaluation research project that would test the intervention.

Additional Readings

Berg, Richard and Peter H. Rossi. *Thinking about Program Evaluation*. Thousand Oaks, CA: Sage, 1998. This is a great book for gaining a good foundation in evaluation research while enjoying a wide range of examples.

Chen, Huey-Tsyh. *Theory-Driven Evaluations*. Newbury Park, CA: Sage, 1990. Chen argues that evaluation research must be firmly based in theory if it's to be meaningful and useful.

Cunningham, J. Barton. *Action Research and Organizational Development*. Westport, CT: Praeger, 1993. This book urges researchers to bridge the gap between theory and action, becoming engaged participants in the evolution of organizational life and using social research to monitor problems and solutions.

Hedrick, Terry E., Leonard Bickman, and Debra J. Rog. *Applied Research Design: A Practical Guide*. Newbury Park, CA: Sage, 1993. This introduction to evaluation research is, as its subtitle claims, a practical guide, dealing straight-out with the compromises that must usually be made in research design and execution.

Rossi, Peter H. and Howard E. Freeman. *Evaluation: A Systematic Approach*. Newbury Park, CA: Sage, 1996. This thorough examination of evaluation research is an excellent resource. In addition to discussing the key concepts of evaluation research, the authors provide numerous examples that might help you guide your own designs.

*Info*Trac: You can find further relevant readings on the World Wide Web at

http://sociology.wadsworth.com

Part 4
Analysis of Data

Analysis of Data

14 Qualitative Data Analysis
15 Quantifying Data
16 Quantitative Data Analysis

In this part of the book, we'll discuss the analysis of data obtained through social scientific research, and we'll examine the steps that separate observation from the final reporting of findings.

Chapter 14 covers qualitative data analysis. We'll begin with the search for patterns and themes and proceed to address the role of theory in approaches to analysis. We'll then cover some common techniques and procedures that are useful aids in bringing order to, and searching for meaning within, a mass of qualitative data. After presenting an example that illustrates this process, we'll look at the use of computers in managing qualitative data.

Chapter 15 addresses the quantification of data that may have been collected through any of the modes of observation discussed in Part 3. We'll look at the powerful impact computers have had in this respect.

The logic of quantitative data analysis is presented in Chapter 16. This chapter is divided into three major segments, Elementary Quantitative Analysis, Multivariate Analysis and The Elaboration Model, and Social Statistics.

We'll begin with an examination of methods of analyzing and presenting the data related to a single variable. Following this, we'll look at the relationship between two variables and learn how to construct and read simple percentage tables. We'll then turn to multivariate analysis and pursue the logic of causal analysis through an examination of the elaboration model developed by Paul Lazarsfeld. Understanding the logic of the elaboration model in the context of contingency table analysis provides a good foundation for understanding other statistical techniques and the patterns of relationships that such techniques are designed to uncover.

Chapter 16 also presents an introduction to some of the more commonly used statistical methods in social science research, including an overview of a more advanced method of multivariate analysis—multiple regression. Rather than merely showing how to compute statistics by these methods (computers can do that), we've attempted to place them in the context of earlier theoretical and logical discussions. Thus, you should come away from this chapter knowing when to use various statistical measures as well as how to compute them.

Chapter 14

Qualitative Data Analysis

Bringing order to a mass of observations obtained through participant observation, in-depth inter-views, focus groups, archival documents, and other qualitative research techniques is a major goal of qualitative analysis. Discerning patterns and finding the underlying meaning in such observations is aided by a number of procedures and techniques such as coding and memoing. The use of computer programs designed to manage qualitative data can help the researcher in this process.

Introduction

There has been a resurgence of attention to qualitative research over the past two decades. This has resulted in a large number of texts devoted to qualitative research methods. How researchers proceed in the gathering, processing, analysis, and interpretation of their data is being told by ever more social scientists. As Miles and Huberman noted in their second edition of *Qualitative Data Analysis* in 1994, more and more practitioners "had begun to explicate their procedures." Their book addressed the need to promote the continued sharing of analysis procedures and to confront the issues of confidence in findings drawn from qualitative research. As they stated:

> [A]s qualitative researchers, we need to keep sharing our craft—that is, the explicit, systematic methods we use to draw conclusions and to test them carefully. We need methods that are credible, dependable, and replicable in *qualitative* terms.
>
> (1994:2)

While the guidelines and strategies described and advocated for conducting qualitative research and analyzing the resulting data vary, there is one theme that emerges as salient: the goal of revealing patterns or themes from the data. Thus, while strategies may differ, how to approach a vast amount of qualitative data and abstract key issues to report has basic commonalities. Although not all qualitative researchers want to summarize and generalize from their data, a substantial number do. It is therefore this task that we shall focus on in this chapter.

As a result of the large number of strategies and techniques that qualitative researchers are increasingly sharing, and the varied approaches to qualitative research we discussed in Chapter 11, the task of qualitative analysis cannot be reduced to a single set of guidelines. Thus our goal here is to present you with some of the common practices (or themes) that recur in these accounts regarding how researchers bring order to their data.

Qualitative data analysis is concerned with how you determine what's important to observe and how you formulate your analytical conclusions on the basis of those observations. We've indicated numerous times that observations and analysis are interwoven processes in qualitative research. Now it's time to say something about that interweaving. In addressing this issue in qualitative analysis, we return to an earlier discussion of inductive logic. Field research, for example, is one place where this mode of reasoning is especially evident and important. Nonetheless, while the use of inductive logic is common in qualitative analysis, it is not the only approach. According to Richard Boyatzis (1998:x), "There are primarily three approaches to developing themes systematically: (a) theory driven, (b) prior data or prior research driven, and (c) inductive."

Although there are those who believe that qualitative research is a craft, and that both gathering data and analyzing it cannot readily be taught, except perhaps through hands-on apprenticeship, there are others who believe that a great deal may be communicated through texts and other books that seek to describe the craft and articulate helpful steps to the new researcher.

Recognizing that the goal for many is to generalize and for some to build explanations or theoretical understanding, a major theme of many texts is the search for patterns and themes. Intertwined with the goal of recognizing and revealing patterns is that of coding and memoing.

Thus, following a general discussion of the search for patterns, we'll briefly look at the role of theory in qualitative analysis. We will discuss grounded theory once again, because many of the basic strategies and ideas advocated in the grounded theory method are used in qualitative data analysis more generally. For example, the major roles of coding and memoing, the idea of building theories from the ground up, the alternation between induction and deduction, the comparative element in the building of theory (constant comparative method) are all central elements of much qualitative analysis. Following this, we move to a more general discussion of processing qualitative data, focusing on coding and memoing in greater detail and providing some examples. This discussion will lead us to an examination of the use of computers in qualitative data analysis and CAQDAS (computer assisted qualitative data analysis software).

Searching for Patterns

As perhaps the most general guide, you're looking especially for *similarities* and *dissimilarities*. (That just about covers everything you're likely to see.) The similarities researchers seek are those patterns of interaction and events that are generally common to what they're studying.

In a study of jay walking, for example, you might notice common patterns of behaviour—behaviour patterns that large numbers of participants in a situation share such as checking for police officers before darting across the street. Once you become

aware of a possibility of a pattern, you should return and check carefully to determine whether the pattern you recognized is indeed widespread. Do all the participants in a religious revival meeting shout "amen" at the appropriate times? Do all prostitutes dress seductively? In this sense, then, the researcher is especially attuned to the discovery of commonalities. As you first notice these, you become more deliberate in observing whether it is occurring in the situation you're observing. If something is occurring repeatedly, you may ask why that should be the case. An explanation may suggest conditions under which you may not observe it, and you may look around for those conditions in order to test your expectations.

On the other hand, the researcher is constantly alert to *differences*. You should be on the watch for deviation from the general ideas you may have noted. Although most of the participants in a religious revival meeting murmur "amen" throughout the leader's sermon, you may note a few who don't. Why do they deviate from the norm? In what other ways do they differ from the other participants? The researcher might find a range of patterns that leads to a typology of behaviours. This might then lead to the search for potential social characteristics that are associated with these different types.

For example, how do different people handle the problem of standing in a line for tickets at a movie theatre? Some stare into space, some strike up conversations with strangers, some talk to themselves, some keep standing on tiptoes to see if the line is really moving, some keep counting their money, some read, and so forth. In such situations, an important part of your initial task as a researcher is to create a classification of behaviours: an organized list of the variety of types. Having done that, you then seek to discover other characteristics associated with those different types of behaviour. Are the "rich-looking" or "poor-looking" moviegoers more likely to re-count their money? Do men strike up more conversations with strangers than women do? Do old people talk to themselves more than young people do? Your purpose is to discover general patterns.

There are numerous suggestions about how a researcher might begin to discover patterns. Let's start with some suggestions by John and Lyn Lofland (1995:127–45) who note six different ways of looking for patterns in the topic of your research. Let's suppose you're interested in analyzing child abuse in a particular neighbourhood. Here are some of the ways you might make sense out of your observations.

1. *Frequencies:* How often does child abuse occur among families in the neighbourhood under study? Of course, we should always be alert to possible differences between actual frequencies and what people are willing to tell us.
2. *Magnitudes:* What are the levels of abuse? How brutal are they?
3. *Structures:* What are the different types of abuse: physical, mental, sexual? Are they related in any particular manner?
4. *Processes:* Is there any order among the elements of structure? Do abusers begin with mental abuse and move on to physical and sexual abuse, or does the order of elements vary?
5. *Causes:* What are the causes of child abuse? Is it more common in particular social classes, different religious or ethnic groups? Does it occur more often during good times or bad?
6. *Consequences:* How does child abuse affect the victims, in both the short and the long term? What changes does it cause in the abusers?

In qualitative research, such as field research or in-depth interview studies, the formulation of theoretical propositions, the observation of empirical events, and the evaluation of theory are typically all part of the same ongoing process. A researcher seldom if ever merely tests a theory and lets it go at that. Rather, many strive to constantly refine their theories, or generalized understandings, over the course of their observations. You ask what each new set of empirical observations represents in terms of general social scientific principles. Your tentative conclusions, so arrived at, then provide the conceptual framework for further observa-

tions. In the course of your observations of jaywalking, for example, it may strike you that whenever a well-dressed and important-looking person jaywalks, others tend to follow suit. Having noticed this apparent pattern, you might pay more attention to this aspect of the phenomenon, thereby testing more carefully your initial impression. You might later observe that your initial impression held true only when the jaywalking "leader" was also middle-aged, for example, or perhaps only when he or she was White. These more specific impressions would simultaneously lead you to pay special attention to the new variables and require that you consider what general principle might be underlying the new observations.

There are a variety of approaches to the discovery of patterns that are suggested in the literature on qualitative research methods and data analysis. As we noted, we cannot cover all of these variations but only provide some general guidelines to get you started. Some of the variation in the strategies and techniques offered depend on the goals of the researcher, their initial approach to their research, and their theoretical orientation.

While a very general goal of research is the discovery of patterns, there are those who desire to provide an idiographic account and do not try to find patterns. However, in the summary of data for presentation, usually patterns are sought for the sake of making generalizations. For some researchers such discovery may be for the purpose of summary and description while for others it may be to provide explanations and build theory from their data. We'll first look at some issues of the role of theory in qualitative analysis and then take a closer look at the process by which patterns are discovered and theories emerge in data analysis.

The Role Of Theory

One of the clearest ways to examine theory building in qualitative analysis is to look once again at the grounded theory method that we discussed in Chapter 11. We'll then take a brief look at the role that theoretical paradigms play in guiding qualitative analysis.

Grounded Theory Method

Grounded theory for Strauss and Corbin (1998:12) means "theory that was derived from data, systematically gathered and analyzed through the research process. In this method, data collection, analysis, and eventual theory stand in close relationship to each other." The key to grounded theory is a combination of grounding concepts in data and researcher creativity.

To better understand the ultimate goal of analysis in this method, let's look at how Strauss and Corbin define theory. Theory is

a set of well-developed categories (e.g., themes, concepts) that is systematically interrelated through statements of relationship to form a theoretical framework that explains some relevant social, psychological, educational, nursing, or other phenomenon. The statements of relationship explain who, what, when, where, why, how and with what consequences an event occurs. Once concepts are related through statements of relationship into an explanatory theoretical framework, the research findings move beyond conceptual ordering to theory.

(1998:22 Italics in the original.)

According to Strauss and Corbin (1998:21), "Theorizing is work that entails not only conceiving or intuiting ideas (concepts) but also formulating them into a logical, systematic, and explanatory scheme." Theory is typically derived from data and explains phenomena. Thus, for the most part, research projects are conducted without an *a priori* theory in mind—the theory emerges from the data. The grounded theory method, however, may also be used to "elaborate and extend existing theory." Under such circumstances, the researcher would, of course, have an existing theory in mind at the start of his or her project.

The process of theory building largely begins as inductive but as concepts are developed and hunches about the way concepts are related begin to form (hypotheses), these are constantly being checked against the data to see if they hold up. Their provisional nature in this regard means the process is recursive—there is an alternation of induction and deduction—a back and forth process between data collection and data analysis. Often, hypotheses will suggest new directions for data collection, concentrating on newly identified contrasts or possibilities. The goal is to make sure the indicators of the concepts are true to the data, and that the enlarging dataset is true to the range of possibilities.

The tools (techniques and procedures) of grounded theory are quite extensive. Coding is a key process and we will discuss this in greater detail below. The coding procedures lead to the development of concepts. Since the concepts are the foundation for building theory, how these are developed is a major element of grounded theory. The coding procedures and other techniques such as constant comparison, help to move the researcher further toward theory development. Concepts lead to broader categories, properties, hypotheses, and ultimately to theory.

Conceptual ordering is important in grounded theory. According to Strauss and Corbin, conceptual ordering refers to the "organizing (and sometimes rating) of data according to a selective and specified set of properties and their dimensions" (1998:15). The case study of private security officers by Micucci (1998), discussed in Chapter 11, is a good illustration of conceptual ordering. The typology he developed from his data represents his organization of the data. He specified three competing work styles among the officers—crime fighters, guards, and bureaucratic cops—and distinguished them in terms of their variation along different dimensions such as age, education, prior experience, differences in orientation to policing functions such as the crime control function and the service function, their relationships with and attitudes toward colleagues and the public, and sources and levels of job satisfaction. Conceptual ordering is a "precursor to theorizing" but may also be the end point of analysis for some researchers, as was the case for Micucci.

The constant alternation of data gathering and conceptualizing advocated in the grounded theory approach is a demanding task that requires systematic persistence. The researcher must be on top of his or her data, coding and memoing at every step. The goal is to continually compare what was learned from the data with what can be learned through further data gathering—checking initial ideas, concept codes, and early indications of relationships among concepts. This process was briefly illustrated in Chapter 11 in the discussion of Conrad's research into the major sources of changes in academic curricula. Thus when Conrad first noticed that academic change was mainly caused by an administrator who was pushing for it, he did not stop there. He went back to reexamine the data to further investigate his initial hypotheses and search for other plausible explanations. This alternation between induction and deduction is the path to theory building in the grounded theory approach to data analysis. Conrad ultimately revised his initial hypothesis in this manner. As we saw, he found the pressure of interest groups was a more telling source of change, because it was the pressure of interest groups that facilitated the role of the administrator as the agent of change. He went on to refine his theory by comparing and integrating the interpretation of data from the different types of universities he studied.

Even for those who are not following the grounded theory method, many of the elements of this approach have been adopted in the analysis of qualitative data. Thus, while not all qualitative researchers aim at developing theory grounded in data, many of the procedures that lead one to this ultimate outcome can prove extremely useful in ordering and summarizing data, and thus in finding patterns.

Theoretical Paradigms and Data Analysis

In Chapter 2 we talked about theoretical paradigms. In Chapter 11 we discussed different approaches to qualitative research that were influenced by such paradigms. We spoke of this as posing different puzzles to solve—thus attempts at solving different puzzles means focusing on different aspects of the data. This has implications for data analysis. For example, if a researcher is concerned with how meaning is conveyed in conversation, as opposed to the specific subject matter conveyed in the content of that conversation—for example an individual's experience as a victim of crime—then how the researcher organizes and analyzes his or her data will differ. While in each case the researcher is analyzing what is said, in the former instance what is being examined is what is often referred to as "talk-in-interaction." In the latter case the words expressed are being examined to determine how the content of what is said informs us about the individual's experience as a victim of crime.

These various approaches may be viewed as asking different questions of the data. These questions are guided by the theoretical orientations of the researchers. This orientation is usually incorporated into the research design. For example, the ethnomethodologist is often concerned with how conversations are managed. Thus, some ethnomethodologists organize their data such that conversation or talk-in-interaction may be assessed with a focus on how naturally occurring talk is managed among individuals. This type of analysis is referred to as **conversation analysis**. The researcher has specific ideas about what he or she wants to learn from the talk or text. Researchers, knowing in advance the types of issues upon which they want to focus, have therefore developed rather elaborate procedures for examining data in conversation analysis.

As Hutchby and Wooffitt (1998:13) state, "conversation analysis is the study of talk." One of the basic assumptions of conversation analysis is "that ordinary talk is a highly organized, ordered phenomenon." Hutchby and Wooffitt prefer the term "talk-in-interaction" rather than that of conversation as the object designated as the focus of study. As they describe in detail, there are specific techniques that have evolved in conversation analysis for the systematic analysis of everyday talk. In particular, there are specific transcription conventions that facilitate the recording of such things as turn-taking and overlap in conversation, gaps and pauses, and laughter and breathiness. Transcription conventions make the analysis of conversation easier and more rigorous. The conventions also help to point the new researcher to important factors that need to be considered in analyzing talk-in-interaction.

In illustrating orderly phenomenon recognizable in conversation and common devices used in such conversations, Hutchby and Wooffitt refer to a study by Drew who uncovered a patterned response to teasing. Drew concluded that a common reaction to being teased is to respond seriously or what he terms a "po-faced" response. According to Hutchby and Wooffitt,

> Drew describes a "continuum" of responses in which there are four main types: "(i) initial serious response...prompted to laugh by others [but] returning to po-faced rejection; (ii) simultaneously laughing at tease and rejecting its proposal; (iii) laughing acceptance, followed by serious rejection of the proposal in the tease; (iv) going along with the tease" (1987:225)
>
> (1998:101–102)

This is not the end point, however. Hutchby and Wooffitt (1998:99) note a sociological goal in the analysis as well—a concern for "the social and interactional functions of identifiable conversational phenomena." Thus, Drew goes on to search for an understanding of why, in the vast majority of cases, a major component of the response to a tease is a serious rejection of it. In searching for an understanding of what he terms "po-faced" or serious responses, he eventually finds a common pattern in the teases, the implication of a mildly negative or deviant identity for the tease recipient. The recipient's serious response, despite the common recognition of the tease, is to negate this implication.

This is only one example of how theoretical paradigms guide a researcher's approach to qualitative data analysis. You will run across many others, for example discourse analysis, which is applied to both conversations and texts. Thus it is an approach that is used to study various forms of communication and does not emphasize naturally occurring talk. It includes the analysis of various forms of talk such as phone interviews or the act of making a sale.

Another example is semiotics. Semiotics is the "science of signs." It refers to the analysis of various forms of symbols—visual and textual. The goal in semiotics is to conduct an analysis that reveals the hidden meanings of such symbols. This interpretation of documents of various forms is often conducted through a content analysis.

Our goal in this section was simply to make you aware of different approaches that are tied to various theoretical paradigms. Our goal in the next section is to discuss the processing and analysis of qualitative data in more general terms.

Processing Qualitative Data

Chapters 11 and 12 dealt with some of the ways researchers generate qualitative data, for example making field observations and recording them. In this chapter we are focusing on what you might do with those recorded observations afterward. In this section we'll briefly discuss some general issues concerning the processing of qualitative data, but as we have noted, there are many strategies and approaches. Thus, before actually undertaking a project, you'd do well to study some of the specific techniques qualitative researchers have developed for a given type of study and data. For example, an excellent source of nitty-gritty, detailed suggestions for field researchers is John and Lyn Lofland's *Analyzing Social Settings* (1995:181–203). Another good source is *Writing Ethnographic Fieldnotes* (1995) by Emerson et al. If you plan to undertake grounded theory, you might do well to read Glasser and Strauss (1967) and Strauss and Corbin (1998). If you want to conduct conversation analysis, a good source to examine is Hutchby and Wooffitt (1998).

Nonetheless, our approach in this section is to provide you with some ideas that will be useful as a starting point for finding order in qualitative data. A mass of raw observations doesn't tell us much of general value about social life. Ultimately, you must analyze and interpret your observations, discerning *patterns* of behaviour, finding the underlying *meaning* in the things you observed. The organization and processing of your notes, for example, is the first step in discovering that meaning.

The steps one takes in processing qualitative data vary. While we speak of steps, it is not a simple linear progression. The procedures of processing and analyzing data are a back and forth alternation between coding and interpretation at ever finer levels. The creation of *analytical* concepts depends on the nature of what you're studying and what you "see" in what you observe. As you begin to develop a sense of the different aspects of what you're observing, you'll want to establish terms or codes so you can recognize and order them.

To introduce the rudiments of the process soon to be more extensively described as coding, let us stress that from the outset you should be prepared to adorn your notes as they accumulate with preliminary codes that will serve as thematic cross-references. Suppose, for example, that we begin to sense that the political movement we are studying has a religious or quasi-religious significance for the people participating in it. We would want to write a memo and also keep track of all data relating to that aspect, perhaps as follows. The term "religious significance" might be the code we would use, and then every time we find an entry in our notes that is relevant to the religious aspect of the movement—say a participant has said that the movement has provided a new meaning to life— we would mark the statement using that code so we could retrieve that segment of our notes when examining the religious aspect of the movement.

Perhaps one of our interests in the political movement concerns the varying degrees of violence considered, proposed, or engaged in by movement members. Sometimes they seem peaceful and willing to compromise; other times they're more oriented toward hard-line aggression. Perhaps we'll want to explain why those differences occur. We might create a code on "Degrees of Violence" and keep tract of all relevant entries from our notes.

These are merely some ideas of analytical assessments. We can't give you a blueprint of what issues will be appropriate in your project—you need to do

that. It's important to keep in mind that this form of making sense of your data is a continuous process. Do not create a coding system at the beginning of the project and stick doggedly to it throughout. Stay flexible and keep modifying your system of codes, as new topics appear to become relevant.

It's now time to look in greater detail at the two core procedures in qualitative data that we mentioned earlier—coding and memoing. The goal of analyzing qualitative data such as field notes and in-depth interview transcripts is well served by considering the processes of coding and memoing, whatever your ultimate approach to analysis might be. The vast majority of researchers, whether their goal is exploration, description, or explanation, seek to communicate a telling and focused story that can be understood by those not directly involved in their research—one that summarizes the material and addresses patterns and themes that are sustained by the data.

Thematic cross-references are the beginnings or rudiments of a more extended process of organizing and analyzing the data, which we are about to describe.

Coding and Memoing

One central means by which the researcher brings order and coherence to a mass of data is through coding. **Coding** refers to the development of concepts and categories in the recognition and ordering of themes. Memoing is tightly intertwined with the coding process. **Memoing** refers to the writing of notes and commentaries concerning ideas, patterns, and themes that occur to the researcher in the process of reading and coding data. Despite the integrative nature of these activities, we will proceed to discuss coding first and then turn to discuss the role of memo writing in qualitative data analysis.

Coding

The process of coding is the identification and labelling of concepts. It is the process by which classification of phenomena occurs. The development of concepts is key to ordering and making sense out of the data. As Strauss and Corbin (1998:103) note, "A concept is a **labelled phenomenon.** It is an abstract representation of an event, object, or action/interaction that a researcher identified as being significant in the data." The goal of this is to "enable researchers to group similar events, happenings, and objects under a common heading or classification." Researchers group such things on the basis of "common characteristics or related meanings" that they share.

Many books concerning the analysis and interpretation of qualitative data discuss the idea of **open coding**. It is one of the initial steps in making sense of the mass of qualitative data that the researcher faces. Strauss and Corbin explain that open coding is the means by which concepts are discovered. As they state:

> to uncover, name and develop concepts, we must open up the text and expose the thoughts, ideas, and meanings contained therein. Without this first analytic step, the rest of the analysis and the communication that follows could not occur. Broadly speaking, during open coding, data are broken down into discrete parts, closely examined, and compared for similarities and differences. Events, happenings, objects, and actions/interactions that are found to be conceptually similar in nature or related in meaning are grouped under more abstract concepts termed "categories." Closely examining data for both differences and similarities allows for fine discrimination and differentiation among categories. In later analytic steps, such as axial and selective coding, data are reassembled through statements about the nature of relationships among the various categories and subcategories. These statements of relationship are commonly referred to as "hypotheses."
>
> (1998:102–03)

Emerson, Fretz, and Shaw (1995:151) speak of open coding and its role in analyzing qualitative data in a similar manner. It is at this early stage in the process where the researcher "entertains all analytic possibilities," trying to identify "as many ideas and themes as time allows...." At this stage the researcher is not concerned with how these ideas or themes will be used or how they may be related to one another. They term the next stage in

the process "focused coding." It is at this stage when the researcher considers the utility of the themes and how they may be related.

As an example of open coding, let's take a brief look at some notes of mine (Benaquisto) from the early stages of a study we've mentioned earlier in this book concerning federal prison inmates in Canada. The box on page 383 contains a segment of notes from an interview with an inmate. The interview was not taped because the inmates indicated discomfort about having what they said recorded. Therefore, recording the interviews would likely have inhibited the inmates from speaking openly and discouraged some from participation altogether. Also, the existence of tape-recorded interviews, which obviously contain the voice of the inmate, added an additional element of risk and hence the maintenance of inmate confidentiality. Instead, notes were taken during the interview. Immediately following the interview, the interviewer recorded what the inmate said in greater detail so the richness of what he said would not be lost. The box entitled "An Illustration of Open Coding" provides an example of a question and an inmate response. The response illustrates the initial coding of the data at an early stage—contained in the left-hand column.

Code-concepts developed in the process of open coding are the labelled phenomena, themes, or ideas that emerge in the examination of the data. Both Emerson et al. and Lofland and Lofland speak of open coding and focused coding as essential steps in the processing and analysis of qualitative data.

As Emerson et al. summarize,

> Qualitative analytic coding usually proceeds in two different phases. In *open coding* the ethnographer reads fieldnotes line-by-line to identify and formulate any and all ideas, themes, or issues they suggest, no matter how varied and disparate. In *focused coding* the fieldworker subjects fieldnotes to fine-grained, line-by-line analysis on the basis of topics that have been identified as of particular interest. Here, the ethnographer uses a smaller set of promising ideas and categories to provide the major topic and themes for the final ethnography.
>
> (1995:143)

An Illustration of Open Coding

Interviewer: If you could change anything about the system, what would you change?

Inmate:
Need for therapy
 	
Young inmates—vulnerable
 	
PEER PRESSURE
 	
  Macho environment
 	
  Therapy—bad rep
 	
Info recorded in prisoner's file
 	
PARANOIA
 	
  Fear of seeking help
  No trust
 	
  Fear of system reprisal
 	
External therapy programs
 	
Increase trust
 	
Residential facilities
	The inmate said that it would be a lot more helpful for some inmates to have therapy type programs to explore some of their issues. He said this was especially true for young people who are more fragile and tend to get bugged by other inmates who are more hardened from spending more time inside. He said that therapy doesn't have a good reputation among the inmates. He described the inmate population as being influenced by "some kind of macho attitude where you're supposed to solve your own problems." He said "what doesn't help when it comes to programs like therapy" is that such programs "have a very bad reputation because whenever you tell something to your psychologist, for example, it's put in the file [the prisoner's record] and can be used against you." He said that as a result "lots of people are paranoid of talking about themselves to the psychologist." He went on to stress that there is essentially no one that the inmate can trust to talk to regarding his personal problems for fear of having information put in his file that could be harmful to his parole board hearing, for instance. What is needed, the inmate added, is some kind of programs on the outside that are brought in on a contract basis and therefore not linked to the prison. He felt that this would make inmates more trusting of the staff working in the prisons and this would make them more likely to work on their issues. He also added that this kind of treatment could be set up in the form of residential facilities that would be funded by the government but where staff would be working independently from the government.

Lofland and Lofland (1995:192–193) describe focused coding as the process of "winnowing out less productive and useful codes and of focusing in on a selected number. This selected or focused set of codes is then applied to an increasing array of data. Categories within the selected codes are elaborated. Other codes are collapsed and yet others are dropped. Some codes begin to assume the status of overarching ideas or propositions that will occupy a prominent or central place in the analysis."

Finally, for Boyatzis, thematic analysis concerns the coding of qualitative data with an eye on reliability and validity—helping to insure that there is consistency of judgment. According to him (1998: x–xi) "A good code should have five elements:"

1. A label
2. A definition of what the theme concerns (i.e., the characteristic or issue constituting the theme)
3. A description of how to know when the theme occurs (i.e., how to "flag" the theme)
4. A description of any qualifications or exclusions to the identification of the theme
5. Examples, both positive and negative, to eliminate possible confusion when looking for the theme

As the process of coding progresses, the coding becomes more systematic and focused. Memoing usually occurs throughout the process of generating and coding qualitative data.

Memoing

The process of coding provides the researcher with a large number of ideas, themes, and potential relationships. Writing down these ideas and insights during the coding process and elaborating upon them is referred to as memoing. Strauss and Corbin (1998:110) provide a general definition of memos as, "The researcher's record of analysis, thoughts, interpretations, questions, and directions for further data collection." They speak of three types of memos that go hand in hand with coding—codes notes, theoretical notes, and operational notes. *Codes notes* indicate the code labels, provide information on the meaning and definition of the codes, and detail information obtained from the different types of coding. *Theoretical notes* concern a wide variety of issues. Such memos elaborate conceptual meanings, connections and relationships among concepts, and layout theoretical propositions, among other things. *Operational notes* concern issues of method and procedure such as how data was collected and situations encountered in the process. Memos therefore serve a variety of purposes.

Drawing on the grounded theory approach to qualitative data analysis, Emerson et al. distinguish two types of memos central to processing and analyzing data:

> Early on in the process of analyzing data, fieldworkers write *initial memos* on a series of discrete phenomena, topics, or categories. Later, as the fieldworker develops a clearer sense of the ideas or themes she wants to pursue, memos take on a more focused character; they relate or integrate what were previously separate pieces of data and analytic points. These *integrative memos* seek to clarify and link analytic themes and categories.
>
> (1995:143)

Lofland and Lofland speak of memo writing in a similar manner, using slightly different terms, and attending more to the role of memos in the final reporting of a study. They too draw on the grounded theory approach. They speak of the elemental memo, the sorting memo, and the integrating memo. The *elemental memo* is "a detailed analytic rendering of some relatively specific matter" (p. 194). The *sorting memo* is written at the stage when the elemental memos are reviewed and key issues and core variables are identified. It is in this stage that the organization and summary of the data takes form. The *integrating memo* makes use of the sorting memos, articulating the relationships and connections among key issues and concepts noted in the sorting memos.

In short, memos are used to elaborate on the codes as one proceeds to assess the data, providing definitions and descriptions. They also summarize potential emerging or discovered relationships among codes. Memos may also concern any subject relevant to the study, such as methodological concerns, ideas for further study, and so forth. Thus, the lengths of memos vary from a sentence to pages.

Whatever the terms used by researchers, the move from identification and clarification of concepts and their definitions to the articulation of relationships between concepts characterizes the progressive stages in memo writing. As the researcher proceeds, the "memos achieve a higher level of abstraction and generalization" (Lofland and Lofland 1995:195). The ultimate goal for many is the development of propositions that speak to questions about specific topics.

It is important to keep in mind that there are typically several different paths a researcher may take with his or her data, because a rich dataset contains various potential propositions that speak to alternative topics and, therefore, will likely produce a number of integrative memos. Thus, choosing which topics to develop and communicate is something most researchers must face.

We have discussed some key elements that many researchers use in various ways in the analysis of their data. This discussion by no means provides a complete account of qualitative data analysis. As we noted, our intent was simply to provide you with a potential starting point for bringing order to data. What we have covered relies heavily on ideas and guidelines articulated in the grounded theory approach. The best way to gain further insights into how to approach qualitative data analysis is to read a variety of authors on the topic and to examine how such analysis is in practice conducted. In the following section we present a brief example of an analysis of real qualitative data.

Bringing Order to Data: An Illustration

In the following example we will again use the Canadian prison inmate data to illustrate some of the steps in an analysis that concerned the reasoning and rationales expressed by offenders when discussing their criminal actions in light of potential consequences. In this brief account it is only possible to illustrate some of the many steps undertaken in the analysis. A fuller version of the analysis and the conclusions drawn from it may be found in Benaquisto 2000.

Coding and memoing were an integral part of the analysis. As I read through the interview data, I noted a large number of initial codes and wrote many preliminary memos. For example, what I found significant in what one inmate was saying was his communication of a demoralized state. He was stressing that it was hard for him to live on the outside—it was easier to be inside. Prison was

comforting in its own way. Trying to live life independently often made him depressed. He couldn't find work. He was uneducated. There were times when he just couldn't handle being independent—being arrested brought him some relief. Some prison environments made him feel secure. He didn't have to deal with the disappointments and hassles of life. At the time of his criminal act and of the interview, he preferred being inside the prison. He mentioned several times that he got the time he needed. He also said that even if he had been given a longer sentence, he would have accepted it. I coded this inmate as desiring prison.

There was another inmate who indicated at length that life behind bars was no better or no worse for him. I coded this person as indifferent to being in prison. There were several others that communicated either the desire to be in prison or an indifference to it. And in each of these cases the inmate expressed that in thinking about the outcome of his actions, he had a high expectation of being caught and did not care. I eventually grouped together these two types and categorized them as Fatalists. As I continued coding the data, a number of different types emerged. These will be discussed in greater detail below.

While the interviews were in progress, it struck me that the vast bulk of inmates were accounting for their behaviour when telling their story of what led to their arrest and ultimate conviction, even without being asked directly. One of my early memos reads as follows:

MEMO: Most inmates seem to attempt to account for themselves and their behaviour without directly being asked when responding to the question concerning what led to the criminal event for which they were imprisoned. They seem to want to explain themselves, even if they don't have rational reasons to present. Accounting for their behaviour is part of their narrative, particularly in light of the consequences of their actions. Also, the vast number of them admits to committing criminal acts, including those for which they were convicted (actually many to acts more severe than those for which they were convicted because often it was a plea bargain).

Each inmate had a narrative. Thus, as the coding progressed, one issue that guided the analysis was the recognition of themes that emerged from the stories the inmates told about their actions leading up to the event that landed them in prison. Following the initial coding and search for themes, a systematic search for commonalities and hence focused coding was undertaken. Eventually, I recognized that there were distinctive similarities among certain types. This took me to a higher level of abstraction. I was able to categorize a number of the themes (what I termed dominant motifs) derived from the inmates' narratives into clusters, reducing the number of conceptual categories for the purpose of summary. As the analysis progressed, I achieved an even higher level of conceptual abstraction and summary based on further similarities among categories. I referred to this final, further reduced set as overarching categories.

A memo that I wrote in the later stages of the analysis illustrates the progression of my thoughts.

> MEMO: There are those who desire prison. Others are not thinking at all about whether they get caught. They are so high on either drugs or alcohol or both how can reason and rationality play a role at all? Those seeking the thrill need the threat and believe they will succeed. They have no intention of getting caught, so they don't consider the consequences per se, just the action. These ways of thinking—reasoning or lack therefore—do not fit well with effectiveness of threat of harsher punishment. Deterrence theory—idea of rational actor weighing costs and benefits of criminal action—not work well. How does this fit with deterrence theory? Counter example: those who were reasoned and calculating about their actions and chances of getting caught (high level drug dealers).

This memo illustrates the gelling of the following idea. The means by which many criminal offenders become involved in criminal activity runs counter to the theory of deterrence, which stresses how one *would* think if he was acting in a calculating and rational way. The data gathered in the interviews with real offenders seemed to contradict many of the findings in support of deterrence theory derived from studies of non-offenders asked to consider hypothetical situations in which they contemplated engaging in criminal acts. Such studies more often concerned how people believed they might think or behave—thus making deliberate decisions independent of "real life" contexts. Such studies seem to represent how members of the middle class—taking a moment to fill out a questionnaire—might think or how students in a classroom respond to the hypothetical costs and benefits of engaging in criminal activities. However, crime control policies are not hypothetical or theoretical. Thus, how the actual offenders "think" about crime and its consequences should be understood and incorporated into the development of penal policies.

When the interviews were complete, I read through them in a focused and systematic way, noting for each inmate whether or not he "accounted for his actions" when describing the events that led to his ultimate conviction. In each case, I also noted what I came to term the dominant rationale that the inmate provided in his narrative for his actions, developed from the initial code-concepts that emerged. In determining the dominant rationale, I looked at what the inmate mentioned first and most often—how much he elaborated upon or repeated a given line of reasoning or thought. I also noted secondary and tertiary rationales when they were present. In this process further themes began to emerge (many I had already identified in memos like the one presented above). There were commonalities among inmate rationales.

I then read through the stories again, once more coding each inmate's story in terms of the dominant "rationale" he provided for his actions. The patterns were emerging more clearly and becoming more refined. Some of the categories of dominant rationales also had an affinity to each other when examined in light of the idea of rationality and reason—weighing costs and benefits—associated with deterrence theory. This meant that a hierarchical structure of concepts might be useful in organizing and making sense of this data.

Thus, from this coding I created a typology or categorization of the rationales the inmates expressed in light of their consideration of the consequences of their actions. The coding of rationale or "criminal reasoning" with respect to deterrence thus emerged from common central motifs in crime stories offered by the inmates. From the point of view of the observer, the themes (dominant motifs) summarize the motivation or inner mental states that led to the crime. From the subject's perspective, it summarizes the reasons offered to explain their action, although, one must keep in mind that reasons and "reasoned thinking" need not coincide.

Simplifying the analysis and argument for the sake of a brief illustration, there were ultimately 12 dominant motifs or themes that emerged: fed up with life; prison is better; extreme intoxication; situational rage/duress; permanent mental incapacity; prideful neutralizers; politically motivated; thrill seekers; calculators; negligence; drug/alcohol addiction; thoughtless greedy. Several distinct dominant motifs could be further grouped on the basis of common themes that linked them at a higher level of abstraction. For example, those fed up with life and prison is better were grouped as Fatalists, as indicated above. The motifs of extreme intoxication, situational rage, and permanent mental incapacity were grouped together under Reduced Mental Capacity on the basis that each of them emphasized how they were unable to think about the consequences, even though this inability to think was attributed to different circumstances. The severe drug addict, the criminally negligent, and the thoughtless greedy were grouped together also. At a higher level of abstraction, the commonality among their stories was how they simply did not think about the consequences despite the fact that they had the ability to do so. Thus they were termed Nonthinkers—or thoughtless criminals. Finally, two other dominant motifs, the prideful neutralizers and politically motivated were grouped as Punishment Neutralizers, because these men had in common a sense that consequences would not apply to them, even though their reasoning as to why the consequences would not apply to them differed.

With this reduced set of six categories, further grouping was yet possible. Those with Reduced Mental Capacity and the Nonthinkers could be grouped at an even higher level of abstraction, each having in common the self-description that they didn't think about the consequences at all when engaging in their criminal act. They were thus grouped under the category Noncalculators. This category brought together those who couldn't think and those who didn't think. In their self-accounts, each of the inmates in the Noncalculator category directly emphasized his disconnection from consequence.

The Punishment Neutralizers were grouped with the Thrill Seekers on the basis of their common overestimation of their ability to escape detection or underestimation of the criminal justice actors' abilities. Given the commonality of their miscalculation of the consequences they were likely to face, despite having consciously taken consequences into account, they were categorized as Miscalculators. The Calculators—those who specifically characterized their thoughts and actions in terms of costs and benefits of committing an offence by weighing their gains against their likelihood of being caught and the potential harshness of the punishment they would receive—remained as a small but prominent category comprised of this single dominant motif.

The end result was four overarching categories that summarized the variety of dominant motifs and therefore criminal reasoning (or nonreasoning) in light of consequences: Noncalculators, Miscalculators, Fatalists, and Calculators. In brief, the paper that emerged spoke to the efficacy of deterrence for such criminal offender types. Focusing on criminal reasoning in light of consequences, these types summarized the mental processing and decision making (or lack of it) that the crime stories revealed.

These categories or types were then assessed in terms of the likelihood that those who comprise them would successfully respond to the threat of even harsher punishments or, what I termed, a policy of enhanced deterrence. In brief, the threat of harsher penalties was likely to prove ineffective for the vast majority, such as the Fatalists who preferred or were indifferent to prison and the Noncalculators—the largest category—comprised of those who didn't consider consequences at all prior to their actions. The small percentage of Calculators (13 percent of the sample) was the exception. Comprised primarily of higher level drug dealers, these men discussed how they consciously weighed the benefits of their criminal acts against the likelihood of the costs of punishment and reasoned that the penalty would likely not be severe enough to outweigh the benefits they would gain from their actions. It seems likely that a real threat of harsher punishment might deter such offenders.

Potentially one category of Noncalculator, the thoughtless greedy might be deterred by harsher punishment as well. These men, who were for the most part first time offenders, indicated that had they thought about the consequences of their actions at the time they engaged in criminal activity, they likely would not have done it—but they hadn't thought about it. Therefore, even for this group harsher punishments would not solve the problem of their lack of thought in the first instance. It seemed clear from what they were saying that had they thought in terms of consequences initially, the current level of punishment would have been sufficient to deter their actions. The bottom line then is that a policy of harsher punishments—enhanced general deterrence—does not look promising as a means of stopping criminal behaviour on the part of the vast majority of criminal offenders we find behind bars in the Canadian federal correctional facilities.

This example briefly illustrates some of the steps involved in the analysis of qualitative data. What ultimately resulted was a coding of "criminal reasoning" or rationale with respect to deterrence that emerged from common motifs or central themes derived from the narratives (crime stories) offered by the inmates. The coding scheme evolved from the themes that first became evident during the interviewing process and were further clarified and systematically pursued in first and second readings of the assembled data.

This is only one example of how a researcher makes sense of qualitative data. In pursuing this theme, there were many issues that emerged during the coding and memoing that were not pursued. Other issues were left for other analyses.

Managing Qualitative Data Using Computers

You may think of computers primarily in connection with the statistical analysis of quantitative data. However, computers have made a powerful contribution to field research and other forms of qualitative research. To begin, any standard word-processing program is a vast improvement over the traditional cut-and-paste technology of the typewriter. Once your qualitative data, such as field notes or interview transcripts, are entered into the computer, you can make complete or partial copies effortlessly, excerpting and reorganizing your notes in any number of ways.

Word-processing systems will search through your notes for specific words and phrases. Enter the word *shout* in such a search routine, and the computer will show you each time that string of letters appears in your notes: *shout, shouting, shouted,* and so on. If you anticipate this tactic when you enter your notes, in fact, you can be even more effective. In addition to the narratives and analyses you might normally write, jot in key code words relevant to your study. For example, you might type in the word *demographics* every time your notes discuss the makeup of the groups you're observing. You could mark all the places that have to do with group leadership or gender discrimination for example. This process of concept-coding is part and parcel of the interpretation of your data. Other, more complex concepts may be coded this way as well.

Many recent word-processing programs have a variety of features that lend themselves to coding and searching textual data. For example, segments of text may be color coded, and notes may be attached to these coded segments of text. Codes and notes may be entered directly into the text and then located using the "find" or "search" function. If you prefer using printed versions of your data and marking your concept codes in the margins, this too is easy to do using a word-processing program.

Once you've entered your notes into the computer, you can review and reprocess them endlessly. Let's say you didn't take our advice about entering code words when you first typed up the notes, or perhaps you didn't anticipate some of the concepts you now wish you had noted. You can go back and enter such codes easily.

Simple word-processing programs may prove sufficient for some in their analysis of qualitative data, particularly if one has a relatively small dataset. Today, however, there are a large number of computer software programs that have been specifically designed for the analysis of qualitative data. We will discuss some of the issues under debate about the desirability of using computer software programs in analyzing qualitative data as well as some of the general, basic capacities of many such programs. We will then briefly discuss some key questions you should consider in choosing a qualitative software package.

Pros and Cons of Using CAQDAS

Some arguments against the use of qualitative data analysis programs centre on a fear that data will not be examined in context because of the code and retrieval process that tends to encourage the examination of qualitative data in isolated segments, such as fragments of text that refer to a particular code or theme. This lack of context means that the richness of a concept may be missed. This in turn contributes to the potential for misapplication of codes. In addition, it has been noted that analysis of isolated data segments is likely to deemphasize elements of process that may be useful in understanding interactions and other potential elements relevant to theory building.

Nonetheless, there are others who find qualitative software packages highly valuable tools in analyzing data. Faced with a vast amount of qualitative data, the organizational efficiency that such tools provide assist the researcher in the mechan-

ical tasks of ordering and managing the data. The coding of data can be done more quickly, and it's easier to make changes in coding that might be required as the research progresses. This makes such changes more likely to occur. The process of retrieving the coded data is faster and more complete. The entire range of illustrative examples is readily available to the researcher and, therefore, a greater amount of illustrative material is likely to be presented in support of interpretations. Such programs facilitate the counting of such supportive evidence as well, for example, the number of times a given idea or opinion was communicated. It should be noted that this latter capacity is also what some have expressed concern about. It has been argued that the ease with which simple counts can be made may encourage ever greater use of them in place of—or will be expected to be included in addition to—more richly descriptive reports, perhaps pushing qualitative research closer to quantitative research in goals and strategies, contributing to the merging of the two approaches.

Overall, it is often said that while the analysis remains the task of the researcher, computer software programs can provide great assistance in the mechanical tasks of managing the large amount of unordered data that is often the result of qualitative data gathering. This in turn assists in bringing order to the data, saving a great deal of time in the mere mechanics of managing large, textual datasets.

Since the researcher is merely using the computer program to assist in the tasks of arranging material—the generation of ideas and concepts (coding), discovery of patterns, refinement of concepts and patterns—the interpretation of the data is still the job of the researcher. These tasks are not computer automated. The analysis of the data remains in the hands of the researcher. Yet, the organizational efficiency of such tools can assist the researcher in taking into account a larger number of factors and hence facilitates the recognition of patterns and relationships. This in turn contributes to emergent theoretical explanations.

Some General Features of CAQDAS

There are a variety of software programs from which to select. In the 1980s, The Ethnograph was a relatively widely used program. As more and more qualitative software programs were produced, however, no one program has become truly dominant. Currently, NUD*IST (Nonnumerical Unstructured Data Indexing Searching and Theorizing), and more recently NVivo (NUD*IST Vivo) appear to have gained recognition.

Many of the programs have free downloadable demonstrations that may be obtained from the Web. For descriptions, tutorials, and demonstrations of a large number of currently available programs go to http://www.scolari.com/. Information on the following qualitative software packages may also be found at the above Web site:

Atlas.ti
BEST
C-I-SAID
Decision Explorer
Diction
The Ethnograph
GBSTAT
HyperRESEARCH
MAXqda
QSR NUD*IST
QSR NUD*IST Vivo (NVivo)
SphinxSurvey
Methodologist's
Toolchest
winMAX

Learning a qualitative software program is an investment of time. Therefore, we suggest that you seriously explore the available features of the different programs before making a choice. What one person finds user-friendly and suitable to their needs, another may not. In addition, different methodological approaches may call for different types of programs with various features that better suit a given approach. For example, a semiotic analyst may have different needs than a conversation analyst or an ethnographer.

Given the variety of packages available, we will not present any single package as illustrative.

Instead, we will briefly review some of the major functions available in such programs in order to give you a general sense of a few of their main features. Each individual program has its own tutorial that provides initial guidance in its use. Typically, however, you will begin your data input by naming your project and then entering or importing data. Such programs accept data for input from standard word-processing programs (the typical way that data is entered into such programs), but data may also be typed directly into the available fields. When importing your data, however, a common requirement is that you save your data in a plain "text" format. This eliminates the formatting commands specific to any given word-processing program. Therefore, elaborate formatting of fieldnotes or interview transcripts in a word-processing program, for example, would not be a good use of time if you plan to import this material into a qualitative software package for data management and analysis.

Each program has various functions for editing the document and coding and linking data in the documents that you import or create. Since coding and retrieving data is central to the process of qualitative data analysis, paying particular attention to these functions when assessing whether a given software package suits you is key. The coding of data allows you to provide a conceptual name for something and then mark the relevant text according to this concept code so that it may be retrieved in connection to the code. For example, if we had a code, racist remarks—referring to all derogatory remarks made about visible minorities—then all such remarks throughout the entire database could be marked, coded under the category racist remarks, and then retrieved using this code.

More specifically, when a concept code is created, there is a place to provide a description or definition of it—that is, a statement of what the code concerns. These codes created to represent our concepts are then used to code the further data. We select the text we want to code—that is, the text that corresponds with the concept—and then we identify the appropriate code by whichever means the given program we are using has arranged. That piece of selected text will then be associated with the code that we applied to it. Such identifications may be altered during the course of our research. In addition, if a given remark or event equally fit under two or more concept codes, say a given statement is coded as a racist remark, but it may equally be coded under hostile relations and tense interactions, that same statement or segment of text may be selected and coded under each of these concept codes as well and thus would be retrieved when any one of the three codes was being examined. The relative ease with which the researcher can use multiple codes for any given segment of text facilitates the possible recognition of an overlap of concept codes, which in turn may assist the researcher in clarifying and refining concepts and relationships between them.

Many, but not all, of the programs also allow the research analyst to arrange codes in a hierarchy, sometimes referred to as a tree. Thus relationships among codes may be maintained in a hierarchical structure. In combination with the typical capacity to incorporate memos into the text, such facilities can be valuable in the movement from descriptive and thematic analyses to examining relationships between concept codes and analytic thoughts in the path toward theory building.

There are a variety of search and retrieve functions that assist you in your data analysis. For example, you might decide to examine all the segments of text you coded as racist remarks, searching for patterns of similarity or difference. The code racist remark would allow you to retrieve and view all such passages for examination in one file location. Such programs usually provide the researcher with further, precise information about the line location of the passage within the larger datafile, making it easier to go back and review the statement in context should that be desired.

Here's an example of two passages that are retrieved from the fieldnote observations in the Canadian prison study (Benaquisto) for the code racist remarks.

> This morning one of the outside staff walked to the guard station in wing X. The person was speaking to the prison guards and the conversation was punctuated by a lot of laughing (but there appeared to be tension in the laughter). In a light-hearted tone, the Black staff member mentioned that he felt "today was his day" and that "God was on his side." In a laughing manner, one of the prison guards mentioned that indeed God was on his side because "he was shitting on his head all the time." This comment was made in reference to that staff member's skin color. The staff member responded to that comment—nervously laughing—by saying that when the guards joked and said "dirty things," they were no longer "playing the game." Although the whole exchange was done in a tone of laughter, it seemed clear that the Black staff member was somewhat resentful of the guard's comment. Nonetheless, the guard continued repeating the joke several times to his other colleagues, stating that it was "a good one." He appeared quite pleased with his sense of humor.

> The following comment by a guard was not directed at anyone in particular but was simply made as a general statement. When one of the guards was making himself some toast, he was looking for white bread. One of the other guards mentioned that there was no more white bread available and that he would have to use brown bread. The guard replied that he did not want brown bread because it was "nigger bread."

The researcher tends to develop a sense of the main themes in his or her data as it is being collected. For example, in field notes or interview data, when certain ideas or topics are repeatedly recognized or raised, these are often considered main themes. Therefore, once the data is entered for coding, the researcher often has a well-developed list of concept codes available for application to the data. It's good to remember, however, that the actual coding of the data is up to you. Thus, care and consistency in the application of these codes is important. In the initial stages of coding, it is often advisable to maintain a rather simple code structure. You can then begin to develop categories and subcategories. As you progress in your coding and analysis, links between and among code categories will develop and may be added. Through this developmental process of coding, patterns begin to emerge.

We'll end this brief review of CAQDAS with a set of questions that Weitzman (2000:810) suggests a researcher should ask when choosing an appropriate software package. As he states, because the issues raised by these questions focus on "matching functions, rather than specific programs, to particular needs, these guidelines can continue to be useful" independent of discussions or illustrations of any given program at a specific point in time.

1. What kind of computer user am I?
2. Am I choosing for one project or for the next few years?
3. What kind of project(s) and databases(s) will I be working with?
4. What kinds of analyses am I planning to do?

In addition to these four questions, he states two crosscutting issues to keep in mind.

- How important is it to you to maintain a sense of "closeness" to your data?
- What are your financial constraints when buying software and the hardware it needs to run on?

Each of these questions is discussed in greater detail to assist you in making a choice. For example, when considering the type of database you will be using or the kind of project you will be working on, you have to think about specific details such as the structure of your data and whether the program provides you with the tools to organize the type of data you plan to use—text, graphics, video, and so forth. If you are working with data that you want to be able to revise, for instance, adding memos or codes and so forth, you should determine if such revisions are easy to make in your database or not.

Another issue that should be addressed when looking at the available features of a qualitative software package concerns the number of data sources from which you will be gathering your data for a given case. For example, if your case is a prison inmate, you will talk to the inmate, but you may also have information from the inmate's file, information gleaned from staff about the inmate, and so forth. Thus you will have multiple data sources per case. Making sure that the program you choose is designed to easily track cases through varied document sources is important. As Weitzman (2000:812) notes, "programs that are good at making links, such as those with hypertext capacity, and that attach 'source tags' telling you where information is coming from" would be particularly useful for those with multiple data sources.

These are only a few of the many issues Weitzman discusses that you would want to consider when choosing a program. The investment of learning a new program can be considerable in terms of both time and money. It is, therefore, worthwhile to read through such guidelines and consider each of the issues carefully when making your selection.

Although books and articles concerning the use of computers in qualitative data analysis may become quickly outdated with the fast pace of change in technology, many such writings deal with issues that are not bound to a given program. Thus, Udo Kelle's edited book on the subject published in 1995 continues to offer useful insights. You can also explore this topic further in Eben Weitzman's chapter discussed above, "Software and Qualitative Research" (2000), which provides a good discussion of what researchers should ask themselves when choosing a software program suitable for their research purposes.

We'll conclude this chapter with the following caution. In all social science research methods, a large gap lies between understanding the skills of data analysis and actually using those skills effectively. Typically, experience is the only effective bridge across the gap. It's worth recalling the parallel between the activities of the scientist and those of the investigative detective. Although fledgling detectives can be taught technical skills and can be given general guidelines, insight and experience separate good detectives from mediocre ones. The same is true of qualitative researchers.

Main Points

- A major goal in the analysis of qualitative data is to reveal themes that emerge from the data.

This process is largely a search for patterns of similarities and differences followed by an interpretation of those patterns.

- In qualitative research, observation, formulation of theoretical propositions, and the evaluation of theory are typically part of a single ongoing process. Many researchers seek to constantly refine their generalized understandings or theories over the course of their observations.

- The use of inductive logic is common in qualitative research. However, qualitative analysis may also be driven by theory, prior data, or prior research.

- Some of the variation in the strategies and techniques offered for the analysis of qualitative data depend on the researchers' goals, their initial approach to their research, and their theoretical orientation.

- Grounded theory refers to building theory that is derived from data. Many of the basic ideas and procedures used in the grounded theory method are used in qualitative data analysis more generally. Searching for themes and patterns using the techniques of coding and memoing, the alternation between induction and deduction, and the constant comparative method are all central elements of many qualitative analyses.

- Theoretical paradigms often guide the analysis of qualitative data. For example, conversation analysis derives from ethnomethodogy and concerns the study of naturally occurring talk. One key assumption of conversation analysts is that ordinary talk is highly organized and ordered. Specific techniques, such as transcription conventions, have been developed by conversation analysts for the systematic study of the devices used in everyday talk.

- Coding and memoing are two key procedures that help researchers organize and process data and discover patterns. The processes of coding and memoing are tightly intertwined.

- Coding refers to applying labels to strips of data that illustrate ideas and concepts and to the continuing process of identifying, modifying, and refining concepts and categories that sustain emerging themes. Memoing refers to writing notes and commentaries on patterns and themes, the meaning of codes, issues of methodology and procedure, and any other ideas that occur to the researcher when reading and coding the data

- Open coding is conducted in the initial stages of a research project when the data is examined closely and the researcher aims to identify as many ideas and themes as he or she can without concern for how these ideas are related or how they will be used.

- As the data gathering and ongoing data processing progresses, coding becomes more focused as the researcher's concerns shift toward how concepts will be used and their relationship to each other.

- Computers can be useful tools in assisting researchers in the management of qualitative data. Many features in common word processing and database programs have proved quite serviceable for some practitioners. There are also a variety of programs designed specifically for use in qualitative data analysis. Such programs facilitate the management of large amounts of unordered data, but the generation and interpretation of concepts and patterns derived from the data remain the job of the researcher.

Review Questions and Exercises

1. Find a research report using the grounded theory approach to qualitative data analysis. Describe the key procedures and techniques used by the researchers to process and analyze their data. Using your own words, summarize the conclusions of the report.

2. Search the Web for the transcription of an interview such as those available in oral history archives. Conduct an open coding of two or three pages of the interview you locate.

3. Using the same interview you located for question (2), write a memo that discusses one of the codes you have applied. Write another memo concerning any initial ideas that occurred to you during your open coding.

Continuity Project

Using your fieldnotes from the participant observation you conducted on campus observing gender equality/inequality (Chapter 11) or the interview you conducted with an elderly female relative or neighbour (Chapter 12), conduct an open coding of your data. In the process of coding, write several memos concerning the ideas that occur to you. When you complete your initial coding of the data, write a memo that explicitly discusses what issues you might like to pursue if you continued to gather data for your project.

Additional Readings

Hutchby, Ian and Robin Wooffitt. *Conversation Analysis: Principles, Practices and Applications.* Cambridge, England: Polity Press, 1998. This book does a good job of introducing the method of conversation analysis. The authors present detailed descriptions of the technique, including illustrations.

Silverman, David. *Interpreting Qualitative Data: Methods for Analyzing Talk, Text and Interaction,* 2nd ed. Thousand Oaks, CA: Sage, 2001. This book brings together theoretical concerns, data-collection techniques, and the process of making sense of what's observed.

Strauss, Anselm and Juliet Corbin. *Basics of Qualitative Research: Techniques and Procedures for Developing Grounded Theory,* 2nd ed. Thousand Oaks, CA: Sage, 1998. This book focuses extensively on coding and memoing, providing numerous definitions and examples.

Weitzman, Eben. "Software and Qualitative Research" in *Handbook of Qualitative Research*, 2nd ed., N. Denzin and Y. Lincoln, eds. Thousand Oaks, CA: Sage, 2000: 803–820. This chapter provides a succinct discussion of issues under debate concerning the use of computer software programs in qualitative research and an excellent summary of issues to consider when choosing a qualitative software program.

InfoTrac: You can find further relevant readings on the World Wide Web at

http://sociology.wadsworth.com

Chapter 15

Quantifying Data

Much social research involves statistical analysis of quantitative data. Today, such analysis is accomplished with the aid of computers. Turning a vast amount of observations into a machine-readable format for computer analysis involves transforming the data into quantitative terms that analysis software can read and process. Thus, data must be coded and then cleaned to rid of any errors that may have occurred in the coding process.

In this chapter . . .

Introduction

What the microscope was to biology and the telescope to astronomy is what the computer has been to quantitative social research. Computers have opened up possibilities of looking at the social world in ways that we could never before view it. Moreover, we are still discovering the ways in which computers can contribute to social science. Computers allow researchers to process and analyze vast amounts of quantitative data.

This chapter describes methods of converting social science data into a *machine-readable form*—a form that can be read and manipulated by computers and similar machines used in **quantitative analysis**. If you conducted a quantitative research project more or less parallel to reading the chapters of this book, your data at this point would be in the form of completed questionnaires, content analysis code sheets, or the like. In the stage covered in this chapter, those data would be recorded on a computer disk, CD-ROM, or some other device for storing information that can be read by the computer.

Computer hardware (equipment) and software (the programs that tell the equipment what to do) are constantly changing. Nevertheless, the logic of using computers for analysis is fundamentally the same independent of the particular hardware and software we might be using. Therefore, we are providing you with an overview of several stages in the evolution of computers in social research. It's useful to know about the earlier equipment and techniques because they reveal the logic of data analysis more clearly than today's more advanced technology—similar to the way learning about the fundamentals of how an automobile works is more easily grasped by looking at an old VW Bug than by taking apart the latest Maserati. We'll then discuss basic steps in quantifying data so you can take advantage of the powerful tools that computers make available to you.

Computers in Social Research

For our purposes, the history of computing in social research began in France in 1801, about the same time the seeds of modern social science itself were germinating. That's the year Joseph-Marie Jacquard created a revolution in the textile industry that would affect the most unlikely corners of life.

To facilitate the weaving of intricate patterns, Jacquard invented an automatic loom that took its instructions from punched cards. As a series of cards passed through the loom's "reader," wooden pegs poked through the holes punched in the cards, and the loom translated that information into weaving patterns. To create new designs, Jacquard needed merely to punch the appropriate holes in new cards, and the loom responded accordingly.

The revolutionary development here was that *information* (for example, a desired weaving pattern) could be *coded* and *stored* in a physical form (holes punched in a card) and subsequently *retrieved* by a machine that "read" the information (provided by the punched holes) and took action based on it. That is still what computers fundamentally do.

The next step in our selective computer history takes place in the United States, during the 1890 census. Following a mandate in the U.S. Constitution, a complete census of the nation's population has been taken every 10 years beginning with the 1790 enumeration of just under four million U.S. citizens. As the new nation's population grew, however, so did the task of measuring it. The 1880 census enumerated a population of over 62 million people—but it took the U.S. Census Bureau *nine years* to finish its tabulations—just short of when they had to begin another census. Clearly, a technological breakthrough was required before the 1890 census was conducted. The bureau sought suggestions.

Herman Hollerith, a former Census Bureau employee who had worked on the 1880 census, had an idea. Now a young engineering instructor at MIT, he proposed to adapt the Jacquard card to the task of counting the nation's population. As local tallies were compiled, they would be punched into cards. Then a tabulating machine of Hollerith's creation would read the cards and determine the population counts for the entire nation.

Hollerith's system was tested in competition with other proposals and found to be the fastest. As a result, the Census Bureau rented $750,000 worth of equipment from Hollerith's new Tabulating Machine Company, and the 1890 population total was reported within six weeks. Hollerith's company, incidentally, continued to develop new equipment, merged with other pioneering firms, and was eventually renamed the International Business Machines Corporation: IBM. By the

1950s, punched cards—commonly called *IBM cards*—were being adapted for the storage and retrieval of social research data.

Most data analyses today are conducted with computers, which electronically store data. A computer can go beyond simple counting and sorting to perform intricate computations and provide sophisticated presentations of the results. Popular computer software programs examine several variables simultaneously and can compute a variety of statistics. Data stored on diskettes, hard drives, or CD-ROMs can be read much faster than punched cards allow, and computers can calculate complex statistics a good deal faster and more accurately than people can. Nonetheless, computer programs simply carry out instructions for doing what people, for example, statisticians, used to do on paper. In fact, the original "computers" *were* human—rooms full of mathematical clerks calculating military ballistics. When machines took over that function, the machines were also called computers.

Computers now process all kinds of information. For example, with the use of word processors, researchers can manipulate text and graphics, making composition, revisions, reorganization, and the incorporation of information from multiple sources easier than ever before. Vast quantities of verbal and quantitative data can be stored in spreadsheets and databases in the form of records that can be displayed, ordered, and analyzed in any number of ways.

Many computer programs today are specially designed to analyze social science data. SPSS is a well-known and commonly used program for analyzing social science data. Other such programs include: ABtab, AIDA, A.STAT, BMDP, CRISP, DAISY, Data Desk, DATA-X, Dynacomp, INTERSTAT, MASS, MicroCase, Microquest, Microstat, Micro-SURVEY, Minitab, POINT FIVE, P-STAT, SAM, SAS, SNAP, STATA, STAT80, Statgraf, Statpak, StatPro, STATS PLUS, Statview, Survey Mate, SURVTAB, SYSTAT, and TECPACS, to name just a few. Whatever program you use, the basic logic of data storage and analysis is the same.

Up until the late 1970s, all computer analyses were perfomed on large, expensive computers—

sometimes called *mainframe computers*—maintained by centralized computer centres, and some analyses still are. To make use of such facilities, a researcher had to supply the data for analysis together with the instructions for the type of analysis desired. And the researcher might have taken the data to the computer centre in the form of cards or a magnetic tape.

Subsequently, two developments improved the process just described. Remote job entry systems placed card readers and printers near the researchers and allowed them to submit jobs and receive their results at locations some distance from the computer centre.

Time sharing was a further advance. In a sense, computers have always operated on a time-sharing basis—several users sharing the same computer. Initially, however, computer facilities were shared in a serial fashion: The computer would run your job, then someone else's, and so forth. More sophisticated computers, however, could perform several different tasks simultaneously. They could read our request, analyze yours, and print out someone else's all at the same time. In fact, the tremendous speed of computers made it possible to sandwich small operations (which may take only one-thousandths of a second) in the middle of larger jobs.

This capacity made it possible for computers to handle requests from hundreds of users simultaneously, often giving the impression that each one had the computer's complete attention. Such interactions with the computer typically involved *computer terminals*—devices that either printed information on paper or displayed their operations on video monitors. The terminals, however, were devices for interacting with the central computer—they were not themselves independent computers.

Today, you're most likely familiar with the next step beyond time sharing. Some networks are local, connecting computers in a single facility or organization (an office, a university, a corporation). Access to these networks is restricted to authorized uses. In the past couple of decades, however, networking and time sharing have gone global via the international networks known collectively as the Internet and the World Wide Web. You and your colleagues share access to an Internet "server" at your campus, and that server talks to other servers all around the world, putting you in seemingly direct contact with anyone connected to any of those other servers. Although this development is revolutionizing communications, it is still a matter of entering, storing, processing, and sharing machine-readable information. The creation of this textbook, for example, involved countless electronic communications. Research and teaching examples were found in electronic forums. Portions of the manuscript were sent electronically for review and comment.

Computer networks greatly increase the resources available to researchers. They make it possible, for example, for a researcher sitting at home in Vancouver to get a copy of a data set maintained on a computer in Paris and to analyze those data using a program maintained on a computer in Toronto. The results of the analysis would be returned to the user in Vancouver, and the results could also be stored for examination by a colleague in Russia. Procedures like this are becoming commonplace; before the end of your career, you'll look back on them as primitive.

The invention of the personal computer or PC (originally called the microcomputer to distinguish it from mainframes and their descendents, minicomputers) put all of this power in the hands of individual researchers. The PC revolution has progressed so rapidly it's easy to lose sight of how much things have changed in a relatively short time. When I (Babbie) was a graduate student at the University of California at Berkeley during the 1960s, the Survey Research Center had an IBM 1620 computer, which occupied approximately the same space as six or seven refrigerators. Its memory capacity was 24K, or 24,000 bytes' (characters') worth of information. The IBM 1620 served the needs of 30 to 40 active researchers, who published numerous books and articles each year.

When I (Benaquisto) was a graduate student at Harvard University in the 1980s, the PC revolution was in its infancy. The first IBM PC was introduced in 1981. These were too expensive for graduate students, but I bought my first PC in 1983—a 4.77 megahertz machine with 64K of random access memory (RAM). I had no hard drive, only a 360K floppy drive that held a 5 ¼ inch disk (a hard cardboard sleeve protecting the flexible plastic that had inspired its name "floppy" disk).

Today, we are working on laptop computers that have 5 to 10 thousand times as much memory as the old 1620 and the first generation IBM PCs. Even most hand-held devices we use today—for example, to store addresses and phone numbers—have several hundred times the memory of the earliest IBM PCs. Presently, most personal computers use hard drives that store data in the billions of bytes (gigabytes). Added to such built-in storage capacity are CD-ROMs, Zip drives, Jaz drives, and other storage devices that vastly expanded the storage capacity of PCs. CD-ROMs can store hundreds of millions of bytes of data on small, thin disks. Originally, the data stored by the manufacturer could only be retrieved, i.e., the "ROM" in CD-ROM stands for "read-only memory." We now have available to us CD Writers—allowing us to write and rewrite to a CD disk or to "burn a CD" as some say.

The value of these technological advances for social researchers has been great. The role played by computers in social research has increased dramatically over the past few decades. The remainder of this chapter discusses the steps and options involved in converting data into machine-readable forms amenable to computer processing and analysis.

Coding

For computers to work their magic, they must be able to read the data you've collected in your research. Moreover, computers are at their best with numbers. If a survey respondent tells you that he or she thinks the biggest problem facing Charlottetown, PEI, today is "the disintegrating ozone layer," the computer can't process that response numerically. You must translate by *coding* the response. We have discussed coding in connection with content analysis (Chapter 10) and again in connection with qualitative data analysis (Chapter

14). Now we'll look at coding specifically for quantitative analysis.

To conduct a quantitative analysis, researchers often must engage in a coding process after the data have been collected. For example, open-ended questionnaire items result in nonnumerical responses, which must be coded before analysis. As with content analysis, the task here is to reduce a wide variety of idiosyncratic items of information to a more limited set of attributes composing a variable. Suppose, for example, that a survey researcher has asked respondents, "What is your occupation?" The responses to such a question would vary considerably. Although it would be possible to assign each occupation reported a separate numerical code, this procedure would not facilitate analysis, which typically depends on several subjects having the same attribute.

The variable *occupation* has many preestablished coding schemes. One such scheme distinguishes professional and managerial occupations, clerical occupations, semiskilled occupations, and so forth. Another scheme distinguishes different sectors of the economy: manufacturing, health, education, commerce, and so forth. Still others combine both. An advantage of using an established coding scheme is the ability to compare your research results with those of other studies. Statistics Canada, for example, has the Standard Occupational Classification, 1991, available at http://www.statcan.ca/english/IPS/Data/12-565-XPE.htm.

The occupational coding scheme you choose should be appropriate to the theoretical concepts being examined in your study. For some studies, coding all occupations as either white-collar or blue-collar might be sufficient. For others, self-employed and not self-employed might be sufficient. Or a peace researcher might wish to know only whether the occupation depended on the defence establishment or not.

Although the coding scheme should be tailored to meet particular requirements of the analysis, one general guideline should be kept in mind. If the data are coded to maintain a great deal of detail, code categories can always be combined during an analysis that does not require such detail. If the data are coded into relatively few, gross categories, however, there's no way during analysis to recreate the original detail. To keep your options open, it's a good idea to code your data in more detail than you plan to use in the analysis.

Developing Code Categories

There are two basic approaches to the coding process. First, you may begin with a relatively well-developed coding scheme, derived from your research purpose. Thus, as suggested previously, the peace researcher might code occupations in terms of their relationship to the defence establishment. Or, you may want to use an existing coding scheme so that you can compare your findings with those of previous research.

As discussed in Chapter 14, the alternative method is to generate codes from your data. Suppose we had conducted a survey of a random sample of adults living in a medium sized town in Canada. In this survey we asked them what project or change over the next year would most benefit their town. Some of the answers they might have given are as follows:

The opening of a new factory
Emergency street phones placed throughout town
Building of a town youth centre
Increase in police presence
Reduction in house taxes
New community centre for the elderly
Initiation of community block parties
Reduction in school taxes
More efficient snow and ice removal

Consider these responses for a moment to see if you can identify any categories represented. Of course, there are several possible coding schemes that a researcher might generate from these responses. Thus, there is no right answer. Let's consider the last response: more efficient snow and ice removal. What category of concern might be represented by this response? One rather clear candidate is "government services." Are there any other responses that might fit into this category?

The following table shows which of the responses could fit into this category.

Community Responses Coded as "Government Services"

	Government Services
Opening of a new factory	
Emergency street phones	X
Building of a town youth centre	X
Increase in police presence	X
Reduction in house taxes	
New community centre for the elderly	X
Initiation of community block parties	
Reduction in school taxes	
More efficient snow and ice removal	X

The last response might equally be viewed in more general terms as a "safety" concern. Thus, if your research interests were focused on community members' concern for safety, the responses might be coded as follows:

Community Responses Coded as "Safety Concerns" and "Non-Safety Concerns"

	Safety Concerns	Non-Safety Concerns
Opening of a new factory		X
Emergency street phones	X	
Building of a town youth centre		
Increase in police presence	X	
Reduction in house taxes		X
New community centre for the elderly		X
Initiation of community block parties		X
Reduction in school taxes		X
More efficient snow and ice removal	X	

There is a gap in the above table. The response, building a town youth centre, has been left uncoded. Non-safety concerns would be the most reasonable place for this response unless we had auxiliary information, such as prominent campaigns emphasizing control of juvenile delinquency or if we had a primary research interest emphasizing the broadest possible notion of safety concerns. Often one can clarify an ambiguous response case by adding a further distinction that groups responses that share a recognizable affinity. This leads to another example of a possible coding scheme. Subdividing non-safety concerns into economic concerns and social concerns results in the following balanced groupings, with the youth centre now grouped with some clear parallel cases.

Non-Safety Concerns Coded as "Economic Concerns" and "Social Concerns"

	Safety Concerns	Economic Concerns	Social Concerns
Opening of a new factory		X	
Emergency street phones	X		
Building of a town youth centre			X
Increase in police presence	X		
Reduction in house taxes		X	
New community centre for the elderly			X
Initiation of community block parties			X
Reduction in school taxes		X	
More efficient snow and ice removal	X		

As this brief illustration may signal, one of the most difficult problems often faced in creating coding schemes is to somehow avoid adding so many codes or creating a scheme of such complexity that it will prove cumbersome or down right unworkable at the stage of analysis when you are trying to produce some form of succinct summary of the entire collection of responses. Although we noted earlier that it might be advisable to preserve some detail in your initial coding scheme so you have some flexibility at the analysis stage, that advice was not intended as a prescription for an initial complex and undigested set of codes. There is no hard and fast rule for the number of code categories one should create, but you may have noticed that most of the examples discussed in this book classify hundreds and even thousands of responses into two or three relatively evenly balanced categories at the stage of analysis. Such a

compact yet complete coding scheme is often an earmark of a high level of research skill.

As you can see from the few examples above, there are a variety of possible ways for coding a set of data. The choices we make reflect both our research purposes and the logic we derive from the data. Over the course of the coding process, it is often necessary to modify the code categories. When such modifications are made, however, all data that has already been classified must be reexamined to determine if the initial classifications of responses must be changed to insure conformity with the modified coding scheme.

Like the set of attributes composing a variable, and like the response categories in a closed-ended questionnaire item, code categories should be both exhaustive and mutually exclusive. Every piece of information being coded should fit into one and only one category. Problems arise whenever a given response appears to fit equally into more than one code category, or when it fits into no category. Such problems indicate a mismatch between your data and your coding scheme.

If you're fortunate enough to have assistance in the coding process, your task would be to refine your definitions of code categories and show your coders how to assign given responses to the proper categories. This is accomplished by explaining the meaning of the code categories and providing several examples of each. To make sure your coders fully understand what you have in mind, code several cases in advance. Then ask your coders to code the same cases, without knowing how you coded them. Compare your coders' work with your own. Any discrepancies will indicate an imperfect communication of your coding scheme to your coders or may indicate flaws in your coding scheme. Even with perfect agreement between you and your coders, however, you should still check the coding of at least a portion of the cases throughout the coding process.

If you're not fortunate enough to have assistance in coding, you should still obtain some verification of your own reliability as a coder. Nobody's perfect, especially a researcher hot on the trail of a finding. Let's say you are studying an emerging cult, and you have the impression that people who don't have a regular family will be the most likely to regard the new cult as a family substitute. The danger is that whenever you discover a subject who reports no family, you'll unconsciously try to find some evidence in the subject's comments that the cult is a substitute for family. If at all possible, then, get someone else to code some of your cases to see if that person makes the same assignments you made.

Codebook Construction

The end product of the coding process is the conversion of data items into numerical codes. These codes represent attributes composing variables, which, in turn, are assigned names and locations within a data file. A *codebook* is a document that describes the locations of variables and lists the assignments of codes to the attributes composing those variables. A codebook serves two essential functions. First, it's the primary guide used in the coding process. Second, it's your guide for locating variables and interpreting codes in your data file during analysis. If you decide to correlate two variables as a part of your analysis of your data, the codebook tells you where to find the variables and what the codes represent.

Figure 15-1 is a partial codebook created from two variables from the General Social Survey conducted by Statistics Canada. Though there is no one right format for a codebook, we've presented some of the common elements in this example. Note first that each variable is identified by an abbreviated variable name: *M42A, RELIGATT.* We can determine the religious services attendance of respondents, for example, by referencing *RELIGATT.* This example uses the format established by the General Social Survey. Other data sets and/or analysis programs might format variables differently. For example, variables may be assigned numerical codes, abbreviated names, a combination of letters and numbers, and so forth. You must, however, have some identifier that will allow you to locate and use the variable in question.

Next, every codebook should contain the full definition of the variable. In the case of a questionnaire, the definition would be the exact wording of the questions asked, because, as we've seen, the wording of questions strongly influences the answers returned. In the case of *M42A,* you know that respondents were read the possible responses. In the case of *RELIGATT,* this variable was derived from a question to which you are

Figure 15-1
A Partial Codebook

M42A	RELIGATT
What is your best estimate of the total income, before deductions, of all household members from all sources during the past 12 months? Was the total household income...(list read to respondents, values 1 and 2)	Religious attendance of the respondent. Derived from M25: Other than on special occasions (such as weddings, funerals or baptisms) how often did you attend religious services or meetings in the last 12 months? Was it... (list read to respondents, values 1–5)
1 Less than $20,000?	1 At least once a week
2 $20,000 and more?	2 At least once a month
5 No income or loss	3 A few times a year
7 Not asked	4 At least once a year
8 Don't know	5 Not at all/never
9 Not stated	7 Not asked
	8 Don't know
	9 Not stated

Source: Statistics Canada, General Social Survey, 2000.

referred, namely M25. We provided you that question's wording and indicated that respondents were read the possible responses from which to choose.

The codebook also indicates the attributes composing each variable. In *RELIGATT* respondents could characterize their religious services attendance as "At least once a week," "At least once a month," and so forth. Finally, notice that each attribute also has a numeric label: "At least once a week" in *RELIGATT* is code category 1, for example. These numeric codes are used in various manipulations of the data: For example, you might decide to combine categories 1 and 2 to create a category for those who attended at least once a month or more and then compare it to those who attended less often than at least once a month by combining categories 3 through 5. It's easier to do this using code numbers than with lengthy names. Other information is often contained in codebooks as well. For example, the frequencies for each variable may be given and the weight to be used with the variable provided.

Coding and Data Entry Options

Years ago, all data entry took the form of manual keypunching, with cards either analyzed by counter-sorters that predated computers or read into computers for more complex analyses. All that has changed. Data are now typically keyed directly into data files stored on computer disks. As before, however, this is intimately related to coding, and there are several methods for effecting this link. Let's look at a few of these possibilities.

Transfer Sheets

The traditional method of data processing involves coding the data and transferring the code assignments to a *transfer sheet* or *code sheet*. Such sheets were traditionally ruled off in 80 columns, corresponding to the data card columns, but they can be adapted to other data configurations appropriate to the data entry method. (Figure 15-2 provides an illustration.) When using this form of data entry, coders write numbers corresponding to the desired code categories in the appropriate columns of the sheets. Each column represents a variable, for example *RELIGATT*. Each row represents a case, for example each respondent in the GSS, and each cell within the column contains a code corresponding to the attribute, for instance 1 = At least once a week, 2 = At least once a month, for a given case on a particular variable. The code sheets are then used for keying data into computer files. This is still a useful technique when particularly complex questionnaires or other data source documents are being processed.

Edge-Coding

Edge-coding is sometimes used to do away with the need for transfer sheets. In *edge-coding*, the

Figure 15-2
A Partial Coding Transfer Sheet

01	02	03	04	05	06	07	08	09	10		71	72	73	74	75	76	77	78	79	80
0	0	1	3	7	8	9	3	1	1		4	5	2	1	1	7	8	7	1	2
0	0	2	4	2	4	2	4	1	2		2	2	5	1	1	2	8	2	2	2
0	0	3	5	6	1	2	3	1	1		1	3	6	2	1	3	9	2	2	3
0	0	4	6	3	4	4	2	2	1		1	4	1	0	3	6	0	4	2	1

outside margin of each page of a questionnaire or other data source document is left blank or is marked with spaces corresponding to variable names or numbers. Rather than transferring code assignments to a separate sheet, the codes are written in the appropriate spaces in the margins. The edge-coded source documents are then used for data entry.

Direct Data Entry

If the questionnaires or other data collection forms have been adequately designed, you can often enter data directly into the computer without using separate code sheets or even edge-coding. A pre-coded questionnaire would contain indications of the column numbers or variable names and the codes to be assigned to questions and responses, and data could be entered directly.

Data Entry by Interviewers

The most direct data entry method in survey research has already been discussed in Chapter 9: computer-assisted telephone interviewing, or CATI. As you'll recall, interviewers with telephone headsets sit at computer terminals, which display the questions to be asked, and type in the respondents' answers. In this fashion, data are entered directly into data files as soon as they're generated. Closed-ended data are ready for immediate analysis. Open-ended data can be entered as well, but they require an extra step.

Let's say the questionnaire asks respondents, "What would you say is the greatest problem facing Canada today?" The computer terminal would prompt the interviewer to ask that question. Then, instead of expecting a simple numerical code as input, it would allow the interviewer to type in whatever the respondent said, for example, "crime in the streets, especially the crimes committed by drug dealers." Subsequently, coders could sit at computer terminals, retrieving the open-ended responses one by one and assigning numerical codes as discussed earlier in this chapter.

Coding to Optical Scan Sheets

Sometimes data entry can be achieved effectively through the use of an *optical scanner*. This machine reads black pencil marks on a special code sheet and creates data files to correspond with those marks. (These sheets are frequently called *op-sense* or *mark-sense* sheets.) Coders can transfer coded data to such special sheets by blacking in the appropriate spaces. The sheets are then fed into an optical scanner, and data files are created automatically. Although an optical scanner provides greater accuracy and speed than manual data entry, it has disadvantages as well. Some coders find it difficult to transfer data to the special sheets. It can be difficult to locate the appropriate column, and once the appropriate column is found, the coder must search for the appropriate space to blacken.

Second, the optical scanner has relatively rigid tolerances. Unless the black marks are sufficiently black, the scanner may make mistakes. Further, researchers have no way of knowing when this has happened until they begin their analysis. And if the op-sense sheets are folded or mutilated, the scanner may refuse to read them at all.

Direct Use of Optical Scan Sheets

Sometimes optical scan sheets can be used a little differently to avoid the difficulties they present. These are the familiar sheets used in multiple-choice exams, for example, on which answers are indicated by black marks in the appropriate spaces. Survey respondents can sometimes be asked to record their responses directly on such sheets. Either standard or specially prepared sheets can be provided with instructions on their use. To answer questions presented with the several answer categories, respondents can be asked to blacken the spaces next to the answers they choose. If such sheets are properly laid out, the optical scanner can read and enter the answers directly. This method may be even more feasible in recording experimental observations or in compiling data in a content analysis.

Connecting with a Data Analysis Program

Different computer programs structure data sets in different ways. In most cases, you'll probably use your data analysis program for data entry. SPSS, for example, will present you with a blank matrix of rows and columns. You can assign variable names to the columns and enter data for each case (such as the responses provided by each survey respondent) on a separate line. Once you're finished, your data will be ready for analysis.

As an alternative, you can often create your data set using some other means (such as a spreadsheet or a word processor) and then import the data into the analysis program. In the case of SPSS, for example, a text file with data items separated by tabs (such as datafile.dat) can be imported and then saved in the SPSS format (such as datafile.sav). Subsequently, you can load the data file as though it had been initially created through SPSS. Most data-analysis programs have similar options.

Data Cleaning

Whichever data-processing method you have used, you'll now have a set of machine-readable data that supposedly represent the information collected in your study. The next important step is the elimination of errors, i.e., "cleaning" the data. *Data cleaning* is the process of detecting and correcting coding errors.

No matter what method of data entry was used or how carefully the data have been entered, some errors are inevitable. Depending on the data-processing method, these errors may result from incorrect coding, incorrect reading of written codes, incorrect sensing of blackened marks, and so forth.

Two types of cleaning should be done: *possible-code cleaning* and *contingency cleaning*.

Possible-Code Cleaning

Any given variable has a specified set of legitimate attributes, translated into a set of possible codes. In the variable *gender*, there will be perhaps three possible codes: 1 for male, 2 for female, and 0 for no answer. For the variable *gender*, say, if a case has been coded 7, it's clear that an error has been made. *Possible-code cleaning* is the process of

checking to see that only the codes assigned to particular attributes (possible codes) appear in the data files.

This can be accomplished in two ways. First, many of the computer programs available for data entry check for errors as the data are being entered. If you tried to enter a 7 for gender in such programs, for example, the computer might "beep" and refuse the erroneous code. Other computer programs are designed to test for illegitimate codes in data files that weren't checked during data entry.

If you don't have access to these kinds of computer programs, you can find some errors by examining the distribution of responses to each item in your data set. Thus if you find your data set contains 350 people coded 1 on gender (for male), 400 people coded 2 (for female), and one person coded 7, you'll probably suspect the 7 is an error. Whenever you discover errors, the next step is to locate the appropriate source document (for example, the questionnaire), determine what code should have been entered, and make the necessary correction.

Contingency Cleaning

Contingency cleaning concerns checking that only those cases that should have data entered for a particular variable do in fact have such data. This type of data cleaning is more complicated. The logical structure of the data may place special limits on the responses of certain respondents. For example, a questionnaire may ask for the number of children that women have had. All female respondents, then, should have a response recorded (or a special code for failure to answer), but no male respondent should have an answer recorded (or should only have a special code indicating the question is inappropriate to him). If a given male respondent is coded as having borne three children, either an error has been made and should be corrected or your study is about to become more famous than you ever dreamed.

Although data cleaning is an essential step in data processing, you can safely avoid it in certain cases. Perhaps you'll feel you can safely exclude the very few errors that appear in a given item—if the exclusion of those cases will not significantly affect your results. Or, some inappropriate contingency responses may be safely ignored. If some men have received motherhood status during the coding process, you can limit your analysis of this variable to women. However, you should not use these comments as rationalizations for sloppy research. "Dirty" data will almost always produce misleading research findings.

Main Points

- The quantification of data is necessary when statistical analyses are desired.
- To analyze quantitative data using computers, the observations describing each unit of analysis must be transformed into standardized, numerical codes that are stored in the computer for retrieval and manipulation by machine.
- In the coding of data, a given variable is assigned a specific identifier in the data storage medium: either a number or an abbreviated name. The attributes of a given variable are represented by numerical codes.
- A codebook is the document that describes the identifiers assigned to different variables and the codes assigned to represent different attributes of those variables.
- Data entry can be accomplished in a variety of ways. Numerical codes may first be recorded on transfer sheets. These transfer sheets would then be used for data entry. Alternatively, edge-coding may be used. With edge-coding, the numerical coding is done in the margins of the original documents such as questionnaires instead of on transfer sheets.
- Data may be transferred to optical-scan sheets (op-sense or mark-sense sheets) where responses are indicated by black marks in the appropriate spaces. These sheets can then be read by optical scanners—machines that read the black marks and transfer the same information to data files.
- Direct use of optical-scan sheets—for example, asking survey respondents to record their responses directly on these sheets—may be used in some research projects to save time and money in data processing.
- Increasingly, data are keyed directly into computer files without the use of coding sheets. The data may be obtained directly from the precoded questionnaire and input into the computer or interviewers may type the respondents' answers directly into data files as the responses are being generated.
- All coding likely involves errors. It's therefore necessary to *clean* the data. Possible-code cleaning refers to the process of checking to see that only those codes assigned to particular attributes—possible codes—appear in the data files. This process guards against one class of data-processing error.
- Contingency cleaning is the process of checking to see that only those cases that *should* have data on a particular variable do in fact have such data. This process guards against another class of data-processing error.

Review Questions and Exercises

1. Find out the data-processing facilities available to social researchers on your campus and describe how survey questionnaires might be processed using those facilities.

2. Create a codebook—with variable and code assignment—for the following questions in a questionnaire:

    a. Did you obtain a high school diploma?
        ☐ Yes → If yes, did you obtain a degree from a higher educational institution
                ☐ Yes   ☐ No
        ☐ No

    b. What do you feel is the most important problem facing your community today?

    c. In the spaces provided below, please indicate the three community problems that most concern you by putting a 1 beside the one that most concerns you, a 2 beside your second choice, and a 3 beside your third choice.

_____Crime

_____Traffic

_____Drug abuse

_____Pollution

_____Prejudice and discrimination

_____Recession

_____Unemployment

_____Housing shortage

3. Write down the first 12 things you see when you walk into your bedroom. Create three different sets of categories that might be used to classify those items.

4. Coding involves grouping data into categories. Suppose that a study report codes people as being either "pro-life" or "pro-choice" on the abortion issue. List some of the different opinions that could have been assigned to each of these summary categories.

Continuity Project

Review the qualitative observations you reported in connection with Chapter 11. Describe how you might code those observations for a quantitative analysis. Discuss the advantages and disadvantages of quantifying your observations.

Additional Readings

Bernstein, Ira H. and Paul Havig. *Computer Literacy: Getting the Most from Your PC.* Thousand Oaks, CA: Sage, 1999. This book provides a quick overview of the various ways social scientists use computers, including many common applications programs.

*Info*Trac: You can find further relevant readings on the World Wide Web at

http://sociology.wadsworth.com

Chapter 16

Quantitative Data Analysis

Quantitative analysis may be descriptive or explanatory, and it may involve one, two, or several variables. We begin our examination of how quantitative analyses are done with some simple but powerful ways to manipulate data in order to reach research conclusions. We then examine the elaboration model to illustrate the fundamental logic of multivariate and causal analysis. Finally, we will acquaint you with a few simple statistics frequently used in social research. Statistics allow researchers to summarize data, measure associations between variables, and draw inferences from samples to populations— and are less painful than you may believe.

In this chapter . . .

Introduction

In the last chapter we discussed how to prepare data for quantitative analysis. It is now time to consider the analysis of such data. We analyze data to discover and substantiate patterns and relationships, test our expectations, and draw inferences.

Most social science analysis falls within the general rubric of **multivariate analysis**, or the examination of several variables simultaneously. The analysis of the simultaneous association among *age, education,* and *prejudice* is an example of multivariate analysis. Multivariate analysis is a general term for the analysis of several variables; it does not refer to a specific form of analysis. Specific techniques for conducting a multivariate analysis include factor analysis, smallest-space analysis, multiple correlation, multiple regression, and path analysis.

The basic logic of multivariate analysis can best be seen through the use of simple tables, called **contingency tables** or *cross-tabulations*. We will first lay the foundation for understanding more complex, multivariate analyses by examining the more fundamental univariate and bivariate modes of analysis and focusing on the construction and understanding of bivariate contingency tables. We will then turn to multivariate analyses using three variable contingency tables. We will proceed to a discussion of the elaboration model—a method for conducting multivariate analysis—and illustrations of the elaboration paradigm. We will then turn to regression analysis. Finally, we will conclude the chapter with a discussion of inferential statistics.

ELEMENTARY QUANTITATIVE ANALYSIS

This section lays the foundation for multivariate analysis by examining more fundamental analytic modes—univariate and bivariate analysis. Along the way we'll develop the basic logic of multivariate analysis through the use of contingency tables.

Univariate Analysis

Univariate analysis is the examination of the distribution of cases of only one variable. We'll begin with the logic and formats for the analysis of univariate data—the simplest form of quantitative analysis.

Distributions

The most basic format for presenting univariate data is called a one-way distribution. This is often laid out in a table which records the number of cases observed for each of the attributes of some

variable. Let's take the General Social Survey data on attendance at religious services, *J22*. Table 16-1 presents the results of an SPSS analysis of this variable.

Let's examine the table, piece by piece. First, if you look near the bottom of the table, you'll see that the sample being analyzed has a total of 12,756 cases. You'll also see that there are different categories of data defined as missing. For 1,825 of the 12,756 respondents, the question was not applicable. No answer was given by 675 respondents and 19 respondents were coded as do not know. These categories total to 2,519 cases defined as missing. So our assessment of Canadian attendance at religious services in 1996 will be based on the 10,237 respondents who answered the question (noted as "valid cases").

Go back to the top of the table now. You'll see that 2,548 people said they attended religious services at least once a week. This number in and of itself tells us nothing about religious practices; it gives us no idea of whether the "average Canadian" goes to church a little or a lot. This number alone does not provide us with sufficient information to determine this.

By analogy, if the spokesperson for some company said that they had 20 women executives, is that a lot or a little? The answer would depend on how the number of women executives compares to the total number of executives that firm employs. If there were 40 executives in total, 20

Table 16-1

Canadian GSS Attendance at Religious Services, 1996

J22	HOW OFTEN DO YOU ATTEND RELIGIOUS SERVICES/MEETINGS				
Value Label	Value	Frequency	Percent	Valid Percent	Cumulative Percent
At least once a week	1	2,548	20.0	24.9	24.9
At least once a month	2	1,216	9.5	11.9	36.8
A few times a year	3	2,202	17.3	21.5	58.3
At least once a year	4	982	7.7	9.6	67.9
Not at all	5	3,289	25.8	32.1	100.0
Not applicable	0	1,825	14.3	Missing	
Do not know (proxy only)	8	19	0.1	Missing	
Not stated	9	675	5.3	Missing	
	Total	12,756	100.0	100.0	
Valid cases	10,237	Missing Cases	2,519		

Source: "Canadian GSS Attendance at Religious Services/Meetings 1996," adapted from the Statistics Canada General Social Survey, Cycle 11, 1996.

would represent one-half or 50 percent female, but if there were 2,000 executives employed by the company, 20 women would mean that women make up only 1 percent of all executives. So our concern would be the proportion or percentage of women executives in that company—the number of women executives relative to a base.

In the case of religious participation, similarly, we need some basis for assessing the 2,548 people who reported that they attended religious services at least once a week. If you were to divide 2,548 by the 10,237 who gave some answer, you would get 24.9 percent, which appears in the table as the "valid percent." If we assess the number in this way, we see that 25 percent of Canadians who are 15 years of age or older reports attending religious services at least once a week. With this further information, we

are now able to make various comparisons among Canadians who attend religious services to varying degrees and those who do not.

A description of the number of times that the various attributes of a variable are observed in a sample is called a *frequency distribution*. It's sometimes easier to see a frequency distribution in a graph. Figure 16-1 was created with SPSS from the GSS data on *J22*. The vertical scale on the left of the graph indicates the percentages selecting each of the answers displayed along the horizontal axis of the graph. Notice how the percentages in Table 16-1 correspond with the heights of the bars in Figure 16-1, with the exception of "Missing—don't know" because on the graph this category combines "do not know" (.1 percent) and "not stated" (5.3 percent).

Figure 16-1
Bar Chart of Canadian General Social Survey, Attendance at Religious Services, 1996

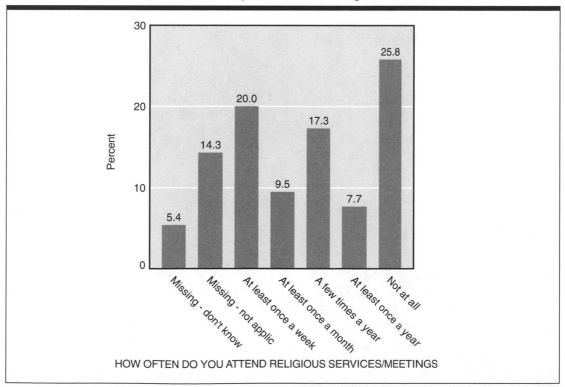

Source: "Bar Chart of Canadian General Social Survey, Religious Service Attendance 1996," adapted from the Statistics Canada General Social Survey, Cycle 11, 1996.

Central Tendency

Beyond simply reporting the overall distribution of values, often referred to as the marginal frequencies or just the *marginals*, you may choose to present your data in the form of an **average** or measure of *central tendency*. This is a way of expressing the "typical" value of a variable. For example, your grade point average expresses the "typical" value of all your grades taken together, even though some of them might be As, others Bs, and perhaps even some C grades. One common way in which a GPA is calculated is by converting the letter grades into their numerical representations, then calculating the arithmetic **mean** by dividing the sum of the values by the total number of cases. The mean is only one way to measure central tendencies or "typical" value. The **mode** (the most frequently occurring attribute), and the **median** (the middle attribute in the <u>ranked</u> distribution of observed attributes) are two other options. Here's how the three averages would be calculated from a set of data.

Suppose you're conducting an experiment that involves teenagers as subjects. They range in age from 13 to 19, as indicated in the following table:

Age	Number
13	3
14	4
15	6
16	8
17	4
18	3
19	3

Now that you've seen the actual ages of the 31 subjects, how old would you say they are in general, or on *average*? Let's look at three different ways you might answer that question.

The easiest average to calculate is the *mode,* the most frequent value. As you can see, there were more 16-year-olds (eight of them) than any other age, so the modal age is 16, as indicated in Figure 16-2.

Figure 16-2 also demonstrates the calculation of the *mean.* There are three steps: (1) multiply each age by the number of subjects who have that age, (2) total the results of all those multiplications, and (3) divide that total by the number of subjects. Figure 16-2 indicates the mean age in this illustration is 15.87.

The *median* represents the "middle" value: Half are above it, half below. If we had the precise ages of each subject (for example, 17 years and 124 days), we'd be able to arrange all 31 subjects in order by age, and the median for the whole group would be the age of the middle subject.

As you can see, however, we don't know precise ages; our data constitute "grouped data" in this regard: For example, three people who are not precisely the same age have been grouped in the category "13 years old."

Figure 16-2 illustrates the logic of calculating a median for grouped data. Because there are 31 subjects altogether, the "middle" subject would be case number 16 if they were arranged by age—15 teenagers would be younger and 15 older. Look at the bottom portion of Figure 16-2, and you'll see that the middle person is one of the eight 16-year-olds. In the enlarged view of that group, we see that case number 16 is the third from the left.

Because we don't know the precise ages of the subjects in this group, the statistical convention here is to assume they're evenly spread along the width of the group. In this instance, the *possible* ages of the subjects go from 16 years and no days to 16 years and 364 days. Strictly speaking, the range, then, is 364/365 days. As a practical matter, it's sufficient to call it one year.

If the eight subjects in this group were evenly spread from one limit to the other, they would be one-eighth of a year apart from each other—a 0.125-year interval. Look at the illustration and you'll see that if we place the first subject half the interval from the lower limit and add a full interval to the age of each successive subject, the final one is half an interval from the upper limit.

What we've done is calculate, hypothetically, the precise ages of the eight subjects—assuming their ages were spread out evenly. Having done this, we merely note the age of the middle subject from the overall list of subjects (case number 16)—16.31—and that is the median age for the group.

Figure 16-2
Three "Averages"

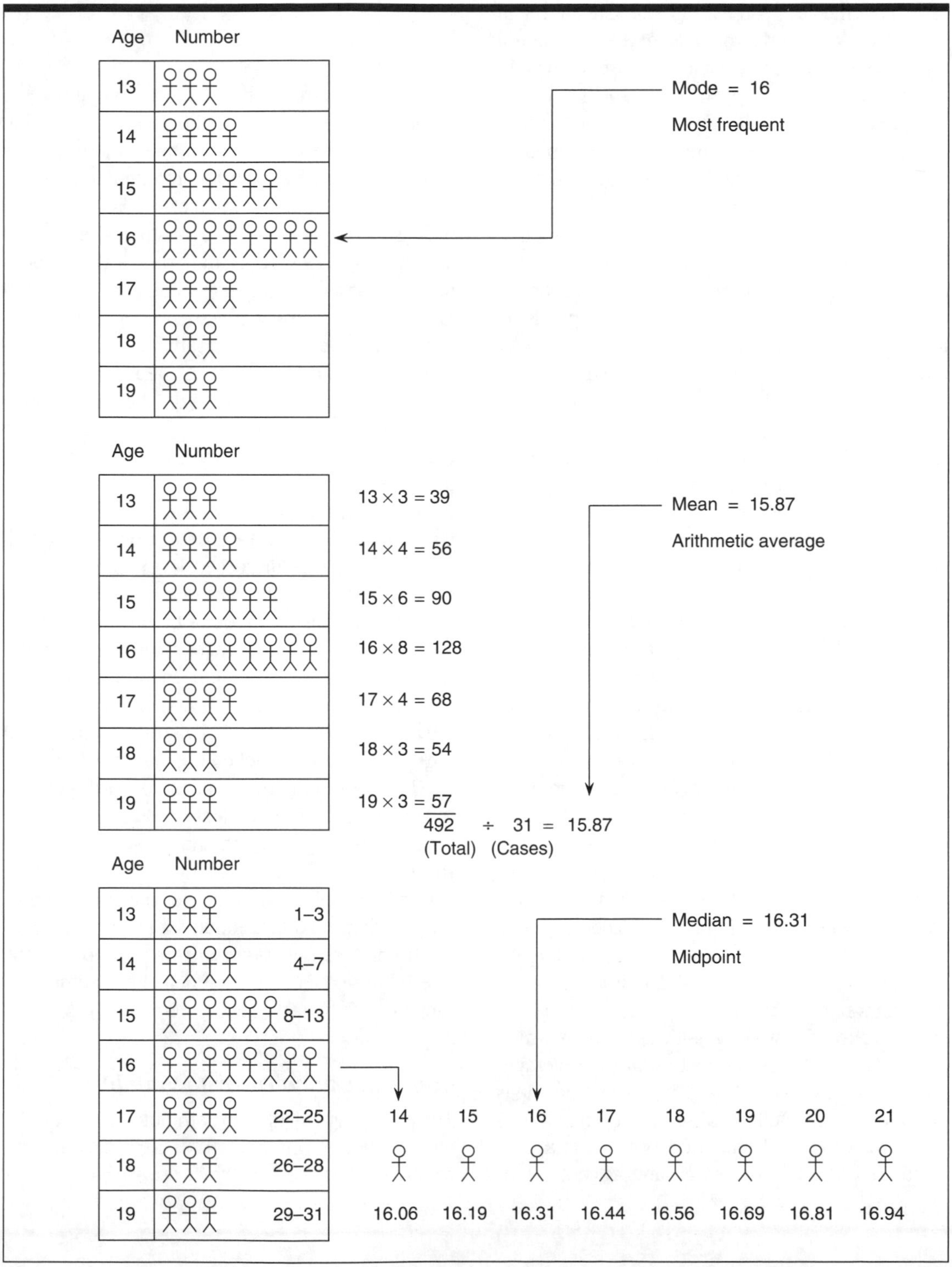

Age	Number	
13		
14		
15		
16		←
17		
18		
19		

Mode = 16

Most frequent

Age	Number	
13		$13 \times 3 = 39$
14		$14 \times 4 = 56$
15		$15 \times 6 = 90$
16		$16 \times 8 = 128$
17		$17 \times 4 = 68$
18		$18 \times 3 = 54$
19		$19 \times 3 = \underline{57}$

$$492 \div 31 = 15.87$$
(Total) (Cases)

Mean = 15.87

Arithmetic average

Age	Number	
13		1–3
14		4–7
15		8–13
16		
17		22–25
18		26–28
19		29–31

Median = 16.31

Midpoint

14	15	16	17	18	19	20	21
16.06	16.19	16.31	16.44	16.56	16.69	16.81	16.94

Whenever the total number of subjects is an even number, of course, there is no middle case. To obtain the median, you merely calculate the mean of the two values on either side of the midpoint of the ranked data. For example, suppose there were one more 19-year-old, giving us a total of 32 cases. The midpoint would then fall between case number 16 and case number 17. The median would therefore be calculated as $(16.31 + 16.44)/2 = 16.38$.

The three measures of central tendency often produce slightly different values, as the above example illustrates. Therefore, which measure of central tendency you choose to report depends on the nature of your data and the goal of your analysis. Whenever means are presented, you should be aware that they are susceptible to extreme values: a few very large or very small numbers. In such circumstances, the different measures of central tendency can produce very different values. It is important, therefore, to be familiar with the distribution of your data when choosing the measure of central tendency to report. For example, if one is attempting to present a relatively accurate picture of the "average" family wealth within a community—in a community where a few families have great wealth—use of the mean, as a measure of central tendency, would likely be misleading. The inequality in the distribution of wealth—the few families with great wealth—would inflate the apparent average. Let's look at a hypothetical example to illustrate. Suppose there were nine families who lived on a block. The families' net worth are distributed as follows: $100,000; $100,000; $105,000; $107,000; $109,000; $110,000; $112,000; $114,000; $30,000,000 (the house on the hill). Clearly, reporting the *mean* ($3,428,556) would be a misleading figure of the average wealth of families on this block; a measure such as *median* family wealth ($109,000) would provide a more accurate picture of the "average" family's net worth in this case. Therefore, it is important to carefully choose among the various measures of central tendency. When it is appropriate to use which of the measures of central ten-

dency is covered in greater depth in statistics courses and textbooks.

Dispersion

Averages offer readers the special advantage of reducing the raw data to the most manageable form: A single number (or attribute) can represent all the detailed data collected in regard to the variable. This advantage comes at a cost, of course, because the reader can't reconstruct the original data from an average. Summaries of the **dispersion** of responses—the way values are distributed around some central value, such as the mean—can somewhat alleviate this disadvantage. The simplest measure of dispersion is the **range**: the distance separating the highest from the lowest value. Thus, besides reporting that our subjects have a mean age of 15.87, we might also indicate that their ages ranged from 13 to 19.

A somewhat more sophisticated measure of dispersion is the **standard deviation**. The logic of this measure was discussed in Chapter 7 as the standard error of a sampling distribution. The standard deviation is an index of the amount of variability in a set of data. A higher standard deviation indicates that the data are more dispersed or spread out around the central value (e.g., the mean). A lower standard deviation indicates that the data are more bunched together.

There are many other measures of dispersion. In reporting intelligence test scores, for example, researchers might determine the **interquartile range**, the range of scores for the middle 50 percent of subjects. If the top one-fourth had scores ranging from 120 to 150, and if the bottom one-fourth had scores ranging from 60 to 90, the researchers might report that the interquartile range was from 90 to 120, or 30 points.

Continuous and Discrete Variables

The preceding calculations are not appropriate for all variables. To understand this point, we must distinguish between two types of variables: continuous and discrete. A *continuous variable* is one where small increments in the values of the variable are logically possible. An example is age, which changes steadily by very small amounts with each increment of time. A *discrete variable* jumps from category to category without intervening steps—intermediate values are illogical or nonsensical. Examples include *gender* or *marital status*—you go from being single to married in one step. One could add other distinct, discrete categories such as separated, but unlike age, there is no natural meaning to small differences

If a discrete variable—a nominal or ordinal variable, for example—were being analyzed, some of the techniques discussed previously would not be applicable. Strictly speaking, only modes should be calculated for nominal data, modes or medians for ordinal data, and modes, medians, or means for interval or ratio data (see Chapter 5). If the variable in question is *religion,* for example, raw numbers (23 respondents in our sample are Catholic) or percentages (7 percent are Catholic) can be appropriate and useful analyses. Calculating the mode would be a legitimate step, and reporting it might be helpful when one religion is predominant—for example, if most of the respondents are Protestants. Reports of mean, median, or dispersion summaries, however, would be inappropriate—they would not make sense.

Detail versus Manageability

In presenting univariate and other data summaries, you'll be constrained by two goals. On the one hand, you should attempt to provide your reader with the fullest degree of detail regarding those data. On the other hand, data summaries should be presented in a manageable form. As these two goals often directly counter each other, you'll find yourself continually seeking the best compromise between them. One useful solution is to report a given set of data in more than one form. In the case of age, for example, you might report the distribution of ungrouped ages *plus* the mean age and standard deviation.

As you can see from this introductory discussion of univariate analysis, this seemingly simple matter can be rather complex. In any event, the lessons of this section will assist us in our consideration of subgroup comparisons and bivariate analyses.

Subgroup Comparisons

Univariate analyses describe the units of analysis of a study and, if they're a sample drawn from some larger population, allow us to make descriptive inferences about the larger population. Bivariate and multivariate analyses are aimed primarily at explanation. Before turning to explanation, however, we should consider the case of subgroup description.

Often, it's appropriate to describe subsets of cases, subjects, or respondents. Table 16-2, for example, presents income data for men and women separately. In addition, the table presents women's earnings as a percentage of men's earnings.

Table 16-2
Mean Earnings of Full-Time, Full-Year Workers by Gender: 1967–1997

Year	Women	Men	Women's Earnings As a Percentage of Men's Earnings
1967	$18,725	$32,057	58.4%
1971	22,614	37,906	59.7
1974	24,762	41,572	59.6
1977	26,299	42,382	62.1
1981	26,638	41,793	63.7
1984	26,992	41,153	65.6
1987	27,761	41,970	66.1
1991	29,360	42,165	69.6
1994	29,967	42,929	69.8
1997	30,915	42,626	72.5

Source: "Mean Earnings of Full-year Workers by Gender: 1967–1997," adapted from the Statistics Canada publication "Women in Canada 2000: A Gender-based Statistical Report," Catalogue 89-503, September 2000.
Earnings expressed in constant 1997 dollars.

In some situations, the researcher presents subgroup comparisons purely for descriptive purposes. More often, the purpose of subgroup descriptions is comparative: Women earn less than men do. In the present case, it's assumed that there is something about being a woman that results in their lower incomes. In such a case, the analysis is based on an assumption of causality: one variable causing another, as in *gender* causing *income.*

When these statistics first came to popular attention, they added legitimacy to the growing outcry over the discrimination against women in the Canadian economy. Both politics and research have focused on the issue ever since, though the discrepancy in male and female earnings has hardly been resolved.

As Table 16-2 shows, in the second half of the 1960s women earned a little over half of what men earned. By the mid-1980s they were earning close to two-thirds what men earned. Women's earnings as a percentage of men's continued to rise in the 1990s, but a large difference between male and female earnings still remains, with the average full-time, year-round female worker earning 72 and one-half cents for each dollar earned by her male counterpart.

Before moving on to the logic of bivariate, causal analysis, let's consider another example of subgroup comparisons—one that will let us address some table-formatting issues.

"Collapsing" Response Categories

"Textbook examples" of tables are often simpler than you'll typically find in published research reports or in your own analyses of data, so this section and the next one address two common problems and suggest solutions.

Let's begin by turning to Table 16-3, which reports data collected in a multinational poll conducted by the *New York Times,* CBS News, and the *Herald Tribune* in 1985, concerning attitudes about the United Nations. The question reported in Table 16-3 deals with general attitudes about the way the UN was handling its job.

Here's the question: How do the people in the five nations in Table 16-3 compare in their support for the kind of job the UN is doing? As you review the table, you may find there are simply so many numbers that it's hard for you to see any meaningful pattern.

Part of the problem with Table 16-3 lies in the relatively small percentages of respondents selecting the two extreme response categories: the UN is doing a *very* good or a *very* poor job. Furthermore, although it might be tempting to merely read the second line of the table—those saying "good job"—that would be improper. Looking at only the second row, we would conclude that West Germany and the United States were the most positive (46 percent) about the UN's performance, followed closely by France (45 percent), with Britain (39 percent) less positive than any of those three and Japan (11 percent) the least positive of all.

This procedure is inappropriate in that it ignores all those respondents who gave the most positive answer of all: "very good job." In a situation like this, you should combine or "collapse" the two ends of the range of variation. In this instance, combine "very good " with "good" and "very poor" with "poor." If you were to do this in the analysis of your own data, it would be wise to add the raw frequencies together and recompute percentages for

Table 16-3

Attitudes Toward the United Nations: "How is the UN doing in solving the problems it has had to face?"

	West Germany	Britain	France	Japan	United States
Very good job	2%	7%	2%	1%	5%
Good job	46	39	45	11	46
Poor job	21	28	22	43	27
Very poor job	6	9	3	5	13
Don't know	26	17	28	41	10

Source: "5-Nation Survey Finds Hope for U.N.," *New York Times,* June 26, 1985, p. 6.

Table 16-4
Collapsing Extreme Categories

	West Germany	Britain	France	Japan	United States
Good job or better	48%	46%	47%	12%	51%
Poor job or worse	27	37	25	48	40
Don't know	26	17	28	41	10

the combined categories, but in analyzing a published table such as this one, you can simply add the percentages as illustrated by the results shown in Table 16-4.

With the collapsed categories illustrated in Table 16-4, we can now rather easily read across the several national percentages that said the UN was doing at least a good job. Now the United States appears the most positive; Germany, Britain, and France are only slightly less positive and are nearly indistinguishable from one another; and Japan stands alone in its quite low assessment of the UN's performance. Although the conclusions to be drawn now do not differ radically from what we might have concluded from simply reading the second line of Table 16-3, we should note that Britain now appears relatively more supportive.

Here's the risk we'd like to spare you. Suppose you had hastily read the second row of Table 16-3 and noted that the British had a somewhat lower assessment of the job the UN was doing than was true of the United States, West Germany, and France. You might feel obliged to think up an explanation for why that was so—possibly creating an ingenious psychohistorical theory about the painful decline of the once powerful and dignified British Empire. Then, once you had touted your "theory" about, someone else might point out that a proper reading of the data would show the British were actually not really less positive than the other three nations. This is not a hypothetical risk. These

types of errors happen frequently, but they can be avoided by collapsing answer categories where appropriate.

Handling "Don't Knows"

Tables 16-3 and 16-4 illustrate another common problem in the analysis of survey data. It's usually a good idea to give people the option of saying "don't know" or "no opinion" when asking for their opinions on issues, but what do you do with those answers in analyzing the data?

Notice there is a good deal of variation in the national percentages saying "don't know" in this instance, ranging from only 10 percent in the United States to 41 percent in Japan. The presence of substantial percentages saying they don't know can confuse the results of tables like these. For example, were the Japanese so much less likely to say the UN was doing a good job simply because so many didn't express any opinion?

Here's an easy way to recalculate percentages, with the "don't knows" excluded. Look at the first column of percentages in Table 16-4: West Germany's answers to the question about the UN's performance. Notice that 26 percent of the respondents said they didn't know. This means that those who said "good" or "bad" job—taken together—represent only 74 percent (100 minus 26) of the whole. If we divide the 48 percent saying "good job or better" by .74 (the proportion giving any

Table 16-5
Omitting the "Don't Knows"

	West Germany	Britain	France	Japan	United States
Good job or better	65%	55%	65%	20%	57%
Poor job or worse	35%	45%	35%	81%	44%

opinion), we can say that 65 percent "of those with an opinion" said the UN was doing a good or very good job (48%/.74 = 65%).

Table 16-5 presents the whole table with the "don't knows" excluded. Notice that these new data offer a somewhat different interpretation than do the previous tables. Specifically, it would now appear that France and West Germany were the most positive in their assessments of the UN, with the United States and Britain a bit lower. Although Japan still stands out as lowest in this regard, it has moved from 12 percent up to 20 percent positive.

At this point, having seen three versions of the data, you may be asking yourself: Which is the *right* one? The answer depends on your purpose in analyzing and interpreting the data. For example, if it's not essential for you to distinguish "very good" from "good," it makes sense to combine them, because it's easier to read the table.

Whether to include or exclude the "don't knows" is harder to decide in the abstract. It may be a very important finding that such a large percentage of the Japanese had no opinion—if you wanted to find out whether people were familiar with the work of the UN, for example. On the other hand, if you wanted to know how people might vote on an issue, it might be more appropriate to exclude the "don't knows" on the assumption that they wouldn't vote or, if they did, that they would likely divide their votes between the two sides of the issue.

In any event, the *truth* contained within your data is that a certain percentage said they didn't know and the remainder divided their opinions in whatever manner they did. Often, it's appropriate to report your data in both forms—with and without the "don't knows"—so your readers can also draw their own conclusions.

Numerical Descriptions in Qualitative Research

Although this chapter deals primarily with quantitative research, the discussions are also relevant to qualitative studies. The findings of in-depth, qualitative studies often can be verified by some numerical testing. Thus, for example, when David Silverman wanted to compare the cancer treat-

ments received by patients in private clinics with those in Britain's National Health Service, he primarily chose in-depth analyses of the interactions between doctors and patients.

> My method of analysis was largely qualitative and . . . I used extracts of what doctors and patients had said as well as offering a brief ethnography of the setting and of certain behavioural data. In addition, however, I constructed a coding form which enabled me to collate a number of crude measures of doctor and patient interactions.
>
> (Silverman 1993:163)

Not only did the numerical data fine-tune Silverman's impressions based on his qualitative observations, but his in-depth understanding of the situation allowed him to craft an ever more appropriate quantitative analysis. Listen to the interaction between qualitative and quantitative approaches in this lengthy discussion.

> My overall impression was that private consultations lasted considerably longer than those held in the NHS clinics. When examined, the data indeed did show that the former were almost twice as long as the latter (20 minutes as against 11 minutes) and that the difference was statistically highly significant. However, I recalled that, for special reasons, one of the NHS clinics had abnormally short consultations. I felt a fairer comparison of consultations in the two sectors should exclude this clinic and should only compare consultations taken by a single doctor in both sectors. This subsample of cases revealed that the difference in length between NHS and private consultations was now reduced to an average of under 3 minutes. This was still statistically significant, although the significance was reduced. Finally, however, if I compared only new patients seen by the same doctor, NHS patients got 4 minutes more on the average—34 minutes as against 30 minutes in the private clinic.
>
> (Silverman 1993:163–64)

This example further demonstrates the special power that can be gained from a combination of approaches in social research. The combination of qualitative and quantitative analyses can be especially potent.

Bivariate Analysis

In contrast to univariate analysis, subgroup comparisons involve two variables. In this respect subgroup comparisons constitute a kind of **bivariate analysis**—the analysis of two variables simultaneously. The purpose of subgroup comparisons, however—like univariate analysis—is largely descriptive. Most bivariate analysis in social research adds another element: determining relationships between the variables themselves. Thus, univariate analysis and subgroup comparisons focus on describing the *people* (or other units of analysis) under study, whereas bivariate analysis focuses on the *variables* and their empirical relationships.

Table 16-6

Religious Service Attendance Reported by Men and Women in 1996

	Men	Women
Weekly or more	21%	28%
Less often	79	72
100% =	(4,910)	(5,327)

Source: "Religious Service Attendance Reported by Men and Women in 1996," adapted from the Statistics Canada General Social Survey, Cycle 11, 1996.
Percentages rounded to the nearest percent.

Table 16-6 could be regarded as an instance of subgroup comparison. It independently describes the religious service attendance of men and women, as reported in the 1996 General Social Survey conducted by Statistics Canada. It shows, comparatively and descriptively, that the women under study attended religious services more often than the men did. However, the same table, seen as an *explanatory* bivariate analysis, tells a somewhat different story. It suggests that the variable *gender* has an effect on the variable *religious service attendance*. In other words, we can view the behaviour as a dependent variable that is partially determined by the independent variable, *gender*.

Explanatory bivariate analyses, then, involve the "variable language" introduced in Chapter 1. In a subtle shift of focus, we're no longer talking about men and women as different subgroups but about *gender* as a variable: one that has an influence on other variables. The theoretical interpreta-

tion of Table 16-6 might be taken from Charles Glock's Comfort Hypothesis as discussed in Chapter 2:

1. Women are still treated as second-class citizens in Canadian society.
2. People denied status gratification in the secular society may turn to religion as an alternative source of status.
3. Hence, women should be more religious than men.

The data presented in Table 16-6 confirm this reasoning. Twenty-eight percent of the women attend religious services at least weekly, compared with 21 percent of the men.

Adding the logic of causal relationships among variables has an important implication for the construction and reading of percentage tables. One of the chief bugaboos for new data analysts is deciding on the appropriate "direction of percentaging" for any given table. In Table 16-6, for example, we've divided the group of subjects into two subgroups—men and women—and then described the behaviour of each subgroup. That is the correct method for constructing this table.

Notice, however, that we could—however inappropriately—construct the table differently. We could first divide the subjects into different degrees of religious service attendance and then describe each of those subgroups in terms of the percentage of men and women in each. This method would make no sense in terms of explanation, however. Table 16-6 suggests that your gender will affect your frequency of religious service attendance. Had we used the other method of construction, the table would suggest that your religious service attendance affects whether you are a man or a woman—which makes no sense. Your behaviour cannot determine your gender.

A related problem complicates the lives of new data analysts. How do you read a percentage table? There's a temptation to read Table 16-6 as follows: "Of the women, only 28 percent attended religious services weekly or more, and 72 percent said they attended less often; therefore, being a woman makes you less likely to attend religious services frequently." This is, of course, an incorrect reading of the table. Any conclusion that *gender*—as a variable—has an effect on religious service attendance must hinge on a comparison between men and women. Specifically, we compare the 28 percent with the 21 percent and note that *women are more likely than men* to attend religious services weekly or more. The comparison of subgroups, then, is essential in reading an explanatory bivariate table.

In constructing and presenting Table 16-6, we have used a convention called *percentage down*. This term means that you can add the percentages down each column to total 100 percent. You read this form of table across a row. For the row labelled "weekly or more," what percentage of the men attends weekly or more? What percentage of the women attends at least weekly?

The direction of percentaging in tables is arbitrary, and some researchers prefer to percentage across. They would organize Table 16-6 so that "men" and "women" were shown on the left side of the table, identifying the two rows, and "weekly or more" and "less often" would appear at the top to identify the columns. The actual numbers in the table would be moved around accordingly, and each *row* of percentages would total 100 percent. In that case, you would read the table down a column, still asking what percentage of men and women attended frequently. The logic and the conclusion would be the same in either case; only the layout of the table would differ.

In reading a table that someone else has constructed, therefore, you need to find out in which direction it has been percentaged. Usually this will be labelled or be clear from the logic of the variables being analyzed. As a last resort, however, you should add the percentages in each column and each row. If each of the columns totals 100 percent, the table has been percentaged down. If the rows total 100 percent each, it has been percentaged across. The rule, then, is as follows:

1. If the table is percentaged down, read across.
2. If the table is percentaged across, read down.

Percentaging a Table

Figure 16-3 reviews the logic by which we create percentage tables from two variables. We've used as variables *gender* and *attitudes toward equality for men and women*.

Here's another example. Suppose we're interested in learning something about newspaper editorial policies regarding the legalization of marijuana. We undertake a content analysis of editorials on this subject that have appeared during a given year in a sample of daily newspapers across the nation. Each editorial has been classified as favourable, neutral, or unfavourable toward the legalization of marijuana. Perhaps we wish to examine the relationship between editorial policies and the communities in which the newspapers are published, thinking that rural newspapers might be more conservative in this regard than urban ones. Thus, each newspaper (hence, each editorial) has been classified in terms of the population of the community in which it is published.

Table 16-7 presents some hypothetical data describing the editorial policies of rural and urban newspapers. Note that the unit of analysis in this example is the individual editorial. Table 16-7 tells us that there were 127 editorials about marijuana in our sample of newspapers published in communities with populations under 100,000. (*Note:* This cutting point is chosen for simplicity of illustration and does not mean that *rural* refers to a community of less than 100,000 in any absolute sense.) Of these, 11 percent (14 editorials) were favourable toward legalization of marijuana, 29 percent were neutral, and 60 percent were unfavourable. Of the 438 editorials that appeared in our sample of newspapers published in communities of more than 100,000 residents, 32 percent (140 editorials) were favourable toward legalizing marijuana, 40 percent were neutral, and 28 percent were unfavourable.

Table 16-7

Hypothetical Data Regarding Newspaper Editorials on the Legalization of Marijuana

Editorial Policy Toward Legalizing Marijuana	Community Size	
	Under 100,000	Over 100,000
Favourable	11%	32%
Neutral	29	40
Unfavourable	60	28
100% =	(127)	(438)

Figure 16-3
Percentaging a Table

A. Some men and women who either favour (=) gender equality or don't (≠) favour it.

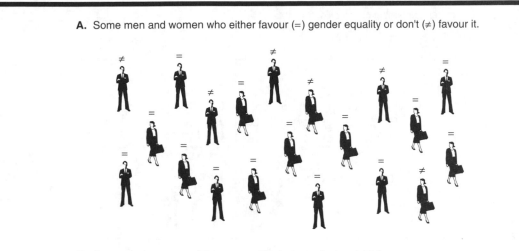

B. Separate the men and the women (the independent variable).

Women   Men

C. Within each gender group, separate those who favour equality from those who don't (the dependent variable).

Women   Men

Figure 16-3

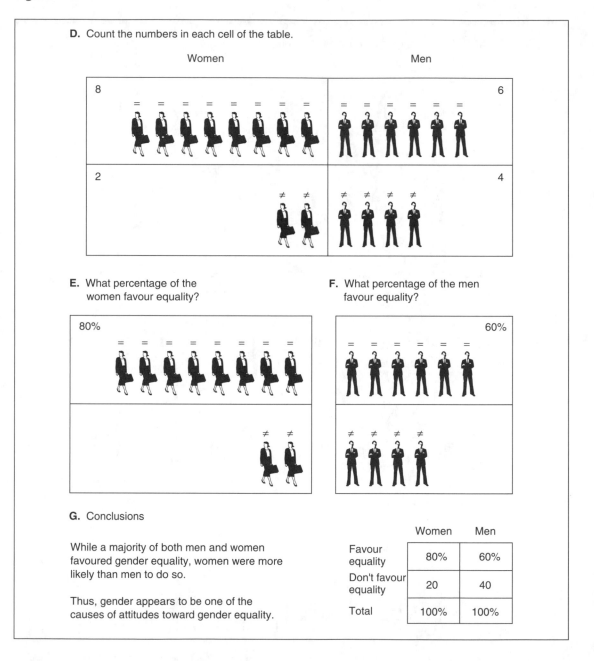

D. Count the numbers in each cell of the table.

E. What percentage of the women favour equality?

F. What percentage of the men favour equality?

G. Conclusions

While a majority of both men and women favoured gender equality, women were more likely than men to do so.

Thus, gender appears to be one of the causes of attitudes toward gender equality.

	Women	Men
Favour equality	80%	60%
Don't favour equality	20	40
Total	100%	100%

When we compare the editorial policies of rural and urban newspapers in our imaginary study, we find, as expected, that rural newspapers are less favourable toward the legalization of marijuana than are urban newspapers. We determine this by noting that a larger percentage (32 percent) of the urban editorials was favourable than the rural ones (11 percent). We might note, as well, that more rural than urban editorials were unfavourable (60 percent compared to 28 percent). Note that this table assumes that the size of a community might affect its newspapers' editorial policies on this issue, rather than that editorial policy might affect the size of communities.

Constructing and Reading Bivariate Tables

Let's review the steps involved in the construction of explanatory bivariate tables:

1. The cases are divided into groups according to their attributes of the independent variable.
2. Each of these subgroups is then described in terms of attributes of the dependent variable.
3. Finally, the table is read by comparing the independent variable subgroups with one another in terms of a given attribute of the dependent variable.

Let's repeat the analysis of gender and attitude on gender equality following these steps. For the reasons outlined previously, *gender* is the independent variable; *attitude toward gender equality* constitutes the dependent variable. Thus, we proceed as follows:

1. The cases are divided into men and women.
2. Each gender subgrouping is described in terms of approval or disapproval of gender equality.
3. Men and women are compared in terms of the percentages approving of gender equality.

In the example of editorial policies regarding the legalization of marijuana, *size of community* is the independent variable, and a *newspaper's editorial policy* the dependent variable. The table would be constructed as follows:

1. Divide the editorials into subgroups according to the sizes of the communities in which the newspapers are published.
2. Describe each subgroup of editorials in terms of the percentages favourable, neutral, or unfavourable toward the legalization of marijuana.

3. Compare the two subgroups in terms of the percentages favourable toward the legalization of marijuana.

Bivariate analyses typically have an explanatory causal purpose. These two hypothetical examples have hinted at the nature of causation as social scientists use it. We'll build on this rather simplified approach in the section covering the elaboration model, where we will look more loosely at the complex nature of causation.

Tables such as the ones we've been examining are commonly called *contingency tables:* Values of the dependent variable are contingent on (depend on) values of the independent variable. Although contingency tables are common in social science, their format has never been standardized. As a result, you'll find a variety of formats in research literature. As long as a table is easy to read and interpret, there's probably no reason to strive for standardization. However, there are several guidelines that you should follow in presenting most tabular data.

1. A table should have a heading or a title that succinctly describes what is contained in the table.
2. The original content of the variables should be clearly presented—in the table itself if at all possible or in the text with a paraphrase in the table. This information is especially critical when a variable is derived from responses to an attitudinal question, because the meaning of the responses will depend largely on the wording of the question.
3. The attributes of each variable should be clearly indicated. Though complex categories will have to be abbreviated, their meaning should be clear in the table and, of course, the full description should be reported in the text.
4. When percentages are reported in the table, the base on which they are computed should be indicated. It's redundant to present all the raw numbers for each category, because these could be reconstructed from the percentages and the bases. Moreover, the presentation of

both numbers and percentages can result in a cluttered table that is more difficult to read.

5. If any cases are omitted from the table because of missing data ("no answer," for example), their numbers should be indicated in the table.

MULTIVARIATE ANALYSIS AND THE ELABORATION MODEL

Our examination of univariate and bivariate modes of analysis have laid the foundation for understanding more complex relationships. Thus, we will now focus on the logic of **multivariate analysis**—the analysis of more than two variables simultaneously. We'll begin by discussing the construction and reading of multivariate tables and then turn to the elaboration model.

Constructing and Reading Multivariate Tables

We can construct multivariate tables on the basis of a more complicated subgroup description by following essentially the same steps outlined for bivariate tables. Instead of one independent variable and one dependent variable, however, we'll have more than one independent variable. Instead of explaining the dependent variable on the basis of a single independent variable, we'll seek an explanation through the use of more than one independent variable.

Let's return to the example of religious service attendance. Suppose we believe that age would also affect such behaviour: Glock's Comfort Hypothesis suggests that older people are more religious than younger people. As the first step in table construction, we would divide the total sample into subgroups based on the attributes of both independent variables simultaneously: younger men, older men, younger women, and older women. Then the several subgroups would be described in terms of the dependent variable, *religious service attendance*, and comparisons would be made. Table 16-8, from an analysis of the 1996 General Social Survey data, is the result.

Table 16-8

Multivariate Relationship: Religious Service Attendance, Gender, and Age

| | How often do you attend religious services/meetings? | | | |
| | Under 40 | | 40 and Older | |
	Men	Women	Men	Women
Weekly or more	16%	20%	26%	36%
Less often	84	80	74	64
100% =	(2,358)	(2,404)	(2,552)	(2,922)

Source: "Multivariate Relationship: Religious Service Attendance, Gender, and Age," adapted from the Statistics Canada General Survey, Cycle 11, 1996.
Percentages rounded to the nearest percent.

Table 16-8 has been percentaged down, and therefore should be read across. The interpretation of this table warrants several conclusions.

1. Among both men and women, older people attend church more often than younger people do. Among women, 20 percent of those under 40 and 36 percent of those 40 and older attend religious services weekly. Among men, the respective figures are 16 and 26 percent.

2. Within each age group, women attend more frequently than men do. Among those respondents under 40, 20 percent of the women attend weekly, compared with 16 percent of the men. Among those 40 and over, 36 percent of the women and 26 percent of the men attend weekly.

3. As measured in the table, age has slightly more of an effect than gender on attendance at religious services.

4. Age and gender have independent effects on attendance at religious services. Within a given attribute of one independent variable, different attributes of the second still affect behaviours.

5. Similarly, the two independent variables have a cumulative effect on behaviours. Older women attend the most often (36 percent), and younger men attend the least frequently (16 percent).

Several of the tables presented in this chapter are somewhat inefficient. When the dependent variable, such as *religious service attendance,* is dichotomous (two attributes), knowing one attribute permits the reader to reconstruct the other easily. Thus, if we know that 20 percent of the women under 40 attend religious services weekly or more, then we know automatically that 80 percent attend less often. So reporting the percentages of women who attend less often is unnecessary. On the basis of this recognition, Table 16-8 could be presented in the alternative format of Table 16-9.

In Table 16-9, the percentages saying they attend religious services weekly or more are reported in the cells representing the intersections of the two independent variables. The numbers presented in parentheses below each percentage represent the number of cases on which the percentages are based. Thus, for example, the reader knows there are 2,404 women under 40 years of age in the sample, and 20 percent of them attend religious services weekly or more. We can calculate from this that 481 of those 2,404 women attend weekly or more and that the other 1,923 younger women (or 80 percent) attend less frequently. This new table is easier to read than the former one, and it doesn't sacrifice any information.

Table 16-9
A Simplification of Table 16-8

| | Percent Who Attend Weekly or More | |
	Men	Women
Under 40	16	20
	(2,358)	(2,404)
40 and Older	26	36
	(2,552)	(2,922)

For another simple example of multivariate analysis, let's return to the issue of gender and income. As you'll recall, there has been a long-standing pattern of women in the labour force earning less than men, and many explanations have been advanced to account for that difference. One explanation is that because of traditional family patterns, women as a group have participated less in the labour force and many only began working outside the home after certain child-rearing tasks were completed. Thus, women as a

group will probably have less seniority at work than men, and income increases with seniority. A study by Drolet (1999) using the 1997 Canadian Survey of Labour and Income Dynamics, however, does not support this. As Table 16-10 shows, women with the same job tenure as men fail to receive comparable earnings.

Table 16-10
Gender, Job Tenure, and Annual Earnings (Full-Year, Full-Time Workers)

| | Average Annual Earnings | | Women/Men |
Job Tenure	Men	Women	Ratio
Less than 1 year	$33,824	$24,438	72.3%
1 to 5 years	39,395	26,733	67.9
6 to 10 years	43,793	31,303	71.5
11 to 19 years	50,211	35,343	70.4
20+ years	56,984	38,574	67.7

Source: "Gender, Job Tenure, and Annual earnings (Full-Year, Full Time Workers)," adapted from the Statistics Canada publication "The Persistent Gap: New Evidence on the Canadian Gender Wage Gap, Catalogue 11F0019, December 1999.

Table 16-10 indicates, first of all, that job tenure does indeed affect earnings. By reading down the first two columns of the table, it can be seen that among both men and women, those with more years on the job earn more. The table also indicates that women earn less than men, regardless of job seniority. This can be seen by comparing average earnings across the rows of the table or by examining the ratio of women-to-men earnings in the third column.

This analysis indicates that the number of years on the job is an important determinant of earnings; it does not provide an adequate explanation for the pattern of women earning less than men. In fact, we see that those women with 20 or more years on the job earn on average less ($38,574) than men with 1–5 years ($39,395).

These data indicate that the difference between men and women's pay is not a matter of men having more time on the job. But then there are other possible explanations for the difference: education, child-care responsibilities, and so forth. The researcher who calculated the information in Table 16-10 also examined some of the other variables that might reasonably explain the male/female difference in pay without representing gender discrimination. In addition to the number of years with current employer, the variables they considered included these:

- Educational background
- Amount of full-year, full-time work experience
- Age of youngest family member
- Marital status
- Part-time status
- Region
- Union status
- Firm size
- Duties
- Amount of influence in budget and staffing decisions
- Type of industry
- Type of occupation

Each of these variables listed here might reasonably affect earnings, and if women and men differ in these regards, could help to account for female/male wage differences. When *all* these variables were taken into account, the researcher was able to account for 49 percent of the discrepancy between the wages of men and women. The remaining 51 percent, then, is a function of other "reasonable" variables and/or gender prejudice. This kind of conclusion can be reached only by examining the effects of several variables at the same time—that is, through multivariate analysis.

We will now delve into multivariate analysis a little more deeply by using the elaboration model to illustrate the fundamental logic of multivariate and causal analysis. Exploring applications of this logic in the form of simple percentage tables provides a foundation for making sense of more complex analytical methods.

The Elaboration Model

In this section we'll focus on a perspective on social scientific analysis that is referred to variously as the **elaboration model**, the interpretation method, the Columbia school, or the Lazarsfeld method. Its many names reflect the fact that it aims at *elaborating* on an empirical relationship among variables in order to *interpret* that relationship in the manner developed by Paul *Lazarsfeld* while he was at *Columbia* University. As such, the elaboration model is one method for doing multivariate analysis. It is a logical approach to data analysis— a systematic way to analyze cross-sectional data— equally applicable to a number of different alternative statistical methods.

Researchers use the elaboration model to understand the relationship between two variables through the simultaneous introduction of additional variables. Though developed primarily through the medium of contingency tables, it may be used with other statistical techniques. Understanding the logic of the elaboration model in the context of contingency table analysis provides a good foundation for understanding other statistical techniques and the types of relationships that are revealed when using them.

We believe that the elaboration model offers the clearest available picture of the logic of causal analysis in social research. This method portrays the logical process of scientific analysis and is particularly accessible when illustrated through the use of contingency tables. Moreover, if you can fully comprehend the use of the elaboration model using contingency tables, you should greatly improve your ability to use and understand more sophisticated techniques.

The Origins of the Elaboration Model

The historical origins of the elaboration model provide a good illustration of how scientific research works in practice. During World War II, Samuel Stouffer organized and headed a special social research branch within the U.S. Army. Of the large number of studies conducted several examined morale in the military. Morale was deemed important because it seemed to affect combat effectiveness. Stouffer and his research staff sought to uncover some of the variables that affected morale. In part, the group sought to confirm empirically some commonly accepted propositions, including the following:

1. Promotions surely affect soldiers' morale, so soldiers serving in units with low promotion rates should have relatively low morale.
2. Given racial segregation and discrimination in the South, African-American soldiers being trained in northern training camps should have higher morale than those being trained in the South.
3. Soldiers with more education should be more likely to resent being drafted into the army as enlisted men than should those with less education.

Each of these propositions made sense logically, and common wisdom held each to be true. Stouffer decided to test each empirically. To his surprise, none of the propositions was confirmed. Stouffer found that soldiers serving in the Military Police (where promotions were the slowest in the army) had fewer complaints about the promotion system than did those serving in the Army Air Corps (where promotions were the fastest in the army). The other proposition fared just as badly. African-American soldiers serving in northern training camps and those serving in southern training camps seemed to differ little if at all in their general morale. And less educated soldiers were more likely to resent being drafted into the army than were those with more education.

Stouffer didn't try to hide the findings or simply run tests of statistical significance and publish the results. He sought an answer to "Why?" He found the answer within the concepts of reference group and relative deprivation. Put simply, Stouffer suggested that soldiers did not evaluate their positions in life according to absolute, objective standards, but rather on the basis of their relative position vis-à-vis others around them. They compared themselves with the people in their reference group, and they felt relative deprivation if they didn't compare favourably in that regard.

Following this logic, Stouffer offered an answer to each of the anomalies in his empirical data. Regarding promotion he suggested that soldiers judged the fairness of the promotion system based on their own experiences relative to others around them. In the Military Police, where promotions were few and slow, few soldiers knew of a less qualified buddy who had been promoted faster than they had. In the Army Air Corps, however, the rapid promotion rate meant that many soldiers knew of less qualified buddies who had been promoted faster than seemed appropriate. Thus, ironically, the MPs said the promotion system was generally fair, and the air corpsmen said it was not.

A similar analysis seemed to explain the case of the African-American soldiers. Rather than comparing conditions in the North with those in the South, African-American soldiers compared their own status with the status of the African-American civilians around them. In the South, where discrimination was at its worst, they found that being a soldier insulated them somewhat from adverse cultural norms in the surrounding community. Whereas southern African-American civilians were grossly discriminated against and denied self-esteem, good jobs, and so forth, African-American soldiers had a slightly better status. In the North, however, many of the African-American civilians they encountered held well-paying defense jobs. And with discrimination being less severe, being a soldier did not help one's status in the community.

Finally, the concepts of reference group and relative deprivation seemed to explain the anomaly of highly educated draftees accepting their induction more willingly than did those with less education. Stouffer reasoned as follows:

1. A person's friends, on the whole, have about the same educational status as that person does.
2. Draft-age men with less education are more likely to engage in semi-skilled production-line occupations and farming than more educated men.
3. During wartime, many production-line industries and farming are vital to the national interest; workers in those industries and farmers are exempted from the draft.
4. A man with little education is more likely to have friends in draft-exempt occupations than a man with more education.
5. When each compares himself with his friends, a less educated draftee is more likely to feel discriminated against than a draftee with more education.

(1949–1950:122–7)

Stouffer's explanations unlocked the mystery of the three anomalous findings. Because they were not part of a preplanned study design, however, he lacked empirical data for testing them. Nevertheless, Stouffer's logical exposition provided the basis for the later development of the elaboration model: understanding the relationship between two variables through the controlled introduction of other variables.

Paul Lazarsfeld and his associates at Columbia University formally developed the elaboration model in 1946. In a methodological review of Stouffer's army studies, Lazarsfeld and Patricia Kendall used the logic of the elaboration model to present hypothetical tables that would have proved Stouffer's contention regarding education and acceptance of induction had the empirical data been available (Kendall and Lazarsfeld 1950).

The central logic of the elaboration model begins with an observed relationship between two variables and the possibility that one variable may be causing the other. In the Stouffer example, the initial two variables were *educational level* and *acceptance of being drafted as fair*. Since the soldiers' education levels were set before they were drafted (and thus before developing any reaction to being drafted) it would seem that *educational level* was the cause, or independent variable, and *acceptance of induction* was the effect, or dependent variable. As we just saw, however, the observed relationship countered what the researchers had expected.

The elaboration model examines the impact of other variables on the relationship first observed. Sometimes this analysis reveals the mechanisms through which the causal relationship occurs. Other times an elaboration analysis disproves the existence of a causal relationship altogether.

In the present example, the additional variable was whether or not a soldier's friends were deferred or drafted. In Stouffer's speculative explanation, this variable showed how it was actually logical that soldiers with more education would be more accepting of being drafted, because it was likely that their friends would have been drafted. Those with the least education were likely to have been in occupations that often brought deferments from the draft, leading those drafted to feel they had been treated unfairly.

Kendall and Lazarsfeld began with Stouffer's data showing the positive association between education and acceptance of induction—Table 16-11. In this and the following tables, "should have been deferred" and "should not have been deferred" represent inductees' judgments of their own situation, with the latter group feeling it was fair for them to have been drafted.

Table 16-11

Summary of Stouffer's Data on Education and Acceptance of Induction

	High Ed.	Low Ed.
Should not have been deferred	88%	70%
Should have been deferred	12	30
	100	100
	(1,761)	(1,876)

Source: Tables 16-11, 16-12, 16-13, and 16-14 are reprinted and modified with the permission of The Free Press, a Division of Simon & Schuster, Inc., from CONTINUITIES IN SOCIAL RESEARCH: Studies in the Scope and Method of "The American Soldier" by Robert K. Merton and Paul F. Lazarsfeld. Copyright © 1950 by The Free Press; copyright renewed 1978 by Robert K. Merton.

Table 16-12

Hypothetical Relationship between Education and Deferment of Friends

Friends Deferred?	High Ed.	Low Ed.
Yes	19%	79%
No	81	21
	100	100
	(1,761)	(1,876)

Table 16-13

Hypothetical Relationship between Deferment of Friends and Acceptance of One's Own Induction

	Friends Deferred?	
	Yes	No
Should not have been deferred	63%	94%
Should have been deferred	37	6
	100	100
	(1,819)	(1,818)

Table 16-14

Hypothetical Data Relating Education to Acceptance of Induction through the Factor of Having Friends Who Were Deferred

	Friends Deferred		No Friends Deferred	
	High Ed.	Low Ed.	High Ed.	Low Ed.
Should not have been deferred	63%	63%	94%	95%
Should have been deferred	37	37	6	5
	100	100	100	100
100% =	(335)	(1,484)	(1,426)	(392)

Kendall and Lazarsfeld then created some hypothetical tables to represent what the analysis might have looked like had soldiers been asked whether most of their friends had been drafted or deferred. In Table 16-12, 19 percent of those with high education hypothetically said their friends were deferred, as compared with 79 percent of the soldiers with less education. Notice that the numbers of soldiers with high and low education are the same as in Stouffer's real data. In later tables, you see that the numbers who accepted or resented being drafted are kept true to the original data. Only the numbers saying that friends were or were not deferred were made up.

Stouffer's explanation next assumed that soldiers with friends who had been deferred would be more likely to resent their own induction than would those who had no deferred friends. Table 16-13 presents the hypothetical data that would have supported that assumption.

The hypothetical data in Tables 16-12 and 16-13 would confirm linkages that Stouffer had specified in his explanation. First, soldiers with low education were more likely to have friends who were deferred than were soldiers with more education. Second, having friends who were deferred made a soldier more likely to think he should have been deferred. Stouffer had suggested that these two relationships would clarify the original relationship between education and acceptance of induction. Kendall and Lazarsfeld created a hypothetical table that would confirm Stouffer's explanation (see Table 16-14).

Recall that the original finding was that draftees with high education were more likely to accept their induction into the army as fair than were those with less education. In Table 16-14, however, we note that level of education has no effect on the acceptance of induction among those who report having friends deferred: 63 percent among both education groups indicate that they accept their induction (that is, they say they should not have been deferred). Similarly, educational level has no significant effect on acceptance of induction among those who reported having no friends deferred: 94 and 95 percent say they should not have been deferred.

On the other hand, among those with high education, the acceptance of induction is strongly related to whether or not friends were deferred: 63 percent versus 94 percent. And the same is true among those with less education. The hypothetical data in Table 16-14, then, would support Stouffer's contention that education affected acceptance of induction only through the medium of having friends deferred. Highly educated draftees were less likely to have friends deferred and, by virtue of that fact, were more likely to accept their own induction as fair. Those with less education were more likely to have friends deferred and, by virtue of that fact, were less likely to accept their own induction.

Recognize that neither Stouffer's explanation nor the hypothetical data denied the reality of the original relationship. As educational level increased, acceptance of one's own induction also increased. The nature of this empirical relationship, however, was interpreted through the introduction of a third variable. The variable, *deferment of friends*, did not deny the original relationship; it merely clarified the mechanism through which the original relationship occurred.

This, then, is the heart of the elaboration model and of multivariate analysis. Having observed an empirical relationship between two variables (such as *level of education* and *acceptance of induction*), we seek to understand the nature of that relationship through the effects produced by introducing other variables (such *as having friends who were deferred*). Mechanically, we accomplish this by first dividing our sample into subsets on the basis of the

test variable, also called the control variable. In our example, having friends who were deferred or not is the test variable, and the sample is divided into those who have deferred friends and those who do not. The relationship between the original two variables (*acceptance of induction* and *level of education*) is then recomputed separately for each of the subsamples. The tables produced in this manner are called the **partial tables**, and the relationships found in the partial tables are called the **partial relationships**, or **partials**. The partial relationships are then compared with the initial relationship discovered in the total sample, often referred to as the **zero-order relationship** to indicate that no test variables have been controlled for.

Although the elaboration model was first demonstrated through the use of hypothetical data, it laid out a logical method for analyzing relationships among variables that have been actually measured. As we'll see, our first, hypothetical example has described only one possible outcome in the elaboration model. There are others.

The Elaboration Paradigm

This section presents guidelines for understanding an elaboration analysis. To begin, we must know whether the test variable is *antecedent* (prior in time) to the other two variables or whether it is *intervening* between them, because these positions suggest different logical relationships in the multivariate model. If the test variable is intervening, as in the case of education, deferment of friends, and acceptance of induction, then the analysis is based on the model shown in Figure 16-4. The logic of this multivariate relationship is that the independent variable (*educational level*) affects the inter-

Figure 16-5
Antecedent Test Variable

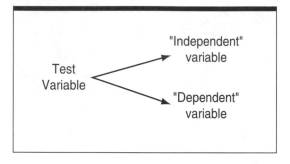

vening test variable (*having friends deferred or not*), which in turn affects the dependent variable (*accepting induction*).

If the test variable is antecedent to both the independent and dependent variables, a different model must be used (see Figure 16-5). Here the test variable affects both the "independent" and "dependent" variables. Realize, of course, that the terms *independent variable* and *dependent variable* are, strictly speaking, used incorrectly in the diagram. In fact, we have one independent variable (the test variable) and two dependent variables. The incorrect terminology has been used only to provide continuity with the preceding example. Because of their individual relationships to the test variable, the "independent" and "dependent" variables are empirically related to each other, but there is no causal link between them. Their empirical relationship is merely a product of their coincidental relationships to the test variable. (Subsequent examples will further clarify this relationship.)

Figure 16-4
Intervening Test Variable

Independent variable ⟶ Test variable ⟶ Dependent variable

Table 16-15
The Elaboration Paradigm

Partial Relationships Compared with Original	Test Variable	
	Antecedent	Intervening
Same	Replication	Replication
Less or none	Explanation	Interpretation
Split*	Specification	Specification

*One partial is the same or greater, and the other is less or none

Table 16-15 is a guide to understanding an elaboration analysis. The two columns in the table indicate whether the test variable is antecedent or intervening in the sense described previously. The left side of the table shows the nature of the partial relationships as compared with the original relationship between the independent and dependent variables. The body of the table gives the technical notations—replication, explanation, interpretation, and specification—assigned to each case. We'll discuss each in turn.

Replication

Whenever the partial relationships are essentially the same as the original relationship, the term **replication** is assigned to the result, regardless of whether the test variable is antecedent or intervening. This means that the original relationship has been replicated under test conditions.

Let's look at an example using real data to illustrate. It has been known for quite some time, as we saw earlier in this chapter, that women earn less money than men—that there is a relationship between *gender* and *income*. We'll look at this bivariate relationship for Canada in 1996 using the General Social Survey. Focusing on full-time employed individuals in the sample, we examined the relationship between *gender* and *personal annual income*. For our purposes, *income* was recoded into a dichotomous variable with two attributes—those earning less than $40,000 annually and those earning $40,000 or greater. Here's what we found.

Table 16-16 shows that women tend to earn less than do men. When we compare the personal annual income of men and women, we see that 59 percent or men and 84 percent of women earn less than $40,000. (In each of the examples in this section, percentages are rounded to the nearest percent.) The difference between women and men is 25 percentage points.

Many researchers have searched, and continue to search, for factors that may provide further understanding of this relationship. One variable that is frequently examined is that of *level of education*. If we believe that issues such as merit impact on the amount of pay one receives, then we might

Table16-16

Personal Annual Income and Gender (employed individuals), 1996

Personal Annual Income	Gender	
	Male	Female
Under $40,000	59%	84%
$40,000 or higher	41	16
	100	100
100% =	(3,695)	(2,958)

Source: "Personal Annual Income and Gender (employed individuals)," 1996, adapted from the Statistics Canada General Social Survey, Cycle 11, 1996.

suspect that *level of education* would affect the relationship between *gender* and *income*, decreasing the strength of the relationship—that is women with higher levels of education should receive pay that is more equivalent to men with higher levels of education. So we might want to see whether the relationship between *gender* and *income* holds or is equally true for men and women of different educational levels. To find out, we will make *level of education* our control or test variable. Of course, there are many other factors that a researcher would examine as well, such as years of service, type of employment, and so forth, however, we will examine only *level of education* presently. *Level of education* was also recoded into a dichotomous variable for illustrative purposes—those who have a high school diploma or less and everyone else (greater than a high school diploma).

Table 16-17 shows the partial relationships when the relationship between *gender* and *income* is examined when controlling for *education level*. We see that *gender* still influences *income* in the same way for those with higher education and for those with lower education. The difference between men and women with lower levels of education is 72 percent versus 95 percent respectively, or 23 percentage points. Compared to the original relationship between gender and income, which shows a 25 percent difference in income between men and women, the difference between men and women with lesser education is nearly the same. For higher levels of education—those with greater than a high school diploma—the

Table 16-17
Education, Personal Annual Income, Gender, 1996

Personal Annual Income	High School Diploma or Less		Greater than High School Diploma	
	Male	Female	Male	Female
Under $40,000	72%	95%	52%	79%
$40,000 or higher	28	5	48	21
	100	100	100	100
100% =	(1,341)	(924)	(2,346)	(2,027)

Source: "Education, Personal Annual Income, Gender, 1996," adapted from the Statistics Canada General Social Survey, Cycle 11,

relationship between *gender* and *income* remains fundamentally the same as the original relationship as well. Comparing men (52 percent) and women (79 percent) with personal annual incomes of less then $40,000, we see a difference of 27 percent. These are the kind of modest, almost negligible, differences that most researchers would call replication. In other words, the relationship between gender and income is substantially the same for those with more and those with less education. Thus, the result represents a replication of the relationship between *gender* and *income* when the variable *education level* is introduced.

Although we see in Table 16-17 that being a man or a woman still influences personal annual income among those with low education and those with higher education, the table also indicates an education effect. For both men and women, those with greater than a high school diploma are more likely to earn $40,000 or higher a year than those with a high school diploma or less—only 28 percent of men with lesser education have incomes of $40,000 compared with 48 percent of men with higher levels of education and for women the increase is from 5 percent to 21 percent.

Researchers frequently use the elaboration model rather routinely in the hope of replicating their findings among subsets of the sample. If we discovered a relationship between education and prejudice, for example, we might introduce such test variables as age, region of the country, race, religion, and so forth to test the stability of the original relationship. If the relationship were replicated among young and old, among people from different parts of the country, and so forth, we would have stronger grounds for concluding that the original relationship was a genuine and general one.

Explanation

Explanation is the term used to describe a *spurious relationship*: an original relationship shown to be false through the introduction of a test variable. This requires two conditions: (1) the test variable must be antecedent to both the independent and dependent variables and (2) the partial relationships must be zero or significantly less than those found in the original. Several examples will illustrate this situation.

There is an empirical relationship between the number of storks in different areas and the birthrates for those areas—the more storks in an area, the higher the birthrate. This empirical relationship might lead one to assume that the number of storks affects the birthrate. An antecedent test variable explains away this relationship, however. Rural areas have both more storks and higher birthrates than do urban areas. Within rural areas, there is no relationship between the number of storks and the birthrate; nor is there a relationship within urban areas.

Figure 16-6 illustrates how the rural/urban variable causes the apparent relationship between storks and birthrates. Part I of the figure shows the original relationship. Notice that all but one of the entries in the box for towns and cities with many storks have high birthrates and that all but one of those in the box for towns and cities with few storks have low birthrates. In percentage form, we say that 93 percent of the towns and cities with many storks also have high birthrates, as contrasted with 7 percent of those with few storks. That's quite a large difference and represents a strong association between the two variables.

Part II of the figure separates the towns from the cities (the rural from urban areas) and examines storks and babies in each type of place separately.

Figure 16-6
The Facts of Life about Storks and Babies

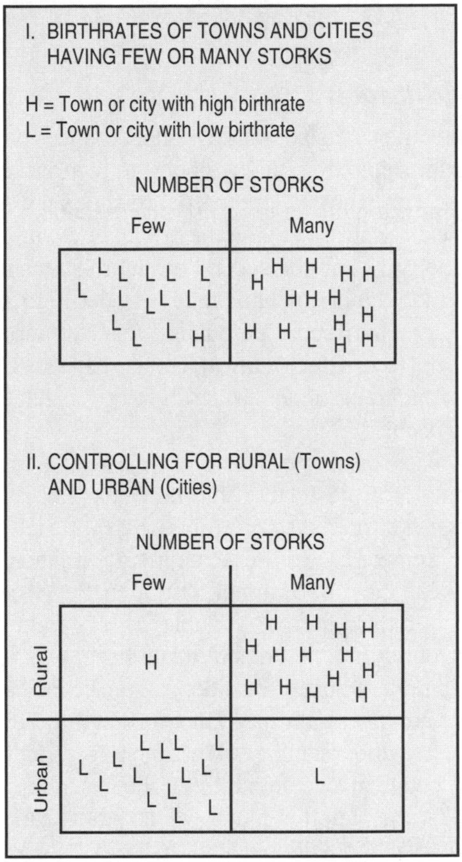

I. BIRTHRATES OF TOWNS AND CITIES HAVING FEW OR MANY STORKS

H = Town or city with high birthrate
L = Town or city with low birthrate

NUMBER OF STORKS

II. CONTROLLING FOR RURAL (Towns) AND URBAN (Cities)

NUMBER OF STORKS

Now we can see that all the rural places have high birthrates, and all the urban places have low birthrates. Also notice that only one rural place had few storks and only one urban place had lots of storks.

Here's a similar example. There is a positive relationship between the number of fire trucks responding to a fire and the amount of damage done. If more trucks respond, more damage is done. One might assume from this fact that the fire trucks themselves cause the damage. However, an antecedent test variable—the size of the fire—explains away the original relationship. Large fires do more damage than small ones, and more fire trucks respond to large fires than to small ones. Looking only at large fires, we would see that the original relationship vanishes (or perhaps reverses itself); and the same would be true looking only at small fires.

Finally, let's take a real research example. Years ago, I (Babbie 1970) found an empirical relationship in the U.S. between the region of the country in which medical school faculty members attended medical school and their attitudes toward Medicare. To simplify matters, only the East and the South will be examined. Of faculty members attending eastern medical schools, 78 percent said they approved of Medicare, compared with 59 percent of those attending southern medical schools. This finding made sense in view of the fact that the South seemed generally more resistant to such programs than the East, and medical school training should presumably affect a doctor's medical attitudes. However, this relationship is explained away when we introduce an antecedent test variable: the region of the country in which the faculty member was raised. Of faculty members raised in the East, 89 percent attended medical school in the East and 11 percent in the South. Of those raised in the South, 53 percent attended medical school in the East and 47 percent in the South. Moreover, the areas in which faculty members were raised related to attitudes toward Medicare. Of those raised in the East, 84 percent approved of Medicare, as compared with 49 percent of those raised in the South.

Table 16-18 presents the three-variable relationship among (a) region in which raised, (b) region of medial school training, and (c) attitude toward Medicare. Faculty members raised in the East are quite likely to approve of Medicare, regardless of where they attended medical school. Those raised in the South are relatively less likely to approve of Medicare, but, again, the region of their medical school training has little or no effect. These data indicate, therefore, that the original relationship between region of medical training and attitude toward Medicare was spurious; it was due only to the coincidental effect of region of *origin* on both region of medical training and on attitude toward Medicare. When region of origin is held constant, as in Table 16-18, the original relationship disappears in the partials.

Table 16-18
Region of Origin, Region of Schooling, and Attitude toward Medicare

		Percentage Who Approve of Medicare	
		Regions in Which Raised	
		East	South
Region of Medical	East	84	50
School Training	South	80	47

Source: Earl R. Babbie, *Science and Morality in Medicine* (Berkeley:University of California Press, 1970:181).

Interpretation

Interpretation is similar to explanation, except for the time placement of the test variable and the implications that follow from that difference. **Interpretation** represents the research outcome in which a test or control variable is discovered to be the mediating factor through which an independent variable has its effect on a dependent variable. The earlier example of education, friends deferred, and acceptance of induction is an excellent illustration of interpretation. In terms of the elaboration model, the effect of education on acceptance of induction is not explained away, it is still a genuine relationship. In a real sense, education differences cause differential acceptance of induction. The intervening variable, deferment of friends, merely helps to interpret the mechanism through which the relationship occurs. Thus an interpretation does not deny the validity of the original causal relationship but simply clarifies the process through which that relationship functions.

Here's another example of interpretation. Researchers have observed that children from broken homes are more likely to become delinquent than are those from intact homes. This relationship may be interpreted, however, through the introduction of *supervision* as a test variable. Among children who are supervised, delinquency rates are not affected by whether or not their parents are divorced. The same is true among those who are not supervised. It is the relationship between broken homes and the lack of supervision that produced the original relationship.

Specification

Sometimes the elaboration model produces partial relationships that differ significantly from each other. For example, one partial relationship is the same as or stronger than the original two-variable relationship and the second partial relationship is less than the original and may be reduced to zero. In the elaboration paradigm, this situation is referred to as **specification,** i.e., we have specified the conditions under which the original relationship occurs.

To illustrate specification, we'll return to our example of the relationship between *gender* and *personal annual income* (Table 16-16). Recall that we attempted to further examine the relationship between these two variables through the introduction of a third, or test, variable, *level of education,* and found that the original relationship was replicated under this test condition. As we've indicated, there are potentially many factors that may help us to better understand or clarify any given relationship between two variables. In the case of *gender* and *income*, another factor we discussed earlier is the impact of traditional family patterns that potentially affect women's labour force participation in numerous ways. If such family patterns interfere with women's labour force participation, one might reason that marital status should help illuminate the difference we found in personal annual incomes between men and women. We might reason that the original relationship should not hold among women who are single and more likely to be without the traditional family responsibilities that married women typically shoulder. Thus, we would expect the difference in income between ever-married men and women to remain the same or increase, while for single men and women the difference should be greatly reduced.

Table 16-19 presents an example of specification. When the test variable of *marital status—*

recoded to a dichotomy of single and married (including common-law, divorced or separated, and widowed)—is introduced, we find that among women who are single, the relationship between *gender* and *income* is substantially reduced. The difference between single men and women is only 7 percent (the difference between men and women in the original two variable relationship is 25 percent). In effect, the table specifies the conditions under which the original relationship holds: among those who are (or were) married. The difference between married men and women is 32 percent; this partial relationship is somewhat stronger than the original two-variable relationship between gender and income. (Note that age is likely related to marital status as well, and therefore, the researcher would continue examining other factors that may affect the relationship between gender and income, as discussed earlier in this chapter.)

The term *specification* is used in the elaboration paradigm regardless of whether the test variable is antecedent or intervening. In either case, the meaning is the same. We have specified the particular conditions under which the original relationship holds.

Table 16-19

Marital Status, Personal Annual Income, Gender, 1996

| Personal Annual Income | Married | | Single | |
	Male	Female	Male	Female
Under $40,000	48%	80%	86%	93%
$40,000 or higher	52	20	14	7
	100	100	100	100
100% =	(2,606)	(2,107)	(1,087)	(851)

Source: "Marital status, Personal Annual Income, Gender, 1996," adapted from the Statistics Canada General Social Survey, Cycle 11, 1996.
"Married" includes married, separated, divorced, common law, and widowed.

Refinements to the Paradigm

The preceding sections have presented the primary logic of the elaboration model as developed by Lazarsfeld and his colleagues. Here we look at

some logically possible variations, some of which can be found in a book by Morris Rosenberg (1968).

First, the basic paradigm assumes an initial relationship between two variables. It might be useful, however, in a more comprehensive model to differentiate between positive and negative relationships. Moreover, Rosenberg suggests using the elaboration model even with an original relationship of zero. Gary F. Koeske (1998) explored the apparent absence of a relationship between *permissive parenting* and *adolescents' reports of psychological and somatic symptoms*. He did not use contingency table analysis; therefore, the example here has been constructed by translating the relationships that he reported into illustrative contingency tables. Thus the example is based on his findings but does not use his data.*

At the top of Table 16-20, the initial contingency table analysis is reported; there is essentially no observed relationship between parental permissiveness and symptoms. Fifty-four percent of adolescents who reported relatively permissive parenting styles reported many symptoms and 58 percent of those reporting less permissive styles claimed many symptoms. There is essentially no observed relationship between parenting style and symptoms. However, a different wrinkle is apparent when warmer and colder parenting styles are introduced as a test factor. *Parental warmth* was found to *suppress* the relationship between parental permissiveness and adolescent symptoms. Among warmer parents, 50 percent of the adolescents reported many psychological symptoms when parental permissiveness was high while only 24 percent reported many symptoms when parental permissiveness was low. The difference is 26 percentage points. Among colder parents 100 percent of the adolescents reported many symptoms when permissiveness was high, but only 75 percent reported many symptoms when permissiveness was low, for a 25 percent difference. Thus the effect of permissiveness, which is not apparent in the original relationship,

---

*Thanks to Steven Rytina for translating this example into a contingency table.

is substantial (about a 25 percent difference) when parental warmth is introduced as a control variable. One can see that warm families produce lower rates of symptoms—within high permissiveness, 50 percent versus 100 percent and within low permissiveness, 24 percent versus 75 percent. Thus the circumstance that warm families are more likely to also be permissive masks the negative consequences that permissiveness can have. Parental warmth, in this case, was a **suppressor variable**, concealing the relationship between parental permissiveness and reports of psychological symptoms by adolescents.

Table 16-20
Example of a Suppressor Variable

I. No Apparent Relationship between Parental Permissiveness and Adolescents' Reports of Psychological Symptoms

	Permissiveness	
Symptoms	High	Low
Many	54%	58%
Few	46	42
	100	100
100% =	(450)	(550)

II. Parental Warmth, Parental Permissiveness, Adolescents' Reports of Psychological Symptoms

	Parental Warmth			
	Warmer		Colder	
	Permissiveness		Permissiveness	
Symptoms	High	Low	High	Low
Many	50%	24%	100%	75%
Few	50	76	0	25
	100	100	100	100
100% =	(419)	(181)	(31)	(369)

Based on constructed data that precisely mirrors the relationships among variables reported by Koeske (1998).

Second, the basic paradigm focuses on partials being the same as or weaker than the original relationship but does not provide guidelines for specifying what constitutes a significant difference between the original and the partials. When you use the elaboration model, you'll frequently find yourself making an arbitrary decision about whether a given partial is significantly weaker than the original. This, then, suggests another dimension that could be added to the paradigm.

Third, the limitation of the basic paradigm to partials that are the same as or weaker than the original neglects two other possibilities. A partial relationship might be stronger than the original. Or, on the other hand, a partial relationship might be the reverse of the original—for example, negative where the original was positive.

Rosenberg provides a hypothetical example of the latter possibility by first suggesting that a researcher might find that working-class respondents in his study are more supportive of the civil rights movement in the U.S. than are middle-class respondents (see Table 16-21). He further suggests that race might be a **distorter variable** in this instance, reversing the true relationship between class and attitudes. Presumably, African-American respondents would be more supportive of the movement than would Whites, but African-Americans would also be overrepresented among working-class respondents and underrepresented among the middle class. Middle-class African-American respondents might be more supportive than working-class African-Americans, however; and the same relationship might be found among Whites. Holding race constant, then, the researcher would conclude that support for the civil rights movement was greater among the middle class than among the working class.

All these new dimensions further complicate the notion of specification. If one partial is the same as the original and the other partial is even stronger, how should you react to that situation? You've specified one condition under which the original relationship holds up, but you've also specified another condition under which it holds even more clearly.

Finally, the basic paradigm focuses primarily on dichotomous test variables. In fact, the elaboration model is not so limited—either in theory or in use—but the basic paradigm becomes more complicated

Table 16-21
Example of a Distorter Variable (Hypothetical)

I. Working-Class Subjects Appear More Liberal on Civil Rights than Middle-Class Subjects

Civil Rights Score	Middle Class	Working Class
High	37%	45%
Low	63	55
	100	100
100% =	(120)	(120)

II. Controlling for Race Shows the Middle Class to be More Liberal than the Working Class

	Social Class			
	Blacks		Whites	
Civil Rights Score	Middle Class	Working Class	Middle Class	Working Class
High	70%	50%	30%	20%
Low	30	50	70	80
	100	100	100	100
100% =	(20)	(100)	(100)	(20)

Source: From THE LOGIC OF SURVEY ANALYSIS by MORRIS ROSEN-BERG. Foreword copyright © 1968 by Basic Books, Inc. Reprinted by permission of Basic Books, a member of Perseus Books, L.L.C.

when the test variable divides the sample into three or more subsamples. And the paradigm becomes more complicated yet when more than one test variable is used simultaneously.

None of this is being said to fault the basic elaboration paradigm. To the contrary, we want to emphasize that the elaboration model is not a simple algorithm—a set of procedures through which to analyze research. Rather, it is primarily a logical device for assisting the researcher in understanding his or her data. A firm understanding of the elaboration model will make a sophisticated analysis easier. However, this model suggests neither which variables should be introduced as controls nor definitive conclusions about the nature of elaboration results. For all these things, you must look to your own ingenuity. Such ingenuity, moreover, will come only through extensive experience. By pointing to oversimplifications in the basic elaboration paradigm, we have sought to bring home

the point that the model provides only a logical framework. You'll find sophisticated analyses far more complicated than the examples used to illustrate the basic paradigm.

At the same time, if you fully understand the basic model, you'll understand other techniques such as correlations, regressions, and factor analyses a lot more easily. The following section of this chapter places such techniques as partial correlations and partial regressions in the context of the elaboration model.

One final note before we turn to our discussion of social statistics. The elaboration paradigm allows researchers to examine various possibilities, helping them to either rule out or provide support for them in turn. Proving hypotheses, however, is not something that researchers can do—there are almost always additional factors that may be considered for examination. Analysis is a continuing process that demands a great deal of ingenuity and perseverance. The image of a researcher carefully laying out hypotheses and then testing them in a ritualistic fashion results only in ritualistic research. The search for understanding and explanation is ongoing. "Scientific proof" is a contradiction in terms. Nothing is ever *proved* scientifically. Hypotheses, explanations, theories, or hunches can all escape a stream of attempts at disproof, but none can be proved in any absolute sense. The acceptance of a hypothesis, then, is really a function of the extent to which it has been tested and not disconfirmed. No hypothesis, therefore, should be considered sound on the basis of one test—whether the hypothesis was generated before or after the observation of empirical data.

SOCIAL STATISTICS

It has been our experience that many students are intimidated by statistics. Sometimes statistics makes them feel they're

A few clowns short of a circus

Dumber than a box of hair

A few feathers short of a duck

All foam, no beer
Missing a few buttons on their remote control
A few beans short of a burrito
About as sharp as a bowling ball
About four cents short of a nickel
Not running on full thrusters*

Many people are intimidated by quantitative research because they feel uncomfortable with mathematics and statistics. And indeed, many research reports are filled with unspecified computations. The role of statistics in social research is quite important, but it's equally important that you see this role in its proper perspective.

Empirical research is first and foremost a logical rather than a mathematical operation. Mathematics is merely a convenient and efficient language for accomplishing the logical operations inherent in good data analysis. *Statistics* is the applied branch of mathematics especially appropriate to a variety of research analyses.

In this section we'll be looking at two types of statistics: *descriptive* and *inferential*. **Descriptive statistics** is a medium for describing data in manageable forms. **Inferential statistics,** on the other hand, assists researchers in drawing conclusions from their observations; typically, this involves drawing conclusions about a population from the study of a sample drawn from it.

Descriptive Statistics

As we've already suggested, descriptive statistics present quantitative descriptions in a manageable form. Sometimes we want to describe single variables, and sometimes we want to describe the associations that connect one variable with another. Let's look at some of the ways to do these things.

Data Reduction

Scientific research often involves collecting large masses of data. Suppose we had surveyed 2,000

people, asking each of them 100 questions—not an unusually large study. We would now have a staggering 200,000 answers! No one could possibly read all those 200,000 answers and reach any meaningful conclusion about them. Thus, much scientific analysis involves the *reduction* of data from unmanageable details to manageable summaries.

To begin our discussion, let's look briefly at the raw data matrix created by a quantitative research project. Table 16-22 presents a partial data matrix. Notice that each row in the matrix represents a person (or other unit of analysis), each column represents a variable, and each cell represents the coded attribute or value a given person has on a given variable. The first column in Table 16-22 represents a person's gender. Let's say a "1" represents male and "2" represents female. This means that persons 1 and 2 are male, person 3 is female, and so forth.

In the case of age, person 1's "3" might mean 30–39 years old, person 2's "4" might mean 40–49. However age had been coded (see Chapter 15), the code numbers shown in Table 16-22 would describe each of the people represented there.

Notice that the data have already been reduced somewhat by the time a data matrix like this one has been created. If age had been coded as suggested previously, the specific answer "33 years old" has already been assigned to the category "30–39." The people responding to our survey may have given us 60 or 70 different ages, but we have now reduced them to six or seven categories.

We earlier discussed some of the ways of further summarizing univariate data: averages such as the mode, median, and mean and measures of dispersion such as the range, the standard deviation, and so forth. It's also possible to summarize the associations among variables.

Measures of Association

A data matrix can also represent the association between any two variables, this time produced by the joint frequency distributions of the two variables. Table 16-23 presents such a matrix. It provides all the information needed to determine the

---

*Thanks to the many contributors to humour lists on the Internet.

nature and extent of the relationship between education and prejudice.

Notice, for example, that 23 people (1) have no education and (2) scored high on prejudice; 77 people (1) had graduate degrees and (2) scored low on prejudice.

Like the raw-data matrix in Table 16-22, this matrix provides more information than can easily be comprehended. A careful study of the table, however, shows that as education increases from "None" to "Graduate Degree," there is a general tendency for prejudice to decrease, but no more than a general impression is possible. For a more precise summary of the data matrix, we need one of several types of descriptive statistics. Selecting the appropriate measure depends initially on the nature of the two variables.

We'll turn now to some of the options available for summarizing the association between two variables. Each measure of association we'll discuss is based on the same model—*proportionate reduction of error* (PRE). To see how this model works, let's assume that we asked you to guess respondents' attributes on a given variable: for example, whether they answered yes or no to a given questionnaire item.

To assist you, let's first assume you know the overall distribution of responses in the total sample—say, 60 percent said yes and 40 percent said no. You would make the fewest errors in this process if you always guessed the modal (most frequent) response: yes.

Second, let's assume you also know the empirical relationship between the first variable and some other variable: say, *gender.* Now, each time we ask you to guess whether a respondent said yes or no, we'll tell you whether the respondent is a man or a woman. If the two variables are related, you should make fewer errors the second time. It's possible, therefore, to compute the PRE by knowing the relationship between the two variables: the greater the relationship, the greater the reduction of error.

This basic PRE model is modified slightly to take account of different levels of measurement—nominal, ordinal, or interval. The following sections will consider each level of measurement and present one measure of association appropriate to each. You should realize that the three measures discussed are only an arbitrary selection from among many appropriate measures.

Nominal Variables

If the two variables consist of nominal data (for example, gender, religious affiliation, race), lambda (λ) would be one appropriate measure. (Lambda is a letter in the Greek alphabet corresponding to *l* in our alphabet. Greek letters are used for many concepts in statistics, which perhaps helps to account for those who say of statistics, "It's all Greek to me.") Lambda is based on your ability to guess values on one of the variables: the PRE achieved through knowledge of values on the other variable.

Imagine this situation. We tell you that a room contains 100 people and we would like you to guess the gender of each person, one at a time. If half are men and half women, you'll probably be right half the time and wrong half the time. But suppose we tell you each person's occupation before you guess that person's gender.

Table 16-22
Partial Raw Data Matrix

	Gender	Age	Education	Income	Occupation	Political Affiliation	Political Orientation	Religious Affiliation	Importance of Religion
Person 1	1	3	2	4	1	2	3	0	4
Person 2	1	4	2	4	4	1	1	1	2
Person 3	2	2	5	5	2	2	4	2	3
Person 4	1	5	4	4	3	2	2	2	4
Person 5	2	3	7	8	6	1	1	5	1
Person 6	2	1	3	3	5	3	5	1	1

Table 16-23
Hypothetical Raw Data on Education and Prejudice

Prejudice	Educational Level				
	None	Grade School	High School	University	Graduate Degree
High	23	34	156	67	16
Medium	11	21	123	102	23
Low	6	12	95	164	77

What gender would you guess if we said the person was a truck driver? Probably you'd be wise to guess "male"; although there are now plenty of women truck drivers, most are men. If we said the next person was a nurse, you'd probably be wisest to guess "female," following the same logic. While you'd still make errors in guessing genders, you'd clearly do better than you would if you didn't know their occupations. The extent to which you did better (the proportionate reduction of error) would be an indicator of the association that exists between gender and occupation.

Table 16-24
Hypothetical Data Relating
Gender to Employment Status

	Men	Women	Total
Employed	900	200	1,100
Unemployed	100	800	900
Total	1,000	1,000	2,000

Here's another simple hypothetical example that illustrates the logic and method of lambda. Table 16-24 presents hypothetical data relating gender to employment status. Overall, we note that 1,100 people are employed, and 900 are not employed. If you were to predict whether people were employed, knowing only the overall distribution on that variable, you would always predict "employed," since that would result in fewer errors than always predicting "not employed." Nevertheless, this strategy would result in 900 errors out of 2,000 predictions.

Let's suppose that you had access to the data in Table 16-24 and that you were told each person's gender before making your prediction of employ-

ment status. Your strategy would change in that case. For every man, you would predict "employed," and for every woman, you would predict "not employed." In this instance, you would make 300 errors—the 100 men who were not employed and the 200 employed women—or 600 fewer errors than you would make without knowing the person's gender.

Lambda, then, represents the reduction in errors as a proportion of the errors that would have been made on the basis of the overall distribution. In this hypothetical example, lambda would equal .67; that is, 600 fewer errors divided by the 900 total errors based on employment status alone. In this fashion, lambda measures the statistical association between gender and employment status.

If gender and employment status were statistically independent, we would find the same distribution of employment status for men and women. In this case, knowing each person's gender would not affect the number of errors made in predicting employment status, and the resulting lambda would be zero. If, on the other hand, all men were employed and none of the women were employed, by knowing gender you would avoid errors in predicting employment status. You would make 900 fewer errors (out of 900), so lambda would be 1.0—representing a perfect statistical association.

Lambda is only one of several measures of association appropriate to the analysis of two nominal variables. You could look at any statistics textbook for a discussion of other appropriate measures.

Ordinal Variables

If the variables being related are ordinal (for example, social class, religiosity, alienation), gamma (γ) is one appropriate measure of associa-

Table 16-25
Hypothetical Data Relating
Social Class to Prejudice

Prejudice	Lower Class	Middle Class	Upper Class
Low	200	400	700
Medium	500	900	400
High	800	300	100

tion. Like lambda, gamma is based on your ability to guess values on one variable by knowing values on another. However, whereas lambda is based on guessing exact values, gamma is based on guessing the ordinal arrangement of values. For any given pair of cases, we guess that their ordinal ranking on one variable will correspond (positively or negatively) to their ordinal ranking on the other.

Let's say we have a group of elementary students. It's reasonable to assume that there is a relationship between their ages and their heights. We can test this by comparing every pair of students: Sam and Mary, Sam and Fred, Mary and Fred, and so forth. Then we ignore all the pairs in which the students are the same age and/or the same height. We then classify each of the remaining pairs (those who differ in both age and height) into one of two categories: those in which the older child is also the taller ("same" pair) and those in which the older child is the shorter ("opposite" pair). So, if Sam were older and taller than Mary was, the Sam–Mary pair would be counted as a "same." If Sam were older but shorter than Mary was, then that pair is an "opposite." (If they are the same age and/or same height, we ignore them.)

To determine whether age and height are related to one another, we compare the number of same and opposite pairs. If the same pairs outnumber the opposite pairs, we can conclude that there is a *positive* association between the two variables—as one increases, the other increases. If the opposite pairs outnumber the same pairs, we can conclude that the relationship is *negative*. If there are about as many same as opposite pairs, we can conclude that age and height are not related to each another, that they are *independent* of each other.

Here's a social science example to illustrate the simple calculations involved in gamma. Let's say you suspect that religiosity is positively related to political conservatism, and if Person A is more religious than Person B, you guess that A is also more conservative than B. Gamma is the proportion of paired comparisons that fit this pattern.

Table 16-25 presents hypothetical data relating social class to prejudice. The general nature of the relationship between these two variables is that as social class increases, prejudice decreases. There is a negative association between social class and prejudice.

Gamma is computed from two quantities: (1) the number of pairs having the same ranking on the two variables and (2) the number of pairs having the opposite ranking on the two variables. The pairs having the same ranking are computed as follows: The frequency of each cell in the table is multiplied by the sum of all cells appearing below and to the right of it—with all these products being summed. In Table 16-25, the number of pairs with the same ranking would be 200(900 + 300 + 400 +

Table 16-26
Gamma Associations among the Semantic Differentiation Items of the Sanctification Scale

	Useful	Honest	Superior	Kind	Friendly	Warm
Good	.79	.88	.80	.90	.79	.83
Useful		.84	.71	.77	.68	.72
Honest			.83	.89	.79	.82
Superior				.78	.60	.73
Kind					.88	.90
Friendly						.90

Source: Helena Znaniecki Lopata, "Widowhood and Husband Sanctification," *Journal of Marriage and the Family* (May 1981): 439–50.

100) + 500(300 + 100) + 400(400 + 100) + 900(100), or 340,000 + 200,000 + 200,000 + 90,000 = 830,000.

The pairs having the opposite ranking on the two variables are computed as follows: The frequency of each cell in the table is multiplied by the sum of all cells appearing below and to the left of it—with all these products being summed. In Table 16-25, the numbers of pairs with opposite rankings would be 700(500 + 800 + 900 + 300) + 400(800 + 300) + 400(500 + 800) + 900(800), or 1,750,000 + 440,000 + 520,000 + 720,000 = 3,430,000. Gamma is computed from the numbers of same-ranked pairs and opposite-ranked pairs as follows:

$$gamma = \frac{same - opposite}{same + opposite}$$

In our example, gamma equals (830,000 – 3,430,000) divided by (830,000 + 3,430,000) or –.61. The negative sign in this answer indicates the negative association suggested by the initial inspection of the table. Social class and prejudice, in this hypothetical example, are negatively associated with one another. The numerical figure for gamma indicates that 61 percent more of the pairs examined had the opposite ranking than the same ranking.

Note that whereas values of lambda vary from 0 to 1, values of gamma vary from -1 through 0 to +1, representing the *direction* as well as the magnitude of the association. Because nominal variables have no ordinal structure, it makes no sense to speak of the direction of the relationship. (A negative lambda would indicate that you made more errors in predicting values on one variable while knowing values on the second than you made in ignorance of the second, and that's not logically possible.)

Table 16-26 is an example of the use of gamma in social research. To study the extent to which widows sanctified their deceased husbands, Helena Znaniecki Lopata (1981) administered a questionnaire to a probability sample of 301 widows. In part, the questionnaire asked the respondents to characterize their deceased husbands in terms of the following semantic differentiation scale:

Characteristic

Positive Extreme								Negative Extreme
Good	1	2	3	4	5	6	7	Bad
Useful	1	2	3	4	5	6	7	Useless
Honest	1	2	3	4	5	6	7	Dishonest
Superior	1	2	3	4	5	6	7	Inferior
Kind	1	2	3	4	5	6	7	Cruel
Friendly	1	2	3	4	5	6	7	Unfriendly
Warm	1	2	3	4	5	6	7	Cold

Respondents were asked to describe their deceased spouses by circling a number for each pair of opposing characteristics. Notice that the series of numbers connecting each pair of characteristics is an ordinal measure.

Next, Lopata wanted to discover the extent to which the several measures were related to each other. Appropriately, she chose gamma as the measure of association. Table 16-26 shows how she presented the results of her investigation.

The format presented in Table 16-26 is called a *correlation matrix*. For each pair of measures, Lopata has calculated the gamma. Good and Useful, for example, are related to each other by a gamma equal to .79. The matrix is a convenient way of presenting the intercorrelations among several variables, and you'll find it frequently in the research literature. In this case, we see that all the variables are quite strongly related to each other, though some pairs are more strongly related than others.

Gamma is only one of several measures of association appropriate to ordinal variables. Again, any introductory statistics textbook will give you a more comprehensive treatment of this subject.

Interval or Ratio Variables

If interval or ratio variables (for example, *age, income, grade point average*, and so forth) are being associated, one appropriate measure of association is Pearson's product–moment correlation *(r)*. The derivation and computation of this measure of association is complex enough to lie outside the scope of this book, so we'll make only a few general comments here.

Like both gamma and lambda, r is based on guessing the value of one variable by knowing the other. For continuous interval or ratio variables, however, it's unlikely that you could predict the precise value of the variable. But on the other hand, predicting only the ordinal arrangement of values on the two variables would not take advantage of the greater amount of information conveyed by an interval or ratio variable. In a sense, r reflects how closely you can guess the value of one variable through your knowledge of the value of the other.

To understand the logic of r, consider the way you might hypothetically guess values that particular cases have on a given variable. With nominal variables, we've seen that you might always guess the modal value. But for interval or ratio data, you would minimize your errors by always guessing the mean value of the variable. Although this practice produces few if any perfect guesses, the extent of your errors will be minimized. Imagine the task of guessing people's incomes and how much better you would do if you knew how many years of education they had as well as the mean incomes for people with 0, 1, 2 (and so forth) years of education.

In the computation of lambda, we noted the number of errors produced by always guessing the modal value. In the case of r, errors are measured in terms of the sum of the squared differences between the actual value and the mean. This sum is called the *total variation*.

To understand this concept, we must expand the scope of our examination. Let's look at the logic of **regression analysis** and discuss correlation within that context.

Regression Analysis

We have referred several times in this text to the general formula for describing the association between two variables: $Y = f(X)$. This formula is read "Y is a function of X," meaning that differences or contrasts in the values of Y accompany or parallel variations in the values of X. Stated more strongly, we might say that X causes Y, so the value of X determines the value of Y. Regression analysis

is a method of estimating from the data the specific function relating Y to X. There are several forms of regression analysis, depending on the complexity of the relationships being studied. Let's begin with the simplest.

Linear Regression

The regression model can be seen most clearly in the case of a *linear regression analysis*, where there is a perfect linear association between two variables. Figure 16-7 is a scattergram presenting in graphic form the values of X and Y as produced by a hypothetical study. It shows that for the four cases in our study, the values of X and Y are identical in each instance. The case with a value of 1 on X also has a value of 1 on Y, and so forth. The relationship between the two variables in this instance is described by the equation $Y = X$; this is called the *regression equation*. Because all four points lie on a straight line, we could superimpose that line over the points; this is the *regression line*.

The linear regression model has important descriptive uses. The regression line offers a graphic picture of the association between X and Y, and the regression equation is an efficient way to summarize that association. The regression model has inferential value as well. To the extent that the regression equation correctly describes the general

Figure 16-7
Simple Scattergram of Values of X and Y

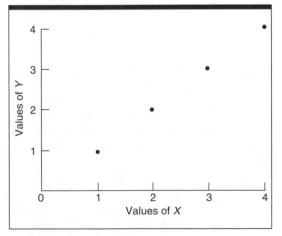

association between the two variables, it may be used to predict other sets of values. If, for example, we know that a new case has a value of 3.5 on X, we can predict the value of 3.5 on Y as well.

In practice, of course, studies are seldom limited to four cases, and the associations between variables are seldom as clear as the one presented in Figure 16-7.

A somewhat more realistic example is presented in Figure 16-8, representing a hypothetical relationship between population and crime rate in small- to medium-sized cities. Each dot in the scattergram is a city, and its placement reflects that city's population and its crime rate. As was the case in our previous example, the values of Y (crime rates) generally correspond to those of X (populations); and as values of X increase, so do values of Y. However, the association is not nearly as clear as it was for the case in Figure 16-7.

In Figure 16-8 we can't superimpose a straight line that will pass through all the points in the scattergram. But we can draw an approximate line showing the best possible linear representation of the several points. We've drawn that line on the graph.

You may recall from algebra that any straight line on a graph can be represented by an equation of the form $Y = a + bX$, where X and Y are values of the two variables. In this equation, a equals the value of Y when X is 0, and b represents the slope of the line. If we know the values of a and b, we can calculate an estimate of Y for every value of X.

We can now say more formally that regression analysis is a technique for establishing the regression equation representing the geometric line that comes closest to the distribution of points on a graph. This regression equation provides a mathematical *description* of the relationship between the variables, and it allows us to *infer* values of Y when we have values of X. Recalling Figure 16-8, we could estimate crime rates of cities if we knew their populations.

To improve your guessing, you construct a *regression line,* stated in the form of a regression equation that permits the estimation of values on one variable from values on the other. The general format for this equation is $\hat{Y} = \hat{a} + \hat{b}(X)$, where $\hat{a}$ and

$\hat{b}$ are estimated from the data, X is any given value on one variable, and $\hat{Y}$ is the corresponding estimated value on the other. The values of $\hat{a}$ and $\hat{b}$ are computed to minimize the differences between actual values of Y and the corresponding estimates $(\hat{Y})$ based on the known value of X. The sum of squared differences between actual and estimated values of Y is called the *unexplained variation* because it represents errors that still exist even when estimates are based on known values of X.

The *explained variation* is the difference between the total variation and the unexplained variation. Dividing the explained variation by the total variation produces a measure of the *proportionate reduction of error* corresponding to the similar quantity in the computation of lambda. In the present case, this quantity is the *correlation squared: r^2*. Thus, if $r = .7$, then $r^2 = .49$, meaning that about half the variation has been explained. In practice, we compute r rather than r^2, because the product–moment correlation can take either a positive or negative sign, depending on the direction of the relationship between the two variables. (Computing r^2 and taking a square root would always produce a positive quantity.) See any other standard statistics textbook for the *method* of computing r, although we anticipate that most readers using this measure will have access to computer programs designed for this function.

Unfortunately, or perhaps fortunately, social life is so complex that the simple linear regression model often does not sufficiently represent the state of affairs. As we saw earlier in this chapter, it's possible, using percentage tables, to analyze more than two variables. As the number of variables increases, such tables become increasingly complicated and hard to read. But the regression model offers a useful alternative in such cases.

Multiple Regression

Very often, social researchers find that a given dependent variable is affected simultaneously by several independent variables. *Multiple regression analysis* provides a means of analyzing such situations. This was the case when Beverly Yerg (1981) set about studying teacher effectiveness in physical

Figure 16-8
A Scattergram of the Values of Two Variables with Regression Line Added (Hypothetical)

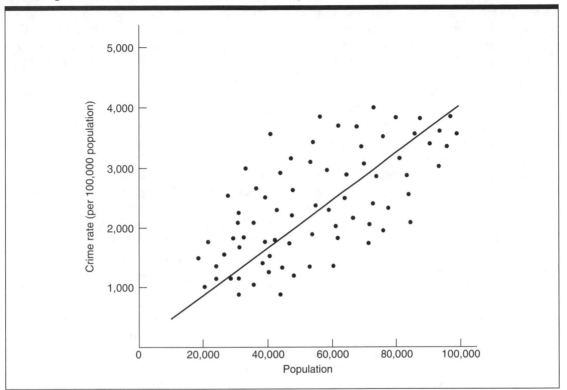

education. She stated her expectations in the form of a multiple regression equation:

$$F = b_0 + b_1 I + b_2 X_1 + b_3 X_2 + b_4 X_3 + b_5 X_4 + e,$$
where

F = Final pupil-performance score
I = Initial pupil-performance score
X_1 = Composite of guiding and supporting practice
X_2 = Composite of teacher mastery of content
X_3 = Composite of providing specific, task-related feedback
X_4 = Composite of clear, concise task presentation
b = Regression weight
e = Residual

(Adapted from Yerg 1981:42)

Notice that in place of the single X variable in a linear regression, there are several X's, and there are also several b's instead of just one. Also, Yerg has chosen to represent a as b_0 in this equation but with the same meaning as discussed previously. Finally, the equation ends with a residual factor (e), which represents the variance in Y that is not accounted for by the X variables analyzed.

Beginning with this equation, Yerg calculated the values of the several b's to show the relative contributions of the several independent variables in determining final student-performance scores. She also calculated the multiple-correlation coefficient as an indicator of the extent to which all six variables predict the final scores. This follows the same logic as the simple bivariate correlation discussed earlier, and it is traditionally reported as a capital R. In this case, $R = .877$, meaning that 77 percent of the variance ($.877^2 = .77$) in final scores is explained by the six variables acting in concert.

Partial Regression

In exploring the elaboration model, we paid special attention to the relationship between two variables when a third test variable was held constant. Thus, we might examine the effect of education on prejudice with age held constant, testing the independent effect of education. To do so, we would compute the tabular relationship between education and prejudice separately for each age group.

Partial regression analysis is based on this same logical model. The equation summarizing the relationship between variables is computed on the basis of the test variables remaining constant. As in the case of the elaboration model, the result may be compared with the uncontrolled relationship between the two variables to clarify further the overall relationship.

Curvilinear Regression

Up to now, we have been discussing the association among variables as represented by a straight line. The regression model is even more general than our discussion thus far has implied.

You may already know that curvilinear functions, as well as linear ones, can be represented by equations. For example, the equation $X^2 + Y^2 = 25$ describes a circle with a radius of 5. Raising variables to powers greater than 1 has the effect of producing curves rather than straight lines. And in the real world there is no reason to assume that the relationship among every set of variables will be linear. In some cases, then, *curvilinear regression analysis* can provide a better understanding of empirical relationships than can any linear model.

Recall, however, that a regression line serves two functions. It describes a set of empirical observations, and it provides a *general* model for making inferences about the relationship between two variables in the general population that the observations represent. A very complex equation might produce an erratic line that would indeed pass through every individual point. In this sense, it would perfectly describe the empirical observations. There would be no guarantee, however, that such a line could adequately *predict* new observations or that it in any meaningful way represented

the relationship between the two variables in general. Thus, it would have little or no inferential value.

Earlier in this book, we discussed the need for balancing detail and utility in data reduction. Ultimately, researchers attempt to provide the most faithful, yet also the simplest, representation of their data. This practice also applies to regression analysis. Data should be presented in the simplest fashion (thus, linear regressions are most frequently used) that best describes the actual data. Curvilinear regression analysis adds a new option to the researcher in this regard, but it does not solve the problems altogether. Nothing does that.

Cautions in Regression Analysis

The use of regression analysis for statistical inferences is based on the same assumptions made for correlational analysis: simple random sampling, the absence of nonsampling errors, and continuous interval data. Because social scientific research seldom completely satisfies these assumptions, you should use caution in assessing the results in regression analyses.

Also, regression lines—linear or curvilinear—can be useful for *interpolation* (estimating cases lying between those observed), but they are less trustworthy when used for *extrapolation* (estimating cases that lie beyond the range of observations). This limitation on extrapolations is important in two ways. First, you're likely to come across regression equations that seem to make illogical predictions. An equation linking population and crimes, for example, might seem to suggest that small towns with, say, a population of 1,000 should produce 123 crimes a year. This failure in predictive ability does not disqualify the equation but dramatizes that its applicability is limited to a particular range of population sizes. Second, researchers sometimes overstep this limitation, drawing inferences that lie outside their range of observation, and you'd be right in criticizing them for that.

The preceding sections have introduced you to some of the techniques for measuring associations among variables at different levels of measure-

Measures of Association and Levels of Measurement

By Peter Nardi
Pitzer College

Note that this table itself is set up with the dependent variables in the rows and the independent variable in the columns, as tables are commonly organized. Also, notice that the levels of measurement are themselves an ordinal scale.

If you want to use an interval/ratio level variable in a crosstab, you must first recode it into an ordinal-level variable.

		Independent Variable		
		Nominal	Ordinal	Interval/Ratio
Dependent Variable	Nominal	*Crosstabs* Chi-square Lambda	*Crosstabs* Chi-square Lambda	
	Ordinal	*Crosstabs* Chi-square Lambda	*Crosstabs* Chi-square Lambda Gamma Kendall's tau Sommers' *d*	
	Interval/Ratio	*Means* *t*-test ANOVA	*Means* *t*-test ANOVA	*Correlate* Pearson *r* Regression (*R*)

ment. Matters become slightly more complex when the two variables represent different levels of measurement. Though we aren't going to pursue this issue in this textbook, we've offered a box by Peter Nardi as a useful resource if you ever have to address such situations.

Other Multivariate Techniques

For the most part, this book has focused on rather rudimentary forms of data manipulation, such as the use of contingency tables and percentages. Multiple regression analysis was briefly discussed. There are many other, more complex multivariate techniques, such as time-series analysis, path analysis, and factor analysis that you will learn about in future statistics courses. Techniques like time-series analysis, for example, allow you to study long-term trends in a regression format. With various forms of regression analysis you can examine time-series data that represent changes in one or more variables over time. You can test factors that might explain the trend in a variable, say crime rates, to determine if factors such as population growth or economic fluctuations, for instance, account for the trend. This type of analysis could permit forecasting of future crime rates. The more you learn about advanced techniques for data manipulation, the more possibilities that are open to you for exploration of your data.

Inferential Statistics

Many, if not most, social scientific research projects involve the examination of data collected from a sample drawn from a larger population. A sample of people may be interviewed in a survey; a sample of divorce records may be coded and analyzed; a sample of newspapers may be examined through content analysis. Researchers seldom if ever study samples just to describe the samples per se; in most instances, their ultimate purpose is to make assertions about the larger population from which the sample has been selected. Frequently, then, you'll wish to interpret your univariate and multi-variate sample findings as the basis for *inferences* about some population.

This section examines *inferential statistics*—the statistical measures used for making inferences to a larger population from findings based on sample observations. We'll begin with univariate data and move to multivariate.

Univariate Inferences

The opening sections of this chapter dealt with methods of presenting univariate data. Each summary measure was intended as a method of describing the sample studied. Now we'll use such measures to make broader assertions about a population. This section addresses two univariate measures: percentages and means.

If 50 percent of a sample of people say they've had colds during the past year, 50 percent is also our best estimate of the proportion of colds in the total population from which the sample was drawn. (This estimate assumes a simple random sample, of course.) It's rather unlikely, however, that *precisely* 50 percent of the population have had colds during the year. If a rigorous sampling design for random selection has been followed, however, we will be able to estimate the expected range of error when the sample finding is applied to the population.

Chapter 7, on sampling theory, covered the procedures for making such estimates, so we'll only review them here. In the case of a percentage, the quantity

$$\sqrt{\frac{p \times q}{n}}$$

where p is a percentage, q equals $1 - p$, and n is the sample size, is called the *standard error*. As noted in Chapter 7, this quantity is very important in the estimation of sampling error. We may say we are confident that in 68 percent of samples, sample estimates (i.e., statistics) are within plus or minus one standard error of the population value; we may say we are confident that in 95 percent of samples, sample statistics are within plus or minus two standard errors of the population parameter; and we may say we are confident that in 99.9 percent of samples, the estimates will fall within plus or minus three standard errors of the true value in the population.

Any statement of sampling error, then, must contain two essential components: the *confidence level* (for example, 95 percent) and the *confidence interval* (for example, plus or minus 2.5 percent). If 50 percent of a sample of 1,600 people say they've had colds during the year, we might say that in theory for samples of this size, the population figure would be between 47.5 percent and 52.5 percent 19 out of 20 times.

In this example we've moved beyond simply describing the sample into the realm of making inferences about the larger population. In doing so, we must take care in several ways.

First, the sample must be drawn from the population about which inferences are being made. A sample taken from a telephone directory cannot legitimately be the basis for statistical inferences about the population of a city, but only about the population of telephone subscribers with listed numbers.

Second, the inferential statistics assume simple random sampling, which is virtually never the case in sample surveys. The statistics assume sampling with replacement, which is almost never done—but this is probably not a serious problem. Although systematic sampling is used more frequently than random sampling, it, too, probably presents no serious problem if done correctly. Stratified sampling, because it improves representativeness, clearly presents no problem. Cluster sampling does present a problem, however, as the estimates of sampling error may be too small. Quite clearly, street-corner sampling does not warrant the use of inferential statistics. Finally, this standard error sampling technique also assumes a 100 percent completion rate (that is, that everyone in the sample completed the survey). This problem increases in seriousness as the completion rate decreases.

Third, inferential statistics are addressed to sampling error only, not *nonsampling error,* such as coding errors or misunderstandings of questions by respondents. Thus, although we might state correctly that between 47.5 and 52.5 percent of the population (95 percent confidence) would *report* having colds during the previous year, we couldn't so confidently guess the percentage who had actually *had* them. Because nonsampling errors are probably larger than sampling errors in a respectable sample design, we need to be especially cautious in generalizing from our sample findings to the population.

Tests of Statistical Significance

There is no scientific answer to the question of whether a given association between two variables is significant, strong, important, interesting, or worth reporting. Perhaps the ultimate test of significance rests with your ability to persuade your audience (present and future) of the association's significance. At the same time, there is a body of inferential statistics to assist you in this regard, called *parametric tests of significance.* As the name suggests, parametric statistics are those that make certain assumptions about the parameters describing the population from which the sample is selected. They allow us to determine the **statistical significance** of associations. "Statistical significance" does not imply "importance" or "significance" in any general sense. If refers simply

to the likelihood that relationships as large as those observed in a sample could be attributed to sampling error alone.

Although **tests of statistical significance** are widely reported in social scientific literature, the logic underlying them is rather subtle and often misunderstood. Tests of significance are based on the same sampling logic discussed elsewhere in this book. To understand that logic, let's return for a moment to the concept of sampling error in regard to univariate data.

Recall that a sample statistic normally provides the best single estimate of the corresponding population parameter, but the statistic and the parameter seldom correspond precisely. Thus, we report the probability that the parameter falls within a certain range (confidence interval). The degree of uncertainty within that range is due to normal sampling error. The corollary of such a statement is, of course, that it is improbable that the parameter would fall outside the specified range *only* as a result of sampling error. Thus, if we estimate that a parameter (99.9 percent confidence) lies between 45 percent and 55 percent, we say by implication that it is extremely improbable that the parameter is actually, say 90 percent if our *only* error of estimation is due to normal sampling. This is the basic logic behind tests of statistical significance.

The Logic of Statistical Significance

We think we can illustrate this logic of **statistical significance** best in a series of diagrams representing the selection of samples from a population. Here are the elements in the logic:

1. Assumptions regarding the independence of two variables in the population study
2. Assumptions regarding the representativeness of samples selected through conventional probability sampling procedures
3. The observed joint distribution of sample elements in terms of the two variables

Figure 16-9 represents a hypothetical population of 256 people; half are women, half men. The diagram also indicates how each person feels about women enjoying equality to men. In the diagram, those favouring equality have open circles; those opposing it have their circles shaded in.

The question we'll be investigating is whether there is any relationship between gender and feelings about equality for men and women. More specifically, we'll see if women are more likely to favour equality than men are, since women would presumably benefit more from it. Take a moment to look at Figure 16-9 and see what the answer to this question is.

The illustration in the figure indicates there is no relationship between gender and attitudes about equality. Exactly half of each group favours equality and the other half opposes it. Recall the earlier discussion of proportionate reduction of error. In this instance, knowing a person's gender would not reduce the "errors" we'd make in guessing his or her attitude toward equality. The table at the bottom of Figure 16-9 provides a tabular view of what you can observe in the graphic diagram.

Figure 16-10 represents the selection of a one-fourth sample from the hypothetical population. In

Figure 16-9

A Hypothetical Population of Men and Women Who Either Favour or Oppose Gender Equality

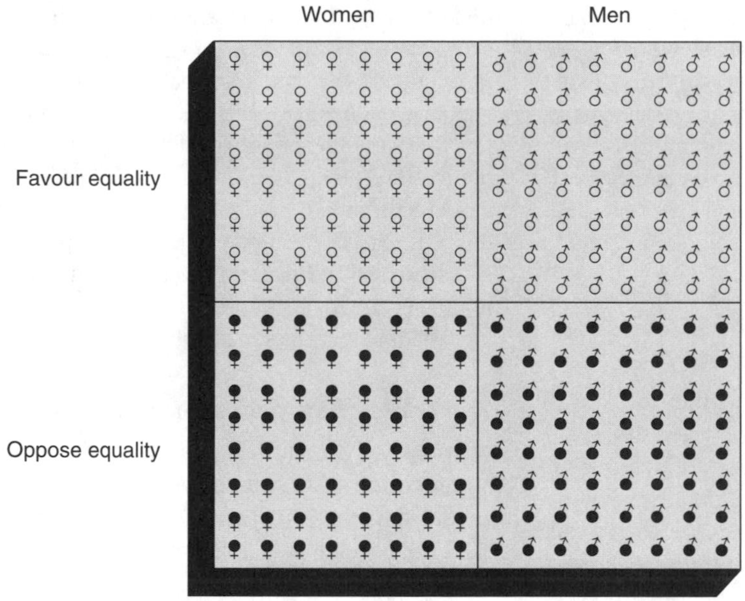

	Women	Men
Favour equality	50%	50%
Oppose equality	50%	50%
	100%	100%

Legend	
♀	Woman who favours equality
♂	Man who favours equality
♀	Woman who opposes equality
♂	Man who opposes equality

terms of the graphic illustration, a "square" selection from the center of the population provides a representative sample. Notice that our sample contains 16 of each type of person: Half are men and half are women; half of each gender favours equality, and the other half opposes it.

The sample selected in Figure 16-10 would allow us to draw accurate conclusions about the relationship between gender and equality in the larger population. Following the sampling logic we saw in Chapter 7, we'd note there was no relationship between gender and equality in the sample; thus, we'd conclude there was similarly no relationship in the larger population—since we've presumably selected a sample in accord with the conventional rules of sampling.

Of course, real-life samples are seldom such perfect reflections of the populations from which they're drawn. It would not be unusual for us to have selected, say, one or two extra men who opposed equality and a couple of extra women who favoured it—even if there was no relationship

Figure 16-10
A Representative Sample

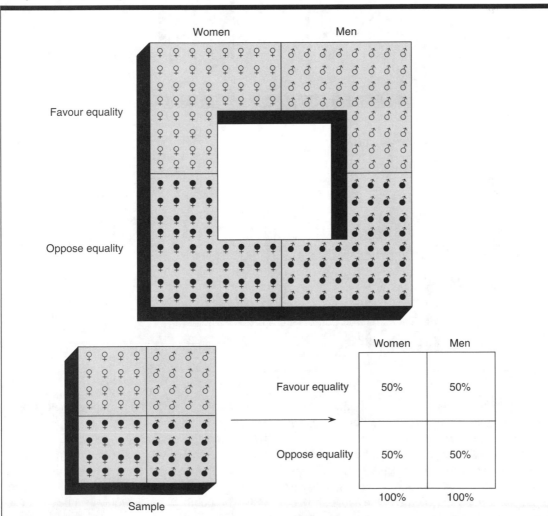

Figure 16-11
An Unrepresentative Sample

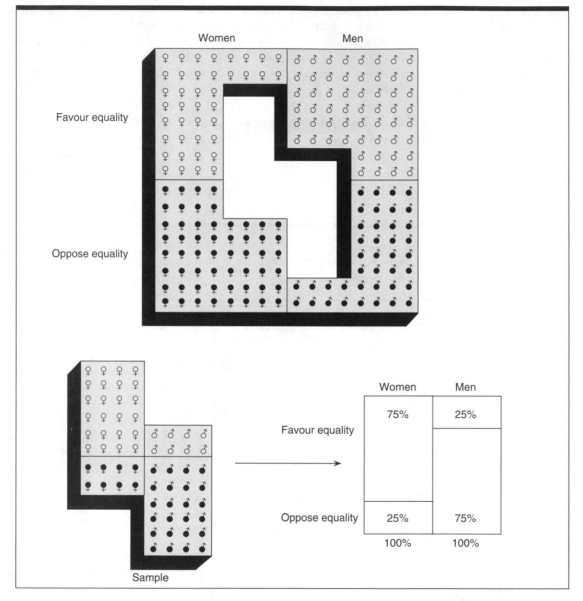

between the two variables in the population. Such minor variations are part and parcel of probability sampling, as we saw in Chapter 7.

Figure 16-11, however, represents a sample that falls far short of the mark in reflecting the larger population. Notice it includes far too many supportive women and opposing men. As the table shows, three-fourths of the women in the sample support equality, but only one-fourth of the men do so. If we had selected this sample from a population in which the two variables were unrelated to each other, we'd be sorely misled by the analysis of our sample.

As you'll recall, it's unlikely that a properly drawn probability sample would ever be as inaccu-

Figure 16-12
A Representative Sample from a Population in Which the Variables Are Related

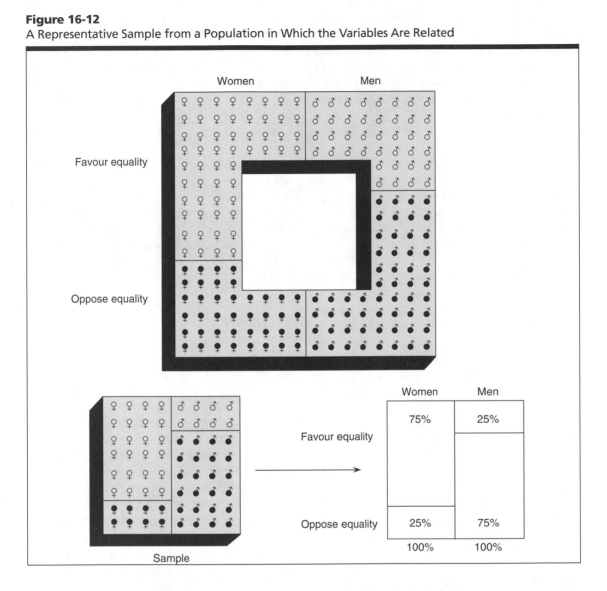

rate as the one shown in Figure 16-11. In fact, if we actually selected a sample that gave us the results this one does, we'd look for a different explanation. Figure 16-12 illustrates the more likely situation.

Notice that the sample selected in Figure 16-12 also shows a strong relationship between gender and equality. The reason is quite different this time. We've selected a perfectly representative sample, but we see that there is actually a strong relationship between the two variables in the population at large. In this latest figure, women are more likely to support equality than men are; that's the case in the population, and the sample reflects it.

In practice, of course, we never know what's so for the total population; that's why we select samples. So if we selected a sample and found the strong relationship presented in Figures 16-11 and 16-12, we'd need to decide whether that finding accurately reflected the population or was simply a product of sampling error.

The fundamental logic of tests of statistical significance, then, is this: Faced with any discrepancy between the assumed independence of variables in a population and the observed distribution of sample elements, we may explain that discrepancy in either of two ways: (1) we may attribute it to an unrepresentative sample, or (2) we may reject the assumption of independence. The logic and statistics associated with probability sampling methods offer guidance about the varying probabilities of varying degrees of unrepresentativeness (expressed as sampling error). More simply put, there is a *high* probability of a *small* degree of unrepresentativeness and a *low* probability of a *large* degree of unrepresentativeness.

The *statistical significance* of a relationship observed in a set of sample data, then, is always expressed in terms of probabilities. "Significant at the .05 level ($p \leq .05$)" simply means that the probability that a relationship as strong as the observed one can be attributed to sampling error alone is no more than 5 in 100. Put somewhat differently, if two variables are independent of one another in the population, and if 100 probability samples were selected from that population, no more than 5 of those samples would provide a relationship as strong as the one that has been observed.

There is, then, a corollary to confidence intervals in tests of significance, which represent the probability of the measured associations being due *only* to *sampling error*. This is called the **level of significance**. Like confidence intervals, levels of significance are derived from a logical model in which several samples are drawn from a given population. In the present case, we assume that there is no association between the variables in the population, and then ask what proportion of the samples drawn from such a population would produce associations at least as great as those measured in the empirical data. Three levels of significance are frequently used in research reports: .05, .01, and .001. These mean, respectively, that the chances of obtaining the measured association as a result of sampling error are 5/100, 1/100, and 1/1,000.

Researchers who use tests of significance normally follow one of two patterns. Some specify in advance the level of significance they will regard as sufficient. If any measured association is statistically significant at that level, they will regard it as representing a genuine association between the two variables. In other words, they're willing to discount the possibility of its resulting from sampling error only.

Other researchers prefer to report the specific level of significance for each association, disregarding the conventions of .05, .01, and .001. Rather than reporting that a given association is significant at the .05 level, they might report significance at the .023 level, indicating the chances of its having resulted from sampling error as 23 out of 1,000.

Chi Square

Chi square (χ^2) is a frequently used test of significance in social science. It's based on the **null hypothesis**: the assumption that there is no relationship between the two variables in the total population. Given the observed distribution of values on the two separate variables, we compute the conjoint distribution that would be expected if there were no relationship between the two variables. The result of this operation is a set of *expected frequencies* for all the cells in the contingency table. We then compare this expected distribution with the distribution of cases actually found in the sample data, and we determine the probability that the discovered discrepancy could have resulted from sampling error alone. An example will illustrate this procedure.

Let's assume we're interested in the possible relationship between church attendance and gender for the members of a particular church. To test this relationship, we select a sample of 100 church members at random. We find our sample is made up of 40 men and 60 women and that 70 percent of our sample report having attended church during the preceding week, whereas the remaining 30 percent say they did not.

If there is no relationship between gender and church attendance, then 70 percent of the men in the sample should have attended church during the preceding week, and 30 percent should have stayed away. Moreover, women should have attended in the same proportion. Table 16-27 (Part I) shows that based on this model, 28 men and 42 women would have attended church, with 12 men and 18 women not attending.

Part II of Table 16-27 presents the observed attendance for the hypothetical sample of 100 church members. Note that 20 of the men report having attended church during the preceding week and the remaining 20 say they did not. Among the women in the sample, 50 attended church and 10 did not. Comparing the expected and observed frequencies (Parts I and II), we note that somewhat fewer men attended church than expected, whereas somewhat more women than expected attended.

Chi square is computed as follows. For each cell in the tables, the researcher (1) subtracts the expected frequency for that cell from the observed frequency, (2) squares this quantity, and (3) divides the squared difference by the expected frequency. This procedure is carried out for each cell in the tables, and the several results are added together. (Part III of Table 16-27 presents the cell-by-cell computations.) The final sum is the value of chi square: 12.70 in the example.

This value is the overall discrepancy between the observed conjoint distribution in the sample and the distribution we should have expected if the two variables were unrelated to one another. Of course, the mere discovery of a discrepancy does not prove that the two variables are related, since normal sampling error might produce discrepancies even when there was no relationship in the total population. The magnitude of the value of chi square, however, permits us to estimate the probability of that having happened.

Degrees of Freedom

To determine the statistical significance of the observed relationship, we must use a standard set of chi square values. This will require the computation of the *degrees of freedom*, which refers to the possibilities for variation within a statistical model. Suppose we challenge you to find three numbers whose mean is 11. There is an infinite number of solutions to this problem: (11, 11, 11), (10, 11, 12), (-11, 11, 33), etc. Now, suppose we require that one of the numbers be 7. There would still be an infinite number of possibilities for the other two numbers.

If we told you one number had to be 7 and another 10, there would be only one possible value

Table 16-27
A Hypothetical Illustration of Chi Square

I. Expected Cell Frequencies	Men	Women	Total
Attended church	28	42	70
Did not attend church	12	18	30
Total	40	60	100
II. Observed Cell Frequencies	**Men**	**Women**	**Total**
Attended church	20	50	70
Did not attend church	20	10	30
Total	40	60	100
III. (Observed − Expected)^2 ÷ Expected	**Men**	**Women**	
Attended church	2.29	1.52	$\chi^2 = 12.70$
Did not attend church	5.33	3.56	$p < .001$

for the third. If the average of three numbers is 11, their sum must be 33. If two of the numbers total 17, the third must be 16. In this situation, we say there are two degrees of freedom. Two of the numbers could have any values we choose, but once they are specified, the third number is determined.

More generally, whenever we're examining the mean of N values, we can see that the degrees of freedom is $N - 1$. Thus in the case of the mean of 23 values, we could make 22 of them anything we liked, but the 23rd would then be determined.

A similar logic applies to bivariate tables, such as those analyzed by chi square. Consider a table reporting the relationship between two dichotomous variables: *gender* (men/women) and *abortion attitude* (approve/disapprove). Notice that the table provides the marginal frequencies of both variables.

Abortion Attitude	Men	Women	Total
Approve			500
Disapprove			500
Total	500	500	1,000

Despite the conveniently round numbers in this hypothetical example, notice there are numerous possibilities for the cell frequencies. For example, it could be the case that all 500 men approve and all 500 women disapprove, or it could be just the reverse. Or there could be 250 cases in each cell, and so forth. Notice there are numerous other possibilities.

Now the question is how many cells could we fill in pretty much as we choose before the remainder is determined by the marginal frequencies? The answer is only one. If we know that 300 men approved, for example, then 200 men would have had to disapprove, and the distribution would need to be just the opposite for the women.

In this instance, then, we say the table has *one degree of freedom*. Now, take a few minutes to construct a three-by-three table. Assume you know the marginal frequencies for each variable, and see if you can determine how many degrees of freedom it has.

For chi square, the degrees of freedom are computed as follows: the number of rows in the table of observed frequencies, minus 1, is multiplied by the number of columns, minus 1. This may be written as $(r - 1)(c - 1)$. For a *three-by-three* table, then, there are *four degrees of freedom*: $(3 - 1)(3 - 1) = (2)(2) = 4$.

In the example of gender and church attendance, we have two rows and two columns (discounting the *totals*), so there is one degree of freedom. Turning to a table of chi square values (see Appendix C), we find that for one degree of freedom and random sampling from a population in which there is no relationship between two variables, 10 percent of the time we should expect a chi square of at least 2.7. Thus, if we selected 100 samples from such a population, we should expect about 10 of those samples to produce chi squares equal to or greater than 2.7. Moreover, we should expect chi square values of at least 6.6 in only 1 percent of the samples and chi square values of 7.9 in only half a percent (.005) of the samples. The higher the chi square value, the less probable it is that the value could be attributed to sampling error alone.

In our example, the computed value of chi square is 12.70. If there were no relationship between gender and church attendance in the church member population and a large number of samples had been selected and studied, then we would expect a chi square of this magnitude in fewer than 1/10 of 1 percent (.001) of those samples. Thus, the probability of obtaining a chi square of this magnitude is less than .001, if random sampling has been used and there is no relationship in the population. We report this finding by saying the relationship is *statistically significant at the .001 level*. Because it is so improbable that the observed relationship could have resulted from sampling error alone, we're likely to reject the null hypothesis and assume that there is a relationship between the two variables in the population of church members.

Most measures of association can be tested for statistical significance in a similar manner. Standard tables of values permit us to determine whether a given association is statistically significant and at what level. Any standard statistics textbook provides instructions on the use of such tables.

Some Words of Caution

Tests of significance provide an objective yardstick against which to estimate the significance of associations between variables. They help us rule out associations that may not represent genuine relationships in the population under study. However, the researcher who uses or reads reports of significance tests should remain wary of several dangers in their interpretation.

First, we've been discussing tests of statistical significance; there are no objective tests of *substantive* significance. Thus, we may be legitimately convinced that a given association is not due to sampling error, but we may be in the position of asserting without fear of contradiction that two variables are only slightly related to each other. Recall that sampling error is an inverse function of sample size—the larger the sample, the smaller the expected error. Thus, a correlation of, say, .1 might very well be significant (at a given level) if discovered in a large sample, whereas the same correlation between the same two variables would not be significant if found in a smaller sample. This makes perfectly good sense given the basic logic of tests of significance: In the larger sample, there is less chance that the correlation could be simply the product of sampling error. In both samples, however, it might represent an essentially zero correlation.

The distinction between statistical and substantive significance is perhaps best illustrated by those cases where there is *absolute certainty* that observed differences cannot be a result of sampling error. This would be the case when we observe an entire population. Suppose we were able to learn the ages of every public official in Canada and also the ages of every public official in Russia. For argument's sake, let's assume further that the average age of Canadian officials was 45 years old compared to, say 46 for the Russian officials. Because we would have the ages of all officials, there would be no question of sampling error.

We would know with certainty that the Russian officials are older than their Canadian counterparts. At the same time, we would say that the difference was of no substantive significance. We'd conclude, in fact, that they were essentially the same age.

Second, lest you be misled by this hypothetical example, realize that statistical significance should not be calculated on relationships observed in data collected from whole populations. Remember tests of statistical significance measure the likelihood of relationships between variables being only a product of sampling error; if there's no sampling, there's no sampling error.

Third, tests of significance are based on the same sampling assumptions we used in computing confidence intervals. To the extent that these assumptions are not met by the actual sampling design, the tests of significance are not strictly legitimate.

While we have examined statistical significance here in the form of chi square, there are several other measures commonly used by social scientists. Analysis of variance and t-tests are two examples you may run across in your studies.

In conclusion, we would like to note that while there are serious problems inherent in too much reliance on tests of statistical significance, at the same time—perhaps paradoxically—we would suggest that tests of significance can be a valuable asset to the researcher—useful tools for understanding data. More generally, we encourage you to use any statistical technique—any measure of association or any test of significance—if it will help you understand your data. Whatever the avenue of discovery, however, empirical data must ultimately be presented in a legitimate manner, and their importance must be argued logically.

Main Points

- Univariate analysis is the analysis of a single variable, thus its purpose is descriptive.
- Data reduction is the process of summarizing the original data to make them more manage-

able while maintaining as much of the original detail as possible. Frequency distributions, averages, grouped data, and measures of dispersion are all ways of summarizing data concerning a single variable.

- Subgroup comparisons can be used to describe similarities and differences among subgroups with respect to some variable. Bivariate analysis focuses on the relationships between variables rather than comparisons of groups.

- Bivariate analysis explores the statistical association between the independent variable and the dependent variable. Its purpose is usually explanatory rather than merely descriptive. The results of bivariate analyses are often presented in the form of contingency tables, constructed to reveal the effects of the independent variable on the dependent variable.

- Multivariate analysis is a method of analyzing the simultaneous relationships among several variables and may also be used to understand the relationship between two variables more fully.

- The elaboration model is a method of multivariate analysis appropriate to social research. It's primarily a logical model that can illustrate the basic logic of other multivariate methods.

- The basic steps in elaboration are as follows: (1) A relationship is observed to exist between two variables; (2) a third variable is held constant in the sense that the cases under study are subdivided according to the attributes of that third variable; (3) the original two-variable relationship is recomputed within each of the subgroups; and (4) the comparison of the original relationship with the relationships found within each subgroup provides a fuller understanding of the original relationship itself.

- The logical relationships of the variables differ depending on whether the test variable is antecedent to the other two variables or intervening between them.

- A zero-order relationship is the observed relationship between two variables without a third variable being held constant or controlled.

- A partial relationship (or "partial") is the observed relationship between two variables within a subgroup of cases based on some attribute of the test or control variable.

- The outcome of an elaboration analysis may be replication (whereby a set of partial relationships is essentially the same as the corresponding zero-order relationship), explanation (whereby a set of partial relationships is reduced essentially to zero when an antecedent variable is held constant), interpretation (whereby a set of partial relationships is reduced essentially to zero when an intervening variable is held constant), or specification (whereby one partial is substantially reduced, ideally to zero, and the other remains about the same as the original relationship or is stronger).

- A suppressor variable conceals the relationship between two other variables; a distorter variable causes an apparent reversal in the relationship between two other variables (from negative to positive or vice versa).

- While the topics discussed in the sections on elementary analysis and the elaboration model are primarily associated with quantitative research, the logic and techniques involved can also be valuable to qualitative researchers.

- Descriptive statistics are used to summarize data under study. Some descriptive statistics summarize the distribution of attributes on a single variable; others summarize the associations between variables.

- Descriptive statistics summarizing the relationships between variables are called measures of association.

- Many measures of association are based on a proportionate reduction of error (PRE) model. This model is based on a comparison of (1) the number of errors we would make in attempting to guess the attributes of a given variable for each of the cases under study—if we knew nothing but the distribution of attributes on that variable and (2) the number of errors we would make if we knew the joint distribution overall and were told for each case the attribute of one variable each time we were asked to guess the attribute of the other.

- Measures of association include lambda (λ) (appropriate for the analysis of two *nominal* variables), gamma (γ) (appropriate for the analysis of two *ordinal* variables), and Pearson's product-moment correlation (*r*) (appropriate for the analysis of two *interval* or *ratio* variables).

- Regression analysis represents the relationships between variables in the form of equations, which can be used to predict the values of a dependent variable on the basis of values of one or more independent variables. Regression equations are computed on the basis of a regression line: that geometric line representing, with the least amount of discrepancy, the actual location of points in a scattergram.

- Types of regression analysis include linear regression analysis, multiple regression analysis, partial regression analysis, and curvilinear regression analysis.

- Inferential statistics are used to estimate the generalizability of findings arrived at through the analysis of a sample to the larger population from which the sample has been selected. Some inferential statistics estimate the single-variable characteristics of the population; others—tests of statistical significance—estimate the relationships between variables in the population.

- Inferences about some characteristic of a population must indicate a confidence interval and a confidence level. Inferences about the generalizability to a population of the associations discovered between variables in a sample involve tests of statistical significance (e.g., chi square). These tests estimate the likelihood that an association as large as the observed one could result from normal sampling error if no such association exists between the variables in the larger population. Computations of confidence levels, confidence intervals, and tests of statistical significance are based on probability theory and assume that conventional probability sampling techniques have been employed in the study.

- Statistical significance must not be confused with substantive significance, the latter meaning that an observed association is strong, important, meaningful, or worth writing home about.

- The level of significance of an observed association is reported in the form of the probability that the association could have been produced merely by sampling error. To say that an association is significant at the .05 level is to say that an association as large as the observed one could not be expected to result from sampling error more than 5 times out of 100.

- Social researchers tend to use a particular set of levels of significance in connection with tests of statistical significance: .05, .01, and .001. This is merely a convention, however.

- Tests of statistical significance, strictly speaking, make assumptions about data and methods that are almost never satisfied completely by real social research. Despite this, the tests can serve a useful function in the analysis and interpretation of data.

Review Questions and Exercises

1. Locate three published examples of "averages." For each, identify the type of average that was calculated and discuss whether it was the appropriate one for the researcher to choose.

2. Construct and interpret a contingency table from the following information: 150 women favour raising the minimum wage and 50 oppose it; 100 men favour raising the minimum wage and 300 oppose it.

3. Using the data in the following table, construct and interpret tables showing the following:
   a. The bivariate relationship between age and attitude toward abortion.
   b. The bivariate relationship between political orientation and attitude toward abortion.

c. The multivariate relationship linking age, political orientation, and attitude toward abortion.

Age	Political Orientation	Attitude Toward Abortion	Frequency
Young	Liberal	Favour	90
Young	Liberal	Oppose	10
Young	Conservative	Favour	60
Young	Conservative	Oppose	40
Old	Liberal	Favour	60
Old	Liberal	Oppose	40
Old	Conservative	Favour	20
Old	Conservative	Oppose	80

4. Review the Stouffer-Kendall-Lazarsfeld example of education, friends deferred, and attitudes toward being drafted. Suppose they had begun with an association between friends deferred and attitudes toward being drafted, and then they had controlled for education. What conclusion would they have reached?

5. In your own words describe the elaboration logic of (a) replication, (b) interpretation, (c) explanation, (d) specification.

6. In your own words, explain the logic of proportionate reduction of error (PRE) measures of associations. Next, explain the purpose of regression analyses.

Continuity Project

Assume that you have undertaken a quantitative study of attitudes toward gender equality. Create a hypothetical bivariate percentage table and interpret its meaning. One of the variables in the table must be an indicator of attitudes toward gender equality, and the other variable must represent a cause of such attitudes. Once you have done this, create a hypothetical multivariate percentage table by adding a third variable that represents a cause of attitudes toward gender quality. Interpret its meaning.

Additional Readings

Babbie, Earl, Fred Halley, and Jeanne Zaino. *Adventures in Social Research*. Newbury Park, CA: Pine Forge Press, 2000. This book introduces you to the analysis of social research data through SPSS for Windows. Several of the basic statistical techniques used by social researchers are discussed and illustrated.

Blalock, Hubert M., Jr. *Social Statistics*. New York: McGraw-Hill, 1979. Blalock's textbook has been a standard for social science students (and faculty) for decades.

Davis, James. *Elementary Survey Analysis*. Englewood Cliffs, NJ: Prentice-Hall, 1971. An extremely well-written and well-reasoned introduction to analysis. In addition to covering the materials just presented in Chapter 16, Davis's book is well worth reading in terms of measurement and statistics.

Healey, Joseph F. *Statistics: A Tool for Social Research*. Belmont, CA: Wadsworth, 1999. An effective introduction to social statistics.

Mohr, Lawrence B. *Understanding Significance Testing*. Newbury Park, CA: Sage, 1990. Here's an excellent and comprehensive examination of the topic: both the technical details of testing statistical significance and the meaning of such tests.

Newton, Rae R. and Kjell Erik Rudestam. *Your Statistical Consultant: Answers to Your Data Analysis Questions*. Thousand Oaks, CA: Sage, 1999. Excellent reader-friendly manual that will answer all sorts of questions you have or will have as soon as you begin to analyze quantitative data.

Rosenberg, Morris. *The Logic of Survey Analysis*. New York: Basic Books, 1968. The most comprehensive statement of elaboration available. Rosenberg presents the basic paradigm and goes on to suggest logical extensions of it. It is difficult to decide which is more important, this aspect of the book or its voluminous illustrations. Both are excellent.

Tacq, Jacques. *Multivariate Analysis Techniques in Social Science Research: From Problem to Analysis*. 1997. Thousand Oaks, CA: Sage. This is a very accessible book for those who want to gain a more statistical grounding for multivariate analysis through the elaboration model. The author uses real research examples from various disciplines to explain why and how to use multivariate analysis.

Ziesel, Hans. *Say It with Figures*. New York: Harper & Row, 1957. An excellent discussion of table construction and other elementary analyses. Though many years old, this is still perhaps the best available presentation of that specific topic. It is eminently readable and understandable and has many concrete examples.

*Info*Trac: You can find further relevant readings on the World Wide Web at

http://sociology.wadsworth.com

Appendix A   *The Research Report*

Introduction

This book has considered the variety of activities that compose the *doing* of social research. In this appendix, we'll turn to an often neglected subject: reporting the research to others. Unless research is properly communicated, all the efforts devoted to previously discussed procedures will go for naught.

The most fundamental guideline is that good social reporting requires good English (or French or whatever language you use). Whenever we ask the figures "to speak for themselves," they tend to remain mute. Whenever we use unduly complex terminology or construction, communication is reduced. Every researcher should read and reread (at approximately three-month intervals) an excellent small book by William Strunk Jr. and E. B. White, *The Elements of Style.** If you do this faithfully, and if even 10 percent of the contents rub off, you stand a good chance of making yourself understood and your findings perhaps appreciated.

Scientific reporting has several functions. First, the report communicates a body of specific data and ideas. The report should provide those specifics clearly and with sufficient detail to permit an informed evaluation. Second, the scientific report should be viewed as a contribution to the general body of scientific knowledge. While remaining appropriately humble, you should always regard your research report as an addition to what we know about social behaviour. Finally, the report should serve the function of stimulating and directing further inquiry.

---

*Fourth ed. (Longman, 2000). Here's another useful reference on writing: R. W. Birchfield, The New Fowler's Modern English Usage, 3rd ed. (New York: Oxford University Press, 1998).

Some Basic Considerations

Despite these general guidelines, different reports serve different purposes. A report appropriate for one purpose might be wholly inappropriate for another. This section deals with some of the basic considerations in this regard.

Audience

Before drafting your report, you must ask yourself who you hope will read it. Normally, you should make a distinction between scientists and general readers. If you are writing the report for the former, you may make certain assumptions about their existing knowledge and may perhaps summarize certain points rather than explain them in detail. Similarly, you may use more technical language than would be appropriate for a general audience.

At the same time, you should remain aware that any science is composed of factions or cults. Terms and assumptions familiar to your immediate colleagues may only confuse other scientists. The sociologist of religion writing for a general sociology audience, for example, should explain previous findings in more detail than would be necessary if he or she were addressing an audience of other sociologists of religion.

Form and Length of Report

Our comments in this section apply to both written and oral reports. Each form, however, affects the nature of the report.

It's useful to think about the variety of reports that might result from a research project. To begin, you may wish to prepare a short *research note* for publication in an academic or technical journal. Such reports are approximately one to five pages long (typed, double-spaced) and should be concise and direct. In only a few pages, you can't present the state of the field in any detail, so your methodological notes must be somewhat abbreviated. Basically, you should tell the reader why you feel a brief note is justified by your findings, and then tell what those findings are.

Often, researchers must prepare reports for the sponsors of their research. These reports may vary greatly in length. In preparing such a report, you should bear in mind the audience for the report— scientific or lay—and their reasons for sponsoring the project in the first place. It is both bad politics and bad manners to bore the sponsors with research findings that have no interest or value to them. At the same time, it may be useful to summarize how the research has advanced basic scientific knowledge (if it has).

Working papers or *monographs* are another form of research reporting. Especially in a large and complex project, you'll find comments on your analysis and the interpretation of your data useful. A working paper constitutes a tentative presentation with an implicit request for comments. Working papers can also vary in length, and they may present all of the research findings of the project or only a portion of them. Because your professional reputation is not at stake in a working paper, feel free to present tentative interpretations that you can't altogether justify—identifying them as such and asking for evaluations.

Many research projects result in papers delivered at professional meetings. Often, these serve the same purpose as working papers. You can present findings and ideas of possible interest to your colleagues and ask for their comments. Although the length of *professional papers* may vary depending on the organization of the meetings, it's best to say too little rather than too much. Although a working paper may ramble somewhat through tentative conclusions, conference participants should not be forced to sit through an oral unveiling of the same. Interested listeners can always ask for more details later, and uninterested ones can gratefully escape.

Probably the most popular research report is the *article* published in an academic journal. Again, lengths vary, and you should examine the lengths of articles previously published by the journal in question. As a rough guide, however, 25 typed pages is a good length. A subsequent section on the organization of the report is primarily based on the structure of a journal article, so we'll say no more at this point, except to indicate that student term papers should follow this model. As a general rule, a term paper that would make a good journal article would also make a good term paper.

A *book*, of course, represents the most prestigious form of research report. It has the length and detail of the working paper, but it's a more polished document. Because publishing research findings as a book gives them greater substance and worth, you have a special obligation to your audience. Although you may still receive some comments from colleagues, possibly leading you to revise your ideas, you must realize that other readers may be led to accept your findings uncritically.

Aim of the Report

Earlier in this book, we considered the different purposes of social research projects. In preparing your report, you should keep these different purposes in mind.

Some reports may focus primarily on the *exploration* of a topic. Inherent in this aim is the tentativeness and incompleteness of the conclusions. You should clearly indicate to your audience the exploratory aim of the study and point to the shortcomings of the particular project. An exploratory report serves to point the way to more refined research on the topic.

Most research reports have a descriptive element reflecting the *descriptive* purpose of the studies they document. You should carefully distinguish those descriptions that apply only to the sample and those that apply to the population. Give your audience some indication of the probable range of error in any inferential descriptions you make.

Many reports have an *explanatory* aim; you wish to point to causal relationships among variables. Depending on the probable audience for your report, you should carefully delineate the rules of explanation that lie behind your computations and conclusions. Also, as in the case of description, you must give your readers some guide to the relative certainty of your conclusions.

Finally, some research reports may *propose action*. For example, the researcher of prejudice may wish to suggest how prejudice may be reduced, on the basis of the research findings. This aim often presents knotty problems, however, because your own values and orientations may interfere with your proposals. Although it's perfectly legitimate for your proposals to be motivated by personal values, you must insure that the specific actions you propose are warranted by your data. Thus, you should be especially careful to spell out the logic by which you move from empirical data to proposed action.

Organization of the Report

Although the organization of reports differs somewhat in terms of form and purpose, a general format for presenting research data can be helpful. The following comments apply most directly to a journal article, but with some modification they also apply to most forms of research reports.

Purpose and Overview

It's always helpful to the reader if you begin with a brief statement of the purpose of the study and the main findings of the analysis. In a journal article, this overview may sometimes take the form of an *abstract* or *synopsis*.

Some researchers find this difficult to do. For example, your analysis may have involved considerable detective work, with important findings revealing themselves only as a result of imaginative deduction and data manipulation. You may wish, therefore, to lead the reader through the same exciting process, chronicling the discovery process with a degree of suspense and surprise. To

the extent that this form of reporting gives an accurate picture of the research process, it has considerable instructional value. Nevertheless, many readers may not be interested in following your entire research account, and not knowing the purpose and general conclusions in advance may make it difficult for them to understand the significance of the study.

An old forensic dictum says, "Tell them what you're going to tell them; tell them; and tell them what you told them." You'd do well to follow this dictum.

Review of the Literature

The next step is to indicate where your report fits in the context of the general body of scientific knowledge. After presenting the general purpose of your study, you should bring the reader up to date on the previous research in the area, pointing to general agreements and disagreements among the previous researchers.

In some cases, you may wish to challenge previously accepted ideas. Carefully review the studies that have led to the acceptance of those ideas, then indicate the factors that have not been previously considered or the logical fallacies present in the previous research.

When you're concerned with resolving a disagreement among previous researchers, organize your review of the literature around the opposing points of view. You should summarize the research supporting one view, then summarize the research supporting the other, and finally suggest the reasons for the disagreement.

Your review of the literature serves a bibliographical function for readers as well, indexing the previous research on a given topic. This can be overdone, however, and you should avoid an opening paragraph that runs three pages, mentioning every previous study in the field. The comprehensive bibliographical function can best be served by a bibliography at the end of the report, and the review of the literature should focus only on those studies that have direct relevance to the present one.

Avoiding Plagiarism

Whenever you're reporting on the work of others, you must be clear about who said what. That is, you must avoid *plagiarism:* the theft of another's words and/or ideas—whether intentional or accidental—and the presentation of those words and ideas as your own. Because this is a common and sometimes unclear problem for university students, let's examine it in some detail. Here are the main ground rules regarding plagiarism:

- You cannot use another writer's exact words without using quotation marks and giving a complete citation, which indicates the source of the quotation such that your reader could locate that quotation in its original context. As a general rule, taking a passage of eight or more words without citation is a violation of federal copyright laws.
- It's also not acceptable to edit or paraphrase another's words and present the revised version as your own work.
- Finally, it's not even acceptable to present another's *ideas* as your own—even if you use totally different words to express those ideas.

The following examples should clarify what is or is not acceptable in the use of another's work.

The Original Work

Laws of Growth

Systems are like babies: once you get one, you have it. They don't go away. On the contrary, they display the most remarkable persistence. They not only persist; they grow. And as they grow, they encroach. The growth potential of systems was explored in a tentative, preliminary way by Parkinson, who concluded that administrative systems maintain an average growth of 5 to 6 percent per annum regardless of the work to be done. Parkinson was right so far as he goes, and we must give him full honors for initiating the serious study of this important topic. But what Parkinson failed to perceive, we now enunciate—the general systems analogue of Parkinson's Law.

The System Itself Tends to Grow At 5 To 6 Percent Per Annum

Again, this Law is but the preliminary to the most general possible formulation, the Big-Bang Theorem of Systems Cosmology.

Systems Tend To Expand To Fill The Known Universe

(Gall 1975:12-14)

Now let's look at some of the *acceptable ways* you might make use of Gall's work in a term paper.

- **Acceptable**: John Gall, in his work *Systemantics,* draws a humourous parallel between systems and infants: "Systems are like babies: once you get one, you have it. They don't go away. On the contrary, they display the most remarkable persistence. They not only persist; they grow."*
- **Acceptable**: John Gall warns that systems are like babies. Create a system and it sticks around. Worse yet, Gall notes, systems keep growing larger and larger.*
- **Acceptable**: It has also been suggested that systems have a natural tendency to persist, even grow and encroach (Gall 1975:12).

Note that the last format requires that you give a complete citation in your bibliography, as we do in this book. Complete footnotes or endnotes work as well.

Here now are some *unacceptable* uses of the same material, reflecting some common errors.

- **Unacceptable**: In this paper, I want to look at some of the characteristics of the social systems we create in our organizations. First, systems are like babies: once you get one, you have it. They don't go away. On the contrary, they display the most remarkable persistence. They not only persist; they grow. [It is unacceptable to quote directly someone else's materials without using quotation marks and giving a full citation.]

---

*John Gall, *Systemantics: How Systems Work and Especially How They Fail* (New York: Quadrangle, 1975), 12.

- **Unacceptable**: In this paper, I want to look at some of the characteristics of the social systems we create in our organizations. First, systems are a lot like children: once you get one, it's yours. They don't go away; they persist. They not only persist, in fact: they grow. [It is unacceptable to edit another's work and present it as your own.]
- **Unacceptable**: In this paper, I want to look at some of the characteristics of the social systems we create in our organizations. One thing I've noticed is that once you create a system, it never seems to go away. Just the opposite, in fact: they have a tendency to grow. You might say systems are a lot like children in that respect. [It is unacceptable to paraphrase someone else's ideas and present them as your own.]

Each of the preceding unacceptable examples is an example of plagiarism and represents a serious offense. Admittedly, there are some "gray areas." Some ideas are more or less in the public domain, not "belonging" to any one person. Or you may reach an idea on your own that someone else has already put in writing. If you have a question about a specific situation, discuss it with your instructor in advance.

We've discussed this topic in some detail because, although you must place your research in the context of what others have done and said, the improper use of their materials is a serious offense. Mastering this matter, however, is a part of your "coming of age" as a scholar.

Study Design and Execution

A research report containing interesting findings and conclusions can be very frustrating when the reader can't determine the methodological design and execution of the study. The worth of all scientific findings depends heavily on the manner in which the data were collected and analyzed.

In reporting the design and execution of a survey, for example, you should always include the following: the population, the sampling frame, the sampling method, the sample size, the data-collec-tion method, the completion rate, and the methods of data processing and analysis. Comparable details should be given if other methods are used. The experienced researcher can report these details in a rather short space, without omitting anything required for the reader's evaluation of the study.

Analysis and Interpretation

Having set the study in the perspective of previous research and having described the design and execution of it, you should then present your data. We will shortly provide further guidelines in this regard. For now, a few general comments are in order.

The presentation of data, the manipulations of those data, and your interpretations should be integrated into a logical whole. It frustrates the reader to discover a collection of seemingly unrelated analyses and findings with a promise that all the loose ends will be tied together later in the report. Every step in the analysis should make sense at the time it is taken. You should present your rationale for a particular analysis, present the data relevant to it, interpret the results, and then indicate where that result leads next.

Summary and Conclusions

Following the forensic dictum mentioned earlier, it's essential to summarize the research report. Avoid reviewing every specific finding, but review all the significant ones, pointing once more to their general significance.

The report should conclude with a statement of what you have discovered about your subject matter and where future research might be directed. Many journal articles end with a statement such as, "It is clear that much more research is needed." This conclusion is probably always true, but it has little value unless you can offer pertinent suggestions about the nature of that future research. You should review the particular shortcomings of your own study and suggest ways those shortcomings might be avoided.

Guidelines for Reporting Analysis

The presentation of data analyses should provide a maximum of detail without being cluttered. You can accomplish this best by continually examining your report to see whether it achieves the following aims.

If you're using quantitative data, present them so the reader can recompute them. In the case of percentage tables, for example, the reader should be able to collapse categories and recompute the percentages. Readers should receive sufficient information to permit them to compute percentages in the table in the opposite direction from that of your own presentation.

Describe all aspects of a quantitative analysis in sufficient detail to permit a secondary analyst to replicate the analysis from the same body of data. This means that he or she should be able to create the same indexes and scales, produce the same tables, arrive at the same regression equations, obtain the same factors and factor loadings, and so forth. This will seldom be done, of course, but if the report allows for it, the reader will be far better equipped to evaluate the report than if it does not.

If you're doing a qualitative analysis, you must provide sufficient details that your reader has a sense of having made the observations with you. Presenting only those data that support your interpretations is not sufficient; you must also share those data that conflict with the way you've made sense of things. Ultimately, you should provide enough information that the reader might reach a different conclusion than you did—though you can hope your interpretation will make the most sense.

The reader, in fact, should be in position to replicate the entire study independently, whether it involves participant observation among heavy metal groupies, an experiment regarding jury deliberation, or any other kind of study. Recall that replicability is an essential norm of science. A single study does not prove a point; only a series of studies can begin to do so. And unless studies can be replicated, there can be no meaningful series of studies.

Integrate supporting materials. We've previously mentioned the importance of integrating data and interpretations in the report. Here is a more specific guideline for doing this. Tables, charts, and figures, if any, should be integrated into the text of the report—appearing near that portion of the text discussing them. Sometimes students describe their analyses in the body of the report and place all the tables in an appendix. This procedure greatly impedes the reader, however. As a general rule, it is best to (1) describe the purpose for presenting the table, (2) present it, and (3) review and interpret it.

Draw explicit conclusions. Although research is typically conducted for the purpose of drawing general conclusions, you should carefully note the specific basis for such conclusions. Otherwise, you may lead your reader into accepting unwarranted conclusions.

Point to any qualifications or conditions warranted in the evaluation of conclusions. Typically, you know best the shortcomings and tentativeness of your conclusions, and you should give the reader the advantage of that knowledge. Failure to do so can misdirect future research and result in a waste of research funds.

We will conclude with a point made at the outset of this appendix: Research reports should be written in the best possible literary style. Writing lucidly is easier for some people than for others, and it's always harder than writing poorly. You are again referred to the Strunk and White book. Every researcher would do well to follow this procedure: Write. Read Strunk and White. Revise. Reread Strunk and White. Revise again. This will be a difficult and time-consuming endeavour, but so is science.

A perfectly designed, carefully executed, and brilliantly analyzed study will be altogether worthless unless you can communicate your findings to others. This appendix has attempted to provide some general and specific guidelines toward that end. The best guides are logic, clarity, and honesty. Ultimately, there is no substitute for practice.

10480	15011	01536	02011	81647	91646	69179	14194	62590	36207	20969	99570	91291	90700
22368	46573	25595	85393	30995	89198	27982	53402	93965	34095	52666	19174	39615	99505
24130	48360	22527	97265	76393	64809	15179	24830	49340	32081	30680	19655	63348	58629
42167	93093	06243	61680	07856	16376	39440	53537	71341	57004	00849	74917	97758	16379
37570	39975	81837	16656	06121	91782	60468	81305	49684	60672	14110	06927	01263	54613
77921	06907	11008	42751	27756	53498	18602	70659	90655	15053	21916	81825	44394	42880
99562	72905	56420	69994	98872	31016	71194	18738	44013	48840	63213	21069	10634	12952
96301	91977	05463	07972	18876	20922	94595	56869	69014	60045	18425	84903	42508	32307
89579	14342	63661	10281	17453	18103	57740	84378	25331	12566	58678	44947	05585	56941
85475	36857	53342	53988	53060	59533	38867	62300	08158	17983	16439	11458	18593	64952
28918	69578	88231	33276	70997	79936	56865	05859	90106	31595	01547	85590	91610	78188
63553	40961	48235	03427	49626	69445	18663	72695	52180	20847	12234	90511	33703	90322
09429	93969	52636	92737	88974	33488	36320	17617	30015	08272	84115	27156	30613	74952
10365	61129	87529	85689	48237	52267	67689	93394	01511	26358	85104	20285	29975	89868
07119	97336	71048	08178	77233	13916	47564	81056	97735	85977	29372	74461	28551	90707
51085	12765	51821	51259	77452	16308	60756	92144	49442	53900	70960	63990	75601	40719
02368	21382	52404	60268	89368	19885	55322	44819	01188	65255	64835	44919	05944	55157
01011	54092	33362	94904	31273	04146	18594	29852	71585	85030	51132	01915	92747	64951
52162	53916	46369	58586	23216	14513	83149	98736	23495	64350	94738	17752	35156	35749
07056	97628	33787	09998	42698	06691	76988	13602	51851	46104	88916	19509	25625	58104
48663	91245	85828	14346	09172	30168	90229	04734	59193	22178	30421	61666	99904	32812
54164	58492	22421	74103	47070	25306	76468	26384	58151	06646	21524	15227	96909	44592
32639	32363	05597	24200	13363	38005	94342	28728	35806	06912	17012	64161	18296	22851
29334	27001	87637	87308	58731	00256	45834	15398	46557	41135	10367	07684	36188	18510
02488	33062	28834	07351	19731	92420	60952	61280	50001	67658	32586	86679	50720	94953
81525	72295	04839	96423	24878	82651	66566	14778	76797	14780	13300	87074	79666	95725
29676	20591	68086	26432	46901	20849	89768	81536	86645	12659	92259	57102	80428	25280
00742	57392	39064	66432	84673	40027	32832	61362	98947	96067	64760	64584	96096	98253
05366	04213	25669	26422	44407	44048	37397	63904	45766	66134	75470	66520	34693	90449
91921	26418	64117	94305	26766	25940	39972	22209	71500	64568	91402	42416	07844	69618
00582	04711	87917	77341	42206	35126	74087	99547	81817	42607	43808	76655	62028	76630
00725	69884	62797	56170	86324	88072	76222	36086	84637	93161	76038	65855	77919	88006
69011	65795	95876	55293	18988	27354	26575	08625	40801	59920	29841	80150	12777	48501
25976	57948	29888	88604	67917	48708	18912	82271	65424	69774	33611	54262	85963	03547
09763	83473	73577	12908	30883	18317	28290	35797	05998	41688	34952	37888	38917	88050
91567	42595	27958	30134	04024	86385	29880	99730	55536	84855	29080	09250	79656	73211
17955	56349	90999	49127	20044	59931	06115	20542	18059	02008	73708	83517	36103	42791
46503	18584	18845	49618	02304	51038	20655	58727	28168	15475	56942	53389	20562	87338
92157	89634	94824	78171	84610	82834	09922	25417	44137	48413	25555	21246	35509	20468
14577	62765	35605	81263	39667	47358	56873	56307	61607	49518	89656	20103	77490	18062
98427	07523	33362	64270	01638	92477	66969	98420	04880	45585	46565	04102	46880	45709
34914	63976	88720	82765	34476	17032	87589	40836	32427	70002	70663	88863	77775	69348
70060	28277	39475	46473	23219	53416	94970	25832	69975	94884	19661	72828	00102	66794
53976	54914	06990	67245	68350	82948	11398	42878	80287	88267	47363	46634	06541	97809
76072	29515	40980	07391	58745	25774	22987	80059	39911	96189	41151	14222	60697	59583
90725	52210	83974	29992	65831	38857	50490	83765	55657	14361	31720	57375	56228	41546
64364	67412	33339	31926	14883	24413	59744	92351	97473	89286	35931	04110	23726	51900
08962	00358	31662	25388	61642	34072	81249	35648	56891	69352	48373	45578	78547	81788
95012	68379	93526	70765	10592	04542	76463	54328	02349	17247	28865	14777	62730	92277
15664	10493	20492	38391	91132	21999	59516	81652	27195	48223	46751	22923	32261	85653
16408	81899	04153	53381	79401	21438	83035	92350	36693	31238	59649	91754	72772	02338
18629	81953	05520	91962	04739	13092	97662	24822	94730	06496	35090	04822	86774	98289
73115	35101	47498	87637	99016	71060	88824	71013	18735	20286	23153	72924	35165	43040
57491	16703	23167	49323	45021	33132	12544	41035	80780	45393	44812	12515	98931	91202
30405	83946	23792	14422	15059	45799	22716	19792	09983	74353	68668	30429	70735	25499
16631	35006	85900	98275	32388	52390	16815	69298	82732	38480	73817	32523	41961	44437
96773	20206	42559	78985	05300	22164	24369	54224	35083	19687	11052	91491	60383	19746
38935	64202	14349	82674	66523	44133	00697	35552	35970	19124	63318	29686	03387	59846
31624	76384	17403	53363	44167	64486	64758	75366	76554	31601	12614	33072	60332	92325
78919	19474	23632	27889	47914	02584	37680	20801	72152	39339	34806	08930	85001	87820

03931	33309	57047	74211	63445	17361	62825	39908	05607	91284	68833	25570	38818	46920
74426	33278	43972	10119	89917	15665	52872	73823	73144	88662	88970	74492	51805	99378
09066	00903	20795	95452	92648	45454	09552	88815	16553	51125	79375	97596	16296	66092
42238	12426	87025	14267	20979	04508	64535	31355	86064	29472	47689	05974	52468	16834
16153	08002	26504	41744	81959	65642	74240	56302	00033	67107	77510	70625	28725	34191
21457	40742	29820	96783	29400	21840	15035	34537	33310	06116	95240	15957	16572	06004
21581	57802	02050	89728	17937	37621	47075	42080	97403	48626	68995	43805	33386	21597
55612	78095	83197	33732	05810	24813	86902	60397	16489	03264	88525	42786	05269	92532
44657	66999	99324	51281	84463	60563	79312	93454	68876	25471	93911	25650	12682	73572
91340	84979	46949	81973	37949	61023	43997	15263	80644	43942	89203	71795	99533	50501
91227	21199	31935	27022	84067	05462	35216	14486	29891	68607	41867	14951	91696	85065
50001	38140	66321	19924	72163	09538	12151	06878	91903	18749	34405	56087	82790	70925
65390	05224	72958	28609	81406	39147	25549	48542	42627	45233	57202	94617	23772	07896
27504	96131	83944	41575	10573	08619	64482	73923	36152	05184	94142	25299	84387	34925
37169	94851	39117	89632	00959	16487	65536	49071	39782	17095	02330	74301	00275	48280
11508	70225	51111	38351	19444	66499	71945	05422	13442	78675	84081	66938	93654	59894
37449	30362	06694	54690	04052	53115	62757	95348	78662	11163	81651	50245	34971	52924
46515	70331	85922	38329	57015	15765	97161	17869	45349	61796	66345	81073	49106	79860
30986	81223	42416	58353	21532	30502	32305	86482	05174	07901	54339	58861	74818	46942
63798	64995	46583	09785	44160	78128	83991	42865	92520	83531	80377	35909	81250	54238
82486	84846	99254	67632	43218	50076	21361	64816	51202	88124	41870	52689	51275	83556
21885	32906	92431	09060	64297	51674	64126	62570	26123	05155	59194	52799	28225	85762
60336	98782	07408	53458	13564	59089	26445	29789	85205	41001	12535	12133	14645	23541
43937	46891	24010	25560	86355	33941	25786	54990	71899	15475	95434	98227	21824	19585
97656	63175	89303	16275	07100	92063	21942	18611	47348	20203	18534	03862	78095	50136
03299	01221	05418	38982	55758	92237	26759	86367	21216	98442	08303	56613	91511	75928
79626	06486	03574	17668	07785	76020	79924	25651	83325	88428	85076	72811	22717	50585
85636	68335	47539	03129	65651	11977	02510	26113	99447	68645	34327	15152	55230	93448
18039	14367	61337	06177	12143	46609	32989	74014	64708	00533	35398	58408	13261	47908
08362	15656	60627	36478	65648	16764	53412	09013	07832	41574	17639	82163	60859	75567
79556	29068	04142	16268	15387	12856	66227	38358	22478	73373	88732	09443	82558	05250
92608	82674	27072	32534	17075	27698	98204	63863	11951	34648	88022	56148	34925	57031
23982	25835	40055	67006	12293	02753	14827	23235	35071	99704	37543	11601	35503	85171
09915	96306	05908	97901	28395	14186	00821	80703	70426	75647	76310	88717	37890	40129
59037	33300	26695	62247	69927	76123	50842	43834	86654	70959	79725	93872	28117	19233
42488	78077	69882	61657	34136	79180	97526	43092	04098	73571	80799	76536	71255	64239
46764	86273	63003	93017	31204	36692	40202	35275	57306	55543	53203	18098	47625	88684
03237	45430	55417	63282	90816	17349	88298	90183	36600	78406	06216	95787	42579	90730
86591	81482	52667	61582	14972	90053	89534	76036	49199	43716	97548	04379	46370	28672
38534	01715	94964	87288	65680	43772	39560	12918	86537	62738	19636	51132	25739	56947

Abridged from *Handbook of Tables for Probability and Statistics,* 2nd ed., edited by William H. Beyer (Cleveland: The Chemical Rubber Company, 1968). Used by permission of The Chemical Rubber Company.

Appendix C
Distribution of Chi Square

				Probability			
df	.99	.98	.95	.90	.80	.70	.50
1	$.0^3157$	$.0^3628$	.00393	.0158	.0642	.148	.455
2	.0201	.0404	.103	.211	.446	.713	1.386
3	.115	.185	.352	.584	1.005	1.424	2.366
4	.297	.429	.711	1.064	1.649	2.195	3.357
5	.554	.752	1.145	1.610	2.343	3.000	4.351
6	.872	1.134	1.635	2.204	3.070	3.828	5.348
7	1.239	1.564	2.167	2.833	3.822	4.671	6.346
8	1.646	2.032	2.733	3.490	4.594	5.528	7.344
9	2.088	2.532	3.325	4.168	5.380	6.393	8.343
10	2.558	3.059	3.940	4.865	6.179	7.267	9.342
11	3.053	3.609	4.575	5.578	6.989	8.148	10.341
12	3.571	4.178	5.226	6.304	7.807	9.034	11.340
13	4.107	4.765	5.892	7.042	8.634	9.926	12.340
14	4.660	5.368	6.571	7.790	9.467	10.821	13.339
15	5.229	5.985	7.261	8.547	10.307	11.721	14.339
16	5.812	6.614	7.962	9.312	11.152	12.624	15.338
17	6.408	7.255	8.672	10.085	12.002	13.531	16.338
18	7.015	7.906	9.390	10.865	12.857	14.440	17.338
19	7.633	8.567	10.117	11.651	13.716	15.352	18.338
20	8.260	9.237	10.851	12.443	14.578	16.266	19.337
21	8.897	9.915	11.591	13.240	15.445	17.182	20.337
22	9.542	10.600	12.338	14.041	16.314	18.101	21.337
23	10.196	11.293	13.091	14.848	17.187	19.021	22.337
24	10.856	11.992	13.848	15.659	18.062	19.943	23.337
25	11.524	12.697	14.611	16.473	18.940	20.867	24.337
26	12.198	13.409	15.379	17.292	19.820	21.792	25.336
27	12.879	14.125	16.151	18.114	20.703	22.719	26.336
28	13.565	14.847	16.928	18.939	21.588	23.647	27.336
29	14.256	15.574	17.708	19.768	22.475	24.577	28.336
30	14.953	16.306	18.493	20.599	23.364	25.508	29.336

continued

For larger values of df, the expression $\sqrt{2\chi^2} - \sqrt{2df - 1}$ may be used as a normal deviate with unit variance, remembering that the probability of χ^2 corresponds with that of a single tail of the normal curve.

Source: We are grateful to the Literary Executor of the late Sir Ronald A. Fisher, F.R.S., to Dr. Frank Yates, F.R.S., and to Longman Group Ltd., London, for permission to reprint Table IV from their book *Statistical Tables for Biological, Agricultural, and Medical Research* (6th Edition, 1974).

Probability

df	.30	.20	.10	.05	.02	.01	.001
1	1.074	1.642	2.706	3.841	5.412	6.635	10.827
2	2.408	3.219	4.605	5.991	7.824	9.210	13.815
3	3.665	4.642	6.251	7.815	9.837	11.341	16.268
4	4.878	5.989	7.779	9.488	11.668	13.277	18.465
5	6.064	7.289	9.236	11.070	13.388	15.086	20.517
6	7.231	8.558	10.645	12.592	15.033	16.812	22.457
7	8.383	9.803	12.017	14.067	16.622	18.475	24.322
8	9.524	11.030	13.362	15.507	18.168	20.090	29.125
9	10.656	12.242	14.684	16.919	19.679	21.666	27.877
10	11.781	13.442	15.987	18.307	21.161	23.209	29.588
11	12.899	14.631	17.275	19.675	22.618	24.725	31.264
12	14.011	15.812	18.549	21.026	24.054	26.217	32.909
13	15.119	16.985	19.812	22.362	25.472	27.688	34.528
14	16.222	18.151	21.064	23.685	26.873	29.141	36.123
15	17.322	19.311	22.307	24.996	28.259	30.578	37.697
16	18.841	20.465	23.542	26.296	29.633	32.000	39.252
17	15.511	21.615	24.769	27.587	30.995	33.409	40.790
18	20.601	22.760	25.989	28.869	32.346	34.805	42.312
19	21.689	23.900	27.204	30.144	33.687	36.191	43.820
20	22.775	25.038	28.412	31.410	35.020	37.566	45.315
21	23.858	26.171	29.615	32.671	36.343	38.932	46.797
22	24.939	27.301	30.813	33.924	37.659	40.289	48.268
23	26.018	28.429	32.007	35.172	38.968	41.638	49.728
24	27.096	29.553	33.196	36.415	40.270	42.980	51.179
25	28.172	30.675	34.382	37.652	41.566	44.314	52.620
26	29.246	31.795	35.563	38.885	42.856	45.642	54.052
27	30.319	32.912	36.741	40.113	44.140	46.963	55.476
28	31.391	34.027	37.916	41.337	45.419	48.278	56.893
29	32.461	35.139	39.087	42.557	46.693	49.588	58.302
30	35.530	36.250	40.256	43.773	47.962	50.892	59.703

Appendix D Normal Curve Areas

z	.00	.01	.02	.03	.04	.05	.06	.07	.08	.09
0.0	.0000	.0040	.0080	.0120	.0160	.0199	.0239	.0279	.0319	.0359
0.1	.0398	.0438	.0478	.0517	.0557	.0596	.0636	.0675	.0714	.0753
0.2	.0793	.0832	.0871	.0910	.0948	.0987	.1026	.1064	.1103	.1141
0.3	.1179	.1217	.1255	.1293	.1331	.1368	.1406	.1443	.1480	.1517
0.4	.1554	.1591	.1628	.1664	.1700	.1736	.1772	.1808	.1844	.1879
0.5	.1915	.1950	.1985	.2019	.2054	.2088	.2123	.2157	.2190	.2224
0.6	.2257	.2291	.2324	.2357	.2389	.2422	.2454	.2486	.2517	.2549
0.7	.2580	.2611	.2642	.2673	.2704	.2734	.2764	.2794	.2823	.2852
0.8	.2881	.2910	.2939	.2967	.2995	.3023	.3051	.3078	.3106	.3133
0.9	.3159	.3186	.3212	.3238	.3264	.3289	.3315	.3340	.3365	.3389
1.0	.3413	.3438	.3461	.3485	.3508	.3531	.3554	.3577	.3599	.3621
1.1	.3643	.3665	.3686	.3708	.3729	.3749	.3770	.3790	.3810	.3830
1.2	.3849	.3869	.3888	.3907	.3925	.3944	.3962	.3980	.3997	.4015
1.3	.4032	.4049	.4066	.4082	.4099	.4115	.4131	.4147	.4162	.4177
1.4	.4192	.4207	.4222	.4236	.4251	.4265	.4279	.4292	.4306	.4319
1.5	.4332	.4345	.4357	.4370	.4382	.4394	.4406	.4418	.4429	.4441
1.6	.4452	.4463	.4474	.4484	.4495	.4505	.4515	.4525	.4535	.4545
1.7	.4554	.4564	.4573	.4582	.4591	.4599	.4608	.4616	.4625	.4633
1.8	.4641	.4649	.4656	.4664	.4671	.4678	.4686	.4693	.4699	.4706
1.9	.4713	.4719	.4726	.4732	.4738	.4744	.4750	.4756	.4761	.4767
2.0	.4772	.4778	.4783	.4788	.4793	.4798	.4803	.4808	.4812	.4817
2.1	.4821	.4826	.4830	.4834	.4838	.4842	.4846	.4850	.4854	.4857
2.2	.4861	.4864	.4868	.4871	.4875	.4878	.4881	.4884	.4887	.4890
2.3	.4893	.4896	.4898	.4901	.4904	.4906	.4909	.4911	.4913	.4916
2.4	.4918	.4920	.4922	.4925	.4927	.4929	.4931	.4932	.4934	.4936
2.5	.4938	.4940	.4941	.4943	.4945	.4946	.4948	.4949	.4951	.4952
2.6	.4953	.4955	.4956	.4957	.4959	.4960	.4961	.4962	.4963	.4964
2.7	.4965	.4966	.4967	.4968	.4969	.4970	.4971	.4972	.4973	.4974
2.8	.4974	.4975	.4976	.4977	.4977	.4978	.4979	.4979	.4980	.4981
2.9	.4981	.4982	.4982	.4983	.4984	.4984	.4985	.4985	.4986	.4986
3.0	.4987	.4987	.4987	.4988	.4988	.4989	.4989	.4989	.4990	.4990

Abridged from Table I of *Statistical Tables and Formulas,* by A. Hald (New York: John Wiley & Sons, Inc., 1952). Used by permission of John Wiley & Sons, Inc.

Appendix E   Estimated Sampling Error

How to use this table: Find the intersection between the sample size and the approximate percentage distribution of the binomial in the sample. The number appearing at this intersection represents the estimated sampling error, at the 95 percent confidence level, expressed in percentage points (plus or minus).

Example: In the sample of 400 respondents, 60 percent answer yes and 40 percent answer no. The sampling error is estimated at plus or minus 4.9 percentage points. The confidence interval, then, is between 55.1 percent and 64.9 percent. We would estimate (95 percent confidence) that the proportion of the total population who would say yes is somewhere within that interval.

Sample Size	Binomial Percentage Distribution				
	50/50	60/40	70/30	80/20	90/10
100	10	9.8	9.2	8	6
200	7.1	6.9	6.5	5.7	4.2
300	5.8	5.7	5.3	4.6	3.5
400	5	4.9	4.6	4	3
500	4.5	4.4	4.1	3.6	2.7
600	4.1	4	3.7	3.3	2.4
700	3.8	3.7	3.5	3	2.3
800	3.5	3.5	3.2	2.8	2.1
900	3.3	3.3	3.1	2.7	2
1000	3.2	3.1	2.9	2.5	1.9
1100	3	3	2.8	2.4	1.8
1200	2.9	2.8	2.6	2.3	1.7
1300	2.8	2.7	2.5	2.2	1.7
1400	2.7	2.6	2.4	2.1	1.6
1500	2.6	2.5	2.4	2.1	1.5
1600	2.5	2.4	2.3	2	1.5
1700	2.4	2.4	2.2	1.9	1.5
1800	2.4	2.3	2.2	1.9	1.4
1900	2.3	2.2	2.1	1.8	1.4
2000	2.2	2.2	2	1.8	1.3

Bibliography

Aliaga, David E. 1994. "Italian Immigrants in Calgary: Dimensions of Cultural Identify." *Canadian Ethnic Studies*, XXVI, No. 2: 141–48.

Anderson, Andy B., Alexander Basilevsky, and Derek P. J. Hum. 1983. "Measurement: Theory and Techniques." Pp. 231–87 in *Handbook of Survey Research,* edited by Peter H. Rossi, James D. Wright, and Andy B. Anderson. New York: Academic Press.

Anderson, Walt. 1990. *Reality Isn't What It Used to Be: Theatrical Politics, Ready-to-Wear Religion, Global Myths, Primitive Chic, and Other Wonders of the Postmodern World.* San Francisco: Harper & Row.

Andorka, Rudolf. 1990. "The Importance and the Role of the Second Economy for the Hungarian Economy and Society." *Quarterly Journal of Budapest University of Economic Sciences* 12, (2): 95–113.

Asch, Solomon. 1958. "Effects of Group Pressure upon the Modification and Distortion of Judgments." Pp. 174–83 in *Readings in Social Psychology,* 3rd ed., edited by Eleanor E. Maccoby, et al. New York: Holt, Rinehart & Winston.

Atkinson, Tom. 1982. "The Stability and Validity of Quality of Life Measures." *Social Indicators Research,* 10:113–132.

Auster, Carol J. 1985. "Manuals for Socialization: Examples from Girl Scout Handbooks 1913–1984." *Qualitative Sociology* 8 (4): 359–67.

Babbie, Earl. 1967. "A Religious Profile of Episcopal Churchwomen," *Pacific Churchman,* January, pp. 6–8, 12.

1970. *Science and Morality in Medicine.* Berkeley: University of California Press.

1990. *Survey Research Methods.* Belmont, CA: Wadsworth.

1994. *The Sociological Spirit.* Belmont, CA: Wadsworth.

Babbie, Earl, Fred Halley and Jeanne Zaino. 2000. *Adventures in Social Research.* Newbury Park, CA: Pine Forge Press.

Bailey, William C. 1975. "Murder and Capital Punishment." In *Criminal Law in Action,* edited by William J. Chambliss. New York: Wiley.

Bailey, William C. and Ruth D. Peterson. 1994. "Murder, Capital Punishment, and Deterrence: A Review of the Evidence and an Examination on Police Killings." *Journal of Social Issues,* 50:53–74.

Baron, Stephen W. 1997. "Canadian Male Street Skinheads: Street Gang or Street Terrorists." *Canadian Review of Sociology and Anthropology.* 34: 125–154.

Bart, Pauline, and Patricia O'Brien. 1985. *Stopping Rape: Successful Survival Strategies.* New York: Pergamon.

B.C. Ministry for Children and Families. 2001. "Measuring Our Success." (http://www.mcf.gov.bc.ca/publications/ measure_success/msbackground.htm, May 28, 2001.

Becker, Howard S. 1997. *Tricks of the Trade: How to Think about Your Research while You're Doing it.* Chicago: University of Chicago Press.

Bednarz, Marlene. 1996. "Push polls statement." Report to the AAPORnet listserv, April 5 [Online]. Available: mbednarz@umich.edu

Belenky, Mary Field, Blythe McVicker Clinchy, Nancy Rule Goldberger, and Jill Mattuck Tarule. 1986. *Women's Ways of Knowing: The*

Development of Self, Voice, and Mind. New York: Basic Books.

Bellah, Robert N. 1957. *Tokugawa Religion.* Glencoe, IL: Free Press.

——— 1967. "Research Chronicle: Tokugawa Religion." Pp. 164–85 in *Sociologists at Work,* edited by Phillip E. Hammond. Garden City, NY: Anchor Books.

——— 1970. "Christianity and Symbolic Realism." *Journal for the Scientific Study of Religion* 9:89–96.

——— 1974. "Comment on the Limits of Symbolic Realism." *Journal for the Scientific Study of Religion* 13:487–89.

Benaquisto, Lucia. 1991. "Outbursts of Repression: Politics and the use of Incarceration." Dissertation.

Benaquisto, Lucia. 2000. "Inattention to Sanctions in Criminal Conduct." Pp. 203–215 in *Crime in Canadian Society.* Sixth Edition. eds. Silverman, Teevan, and Sacco. Toronto: Harcourt Brace & Co.

Benaquisto, Lucia and Philippe Couton. 2001. "The Liberal Use of Repression: Enhanced Judicial Penetration and the Establishment of the French Third Republic" paper presented at the American Sociological Association Meetings, Anaheim, CA.

Benton, J. Edwin, and John L. Daly. 1991. "A Question Order Effect in a Local Government Survey." *Public Opinion Quarterly* 55:640–42.

Berg, Bruce L. 2001. *Qualitative Research Methods for the Social Sciences.* 4th ed. Boston: Allyn and Bacon.

Berg, Richard, and Peter H. Rossi. 1998. *Thinking about Program Evaluation.* Thousand Oaks, CA: Sage.

Bernstein, Ira H. and Paul Havig. 1999. *Computer Literacy: Getting the Most from Your PC.* Thousand Oaks, CA: Sage.

Beveridge, W. I. B. 1950. *The Art of Scientific Investigation.* New York: Vintage Books.

Bian, Yanjie. 1994. *Work and Inequality in Urban China.* Albany: State University of New York Press.

Birchfield, R. W. 1998. *The New Fowler's Modern English Usage.* 3rd ed. New York: Oxford University Press.

Black, Donald. 1970. "Production of Crime Rates." *American Sociological Review* 35 (August): 733–48.

Blalock, Hubert M., Jr. 1979. *Social Statistics.* New York: McGraw-Hill.

Bohrnstedt, George W. 1983. "Measurement." Pp. 70–121 in *Handbook of Survey Research,* edited by Peter H. Rossi, James D. Wright, and Andy B. Anderson. New York: Academic Press.

Bolstein, Richard. 1991. "Comparison of the Likelihood to Vote among Preelection Poll Respondents and Nonrespondents." *Public Opinion Quarterly* 55:648–50.

Bottomore, T. B., and Maximilien Rubel, eds. [1843] 1956. *Karl Marx: Selected Writings in Sociology and Social Philosophy.* Translated by T. B. Bottomore. New York: McGraw-Hill.

Boyatzis, Richard E. 1998. *Transforming Qualitative Information: Thematic Analysis and Code Development.* Sage Publications, Thousand Oaks:CA.

Bradburn, Norman M., and Seymour Sudman. 1988. *Polls and Surveys: Understanding What They Tell Us.* San Francisco: Jossey-Bass.

Bright, Robert, Elaine Coburn, Julie Faye, Derek Gafijczuk, Karen Hollander, Janny Jung, and Helen Syrmbros. 1999. "Mainstream and Marginal Newspaper Coverage of the 1995 Quebec Referendum: An Inquiry into the Functioning of the Canadian Public Sphere." *Canadian Review of Sociology and Anthropology,* 36:313–330.

Brownlee, K. A. 1975. "A Note on the Effects of Nonresponse on Surveys." *Journal of the American Statistical Association* 52 (227): 29–32.

Bucharski, Dawn, Larry Brockman, and Delores Lambert. 1999. "Developing Culturally Appropriate Prenatal Care Models for Aboriginal Women." *The Canadian Journal of Human Sexuality,* 8:151–154.

Burawoy, M., A. Burton, A. A. Ferguson, K. J. Fox, J. Gamson, N. Gartrell, L. Hurst, C. Kurzman, L. Salzinger, J. Schiffman, and S. Ui, eds. 1991.

Ethnography Unbound: Power and Resistence in the Modern Metropolis. Berkeley, CA: University of California Press.

Campbell, Donald, and Julian Stanley. 1963. *Experimental and Quasi-Experimental Designs for Research.* Chicago: Rand McNally.

Campbell, Marie L. 1998. "Institutional Ethnography and Experience As Data." *Qualitative Sociology*, 21:55–73.

Casley, D. J., and D. A. Lury. 1987. *Data Collection in Developing Countries.* Oxford: Clarendon Press. Census Bureau. *See* U.S. Bureau of the Census.

CCJS: Canadian Centre for Justice Statistics. 1999. *The Juristat Reader*. Toronto: Thompson Educational Publishing, Inc.

Chafetz, Janet. 1978. *A Primer on the Construction and Testing of Theories in Sociology.* Itasca, IL: Peacock.

Chan, Kwok B. 1983. "Coping with Aging and Managing Self-Identity: The Social World of the Elderly Chinese Women." *Canadian Ethnic Studies,* 15:36–50.

Chen, Huey-Tsyh. 1990. *Theory-Driven Evaluations.* Newbury Park, CA: Sage.

Chossudovsky, Michel. 1997. *The Globalization of Poverty. Impacts of IMF and World Bank Reforms.* London: Zed Books.

CNEWS. 2001. "Decision 2000 Results." http://www.canoe.ca/CNEWSElection2000 News/001027_flash2.html, January 27, 2001.

Cohn, Werner. 1976. "Jewish Outmarriage and Anomie: A Study of the Canadian Syndrome of Polarities." *Canadian Review of Sociology and Anthropology*, 13:90–105.

Coldevin, Gary O. 1976. "Some Effects of Frontier Television in a Canadian Eskimo Community." *Journalism Quarterly*, 53:34–39.

Collins, G. C., and Timothy B. Blodgett. 1981. "Sexual Harassment . . . Some See It . . . Some Won't." *Harvard Business Review,* March–April, pp. 76–95.

Conrad, Clifton F. 1978. "A Grounded Theory of Academic Change." *Sociology of Education*, 51:101–12.

Cook, Thomas D., and Donald T. Campbell. 1979. *Quasi-Experimentation: Design and Analysis Issues for Field Settings.* Chicago: Rand McNally.

Cooper, Harris M. 1998. *Synthesizing Research: A Guide for Literature Reviews.* 3rd Ed. Newbury Park, CA: Sage.

Craig, R. Stephen. 1992. "The Effect of Television Day Part on Gender Portrayals in Television Commercials: A Content Analysis." *Sex Roles* 26 (5/6): 197–211.

Cunningham, J. Barton. 1993. *Action Research and Organizational Development.* Westport, CT: Praeger.

Davis, Fred. 1973. "The Martian and the Convert: Ontological Polarities in Social Research." *Urban Life* 2 (3): 333–43.

Davis, James A. 1971. *Elementary Survey Analysis.* Englewood Cliffs, NJ: Prentice-Hall. 1985. *The Logic of Causal Order.* Beverly Hills, CA: Sage.
1992. "Changeable Weather in a Cooling Climate atop the Liberal Plateau: Conversion and Replacement in Forty-Two General Social Survey Items, 1972–1989." *Public Opinion Quarterly* 56:261–306.

Devault, Majorie L. 1999. *Liberating Method: Feminism and Social Research.* Philadelphia: Temple University Press.

Dillman, Don A. 1978. *Mail and Telephone Surveys: The Total Design Method.* New York: Wiley.

Dillman, Don A. 1991. "The Design and Administraiton of Mail Surveys." *Annual Review of Sociology*, 17:225–49.

Donald, Marjorie N. 1960. "Implications of Nonresponse for the Interpretation of Mail Questionnaire Data." *Public Opinion Quarterly* 24:99–114.

Doyle, Sir Arthur Conan. [1891] 1892. "A Scandal in Bohemia." First published in *The Strand,* July 1891. Reprinted in *The Original Illustrated Sherlock Holmes.* Secaucus, NJ: Castle, pp. 11–25.

Drolet, Marie. 1999. "The Persistent Gap: New Evidence on the Canadian Gender Wage Gap." *Statistics Canada*: Income Statistics Division. 75F0002MIE-99008.

Durkheim, Emile. [1893] 1964. *The Division of Labor in Society.* Translated by George Simpson. New York: Free Press.

[1897] 1951. *Suicide.* Glencoe, IL: Free Press.

Ellison, Christopher G., and Darren E. Sherkat. 1990. "Patterns of Religious Mobility among Black Americans." *Sociological Quarterly* 31 (4): 551–68.

Emerson, Robert M., Kerry O. Ferris, and Carol Brooks Gardner. 1998. "On Being Stalked." Social Problems, 45:289–314.

Emerson, Robert M., Rachel I. Fretz, and Linda L. Shaw. 1995. *Writing ethnographic fieldnotes.* Chicago: University of Chicago Press.

Erickson, Patricia. 1998. "Neglected and Rejected: A Case Study of the Impact of Social Research on Canadian Drug Policy." *Canadian Journal of Sociology,* 23:263–280.

Fedoroff, J. Paul, and Beverley Moran. 1997. "Myths and Misconceptions about Sex Offenders." *The Canadian Journal of Human Sexuality,* 6:263–276.

Feick, Lawerence F. 1989. "Latent Class Analysis of Survey Questions That Include Don't Know Responses." *Public Opinion Quarterly* 53:525–47.

Feldman, Linda, Philippa Holowaty, Linda Shortt, Bart Harvey, Katherine Rannie, and Alykhan Jamal. 1997. "A Comparison of the Demographic, Lifestyle, and Sexual Behaviour Characteristics of Virgin and Non-Virgin Adolescents." *The Canadian Journal of Human Sexuality,* 6:197–209.

Festinger, L., H. W. Reicker, and S. Schachter. 1956. *When Prophecy Fails.* Minneapolis: University of Minnesota Press.

Forster, Christina A., Brian Evans and Ronald J. Fisher. 1990. "Evaluation of a Pilot Project in Service Coordination." *Evaluation Review,* 14:616–31.

Foschi, Martha, G. Keith Warriner, and Stephen D. Hart. 1985. "Standards, Expectations, and Interpersonal Influence." *Social Psychology Quarterly* 48 (2): 108–17.

Fowler, Floyd J., Jr. 1995. *Improving Survey Questions: Design and Evaluation.* Thousand Oaks, CA: Sage Publications.

Fox, Katherine J. 1991. "The Politics of Prevention: Ethnographers Combat AIDS among Drug Users." Pp. 227–49 in *Ethnography Unbound: Power and Resistence in the Modern Metropolis,* eds. M. Burawoy, A. Burton, A. A. Ferguson, K. J. Fox, J. Gamson, N. Gartrell, L. Hurst, C. Kurzman, L. Salzinger, J. Schiffman, and S. Ui. Berkeley, CA: University of California Press.

Gall, John. 1975. *Systemantics: How Systems Work and Especially How They Fail.* New York: Quadrangle.

Gallup, George, Jr., Burns Roper, Daniel Yankelovich, et al. 1990. "Polls that Made a Difference." *Public Perspective,* May–June, pp. 17–21.

Gamson, William A., Bruce Fireman, and Steven Rytina. 1982. *Encounters with Unjust Authority.* Homewood, Illinois: The Dorsey Press.

Gans, Herbert J. 1962. *Urban Villagers.* New York: Free Press.

Gans, Herbert J. 1967. *The Levittowners.* New York: Random House.

Garant, Carol. 1980. "Stalls in the Therapeutic Process." *American Journal of Nursing,* December, pp. 2166–67.

Gartner, Rosemary and Ross Macmillan. 2000. "Victim–Offender Relationship and Reporting Crimes of Violence against Women." Pp. 128–139 in *Crime in Canadian Society.* Sixth Edition. eds. Silverman, Teevan, and Sacco. Toronto: Harcourt Brace & Co.

Gaventa, John. 1991. "Towards a Knowledge Democracy:Viewpoints on Participatory Research in North America." Pp. 121–131 *in Action and Knowledge: Breaking the Monopoly with Participatory Action-Research,* eds. O. Fals-Borda and M. A. Rahman. New York: Apex Press.

Gillis, A. R. 1994. "Literacy and the Civilization of Violence in 19th-Century France." *Sociological Forum,* 9:371–401.

Gillis, A. R. 1989. "Crime and State Surveillance in Nineteenth-Century France." *American Journal of Sociology,* 95:307–341.

Gillis, A. R. 1996. "So Long as They Both Shall Live: Marital Dissolution and the Decline of Domestic Homicide in France, 1852–1909." *American Journal of Sociology,* 101:1273–1305.

Glaser, Barney, and Anselm Strauss. 1967. *The Discovery of Grounded Theory*. Chicago: Aldine.

Glock, Charles Y., Benjamin B. Ringer, and Earl R. Babbie. 1967. *To Comfort and to Challenge*. Berkeley: University of California Press.

Goffman, Erving. 1961. *Asylums: Essays on the Social Situation of Mental Patients and Other Inmates*. Chicago: Aldine.
1963. *Stigma: Notes on the Management of a Spoiled Identity*. Englewood Cliffs, NJ: Prentice-Hall.
1974. *Frame Analysis*. Cambridge, MA: Harvard University Press.

Gomme, Ian M. and Mary P. Hall. 1995. "Prosecutors at Work: Role Overload and Strain." *Journal of Criminal Justice*, 23: 191–200.

Goyder, John. 1985. "Face-to-Face Interviews and Mailed Questionnaires: The Net Difference in Response Rate." *Public Opinion Quarterly* 49:234–52.

Goyder, John. 1987. *The Silent Minority: Nonrespondents on Sample Surveys*. Cambridge: Polity Press.

Goyder, John. 1982. "Further Evidence on Factors Affecting Response Rates to Mailed Questionnaires." *American Sociological Review*. 47:550–53.

Gray, George and Neil Guppy. 1999. *Successful Surveys: Research Methods and Practice*. Second Edition. Toronto: Harcourt Brace Canada.

Grenier, Marc. 1994. "Native Indians in the English-Canadian Press: The Case of the 'Oka Crisis'." *Media, Culture & Society*, 16:313–36.

Groves, Robert M. 1990. "Theories and Methods of Telephone Surveys." Pp. 221–40 in *Annual Review of Sociology* (Vol. 16), edited by W. Richard Scott and Judith Blake. Palo Alto, CA: Annual Reviews.

Gubrium, Jaber F. and James A. Holstein. 1997. *The New Language of Qualitative Method*. New York: Oxford University Press.

Harlton, Shauna-Vi, Norah Keating, and Janet Fast. 1998. "Defining Eldercare for Policy and Practice: Perspectives Matter." *Family Relations*. 47:281–288.

Hartnagel. Timothy F. 1997. "Crime Among the Provinces: The Effect of Geographic Mobility." *Canadian Journal of Criminology*, 39:387–402.

Healey, Joseph F. 1999. *Statistics: A Tool for Social Research*. Belmont, CA: Wadsworth.

Hedrick, Terry E., Leonard Bickman, and Debra J. Rog. 1993. *Applied Research Design: A Practical Guide*. Newbury Park, CA: Sage.

Hempel, Carl G. 1952. "Fundamentals of Concept Formation in Empirical Science." *International Encyclopedia of United Science II*, no. 7.

Henry, Frances and Effie Ginzberg. 1988. "Racial Discrimination in Employment" Pp. 214–220 in *Social Inequality in Canada: Patterns, Problems, Policies*, edited by James Curtis, E. Grabb, N. Guppy, S. Gilbert. Prentice Hall.

Heritage, Johen, and David Greatbatch. 1992. "On the Institutional Character of Institutional Talk." In *Talk at Work*, edited by P. Drew and J. Heritage. Cambridge, England: Cambridge University Press.

Hirschi, Travis, and Hanan Selvin. 1973. *Principles of Survey Analysis*. New York: Free Press.

Hoover, Kenneth R. 1992. *The Elements of Social Scientific Thinking*. New York: St. Martin's Press.

"How Poll Was Done." 1999. *New York Times*. February 3, p. A14

Howell, Joseph T. 1973. *Hard Living on Clay Street*. Garden City, NY: Doubleday Anchor.

Howlett, Michael. 1986. "Acts of Commission and Acts of Omission: Legal–Historical Research and the Intentions of Government in a Federal State." *Canadian Journal of Political Science*, 19:363–70.

Hoy, Claire. 1989. *Margin of Error: Pollsters and the Manipulation of Canadian Politics*. Toronto: Key Porter.

Hughes, Karen D. and Graham S. Lowe. 2000. "Surveying the 'Post-Industrial' Landscape: Information Technologies and Labour Market Polarization in Canada." *The Canadian Review of Sociology and Anthropology*, 37:29–53.

Humphreys, Laud. 1970. *Tearoom Trade: Impersonal Sex in Public Places*. Chicago. Aldine.

Hutchby, Ian and Robin Wooffitt. 1998. *Conversation Analysis: Principles, Practices and Applications*. Cambridge, England: Polity Press.

Indrayan, A., M. J. Wysocki, A. Chawla, R. Kumar, and Singh. 1999. "Three-Decade Trend in Human Development Index in India and Its Major States." *Social Indicators Research* 46 (1): 91–120.

Iversen, Gudmund R. 1991. *Contextual Analysis.* Newbury Park, CA: Sage.

Jasso, Guillermina. 1988. "Principles of Theoretical Analysis." *Sociological Theory* 6:1–20.

Jendrek, Margaret Platt. 1985. *Through the Maze: Statistics with Computer Applications.* Belmont, CA: Wadsworth.

Johnson, Jeffrey C. 1990. *Selecting Ethnographic Informants.* Newbury Park, CA: Sage.

Jones, James H. 1981. *Bad Blood: The Tuskegee Syphilis Experiments.* New York: Free Press.

Jones, Stephen R. G. 1990. "Worker Independence and Output: The Hawthorne Studies Reevaluated." *American Sociological Review* 55 (April): 176–90.

Kahane, Howard. 1992. *Logic and Contemporary Rhetoric.* Belmont, CA: Wadsworth.

Kalton, Graham. 1983. *Introduction to Survey Sampling.* Newbury Park, CA: Sage.

Kaplan, Abraham. 1964. *The Conduct of Inquiry.* San Francisco: Chandler.

Kasof, Joseph. 1993. "Sex Bias in the Naming of Stimulus Persons." *Psychological Bulletin* 113 (1): 140–63.

Kay, Fiona. 1997. "Flight from Law: A Competing Risks Model of Departures from Law Firms." *Law & Society Review,* 31:301–335.

Kelle, Udo, ed. 1995. *Computer-Aided Qualitative Data Analysis: Theory, Methods, and Practice.* Thousand Oaks, CA: Sage.

Kendall, Patricia L., and Paul F. Lazarsfeld. 1950. "Problems of Survey Analysis." Pp. 133–96 in *Continuities in Social Research: Studies in the Scope and Method of "The American Soldier,"* edited by Robert K. Merton and Paul F. Lazarsfeld. New York: Free Press.

Khayatt, Didi. 1995. "Compulsory Heterosexuality: Schools and Lesbian Students." Pp. 149–63 in *Knowledge, Experience, and Ruling Relations: Studies in the Social Organization of Knowledge,* eds. M. Campbell and A. Manicom. Toronto, ON: University of Toronto Press.

Kish, Leslie. 1965. *Survey Sampling.* New York: Wiley.

Koeske, Gary F. 1998. "Suppression in the Study of Parenting and Adolescent Symptoms: Statistical Nuisance and Nonsense, or Scientific Explanation?" *Journal of Social Service Research* 24: 111–130.

Kong, Rebecca. 2000. "Canadian Crime Statistics." Pp. 63–95 in *Crime in Canadian Society.* Sixth Edition. eds. Silverman, Teevan, and Sacco. Toronto: Harcourt Brace & Co.

Krahn, Harvey and Jeffrey W. Bowlby. 1997. "Good Teaching and Satisfied University Graduates." *The Canadian Journal of Higher Education.* XXVII: 157–180.

Krueger, Richard A. 1988. *Focus Groups.* Newbury Park, CA: Sage.

Kuhn, Thomas. 1970. *The Structure of Scientific Revolutions.* Chicago: University of Chicago Press.

Kvale, Steinar. 1996. *InterViews: An Introduction to Qualitative Research Interviewing.* Thousand Oaks, CA: Sage.

Laxer, Gordon. 1989. "The Schizophrenic Character of Canadian Political Economy." *Canadian Review of Sociology and Anthropology.* 26:178–192.

Lazarsfeld, Paul F. 1955. "Foreword." In *Survey Design and Analysis,* by Herbert Hyman. New York: Free Press.
——— 1959. "Problems in Methodology." In *Sociology Today,* edited by Robert K. Merton. New York: Basic Books.

Lazarsfeld, Paul F., and Morris Rosenberg, eds. 1955. *The Language of Social Research.* New York: Free Press.

Lenton, Rhonda, Michael D. Smith, John Fox, and Norman Morra. 1999. "Sexual Harassment in Public Places: Experiences of Canadian Women." *The Canadian Review of Sociology and Anthropology,* 36:517–540.

Lever, Janet. 1986. "Sex Differences in the Complexity of Children's Play and Games." Pp. 74–

89 in *Structure and Process,* edited by Richard J. Peterson and Charlotte A. Vaughan. Belmont, CA: Wadsworth.

Lewis, Jacqueline. 1998. "Learning to Strip: The Socialization Experiences of Exotic Dancers" *The Canadian Journal of Human Sexuality,* 7: 51–66.

Li, Peter S. 1985. "The Use of Oral History in Studying Elderly Chinese-Canadians." *Canadian Ethnic Studies,* 17: 67–77.

Linton, Ralph. 1937. *The Study of Man.* New York: D. Appleton-Century.

Literary Digest. 1936a. "Landon, 1,293,669: Roosevelt, 972,897." October 31, pp. 5–6.
1936b. "What Went Wrong with the Polls?" November 14, pp. 7–8.

Lofland, John, and Lyn H. Lofland. 1995. *Analyzing Social Settings: A Guide to Qualitative Observation and Analysis.* Belmont, CA: Wadsworth.

Lopata, Helena Znaniecki. 1981. "Widowhood and Husband Sanctification." *Journal of Marriage and the Family,* May, pp. 439–50.

Lynd, Robert S. and Helen M. Lynd. 1929. *Middletown.* New York: Harcourt, Brace.

Lynd, Robert S. and Helen M. Lynd. 1937. *Middletown in Transition.* New York: Harcourt, Brace.

Maclean's. 2000–2001. "We are Canadian." Dec. 25, 2000/Jan. 1, 2001, volume 113, no. 52.

MacKenzie, David. 1986. *Inside the Atlantic Triangle: Canada and the Entrance of Newfoundland into Confederation 1939–1949.* Toronto, ON: University of Toronto Press.

Madison, Anna-Marie. 1992. "Primary Inclusion of Culturally Diverse Minority Program Participants in the Evaluation Process." *New Directions for Program Evaluation,* no. 53, pp. 35–43.

Marshall, Catherine, and Gretchen B. Rossman. 1995. *Designing Qualitative Research.* Thousand Oaks, CA: Sage.

Martin, David W. 1996. *Doing Psychology Experiments.* 4th ed. Monterey, CA: Brooks/Cole.

Marx, Karl. [1867] 1967. *Capital.* New York: International Publishers.
[1880] 1956. *Revue Socialist,* July 5. Reprinted in *Karl Marx: Selected Writings in Sociology and Social Philosophy,* edited by T. B. Bottomore and Maximilien Rubel. New York: McGraw-Hill.

Maxwell, Joseph A. 1996. *Qualitative Research Design.* Thousand Oaks, CA: Sage.

McGrane, Bernard. 1994. *The Un-TV and the 10 mph Car: Experiments in Personal Freedom and Everyday Life.* Fort Bragg, CA: The Small Press.

McIver, John P., and Edward G. Carmines. 1981. *Unidimensional Scaling.* Newbury Park, CA: Sage.

Meadows, Donella H., Dennis L. Meadows, and Jørgen Randers. 1992. *Beyond the Limits: Confronting Global Collapse, Envisioning a Sustainable Future.* Post Mills, VT: Chelsea Green.

Meadows, Donella, Dennis L. Meadows, Jørgen Randers, and William W. Behrens, III. 1972. *The Limits to Growth.* New York: Universe Books.

Menard, Scott. 1991. *Longitudinal Research.* Newbury Park, CA: Sage.

Merton, Robert K. 1938. "Social Structure and Anomie." *American Sociological Review* 3: 672–82.
1957. *Social Theory and Social Structure.* Glencoe, IL: Free Press.

Merton, Robert K., and Paul F. Lazarsfeld, eds. 1950. *Continuities in Social Research: Studies in the Scope and Method of "The American Soldier."* New York : Free Press.

Micucci, Anthony. 1998. "A Typology of Private Policing Operational Styles." *Journal of Criminal Justice.* 26:41–51.

Miles, Matthew B., and A. Michael Huberman, A. M. 1994. *Qualitative Data Analysis.* 2nd edition. Thousand Oaks, CA: Sage Publications.

Milgram, Stanley. 1969. *Obedience to Authority.* New York, NY: Harper Colophon Books.

Miller, Delbert. 1991. *Handbook of Research Design and Social Measurement.* Newbury Park, CA: Sage.

Mohr, Lawrence B. 1990. *Understanding Significance Testing.* Newbury Park, CA: Sage.

Mooney, Linda A., David Knox, Caroline Schacht, and Adie Nelson. 2001. *Understanding Social*

Problems. First Canadian Edition. Scarborough, ON: Nelson Thomson Learning.

Morgan, David L., ed. 1993. *Successful Focus Groups: Advancing the State of the Art*. Newbury Park, CA: Sage.

Morgan, David L. 1997 *Focus Groups as Qualitative Research* (2nd edition). Thousand Oaks, CA: Sage Publications.

Mosher, Clayton and John Hagan. 1994. "Constituting Class and Crime in Upper Canada: The Sentencing of Narcotics Offenders, circa 1908–1953." *Social Forces*, 72:613–41.

Moskowitz, Milt. 1981. "The Drugs That Doctors Order." *San Francisco Chronicle,* May 23, p. 33.

Mullins, Mark R. 1988. "The Organizational Dilemmas of Ethnic Churches: A Case Study of Japanese Buddhism in Canada." *Sociological Analysis*, 48:217–233.

Newton, Rae R. and Kjell Erik Rudestam. 1999. *Your Statistical Consultant: Answers to Your Data Analysis Questions*. Thousand Oaks, CA: Sage.

Nicholls, William L., II, Reginald P. Baker, and Jean Martin. 1997. "The Effect of New Data Collection Technology on Survey Data Quality." In *Survey Measurement and Process Quality*, edited by Lars Lyberg, P. Biemer., M. Collins, C. Dippo, N. Schwarz, and D. Trewin. New York: Wiley-Interscience.

Noh, Samuel and William R. Avison. 1996. "Asian immigrants and the stress process: a study of Koreans in Canada." *Journal of Health & Social Behavior*, 37:192–206.

Oakley, Ann. 1981. "Interviewing Women: A Contradiction in Terms." In *Doing Feminist Research*, edited by Helen Roberts. London: Routledge & Kegan Paul.

O'Neill, Harry W. 1992. "They Can't Subpoena What You Ain't Got." *AAPOR News* 19 (2): 4, 7.

Osborne, Geraint B. 1999. "Scientific Research Using Canadian Federal Inmates As Subjects, 1955–1998: A Bibliographic Search." Her Majesty The Queen In Right Of Canada, as represented by the Minister of the Department of the Solicitor General of Canada.

Øyen, Else, ed. 1990. *Comparative Methodology: Theory and Practice in International Social Research*. Newbury Park, CA: Sage.

Parr, Janet. 1998. "Theoretical Voices and Women's Own Voices: The Stories of Mature Women Students." Pp. 87–102 in *Feminist Dilemmas in Qualitative Research: Public Knowledge and Private Lives*. eds. Jane Ribbens and Rosalind Edwards. Thousand Oaks, CA: Sage Publications.

Patton, Michael Quinn. 1987. *How to Use Qualitative Methods in Evaluation*. Newbury Park: CA. Sage Publications.

Payne, Charles M. 1995. *I've Got the Light of Freedom: The Organizing Tradition and the Mississippi Freedom Struggle*. Berkeley: University of California Press.

Perinelli, Phillip J. 1986. "Nonsuspecting Public in TV Call-In Polls." *New York Times,* February 14, letter to the editor.

Polivka, Anne E., and Jennifer M. Rothgeb. 1993. "Redesigning the CPS Questionnaire." *Monthly Labor Review* 116 (9): 10–28.

Ponting, J. Rick. 1988. "Public Opinion on Aboriginal Peoples' Issues in Canada." *Canadian Social Trends*, winter:9–17.

Population Communications International. 1996. *International Dateline* [February]. New York: Population Communications International.

Potvin, Louise, François Champagne, and Claire Laberge-Nadeau. 1988. "Mandatory Driver Training and Road Safety: The Quebec Experience." *American Journal of Public Health*, 78:1206–1209.

Powell, Elwin H. 1958. "Occupation, Status, and Suicide: Toward a Redefinition of Anomie." *American Sociological Review* 23:131–39.

Presser, Stanley, and Johnny Blair. 1994. "Survey Pretesting: Do Different Methods Produce Different Results?" Pp. 73–104 in *Sociological Methodology 1994,* edited by Peter Marsden. San Francisco: Jossey-Bass.

Redfield, Robert. 1941. *The Folk Culture of Yucatan*. Chicago: University of Chicago Press.

Reimer, Bill. 2001. "A Sample Frame for Rural Canada: Design and Evaluation." June, unpublished.

Reinharz, Shulamit. 1992. *Feminist Methods in Social Research*. New York: Oxford University Press.

Renaud, Cheryl A. and E. Sandra Byers. 1999. "Exploring the Frequency, Diversity, and Content of University Students' Positive and Negative Sexual Cognitions." *The Canadian Journal of Human Sexuality*, 8:17.

Riecken, Henry W., and Robert F. Boruch. 1974. *Social Experimentation: A Method for Planning and Evaluating Social Intervention*. New York: Academic Press.

Roberts, Julian V. and Robert J. Gebotys. 1992. "Reforming Rape Laws: Effects of Legislative Change in Canada." *Law and Human Behavior*. 16:555–73.

Roethlisberger, F. J., and W. J. Dickson. 1939. *Management and the Worker*. Cambridge, MA: Harvard University Press.

Rogers, Everett M., Peter W. Vaughan, Ramadhan M. A. Swalehe, Nagesh Rao, and Suruchi Sood. 1996. "Effects of an Entertainment-Education Radio Soap Opera on Family Planning and HIV/AIDS Prevention Behavior in Tanzania." Report presented at a technical briefing on the Tanzania Entertainment-Education Project, Rockefeller Foundation, New York, March 27.

Rollings-Magnusson, Sandra. 2000. "Canada's Most Wanted: Pioneer Women on the Western Prairies." *Canadian Review of Sociology and Anthropology*, 37:223–238.

Rosenberg, Morris. 1968. *The Logic of Survey Analysis*. New York: Basic Books.

Rosenthal, Robert, and Leonore Jacobson. 1968. *Pygmalion in the Classroom*. New York: Holt, Rinehart & Winston.

Rossi, Peter H., and Howard E. Freeman. 1996. *Evaluation: A Systematic Approach*. Newbury Park, CA: Sage.

Rubin, Herbert J., and Riene S. Rubin. 1995. *Qualitative Interviewing: The Art of Hearing Data*. Thousand Oaks, CA: Sage.

Ryan, Joan. 1995. *Doing Things the Right Way : Dene Traditional Justice in Lac La Martre, N.W.T.*, Calgary: University of Calgary Press and the Arctic Institute of North America.

Sacks, Jeffrey J., W. Mark Krushat, and Jeffrey Newman. 1980. "Reliability of the Health Hazard Appraisal." *American Journal of Public Health*, July, pp. 730–32.

Saint-Pierre, Yves. 1993. Statistics Canada's Internet Site. http://www.statcan.ca/english/IPS/Data/75F0002MIE93013.htm May 4, 2001.

Sanders, William B. 1994. *Gangbangs and Drive-bys: Grounded Culture and Juvenile Gang Violence*. New York: Aldine De Gruyter.

Scarce, Rik. 1990. *Ecowarriors: Understanding the Radical Environmental Movement*. Chicago: Noble Press.

Schatzman, Leonard and Anselm L. Strauss. 1973. *Field Research: Strategies for a Natural Sociology*. Englewood Cliffs N.J.: Prentice-Hall:

Schifiett, Kathy L., and Mary Zey. 1990. "Comparison of Characteristics of Private Product Producing Organizations and Public Service Organizations." *Sociological Quarterly* 31 (4): 569–83.

Shaffir, William B., and Robert A. Stebbins, eds. 1991. *Experiencing Fieldwork: An Inside View of Qualitative Research*. Newbury Park, CA: Sage.

Shaver, Kelly G. 1985. *The Attribution of Blame: Causality, Responsibility, and Blameworthiness*. New York: Springer-Verlag.

Sheatsley, Paul F. 1983. "Questionnaire Construction and Item Writing." Pp. 195–230 in *Handbook of Survey Research,* edited by Peter H. Rossi, James D. Wright, and Andy B. Anderson. New York: Academic Press.

Silverman, David. 1993. *Interpreting Qualitative Data*. Newbury Park, CA: Sage.

Silverman, David. 2001. *Interpreting Qualitative Data: Methods for Analyzing Talk, Text, and Interaction*. 2nd Ed. Thousand Oaks, CA: Sage.

Silverman, David. 1999. *Doing Qualitative Research: A Practical Handbook*. Thousand Oaks, CA: Sage.

Silverman, Robert A., James J. Teevan, and Vincent F. Sacco. 2000. "Introduction." Pp. 1–10 in *Crime in Canadian Society*. Sixth Edition. eds. Silverman, Teevan, and Sacco. Toronto: Harcourt Brace & Co.

Simon, Rita J. 1998. *Abortion: Statutes, Policies, and Public Attitudes the World Over*. Westport, CT: Praeger.

Sintonen, Teppo. 1993. "Life Course and Ethnicity: Experiences of Canadian Finns Who Immigrated to Canada in the 1920s. *Canadian Ethnic Studies/Etudes Ethniques au Canada*, 25:76–89.

Smart, Reginald G., Edward M. Adlaf, and Gordon W. Walsh. 1993. "Declining Drug Use in Relation to Increased Drug Education: A Trend Study 1979–1991." *Journal of Drug Education*, 23:125–132.

Smith, Andrew E., and G. F. Bishop. 1992. *The Gallup Secret Ballot Experiments: 1944–1988.* Paper presented at the annual conference of the American Association for Public Opinion Research, St. Petersburg, FL, May.

Smith, Dorothy E. 1987. *The Everyday World as Problematic: A Feminist Sociology*. Boston: Northeastern University Press.

Smith, Eric R. A. N., and Peverill Squire. 1990. "The Effects of Prestige Names in Question Wording." *Public Opinion Quarterly* 54:97–116.

Sorensen, Marianne and Harvey Krahn. 1996. "Attitudes Toward Immigrants: A Test of Two Theories. *The Alberta Journal of Educational Research*. XLII: 3–18.

Sorokin, Pitirim A. 1937–1940. *Social and Cultural Dynamics,* 4 vols. Englewood Cliffs, NJ: Bedminster Press.

Sosteric, Mike. 1996. "Subjectivity and the Labour Process: A Case Study in the Restaurant Industry." *Work, Employment & Society*, 10:297–318.

Srole, Leo. 1956. "Social Integration and Certain Corollaries: An Exploratory Study." *American Sociological Review* 21:709–16.

Statistics Canada. June 2001. "2000 General Social Survey, Cycle 14: Access to and use of Information and Technology." Catalogue no. 12M0014GPE.

Statistics Canada. 2000. "Women in Canada." Catalogue no. 89-503-XPE.

Statistics Canada. 1996. *General Social Survey*, Cycle 11.

Statistics Canada. 1996. "About 1996 Census Tables on the Internet: Definitions." Statistics Canada's Internet Site, July 27, 2001. (http://www.statcan.ca:80/english/census96/define.html.

Statistics Canada. 1996. "Agriculture Census 96." Statistics Canada's Internet Site, May 16, 2001. http://www.statcan.ca/english/concepts/question.htm.

Statistics Canada. "Canadian Statistics: Births and Birth rate." CANSIM, Matrix 5772 and Catalogue no. 91-213-XB. Statistics Canada's Internet Site, December 13, 2000. http://www.statcan.ca/english/Pgdb/People/Population/demo04b.htm

Statistics Canada. 1997. "Focus groups and interviews: Aboriginal identity question and other issues for the 2001 Census short form questionnaire."

Statistics Canada's Internet Site, May 4, 2001 http://www.statcan.ca/english/IPS/Data/92F0096XIE.htm.

Statistics Canada. 1983. "Historical Statistics of Canada" (second edition), jointly produced with the Social Science Federation of Canada. Statistics Canada's Internet Site. http://www.statcan.ca/english/freepub/11-516-XIE/sectiona/toc.htm

Statistics Canada. Toronto Area Survey 1991, conducted by the Institute for Social Research at York University. Statistics Canada's Internet Site, May 4, 2001. http://www.statcan.ca/english/edu/prototype/data_collection/dpart4.htm

Steele, Stephen F., and Joyce Miller Iutcovich, eds. 1997. *Directions in Applied Sociology.* Arnold, MD: Society for Applied Sociology.

Stevahn, Laurie. David W. Johnson, Roger T. Johnson, Kathy Green, and Anne Marie Laginski. 1997. "Effects on High School Students of Conflict Resolution Training Integrated into English Literature." Journal of Social Psychology, 137:302–315.

Stouffer, Samuel, et al. 1949, 1950. *The American Soldier,* 3 vols. Princeton, NJ: Princeton University Press.

Strauss, Anselm, and Juliet Corbin. 1998. *Basics of Qualitative Research: Techniques and Procedures for Developing Grounded Theory*. 2nd ed. Thousand Oaks, CA: Sage.

Strunk, William Jr., and E. B. White. 2000. *The Elements of Style*. Fourth ed. NY: Longman.

Sudman, Seymour. 1983. "Applied Sampling." Pp. 145–94 in *Handbook of Survey Research*, edited by Peter H. Rossi, James D. Wright, and Andy B. Anderson. New York: Academic Press.

"Support for death penalty plunges." 2001. *The Globe and Mail*, by Colin Freeze, February 16, p. 1.

Swalehe, Ramadhan, Everett M. Rogers, Mark J. Gilboard, Krista Alford, and Rima Montoya. 1995. "A Content Analysis of the Entertainment-Education Radio Soap Opera 'Twende na Wakati' (Let's Go with the Times) in Tanzania." Arusha, Tanzania: Population Family Life and Education Programme (POFLEP), Ministry of Community Development, Women Affairs, and Children, November 15.

Tacq, Jacques. 1997. *Multivariate Analysis Techniques in Social Science Research: From Problem to Analysis*. Thousand Oaks, CA: Sage Publications.

Takeuchi, David. 1974. "Grass in Hawaii: A Structural Constraints Approach." M.A. thesis, University of Hawaii.

Tandon, Rajesh, and L. Dave Brown. 1981. "Organization-Building for Rural Development: An Experiment in India." *Journal of Applied Behavioral Science*, April–June, pp. 172–89.

Terkel, Studs. 1970. *Hard Times: An Oral History of the Great Depression*. New York: Pantheon Books.

The Daily. 2000. "Women in Canada." *Statistics Canada*, September 14. http://www.statcan.ca/Daily/English/000914 /d000914c.htm (January 24, 2001).

Thomas, W. I., and Florian Znaniecki. 1918. *The Polish Peasant in Europe and America*. Chicago: University of Chicago Press.

Thompson, Paul. 2000. *The Voice of the Past: Oral History*. 3rd Ed. Oxford: Oxford University Press.

Tiano, Susan. 1994. *Patriarchy on the Line: Labor, Gender, and Ideology in the Mexican Maquila Industry*. Philadelphia, PA: Temple University Press.

Tomm, Winnie. ed. 1989. *The Effects of Feminist Approaches on Research Methodologies*. Waterloo, ON: Wilfrid Laurier University Press.

Tourangeau, Roger, Kenneth A. Rasinski, Norman Bradburn, and Roy D'Andrade. 1989. "Carry-over Effects in Attitude Surveys." *Public Opinion Quarterly* 53:495–524.

Tremblay, Manon. 1998. "Do Female MPs Substantively Represent Women? A Study Of Legislative Behaviour in Canada's 35th Parliament." *Canadian Journal of Political Science*, 31:435–65.

Tuckel, Peter S., and Barry M. Feinberg. 1991. "The Answering Machine Poses Many Questions for Telephone Survey Researchers. *Public Opinion Quarterly* 55:200–17.

Turner, Jonathan H., ed. 1989. *Theory Building in Sociology: Assessing Theoretical Cumulation*. Newbury Park, CA: Sage.

Turner, Terisa E., Wahu M. Kaara and Leigh S. Brownhill. 1997. "Social Reconstruction in Rural Africa: A Gendered Class Analysis of Women's Resistance to Export Crop Production in Kenya." *Canadian Journal of Development Studies*, 18:213–238.

United Nations. 1995. *Human Development Report 1995*, New York: United Nations Development Program. [Summarized in Population Communication International. 1996. *International Dateline*, February, pp. 1–4.]

U.S. Bureau of the Census. 1996. *Statistical Abstract of the United States, 1995*. CD-ROM CD-SA-95, issued April.
1999. *Statistical Abstract of the United States*. Washington, DC: U.S. Government Printing Office.

Walker, Jeffery T. 1994. "Fax Machines and Social Surveys: Teaching an Old Dog New Tricks." *Journal of Quantitative Criminology* 10 (2): 181–88.

Walker Research. 1988. *Industry Image Study*, 8th ed. Indianapolis, IN: Walker Research.

Wallace, Walter. 1971. *The Logic of Science in Sociology.* Chicago: Aldine.

Wallace, William A. 1972. *Causality and Scientific Explanation.* Ann Arbor: University of Michigan Press.

Warriner, Keith, John Goyder, Heidi Gjertsen, Paula Hohner, and Kathleen McSpurren. 1996. "Charities, No; Lotteries, No; Cash, Yes: Main Effects and Interactions in a Canadian Incentives Experiment." *Public Opinion Quarterly*, 60:542–562.

Webb, Eugene J., Donald T. Campbell, Richard D. Schwartz, and Lee Sechrest. [1966] 2000. *Unobtrusive Measures* (Revised Edition). Thousand Oaks, CA: Sage Publications.

Weber, Max. [1905] 1958. *The Protestant Ethic and the Spirit of Capitalism.* Translated by Talcott Parsons. New York: Scribners.
[1925] 1946. "Science as a Vocation." Pp. 129–56 in *From Max Weber: Essays in Sociology,* edited and translated by Hans Gerth and C. Wright Mills. New York: Oxford University Press.
[1934] 1951. *The Religion of China.* Translated by Hans H. Gerth. New York: Free Press.
[1934] 1952. *Ancient Judaism.* Translated by Hans H. Gerth and Don Martindale. New York: Free Press.
[1934] 1958. *The Religion of India.* Translated by Hans H. Gerth and Don Martindale. New York: Free Press.

Weber, Robert Philip. 1990. *Basic Content Analysis.* Newbury Park: Sage.

Weiss, Carol. 1972. *Evaluation Research.* Englewood Cliffs, NJ: Prentice-Hall.

Weitzman, Eben. 2000. "Software and Qualitative Research" Pp. 803–820 in *Handbook of Qualitative Research,* 2nd ed., eds. N. Denzin and Y. Lincoln. Thousand Oaks, CA: Sage Publications.

Whyte, W. F., D.J. Greenwood, and P. Lazes. 1991. "Participatory Action Research: Through Practice to Science in Social Science." Pp. 19–55 in *Participatory Action Research,* edited by W. F. Whyte. New York: Sage Publications.

Wilson, Robin J., Lynn Steward, Tania Stirpe, Marianne Barrett, and Janice E. Cripps. 2000. "Community–based sex offender management: Combining parole supervision and treatment to reduce recidivism. *Canadian Journal of Criminology*, 42:177–188.

Wolcott, Harry F. 1995. *The Art of Fieldwork.* Walnut Creek, CA: AltaMira Press.

Wolf, Daniel R.. 1990. *The Rebels: A Brotherhood of Outlaw Bikers.* Toronto: University of Toronto Press.

Wolf, Daniel R. 1991. "High-Risk Methodology: Reflections on Leaving an Outlaw Society." Pp. 211–13 in *Experiencing Fieldwork: An Inside View of Qualitative Research,* edited by William B. Shaffir and Robert A. Stebbins. Newbury Park, CA: Sage.

Yerg, Beverly J. 1981. "Reflections on the Use of the RTE Model in Physical Education." *Research Quarterly for Exercise and Sport,* March, pp. 38–47.

Yinger, J. Milton, et al. 1977. *Middle Start: An Experiment in the Educational Enrichment of Young Adolescents.* London: Cambridge University Press.

Young, Kevin, and Laura Craig. 1997. "Beyond White Pride: Identity, Meaning and Contradiction in the Canadian Skinhead Subculture." *Canadian Review of Sociology and Anthropology*, 34:175–206.

Young, Shelley. 1997. "The use of normalization as a strategy in the sexual exploitation of children by adult offenders." The Canadian Journal of Human Sexuality, 6:285–95.

Ziesel, Hans. 1957. *Say It with Figures.* New York: Harper & Row.

Zimbardo, Philip G. and Ken Musen. 1992. *Quiet Rage: The Stanford Prison Experiment.* Harper Collins College Publishers.

Glossary

attributes Characteristics of persons or things. See *variables* and Chapter 1.

average An ambiguous term generally suggesting typical or normal. The *mean, median,* and *mode* are specific examples of mathematical averages referred to as measures of central tendency. (Chapter 16)

bias (1) That quality of a measurement device that tends to result in a misrepresentation of what is being measured in a particular direction. For example, the questionnaire item "Don't you agree that the prime minister is doing a good job?" would be *biased* in that it would generally encourage more favorable responses. See Chapter 9 for more on this topic. (2) The thing inside you that makes other people or groups seem consistently better or worse than they really are. (3) What a nail looks like after you hit it crooked. (If you drink, don't drive.)

binomial variable A variable that has only two attributes is binomial. Gender would be an example, having the attributes *male* and *female.* (Chapter 7)

bivariate analysis The analysis of two variables simultaneously, for the purpose of determining the empirical relationship between them. The construction of a simple percentage table or the computation of a simple correlation coefficient would be examples of bivariate analyses. (Chapter 16)

Bogardus social distance scale A measurement technique for determining the willingness of people to participate in social relations—of varying degrees of closeness—with other kinds of people. It's an especially efficient technique in that several discrete answers may be summarized

without losing any of the original details of the data. (Chapter 6)

case study A focussed, detailed investigation of a single instance of some social phenomenon like a town, an industry, a community, an organization, or a person. (Chapter 11)

census (1) An enumeration of the characteristics of some population. A *census* is often similar to a survey, with the difference that the census collects data from all members of the population and the survey is limited to a sample. (Chapter 4) (2) What sober-minded folks always want to bring you to.

cluster sample (1) A multistage sample in which natural groups (clusters) are sampled initially, with the members of each selected group being subsampled afterward. For example, you might select a sample of Canadian universities from a directory, get lists of the students at all the selected schools, then draw samples of students from each. (Chapter 7) (2) Pawing around in a box of macadamia nut clusters to take all the big ones for yourself.

codebook (1) The document used in data processing and analysis that tells the location of different data items in a data file. Typically, the codebook identifies the locations of data items and the meaning of the codes used to represent different attributes of variables. (Chapter 15) (2) The document that cost you 38 boxtops just to learn that Captain Marvelous wanted you to brush your teeth and always tell the truth. (3) The document that allows government intelligence agents to learn that Captain Marvelous wants them to brush their teeth.

coding (1) The process whereby raw data are transformed into standardized form suitable for machine processing and analysis. (Chapters 10 and 15) (2) A key procedure used by researchers in organizing and processing qualitative data, coding refers to applying labels to strips of data that illustrate ideas and concepts and to the continuing process of identifying, modifying, and refining concepts and categories that sustain emerging themes and patterns. (Chapter 14)

cohort study A study in which some specific group is studied over time although data may be collected from different members in each set of observations. A study of the occupational history of the class of 1970, in which questionnaires were sent every five years, for example, would be a cohort study. (Chapter 4)

conceptualization (1) The mental process whereby fuzzy and imprecise notions (concepts) are made more specific and precise. So you want to study prejudice. What do you mean by prejudice? Are there different kinds of prejudice? What are they? See Chapter 5, which is all about conceptualization, and its pal, *operationalization*. (2) Sexual reproduction among intellectuals.

confidence interval (1) The range of values within which a population parameter is estimated to lie. A survey, for example, may show 40 percent of a sample favoring Candidate A (poor devil). Although the best estimate of the support existing among all voters would also be 40 percent, we would not expect it to be exactly that. We might, therefore, compute a confidence interval (such as from 35 to 45 percent) within which the actual percentage of the population probably lies. Note that we must specify a *confidence level* in connection with every confidence interval. (Chapters 7 and 16) (2) How close you dare to get to an alligator.

confidence level (1) The estimated probability that a population parameter lies within a given *confidence interval.* Given an appropriately constructed confidence interval, such as plus or minus two standard errors around the mean, we may state that in 95 percent of all samples the true population value will be inside the constructed

interval. (Chapters 7 and 16) (2) How sure you are that the ring you bought from a street vendor for ten dollars is really a three-carat diamond.

construct validity The degree to which a measure relates to other *variables* as expected within a system of theoretical relationships. (Chapter 5)

content analysis A social research method appropriate for studying human communications through social artifacts such as books, magazines, songs, poems, or paintings. (Chapter 10)

content validity The degree to which a measure covers the range of meanings included within a concept. (Chapter 5)

contingency question A survey question intended for only some respondents, determined by their responses to some other question. For example, all respondents might be asked whether they belong to the Cosa Nostra, and only those who said yes would be asked how often they go to company meetings and picnics. The latter would be a *contingency question.* (Chapter 9)

contingency table (1) A format for presenting the relationships among variables in the form of percentage distributions. See Chapter 16 for several illustrations of it and for guides to doing it. (2) The card table you keep around in case your guests bring their seven kids with them to dinner.

control group (1) In experimentation, a group of subjects to whom no experimental stimulus is administered and who should resemble the experimental group in all other respects. The comparison of the control group and the experimental group at the end of the experiment points to the effect of the experimental stimulus. (Chapter 8)

control variable A variable that is held constant in an attempt to clarify further the relationship between two other variables. Having discovered a relationship between education and prejudice, for example, we might hold gender constant by examining the relationship between education and prejudice among men only and then among women only. In this example, gender would be the control variable *(also called the test variable).* (Chapter 16)

conversation analysis The study of conversation or talk-in-interaction with a focus on how talk, particularly naturally occurring talk, is managed among individuals. One key assumption of conversation analysts is that everyday talk is highly organized and ordered. Specific techniques, such as transcription conventions, have been developed by conversation analysts for the systematic and detailed study of the devices used in ordinary talk. (Chapter 14)

correlation A correlation exists between two variables when they are observed to be related; that is, when one occurs or changes, so does the other. For example, weight and height are said to be correlated because of the association between increases in height and increases in weight. Correlation alone does not establish a particular causal relationship. The mere fact of association does not tell us which variable causes the other, or, indeed, whether there is any causal relationship between them. Nonetheless, correlation is one of several criteria of causality. (Chapter 3)

criterion-related validity The degree to which a measure relates with some external criterion. For example, the validity of occupational qualifying examinations is shown in their ability to predict future evaluations of the individuals' job performances. (Chapter 5)

cross-sectional study A study based on observations representing a single point in time. Contrasted with a *longitudinal study*. (Chapter 4)

debriefing Interviewing subjects following their participation in the research project to learn about their experiences and reactions to their participation. Negative reactions can be a special concern. If it is determined that participation generated any problems for the subject, there is an attempt to correct such problems. See Part 3, Introduction.

deduction (1) The logical model in which specific expectations of *hypotheses* are developed on the basis of general principles. Starting from the general principle that all deans are meanies, you might anticipate that this one won't let you change courses. This anticipation would be the result of deduction. See also *induction* and Chapters 1, 2 and 3. (2) What Revenue Canada said

your good-for-nothing moocher of a brother-in-law technically isn't. (3) Of a duck.

dependent variable (1) A variable assumed to depend on or be caused by another (called the independent variable). If you find that *income* is partly a function of amount of formal education, *income* is being treated as a dependent variable. See Chapter 1 and *independent variable*. (2) A wimpy variable.

descriptive statistics Statistical computations describing either the characteristics of a sample or the relationship among variables in a sample. Descriptive statistics merely summarize a set of sample observations, whereas *inferential statistics* move beyond the description of specific observations to make inferences about the larger population from which the sample observations were drawn. (Chapter 16)

dichotomous variable A variable having only two categories. Also called *binomial variable*. (Chapter 8)

dimension A specifiable aspect or facet of a concept. (Chapter 5)

dispersion The distribution of values around some central value, such as an *average*. The *range* is a simple example of a measure of dispersion. Thus, we may report that the *mean* age of a group is 37.9, and the *range* is from 12 to 89. (Chapter 16)

distorter variable A control variable that causes an apparent reversal in the relationship between two other variables (from negative to positive or vice versa). (Chapter 16)

ecological fallacy Erroneously drawing conclusions about individuals based solely on the observation of groups. (Chapter 4)

elaboration model A method for conducting multivariate analysis, the elaboration model is a logical approach to dissecting the relationship between two variables through the simultaneous introduction of a third variable, usually referred to as a control or test variable. Though developed primarily through the medium of contingency tables by Paul Lazarsfeld, it may be used with other statistical techniques. For various outcomes of an elaboration analysis see *replication, specification, explanation,* and *interpretation.* Also see Chapter 16.

element The unit that may be selected in a sample. Thus elements are the units of which the population is comprised for a given study. (Chapter 7)

EPSEM (Equal probability of selection method) A sample design in which each member of a population has the same chance of being selected into the sample. (Chapter 7)

experimental group In experimentation, a group of subjects to whom an experimental stimulus is administered, as compared with the *control group,* which receives no experimental stimulus. (Chapter 8)

explanation When used in connection with the elaboration model, this is a technical term that represents the research outcome in which an antecedent test variable reveals the original (zero-order) relationship between two variables to be *spurious*. In other words, the original relationship disappears—is explained away—when the antecedent test variable is introduced. (Chapter 16)

extended case method A research technique developed by Michael Burawoy which uses case study observations for the purpose of discovering flaws in, and then modifying, existing social theories. Thus the technique emphasizes rebuilding or improving theory rather than approving or rejecting it. (Chapter 11)

external invalidity Refers to the possibility that conclusions drawn from experimental results may not be generalizable to the "real" world. See Chapter 8 and *internal invalidity.*

external validation The process of testing the *validity* of a measure, such as an index or scale, by examining its relationship to other, presumed indicators of the same variable. If the index really measures prejudice, for example, it should correlate with other indicators of prejudice. See Chapter 6 for a fuller discussion of this topic and for illustrations.

face validity (1) That quality of an indicator that makes it seem a reasonable measure of some variable. That the frequency of church attendance is some indication of a person's religiosity seems to make sense without a lot of explanation. It has face validity. (Chapter 5) (2) When your face looks like your driver's license photo (rare).

focus group An interviewing method where a number of subjects are brought together to discuss a specific topic or issue. A focus group is typically led by a moderator who helps to facilitate discussion and ensures that no person dominates the conversation, while interfering as little as possible in the discussion. (Chapter 12)

frequency distribution (1) A description of the number of times the various attributes of a variable are observed in a sample. The report that 53 percent of a sample were men and 47 percent were women would be a simple example of a frequency distribution. Another example would be the report that 15 of the cities studied had populations under 10,000, 23 had populations between 10,000 and 25,000, and so forth. (Chapter 16) (2) A radio dial.

generalizability (1) That quality of a research finding that justifies the inference that it represents something more than the specific observations on which it was based. Sometimes this involves the generalization of findings from a sample to a population. Other times, it's a matter of concepts: If you discover why people commit burglaries, can you generalize that discovery to other crimes as well? See Part 4, Introduction, and Chapters 4, 7, 8 and 16. (2) The likelihood that you will ever be a general.

grounded theory An inductive approach to social research that attempts to derive theory from an analysis of the patterns, themes, and common categories discovered in observational data. This differs from *hypothesis testing*, in which theory is used to generate hypotheses to be tested through observations. Barney Glaser and Anselm Strauss introduced the grounded theory method (GTM), an inductive approach to research in which theories emerge from the data. (Chapters 11 and 14)

Guttman scale (1) A type of composite measure used to summarize several discrete observations and to represent some more general variable. (Chapter 6) (2) The device Louis Guttman weighs himself on.

Hawthorne effect A term coined in reference to a series of productivity studies at the Hawthorne plant of the Western Electric Company in Chicago, Illinois. The researchers discovered that their presence affected the behaviour of the workers being studied. The term now refers to any impact of research on the subject of study. (Chapter 8)

hypothesis An expectation about the nature of things derived from a theory. It is a statement of something that ought to be observed in the real world if the theory is correct. Derived from propositions, it is a specified, testable expectation about empirical reality. See *deduction* and also Chapter 2.

hypothesis testing The determination of whether the expectations that a *hypothesis* represents are, indeed, found to exist in the real world. (Chapter 2)

idiographic An approach to explanation in which we seek to exhaust the idiosyncratic causes of a particular condition or event. Imagine trying to list all the reasons why you chose to attend your particular university. Given all those reasons, it's difficult to imagine your making any other choice. By contrast, see *nomothetic*. See also Chapters 1 and 2.

independent variable (1) A variable with values that are not problematical in an analysis but are taken as simply given. An independent variable is presumed to cause or determine a *dependent variable*. If we discover that religiosity is partly a function of gender—women are more religious than men—*gender* is the independent variable and *religiosity* is the dependent variable. Note that any given variable might be treated as independent in one part of an analysis and dependent in another part of it. *Religiosity* might become an independent variable in the explanation of crime. See Chapter 1 and *dependent variable*. (2) A variable that refuses to take advice.

index A type of composite measure that summarizes and rank-orders several specific observations and represents some more general dimension. Contrasted with *scale*. (Chapter 6)

indicator An observation that we choose to consider as a reflection of a variable we wish to study. Thus, for example, attending church might be considered an indicator of religiosity. (Chapter 5)

induction (1) The logical model in which general principles are developed from specific observations. Having noted that Jews and Catholics are more likely to vote Liberal than Protestants are, you might conclude that religious minorities in Canada are more affiliated with the Liberal party and explain why. This would be an example of induction. See also *deduction* and Chapters 1, 2 and 3. (2) The culinary art of stuffing ducks.

inferential statistics The body of statistical computations relevant to making inferences from findings based on sample observations to some larger population. See also *descriptive statistics* and Chapter 16. (Not to be confused with infernal statistics, a characterization sometimes invoked by frustrated statistics students.)

informant Someone well versed in the social phenomenon that you wish to study and who is willing to tell you what he or she knows. If you were planning participant observation among the members of a religious sect, you would do well to make friends with someone who already knows about them—possibly a member of the sect—who could give you some background information about them. Not to be confused with a *respondent*. See Chapters 7 and 11.

institutional ethnography A research technique that uses the personal experiences of individuals (especially women and other oppressed people) to uncover the institutional power relations that structure and govern their experiences. (Chapter 11)

internal invalidity Refers to the possibility that the conclusions drawn from experimental results may not accurately reflect what went on in the experiment itself. See Chapter 8 and also *external invalidity*.

interpretation When used in connection with the elaboration model, this is a technical term that represents the research outcome in which a test or control variable is discovered to be the mediating factor through which an independent variable has its effect on a dependent variable. (Chapter 16)

interval measure A level of measurement describing a variable whose attributes are rank-ordered and have equal distances between adjacent attributes. The Celsius temperature scale is an example of this, since the distance between 17 and 18 is the same as that between 39 and 40. See also Chapter 5 and *nominal measure, ordinal measure,* and *ratio measure.*

interview A data-collection encounter in which one person (an interviewer) asks questions of another (a *respondent*). Interviews may be conducted face-to-face or by telephone. See Chapter 9 for more information on interviewing as a method of survey research and Chapter 12 for more information on qualitative interviewing.

judgmental sample (1) A type of *nonprobability sample* in which you select the units to be observed on the basis of your own judgment about which ones will be the most useful or representative. Another name for this is *purposive sample.* (Chapter 7) (2) A sample of opinionated people.

latent content (1) As used in connection with content analysis, the underlying meaning of communications as distinguished from their *manifest content.* (Chapter 10) (2) What you need to make a latent.

level of significance (1) In the context of *tests of statistical significance,* the degree of likelihood that an observed, empirical relationship could be attributable to *sampling error.* A relationship is significant at the .05 level if the likelihood of its being only a function of sampling error is no greater than 5 out of 100. (Chapter 16) (2) Height limits on outdoor advertising.

Likert scale A type of composite measure developed by Rensis Likert in an attempt to improve the levels of measurement in social research through the use of standardized response categories in survey *questionnaires* to determine the relative intensity of different items. Likert items are those using such response categories as strongly agree, agree, disagree, and

strongly disagree. Such items may be used in the construction of true Likert scales as well as other types of composite measures. (Chapter 6)

longitudinal study A study design involving the collection of data at different points in time, as contrasted with a *cross-sectional study.* See also Chapter 4 and *cohort study, panel study,* and *trend study.*

macrotheory A theory aimed at understanding the "big picture" of institutions, whole societies, and the interactions among societies. Karl Marx's examination of the class struggle is an example of macrotheory. By contrast, see *microtheory.* (Chapter 2)

manifest content (1) In connection with content analysis, the concrete terms contained in a communication, as distinguished from *latent content.* (Chapter 10) (2) What you have after a manifest bursts.

matching In connection with experiments, the procedure whereby pairs of subjects are matched on the basis of their similarities on one or more variables; then one member of the pair is assigned to the *experimental group* and the other to the *control group.* (Chapter 8)

mean (1) An *average* computed by summing the values of several observations and dividing by the number of observations. If you now have a GPA of 4.0 based on 10 courses, and you get an F in this course, your new grade point (mean) average will be 3.6. (Chapter 16) (2) The quality of the thoughts you might have if your instructor did that to you.

measures of association Descriptive statistics summarizing the relationships between variables. (Chapter 16)

median (1) An *average* representing the value of the "middle" case in a rank-ordered set of observations. If the ages of five men were 16, 17, 20, 54, and 88, the median would be 20. (The *mean* would be 39.) (Chapter 16) (2) The dividing line between safe driving and exciting driving.

memoing The process of writing memos concerning the ideas and insights developed during the collection and analysis of qualitative data. Memos are the researcher's record of methodological concerns, descriptions and definitions of concepts, emerging or discovered relationships among codes, ideas for further study, or any other subject relevant to the study. The procedure helps the researcher to organize and process qualitative data and to discover patterns. (Chapter 14)

microtheory A theory aimed at understanding social life at the intimate level of individuals and their interactions. Examining how the play behaviour of girls differs from that of boys would be an example of microtheory. By contrast, see *macrotheory*. (Chapter 2)

mode (1) An *average* representing the most frequently observed value or attribute. If a sample contains 1,000 Protestants, 275 Catholics, and 33 Jews, Protestant is the modal category. (Chapter 16) (2) Better than apple pie à la median.

multiple regression analysis A statistical analysis that provides a means of analyzing the simultaneous impact of two or more independent variables on a single dependent variable. The analysis produces an equation that represents the several effects of the multiple independent variables on the dependent variable. (Chapter 16)

multivariate analysis The analysis of the simultaneous relationships among several variables. Examining simultaneously the effects of age, gender, and social class on religiosity would be an example of *multivariate analysis.* (Chapter 16)

nominal measure A level of measurement describing a variable whose attributes only have the characteristics of being jointly exhaustive and mutually exclusive, that is, the attributes are merely different from each other, as distinguished from *ordinal, interval,* or *ratio measures.* Gender is an example of a nominal measure. (Chapter 5)

nomothetic An approach to explanation in which we seek to identify a few causal factors that generally impact a class of conditions or events. Imagine the two or three key factors that determine which universities students choose, such as proximity, reputation, and so forth. By contrast, see *idiographic.* (See also Chapters 1 and 2.)

nonprobability sample A sample selected in some fashion other than any suggested by probability theory. Examples include *judgmental (purposive), quota,* and *snowball samples.* (Chapter 7)

nonsampling error (1) Those imperfections of data quality that are a result of factors other than sampling error. Examples include misunderstandings of questions by respondents, erroneous recordings by interviewers and coders, and keypunch errors. (Chapter 16) (2) The mistake you made in deciding to interview everyone rather than selecting a sample.

null hypothesis (1) In connection with *hypothesis testing* and *tests of statistical significance,* that *hypothesis* that suggests there is no relationship among the variables under study. You may conclude that the variables are related after having statistically rejected the null hypothesis. (Chapter 16) (2) An expectation about nulls.

open coding The process of closely examining the data in the initial stages of a qualitative data analysis with the aim of identifying and labeling as many ideas, concepts, and themes as the researcher can without concern for how these ideas or concepts are related or how they will be used. (Chapter 14)

operational definition The concrete and specific definition of something in terms of the operations by which observations are to be categorized. The operational definition of "earning an A in this course" might be "correctly answering at least 90 percent of the final exam questions." (Chapters 2 and 5)

operationalization (1) One step beyond *conceptualization.* Operationalization is the process of developing *operational definitions*, which specify the exact operations involved in measuring a variable. (Chapter 2) (2) Surgery on intellectuals.

oral history A method that uses in-depth interviews as a means of gathering data about the past from individuals' recollections, typically focussing on specific events or periods of time. (Chapter 12)

ordinal measure A level of measurement describing a variable with attributes you can rank-order along some dimension. An example would be socioeconomic status as composed of the attributes high, medium, low. See also Chapter 5 and *nominal measure, interval measure,* and *ratio measure.*

panel study A type of *longitudinal study,* in which data are collected from the same set of people (the sample or panel) at several points in time. (Chapter 4)

paradigm (1) A model or framework for observation and understanding, which shapes both what we see and how we understand it. The conflict paradigm causes us to see social behaviour one way, the interactionist paradigm causes us to see it differently. (Chapter 2) (2) $0.20

parameter The summary description of a given variable in a population. (Chapter 7)

partial See *partial relationship.*

partial relationship In the elaboration model, this refers to the relationship between two variables when examined in a subset of cases defined by a third (test) variable. Thus the zero-order relationship (original two variable relationship) is recomputed separately for each of the subsamples defined by the test variable. For example, beginning with a zero-order relationship between *income* and attitudes *toward gender equality*, we might want to control for *gender*, that is, see whether the relationship holds true among both men and women. The tables produced in this manner—one showing the relationship found among men and the other showing the relationship found among women—are called the partial tables, and the relationships within these partial tables are called partial relationships, or partials. (Chapter 16)

participatory action research In this approach to social research, the researcher serves as a resource to those being studied, typically disadvantaged groups, with the aim of increasing their ability to act effectively in their own interest. Counter to the conventional status and power differences between researchers and subjects, those under study are given control to define their problems, define the remedies they desire, and take lead in designing the research that will help them realize their aims. (Chapter 11)

population The theoretically specified aggregation of the elements in a study. (Chapter 7)

PPS (probability proportionate to size) (1) This refers to a type of multistage *cluster sample* in which clusters are selected, not with equal probabilities (see *EPSEM*) but with probabilities propor-

tionate to their sizes—as measured by the number of units to be subsampled. (Chapter 7) (2) The odds on who gets to go first: you or the 275-pound fullback.

probability sample The general term for samples selected in accord with probability theory, typically involving some random selection mechanism. Specific types of probability samples include *EPSEM, PPS, simple random sample,* and *systematic sample.* (Chapter 7)

probe A technique employed in interviewing to solicit a more complete answer to a question. It is a nondirective phrase or question used to encourage a respondent to elaborate on an answer. Examples include "Anything more?" and "How is that?" See Chapters 9 and 12 for discussions of interviewing.

purposive sample See *judgmental sample* and Chapter 7.

qualitative analysis (1) The nonnumerical examination and interpretation of observations, for the purpose of discovering underlying meanings and patterns of relationships. This is most typical of field research and historical research. (Chapter 14) (2) A classy analysis.

qualitative interview In contrast to a survey interview, a qualitative interview allows the researcher to pursue issues in depth and gives the respondent more freedom to direct the flow of conversation. The researcher typically has a general plan of inquiry but not a standardized set of questions that must be rigidly followed. Respondents' answers to initial questions shape a researcher's subsequent questions. (Chapter 12)

quantitative analysis (1) The numerical representation and manipulation of observations for the purpose of describing and explaining the phenomena that those observations reflect. (Chapters 15 and 16) (2) A BIG analysis.

questionnaire A document containing questions and other types of items designed to solicit information appropriate to analysis. *Questionnaires* are used primarily in survey research but also in experiments, field research, and other modes of observation. (Chapter 9)

quota sample A type of nonprobability sample in which units are selected into the sample on the basis of prespecified characteristics, so that the total sample will have the same distribution of characteristics assumed to exist in the population being studied. (Chapter 7)

random selection In sampling, a method where each element has an equal chance of selection independent of any other event in the selection process. (Chapter 7)

randomization The procedure of randomly assigning experimental subjects to *experimental* versus *control groups*. Not to be confused with probability sampling techniques such as a simple random sample. (Chapter 8)

range (1) A measure of *dispersion,* composed of the highest and lowest values of a variable in some set of observations. In your class, for example, the range of ages might be from 17 to 37. (Chapter 16) (2) Recreation area for deer and antelope.

ratio measure A level of measurement describing a variable whose attributes have all the qualities of *nominal, ordinal,* and *interval measures* and in addition are based on a "true zero" point. Age is an example of a ratio measure.(Chapter 5)

regression analysis (1) A method of data analysis in which the relationships among variables are represented in the form of an equation, called a *regression equation.* See Chapter 16 for a discussion of the different forms of *regression analysis.* (2) What seems to happen to your knowledge of social research methods just before an exam.

reification The process of regarding things that are not real as real. (Chapter 5)

reliability (1) That quality of measurement method that suggests that the same data would have been collected each time in repeated observations of the same phenomenon. In the context of a survey, we would expect that the question "Did you attend religious services last week?" would have higher reliability than the question "About how many times have you attended religious services in your life?" This is not to be con-

fused with *validity.* (Chapter 5) (2) Quality of repeatability in untruths.

replication Generally, the duplication of an experiment with the possibility of confirming results or reducing or exposing error. In addition, it is a technical term used in the elaboration model to refer to the empirical outcome of the persistence of the observed initial relationship between two variables when a control variable is held constant. This supports the idea that the original, zero-order relationship is genuine. (Chapters 1 and 16)

representativeness (1) That quality of a sample of having the same distribution of characteristics as the population from which it was selected. By implication, descriptions and explanations derived from an analysis of the sample may be assumed to represent similar ones in the population. Representativeness is enhanced by *probability sampling* and provides for *generalizability* and the use of *inferential statistics.* (Chapter 7)

respondent A person who provides data for analysis by responding to a survey *questionnaire.* (Chapter 9)

response rate The number of people participating in a survey divided by the number selected in the sample, in the form of a percentage. This is also called the "completion rate" or, in self-administered surveys, the "return rate": the percentage of questionnaires sent out that are returned. (Chapter 9)

sampling error The degree of error to be expected for a given probability sample design. Probability theory gives us a formula for estimating sampling error—how closely the sample statistics will tend to cluster around the true values in the population. See Chapter 7 for the formula to determine sampling error.

sampling frame That list or quasi list of units composing a population from which a sample is selected. If the sample is to be *representative* of the population, it's essential that the sampling frame include all (or nearly all) members of the population. (Chapter 7)

sampling interval The standard distance between elements selected from a population for a sample. (Chapter 7)

sampling ratio The proportion of elements in the population that are selected to be in a sample. (Chapter 7)

scale (1) A type of composite measure composed of several items that have a logical or empirical structure among them. Examples of *scales* include *Bogardus social distance, Guttman, Likert,* and *Thurstone scales.* Contrasted with *index.* See also Chapter 6. (2) One of the less appetizing parts of a fish.

secondary analysis (1) A form of research in which the data collected and processed by one researcher are reanalyzed—often for a different purpose—by another. This is especially appropriate in the case of survey data. Data archives are repositories or libraries for the storage and distribution of data for secondary analysis. (Chapter 9) (2) Estimating the weight and speed of an opposing team's linebackers.

semantic differential A questionnaire format in which the respondent is asked to rate something in terms of two, opposite adjectives (e.g., rate textbooks as "boring" or "exciting"), using qualifiers such as "very," "somewhat," "neither," "somewhat," and "very" to bridge the distance between the two opposites. (Chapter 6)

semiotics The science of signs. It refers to the analysis of various forms of visual and textual symbols with the goal of revealing the hidden meanings of such symbols—often conducted through the use of content analysis. (Chapter 14)

simple random sample (1) A type of *probability sample* in which the units composing a population are assigned numbers. A set of random numbers is then generated, and the units having those numbers are included in the sample. Although probability theory and the calculations it provides assume this basic sampling method, it's seldom used, for practical reasons. An equivalent alternative is the *systematic sample* (with a random start). (Chapter 7) (2) A random sample with a low IQ.

snowball sample (1) A *nonprobability sampling* method often employed in field research whereby each person interviewed may be asked to suggest additional people for interviewing. (Chapter 7) (2) Picking the icy ones to throw at your methods instructor.

specification In general terms it is the process through which concepts are made more specific. In the context of the elaboration model the term is used in a technical sense to represent the elaboration outcome when the partial relationships revealed by controlling for the test variable differ significantly from each other. For example, one partial relationship is the same as or stronger than the zero-order relationship, and the other partial relationship is less than the original and may be reduced to zero. Thus an initially observed relationship between two variables is replicated among some subgroups created by the test variable but not among others. When this outcome is found, you will have specified the particular conditions under which the original relationship holds, for example among the elderly but not among children. (Chapter 16)

spurious relationship An observed association (statistical correlation) between two variables that is shown to be caused by some third variable. For example, there is a positive correlation between ice cream sales and deaths due to drowning: the more ice cream sold, the more drownings. However, there is no direct link between ice cream and drowning. The third variable at work here is season or temperature. Most drowning deaths occur during summer, the peak period for ice cream sales. (Chapters 3 and 16)

statistic The summary description of a variable in a sample, used to estimate a population parameter. (Chapter 7)

statistical significance (1) A general term referring to the likelihood that relationships observed in a sample could be attributed to sampling error alone. See *tests of statistical significance* and Chapter 16. (2) How important it would really be if you flunked your statistics exam. You could always be a poet.

stratification The grouping of the units composing a population into homogeneous groups (or strata) before sampling. This procedure, which may be used in conjunction with *simple random,* *systematic,* or *cluster sampling,* improves the representativeness of a sample, at least in terms of the stratification variables. (Chapter 7)

study population That aggregation of elements from which a sample is actually selected. (Chapter 7)

suppressor variable In the elaboration model, a test variable that conceals a true zero-order relationship. (Chapter 16)

systematic sample (1) A type of *probability sample* in which every *k*th unit in a list is selected for inclusion in the sample—for example, every 25th student in the university directory of students. You compute *k* by dividing the size of the population by the desired sample size; *k* is called the *sampling interval.* Within certain constraints, systematic sampling is a functional equivalent of *simple random sampling* and usually easier to do. Typically, the first unit is selected at random. See *snowball sample* and Chapter 7. (2) Picking every third one whether it's icy or not.

test variable See *control variable.*

tests of statistical significance (1) A class of statistical computations that indicate the likelihood that the relationship observed between variables in a sample can be attributed to sampling error only. See *inferential statistics* and Chapter 16. (2) A determination of how important statistics have been in improving humankind's lot in life. (3) An examination that can radically affect your grade in this course and your GPA as well.

theory A systematic explanation for the observations that relate to a particular aspect of life: juvenile delinquency, for example, or perhaps social stratification or political revolution. (Chapters 1 and 2)

Thurstone scale A type of composite measure, constructed in accord with the weights assigned by "judges" to various indicators of some variables. (Chapter 6)

trend study A type of *longitudinal study* in which a given characteristic of some population is monitored over time. An example would be the series of Gallup Polls showing the political-candidate preferences of the electorate over the course of a campaign, even though different samples were interviewed at each point. (Chapter 4)

typology (1) The classification (typically nominal) of observations in terms of their attributes on two or more variables or concepts. The classification of newspapers as liberal-urban, liberal-rural, conservative-urban, or conservative-rural would be an example. (Chapters 6 and 14) (2) Apologizing for your neckwear.

units of analysis The *what* or *whom* being studied. In social science research, the most typical units of analysis are individual people. (Chapter 4)

univariate analysis The analysis of a single variable, for purposes of description. *Frequency distributions, averages,* and measures of *dispersion* would be examples of univariate analysis, as distinguished from *bivariate* and *multivariate analysis.* (Chapter 16)

validity A term describing a measure that accurately reflects the concept it is intended to measure. For example, your IQ would seem a more valid measure of your intelligence than would the number of hours you spend in the library. Though the ultimate validity of a measure can never be proven, we may agree to its relative validity on the basis of *face validity, criterion validity, content validity, construct validity, internal validation,* and *external validation.* This must not be confused with *reliability.* (Chapter 5)

variables Logical groupings of *attributes.* The variable *gender* is made up of the attributes *male* and *female.* (Chapters 1 and 2)

weighting (1) A procedure employed in connection with sampling whereby units selected with unequal probabilities are assigned weights in such a manner as to make the sample *representative* of the population from which it was selected. When all cases have the same chance of selection no weighting is necessary. (Chapter 7)

zero-order relationship The relationship between two variables when no test variables are being held constant, i.e. controlled for. (Chapter 16)

Chapter-Opening Photo Credits

Chapter 1   © AFP/CORBIS/MAGMA
Chapter 2   © PhotoDisc, Inc.
Chapter 3   © PhotoDisc, Inc.
Chapter 4   © CORBIS/MAGMA
Chapter 5   © PhotoDisc, Inc.
Chapter 6   © CORBIS/MAGMA.
Chapter 7   © Stephen MacGillivray/CP Picture Archive
Chapter 8   © PhotoDisc, Inc.
Chapter 9   © PhotoDisc, Inc.
Chapter 10   © PhotoDisc, Inc.
Chapter 11   © Liba Taylor/CORBIS/MAGMA.
Chapter 12   © PhotoDisc, Inc.
Chapter 13   © PhotoDisc, Inc.
Chapter 14   © PhotoDisc, Inc.
Chapter 15   © PhotoDisc, Inc.
Chapter 16   © PhotoDisc, Inc.

Index